CISTERCIAN STUDIES SERIES: NUMBER SEVENTY-NINE

THE SPIRITUALITY OF THE CHRISTIAN EAST
A Systematic Handbook

CISTERCIAN STUDIES SERIES: NUMBER SEVENTY-NINE

THE SPIRITUALITY OF THE CHRISTIAN EAST
A Systematic Handbook

by
Tomáš Špidlík, SJ

Translated by
Anthony P. Gythiel

α
Cistercian Publications
www.cistercianpublications.org

LITURGICAL PRESS
Collegeville, Minnesota
www.litpress.org

A translation of Tomáš Špidlík, SJ, *La spiritualité de l'Orient chrétien*, Orientalia Christiana Analecta 206. Rome: Pontificium institutum orientalium studiorum, 1978.

© Translation copyright, Cistercian Publications, 1986

The editors of Cistercian Publications express their appreciation to Dr. Anthony P. Gythiel for not only capably and painstakingly translating this work but also for locating English translations of texts and studies cited by the author.

A Cistercian Publications title published by Liturgical Press

Cistercian Publications
Editorial Offices
Abbey of Gethsemani
3642 Monks Road
Trappist, Kentucky 40051
www.cistercianpublications.org

© 2008 by Order of Saint Benedict, Collegeville, Minnesota. All rights reserved. No part of this book may be reproduced in any form, by print, microfilm, microfiche, mechanical recording, photocopying, translation, or by any other means, known or yet unknown, for any purpose except brief quotations in reviews, without the previous written permission of Liturgical Press, Saint John's Abbey, P.O. Box 7500, Collegeville, Minnesota 56321-7500. Printed in the United States of America.

Library of Congress Cataloging-in-Publication Data

Spidlik, Tomas.
    The spirituality of the Christian East.
    (Cistercian studies series: no. 79)
    Translation of: La spiritualité de l'Orient chrétien
    Includes bibliographies and index.
    1. Spirituality—Eastern churches. 2. Eastern churches—Doctrines.
I. Title. II. Series.
BX106.2.S5513   1986   231'.15   84-29348
ISBN 0-87907-879-0   (pb 0 87907 979 7)

CONTENTS

INTRODUCTION 1

CHAPTER 1. SOURCES 5

1. COMMON SOURCES 5
   Scripture, 5. The Tradition of the Church, 6.
   Christianity and Cultural Traditions, 8. The Judaeo-
   Christian Environment, 8. Hellenism, 9. The Fathers
   and Philosophy, 10. 'Heterodox' Authors, 11.

2. THE SPIRITUAL LITERATURE OF THE VARIOUS CHURCHES 11
   Greek and Byzantine, 11. Coptic, 13. Ethiopian, 14.
   Syrian, 14. Armenian, 15. Georgian, 16. Russian, 17.

3. THE TRENDS OF EASTERN SPIRITUALITY 17
   Distinguishing Criteria, 17. 'Practical' Primitive
   Spirituality, 18. Intellectualized Spirituality and the
   Origin of Mysticism, 19. Experiencing God, the
   Mysticism of the Heart, 20. Cosmic Spirituality; The
   Veneration of Images, 20. The Cenobitic Trend,
   Ecclesial Spirituality, 21. Names Applied to Spiritual
   Doctrine, 22.

CHAPTER 2. LIFE IN GOD 29

1. IN THE HOLY SPIRIT 29
   Spiritual, 29. The Personal Indwelling of the Spirit, 30.
   'One Spirit with the Lord', 31. 'The Soul of the Human
   Soul', 32. The Effects of the Spirit in the Soul, the
   Body, and Creation, 32. The Christian Life a Progressive
   'Spiritualization', 33.

2. THROUGH JESUS CHRIST 34
   The Christian Life as Christological, 34. Names of
   Christ, 34. The Unifying Activity of Christ, 36. Devotion
   to Christ, 37. Devotion to the Humanity of Christ, 38.
   The Imitation of Christ, 39. Imitating the Saints, 41.

3. TO THE FATHER 42
   The Problem of God in Ancient Greek Thought, 42.
   The God of Christian Revelation: The Father, 43. The
   'Super-essential Unity' within the Trinity, 44.
   Deification, 45. Equivalent Expressions, 47.

CHAPTER 3. THE NEW LIFE 55

1. THE IMAGE AND LIKENESS OF GOD 55
   The Importance of the Question, 55. The Theme of the
   Image in Scripture and Hellenistic Philosophy, 55. Man,
   'the Image of God', of the Trinity, 56. 'After' the Image
   of God, 57. The Distinction between Image and Likeness, 58. From the Image to the Likeness, 59. The Place
   of the Image, 59. Is the Image of God the Soul Alone or
   the Whole Man or Only 'The Spirit'?, 60. The Image
   and Evil, 61.

2. THE NATURAL LIFE 62
   Natural Law, 62. The Word 'Nature' in West and East, 63.
   The Happy Life, 64. Eternal Life, 65. The Soul's
   Salvation, 66. The Body, 66. 'Spiritual Selfishness',67.

3. PROGRESS IN THE SPIRITUAL LIFE 68
   The Need for Progress, 68. Names of the Degrees, 68.
   Praktikē, Physikē, Theologikē, 70. The Meaning of the
   Degrees in the Spiritual Life, 71.

4. THE CONSCIOUSNESS OF GRACE 71
   A Direct Experience of the Spirit?, 71. Orthodox
   Opposition to the Messalian Thesis, 72. Spiritual Feelings.
   'A Sign of the Quickening of the Soul', 72. The Indirect
   Experience, Through Signs, 73. The Outstanding Sign
   of the Spirit: Charity Manifested in Martyrdom, 75. The
   'True Gnostic', 76.

CHAPTER 4. CHRISTIAN ANTHROPOLOGY 87

1. SELF-KNOWLEDGE 87
   The Moral Aspect of Self-knowledge, 87. Humility, 88.
   The Psychological Aspect of Self-knowledge, 90. Inner
   Man-Outer Man, 90. Body-Soul-Spirit, 91. Various
   Aspects of the 'Trichotomy', 92.

Contents vii

2. THE SPIRIT AND THE SOUL 94
   Living according to the Spirit, 94. The Spiritual Sense, 94.
   Conscience, 95. The Nature of the Soul, 96. The Divine
   Origin of the Soul, Its Spirituality, 96. The Immortality
   of the Soul, 97. The Greek Concept of Freedom, 98.
   Christian Freedom, 99. 'Structural Freedom' and
   Freedom of Choice: *eleutheria* and *proairesis*, 100. 'To
   Save Oneself, 'One Need Only Will It', 101. The Parts
   and Faculties of the Soul, 102.

3. THE HEART 103
   Its Importance in Eastern Spirituality, 103. The Point of
   Contact Between God and Man, 104. The Heart—Principle
   of Human Integration, 105. The Feelings of the
   Heart, 106. Attention to the Heart, 107.

4. THE BODY 107
   The Body in Antiquity and in Scripture, 107. The Body
   in the Fathers and Spiritual Writers, 108. The Orthodox
   Reaction Against Dualism, 109. The Mysterious Union of
   Body and Soul, 110. Aphorisms about the Body, 111.
   Sex, 112. Illness, 113. Death, 113.

CHAPTER 5. SPIRITUAL COSMOLOGY 125

1. THE WORLD AND DIVINE PROVIDENCE 125
   The Problem of the World in Antiquity, 125. The
   World in Scripture, 126. The Goodness and the Beauty
   of the World Created for Man, 127. The Unity of the
   Deified World, 128. Divine Providence or Fate?, 130.
   The Divine *Oikonomia*, 131. Definitions and the Purpose
   of Providence. Distinctions, 132. Personal Providence
   and the Law of the World, 133. Surrender to
   Providence, 134.

2. EVIL AND PROVIDENCE 135
   The Problem of Evil, 135. Refutation of False Opinions
   about the Origin of Evil, 136. *Proairesis* (Intention,
   Choice)—The Source of Evil, 136. Divine Providence
   within Evil, 137. The Benefits of Suffering to the
   Sinner, 137. The Sufferings of the Just, 138. Christlike
   Suffering, 139. Divine *Paideia*, 139. 'No One is Harmed
   Except By His Own Hand' (Chrysostom), 140.

3. THE COSMIC VOCATION OF MAN   140
The Human Mission, 140. The Purification of the World and its Progressive Deification, 141. The History of the World, 142. The World of the Past has Gone, 143. *Apokatastasis* (Universal Salvation) or the Progressive Concept? 144.

CHAPTER 6. SPIRITUAL SOCIOLOGY   151

1. THE UNIVERSALITY OF CHRISTIAN LOVE   151
Man—a Social Being, 151. Love of God and Love of Neighbor, 152. The General Principle: Love's Universality, Perpetuity, and Equality, 153. The Difficulty of Application; The Order of Charity, 153. The Plurality of Nations, 154. Christian Cosmopolitanism, 155. Russian Messianism, 156.

2. UNITY IN THE BODY OF CHRIST   157
The Church, 157. The Heavenly Church, 158. Devotion to the Mother of God, 158. The Monastic Brotherhoods, 159. Praises of the Common Life, 160. Friendship, 161. The Family, 162. The State Society, 162.

3. MAN'S CONCRETE OBLIGATIONS IN SOCIETY   164
Negative Principle and Positive Principle, 164. The Example of the Christian Life, 165. Brotherly Correction—An Act of Charity, 165. The Service of the Word, 166. Almsgiving, 167. The Obligation to Work, 168. The Practice of Charity in the Monasteries, 169. The Monks' Apostolate, 169. Educating the Young, 170.

CHAPTER 7. NEGATIVE PRAXIS   177

1. PRAXIS   177
The Spiritual Life—The Work of God, 177. The Term *Praxis*, 178. Asceticism, 179. Self-denial, Renunciation, 180. The Stripping of Self, 181. Mortification, 181. Chastity, 182.

2. PURIFICATION FROM SIN   182
Purification, 182. The State of Sin, 183. Full Responsibility for Sin, 184. Sin as Ignorance, 185. Transgressing the Commandments, Offending God, 186. The Distinction Between Sins, 187. The Consequences of Sin, 188. The Social and Cosmic Dimensions of Sin, 188.

Contents ix

3. REPENTENCE 189
   Exhortations to Repentance, 189. Essential Elements of Repentance, 190. Sacramental Repentance, 191. Disciplines and Acts of Repentance, 192.

4. PENTHOS 193
   Perpetual Compunction, 193. Causes of Compunction, 194. The Effects of *Penthos* and Ways of Obtaining It, 196.

CHAPTER 8. THE FLIGHT FROM THE WORLD AND THE RENUNCIATION OF THE FLESH — 205

1. THE CHRISTIAN IS NOT OF THIS WORLD 205.
   Flight from the World in Greek Thought, 205. Flight from the World in Christianity, 206. Various Aspects of Flight from the World, 206. Poverty, 208. A Double Spirituality? 210.

2. THE SOLITARY LIFE 211
   Affective and Effective Flight from the World, 211 Flight from the World in the Hesychast Tradition, 211. In Praise of the Eremitic Life, 212. Various Forms of the Eremitic Life, 213.

3. FLIGHT FROM THE WORLD IN CENOBITISM 214
   Life in Common, Separated from the World, 214. Guests, 214. Relatives, 215. Silence, 215. Abstaining from Laughter, 216. Flight from Divisions, Unanimity, 217.

4. RENUNCIATION OF THE FLESH 217
   Temperance – The Broad and Narrow Meanings, 217. The Pauline Basis of the Doctrine of Renunciation of the Flesh, 218. Chastity, 219. Marriage, 219. Virginity, 220. Widowhood and Second Marriage, 221. The Preservation of Chastity, 222. Flight from Women and 'Beardless Youths', 222. Bodily Mortifications, 223. Fasting, 223.

CHAPTER 9. SPIRITUAL WARFARE 233

1. THE STRUGGLE AGAINST DEMONS 233
   The Visible and Invisible War, 233. The Necessity of Warfare, 234. The Enemy, 234. The Power of Demons, 235. Exorcism, 236.

2. LOGISMOI — 237
   The Struggle against Evil Thoughts, 237. The Term *Logismos*, 238. The Definition of *Logismos*, 239. 'Passionate' Thoughts, 239. The Origin of Evil Thoughts, 240. The Degrees of Penetration by an Evil Thought into the Heart, 241.

3. CUSTODY OF THE HEART — 242
   'The Elimination of Thoughts', 242. The Method of Fighting Hostile Thoughts, 243. The Discernment of Spirits, 244. Discernment as a Gift of God, a Spiritual Art, and the Fruit of Experience, 244. The 'Psychological Rules': How Spirits Act, 245. The Manifestation of Thoughts, 246. Examination of Conscience, 247.

4. THE EIGHT EVIL THOUGHTS — 248
   The Theory of the Eight Evil or 'Generic' Thoughts, 248. The Sequence of *Logismoi* and the Latin List, 248. Gluttony, 249. Fornication, 250. Avarice, 250. Melancholy, 251. Anger, 251. Acedia, 252. Vainglory, 254. Pride, 254. The Root of All Evil Thoughts: Love of Self, 255. Self-will, 256.

CHAPTER 10. PURIFICATION OF THE PASSIONS — 267

1. 'DISEASES OF THE SOUL' — 267
   Philosophic Theories about the Passions, 267. Christian Writers of the East, 268. Passions, Feelings, and Human Corruptibility, 269. Transformation of the Passions, 269.

2. APATHEIA — 270
   Biblical Zeal, 270. The Peaceful State—the Greek Philosophic Ideal, 270. The Christian Adaptation of the Ideal, 271. The Impassibility of God, 272. The Quality of the Risen Body, 272. Evagrius: Men Like Angels, 273. The Messalians, 273. *Apatheia*: Not the Absence of Suffering or Feeling, 274. *Apatheia*: Not the Absence of Passionate Thoughts, 274. *Apatheia*: An Inner Force Capable of Resisting the Passions, 275. *Apatheia* and Love, 275. *Apatheia* and *Gnosis*, 275. *Apatheia* and Sinlessness, 276. The Signs of *Apatheia*, 276. The Condemnation of *Apatheia* by the West, 277.

CHAPTER 11. POSITIVE PRAXIS — 283

1. THE WILL OF GOD — 283
   Obedience to the Will of God, 283. Obedience to the Spiritual Father, 284. Hierarchical Obedience, 285.

Contents   xi

  Obedience to a Person or to a Written Law? 285.
  Obedience to Divine Commandments, 286. Precepts
  and Counsels, Christian and Monastic Spirituality, 287.

2. THE 'PATH OF VIRTUE'   288
  The Virtuous Life, 288. Axioms on the Virtues, 289.
  Virtue is the Only Good, Vice the Only Evil; Everything
  Else is Indifferent, 289. Virtue: The Mean Between Two
  Extremes, 289. Virtue is its Own Reward (*Virtus sibi ipsi
  premium*), 290. Virtue: Likeness to God and Participation
  in Christ, 290. The Difficulty and Ease of the Virtuous
  Life, 291. The Oneness of the Virtues, 291. The
  Division Between the Virtues, 293. The Genealogy of
  the Virtues, 294.

3. CHARITY   295
  Perfection in Charity, 295. Three Objections, 296. Greek
  Terms, 297. 'Love' in Greek Philosophy, Summarized in
  Three Points, 297. Christian Teaching, 297. *Eros*
  and *Agape, Amor Concupiscentiae* and *Amor
  Benevolentiae*, 298. The 'First Commandment', 299.
  The 'Love of God': *Eros* or *Agapē*? 299.

CHAPTER 12. PRAYER   307

1. THE ESSENCE OF PRAYER   307
  The Excellence and Necessity of Prayer, 307. To Whom
  do We Pray? 307. Definitions of Prayer, 308. The
  Prayer of Supplication, 309. The Ascent of the Spirit
  to God, 310.

2. THE DEGREES AND THE TYPES OF PRAYER   311
  The Degrees of Prayer, 311. Liturgical Prayer, 312.
  Icons, 313. The Symbolism of the Church Building, 314.

3. UNCEASING PRAYER   315
  Pray without Ceasing (1 Th 5:17), 315. Ejaculatory
  Prayers, 316. The Jesus Prayer, 316. Three Stages in the
  Jesus Prayer, 317. The 'Psychosomatic', 'Scientific'
  Method, 318. The Russian Pilgrim, 318. Reflections on
  the Jesus Prayer, 319.

CHAPTER 13. CONTEMPLATION   327

1. THE NATURE OF CONTEMPLATION   327
  Definition and Terms, 327. *Theōria* and *Gnōsis*, 327.
  'The Contemplative East', 328. The Incomprehensibility
  of God, 329.

xii   *Contents*

2. THE OBJECT OF CONTEMPLATION   329
   Not the 'Surface' of Things, 329. Not the Philosophic
   Logos, 330. The *Theoteles Logos*, 330.

3. THE ORGAN OF CONTEMPLATION   331
   Beginning with the senses, 331. The *Nous*—the Divine
   Faculty, 332. The Deified and Purified *Nous*, 332.
   Praxis Leads to *Theōria*, 333. No True Knowledge
   Without Love, 334. From Faith to *Gnosis*, 335.

4. PROGRESS IN CONTEMPLATION   335
   The Degrees, 335. Natural Contemplation, 336. The
   Contemplation of Invisible Beings, 337. The
   Contemplation of Providence and Judgment, 337.
   Theologia, 338. Ecstasy, 339.

5. THE EFFECTS OF CONTEMPLATION   340
   Unceasing Remembrance of God, 340. Transformation
   and Holiness, 341. The Glory of God, 342.

                     CONCLUSION   351

                     TABLE OF ABBREVIATIONS   357

                     A SELECTED BIBLIOGRAPHY   359

                     AN INDEX OF USEFUL TEXTS   415

                     TOPICAL INDEX   445

                     NAMES INDEX   466

INTRODUCTION

Spiritual Theology: the very term—made up of the three words most sacred to Christians: *Theos, Logos, Spiritus*—contains a juxtaposition to be reflected upon. It is true that words, like garments, become shopworn after long use. What a delight it is to come upon words once more adorned in their ancient splendor.

Such is the case with the word 'theology'. The ancient christian East understood the practice of theology only as a personal communion with *Theos*, the Father, through the *Logos*, Christ, in the Holy Spirit—an experience lived in a state of prayer.[1] Consequently, it possessed no handbooks of 'spiritual theology' as we have them today; but manuals of instruction and nigh exhaustive treatises on prayer abounded. Theophane the Recluse, the greatest writer in the Russian spiritual tradition, emphasized this strongly by saying: 'Let us hope that someone will collect the prayers written by the holy Fathers, for they would make a true handbook of salvation.'[2]

It is, on the other hand, true that beginners in the life of the Spirit and of prayer are always in need of instruction. It was imperative they be given sound teaching, examples, and rules of conduct. May we not call Athanasius' *Life of Antony* the first handbook of asceticism and mysticism? *The Sayings of the [Desert] Fathers* are still more complete collections. They are presented in the form of aphorisms, a literary genre for which the East showed a distinct preference. Grouped by Centuries (hundreds), they contain spiritual 'sentences'[3] which are short, easy to remember, and clear, but also respectful of mystery. These sayings were learned by heart, ruminated, interpreted: and thus a spiritual tradition arose. Eastern Christendom began to take on its own character with certain unique features that early distinguished it from the Latin West. Various trends emerged in the East itself: ethnic, geographic, or historical areas developed their unique character. Within the Church universal, the true 'tradition' consists of *traditions*.

Nowadays 'spirituality', including its historical trends, is studied in a systematic manner. The ascetics of old would have said that it has become the object of 'simple knowledge',[4] which unfortunately complicates its spiritual simplicity. On the one hand, the christian East no longer appears [to Westerners] a virgin *terra incognita*. That gives us some satisfaction, but what pleases us still more is that nowadays no one any longer feels a need to build a dividing wall between the heirs of the two parts of the ancient Roman empire. On the other hand, one hardly dares speak in general terms about 'the spirituality of the christian East'. We realize that we must take its marked diversities into account.

Up till now all attempts to write a handbook on Eastern spirituality have ended in failure. And yet many want to have such a text to consult in their teaching, as a basis for further study, or as an introduction.

The courses of Irénée Hausherr, late professor at the Pontifical Oriental Institute in Rome and a Western pioneer in teaching Eastern spirituality, lie at the heart of the present undertaking. In his article on the Greek church (*Grecque, Église*),[5] Jean Kirchmeyer used Hausherr's typewritten syllabi. Relying heavily upon the work of our predecessors, we have devoted ourselves to the same task, but on a broader basis, by making use of our own course preparations and the publications we have already devoted to the subject.

A comprehensive study? That would be pretending too much. From the outset, our intention has been not to go beyond the confines of a handbook. As a prisoner, so to speak, of our constant desire to condense, we have too often had to put aside some of the loveliest texts, and not without regret; we were not always able to take certain nuances into account; we had to withhold our own opinion on some problem or other. Composing a handbook on the spiritual life is not altogether different from writing a work on art, music, or painting. A real manual must not start from a rigid framework or pretend that the rules it proposes are complete, infallible, and always and everywhere valid. Yet such 'rules', precisely because they are rules, are usually the result of a long experience lived first by those who had a sense of the beautiful and then by larger groups and circles. In this manner the original experience evolves into a tradition.

An analogy with sacred iconography is striking. Russian icons show a surprisingly rich combination of colors, and the register of feelings which they evoke varies greatly, while the lines and forms are almost always unchanging, as the iconographic canon demands. For a Western artist, to grow and become more skilled means to respond to the irresistible impulse to invent new forms, to 'restructure'. By contrast, the icon painter is happy to find unchangeable prototypes, an art form well protected against all individual expressions of personality.

In the same spirit the Eastern monks felt no need to 'reform' St Basil or 'modernize' St John Climacus. Yet over the centuries, their fidelity to the direction pointed out by the Fathers did not prevent them from adding a new coloring to Basilian or 'Sinaitic' outlines—a coloring they personally liked or one given to them, even imposed, by the palette of their ethnic surroundings. This approach unquestionably deserves more than a general overview, and will be the subject of a later publication. Before all else, we indispensibly need a preparation: it is our hope that this handbook, in sketching a general outline, will answer that need.

If a treatise on spirituality is to be a treatise on the Holy Spirit, any pretense of offering an exhaustive study would manifest nothing less than heresy. For this reason we appropriate the conclusion of St Basil, writing on the same topic:

> If you find what I have said unsatisfactory,...pray do not hesitate to pursue the investigation with all diligence and add to your information by asking questions, but not in a spirit of controversy. Either through me or through others the Lord will supply what is missing, according to the knowledge given to the worthy by the Holy Spirit.[6]

4 *Introduction*

Notes

1. See below, Chapter 13, *Theologia*.
2. Načertanie christianskogo nravoučenija *[Christian Moral Teaching]* (Moscow, 1895) 411; *Théophane le Reclus*, 239.
3. See Irénée Hausherr, 'Centuries'; DS 2/1 (1953) col. 416–18.
4. See below, Chapter 7, '*Sin as Ignorance*'.
5. DS 6: col. 808–72.
6. *De spiritu sancto*; PG 32: 217C. Annotated critical edition, SCh17 (1954). [English translation by B. Jackson, LNPF ser. 2, vol 8 (1895, rpt 1978); revised trans. by D. Anderson, *On the Holy Spirit* (New York: St Vladimir's Seminary Press, 1980). We gratefully acknowledge the assistance of Ms Barbara Mainz and of the Wichita State University Office of Research and Sponsored Programs in locating English translations of the various texts cited throughout this book —tr.]

1
SOURCES

1. COMMON SOURCES

Scripture

THE WORD OF GOD and the life of the believer are intimately connected. For the Word of God which reveals God's glory also inseparably reveals God's commandments: the believer must therefore bring his life into harmony with the Word.[1] The *novellae* of Justinian the Emperor, the advice given by Barsanuphius, the mystical secrets imparted by Symeon the New Theologian and others all witness uniformly to a submission to the rule of life, Scripture. But it was St Basil in particular who affirmed an immutable principle: that every word and action must be checked against the witness of Scripture,[2] for here he sought the *logion* (short rule) and the *politeia* (special instruction) to save his soul.[3]

Among contemplatives, one notices the symbolism of spiritual food, of eating Scripture: a biblical symbolism, certainly, but one which Origen inserted into the tradition. To him, Scripture and the Eucharist were intimately connected.[4] Since Scripture is one of the 'indwellings' of the divine *Logos*, a meditative reading of the sacred books helps, little by little, to unlock the divine secret hidden in our heart.[5]

Although the Desert Fathers did not often quote Scripture, they lived by it and were saturated with it.[6] A detailed study of *typica* and hagiographic texts gives us specific information about the monks' constant attention to Scripture. Seraphim of Sarov, for example, read the entire New Testament once a week.[7]

Reciting Scripture from memory was an activity practised and recommended by the ascetics.[8] Deeply imbued with sacred texts, some monks devoted themselves to repeating them ceaselessly for meditation[9] and used them for the spiritual guidance of others.[10] Ruminating certain passages in search of the spiritual sense often gives them a new flavor. 'While reading Scripture', Paul Evdokimov states, 'the Fathers read not words, but the living Christ, and Christ spoke to them. They consumed words in the manner of the Eucharistic bread and wine, and the word appeared to them in its Christ dimension'.[11] Accordingly, the inspiration and the divine nature of sacred texts were for the Fathers two concepts of equal value. The power of the Spirit is active in the world every time scriptural texts, especially the Psalms, are recited.[12]

Filled with mystery, Scripture is beyond human understanding. That is why purity of life is essential to reading it. We need only recall the example of St Dosithy who 'indeed began to understand certain passages from Scripture because of his purity'.[13] In the beautiful words of Evdokimov, the "incarnation" of Scripture presupposes a reaction by the one who is acted upon, a permeation, a *perichoresis* following the example of the two natures in Christ'.[14]

The Tradition of the Church

Eastern writers' esteem for the tradition of the Fathers is well known. We may cite an example from the *Spiritual Meadow* by John Moschus: 'If you find a maxim by Saint Athanasius and you have nothing to write it on, write it on your cloak!'[15]

The Fathers clearly distinguished two sources of faith: Scripture, and 'the mysteries of the Church which Scripture does not proclaim'.[16] They insisted on the need for the living, oral tradition.[17] Once the teaching of the Fathers was written down it in turn became 'divine Scripture'. Joseph of Volokolamsk, an ardent traditionalist, found this broadening of the term 'sacred Scripture' legitimate: 'We have received the testimony of Scripture, that is, of the Old Testament and the Prophets, of the holy Gospel and of the Apostles, and furthermore of all the writings left by the Fathers and Doctors of the Church.'[18] All were of equal value, for 'whoever writes in his own day for the Church is moved by the Holy Spirit'.[19]

The result was an occasionally excessive regard for books on spirituality,[20] a reluctance to express one's own opinion,[21] a duty-bound compulsion to adhere only to the compilations of 'Scripture',[22] because one felt unworthy of direct inspiration by the Holy Spirit.[23] Against such a bookish mentality there had to be a repeated insistence once again on living tradition, which implies 'the unceasing action of the Holy Spirit—an activity which can only find its fulfillment and come to fruition in the Church'.[24]

Consequently, when speaking of the 'traditionalism' of the Eastern Church one should keep in mind that for Eastern Christians, tradition means 'the life of the Church in which each one of her members can share according to his capacity. To be in the tradition means to share the experience of the mysteries revealed to the Church.'[25]

This living tradition cannot be separated from the prayer of the Church. This is why there is a close connection between dogma and devotion, which are inseparable in the consciousness of the Church.[26] St Irenaeus made the equation by stating that 'our doctrine is in agreement with the Eucharist and is confirmed by the Eucharist'.[27] In the words of Theodore the Studite, 'the liturgy recapitulates the economy of salvation.'[28]

Within this context the term 'Fathers' also received a wider meaning than is the case in modern patrologies. In the opinion of the spiritual writers, the 'divinely-inspired Fathers' were, as far as content was concerned, the monks of the desert and their heirs. Preference was given to the ascetical writings of the great Doctors of the Church. That the 'patristic age' had ended was scarcely credited. One of the great patristic anthologies is the *Synagogē* by Paul Evergetinos. Although he particularly venerated the moderns—in his view, Athanasius of Sinai, Euthymius the Younger, and others—could also be called 'Fathers', provided their holiness was visible. He viewed all of them as 'God-bearers' (*theophoroi*) and included their words as inspired Scripture.[29] The biographer of Symeon the New Theologian wrote of his hero that, 'His thought was like that of the Apostles, for he was animated by the movement of the Holy Spirit.... The faithful learned from his inspired writings.'[30]

Chapter One

Christianity and Cultural Traditions

Some historians study the teaching of Christianity[31] in connection with its judaic antecedents.[32] Others concentrate on how Christianity encountered cultures and civilizations that helped shape it or, on the contrary, were hostile to it.[33] Still others pay particular attention to pre-existing religious beliefs and practices, generally in order to point out comparisons and parallels.[34]

It should be clear that the difficulty cannot be approached by means of a parallel which puts both 'systems' side by side. Nor is it enough to view the Christianity of some group as the result of syncretism. We do not want to speak of how Christianity 'adapted' itself to the Greek, Syrian, or Russian environment. If a term is needed, it would be best to speak of a progressive 'incarnation' of the divine life into the traditions and the concrete humanity of various cultures, an incarnation accomplished by Christ in the Spirit. This is a progressive and dynamic 'deification'. How deeply the various cultures espouse progressive christianization depends on the depth of their moral and spiritual convictions.

To contrast Hebrew with Greek reflection, to understand the African attitude toward reality is undoubtedly useful. Yet one should avoid any direct comparisons between 'Christianity' on the one hand and, on the other, Greek, Egyptian, or Slavic thought. For the christian life in its full sense becomes incarnated in these human situations.

This should not prevent us from comparing the various 'incarnations' to one another: the oldest, the judaic form, to that of the hellenistic world; or the Armenian to the Georgian, and so on. No one doubts that a comparison between judaeo-christian religion and hellenized Christianity holds a special interest to those trying to understand the characteristics of the spirituality of the christian East.

The Judaeo-Christian Environment

Christianity appeared on the scene as a movement within Judaism. Christian theological concerns and institutions owe a great deal to this original environment. Today we realize more and more how the ancient semitic way of viewing reality and the problems of the spiritual life differed from that of the greco-roman world. Our attention is drawn, for example, to the contrast between dynamic and static thought, between the subjective and the objective, between a concern for matter and a concern for form, between an accoustic and a visual sensibility, and between the concrete and the abstract.[35]

On the other hand, we discover that judaeo-christian theology is indeed a theology in the true sense of the word: an attempt to create a total overview, an abiding concern to indicate that all the events in the life of Christ and of the Church are realizations of God's eternal plan. Judaeo-christian theology is a theology of history but it has a cosmic character: the activity of the Word, prefigured in the history of Israel, fills all the spiritual space there is, and all of creation. Several elements of this primitive theology have passed into the tradition of the Greek Fathers, and they continue to live especially among Christians of semitic extraction — Syrians, Ethiopians — and also among Armenians.[36]

Hellenism

Christianity had its roots in a judaic world already in contact with Hellenism and no doubt already partly hellenized. To oversimplify, we may say that primitive Christianity grew on the eastern shores of the mediterranean basin and in a Greek (and, soon, a greco-roman) setting.

In such a cultural and spiritual climate, the Fathers were exposed in the schools above all to philosophic doctrines which, more than anything else, created the atmosphere in which they lived: an eclectic philosophy, some sort of philosophic-religious *koinē*, a mixture of popularized Stoicism, Pythagoreanism, Middle Platonism, and later Neoplatonism. When compared to that of the classical era, this type of philosophy presents a character of its own, a specifically moral and religious orientation.

The influence of this type of philosophy on the development of christian dogma has been amply demonstrated.[37] Here we ask ourselves whether and to what extent the spiritual teaching and the practice of Christianity received the imprint of Hellenism.[38] We must think in terms of a subtle interplay of action and reaction rather than of a systematic influence. The Fathers were Greeks who became Christians. Yet, it is evident that the 'christianization' of a person, still more of a cultural climate, admits of innumerable shades and degrees.

The Fathers and Philosophy

Many early writers were deeply engaged in stressing the gulf between the wisdom of the world and the wisdom of God (Cf. Rm 1:18, 2:14 ff). Was pagan philosophy not the realm of the demon, of error?[39] Was it not, at least, a vanity,[40] the realm of opinion,[41] 'merely a human tradition'?[42] Yet halfway through the second century, Justin Martyr, a converted philosopher, continued to be enamored of the philosophies of his day.[43] At Alexandria, the chief intellectual center of the empire, the capital of Hellenism and Judaism, the crossroads of all types of Eastern wisdom, the problem became acute. Clement of Alexandria clearly saw the insufficiency, even the danger, of an entirely negative attitude.[44] Origen's most original contribution was his ability to synthetize two contradictory attitudes which had existed before his time. First, he unmasked an idolatrous thrust in the wisdom of the pagan philosophers: the philosopher idolizes the creation of his own mind; he makes his own truth instead of accepting it from God. For Christians the danger was very real: 'Philosophy is a golden ingot.'[45] On the other hand, Origen was convinced that by rejecting pagan philosophy altogether the Christian would be somehow condemned to remain poverty-stricken in the midst of wealth in that he would not be allowed to use his human power of reasoning and articulation to defend, communicate, and explore such wealth.[46]

Subsequently, one finds them admitting that philosophy was useful as a preparation for the revelation of the Gospel,[47] though some also stated that the revelation of Scripture is a light which, like the sun, overwhelms and dims the lamplight of philosophy.[48] Finally, spiritual writers felt a real fear of the 'golden ingot' of rational constructs, because they understood the essential difference between 'mere' knowledge and 'spiritual' knowledge, and the danger of mistaking the former for true knowledge.[49] They were confronted by the ambiguity of the [later] formula *Fides quaerens intellectum*,[50] knowing full well that faith seeks *gnōsis*, contemplation.[51]

'Heterodox' Authors

Declared 'heretics' often became masters of the spiritual life in christian communities which condemned their theological errors but were quite unable to reproach them for their ascetic and mystical points of view. Greek literature offers famous examples: from the beginning of the sixth century Origen was given the epithet 'impious'. And yet, the more one studies the history of spirituality the more one becomes aware of his influence. The *Spiritual Homilies* of pseudo-Macarius might contain condemned propositions from the *Ascetic Book* of the Messalians, and yet they have delighted christian souls for centuries.[52] Isaac of Nineveh, the great mystic held in high honor by the Byzantines and the Russians, was a Nestorian bishop.[53] Abba Isaiah, included in the *Philokalia*, was a Monophysite.[54]

Spirituality is living dogma.[55] Nonetheless, spiritual doctrine does not consist of abstract deductions. The truth of spiritual knowledge possesses a different hierarchy of principles than that which can be deduced from an *a priori* speculative synthesis. Doctrinal heresy consists in 'the choices' made from among the truths of faith. The spiritual teaching of an 'heretic' will be wrong if it is based upon such a choice. For the true spiritual writer this is impossible because he follows the principle that *praxis*, the observance of all the commandments and especially that of charity, proves the correctness of *theōria*, of spiritual knowledge.[56]

2. THE SPIRITUAL LITERATURE OF THE VARIOUS CHURCHES

Greek and Byzantine

The first Greek spiritual writers were, of course, the ancient Fathers. The christian East has never forgotten them. Let us be satisfied with a few observations for those who approach patristics today from that angle.

The space devoted to a work in handbooks on patristics is not always indicative of its real influence; the ascetics often read and reread booklets which are scarcely mentioned in patristic manuals: *centuries*, that is, collections of sayings grouped by hundreds.¹ Furthermore, complete works were not always available. Instead there were collections of homilies,² *florilegia* (especially the *Pandects* by Nikon of the Black Mountain,³ the *Synagogē* by Paul Evergetinos⁴ and more recently the *Philokalia* by Nicodemus the Hagiorite⁵). Every church, every spiritual movement, and almost every monastery has its Fathers at its disposal, writers chosen by ideological criteria or by simple convenience.

Let us mention a few works which are indispensable for an understanding of spirituality: Origen's treatise *On Prayer*, Athanasius' *Life of Antony*, *The Sayings of the [Desert] Fathers*, the *Lausiac History* by Palladius, the *Spiritual Meadow* by John Moschus, the *Philotheus* (or *Religious History*) by Theodoret of Cyrus, the *Rules* by Basil the Great, the *Life of Moses* and the *Homilies on the Song of Songs* by Gregory of Nyssa, *Chapters on Prayer* and the *Praktikos* by Evagrius Ponticus, *One Hundred Chapters on Spiritual Perfection* by Diadochus of Photice, the *Four Centuries on Charity* by Maximus the Confessor, and the *Ladder of Paradise* by John Climacus. Among the Western Fathers the *Dialogues* of Gregory the Great were read in the East, hence his surname Gregory Dialogos. Cassian, who wrote in Latin, had nonetheless an Eastern background.

The first great name to present itself in Byzantine times is Theodore the Studite (d. 826), a reformer of monastic life 'according to the Fathers', in the spirit of Basilian cenobitism.⁶ Not much ascetical literature was produced during the ninth and tenth centuries. Into this environment, threatened with aridity, came a seed of renewal from Syrian-speaking Persia: the Greek version of Isaac of Nineveh. It was, in fact, the contemplative doctrine of Evagrius returned to his own people.⁷

The eleventh century has given us a few famous *typica* (of the monastery of Evergetis, by Pacourianos, Alexis of Studios, and Michael Attaliate), important documents for monasticism,⁸ as well as an illustrious name in the history of mysticism, Symeon the New Theologian (d. 1022). Especially since the fourteenth century he has received due honor, along with his disciple-biographer, Nicetas Stethatos.⁹

At the beginning of the fourteenth century Gregory of Sinai¹⁰ ushered in the most famous mystical revival of all Byzantine history, Athonite hesychasm.¹¹ In his theological synthesis, Gregory

Palamas (d. 1359) posited man's deification, of which the 'Taborite light' would be the manifestation.[12] Among his adherents a place of honor was given to Nicholas Cabasilas, whose work the *Life in Christ* is considered one of the great masterpieces of Byzantine spirituality.[13]

For the centuries that follow we will limit ourselves to citing the titles and authors which the editors of the *Philokalia* deemed worthy of being included in their collection: the *Hagioritic Tome* drawn up by Philotheus Coccinos, the *Century* by Callistus and Ignatius of Xanthopoulos, Symeon of Thessalonica, and a few others.

For two hundred years the most widespread manual on asceticism was *The Salvation of Sinners* by Agapios Landos (d. 1664).[14] At the end of the eighteenth century the Greek church experienced a profound spiritual renewal, the main architects of which were Macarius of Corinth (d. 1805) and Nicodemus of Naxos, surnamed the Hagiorite (d. 1809). They published the *Philokalia of Neptic Saints*,[15] a collection of particularly significant texts on prayer and the hesychast life ranging from the Desert Fathers to the theoreticians of the neo-hesychast method. The impact of this famous anthology was especially felt in nineteenth-century Russia.[16] Very popular even to our day has been *Unseen Warfare* by the same Nicodemus the Hagiorite: it is a Greek adaptation of Lorenzo Scupoli's *Spiritual Warfare*.[17]

Coptic[18]

From the second to the fifth century, Egypt was the chosen land of a christian spirituality expressed in Greek. Alongside this learned and especially Alexandrian spirituality, however, there developed in Christian Egypt a native form expressed in Coptic, the final evolution of ancient Egyptian existing in various dialects. From the literary point of view the principal dialect was that of the South, Sahidic. The dialects of Middle Egypt—Sahidic, Akhimic, Sub-Akhimic, and Fayumic—were used in the composition of numerous apocryphal texts and Manichean writings. Bohairic, the dialect of Nitria, developed last as a literary language, especially when translations were made from Sahidic manuscripts for the monastery of St Macarius, which became the center of the Egyptian church in the ninth and tenth centuries. After that, Coptic had to compete more and more with Arabic.

In numerous Old and New Testament Apocrypha it is often hard to distinguish between texts of Gnostic, Manichaean, and orthodox origin. A taste for the marvellous, combined with aspirations to the highest forms of christian heroism, was satisfied through hagiographic texts. In Coptic manuscripts, writings of monastic origin occupy an important place, for Coptic was the only language known by the majority of ancient monks. Nonetheless, it is true that Coptic contains a great number of Greek loan-words.

Ethiopian

During the Axumite era (fifth-seventh centuries) translations were made from Greek originals. Original texts were produced more abundantly 1) under Abuna Salama (metropolitan from 1350 to 1390) who gave an impetus to hagiographic writings; 2) in the reign of Zar'a Yakob(1434–1468) who gave a rule of faith to his people and legislated in the name of the Church; 3) during the seventeenth century when the arrival of Jesuit missionaries gave rise to theological discussions; 4) finally, during the Monophysite reaction of the eighteenth century.

Ethiopian literature often expresses the unique mentality of the country. Its spiritual teaching is found disseminated among Acts of the Martyrs, biographies of founders, apocryphal writings, liturgical hymns, and even legal codes. Devotion to Mary, which was one of the glories of the Ethiopian church, gave rise to a beautiful affective poetry. *The Book of the Miracles of Mary (Ta'amra Mâryâm)*, of French origin and translated into Arabic, spread to Egypt and Ethiopia during the thirteenth century, and remains a favorite text to this day. Apocryphal and apocalyptic texts have always had great success in Ethiopia; they continue the tradition of Scripture in form and thought, which gives this type of writing a great advantage.[19]

Syrian

The name Syrian is given not only to the inhabitants of Syria but also to those whose ritual used, or uses, Syriac; the Jacobites, the Nestorians, the Maronites, the Syro-Malabarese. Most of their authors wrote in Syriac, although after the Arab conquest several were led to adopt the language of the conqueror. Syrian spiritual literature is extremely rich.[20]

Among the Syrian Church Fathers the two most illustrious names come from the fourth century: Aphraates (Aphrahat)[21] and Ephrem.[22] John the Solitary (of Apamea)[23] distinguished himself in the fifth century. The most notable writers of the sixth century were James of Sarug,[24] Philoxenes of Mabbug,[25] and Stephen Bar Soudaili.[26] In the seventh century we find James of Edessa[27] and Dadišo Quatraya[28] whose book, *The Solitude of Seven Weeks*,[29] is an almost complete treatment of asceticism and mysticism. The writings of Isaac of Nineveh (who died at the end of the seventh century)[30] were highly successful in the monastic circles of nearly all Eastern churches. He was a true mystic who in his personal search of God profited from the spiritual experience of others, especially Evagrius Ponticus, the unrivalled master. We may also cite John of Dalyatha (eighth century),[31] James bar Salibi (d. 1171),[32] John son of Abu Zakarija,[33] a thirteenth-century Arab author, and many others.

Syrian ascetical teaching goes back to primitive spirituality with no loss of originality. It was based on the hope of 'the life following the Resurrection' (John the Solitary). Their concern with precision led several authors to what may be called a scientific description of the movements of the soul, of the passions, and of states of prayer. Certainly, their psychological observations were generally more refined than those of the Greeks.

Their sacred hymnography and the metrical homilies (*memrē*) contain passages which are among the most beautiful christian poetry ever written. Their many commentaries on the books of the Old and New Testament urgently invite one to look upon the mysteries of Scripture with the eyes of a child. The deeds of the patriarchs, the imagery of the Church as the bride of Christ, and rules for daily living were explored in terms of their Christ typology.

Armenian

Armenian literature extends from Mesrob (d. 441) to the present. Like Syrian literature, it was essentially religious. The Armenians did a great deal of translating, especially during the fifth, eighth, and eleventh centuries. After the early fifth century, however, their authors also composed original texts. In the tenth century, the greatest of them, Gregory of Nareg—called 'the Armenian Pindar'—wrote a *Commentary on the Song of Songs*,[34] taking his inspiration from the Greek Fathers and the panegyrists. His main work, however, which the Armenians through autonomasy call 'the Nareg', consists of a collection of ninety-two *Sacred Elegies* or elevations—prayers, we would say.[35]

For Armenian literature the thirteenth century marked the end of good times. It was only during the eighteenth century that schools and printing houses spread across Europe and gave some luster back to literature. For the Armenians the true renewal, however, only came with the Mechitarists.[36]

The general features of Armenian spirituality arise from the vicissitudes of history: catastrophes are hardly conducive to the development of great theological syntheses. Monasticism followed St Basil and was deeply attached to the liturgy. A predilection for the traditional and the practical followed from this and above all a great number of hymns, prayers, and elevations to God, some of which are among the most beautiful within the mystical tradition anywhere.[37]

Georgian

Georgian spiritual literature is largely composed of translations from Greek, Armenian, Syriac, and Arabic. At the beginning of the seventh century the Georgian church broke its ties with the Armenian, and has since then followed Chalcedonian orthodoxy and Byzantine literature.

During the 'Golden Age' from the establishment of the monastery of Iviron on Mount Athos in 980 to the middle of the thirteenth century, Georgian literature was enriched with innumerable versions of ascetical texts by the active translators of the Athonite school and their followers: Euthymius the Hagiorite (d. 1028),[38] St George the Hagiorite (d. 1065), Theophilus (eleventh-twelfth centuries), Ephrem Mtsirē ('the minor', *fl.* 1100), Arsenius of Iqualto (d. *c.* 1130), John Petritsi (d. *c.* 1125), and others.

In narrative literature a certain number of works dependent on the Greek tradition are worthy of note: for instance, *The Lives of the Syrian Fathers* — the thirteen monks who introduced monasticism into Georgia — and, in the sixth century, the legend of *Barlaam and Joasaph*. Even though it remained within the fold of Chalcedonian orthodoxy, the Georgian church nonetheless retained certain Eastern non-byzantine traits by which it was able to maintain its individuality.[39]

Russian

Russian spirituality sprang from the traditions of the ancient Fathers and from Byzantine trends. It came under Western influence at the beginning of the seventeenth century. Over the centuries these traditions merged and were adapted to the needs of the peoples' mentality. The most ancient sources of Russian spirituality are the numerous, and much recopied biographies of saints. Monasticism became popular at the beginning of the eleventh century. The exemplary lives of the first ascetics of Kiev were early collected in the *Pechersky Paterikon*.[40] Monastic *Rules* appeared later, especially those of Nilus of Sora (d. 1508)[41] and Joseph of Volokolamsk (d. 1515).[42] The monks gave Russia its best writers: Dmitri of Rostov (d. 1709),[43] Tikhon of Zadonsk (d. 1783),[44] Paisius Velichkovsky (d. 1794),[45] and Theophane the Recluse (d. 1804).[46]

It should be noted that the works of modern Russian authors and thinkers have a basically religious character: Dostoevsky (d. 1888), Soloviev (d. 1900), and Florensky (d. probably in 1946).

To grasp the distinctive features of Russian spirituality, however, we must pay special attention to the living traditions of popular piety, the teaching of spiritual directors (the famous *startzy*), and the rituals and customs of the Church in the various areas.

3. THE TRENDS IN EASTERN SPIRITUALITY

Distinguishing Criteria

In the West, schools of spirituality are differentiated by, for example, religious order or country. There are no religious orders in the East, and although the countries are different the issues of ethnicity have not encroached too much upon spiritual teaching. The same criteria can therefore not be used in the East as in the West to distinguish between schools.[1]

Yet, to identify 'Eastern spirituality' with some coordinated system of common principles would be a very serious mistake. The same terminology often covers a variety of meanings ranging from an exaggerated mysticism to a sterile moralizing, all the while passing along the middle road, in itself broad enough, of spiritual orthodoxy.

Spirituality encompasses all of life and develops within history. But an eventless history or a history of ideas without either innovation or discussion would be an absence of history. History does not follow a prefabricated plan. One observes and admires it, discerning within it the manifold wisdom of God (Cf. Eph 3:10). On the other hand, one explores a forest by blazing trails in various directions. Could something similar be done on the terrain of spirituality? Where is the distinguishing criterion to be found? Once external circumstances are removed, what remains is the intrinsic character of the spiritual life itself, that is, the divine life which actualizes human life—a life which is inserted in the created order and develops historically.

Full and perfect deification may be viewed as the unique goal of human existence. And yet, the manner in which this goal is envisaged and achieved will vary according to one's understanding of human life itself: whether we feel we can fully develop our powers through external action or deepen our capacity to know God by reflecting on him in mind or heart, alone or with the help of the visible cosmos and human society.

It is this perspective—at once anthropological, cosmological, and sociological—which we have chosen in order to outline the five basic trends of Eastern spirituality. History clearly shows that the distinguishing criteria are not mere abstractions: concrete events have proven that these trends are real.

'Practical' Primitive Spirituality

Christianity appeared first as a judaic movement. Theological themes and christian institutions owe a great deal to their place of origin.[2] The relationship between God and his people was molded by the framework of the Covenant—a relationship which called not for abstract speculation but for observance of the commandments.[3] Christians believed and lived their faith in quiet obedience to the gospel tradition as long as no philosophers stepped forward to attempt to put Christianity into a systematic mold. This period continued a longer or shorter time depending on the region. It lasted longer in areas which Christianity penetrated before hellenistic philosophy: Syria and the Syriac-speaking territories (Aphrahat, Ephrem, and, at the beginning of the sixth century, James of Sarug). There, a discreet, balanced psychology is found together with a miraculously complete dogmatic teaching, and an ethic fully permeated with charity. This 'practical' trend never disappeared altogether and found enthusiastic followers among the great spiritual masters of the East.

Intellectualized Spirituality and the Origin of Mysticism

Such a concept was not to satisfy thinkers steeped in the type of Hellenism that long before had heard from Anaxogoras himself that the end of life consists of *theōria*, knowledge, understanding, contemplation—an axiom preserved by Clement of Alexandria.[4] Thus arose the surprising phenomenon that faith and works do not directly lead to perfection but serve as an intoduction to the one *praxis* fully suited to humans, contemplation.

Although Evagrius in the fourth century established the framework of *theōria*, he did not give final shape to its content. Many others also contributed to it. The richness of a long contemplative tradition allowed Macarius of Corinth (d. 1805) and his friends to compile the famous *Philokalia*,[5] 'the very instrument of *theosis*', Nicodemus the Hagiorite said in the Prologue.[6]

The question sometimes arises whether the Greek Fathers' enthusiasm for *theōria* stemmed from Scripture or was inherited from philosophy.[7] One thing is certain: contemplative Christians faced a serious problem from the outset. Was the experience of the divine to be situated only on the plane of reason or was it possible to consider a direct contact with God, beyond any intermediate concept or image?[8] It was realized more and more that 'spiritual' reality in the christain sense could not be identified with the 'intellectual' in the greek sense.[9] The traditional picture of Moses ascending Mount Sinai may help clarify the issue. One climbs with great difficulty from one intellectual concept to another and once the most sublime level of speculation has been reached one discovers that God is still far away; thereupon one chooses another path, that of 'ignorance' and that of 'love' or 'ecstasy'.[10]

Experiencing God, The Mysticism Of The Heart

Is the experience of the Spirit reserved solely for mystical states? The term 'experience' is one of the key words of twentieth century thought: man is a psychological consciousness, an apperception grasping all inner reality. Does that also include the spirit of God?[11]

Aspirations towards a conscious experience of grace were not unknown in the ancient East.[12] Some writers even went so far as to state forcefully that to stop feeling the activity of the Holy Spirit amounted to losing the Spirit: 'Just as a pregnant woman feels the child moving in her womb, so we know that the spirit of God dwells in us on account of the joy, the happiness, and the exultation we feel in our heart.'[13]

The Messalians, who had insisted too strongly on the need to feel the state of grace sensibly, were condemned toward the close of the fourth century.[14] Orthodox authors never dreamed of denying the transcendence of God and the mysterious nature of his presence in man. If vivid feelings are not the sole and infallible manifestation of the divine life in man, 'they are nevertheless a sign of perfect spiritual health', noted Theophane the Recluse.[15]

Diadochus of Photice opposed the Messalians, and yet among the terms he frequently used are *aisthēsis* (sensation), *peira* (experience), and *plērophoria* (fullness).[16] Terms such as these were commonly used by all writers whose favorite texts were the *Spiritual Homilies* of pseudo-Macarius, by the hesychasts and all those who insisted on the value of the heart in the spiritual life.[17]

Cosmic Spirituality. The Veneration Of Images

The mysticism of the intellect condemned images and sensory expressions. For it the world of matter was a source of distraction.

For the eye of the mind to be opened,[18] the bodily eye had to be closed. The moment the gnostic's spiritual eye was illumined by faith and his gaze purified of all attachment to matter, however, he reverted to that earlier blessed state in which his surroundings were no longer a perilous temptation but a voice telling him of the Creator.[19]

All great contemplatives have expounded the principles of *theōria physikē* (natural contemplation),[20] but it was most frequently the unlearned ascetics, 'the pilgrims', who intently lived 'the Paschal joy of the Eastern Church',[21] and succeeded in retaining a vivid remembrance of God and Christ everywhere and in the presence of all creatures.[22] This, too, was the aim of Eastern iconography: to decipher the meaning of the visible forms we see, in order to grasp their divine meaning.[23]

The Cenobitic Trend, Ecclesial Spirituality

Those who best represent the contemplative tradition of the East, the hesychasts,[24] were convinced that perfect prayer flourished only in the desert, in solitude. All of reality, however, has been rehabilitated by the crucifixion of Christ. The Christian should therefore not exclude another possibility, that of living among men and holding converse with them while raising their minds to God, of being open to many human ideas and individual desires while making sure they do only the will of God.

In a way we can agree with Cassian's statement[25] that the cenobitic life dates back to the days of the Apostles and that the early christian community was a type of this life.[26] Yet cenobitism proper originated with Pachomius (d. 346) and had St Basil as its great legislator.[27] The ideal set forth by the Basilian *Rules* was to remain virtually unchanged in the East. The legislation of Justinian I contributed to such permanence, as did the later 'Studite reform' which exercised a profound influence on Byzantine and Russian monasticism and was inspired by 'fidelity to the Fathers'.[28] One has only to survey the history of Eastern monasticism[29] to realize how greatly its regulations, customs, terminology, and law are dependent upon the work of these great legislators.

Basilian cenobitism presupposed an evangelical life in common where the presence of others would not endanger one's union with God but would on the contrary, be of great help in not straying from it.[30] Furthermore, what was valid for the monastery became an ideal for the entire Church.[31] Consequently, among Christians there will always be those who speak fervently of the obligation to live within the Church, to think with her and participate fully in her life, because 'it has pleased God to entrust to her and her alone whatever is necessary to salvation'.[32]

Names Applied to Spiritual Doctrine

In order to bring light and coherence to life, the inspired word, the 'wisdom of God' (Cf. 1 Co 1:30), broke into the history of ideas during an age thoroughly imbued with the Greek spirit and its ideal of *philosophia*. Consequently, the Fathers presented the true Christians who lived their faith as perfect models of philosophers[33] and the *philosophic life* as not unlike the perfect life of ascetics.[34] *Asceticism* and *mystical* are terms of ancient Greek origin.[35] Only recently, however, have they appeared in the East as titles of works that systematically deal with the spiritual life.[36]

According to the accepted meaning of the term today, *theology* is the all-encompassing study of faith which deals with all of revelation and the faith corresponding to it.[37] A distinction has often been made between the two branches of this science: one deals with God himself; the other with God's works (*de operibus divinis*). Spiritual theology belongs to the second branch since man's sanctification is one of the 'works' of God. Such terminology does not correspond to the ancient tradition of the Greek Fathers. For them, *theologia* was 'knowledge of the Holy Trinity',[38] God's works belong to the *oikonomia*.[39] Following this tradition, we shall therefore speak not of 'spiritual theology' but of 'spiritual teaching' or, even better, of the teaching of spiritual writers, because true 'spiritual knowledge' is the result not of teaching but of personal prayer.[40]

Notes

1. COMMON SOURCES

1. See *The Shepherd of Hermas*, Vision I.3.3–4 and *passim*.
2. See Jean Gribomont, 'Les Règles Morales de saint Basile et le Nouveau Testament', *Studia Patristica* 1, TU 63 (Berlin, 1957) 416–26; *id.*, 'Obéissance

et Evangile selon saint Basile le Grand', *La vie spirituelle*, Suppl. VI (1952) 192–215; T. Špidlík, *La Sophiologie de S. Basile*, 167ff.
3. See Irénée Hausherr, *Noms du Christ et voies d'oraison*, OCA 157 (1960), 162ff. [English translation by Ch. Cummings, *The Name of Jesus*, CS 44 Kalamazoo, 1978].
4. *Homilies on the Hexateuch, Ex.* 13.3; ed. Baehrens, GCS 6: 274; see Henri de Lubac, *Histoire et Esprit* (Paris, 1950) 355ff.
5. de Lubac, 349.
6. See Louis Leloir, 'La Bible et les Pères du désert d'après les deux collections arméniennes des Apophthegmes', in *La "Bible et les Pères"* (Paris: Presses Universitaires de France, 1971) 112–34.
7. See E. Posseljanin, *Russkie podvižniki XIX-ogo věka* [*Russian Ascetics of the Nineteenth Century*] (St Petersburg, 1910) 272.
8. See *Historia monachorum* 2; PL 21:406B [English translation by Norman Russell, *Lives of the Desert Fathers*, CS 34 (1981); Palladius, *Historia Lausiaca* 10.17; Pg 34: 1033, 1041 [English translation by Robert T. Meyer, ACW 34 (Washington-London, 1965)]; Athanasius, *Vita Antonii* 3; PG 26:835A. [English translation by M. M. Müller, *Early Christian Biographies*, FC 15 (Washington, 1952)].
9. See Heinrich Bacht, '"Meditari" in den ältesten Mönchsquellen', *Geist und Leben* 28 (1955) 360–73; Hausherr, *Noms du Christ*, 171; René Draguet, *Les Pères du désert* (Paris, 1949) 155; Špidlík, *Théophane le Reclus*, 267.
10. See T. Špidlík, 'L'autorità del libro per il monachesimo russo', in *Monachesimo orientale*, OCA 153 (1958) 169ff.
11. *La femme et le salut du monde* (Tournai-Paris, 1958) 12.
12. See de Lubac, *Histoire et Esprit*, 299ff., Abba Marcel in John Moschus, *Le pré spirituel* 152; SCh 12 (1946) 204ff.
13. *Vie de saint Dosithée* 12; SCh 92 (1963) 143.
14. *La femme et le salut du monde*, 13.
15. N. 40; SCh 12 (1946) 84.
16. Basil, *Tractatus de spiritu sancto* 27; PG 32:193A.
17. See Špidlík, *La sophiologie de S. Basile*, OCA 162: 172ff.
18. See *Joseph de Volokolamsk: un chapitre de la spiritualité russe*, OCA 146 (Rome, 1956) 10. [For an English translation of the Rule, consult *The Monastic Rule of Iosif Volotsky*, trans. David M. Goldfrank, CS 36 (1983).]
19. *Joseph de Volokolamsk*.
20. See Špidlík, 'L'autorità del libro', OCA 153; 159–79; *id.*, 'Der Einfluss Cyrillo-methodianischer Uebersetzungen auf die Mentalität der russischen Mönche', in Franz Zagiba, *Annales Instituti Slavici, Acta Congressus . . . Salisburgensis* I.4 (Wiesbaden, 1968) 95–102; *id.*, 'La spiritualità di monaci greci in Italia. Alcuni aspetti particolari', in *La Chiesa greca in Italia . . .* (Padua, 1973) 1201–4.
21. See *Joseph de Volokolamsk*, 95
22. See 'L'autorità del libro', 167ff.
23. See *Joseph de Volokolamsk*, 9.
24. Vladimir Lossky, *In the Image and Likeness of God* (Crestwood, New York: St Vladimir's Seminary Press, 1967) 198.
25. Lossky, *The Mystical Theology of the Eastern Church* (London, 1957) 236.
26. Lossky, *In the Image and Likeness of God*, 196.
27. *Adversus haereses* IV.18.5; SCh 100 (1965).
28. *Antirrheticos* I.38; PG 99:339C.

Chapter One

29. See Irénée Hausherr, 'Paul Evergetinos a-t-il connu Syméon le Nouveau Théologien?', OCP 23 (1957) 58–79; *id.*, *Etudes de spiritualité orientale*, OCA 183 (Rome, 1969) 262–83.
30. *Id.*, 'Syméon le Nouveau Théologien', *Or. Christ.* 12 (Rome, 1928) 97.
31. See Wilhelm Classen, *Eintritt des Christentums in die Welt: der Sieg des Christentums auf dem Hintergrunde der untergehenden antiken Kultur* (Gotha, 1930); Michel Spanneut, *Le Stoïcisme des Pères de l'Eglise de Clément de Rome à Clément d'Alexandrie* (Paris, 1957) 57ff.
32. See Rudolf Bultmann, *Das Urchristentum im Rahmen der antiken Religionen*, in Erasmus Bibliothek (Zürich, 1949).
33. See A. Causse, *Essai sur le conflit du christianisme primitif et de la civilisation* (Paris, 1920); L. Rougier, *Celse ou conflit de la civilisation antique et du christianisme primitif* (Paris, 1926).
34. T. Zielinski, *La Sibylle, trois essais sur la religion et le christianisme*, in the collection *Christianisme*, ed. Paul-Louis Couchoud (Paris, 1924); Martin P. Nilsson, *A History of Greek Religion*, vol. 2, trans. F. Fielden, (New York, 1964); Mircea Eliade, *History of Religions* (Chicago, 1959).
35. See Thorleif Boman, *Das hebräische Denken im Vergleich mit dem griechischen* (5th ed., Göttingen, 1968).
36. See above, *Syrian*.
37. See Aloys Grillmeier, 'Hellenisierung-Judaisierung des Christentums als Deuteprinzipien der Geschichte des kirchlichen Dogmas', *Scholastik* 33 (1958) 321–35, 528–58.
38. Hausherr contrasts what he calls 'primitive spirituality' to 'intellectualized spirituality', the heir of a Platonic psychology aspiring to contemplation; see below, 'Intellectualized Spirituality'.
39. To Tertullian, philosophy was the parent of heresies. He sharply condemned the various leaders of schools, especially in *De praescriptione*. [For a translation, see *The Prescription Against Heretics*, ANF 3 (rpt Grand Rapids, 1978) 244–65].
40. See *La sophiologie de S. Basile*, 142: 'Renouncing outside wisdom'.
41. *Ibid.*, 143f.
42. Basil's *Moralia* are excerpts from Holy Scripture designed to discourage following 'human traditions' (12.2; PG 31:724A).
43. See N. Hyldahl, *Philosophie und Christentum. Eine Interpretation der Einleitung zum Dialog Justin*. Acta Theologica Danica 9 (Copenhagen, 1966).
44. See Eugène de Faye, *Clément d'Alexandrie*, 2d ed., (Paris, 1906); see GCS 4: 790ff. (*Indices*).
45. In Librum Jesu Nave *Homilia* 7.7; GCS 7:334, 5.
46. See Henri Crouzel, *Origène et la philosophie* (Paris, 1962).
47. See Basil's famous *Ad adolescentes: sermo de legendis libris gentilium*; PG 31:464–589. [English trans., F. M. Padelford, *Address to Young Men on the Right Use of Greek Literature*: Essays on the Study and Use of Poetry by Plutarch and Basil the Great (New York, 1902) 97–120].
48. See Clement of Alexandria, *Stromata* V.26.6; GCS 2:345, 8ff.
49. See below, Chapter 7, *Sin as Ignorance*.
50. See Max Seckler, 'Foi', *EF* II, 148.
51. See Chapter 13, *From Faith to Gnosis*.
52. Hermann Dörries, *Symeon von Mesopotamien. Die Ueberlieferung der messalianischen 'Makarios' Schriften* (Leipzig, 1941).
53. E. Khalifé-Hachem, 'Isaac de Ninive', DS 7/2: 2041–54.
54. Lucien Regnault, 'Isaïe de Scété ou de Gaza', DS 7/2; 2083–95.

55. Hausherr, 'Dogme et spiritualité orientale', OCA 183 (Rome, 1969) 145–79; K. Hörmann, *Leben in Christus. Zusammenhänge zwischen Dogma und Sitte bei den Apostolischen Vätern* (Vienna, 1952).
56. See below, *Conclusion*.

2. THE SPIRITUAL LITERATURE OF THE VARIOUS CHURCHES

1. See Irénée Hausherr, 'Centuries', DS 2/1: 416–18.
2. See Réginald, Grégoire, 'Homiliaires orientaux', DS 7/2: 606–17.
3. The first chapters have been edited by V. N. Beneševič (St Petersburg, 1917); see Charles de Clercq, *Les textes juridiques dans les Pandectes de Nicon de la Montagne Noire*. Codif. can. orient., Fonti, II, 30 (Venice, 1942).
4. (Constantinople, 1861; 5th ed., Athens, 1957).
5. First published at Venice, 1782; the most recent edition was published at Athens, 1957. The most complete Russian edition is by Theophane the Recluse (Moscow, 1884–1905); for other Russian translations, see Un moine de l'Église d'Orient, *La prière de Jésus* (Chevetogne, 1963) 56ff, and I. Smolitsch, *Kleine Philokalie* (Cologne) 19ff. A complete English translation is now in the process of publication under the direction of G. E. H. Palmer, Philip Sherrard, and Kallistos Ware, *The Philokalia. The Complete Text* (London: Faber & Faber, 1979–). Other modern language translations offer only excerpts: in English, E. Kadloubovski and G. E. H. Palmer, *Writings from the Philokalia on Prayer of the Heart* (London, 1951), and *Early Fathers from the Philokalia* (London, 1954); in German, Matthias Dietz, *Kleine Philokalie* (Cologne), introduction by I. Smolitsch; in French, *Petite Philocalie de la prière du coeur* (Paris, 1953); in Italian, G. Vannucci, *La Filocalia* (Florence, 1963²)
6. Hausherr, *Saint Théodore Studite. L'homme et l'ascète (d'après ses Catéchèses)*, OCA 22, vol.6/1 (Rome, 1926).
7. See above, *Armenian*.
8. See Emil Herman, 'Ricerche sulle istituzioni monastiche bizantine', *OCP* 6 (1940) 293–375; Špidlík, 'Bizantino monachesimo', DIP 1 (1974) 1466ff.
9. Edited and translated into French in SCh 51, 81, 96, 104, 113, 122, 156, 174. [*The Catechetical Discourses* of Symeon the New Theologian have been translated by C. J. deCatanzaro in The Classics of Western Spirituality (New York: Paulist Press, 1982); *The Practical and Theological Chapters and The Three Theological Discourses* by Paul McGuckin, Cistercian Studies Series 41 (1982)]
10. Jean Darrouzès, 'Grégoire le Sinaïte', DS 6: 1011–14.
11. Pierre Adnès, 'Hésychasme', DS 7/1: 381–99; see below, Chapter 8, *The Solitary Life*.
12. See John Meyendorff, *St. Grégoire Palamas et la mystique orthodoxe* (Paris, 1959). [English trans. A. Fiske, *St. Gregory Palamas and Orthodox Spirituality* Crestwood, 1974], see Chapter 13, *The Glory of God*.
13. Nicholas Cabasilas, *The Life in Christ*; PG 150:491–726; English tr. by C. deCatanzaro (Crestwood, N.Y., 1974); French tr. by S. Broussaleux (Chevetogne, 1960, 2d ed.); German tr. by E. von Ivánka (Klosterneuburg, 1958); Italian tr. with an edition of the Greek text by U. Neri (Turin, 1971).
14. Venance Grumel, 'Agapios Landos', DS 1 (1937) col. 248–50; I. Hausherr, 'Dogme et spiritualité orientale', RAM 23 (1947) 26ff; *id., Études de spiritualité orientale*, OCA 183 (1969) 168ff.

26   Chapter One

15. See above.
16. Un moine de l'Eglise orthodoxe Roumaine (Scrima), 'L'avènement philocalique dans l'Orthodoxie roumaine', *Istina* (1958) 295-328, 443-74.
17. See Marcel Viller, 'Nicodème l'Agiorite et ses emprunts à la littérature spirituelle occidentale. Le combat spirituel et les Exercices de S. Ignace dans l'Eglise byzantine', RAM 5 (1924) 174-77; Theophane the Recluse made a Russian translation and adaptation of *Unseen Warfare* (Moscow, 1892), and an English translation of this Russian version was made by E. Kadloubovsky and G. E. H. Palmer, *Unseen Warfare* (London: Faber & Faber, Crestwood: St Vladimir's, 1952).
18. Antoine Guillaumont, 'Copte (littérature spirituelle)', DS 2/2: 2266-78 (bibliogr.); see below, *Bibliography*: Copts.
19. See the *Bibliography*.
20. See the *Bibliography*.
21. Hausherr, 'Aphraate (Afrahat)', DS 1: 746-752.
22. Edmund Beck, Demetrios Hemmerdinger, Iliadou, and Jean Kirchmeyer, 'Ephrem'; DS 4/1: 788-822.
23. Bruce Bradley, 'Jean le Solitaire (d'Apamée)', DS 8: 764-72.
24. François Graffin, 'Jacques de Saroug', DS 8: 56-60.
25. Hausherr, 'Contemplation et sainteté. Une remarquable mise au point par Philoxène de Mabboug (d. 523)' RAM 14 (1933) 171-95; *id.*, 'Hésychasme et prière', OCA 176 (Rome, 1966) 15-37; E. Lemoine, 'La spiritualité de Philoxène', *L'Orient Syrien* 2 (1957) 351-66.
26. A. Guillaumont, 'Etienne Bar Soudaïlî', DS 4/2: 1481-88.
27. F. Graffin, 'Jacques d'Edesse', DS 8: 34-35.
28. A Guillaumont, 'Dadišo Quatraya', DS 3: 2-3; ed. *Commentaire du livre d'Abba Isaïe*, CSCO 326-27; in Syriac, 144-45.
29. Ed. by Alphonse Mingana, *Woodbrook Studies*, vol 7 (Cambridge, 1934) 201-48; English tr. 76-143.
30. E. Khalifé-Hachem, 'Isaac de Nineve', DS 7/2: 2041-54.
31. Robert Beaulay, 'Jean de Dalyatha', DS 8: 449-52.
32. F. Graffin, 'Jacques (Denys) Bar Salibi (d. 1171)', DS 8: 29-30.
33. Pierre du Bourguet, 'Jean, fils d'Abou Zakariya', DS 8: 256.
34. (Venice, 1779-1827).
35. SCh 8 (1961); see I. Kechichian, 'Grégoire de Narek', DS 6: 927-32.
36. Raymond Janin, 'Mekhitar, Mekhitaristes', DThC 10 (1928) col. 495-502. Paul Krüger, 'Die armenische Mechitaristen und ihre Bedeutung', *Ostkirchliche Studien* 16 (1967) 3-14.
37. See below, *Bibliography*.
38. See Jean Kirchmeyer in DS 4 (1961) 1722-23.
39. See below, *Bibliography*.
40. Ed., Dimitry-Ivan Abramovič (St Petersburg, 1911); Reprint by D. Tschiževskij, *Slavische Propyläen* 2 (Munich, 1964).
41. Fairy von Lilienfeld, *Nil Sorskij und seine Schriften. Die Krise der Tradition in Russland Ivans III* (Berlin, 1962); George Maloney, *The Spirituality of Nil Sorsky* (Westmalle, 1964).
42. Spidlík, *Joseph de Volokolamsk. Un Chapitre de la spiritualité russe*, OCA 146 (Rome, 1956); *id.*, in DS 8: 1408-11. [English tr. by David M. Goldfrank, *The Monastic Rule of Iosif Volotsky*, CS 36 (1982).]
43. Ivan Kologrivof, *Essai sur la spiritualité en Russie* (Bruges, 1953) 291-328; *id.*, in DS 3: 982-85.

Sources

44. Id., *Essai*, 329-78; N. Gorodetsky, *The Humiliated Christ in Modern Russian Thought* (London, 1938); S. Janežič, *Imitazione di Cristo secondo Tichon Zadonskij* (Trieste, 1962).
45. Kologrivof, *Essai*, 379-97; M. Schwarz, 'Un réformateur du monachisme du XVIIIe siècle: Paisios Veličkovskij', *Irénikon* 11 (1934) 561-72; C. Hainsworth, *Staretz Paisy Veličkovsky (1722-1794). Doctrine of Spiritual Guidance* (Rome, 1976).
46. Špidlík, *Théophane le Reclus*.
47. Kologrivof, *Essai*, 398ff.; von Lilienfeld, *Hierarchen und Starzen der russischen orthodoxen Kirche*, Aufsätze der Zeitschrift des Moskauer Patriarchats (Berlin, 1966).

3. THE TRENDS OF EASTERN SPIRITUALITY

1. See Irénée Hausherr, 'Les grand courants de la spiritualité orientale', OCP 1 (1935) 114-38; Špidlík, 'Spiritualität des östlichen Christentums', in *Handbuch der Ostkirchenkunde*, 483-502.
2. See above, Chapter 1.
3. See *Grégoire de Nazianze*, 4ff.
4. *Stromateis* II, 130.2; GCS 2, p. 184; ANF 2; p. 131.
5. See above, part 2, note 4.
6. Vol. I (Athens, 1957) xxiii.
7. Patricius van der Aalst, 'Contemplation et Hellénisme', *Proche-Orient Chrétien* 14 (1964): 151-68; *Grégoire de Nazianze*, 9ff.
8. See Henri Crouzel, *Origène et la "connaissance mystique"* (Bruges, 1962), 373; see below, Chapter 13, *Ecstasy*.
9. See below, Chapter 2.1, and ch. 4, *Various Aspects of the Trichotomy*.
10. Roger Leys, *L'image de Dieu chez saint Grégoire de Nysse* (Brussels, 1951) 28ff; see Ch. 13, *Ecstasy*.
11. See Jean Mouroux, *L'expérience chrétienne*, Théologie 26 (Paris, 1952) chaps. 5-6; Augustin Léonard, 'Expérience spirituelle', DS 4/2: 2004-6.
12. Hausherr, 'Les grand courants', 126ff.
13. *Id.*, 'Vie de Syméon le Nouveau Théologien', *Orient. Christ.* 12 (1928) lxxiv; see 'Hieronymus Graecus'; PG 40: 860-65.
14. Hausherr, 'L'erreur fondamentale et la logique du Messalianisme', OCP 1 (1935) 238-60; *Études*, OCA 183 (1969) 64-96.
15. See *Théophane le Reclus*, 98ff.
16. See E. des Places, 'Diadoque de Photicé', DS 3: 825; F. Dörr, *Diadochus von Photike und die Messalianer, Ein Kampf zwischen wahrer und falschen Mystik im fünften Jahrhundert*, Freiburger theologische Studien 47 (Freiburg-im-Breisgau, 1937) 50.
17. See A. Guillaumont, 'Le "coeur" chez les spirituels grecs à l'époque ancienne', DS 2/2: 221-88; cf. Chapter 4, THE HEART.
18. Following Plato (*Politicus* 383d) and Proclus (*Alcibiades* II. 90), Celsus resumes this generally admitted principle (Origen, *Contra Celsum* VII.36; PG 11:1472A); see Špidlík, *Grégoire de Nazianze*, 30ff.
19. See Špidlík, *La sophiologie de S. Basile*, 225.
20. See below, Chapter 13, *The Degrees* [of Contemplation].
21. See Chapter 7, *Chastity*, and 8, *A Double Spirituality?*
22. See Basil, *Homilia 5 in Hexaemeron*, 2; PG 29:97C FC 46 (1963) 68ff.

23. See Chapter 12, *Icons*.
24. See Chapter 8, . . . *Hesychast Tradition*.
25. *Conferences* 18.5-6; Sch 64 (1959) 14ff; LNPF 11: 481-83.
26. See Chapter 6; *Praises of the Common Life*.
27. See Gribomont, *Histoire du texte des Ascétiques de S. Basile* (Louvain, 1953).
28. See Julien Leroy, 'La réforme studite', in *Monachesimo orientale*, OCA 153 (1958) 181-214.
29. See Placide de Meester, *De monachico statu iuxta disciplinam byzantinam* (Rome, 1942).
30. See Chapter 6, *Praises of the Common Life*.
31. *Ibid.*, UNITY . . . , *The Church*
32. Theophane the Recluse, *Pima k raznym licam* (*Letters to Various Persons*) (Moscow, 1892) 236.
33. See Gregory of Nazianzus, *Oratio* 18.9; PG 35:996AB.
34. See Špidlík, *Grégoire de Nazianze*, 139, note 1 (bibliography); G. Bardy, '"Philosophie" et "philosophe" dans le vocabulaire chrétien des premiers siècles', RAM 25 (1949) 97-108; A. Malingrey, '*Philosophia*'. *Etude d'un groupe de mots dans la littérature grecque des Présocratiques au IVe siècle après J.-C.* (Paris, 1961).
35. See Chapter 13, *Ecstasy*.
36. See, for example, the Russian Sergei Michel Zarin, *Asketism po pravoslavnochristianskomu učeniju* [*The Ascetic Doctrine according to Orthodox Christian Teaching*] (St Petersburg, 1907).
37. See Heinrich Fries, 'Théologie', in EF 4:312.
38. See Chapter 13, *The Degrees, Theologia*.
39. See Chapter 5, *Definitions and the Purpose of Providence, The History of the World*.
40. See Chapter 7, *Sin as Ignorance*.

2

LIFE IN GOD

1. IN THE HOLY SPIRIT

Spiritual

THE TERM SPIRITUAL IS SO FAMILIAR that one would hardly dream of defining it. Nonetheless, a complex reality lies hidden under such apparent simplicity. The concept has its history and includes gradations of meaning ranging from its bad sense, an heretical exaggeration, to its weakened and almost secularized use.[1]

In Scripture, the spirit is the breath of life.[2] The hellenistic philosophers stressed, though not always, the immaterial character of the term. Yet all of them viewed the spirit as the principle which gave a general orientation to human activity. It can be said that this 'vital sense', *sens vital,* is more in keeping with the vocabulary of Scripture. Yet, the decisive characteristic of the concept of spirit in Scripture, as distinguished from that found in philosophic reflection, lies in its immediate association with the person of God (and not as the more or less divine element in the human person). The spirit of God in action is manifested ever more and more in the history of salvation; in St Paul it becomes the foundation of the christian life: 'the spirit of God', 'the spirit of Christ', 'the spirit of the Lord', and the Holy Spirit.[3]

While speaking of the activity of the Spirit of God, St Paul once lists the Christian's 'Spirit, soul, and body' (1 Thess 5:23). Thus the Fathers found themselves with a trichotomic formula of which the biblical *pneuma* was the most important element. The formula became traditional in the East.[4]

It was Irenaeus' great contribution to have eliminated the gnostics' concept of the purely spiritual man (in the sense of being 'incorporeal'). He clearly distinguished this gift, which scholastic theologians would call supernatural, from the in-breathing which created man as animal:

> The perfect man consists of three elements: flesh, soul, and Spirit. One preserves and fashions—this is the Spirit; the other is united and formed—that is the flesh; that which is between these two is the soul, which sometimes, when it follows the Spirit, is raised up by it. But sometimes it sympathizes with the flesh and falls into carnal lusts. Many do not have the Spirit who preserves and fashions: these are called flesh and blood by St Paul.... But all those who fear God and trust in his Son's advent and who through faith establish the Spirit of God in their hearts, such men as these shall be properly called 'spiritual' because they possess the Spirit of the Father who purifies man and raises him up to the life of God.[5]

A careful study would show that such faith in the Spirit became more explicit later on: man is qualified as *pneumatikos* (spiritual) through the operation of the Spirit (*apo tēs tou Pneumatos energeias*).[6]

The Personal Indwelling of the Spirit

When tracing the evolution of the doctrine of the Holy Spirit in primitive Christianity, one finds that pronouncements on the divinity of the Spirit were more precise than those dealing with his personhood. Only with the First Council of Constantinople (381) did a definition confirm the identity in nature between the Spirit, the Son, and the Father, and consequently his personhood and divinity.[7] Such development can be seen, for example, in the works of Ephrem. In such early writings as *De paradiso* and the *Sermones de fide* the person of the Holy Spirit appears very little. It is only in the hymns *De fide* that an ode is addressed to him.[8]

Once the personhood of the Holy Spirit had been established a second problem became the subject of theological controversy: is the salvific activity of the third divine Person in the Church and in every human being exclusively proper (*proprium*) to the Holy Spirit, or is it exercised together with the other two Persons and thus only attributed to him (*appropriato*)? Western theology spoke of an uncreated gift, which is the indwelling of the Holy Spirit in us, and of a created gift, which imparts a new quality to the soul and forms the true basis for new relationships in grace with the Holy Spirit, but which is the result of a divine activity *ad extra* shared by the three Persons.[9]

It is generally recognized that the Greek Fathers and Eastern thinkers as a whole presented the Holy Spirit as the principal and true author of man's sanctification and that they spoke of a personal communion, a 'participation' in the divine life, while Latin scholasticism more readily viewed grace as a supernatural habit, a created gift.[10]

'One Spirit With The Lord'[11]

The presence of an invisible Breath in the human soul created a third problem: does the Holy Spirit not remain outside our human soul? As the difference between the Holy Spirit and the creature was clarified, the Holy Spirit came to be looked upon as an entirely distinct indweller. The *Spiritual Homilies* of pseudo-Macarius are eloquent witness to this[12] (according to the Messalians, this 'divine guest' could even co-exist with the demon in the same soul).[13]

It became necessary to insist on the distinction. The mystery of the love of God is a mystery of union, but also one of distinction. The soul does not get lost in some *nirvana*. On the contrary, it affirms its personality and develops it to the highest degree. On the other hand, however, the ancient freedom of expression stressed, often in an awkward and unclear manner, the nearness of the Spirit, or better, the transformation of the Christian and his entrance into the personal life of God.[14] In Aphraates of Syria, for example, the Spirit of Christ is given so abundantly that it becomes what is most spiritual in us, our true self.[15] And thus the wicked 'shall be cut asunder', as Basil said, cutting asunder meaning 'complete separation from the Spirit'.[16]

The great mystery of the christian life — a life which is a participation in the divine Unity and Trinity — is that of the many relationships between man's spirit and the Spirit of God. At times the two seem so united that they seem to be one; then the two become separated by an infinite distance. The soul envisions herself in an abyss of weakness and ignorance only to feel suddenly strong again, illumined, bearing within herself 'the intelligible light, the source of all sanctification'.[17]

'The Soul of the Human Soul'

There are images of the Holy Spirit which express his arrival from outside as, for example, the archaic formula 'the angel of the Holy Spirit',[18] or that of the Giver.[19] By contrast, when Basil wrote that the Spirit is Light, he explained: 'And as the power of seeing is in the healthy eye,[20] so the operation of the Spirit is in the purified soul....'[21] as 'the art is potentially in the artist'.[22]

Basil did not hesitate to call the Spirit our *eidos* (which may be translated as 'formal cause').[23] Origen defined man's union with him as *anakrasis* (a commingling).[24] In the trichotomy[25] as explained by Irenaeus, the Spirit must be united with the soul and through it with the body in order for there to be a complete man.[26] It is in connection with such reflections that the following statement by Theophane the Recluse acquires deep meaning: 'The Spirit is like the "soul of the human soul"'.[27] 'On the day of Pentecost', Evdokimov writes, 'he comes down in person and is active inside creation; he operates as the *inner reality* of human nature.'[28]

The Effects of the Spirit in the Soul, the Body, and Creation

The activity of the Holy Spirit, like that of the Son, is expressed through the names given to him by the Church.

— He is the Sanctifier. In Origen we find a formula destined to become highly developed in the theology of Basil and Athanasius: through participation in the Holy Spirit creatures who are not holy by nature can become holy.[29]

— He is the Life-Giver, as the Creed states,[30] the Breath of life; the Antiphon (in tone 4) of Byzantine Sunday Matins states that 'through the Holy Spirit every soul is quickened...., and made resplendent by the Triune Unity in mystic holiness'.

Life in God

— He is the Enlightener. Verse 10 of Psalm 35, 'In thy light shall we see light' is explained by Basil: 'By the illumination of the Spirit we shall see the true light which enlightens every one who comes into the world' (Jn 1:9).[31]

— As Purifier, the Spirit forgives sins,[32] and purifies the flesh in asceticism and virginity.[33] He imparts strength to martyrs,[34] gives tears to penitents,[35] causes men to observe the commandments, and teaches all the virtues.[36]

The drawing near of man's spirit to God occurs especially in prayer, which must therefore be made 'in the Spirit'.[37] In this sense each prayer contains an implied *epiklesis* (invocation) so that it may be uttered by the power of the Holy Spirit. Since the most excellent prayer is the eucharistic prayer, however, this invocation is made explicitly in Eastern liturgies.[38]

By way of summary, we need only say that the Holy Spirit leads us into Christ. His activity aims at reproducing in us the life of the Saviour.[39] He unites all the faithful in the one Body of Christ which is the Church;[40] he sheds his light upon all creation.[41]

The Christian Life as a Progressive 'Spiritualization'

Summarizing the traditional teaching, Theophane the Recluse stated that, 'The essence of the spiritual life, the life in Christ, consists in the transformation of soul and body and their translation into the sphere of the Spirit, that is, in the spiritualization of soul and body.'[42]

The spiritual life has, furthermore, a decisive effect upon our relationships with our neighbor and also with non-rational nature, the whole cosmic order. Placed in the visible world, man achieves his spiritual goal through 'cosmic spiritualization'.[43] We, therefore, 'may describe the ultimate end of the world process as the spiritualization of reasonable creatures through moral order and of the others through some order which is different...'.[44]

This spiritual progress is slow, but it corresponds to everyone's 'natural' make-up: 'The man hidden deep in the heart (2 Co 4:16; the Spirit in Theophane's view) is born and grows. We feel him. His development occurs by means of the same elements that have constituted him since birth.'[45]

Seraphim of Sarov, the popular Russian thaumaturge, explained this mystery to his spiritual son by saying:

> They [the priests] tell you: 'go to church, observe the commandments, do good. That is the goal of your christian life.' They did not speak as they should have. Prayer, fasting, vigils, and all other christian works, however excellent they might be, do not in themselves constitute the goal of the christian life; they are but the indispensable means of attaining that end. The true end of the christian life is the acquisition of the Spirit of God....of the grace of the Holy Spirit.[46]

2. THROUGH JESUS CHRIST

The Christian Life as Christological

'Whatever is innate in the human soul', Origen wrote, 'has been sown there by God the Word who was in the beginning with God; this is all the seed of the kingdom of God.'[1] One could not imagine a more intimate union than the one which leads to the type of identification so well expressed by Gregory of Nazianzus in his Easter Oration:

> Yesterday I was crucified with him; today I am glorified with him; yesterday I died with him; today I am quickened with him; yesterday I was buried with him; today I rise with him .... We have become like Christ, for Christ became like us. We have become gods through him, for He became man for us.[2]

Consequently, 'the Saviour is more closely united to us than our own soul'.[3]

Faced with this mystery, the Greek Fathers, in their polemical treatises as well as their homilies, thought primarily in theological terms. What they ordinarily asked of Christians was belief in Christ's divinity and his mission.

Names of Christ

The Fathers did not hesitate to express the mystery of Christ by means of philosophic concepts, those of Neoplatonism,[4] for example, although their value remained very limited. The excessive use of them, moreover, always led to heresy. The main error, Gregory of Nazianzus believed, was that of constructing far-reaching speculations on the basis of a few terms. As it happens, Scripture designates the Only-begotten by numerous names: 'God, the Son, Image, Vapor, Emanation, Effulgence, Creator, King, Head, Law, Door, Foundation, Rock, Pearl, Peace, Righteousness, Sanctification, Redemption, Man, Servant, Shepherd, Lamb, High Priest, Sacrifice, Firstborn before creation, Firstborn of the dead, of the Resurrection.'[5]

How can these be classified or put in order, how can a choice be made from among them? If he felt obliged to indicate a preference, each author listed first the name that seemed to him to evoke the greatest response:

—*Jesus*-Saviour. Most predominant in Eastern monastic circles was *penthos*, compunction.[6] Tenderness towards Jesus stemmed from it. An anonymous writer states in the *Philokalia*: 'Nevertheless, [the inspired Fathers] have prescribed that we who are beginners and imperfect should also say the words "have mercy on us" [after invoking the sweet name of Jesus]'.[7]

It has been said that in the Eastern Church the incarnation was never viewed in function of the redemption and that the Word would have become man regardless.[8] The fear was that the term redemption sounded too legalistic.[9] Clearly, the christian doctrine of redemption stands out sharply from all other nonbiblical concepts of redemption and from everything that would render belief in creation useless. That is why the Orthodox Church views redemption as the restoration and fullness of creation, its 'recapitulation'[10] its liberation, its sanctification,[11] and its deification.[12]

—*Jesus*-Light, *Wisdom*. Christ forever opened 'the gates of light to those who were the sons of darkness and of night and had devoted themselves to becoming the sons of light and of the day'.[13] For the Greek Fathers the misery of the sinner consists in 'ignorance'.[14] On this basis we better understand the great importance they attached to the revelatory function of the Word become flesh. The tradition retained the full run of scriptural names: Truth, Wisdom, Master, the Word, the Light.[15]

Chapter Two

The Unifying Activity of Christ

There can be no greater difference than the one which exists between the Creator and the created. And yet, the mystery of Jesus Christ appears as the perfect union of the two, and this is why he is essentially the Unifier.

The need for a 'mediator' was seen even in Greek philosophy. How could two antithetical realities—the material and the spiritual—be reconciled?[16] A serious problem. If God must remain transcendent, indifferent to everything under him,[17] then the transition from the divine to the human cannot be conceived of without some intermediary.[18] It is along such philosophical lines that a carefully developed doctrine of the Logos-mediator, *organon theou* (the instrument of God), is found in Philo.[19]

A similar notion could not be applied to Christ. The New Testament does not often use the term 'mediator'. One also looks for it in vain in the Apostolic Fathers and the Apologists.[20] Jesus Christ does not stand *between* God and his people, nor is he God's representative, as an angel could be, but he is himself 'the author of eternal salvation' (Heb 5:9).

We do not wish to diminish the value of Christ's mediation, quite the contrary. We realize, however, that such a doctrine differs from ancient teaching in two respects:

1) in the philosophical systems it was God who, because of his absolute transcendence, needed a mediator to communicate with the world. By contrast, in Scripture such communication is made possible only by virtue of God's condescension. Jesus stands explicitly on the side of God. It is God himself who performs the work of salvation through the man Jesus Christ, his Son.

2) This salvation could become effective only by means of a complete taking on by God of the human condition. The axiom 'What is not assumed cannot be saved,' which underlines the development in Irenaeus,[21] is already found explicitly in Origen: 'The whole man would not have been saved unless he had taken upon him the whole man.'[22] The union between the human and the divine is a 'mixture' (*mixis*), a 'blending' (*krasis*),[23] but of a special type: indeed, the two natures remain unconfused. Christ is the only one to bring about the encounter of the divine transcendence with the human finite, without sacrificing the one or

ignoring the other.[24] Jesus belongs authentically to the two orders of existence, that of God and that of man. 'God and man have become one.'[25] The mystery of mediation is therefore the mystery of union, realized by the Son who is 'one' with the Father.

It is a social unity: Christ is the new and true Adam of mankind (Rm 5:12-21), the head of the body of the Church (Col 1:18). The Pauline affirmation of the Body of Christ is found frequently in patristic texts.[26] Nicholas Cabasilas summarized the tradition when he wrote that 'We are joined to him in the same body and share his life and are his members'.[27] Then, he also added a new expression: Christ is the heart of the mystical body, the intimate principle of the life forces of the Church and each individual Christian.[28]

In and through the Firstborn of all creation (Col 1:15), the sanctification of the world ultimately results in the unity of the created order. The Fathers called this last state *apokatastasis* (the final restoration of things),[29] a term which may be explained by the simple statement of Irenaeus: 'In him, all became one'.[30] Maximus the Confessor often pondered the consequences for the world of the victory of Christ over the forces of disunity.[31] For him, 'Christ is the center where all lines converge.'[32] Byzantine architecture placed the icon of the *Pantocrator* high in cupolas, where it was seen as the center of all iconography and of the cosmic orb.[33]

In Russian thought[34] the concept of Christ as the principle of unity is often found in various guises: as the unity of the visible world (G. S. Skovorodà, † 1794), of human society (Chaadaev, † 1856), of the Church (Chomiakov, † 1860), of human history (Belinsky, † 1848), of human cultures (V. Ivanov, † 1949), of the entire cosmic evolution (Soloviev, † 1900). 'If one were to deny the reality of this event [Christ's Incarnation] the entire meaning and the finality of the universe would collapse', wrote Soloviev.[35]

Devotion to Christ

Spirituality is lived dogma. That is why even in the midst of discussions that divide opponents we experience a spontaneous transition to personal attitudes closer to what we may call a devotion common to all Christians. Strictly speaking one should not pray 'to Christ' but 'through Christ', as Origen warned us,[36] and yet he did not follow this rule himself.[37]

It comes as no surprise that Christians love Christ. But how? Ancient liturgies praised him, thanked him, worshipped and implored him. Tenderness and intimacy began to be emphasized only with some reservations in the early days: by the martyrs, by pilgrims to Jerusalem, in Syriac religious poetry.[38] Yet even the Byzantines have 'An Office of the Most Sweet Jesus' which antedates the *Jubilus* attributed to St Bernard',[39] the *Jesou glykytate*. From the entire tradition let us cite at least one, anonymous, writer included in the *Philokalia*, who greatly praised the excellence of the famous 'Jesus prayer'[40]:

> This is the doctrine that has been handed down to us by our inspired Fathers. . . . ; The whole effort of their lives was to fill themselves with the sweetness of Jesus. Their whole hunger was for Jesus. This is what filled them with indescribable spiritual joy. By calling on the sweet name of Jesus they received special charisms and were elevated above the cares of the flesh and of the world.[41]

Devotion to the Humanity of Christ

There are two paths which can lead to a tender love for the Saviour: the sweetness of God[42] because he is God; and his human amiability, because no man has ever spoken as did he. These two paths ultimately merge, for Christ is a single divine-human person.

The heresy of Docetism led the orthodox writers to reaffirm the reality of Christ's existence on earth.[43] Yet, it was theological reflection which led them to pay more attention to the nature of man which the Word did not scorn. Can we, however, say that the Fathers' preoccupation with this was 'devotion' to this human nature, or that they took a predominantly dogmatic view of it? In this sense, Vladimir Lossky states, 'the cult of the humanity of Christ is foreign to the Eastern tradition'.[44]

It is undeniably difficult to speak of an explicit devotion to the humanity of Christ during the early centuries. Their prayer was addressed to 'Christos as if to a god,' according to Pliny the Younger's witness in his famous Letter to Trajan.[45] One thing astonished the pagans greatly; that such religious homage was being addressed to a crucified man.[46]

It is also true that the function of the liturgy was to stress the divinity of Christ. At the same time, various feasts gave christain poets an opportunity to compose hymns in honor of the God-Man. Pilgrims had the opportunity of visiting the localities of Christ's life and of venerating in particular the instrument of salvation, the cross, and later the 'holy face'.[47]

Slowly, Christian piety agreed to view Christ in his humiliations as a human being. John of Damascus justified this adoration:

> Christ, therefore, is one, perfect God and perfect man. Along with the Father and the Spirit, we worship him in one adoration together with his immaculate body, for to us his body is not unworthy of adoration. In fact, it is adored in the one Person of the Word. We do not do homage to what is created. We worship him not as mere flesh, but as flesh united with the godhead.[48]

The Imitation of Christ

The theme of the imitation of Christ occupies an important place in the history of spirituality,[49] even though in their reaction to medieval piety, the Reformers in the West replaced the concept of 'imitation', which they viewed as an arrogant human effort, with 'a following' of Christ in response to his call.[50]

Lossky believed that in the spiritual life of the Eastern Church, 'The way of the imitation of Christ is never practised.... Indeed, this way seems to have a certain lack of fullness; it would seem to imply a somewhat external attitude toward Christ'. Eastern spirituality 'may instead be defined as a *life in Christ*'.[51]

Indeed, unlike the Greek world, which attached great importance to imitation in its philosophic reflection (Plato)[52] or in its view of art as a copy of nature (Plato and Aristotle), or in its pedagogy (the attractive value of the example), Scripture seems to ignore the virtues of *mimēsis*. In fact, this concept is viewed from a different perspective: as ancient nomads, the Hebrews preferred the theme of the way, the road. Man must walk 'in Yahweh's footsteps'.[53]

The theme of imitation is found in pauline thought,[54] but it seems to have been developed there mainly as an ethical ramification of a more fundamental principle, namely, the union of the believer with Christ, which is expressed especially by the formula *in Christ* (used approximately 165 times), and by verbs beginning with *syn* (to die with, to be with....).[55]

It is very possible that the West, more inclined towards activity, viewed conformity to Christ in an ascetic and moral rather than an ontological and mystical sense.[56] If Christ is God, however, he cannot be imitated as a human hero. The participaion between him and his imitators is of an entirely different nature: it assumes a basically sacramental and ecclesiastical character.

If one book ever brought out the difference between life *in* Christ and the imitation *of* Christ, it is certainly *The Life in Christ* by Nicholas Cabasilas. With all the simplicity we could ask for, the author affirms that there is, not opposition, but rather a true identity between the two: 'To imitate Christ and to live *according* to him is to live *in* Christ; this life is the work of the free will when it obeys God's purposes.'[57]

The concept of imitation seems therefore sufficiently clear. 'The Christian', wrote John Climacus, 'is one who imitates Christ in thought, word, and deed, as far as is possible for human beings.'[58] The imitation of Christ is linked to the doctrine of the image and the likeness. It coincides with the progressive realization of 'the likeness'.[59]

Another question must also be asked. For Origen, to follow Christ meant to cultivate the virtues, of which he gave a list: knowledge, wisdom, truth, righteousness....'.[60] These are the attributes of the divine Logos. We know that the West chose to imitate the Word made flesh as he was seen in the mysteries of his life on earth.[61] Origen adopted the same point of view toward the end of his life.[62] For Gregory Nazianzen, to imitate Christ meant trying to become 'all that he became for us'.[63] Every detail of the mysteries he evoked in his orations called for a participation: 'Guided by the star, we ran to him, and with the magi we worshipped, and with the shepherds we were illumined, and with the angels we glorified him...'.[64]

This corresponds well to the essence of the liturgical *anamnesis (commemoration), Christ living in the ritual of the Church:* 'At Christmas he is truly born, just as at Easter he truly dies.'[65]

Being conscious of the absolute oneness of Christ, the Christian will avoid the pitfalls of mimicry and formalism. It is not a matter of repeating the physical gestures of Christ but of imitating their spiritual intent, of using the sentiments of Christ as models for our feelings.[66] The imitation of Christ will therefore vary according to each person's vocation.

Imitating the Saints

The Christians of the first centuries were aware that Christ had outstanding imitators and that it was especially because of them that the Church had become a light to the nations.

'Examples' had played an important role in the moralizing literature of the ancients, especially in the tradition stemming from the Cynic-Stoic diatribe.[67] To what degree could a Christian make use of examples taken from secular history? The question is related to the problem of the connections between ancient culture and Christianity.[68] Confronted with such secular heroes, christians did not take long to tap the treasury of examples in the Old and the New Testaments, examples that soon became traditional: Abraham, Moses, Elijah, John the Baptist. The Apostles became the great models. St Paul expressly exhorted his audience to imitate him, as he imitated Christ (1 Th 1:6).

It comes as no surprise therefore that the christian tradition always considered the reading of the lives of the saints as 'useful to the soul' (*psychōphelēs*).[69] Its early documents, such as *The Life of Antony* and the *Sayings of the Fathers* originated in a desire to have models that could be followed, as is stated in the Prologue to the *Sayings*: 'In this work are kept the virtuous deeds and the admirable way of life and the sayings of the holy and blessed Fathers, to instruct us and to stimulate us to emulation.'[70] They are not, however, to be imitated externally, as John Climacus noted.[71]

3. TO THE FATHER

The Problem of God in Ancient Greek Thought

Every living religion has a personal view of God; in this aspect the idea of God the Father is not unique to the revelation of Scripture.[1] This truth does not affect the question of whether reflections drawn from a religious philosophy are capable of developing and perfecting the concept 'personal'.

Christianity arose at a time when the greco-roman world was experiencing a deep religious need. All philosophies desired to ascend to God, the source of felicity, the ideal of the Good and the Beautiful.[2] Even though they varied, the schools of philosophy held one tenet in common, happiness.[3] Plato defined the aim of human life as blessedness, the active state of knowing, whereby the mind contemplates the truest being, God.[4]

Since like alone knows like,[5] the desire to know God urges man to imitate him. 'God ought to be to us the measure of all things', Plato said, 'And he who would be dear to such a being must, to the utmost of his might and as far as is possible, be like him and such as he is.'[6] The Fathers were to adopt such reflections and accentuate them.

The most important common ground between religion and philosophy was that in the latter the question of God is intimately related to the question of being. The fact of penetrating the being of a limited being always stirred the Greeks to a burning desire for limitless Being. *Theologia*[7] thereby became one of the three essential parts of philosophy, the crown of human thought.[8]

Such a philosophical approach, however, never fails to create serious problems for a living religion. Expressed in rational concepts, the supreme being in its perfection is presented as an 'Idea', a transcendent unmoved mover unable to communicate with the world, or as a universal law immanent in the events of the world, like blind destiny. In such a context, prayer—the essential act of worship—might be an ascent of the mind to God[9] (for being is essentially intelligible), but never a dialogue.

A strange contradiction resulted from all this. God was to be man's happiness and yet he did not free man from the dangers that terrified him in one particular area: death, loneliness, and *fatum.* Finally, would the ideal of imitating God not lead to the odious *mega phronein* (mega-thinking), the *hubris* (pride), the lack of moderation that spells the ruin of a limited being wanting to mimic the being of God?[10]

The God of Christian Revelation: The Father

Scripture brings us into a new climate; we believe in 'God the Father Almighty, creator of heaven and earth'. He is also the first principle of all that exists, though in an essentially different way. Scripture contains no treatise on God, but it invites man to hear him speak and to respond to him. This God is 'the author of all that happened, happens, and will happen' (Jdt 9:5,4). This means that human history does not unfold according to the impulse of a blind eternal Law but according to the will of a living Person who shows his fatherly care for his children (Cf. Ps 27:10), and who, in Jesus Christ, adopts all humankind as his true children (Ga 4:5 ff.).[11]

Good and evil, life and death, poverty and wealth all come from God (Si 11:14). The 'God of gods' (Dt 10:17) can snatch his people from death (Ex 3:7) by removing man from the power of evil (1 Jn 5:18). Cries of loneliness (Cf. Pss 42-43) rise up only in moments when the waiting in faith is being tested. Finally, Christ gave the commandment, 'Be perfect as your heavenly Father is perfect' (Mt 5:48). This is not presumption but rather the obligation of a 'child', and the child is presented as the model of humility (Mk 10:15 ff.).

On only one point did the Christians seem to be at a disadvantage. Following Plato, the Fathers spoke of the blessedness that results from knowing God: 'There is nothing on earth that gives so much pleasure as the knowledge of God', wrote Evagrius.[12] In Scripture, however, the name of God carries with it an inaccessible mystery precisely because he is the Father, a free Person, sovereignly independent.[13] The Gospel, on the other hand, is 'the revelation of this mystery wrapped in silence from eternity, but made manifest to us today' (Rm 16:25 ff). The Inaccessible makes himself known to his children through grace in Jesus Christ.

Chapter Two

The 'Super-essential Unity' within the Trinity

When Christ revealed the identity of the Father and of God, he placed this revelation within another, still more inaccessible, mystery, that of the Trinity. God is Father because he has a Son who is God, Jesus Christ (Jn 1:18). The basic principle of divine 'fatherhood' was thereby transposed to a level which surpasses merely human thought.[14]

The divine Trinity is the fundamental mystery of the christian faith. It is the one starting-point from which the other elements of the christian faith can be understood. For the Greeks, the perfection of knowledge consisted of *theologia*,[15] the aim of which is 'knowledge of the Father, the Son, and the Holy Spirit,' according to the testimony of Origen.[16] In the opinion of Gregory Nazianzen the grace of the kingdom of heaven consists in 'the Holy Trinity uniting itself wholly to the whole soul'.[17]

Two different concepts are found in the exposition of trinitarian faith, though it would not be right to exaggerate their difference: the 'Alexandrian-Latin' view and the so-called 'Greek' view.[18] The teaching of the Western doctors goes back to Augustine and Boethius: in God everything is one to the extent that there is no opposition of relations.[19] Consequently, God is the unity of the Father, the Son, and the Holy Spirit. By contrast, the texts of the Greek Fathers (and of the Latin liturgy) remained faithful to the terminology of the New Testament: the expression *ho theos* is reserved for the father of Christ (Rm 5:6, 2 Co 11:31, Eph 1:3). The Father Almighty is the creator of heaven and earth, and hence the principle of cosmic unity in the extra-divine universe. This Father, however, is also the source of intra-divine unity. The Son and the Spirit are one in the Father. And since the function of the divine Persons corresponds to the place each occupies in the bosom of the Trinity, the salvific value of the mystery of the Trinity is manifested. It is the Father who is the ground of human divinization.

Spiritual writers have always preferred the 'greek' way expressed in traditional formulas which summarize it in two movements, one downward: the Father creates man through the Son and sanctifies him in the Spirit; the other upward: man gives glory to the Father through the Son in the Holy Spirit.[20] This is the 'royal highway' of human deification.[21] St Basil wrote: 'Thus the way of the knowledge of God lies in the One Spirit through the One Son to the One Father, and conversely, natural goodness, inherent holiness, and royal dignity extend from the Father through the Onlybegotten to the Spirit.'[22]

This approach created no religious problems as did the 'latin' concept where the Persons remain in the background. However, it had to wrestle with the problem of the oneness of God which seemed to be unveiled here in an entirely new and mysterious manner, as the unifying force of divine love.

The dialectic of the one and the many has been an enduring and fascinating theme in philosophy from the outset. In the beginning, Thales posited the material unity (water) of the world. Parmenides conceived the philosophy of one identical being. The principle of unity is found in Plato and Aristotle, in Stoicism, and most emphatically in Plotinus.[23]

Philosophic reflection, in its various ways of understanding reality, became an ally of religion and mysticism and of the ways by which they represented the unity of, and union with, divinity. Greek and oriental themes were both part of this as well.

By the same token, it seems clear that of all these attempts only the christian revelation teaches the highest and most intense union as embracing that which in the finite realm divides and is a principle of division: the personality, freedom. For Christians, unlike the others, all things are one in the free and loving person of the Father. Such unity is inconceivable to the human mind: it is a 'super-essential unity' (*he hyper henarchian henotēs, unitas super principium unitatis*), as Dionysius the pseudo-Areopagite stated so well.[24]

Deification

Every movement of the Holy Spirit, who dwells within us, aims at bringing us into a living communion with Christ and with the Father,[25] at 'deifying' us. In spite of the serious liabilities attached to it, the terminology of 'deification' and 'divinization' (*theōsis, theopoēisis*) was to impose itself upon the Fathers as capable of expressing the newness of the condition to which man had been restored through the Incarnation of the Son of God.[26] The deification of man corresponds to the 'man-becoming' of God.[27] It deals with a mysterious exchange by which 'each takes on the qualities of the other'.[28]

Whereas the Old Testament was keen to preserve the absoute transcendence of God, ancient Greek religious thinking fluctuated between a sense of the human condition beyond which one was not supposed to venture,[29] and assimilation to the deity, the consciousness of belonging to God's people. 'You are a fragment of God; you have within you a part of him', wrote Epictetus.[30] St Paul was to reaffirm before the Areopagus the assertion of Aratos the poet, 'and we are of his [God's] race' (Ac 17:28).

Among Christians, Ignatius of Antioch told his correspondents that they were 'God bearers' (*theophoroi*),[31] 'full of God' (*theou gemete*).[32] But it was left to Clement of Alexandria to give this doctrine adequate expression through the use of the terminology of deification: 'the Word of God became man in order that you may learn from man how man may become God.'[33]

Athanasius, even though he clearly identified sonship and deification, took great care to note that this assimilation was not identification: it does not make us 'as the true God or his Word, but as it has pleased God who has given us that grace'.[34] In Dionysius the pseudo-Areopagite, deification became part of the neoplatonic scheme of the return to God. Maximus the Confessor made use of Aristotelian and Platonic logic and physics for his theological vision of the cosmos, the basis of which was deification, which is 'the fulfillment of time and of the ages and of everything they contain'.[35] Symeon the New Theologian insisted on the need to become conscious of this participation in the divine, and this was his new contribution.[36] Two centuries later, Gregory Palamas was to use deification as the decisive argument of his theological synthesis.[37] In our day, it is Eastern theologians who have made this doctrine familiar again in the West.[38] Moreover, the 'sophiological' or 'sophianic' theories[39] are also expressions of it.

The language of deification expressed serveral themes: man's creation in the image and likeness of God; adoptive sonship; the imitation of God and Christ; contemplation, charity, the virtues, and prayer.

Life in God

Equivalent Expressions

Terms are less important than the reality they signify. Indeed, many authors used neither *theōsis* nor *theopoēsis* but chose to keep to the language of Scripture.

Adoptive sonship. Cyril of Alexandria distinguished a double kinship of humanity with the Son: 'In him and through him we are sons of God naturally (*physikōs*) and by grace (*kata charin*)'.[40] Somewhat diagrammatically, John Chrysostom stated that under Mosaic Law the divine sonship was only nominal, while it became reality under the new Law.[41]

Regeneration. Although the concept of adoption has a legal origin, more vital was the ever new birth of 'the Word in the hearts of the saints'.[42] This 'remaking' (*anastoicheoun*) of human nature is effected by the Incarnation.[43]

Anointing. Christ is the *Anointed*; the communication of divine holiness to human nature is an 'anointing.[44]

Kinship (*syngeneia, gnēsios*) with God.[45]

Community (*koinōnia*)[46]

Familiarity (*oikeotēs parrhēsia*)—originally, 'freedom of speech'.[47]

New Covenant.[48]

Connaturality with God: 'The connaturality with God, like him who is born of God and remains in the things divine, and (in the words of Macarius the Great) has already passed into the world to come.'[49]

Conjunction (*synaphē, synapheia*).[50]

Bond (*syndesmos*)[51]

The Image of Betrothal[52]

Mixture (*krasis*)[53] and *participation* (*metochē, methexis, metousia*).[54] On account of their philosophical nature, these two terms were used to express the substantial, assimilating presence of the three divine Persons communicating themselves to the believer.

Image of God, eternal life, and *salvation* demand a fuller explanation.

Notes

1. IN THE HOLY SPIRIT

1. See Gerard Verbeke, *L'évolution de la doctrine du Pneuma, du stoïcisme à saint Augustin* (Paris-Louvain, 1945); Irénée Hausherr, *Direction spirituelle en*

48 Chapter Two

Orient autrefois, OCA 144 (Rome, 1955), especially the history of the word *pneumatikos*, 45–55; DS 3:1015 ff., 1025, 1049 ff.; DS 2:1833.
2. Gn 2:7; Jb 27:3, 33:4, 12:10; Ps 104:29ff.
3. I. Hermann, 'Esprit-Saint, Etude biblique', EF 2:18–24.
4. See Jean Gribomont, 'L'Esprit sanctificateur dans la spiritualité des Pères grecs', DS 4/2:1257–72; see Chapter 4, *Inner Man-Outer Man*.
5. *Adversus haereses* V.9.1–2; PG 7:1144–45; ed. W. Wigan Harvey (Cambridge, 1857) vol. 2:342–43. Paul Galtier, *Le Saint-Esprit en nous d'après les Pères grecs* (Rome, 1946). Adhémar d'Alès, 'La doctrine de l'Esprit Saint en saint Irénée', RSR 14 (1924) 497–538.
6. *De prophetiarum obscuritate* II. 5; PG 56:183A; I. Tugij, *Tajna christianskoj žizni* [*The Mystery of the Christian Life*] (Optina Pustyň, 1908).
7. See Otto Semmelroth, 'Esprit-Saint. Histoire dogmatique', EF 2:26ff.
8. *De fide* 10.9; ed. J. S. Assemani, *Ephraem Syri Opera omnia quae extant graece, syriace, latine* (Rome, 1732–46) vol. 3:23.
9. See Semmelroth, p. 27.
10. See Galtier, *Le Saint-Esprit en nous d'après les Pères grecs, Analecta Gregoriana*, theol. series 35 (Rome, 1946) (Reviewed by Gerard Philips, 'Le Saint-Esprit en nous. A propos d'un livre récent', *Ephemerides Theologicae Lovanienses* 24 [1948] 127–35); Gribomont, 'Esprit sanctificateur dans la spiritualité des Pères grecs', DS 4/2: 1257–72.
11. Pseudo-Macarius, *De caritate* 24; PG 34:928B; Špidlík, *Théophane le Reclus*, 32.
12. See, for example, *Homilia* I.3 (PG 34: 452ff), *Hom.* VI.6 (521CD), *Hom.* XV.1–2 (576) etc; [English translation by George A. Maloney, *Intoxicated with God. The Fifty Spiritual Homilies of Macarius* (Denville, 1978).]
13. Hausherr, 'L'erreur fondamentale et la logique du Messalianisme', OCP 1 (1935) 168ff; *Etudes de spiritualité orientale*, OCA 183 (Rome, 1969) 68ff.
14. *Théophane le Reclus*, 5ff.
15. *Demonstration* 6.14; ed. Jean Parisot, *Patrologia syriaca* I: col. 293. See J. Gribomont, in DS 4/2: 1266.
16. *De spiritu sancto* 16; PG 32:141C; LNPF ser. 2, vol. 3:25.
17. See Špidlík, *La sophiologie de S. Basile*, 196.
18. See Jules Lebreton, *Histoire du dogme de la Trinité*, vol. 2 (Paris, 1928) xiv–xxi, and G. L. Prestige, *God in Patristic Thought* (London, 1936) 80–86. This term may be explained by going back to Jewish categories of thought, and expresses the distinct personality of the Spirit but especially his mission for the salvation of the Church and the holiness of Christians; see Jean Daniélou, *Théologie du Judéo-Christianisme* (Paris, 1958) 177–78 [English translation by John A. Baker, *The Theology of Jewish Christianity* (London-Chicago, 1964).
19. See Gregory of Nyssa, *Adversus Macedonianos de spiritu sancto*. III. 1; ed. F. Mueller, 109, 16–20.
20. Basil, *De spiritu sancto* 26; PG 32: 180C; LNPF, ser. 2, vol. 3: 38.
21. *Ibid.*
22. *Ibid.*, 180D; 38.
23. *Ibid.*, 180BC; 23.
24. *De oratione* 10.2; PG 11:445C; GCS 2; p. 320, 13.
25. See Chapter 4, *Inner Man-Outer Man*.
26. *Adversus Haereses* V. 6.1; PG 7:1138A.
27. *Cto jest' duchovnaja žizň i kak na nee nastroitsija* [*What the Spiritual Life is and How to Begin It*] (Moscow, 1897); *Théophane le Reclus*, 33.

Life in God 49

28. 'L'Esprit Saint et l'Eglise d'après la tradition liturgique', *L'Esprit Saint et l'Eglise, Actes du symposium*——(Paris: Librairie Fayard, 1969) 98.
29. *De principiis* I.8.3; PG 11:178C; GCS 5: p. 100; see Paul Galtier, *Le Saint-Esprit*, 1ff.
30. See Ignazio Ortiz de Urbina, *Nicée et Constantinople* (Paris, 1963) 182–92; J. N. Kelly, *Early Christian Creeds* (London, 1950) 276–332.
31. Basil, *De spiritu sancto* 18; PG 32: 153B; LNPF, ser. 2, vol. 8: 29.
32. Pseudo-Basil, *Adversus Eunomium* 5; PG 29: 717.
33. See Methodius of Olympus, *Symposium* 1.3; PG 18:44B; GCS, p. 12 [English tr. by Herbert Musurillo, *The Symposium: a Treatise on Chastity*, ACW 27 (1958)]
34. Cyril of Jerusalem, *Catecheses* 16.12; PG 33:933; [English trans. of Catech. Lecture XVI; LNPF, ser. 2, vol. 7: 12ff.]
35. *Ibid.*, cf. J. Gribomont, in DS 4/2:1269.
36. *Ibid., cf. Basil, Short Rules* 204; PG 31:1217B.
37. See Origen, *De oratione* 2; PG 11:421; *Théophane le Reclus*, 239: prayer is the 'breathing of the Spirit'.
38. See Sévérien Salaville, 'Epiclèse eucharistique', *Catholicisme* IV (1956) col. 302–307.
39. See Paul Evdokimov, 'L'Esprit Saint et l'Eglise' 97:'The sanctifying action of the Spirit preceeds every act during which the spiritual becomes embodied, incarnated, Christophanic'.
40. Basil, *De spiritu sancto* 26; PG 32:181AB.
41. Michel Spanneut, *Le stoicisme des Pères de l'Église de Clément de Rome à Clément d'Alexandrie* (Paris, 1957) 332ff.
42. *Pisma o duchovnoj žizni* [Letters on the Spiritual Life] (Moscow, 1903) 247; *Théophane le Reclus*, 196.
43. See Vladimir Soloviev, *Duchovnyja osnovy žizni*, oeuvres, (St Petersburg, n.d., rept Brussels, 1966) vol. 3:353 [English trans. Donald Attwater, *God, Man and the Church: The Spiritual Foundations of Life* (London, 1938)]; Ivan Kologrivof, *Essai sur la sainteté en Russie* (Bruges, 1953) 13ff.
44. *Pisma k ranzym licam u litsam u raznuikh predmetakh verui zizni* [Letters to Various Persons on Various Subjects of Faith and Life] (Moscow, 1892) 376.
45. Theophane, *Pisma k raznym licam* 86, 160, p. 464.
46. See Kologrivof, *Essai*, 432.

2. THROUGH JESUS CHRIST

1. *In Matthaeum Commentarium.* Series 10.2, Klostermann, GCS 10:2; see above, Chapter I, *Hellenism ff.*
2. *In sanctum Pascha, oratio* 1.4–5; PG 35:397BC; LNPF, ser. 2, vol. 7: 203.
3. Nicholas Cabasilas, *The Life in Christ* 7; PG 150:712A (see note 57 below).
4. See Henri Crouzel, *Théologie de l'image de Dieu chez Origène* (Paris, 1956) 33ff.
5. Gregory of Nazianzus, *Oratio* 40.4; PG 36:361C–364C; *Oratio* 2.98; PG 35:500BC.
6. See Chapter VII, *Penthos.*
7. Vol. 5 (Athens, 1963) p. 66.
8. Myrrha Lot-Borodine, 'La doctrine de la "déification" dans l'Eglise grecque

50 Chapter Two

jusqu'au 11ᵉ siècle', *Revue d'histoire des religions* 105 (1932) 30, note 1; see P. Evdokimov, *La femme et le salut du monde* (Tournai-Paris, 1958) 35.
9. Evdokimov, 'L'Esprit Saint', 67; see Bernhard Schultze, 'Probleme der orthodoxen Theologie', in *Handbuch der Ostkirchenkunde*, 156ff.
10. See L. Regnault in DS 7/2 (1971) col. 1949ff.
11. See G. Aulén, *Christus Victor*, trans, A. G. Hebert (London, 1931).
12. See below, 'Deification'.
13. Origen, *Contra Celsum* 2.67; PG 11:901C; GCS 2:349; ANF (rept. 1979) vol. 4:458.
14. See Chapter VII, 'Sin as Ignorance'.
15. See Jean Kirchmeyer in DS 6:825.
16. See Špidlík, *Grégoire de Nazianze*, 85.
17. See Aristotle, *Nicomachean Ethics*, I.5.1997.
18. See *Grégoire de Nazianze*, 87.
19. See Hermann Kleinknecht, 'Die logoi des Philo von Alexandria', Gerhard Kittel, *Theologisches Wörterbuch zum Neuen Testament* (Stuttgart, 1933f) 4, p. 87ff.
20. See Franz Josef Schierse, 'Médiateur', EF III, 46–49.
21. *Adversus haereses* II.22.4 (PG 7:784A); V.14, 1–4 (1160–1163).
22. *Dialogue with Heraclides*, tr. J. E. L. Oulton and Henry Chadwick, *Alexandrian Christianity*, Library of Christian Classics (Philadelphia, 1954) 442.
23. See Špidlík, *Grégoire de Nazianze*, 94 *Oratio* 38.13; PG 35:325B.
24. See Cyril of Alexandria, *Thesaurus* 32; PG 75:504C, and the definition of the Council of Chalcedon in 451, in Denziger, *Enchiridion Symbolorum*, nn. 301–302.
25. Gregory of Nazianzus, *Oratio* 2.23; PG 35:432BC.
26. See Robert Brunet in DS 4/1:396ff.
27. *The Life in Christ* 1; PG 150:501C.
28. *Ibid.*, col. 596ff.; 620C; 621AB; see Sévérien Salaville, DS 2/1:7.
29. See Chapter V, '*Apokatastasis*'.
30. *Oratio* 2.23; PG 35:433A.
31. See Lars Thunberg, *Microcosm and Mediator, The Theological Anthropology of Maximus the Confessor* (Lund, 1965).
32. *Mystagogia* 1; PG 91:668. [English tr. by Julian Stead, *The Church, the Liturgy, and the Soul of Man* (Still River: St Bede's Publications, 1982).]
33. See Çarmelo Capizzi, *Pantocrator*, OCA 170 (Rome, 1964).
34. See Špidlík, 'Gesu nella pietà dei Cristiani Orientali', in E. Ancilli, *Gesu Cristo — mistero e presenza* (Rome, 1971) 385–408; *id.*, *I grandi mistici russi* (Rome, 1977) 327–44.
35. Soloviev, *The Justification of the Good*, tr. N. Duddington (London, 1918) II (chap. III):186.
36. *De oratione* 15–16; PG 11:464 ff; see Ephrem, *De virginitate* 31, 2; ed. (in Syriac) by I. E. Rahmani (Scharfen, 1907) 88.
37. See, for example, his *Homilies on Luke* (12–17, PG 13:1828–47) where we see an almost familiar intimacy with the child Jesus: 'let us pray to God Almighty, let us pray even to this Child Jesus with whom we desire to speak, while holding him in our arms' (col. 1839C).
38. See Hausherr, *Noms du Christ et voies d'oraison*, OCA 157 (Rome, 1960) 96ff. [*The Name of Jesus*, 81ff.]
39. This is the title of an article by Salaville, RAM 25 (1949) 247–59.
40. See Chapter XII, 'The Prayer to Jesus'.

41. Vol. 5 (Athens, 1963) p. 66; see Hausherr, *Noms* 279ff.
42. Jozef Ziegler, *Dulcedo Dei. Ein Beitrag zur Theologie der griechischen und lateinischen Bibel* (Münster, 1937).
43. See Ignatius, Polycarp, later Tertullian, *De carne Christi* 6; PL 1:809; see Gustave Bardy, 'Docétisme', DS 3:1461–68.
44. *The Mystical Theology of the Eastern Church* (London, 1957) 243.
45. *Lettres* x. 96; coll. Budé, vol 4, ed. M. Durry, (Paris, 1947) 96 [English translation by I. D. Lewis, *The Letters of The Younger Pliny* (London, 1879) 377–80.]
46. Arnobius, *Adversus nationes* I. 36; ed. A. Reifferscheid, CSEL 4, (1875) 23.
47. See Jean Augustin Robilliard in DS 5:26–33.
48. *De fide orthodoxa* III.8; PG 94:1013ff.
49. See DS 7/2: 1536–1601.
50. See DS 7/2: 1536.
51. *The Mystical Theology of the Eastern Church*, 243, 215.
52. See below, 3. *To The Father*.
53. Robert Koch, 'L'imitation de Dieu dans la morale de l'ancien Testament', in *Studia moralia*, vol. 2 (Rome, 1964) 73–88.
54. See DS 7/2: 1539ff.
55. The list is in the Lucien Cerfaux, *Le chrétien dans la théologie paulinienne* (Paris, 1962) 311.
56. See L. B. Gillon, 'L'imitation du Christ et la morale de saint Thomas', *Angelicum* 36 (1959) 270–75.
57. *The Life in Christ* VIII: PG 150–721D; trans. C. J. deCatanzaro, (New York, 1974) 226.
58. *Scala Paradisi* 1; PG 88:633B.
59. See Chapter III, *The Distinction between Image and Resemblance*,
60. This is the doctrine of Book I of his *Commentary on John*; see Margherite Harl, *Origène et la fonction révélatrice du Verbe incarné* (Paris, 1958) 290.
61. See, for example, Cardinal Bérulle, *Oeuvres de piété*, n. 54 (77) (Paris, 1944) 202.
62. See Harl, *Origène* 291.
63. *Oratio* 1.5; PG 35:400A; *Grégoire de Nazianze*, 107ff.
64. *Oratio* 39.14; PG 36:349C; LNPF, ser. 2, vol 7:357.
65. Sergei Nikol Bulgakov, *The Orthodox Church* (London, 1935) 150; cf. Boris Bobrinskij, in Serge Verchovskoj, *Pravoslavie v žizni* (New York, 1935) 244ff.
66. See Gregory of Nazianzus, *Oratio* 19.13 (PG 35:1060AB) 42.13 (PG 36:473A).
67. See A. Olttramare, *Origines de la diatribe romaine* (Lausanne, 1926).
68. Hélène Pétré, 'Exemplum–époque patristique', DS 4/2 (1961) col. 1886–92.
69. See PG. 65:73C; *duśepoleznaja* in Russian.
70. *Ibid.*, 72A. [*The Sayings of The Desert Fathers*, CS59 (1975) xviii]
71. See *Scala Paradisi* 1; PG 88:623B.

3. TO THE FATHER

1. Henrich Fries, 'Dieu', EF I:341.
2. See René Antoine Gauthier, 'Eudémonisme', DS 4/2:1660–74; Spanneut, *Le stoïcisme des Pères*, 37.

52 Chapter Two

3. See Aristotle, *Eudemian Ethics* I.1; ed. A. F. Didot *Opera Omnia* (Paris: Firmin-Didot, 1850–1931) vol. 2:184.
4. A. J. Festugière, *Contemplation et vie contemplative selon Platon* (Paris, 1936) 289ff.
5. See Chapter 7, *Purification*, and 13, *The Deified and Purified Nous*.
6. *Laws* IV, 716c.
7. Plutarch, *Quaestiones conviviales* I. 1. 4.5; edd. Th. Dochner and Fr. Dübner *Plutarchus, Opera* (Paris, 1846–82) vol. 2: 743.
8. See Grégoire de Nazianze, 134ff; cf. Chapter 13, Theologia.
9. See Chapter 12, *The Ascent of the Spirit to God*.
10. Herodotus, *Historia* VII. 10.55; see Chapter 4, *The Moral Aspect of Self-knowledge*.
11. Juan Alfaro, 'Dieu-Père', EF I, 355–63.
12. *Kephalaia gnostica* III. 64, ed. Antoine Guillaumont, 123–25.
13. See Karl Rahner, 'Mystère', EF III, 163.
14. See Špidlík, 'La libertà come riflesso del mistero trinitario nei Padri Greci', *Augustinianum* 13 (1973) 515–23.
15. See Chapter 13, Theologia.
16. *Homily on Numbers* 10, 3; SCh 29 (1951) 199.
17. Oratio 16.9 *In patrem tacentem*; PG 25:945C (See the commentary by Maximus the Confessor, *Ambigua*, PG 91:1088AD); Oratio 8.23; PG 25:816C.
18. Michael Schmaus, 'Trinité', EF IV, 369.
19. The council of Florence; H. Denziger, *Enchiridion Symbolorum*, 703 (Freiburg/Br., 1963 ed.), p. 1330)
20. Basil, *De spiritu sancto* 16; PG 32;137b, LNPF, ser. 2, 8:23.
21. See Lot-Borodine in RHR 106 (1933): 35.
22. *De spiritu sancto* 18; PG 32:153B, tr. LNPF, ser. 2, 8:29; Cyril of Alexandria, *De incarnatione Unigeniti*, PG 75:1129B; ed. P. E. Pusey, *S.P.N. Cyrilli Archiepiscopi Alexandrini, De recta fide, De incarnatione Unigeniti . . .* (Oxford, 1868–77, 2nd edn. Brussels, 1965) p. 96: 'We are the sons of God through the Son in the Spirit'; see DS 4/2:1263.
23. Heinrich Fries, 'Unité', EF IV, 376–87.
24. *De divinis nominibus II.4; PG 3:641A; ibid.*, II. 1; 637: *tēn hyperēnomenēn enada*; see Albert van den Daele, *Indices Pseudo-Dionysiani* (Louvain, 1941) 139: *hyperennoomai*. by C. E. Rolt, *The Divine Names and Mystical Theology* (London: SPCK, 1977).]
25. See above.
26. See Irénée Henri Dalmais in DS 3:1376.
27. See Irenaeus, *Adversus haereses* III.19.1; PG 7:939B.
28. Theodore of Ancyra, *In nativitatem* 5; PG 77: 1356BC.
29. *The Iliad*, V. 441–42: 'Never the same — Apollo tells Diomedes — is the race of the gods who are immortal and men who walk upon the earth'.
30. Arrian's *Discourses* of Epictetus II.8.11; ed. H. Schenkl, *Epicteti Dissertationes ab Arriano litteris mandatae* (Leipzig, 1898).
31. *Letter to the Ephesians* 9.2.
32. *To the Magnesians* 14.1.
33. Protrepticus 1.8; SCh 2bis (1949) 63. [Tr. *Exhortation to the Greeks* I.8; ANF, vol. 2, 174.]
34. *Against the Arians* III. 19; PG 26:361C–364A; LNPF, 4: 404; cf. 24–25 (col. 373–376); *De decretis* 31; PG 25:473.
35. *Quaestiones ad Thalassium* 59; PG 90:608D–609A.

Life in God

36. See Chapter 3, *The Consciousness of Grace*.
37. See Georgios I. Mantzarides, *The Doctrine on the divinisation of man in Gregory Palamas* (in Greek) (Thessalonica, 1963).
38. See Lot-Borodine, RHR 106, Introd. by Jean Daniélou.
39. See Chapter 5, *The Unity of The Deified Word*, and 13, *The Theoteles Logos*.
40. *De incarnatione Unigeniti*; PG 75:1229B; see L. Janssens, 'Notre filiation divine d'après saint Cyrille d'Alexandrie', in *Ephemerides Theologicae Lovanienses* 15 (1938) 233–78.
41. *In Joannem* 14.2; PG 59:93C; *Ad Romanos homiliae* 14.2, PG 60: 526BD; see Jean Kirchmeyer in DS 6/1: 840.
42. *Ad Diognetum* 11.4. [Tr. in FC 1:357ff.]
43. John Chrysostom, *In Joannem* 14.2; PG 59:93B; Cyril of Alexandria, *In Joelem* 28; PG 71:380AB; ed. Pusey, vol. 1:338.
44. See Kirchmeyer in DS 6: 836ff; Ignace de la Potterie, 'L'onction du chrétien par la foi', in *La vie selon l'Esprit*, Unam Sanctam 55 (Paris, 1965) 107–67.
45. See Edouard des Places, *Syngeneia. La parenté de l'homme avec Dieu d'Homère à la Patristique* (Paris, 1964).
46. See DS 6:836.
47. Irenaeus, *Adversus haereses* III.18.7; PG 7:937AB; Jean Daniélou, *Platonisme et théologie mystique*, 2d ed. (Paris, 1953) 110–23.
48. Heb 9:15 and 12:24; used frequently by Ethiopian authors.
49. Theophan the Recluse, *Načertanie christianskogo nravoučenija* [*Christian Moral Teaching*] (Moscow, 1895), 309; Pseudo-Macarius, *De charitate* 18–19; PG 34:929ff.
50. See DS 6:836.
51. *Ibidem*.
52. *Ibid.*: 858–59.
53. See J. Stoffels, *Die mystische Theologie Makarius des Aegypters und die ältesten Ansätze christlicher Mystik* (Bonn, 1807) 160ff.
54. See DS 6: 839.

3

THE NEW LIFE

1. THE IMAGE AND LIKENESS OF GOD

The Importance of the Question

THE RELATIONSHIP OF THE IMAGE to the model has a special importance in the thought of the Eastern Fathers. It lies at the heart of allegorical exegesis: the Old Testament contains the shadow of true reality, the New Testament bears its image, but the reality itself will be found only in the world to come. The same holds true for the visible world: things are copies of eternal models.[1] It has been noted that the Western mind examines the efficient cause (*causa efficiens*) whereas the Eastern concentrates on the *causa exemplaris*, pondering the meaning of emerging facts.[2]

Among these many relationships there was one of crucial importance: man who belongs to the world of reason and dominates the visible world is made in the image of God, the ruler of the intelligible world.[3] Even though man's creation in the image of God has never been questioned, there has existed a wide divergence of opinion about the nature of this image. In the fourth century pseudo-Caesarius echoed this lack of consensus.[4] Nowhere, moreover, do the Fathers present an organic theology of the image: they offer elements of a synthesis, but the synthesis itself is missing.[5]

The Theme of the Image in Scripture and Hellenistic Philosophy

Both in content and certainly terminology, this theme goes back to a twofold source, one scriptural, the other philosophic.

There are several passages in Scripture which speak, in various contexts, of the image of God.[6] The basic text is Genesis 1:26–27, describing the creation of man. The weight of the description is derived not so much from the term 'image' (the Semitic mentality is not 'formal'), as from the context of the revelation proper to Scripture: man is 'on the side' of God. Adam comes from God just as he begets children himself (Cf. Lk 3:38).[7] A study of the pauline theology of Christ as the image of God allows us to divide the texts into two groups, one which presents Christ as the image of God,[8] the other which deals with Christ as the model for Christians.[9]

The Fathers based their themes of the image on Scripture but amplified them with the help of abundant materials taken from Greek philosophy. Indeed, the very concept of assimilation (*homoiōsis, exomoiōsis*) is derived from Plato. According to the famous formulation in the *Theaetetus*,[10] the duty of the sage was 'to fly away from earth to heaven as quickly as possible; and to fly away is to become like God as far as this is possible; and to become like him is to become holy, just, and wise'.[11] This idea became a commonplace in Stoic circles and in Neoplatonism; it occupied an important place in the hermetic writings,[12] and is intimately linked to the thought of Plotinus.[13]

In this Greek doctrine of the likeness there were elements which the Christian could incorporate: the spiritual character of the image (although, on the other hand, the term 'spiritual' remained ambiguous),[14] the dynamic attraction of the image which prompted the soul to reascend to God, and the relationship between contemplation and likeness. There were, however, elements which could not be assimilated: the necessary character of the generation of the image in Plotinus, and the danger of subordinationism in the generation of the Word. The hellenistic speculations about the image therefore required serious adaptation in christian circles. Let us consider the main points on which the Fathers insisted.

Man 'the Image of God', of the Trinity

In the Book of Wisdom (2:23) man is not only 'in' the image of God, he is 'the image of God' properly. Gregory of Nyssa, who in his anti-Arian polemic stressed the perfect equality of the three persons, preferred to speak as follows: God is always the archetype in whose *image man is said to have been created*.[15]

The efforts of an Augustine to discern within the human mind a replica of the life of the three persons was, however, largely alien to traditional Eastern concerns.[16] Elements of this doctrine are supposedly found in Gregory of Nyssa; it is present indeed in the undoubtedly apocryphal *De eo qui sit ad imaginem* which is attributed to him[17] and especially in the *Commentary on the Hexaemeron* by Athanasius of Sinai.[18] Ephrem illustrated the Trinity by means of the three constituent elements of the human person; while the spirit corresponds to the Father, however, it was the human body (the third element) which became a parallel to the Holy Spirit.[19] Gregory Palamas came close to the Augustinian concept but did not develop it systematically.[20]

The trinitarian meaning of the concept of the image is certainly found in the East, but it was applied in a social sense to the Church, the human collectivity united in divine unity.[21]

'After' the Image of God

The expressions 'in the image of God', "after" God's image' (*kat' eikon*) and 'the image of God' are not synonymous. 'In' the image sounds as if God first created an image-prototype in terms of which he would then have created man. This intermediate image could be wisdom (Ws 7:26) or the Logos.[22] Christ, however, is the true archetype according to which man is created and re-created; he is 'in the form of God' (Ph 2:6), "the image of God" (2 Co 4:4). The entire tradition on this point may be summarized by saying that man is in the image of the Word and that he is the image of God through the mediation of the Word. He is therefore 'an image of the image'.[23]

This general statement, however, includes rather divergent interpretations depending on whether the image was conceived as a visible or an invisible reality. There is no doubt that Irenaeus thought the God-man was the model according to which Adam was created by God, and that man was thereby made like to 'the invisible Father through means of the visible Word'.[24] The Alexandrians (Origen, Athanasius, Evagrius, and others), in return, espoused the Philonian concept of an invisible image which they applied to the Word.[25] That this insistence on invisibility ran the risk of minimizing the humanity of Christ was revealed more clearly after the soteriological disputes. The outcome was the balanced synthesis of Maximus the Confessor.[26]

In addition, the term 'spiritual' has also become better understood over the years, as is indicated by a recent text of Paul Evdokimov: 'What distinguishes man from the angels is that he is made in the image of the Incarnation. The purely "spiritual" becomes incarnated and penetrates all of nature through its "lifegiving" energies....'.[27]

The Distinction Between Image and Likeness

Clement of Alexandria was the first to inquire into the origin of this distinction.[28] It is neither Platonic, no matter what Clement believed,[29] nor Stoic, nor Philonian. It is based on the commentary of Genesis (1:26–27). The distinction in Hebrew between the two expressions *be selem* and *ke demut* ought not to be exaggerated; it is a matter of 'resembling image' (in our image, after our likeness). The Septuagint, however, made these into a coordinate expression, 'in our image *and* likeness'. The words *eikōn* and *homoiōsis* were introduced here by the translator. At that time, under the influence of Plato and his disciples, *eikōn* could mean participation in a sensible mode whereas *homoiōsis* referred to the perfect spiritual resemblance toward which man must strive.

Several authors—not only those who used a Semitic language but also certain Greeks—did not take this nuance into account and did not distinguish between image and likeness: Athanasius of Alexandria, Didymus, the Cappadocians, pseudo-Macarius, and others. Yet Irenaeus made systematic use of this distinction. For him the couplet image-likeness corresponded to the pauline couplet fleshly man-spiritual man;[30] it was therefore the Holy Spirit who for him established 'the likeness' to God.[31] Origen, followed by one strand of the Eastern tradition, utilized the dynamic character of the image. The image is but incipient deification: its goal is to become as like God as possible. This ascension from 'image to likeness' will be completed in the glory of the risen body (Cf 1 Jn 3:2) and in conformity with Christ's prayer (Jn 17:21), in unity.[32]

From the Image to the Likeness

According to Origen's interpretation, 'man received the dignity of God's image at his first creation' — on this connection others speak of baptism[33] — but he must acquire the perfection of this likeness 'for himself by his own diligence in the imitation of God'.[34] The image is like a seed: 'the soul conceives by this seed of the Word and the conceived Word is formed in it'[35] in conformity with the virtues of Christ.[36]

Progress in the spiritual life develops from *praxis* to *theōria*.[37] The Alexandrians who saw the image in the *nous* (intelligence) accentuated a transforming contemplation which is also rooted in the image of God in the soul.[38] Origen explained this in the numerous texts where he commented on 2 Co 3:18. He gave an active meaning to the word *katoptizomenoi*, 'looking as in a mirror, contemplating', and interpreted it in the hellenistic manner as a vision which transforms.[39]

It goes without saying, of course, that those who identified the image with the likeness did not in the least deny spiritual progress.

The Place of the Image

Great diversity of opinion existed on this point.[40] Since the monks avoided theological discussions Abba Sopatrus admonished them in the *Sayings*: 'Do not allow a woman to enter your cell and do not read apocryphal literature. Do not speculate on the image.'[41] Even the great theologian Epiphanes wrote that 'one should categorically not seek to define where the image is actualized'.[42]

Of course, the answers varied depending on one's point of view, manner of analysis, and the way in which the question was asked. There were three aspects which were of especially burning interest to christian writers:

1) If man *is* the image of God, then the question about the place of the image would become an examination of the true nature of man.

2) Western theology asked a special question: *de sede gratiae*. The traditional answer was that grace resided primarily in the soul

and secondarily in the body. An answer of this type was suggested by the very question about the 'place' of the image.

3) From the practical standpoint, which was what interested ascetical writers, the question became: which human attribute is most godlike? This is the one that should be cultivated.

Is the Image of God the Soul Alone or the Whole Man or Only 'The Spirit'?

The Alexandrian position is well known. Since God is spirit, man is the image of God insofar as he is joined to that spirit.[43] Origen's criticism touched not only those who saw the image only in the body but also those who, like Irenaeus, located it in the entire human composite.[44] This doctrine of the incorporeal character of being in the image coincided with Origen's continued struggle in favor of the allegorical sense of Scripture and of the spirituality of God.[45]

Man is undoubtedly spiritual, but his composite character cannot be denied. That is why Irenaeus, and still more the Syrian exegetes, made the body a part of their definition of the image.[46] Maximus the Confessor emphasized this integration very strongly[47] when he described the effects of the image on the various levels of the human being. In the words of Vladimir Lossky, 'Man created "in the image" is the person capable of manifesting God to the extent to which his nature allows itself to be transformed by deifying grace'.[48]

The mystics approached the question from a different angle. They often searched for the *apex mentis*,[49] the mysterious abode wherein the Holy Spirit indwells the human being, the place where God and man meet.[50] It had to be in the noblest part of the soul: the *nous* (intelligence), *logos* (*mens*), *hēgemonikon* (the ruling part) (the *principale cordis* in Rufinus), the heart, or simply the spirit (*pneuma*).[51] The image of God was therefore to be found in that part of the soul which is influenced by the mind, where it becomes one spirit with the *Pneuma*.[52]

Since the soul becomes conformed to the Spirit according to the degree of its 'spiritualization', Cyril of Alexandria identified the image of God with sanctification (*hagiasmos*).[53] When the question was viewed from this perspective, there arose a great diversity of opinions that were not mutually exclusive. The image of God could be discerned in all the virtues and prerogatives of the spiritual man. He resembles God through his freedom,[54] *apatheia* (impassibility),[55] gnosis,[56] mercy,[57] and immortality.[58]

The Alexandrian view insisted on spirituality, whereas the Antiochenes saw man in God as possessing universal dominion[59] (which is nothing but an expression of his freedom). The concept of lordship over the universe is basically Semitic, in spite of its Stoic accretions. The Fathers set it within a theological perspective: in the created order man prolongs the work of God. This mission is indicated by man's upright posture, 'by the fact that he is the leader' (*kata to archikon*), as Diodore of Tarsus stated, concluding on a note that bears witness to the same Semitic mentality: 'St Paul is therefore fully justified in stating that man alone is the image and reflection of God, and woman the reflection of man'.[60]

The Image and Evil

On the one hand, a series of texts mention the 'loss' of the image through sin: 'a hardened heart ... no longer receives the imprint of the divine image'.[61] On the other hand, the image is always present, but in a manner which is hard to define with precision. The image has only been obscured. Once evil is removed, qualities of the image reappear on their own, veiled only[62] by 'some ugly mask'.[63] According to Origen's well-known idea, our sins impose on us images of the terrestrial (the devil),[64] of beasts (the descent of the *logika* [reasonable] into *aloga* [the animals][65], of Caesar (a symbol of the demon, according to Origen, who was borrowing from another tradition).[66] The coexistence of two images causes the sinner to be inwardly divided. Catharsis will allow him to recover his original purity.[67] Clearly good and evil cannot dwell together under the same aspect in the soul. To believe that they could was the error of the Messalians.[68]

And so there was a fluctuation between the 'lost image' and the likeness that was 'dimmed' or 'covered over' (now and then, the two occur next to one another in the same text). These variations on the level of expression did not preclude coherent thought on the deeper plans of spiritual meaning. Created in the divine life man retains a nostalgia for it when he is separated from it through sin.

2. THE NATURAL LIFE

Natural Law

In Stoicism virtue consisted essentially in adhering to the world-order, an expression of the divine will of which everyone's inner *logos* forms a part. Life had to be lived in harmony with this logos: *homologoumenos zēn* (living according to reason), as Zeno said. Since *logos* and *physis* were synonymous, Cleanthes added: living in consonance with nature.[1] Panaetius further enlarged the expression: *to zen kata tas dedomenas hemin ek physeōs aphormas*[2] (to live according to the means given us by nature). He thereby humanized morality: one must live according to all the tendencies which nature has placed in man and not only according to the *logos*, as Chrysippus understood it.[3]

Set apart from the nations, the Jewish people were placed by God under a positive law revealed by God himself, the Mosaic Law. Philo, however, indicated its relation to the natural law:[4] by virtue of this conformity to Universal law, the Hebrew sage was the Living Law.[5]

The concept of natural law in the moral sense is found in Justin and Irenaeus, but it was Clement of Alexandria who stated explicitly that 'the law of nature and the law of revelation are one and come from God'.[6]

The term 'nature', was not, however, always uniform. For the pre-Socratics nature meant chiefly whatever was not specifically human: visible nature.[7] Stoic philosophy attributed a concrete and real existence to nature. And since the Fathers had more reason still to affirm the concrete solidarity of mankind, they easily used expressions such as: Christ saved 'human nature', that is, all human persons.[8]

For their part, however, Christians generally adopted the Platonic and Aristotelian concept. While examining the nature of the soul, Plato defined nature as the 'capacity' a thing has 'of acting or being acted upon'.[9] The Aristotelian definition followed the same line.[10] This meaning corresponds to the origin of the words *physis* in Greek and *natura* in Latin, of terms designating growth, generation, and origin. Nature was the principle (*archē*) inherent in the things themselves, whereas that which existed

The New Life 63

through 'art' (*technē*) had to be begun by an outside force. Christians believed in creation. Nature was therefore what God has sown: it was up to man to cultivate it.[11] Nature was a powerful force.[12]

The Word 'Nature' in West and East

In Western theology, the spiritual man is a 'natural' man to whom grace has been added. Human nature (*natura pura*) includes the intellectual and the animal life, and to this the spiritual life (the supernatural) has been added and somehow superimposed on a purely human economy.

In the East, the expression, man 'in the image of God' (that is, with the grace of the Spirit) defines exactly what man is 'by nature'. 'By his creation man shares the nature of God',[13] Evdokimov states, and so 'charismatism is intrinsic to human nature'.[14] What the West calls 'natural-supernatural' is simply called 'human-divine', or 'created-uncreated' by Eastern authors.[15] Consequently, for man 'the natural' (*kata physin*) consists of whatever is for him a true good: charity, faith, the virtues, *gnosis,* and so on. Wickedness is sin, evil thoughts, the passions—all these are 'against nature' (*para physin*).[16]

Ephrem explained that it is not man's nature which is corrupted, but his habits, and that this corruption has altered nature. Only deliverance from sin allows the appropriate use of nature.[17] And we read in Evagrius: 'When we were created at the beginning, seeds of virtue existed naturally in us but no malice at all...'.[18] The demons have hounded us from 'the state which is rightfully ours'.[19]

To Eastern theologians, conversion is a return to our 'first nature..., the only one willed by God.'[20] Unlike theologians in the West, they do not speak of *natura lapsa* (fallen nature). Part III, Chapter 54, of *The Imitation of Christ*, which cautions man to heed not 'nature' but the voice of 'grace', is therefore hard for them to understand.

There existed, however, various modes of expression even in the East.[21] In the *Spiritual Meadow* of John Moschus (where an anti-Evagrian attitude is clearly present) Abba Marcellus says: 'Brothers, nature excites the passions, but the intensity of ascetical effort quenches them'.[22] Theodoret (who reflects the Antiochene current) spoke of a 'nature full of passions'.[23] The transition to the pejorative sense is explained by the fact that when we consider concrete, existing nature, then each person identifies it with his own 'character'.[24] After that, it becomes difficult not to see one's present, fallen state. Even a Greek, Gregory Nazianzen, recommended 'doing violence [*ekbiazein*] to nature'.[25] It is perhaps in this sense that one has to understand the texts by Athanasius[26] and John of Damascus that explain the fall as a transition from the *hyper physin* to the *kata physin*.[27] A few texts by pseudo-Macarius even remind one of the Latin *natura pura*, when he states that nature is capable of fellowship both with wickedness and with the Holy Spirit.[28]

In general, however, the East defended the basic goodness of 'nature' because the authors were always fighting traces of Manichaeism, Messalianism, and other dualistic systems. In the West, by contrast, the main heresy was Pelagianism, which deemphasized divine grace. Augustine therefore devoted himself to demonstrate convincingly how nature had been weakened and corrupted by sin. One and the same teaching results, consequently, under a noticeable difference in terminology. This striking difference must be noted in a study of the texts.

The Happy Life

The Fathers' theology of blessedness has points indisputably in common with Greek eudemonism.[29] They often stated explicitly that they had borrowed the expression 'the happy life', *vita beata*, from the philosophers to indicate what Scripture meant by eternal life. They certainly were quick to add that the prophets had spoken of blessedness even before the philosphers had, and that Christ and David began their teaching with the same word, 'blessed'.[30] The phrase 'inexpressible joy' in the First Letter of Peter (1:8) has had a long history in spiritual literature.[31]

As to terminology, the Septuagint avoided the greek terms of the *eudaimonia* group; it used *makarios* and words of the same family exclusively. Aristotle considered these expressions identical.[32] Nevertheless, in order to understand the scope and meaning of the many maxims of Wisdom on true happiness they should be set in the religious climate in which they were uttered. The Beatitudes of Christ (Mt 5:2-12, Lk 6:20-26) present a program of christian blessedness based on a radical reversal of values which is made possible through Jesus, who is himself the highest value. One must however admit that christian 'eudemonism' never took on a systematic form, but has been expressed instead through images and symbols.

Eternal Life

The living God[33] calls man to eternal life in him. He is 'the fountain of life' (Ps 36:10). Christ is the source of life (Jn 5:26) and bestows it abundantly (Jn 10:10); He is the life (Jn 14:6, 11:25). The passage from death to life is repeated in the one who believes in Christ (Jn 5:24). Yet, this life will not reach perfection until the day when the risen and glorified body will be part of it, when 'Christ, our life' (Col 3:4) will be manifested.

This 'eternal life' (*zoē* as distinguished from *bios*, temporary life) will be complete only in eternity, in the age which is to come. One speaks of the eschatologism of the Eastern Church[34] which focuses its main attention on the *eschata* (last things), the events to come. This can be expressed even under the form of mutual rebukes. On the one hand, the West may be guilty of being too absorbed with the works of this world which passes away; Eastern Christians, on the other hand, are accused of lacking interest in social and charitable activities.[35]

Of course, Christianity is essentially 'eschatological'. We should live in the expectation of the 'restoration of all things' (Ac 3:21). The last things, however, are already rooted in this life on earth. Consequently, it is possible to focus attention on one or another aspect of *zoē*. There will be times when everything is centered around 'waiting'; there will be others when the kingdom of God seems to be so present that someone already perceives 'heaven on earth'; finally, there are people who concentrate with such intensity on the work to be done in this life that meditation on the last things becomes almost secondary.

In sermons to the people, especially in times of present or expected calamities, the things to come were always the theme chosen to move the audience.[36] By contrast, there were among the preachers those whom we can readily call 'moralists' or 'practical'. who considered it a special grace 'to be able to work for the true and living God',[37] 'to be capable of serving God' in the present life.[38] But the aim of the contemplatives is 'to see God', to imitate the angelic spirits,[39] to change the desert into paradise,[40] to be translated even now into the world to come. In the sense of being more contemplative, Eastern spirituality is more 'eschatological' than is that of the West. But it never forgot that one arrives at *theōria* through *praxis*. Christian eschatologism may not degenerate into passive, quiet expectation.

The Soul's Salvation

Scripture moves easily from the term 'life' to 'soul'.[41] Ultimately, the 'salvation of the soul' is the victory of eternal life.[42] God saves us, Christ is our Saviour (Lk 2:11), the Gospel brings salvation to all believers (Rm 1:16). Salvation is therefore a key term of scriptural language.[43] It was into these biblical terms of salvation (*sotēria*) that the great Doctors of the Church, liturgical texts, and monastic literature chose to translate the mystery of the spiritual life.[44]

In Hebrew the idea of salvation is expressed by a whole group of root-words referring to the same basic experience: to be saved meant to be rescued from imminent peril.[45] In Greek the verb *sozo* and its derivatives (*sotēria, sotērios, sotēr*) were used to convey the same idea of deliverance from danger and of being healed of a deadly illness, but also of keeping one's integrity, preserving one's health, seeing to one's well-being (*saos* connotes that which is intact). On account of this semantic polyvalence, the terminology of 'salvation' covered a complex reality. The person with any infirmity whatever was unhealthy. Complete salvation meant that at no time in life did one fail to acquire a degree of possible perfection. Salvation and 'perfection' were equivalent. Moreover, the term 'perfection' (*teleōsis* or *teleōtēs*) is rare in the ancient Fathers, as it is in the New Testament.[46]

The Body

It seemed easy to compare 'the salvation of the soul' inculcated by the Gospel to the doctrine of the philosophers as it was expressed, for example, by Epictetus: the soul is our true and greatest good; aside from it there is neither good nor evil.[47]

In a tract addressed to young men on how best to profit from hellenistic writings, Basil commented especially on the moral consonance between the gospel and philosophy: 'We should give the greatest care to our soul and through philosophy deliver it as it were from prison, from the bond that ties it to the passions of the body';[48] The danger of such a viewpoint is considerable, but it would be more dangerous to understand the expressions of the Fathers and the ascetics in a purely philosophical sense. If they called the work of salvation the *psychōn iatreia* (the healing of souls) and compared it to the healing of the body,[49] the contrast was transposed to a level higher than that of philosophy.[50]

'Spiritual Selfishness'

Advocates of the doctrine of 'disinterestedness'[51] claimed that the primacy of charity is saved through the denial of self. The ancient maxim of the monks, 'pay attention to yourself!' 'and to your soul'[52] would in their eyes therefore be only a very imperfect expression of the christian life. The masters of the spiritual life, however, clearly distinguished between inordinate self-love (*philautia*), which is carnal, from true love of self, which is spiritual. Total disinterestedness is impossible and can lead to mistaken conclusions.[53] The salvation of one's own soul does not rule out charity; on the contrary, it presupposes it, for charity is the soul's, even life's, most precious ornament.[54] For this reason the monks were often deeply involved in social activity, especially during periods of particular need;[55] they did not sidestep the apostolate, preaching, or teaching.[56]

On the other hand, we must admit that their understanding of brotherly love differed somewhat from that of the modern mind. Their love was directed more to their neighbor's soul than to his corporal needs; to pray for someone and do penanace they considered worth more than ministering to him in sickness. Dadišo Quatraya stated this traditional monastic conviction when he described 'the war of the passions and the demons with those in solitary retreat with a view to the love of God and man ... with a view to the love of God and neighbor'.[57]

3. PROGRESS IN THE SPIRITUAL LIFE

The Need for Progress

St Paul proclaims the need for spiritual growth with such words as *auxanein* (2 Co 9:10), *auxēsis* (Eph 4:16), and *bathmos* (1 Tm 31:13). 'Let us grow in all manner of charity in him who is our head, Christ' (Eph 4:15), '... until Christ be formed in you' (Ga 4:19). The word *morphōsis* (a shaping, in the biological and plastic sense of the term) takes into account both increase and the stages of grace in unending completion.

The gnostics divided men into more or less static, definitive categories (*hylikoi*—the somatic; *psychikoi*—the psychic; and *pneumatikoi*—the pneumatic). Irenaeus, by contrast, was concerned to give an overview of revelation while attempting to demonstrate its continuity as well as its innovations. The true God is the eternal God who prevents the world from growing old because he is *life*, because he re-creates incessantly as he has created from the beginning.[58]

Origen considered the organic growth of the creature endowed with reason based on the dynamic character of the image-likeness theme.[59] As to turning away from sin, Basil insisted a little too much on rapid change.[60] We may note here the influence of the Stoics, who hardly admitted the concept of moral progress because the *logos* does not admit of degrees (the *logos* is right, or it is not).[61] Abrupt conversions are also typical of the Russian mentality.[62] Yet the general opinion of the spiritual masters was that of a continuous *prokopē* (progress),[63] *apo mikrōn pros ta megala* (from the small to the great).[64] Grace was like a seed sown in the heart. Consequently, there existed well-ordered and distinct degrees allowing the humble person to ascend on high.[65] To trace human progress in a given virtue—in humility, charity, prayer, self-denial, *apatheia,* and so on[66]—writers often listed highly developed degrees, but they only reflected the integral growth of our life in God.

Names of the Degrees

The most frequent division made was between beginners (or novices), advanced, and perfect: 'There are three degrees according to which man may progress: the one for beginners, the intermediate, and the perfect.'[67]

The beginning of life was called infancy (*nēpion*), adolescence (*neaniai*) followed later and finally came full maturity or old age (Cf 1 Co 3:1-2; Eph 4:13). Every christian language has used the term 'old man' to designate someone experienced in the spiritual life: *geron, senex, saba, khello* or *hello, cer, starets, beri* (cf. the Arab *sheikh*).[68] The term *paidogeron* (child-old man), *puer-senex*, clearly indicated that spiritual growth was often more advanced than physical age.[69]

The Christian is on his way to God. This road is described at length in Origen's twenty-seventh *Homily on Numbers*.[70] Its forty-two stopping-points in the desert correspond to the forty-two generations enumerated by Matthew[71] and signify a deeper penetration into the mysteries of God.[72] This was also the thematic concept of Gregory of Nyssa's *Life of Moses*,[73] which gives a description of the perfect life by means of the structure of Exodus—an idea later used by Abba Isaiah of Gaza,[74] Philoxenes of Mabbug,[75] and many others.[76] To indicate progress in the life of prayer they used, above all, the mountain of vision and of the love of God which one goes up step by step.[77]

Jacob's dream (Gen 28:12-13) was to remain the great symbol of the spiritual ladder and to be used endlessly,[78] by Aphrahat, *The Book of Degrees*, James of Sarug, and others. The Syrian Jacobites loved to compose *seblata* or 'ladder' hymns. Many of the medieval manuscripts of John Climacus (John of the Ladder, from his famous *Climax*) contain miniatures which show graphically the ascent up the ladder of virtues.[79]

As man progresses, his attitude towards God changes: he passes from slavery to the rank of child (Cf Ga 4:7). In order to maintain a triad, Clement of Alexandria distinguished between the slave, the faithful servant, and the son.[80] Depending on the virtue which dominated each of the three stages a distinction was made between 'the instruction accompanied by fear', 'hope by reason of which we desire the best, and finally the love which assures perfection'.[81]

While Evagrius wanted to be 'detached from concern with body and soul' and live 'according to the intellect',[82] John the Solitary saw growth as beginning with the practice of the virtues proper to the body, then moving to those of the soul, in order finally to serve God in spirit. The general framework of his spiritual teaching is therefore the division of men into somatic, psychic, and pneumatic.[83] On that score he viewed himself as a faithful follower of St Paul (1 Co 3:3), and was followed by Philoxenes and Isaac of Nineveh.[84]

The principle of the three stages — purgative, illuminative, and unitive — is found in Plato.[85] This division became famous in the West through Dionysius the pseudo-Areopagite, who associated it with the triads of the church hierarchy: the ministers purifiy, the priest enlightens, and the bishop makes perfect; the initiates are purified, the holy people are illuminated, and the monks are perfect.[86]

A mystic like Gregory of Nyssa taught that the ascension of the soul towards God takes place first *in the light*, and afterwards *in the cloud*, until finally the perfect contemplate God *in the darkness*.[87]

Praktikē, Physikē, Theologikē

This scheme, of Stoic origin and encountered, for example, in Seneca (*moralem, naturalem, rationalem*),[88] is found in Albinus, from whom Origen may have taken it.[89] What was at first a simple classification of disciplines became a way of distinguishing between the degrees of the spiritual life.

A good indication of this evolution is found in Origen. He associates each of the three disciplines with one of the three books attributed to Solomon, differentiating between *ethikē* (the Book of Proverbs), *physikē* (The Book of Ecclesiastes), and *epoptikē* or *theologia* (The Song of Songs).[90] This division had already had a long history when Evagrius borrowed it and gave it a precise, technical meaning, one which through him, and after him, was destined to become classic in byzantine spiritual literature: 'Christianity is the dogma of Christ our Saviour. It is composed of *praktikē*, of the contemplation of the physical world, and of the contemplation of God' (*ek praktikēs kai physikēs, kai theologikēs*).[91]

The last two together form *gnostikē*, so that the tripartite scheme may be reduced to two terms, *praxis-gnosis* (practical — *ta praktika*— and gnostic chapters — *ta gnostika*)[92] which leads back to the old division, *praxis-theōria*.[93] In the tenth century Symeon the New Theologian wrote *The Practical and Theological Chapters*[94] in which 'theology' was the height of gnosis (or *theōria*) and *physikē* its first degree.[95]

The Meaning of the Degrees in the Spiritual Life

This is an idea typical of Scripture: the word of God, the Law, the prophets, the times are being fulfilled.[96] No stage is definitive. Far from ever taking satisfaction in their acquired perfection, the ascetics outdid each other in repeating that they were only beginners.[97] Progress was *atelestos*, without end.[98] One must always remount the ladder toward God.[99]

But two dangers need to be avoided during the ascent: 1) placing oneself on a higher step before passing through the preceding ones (for example, to seek *theōria* without *praxis*)[100]; 2) believing that the lower steps can be dispensed with because one practises the higher. The first steps have not been abolished: rather they are subsumed in the second. Moreover, the dynamics of the spiritual life involve an unceasing ascent that always leads back to the original starting point.[101] Even the mystical height is realized through infinite progress. Gregory of Nyssa taught that the soul that has subdued the agitation of the passions obtains stability on the rock, Christ. The soul, however, 'uses its stability as if it were a wing'.[102] It is viewed not as immobility but as the quiet flow of a river.[103] It is a 'stable movement', an *epektasis*.[104]

4. THE CONSCIOUSNESS OF GRACE

A Direct Experience of the Spirit?

Life is intimately linked to consciousness. But 'eternal life' is the hidden, mysterious life of God. We must therefore ask whether this life belongs to the realm of consciousness, whether it forms an observable part of the christian experience.

In nineteenth and twentieth century philosophy the word experience has been a key term.[105] By modern definition, 'experience is the direct, immediate presence of anything showing itself to us'.[106] Experience is thereby contrasted to the way of knowing by which reality is not directly present to the consciousness but becomes present in an indirect, mediate way through instruction, by means of abstract ideas.[107]

In the area of the christian life, Vladimir Lossky affirms that 'the Eastern tradition has never made a sharp distinction between mysticism and theology; between personal experience of the divine mysteries and the dogma affirmed and taught by the Church.[108] It is only the fallen mind 'turned Kantian' which is always ready to push the authentic christian experience back 'into the realm of objects of faith' (that is, the teaching of doctrine). It is a tendency of 'the anti-gnosis, the anti-light, the opposition to the Holy Spirit'.[109]

Orthodox Opposition to the Messalian Thesis

In the East the question of religious experience was always lively. The Messalians had insisted on the need for a conscious awareness of being in the state of grace. They were condemned toward the end of the fourth century, having gone too far. In keeping with their view of evil (they confused temptation with sin), they ignored or refused to admit a divine activity not present to consciousness. Consequently, baptism they considered inefficacious beause it changed nothing in the psychological state of the person baptized.[110] The reaction of the orthodox (Diadochus of Photice, Mark the Ascetic) was unambiguous: 'from the instant we are baptized, grace is hidden in the depths of the intellect, concealing its presence from the perception of the intellect itself'.[111] Direct experience of the Spirit's presence could therefore not be identified with any degree of deification.[112]

The answer to a related question concerning the certainty of salvation was also negative. The greatest of the cenobiarchs seem to have feared that their monks might have illusions about the certainty of their salvation. Theodore the Studite often adverted to this in his catecheses.[113]

Spiritual Feelings. 'A Sign of the Quickening of the Soul'[114]

Although spiritual feelings are not the only manifestation of the divine life in man, they are nonetheless a sign of spiritual health, thought Theophane the Recluse.[115] The final victory is gained only the moment one begins to experience feelings which are contrary to temptations, when one relishes nothing except the divine. The terms *anaisthētos, anaisthētein, anaisthēsia* (insensibility) usually carry a pejorative meaning. They signify obtuseness, slackness in spiritual matters, complete tepidity.[116] John Climacus describes this vice at length in a chapter entitled, 'On insensitivity: the death of the soul before the death of the body'.[117]

Others speak of *sklērokardia*, 'the sclerotic heart', or of *pōrōsis*, callousness, *duritia cordis, obduratio* (Is 6:9-10). This is a disease which begins with a 'darkening of the heart'.[118] It is a trial orchestrated by Satan, keen to create despondency, *accidie*, in the soul.[119] So said Diadochus of Photice, Dorotheus, John Climacus, Symeon the New Theologian, and others.[120]

Yet even those who ardently desired 'spiritual feelings' (the school of feeling)[121] could not deny that 'a sense of the divine' is subject to multiple variations. According to the explanation given by Theophane the Recluse (who summarizes typical passages in Diadochus of Photice), God most frequently instructs man according to the following pattern:

1) grace is present from the beginning; it is almost inseparable from man, forming as it were one substance with him;

2) at the beginning of the spiritual life grace often makes its presence felt as a consolation, a reward for labour;

3) Later, it often withdraws and God lets his saints suffer;

4) at the end, when the period of purification is over, God again grants his comfort and the fulness of the Holy Spirit.[122]

And yet, Theophane warns that 'Only the grace of God causes feelings that are truly holy. And when the grace of God gives something, it gives to whom, how, and when it chooses'.[123] Anyone who wants to arrive too quickly at the inner experience of grace is in danger of experiencing false and deceptive feelings.[124]

The Indirect Experience, Through Signs

Symeon the New Theologian said: 'The soul is invisible; whether it is healthy or not cannot be seen.... There are, however, visible signs which render its state manifest to all.'[125] The Holy Spirit bears fruit (Cf. Ga 5:22), and, as Nicetas Stetathos said, where the fruit can be seen there God resides.[126] What are these fruits? For St Paul life in the Spirit is not yet an intuitive understanding of the Spirit. It is a life of faith which nonetheless creates an authentic experience through signs, the certainty of a concrete presence. The charisms, such as the gift of tongues or of healing (1 Co 12:28 ff., 14:12) make one aware of a personal presence, of one who is 'indwelling' (Rm 8:11), who 'bears witness' (8:16), who 'joins himself to our spirit' (8:16) and 'cries in our heart' (Ga 4:6).

These signs are extremely varied. When reading the *Lives* of the saints we get the impression that the miraculous, the extraordinary, and the unusual are stressed. The farther removed we are from ancient times the greater becomes the reputation of the 'God-bearing Fathers who even raised the dead, performed great miracles, and received power against demons'.[127] Yet, such miraculous deeds are only mentioned as signs of God's approval of the life of our great ancestors in the monastic life, for 'in those days charity reigned'.[128] An admonition of this type can already be seen in Antony's *Great Discourse*; those who boast not about their virtue but about working miracles he reminds that this ability is only a gift and that it is our virtuous and disciplined life that causes our names to be written in heaven.[129]

A miracle certainly manifests the power of prayer,[130] but not directly a person's holiness. Nicolas Cabasilas explained this clearly: the soul who lives in Christ the Exemplar concurs with sacramental grace and is transformed; this transformation, which is perfection in virtue and true holiness, resides in the will and not in miracles or extraordinary gifts.[131] When it came to visions, without banishing them altogether, most spiritual masters had deep reservations about them.[132] We need only remember the horror with which the Byzantines and Syrians spoke of the Euchitae, from Ephrem to the Palamites. Indeed, the Messalians (Euchites) laid great value on the advent of the Spirit *aisthētos kai oratōs* (sensibly and visibly).[133] Pseudo-Macarius resorted to a classification of these phenomena, differentiating in *Homily VII* between sense knowledge (*aisthēsis*), vision (*orasis*), enlightenment (*phōtismos*), and revelation (*apokalypsis*).[134]

That is why we find in Philoxenes of Mabbug an absolute rejection of corporeal visions and the alleged revelations based on them. His statement is categorical and is placed in the mouth of St Paul: 'Indeed all the contemplations which words can express in the realm of corporeal beings are phantoms of the soul's thinking, and not of grace. Therefore, let Your Holiness be reminded of this, and be very wary of the phantasies of deep [subconscious?] thoughts.'[135] Philoxenes mentions an anecdote which made the rounds in Eastern monastic circles.[136] The devil appeared in human form to a hermit and said: 'I am Christ'. To which the solitary replied: 'I do not want to see Christ in this world'. Visions can only fling one into deplorable illusions; they lead to heresy and suicide.[137]

The obligation to keep extraordinary charisms secret was instilled, even when they were genuine.

> One day when Abba Tithoes was sitting down, a brother happened to be beside him. Not realizing this, he began to groan unconsciously, without being aware that the brother was beside him, for he was in ecstasy. Afterwards he made a prostration before him and said to him, 'Forgive me, brother; I have not yet become a monk, for I groaned in front of you.[138] The same thing happened to John the Dwarf, and his excuse was, 'Forgive me, for I have not yet learned the catechism'.[139]

The Outstanding Sign of the Spirit: Charity Manifested in Martyrdom

Among the charismatic activities which reveal the dynamic presence of the Holy Spirit charity comes first (1 Co 12:13– 14:1). It is the epitome of christian perfection.[140] But how can the perfection of charity be demonstrated? 'No one can acquire its perfection as long as he is on earth, save only the saints who have arrived at martyrdom and the perfect confession', Diadochus said.[141]

That martyrdom is an expression of fidelity to God had already been affirmed by Judaism.[142] For the early Christians, martyrdom was proof of God's presence.[143] Ignatius of Antioch has given us the elements of a theology, even a mystique, of martyrdom.¹⁴⁴ Irenaeus considered it a demonstration of perfect charity which could not be achieved without the presence of the Spirit: 'The martyrs bear their witness, and despise death, not after the infirmity of the flesh, but because of the readiness of the Spirit.'¹⁴⁵

The testimony of blood exemplified a limited situation. On the other hand, the Christian was called to bear witness to the love of God without regard to the circumstances of place and time. A twofold martyrdom was recognized very early. It was said of Attalus the Martyr that before his death in 1777, he was a martyr to the truth' through his christian involvement.¹⁴⁶ It was Origen who popularized the phrase 'martyrdom of conscience' (*martyrion tes syneidēseōs*).¹⁴⁷

It became more and more customary to assimilate to martyrs the men and women who had chosen 'the narrow path' of asceticism, the monks.¹⁴⁸ Antony's spiritual experience clearly shows how the asceticism of the desert spontaneously became a substitute for the quest of martyrdom — one which allowed the saintly martyr to become 'a daily martyr to his conscience and an athlete in the contests of faith'.¹⁴⁹ The spiritual authors never failed to point out the analogies between martyrdom and the monks' asceticism.¹⁵⁰ By his profession, the monk 'bears the cross'; his habit reminds him of this, said Theodore the Studite.¹⁵¹

But short of violent martyrdom and rigorous asceticism, the authentic christian life remains a valid argument for the presence of the Spirit. For 'the Spirit is preserved through faith and a pure life' (*dia tēs pisteōs kai tēs hagnēs anastrophēs*), Irenaeus said.¹⁵² Faith is a gift of the Spirit (1 Co 12:3) and the virtues are a participation in Christ,¹⁵³ and hence a sure sign of God's presence. For John Climacus perfect chastity above all, manifests 'the Maker of Nature' by its victory over 'nature'.¹⁵⁴

The 'True Gnostic'

Once the 'spiritual' has become, in the nomenclature of Clement of Alexandria, a 'true gnostic'¹⁵⁵ it is sensible to ask whether 'true *gnōsis*' is a sure sign of the presence of the Spirit. We are not speaking of the pseudo-*gnōsis* well known from the polemics of Irenaeus. Unless it is infused by the Holy Spirit as a reward for the

The New Life

ascetic life, *gnōsis* is not recommended to the spiritual man. The false *gnōsis* which leads to boasting and makes man fall away from charity inspires its owners with a pretended perfection. It is better to be unlettered (*idiota*),[156] and to walk in union with God through charity.[157]

The true gnosis is *theōria*, christian contemplation.[158] Yet it is not the same as holiness, according to Philoxenes of Mabbug, one of the rare authors of antiquity to deal with this subject.[159]

There also existed a special *gnōsis* given to the prophets whose ancient titles were 'seer' (1 Wi 9:9) and 'visionary' (Am 7:12). The description of this gift in St Paul (1 Co 12) and later in the *Didache* or the *Shepherd of Hermas* hardly differs from the description given by Irenaeus: 'we have heard many brethren in the Church who possessed prophetic gifts, and who through the Spirit spoke all kinds of languages and who for the benefit of all brought to light the hidden things of men'.[160]

Montanism, at its beginning in the second century, was a typical example of the illuminist conception of a 'new prophecy' which was opposed to hierarchy. By reason of its content and its psychological conditions it was viewed as contrary to the faith.[161] This 'new prophecy', as it styled itself,[162] nearly succeeded in discrediting the very gift of prophecy. In the West, the title 'prophet' disappeared from the Church. In the East, the title was still attached some centuries later, to the name of the great spiritual directors, as to Zeno the Prophet in the fifth century.[163] In the sixth century Dorotheus found two remarkable old men in a monastery, Barsanuphius and 'Abba John, surnamed the Prophet, because of the gift of discernment (*to dioratikon charisma*) he had received from God'.[164]

The charism of *diorasis* remained therefore a sign of the Spirit and was composed of two main elements: a knowledge of the mysteries of God (theology) and an understanding of the secrets of the heart (*cardiognosis*). It was a spiritual perspicuity that saw through the flesh, through time, and through space (*proorasis*).

There were great 'dioratics' among the spiritual directors of the *startzy* in Russia, for example.[165] It is a divine gift because 'only (God) is *kardiognōstēs* (knows men's hearts)'.[166] On the other hand, such clear-sightedness was a natural reward for purity of soul, according to the declaration of St Antony: 'I believe that, when a soul is perfectly pure and has persevered in its natural state, it becomes clear sighted and is able to see more and further than the evil spirits.'[167]

What characterized a spiritual man above all else was diakrisis — the discernment of spirits.[168] For Origen it was one of the marks of holiness: 'So, then, the soul progresses when it comes to the place where it begins to distinguish between visions; and it is proved to be spiritual if it knows how to discern them all.'[169]

Notes

1. THE IMAGE AND LIKENESS OF GOD

1. See Chapter 13, *Natural Contemplation*.
2. Yves Congar, *Les chrétiens désunis. Principes d'un 'Oecuménisme' catholique*. Unam Sanctam 1 (Paris, 1937) 252.
3. The theme of the image of God in man has been the subject of often important monographs.
4. *Quaestiones et responsiones* 155–172; PG 38:1108-37.
5. See, for example, Jean Philopon, *De opificio mundi* 6, ed. G. Reichart (Leipzig, 1897) p. 229–82.
6. Ws 7:24-28, Rm 8:29, 2 Co 4:4, Col 1:15, Heb 1:3, 1 Jn 3:2. On these texts, see F. W. Eltester, *Eikôn im Neuen Testament* (Berlin, 1958); J. Jervell, *Imago Dei. Gen. 1.26 f. im Spätjudentum, in der Gnosis und in den paulinischen Briefen* (Göttingen, 1960); Paul Lamarche, 'Image et ressemblance dans l'Ecriture Sainte', DS 7/2:1402-6.
7. See DS 7/2:1402.
8. 2 Co 4:4, Col 1:15.
9. I Co 15:49, 2 Co 3:18, Rm 8:29, Col 3:10; see B. Rey, *Créés dans le Christ Jésus. La création nouvelle selon saint Paul* (Paris, 1966) 226ff.
10. '175ab.
11. See also *Republic* VI.13.500c and X.12.613AB: *Laws* IV.716cd.
12. *Corpus Hermeticum*, eds. A. D. Nock and A.-J. Festugière (Paris, 1945) 9, 11.
13. See P. Aubin, 'L'image dans l'oeuvre de Plotin', RSR 41 (1953) 348ff.
14. See Chapter 1. *Cosmic Spirituality*, and 4, *Various Aspects of Trichotomy*.
15. *De hominis opificio*; PG 44:140C; cf Roger Leys, *L'image de Dieu chez saint Grégoire de Nysse* (Brussels, 1951) 96.
16. See J. Kirchmeyer in DS 6:816.
17. PG 44:1327-1346, and especially in PG 89:1143-50.
18. VI; PG 89:931A-932A, in Greek in the Parisinus gr. 861.
19. *Hymnes de fide* 18.4-5, ed. E. Beck, CSCO 154 (Syr. 73).
20. *Capita physica* 36-40; PG 150:1144-49; see J. Meyendorff, *Introduction à l'étude de Grégoire Palamas* (Paris, 1959) 316. [translated by G. Lawrence, *A Study of Gregory Palamas* (London, 1964].

21. See Špidlík, 'La Trinità nella spiritualità della Chiesa Orientale', in Ermanno Ancilli, *Il mistero del Dio vivente*, Collana della 'Revista di vita spirituale', Teresianum, vol. 3 (Rome, 1968) 230–45.
22. See Philo of Alexandria, *Legum allegoriae* 3.96; *De confusione linguarum* 146–47; *De opificio mundi* 24–25; *Quis rerum divinarum haeres* 230–31.
23. See J. Kirchmeyer in DS 6:815. In his theology, Athanasius makes constant use of it: R. Bernard, *L'image de Dieu d'après saint Athanase* (Paris, 1952) 21ff.
24. *Adversus haereses* V.16.1–2; PG 7:1167–68; see also IV.33.4; col. 1075b, and *Epideixis* 22; PO 12:676.
25. This is Origen's customary opinion; see H. Crouzel, *Théologie de l'image de Dieu chez Origène* (Paris, 1956) 71ff.
26. See *Ambigua*; PG 91:1081–85.
27. *La femme et le salut du monde* (Tournai-Paris, 1958) 59.
28. *Stromata* II.22.131.6; SC 38 (1954) 133.
29. *Ibid.*, 131.2.
30. *Adversus haereses* V.10.12; PG 7:1148–49; see M. Aubineau, 'Incorruptibilité et divinisation selon saint Irénée', RSR 44 (1956) 25–52; Antonio Orbe, 'El hombre ideal en la teologia de S. Ireneo', *Gregorianum* 43 (1962) 449–91.
31. *Adversus haereses* V.6.1; PG 7:1137.
32. *De principiis* III.6.1; GCS 5: p. 281, 3 ff.; Henri Crouzel, *La théologie de l'image de Dieu chez Origène*, 254.
33. The disagreement is often more apparent than real, baptism restoring a reality which man had originally received but then lost. See Diadochus of Photice, *Cent chapitres gnostiques* 89; SCh 5bis (1955) 149ff., and Introduction, p. 34ff. [English translation in *The Philokalia. The Complete Text*, vol. I (London: Faber & Faber, 1980) p. 288].
34. *De principiis* III.6.1; GCS 5:280; PG 11:333C; tr. G. W. Butterworth [*On First Principles* (New York, 1966) 245]; see also *Entretien avec Héraclite* 15–16, SC 67 (1960), 89.
35. Origen, *Homilia in Leviticus* 12.7; GCS 6:466, 23 ff.
36. See Chapter XI, *Virtue, likeness to God*. . . .
37. See Chapter 13, *No True Knowledge Without Love*.
38. Gregory of Nyssa, *De beatitudinibus* 6; PG 44:1272B; see below.
39. Origen, *Fragmenta in Lamentationes Jeremiae* 116; GCS 3, p. 276, 16 ff; see H. Crouzel, *Théologie de l'image de Dieu chez Origène*, 232ff, 60ff.
40. See Caesarius Nazianzenus (?), *Dialogus* III, interr. 155–59; PG 38:1107ff (Caesarius enumerates still other opinions); Roger Leys, *L'image de Dieu chez saint Grégoire de Nysse*, 59–93.
41. *Apophthegmata Patrum*, Daniel 7; PG 65:157B [CS 59:44].
42. *Panarion* 70.2.7; GCS 3; 234.
43. See Clement of Alexandria, *Protrepticus* 10.98.4; GCS 1:71; *Stromata* VI.91.72, and 14.112.4; GCS 2:462 and 488.
44. *Contra Celsum* VI.63; GCS 2:133, 23ff.
45. See *Selecta in Genesim* I.26–27; PG 12:93BC.
46. *Adversus haereses* V.6.1–2; PG 7:1136–39; Cf. the Pseudo-Clementine Hom. III.20.3, IX.3.1, and X.3.3; CGS 1:64, 132ff. Thus Eustathius Antiochenus, Eusebius of Emesa, Severianus of Gabala, Diodorus of Tarsus, John Chrysostom, and partially Theodorus of Mopsuestia (texts in DS 6:818).
47. *Ambigua*; PG 91:1181–85.
48. *In the Image and Likeness of God* (New York, 1974), 139.
49. See Heribert Fischer, 'Fond de l'âme, chez Eckhart', DS 5:650ff.

50. See Špidlík, *Théophane le Reclus*, 296.
51. H. Crouzel, *Théologie de l'image de Dieu chez Origène*, 157.
52. *Ibid.*, 157.
53. See Walter Burghardt, *The Image of God in Man according to Cyril of Alexandria* (Maryland, 1957) 65ff.
54. Gregory of Nyssa, *De opificio hominis* 16; PG 44:184B.
55. *Ibid.*; col. 137B.
56. See Maximus the Confessor, *Capita ducenta ad theologiam et oeconomiam spectantia* 3.55; PG 90:1284C.
57. See Origen, *Homilia in Leviticum* 4.3; PG 12:436B; Špidlík, *Joseph de Volokolamsk*, 73.
58. See Maximus the Confessor, (note 56 above).
59. See Hilda C. Graef, 'L'image de Dieu et la structure de l'âme', VS, Suppl. n. 22 (1952) 331–39.
60. The passage has come down to us in the *Catena* of Nicephorus, *In Genesim* 1.26; PG 33:1564ff (= *Fragmenta in octatenchum* by Diodorus of Tarsus, who copied the *Catena*); see Theodoret, *Quaestiones in Genesim, Interr.* 20; PG 80:108ff.
61. Origen, *In Romanos* II.4; PG 14:875A; see Crouzel, *Théologie de l'image*, 206; R. Leys, *L'image de Dieu chez saint Grégoire de Nysse*, 112.
62. See Leys, 112, Crouzel, 209.
63. Gregory of Nyssa, *De hominis opificio* 18; PG 44:193.
64. *In Johannem* 19.21(5); GCS 4; 322, 18; Crouzel, *Théologie de l'image*, 183.
65. *Fragmenta* of the *Selecta in Ezechielem, in Ez.* 8.9; PG 13:797B; Crouzel, 197.
66. *Matthaeum* 13.10; GCS 10; 207,20ff; Crouzel, 195.
67. See Chapter VII, *Purification*.
68. Irénée Hausherr, 'L'erreur fondamentale et la logique du messalianisme', OCP 1 (1935) 328–60; *Études de spiritualité orientale*, OCA 183 (Rome, 1969) 64–96.

2. THE NATURAL LIFE

1. Arnim, SVF III, 1–9, pp. 3–7; Max Pohlenz, *Die Stoa. Geschichte einer geistigen Bewegung*, vol. I (Göttingen, 1948–49) 116–18; Michel Spanneut, *Le stoïcisme des Pères de l'Église*, 241.
2. See Pohlenz, 200. Clement of Alexandria gives all these definitions word-for-word in *Stromata* II.129.1–8; GCS 2:183; SCh 38 (1954) 130.
3. See Spanneut, 241.
4. *De vita Moysis* II.48; [translation by A. J. Malherbe and Everett Ferguson, *The Life of Moses* (Kalamazoo-New York, 1978).]; A. J. Festugière, *La révélation d'Hermès Trismégiste* (Paris, 1944–45) vol. 2:539.
5. *De opificio mundi* 3; *De Abraham* 5; *De virtutibus* 194.
6. *Stromata* I.182.1; GCS 2:111, 18.
7. Helmut Kuhn, 'Nature, Etude philosophique', EF III: 189–94; see Gregory of Nazianzus, *Carminum Liber* I.II.2. verses 534 ff., PG 37:620.
8. Henri de Lubac in *Catholicisme* (5th ed., Paris, 1952) 329–409.
9. *Phaedrus* 270c.
10. *Politics* I, 252b, 32ff.

The New Life 81

11. See Gregory of Nazianzus, *Oratio* 2.17; PG 35:425C.
12. *Id.*, *Oratio* 22.1; PG 35:1132.
13. *La femme et le salut du monde* (Tournai-Paris, 1958) 68; See Jean Daniélou, *Platonisme et théologie mystique* (Paris, 1944) 63.
14. Evdokimov, *La femme*, 67.
15. See R. Leys, *L'image de Dieu chez saint Grégoire de Nysse*, 100ff.
16. Hausherr, *Philautie*, OCA 137 (Rome, 1952) 134 ff; *id.*, 'L'imitation de Jésus-Christ dans la spiritualité byzantine', in *Mélanges* . . . *F. Cavallera* (Toulouse, 1948) 239 ff; *Études de spiritualité orientale* OCA 183 (1969) 225 ff.
17. See *De paradiso* 7.18, ed. J. S. Assemani, *Opera omnia quae extant graece* (Rome, 1732–46) vol. 3: 584c; [Beck, *Des heiligen Ephraem des Syrers Hymnen De Paradiso und Contra Julianum*,] OSCO *Scr. syr.* 78 (Louvain, 1957) 70.
18. *Kephalaia gnostica* I.39, ed. Antoine Guillaumont, p. 639; see *Le traité pratique* 57; SCh 171 (1971 635.
19. *Praktikos* 43; SCh 171: 601 [translated by J. E. Bamberger, *Evagrius Ponticus: Praktikos and Chapters on Prayer* CS4 (Kalamazoo, 1978).]
20. Evdokimov, *La femme*, 142.
21. See Theodoret of Cyrus; PG 84:1164ff., (Index, *physis*).
22. PG 87:3020C, ed. SCh 15 (1946) p. 206.
23. Theodoret, PG 82:1288B; Maximus the Confessor, *Ad Thalassium*, *quaestio* 21; PG 90:317A.
24. Gregory of Nazianzus, *Carminum Liber* I.II.24, verse 3; PG 37:946; II.II.5, verses 117–19; col. 1529; Pseudo-Macarius, *Hom.* 26.5; PG 34:677AB.
25. Gregory of Naz., *Carminum Liber* I.II.32. verse 123; PG 27:925.
26. *De incarnatione Verbi* 4; PG 25:104B; see Louis Bouyer, *L'incarnation et l'Église-Corps du Christ dans la théologie de saint Athanase* (Paris, 1943) 36ff.
27. *Dialogus contra Manicheos* 71; PG 94:1569C.
28. See *Homilia* 17.4; PG 34:625D and 27.19; 708A.
29. René Antoine Gauthier, 'Eudémonisme', DS 4/2: 1660–74.
30. Basil, *In Psalmos* 1.3; PG 29:216A; Špidlík, *La sophiologie de S. Basile*, 1; see Ambrose, *De Jacob et beata vita* III.1.1; PL 14:615A.
31. See *Vita Antonii* 36; PG 26:896C; Evagrius, *Le traité pratique* 12, Sch 171: 526 [CS4:18–19]; Diadochus, *Cent chapitres* 59 and 91, SCh 5ter (1966) 119 and 152.
32. *Rhetoric* I.9.1376b, 33–34.
33. Josh 3:10, Ps 42:3, and others.
34. See Nikolai Serge Arseniev, *Duša pravoslavija. Radost voskresenija i preobraženie tvari* [*The Soul of Orthodoxy. The Joy of the Resurrection and the Transfiguration of the Creature*] (Novyi Sad, 1927); Stefan Zankow, *Das orthodoxe Christentum des Ostens, sein Wesen und seine Gestalt* (Berlin, 1928); Hermegild Biedermann, *Der eschatologische Zug in der ostkirchliche Frömmigkeit*, Das östliche Christentum, Neue Folge 8 (Würzburg, 1949).
35. See the opinion of V. Soloviev in Michel d'Herbigny, *Un Newman russe, Vladimir Soloviev* (1853–1900) (Paris, 1934) 263. [English trans. by A. M. Buchanan, *Vladimir Soloviev: A Russian Newman (1853–1900)* (London, 1918) 146.]
36. See Špidlík, *Joseph de Volokolamsk*, 58 ff; see Chapter V, *The World of the Past Has Gone*.
37. *Joseph of Volokolamsk*, 27.
38. Theodore the Studite, *Letters* II.134; PG 99:1432B.
39. See Cassian, *Collationes* 10.7; CSEL 13; 293ff.

40. See Garcia M. Colombás, *Paradis et vie angélique* (Paris, 1961).
41. See Chapter IV, *The Divine Origin of The Soul*.
42. Jm 1:21, 5:20, 1 P 1:9, Heb 10:39.
43. Colomban Lesquivit and Pierre Grelot, 'Salut', VTB, col. 1185–92.
44. See J. Kirchmeyer in DS 6:808–12.
45. VTB, col. 1185.
46. P. J. du Plessis, *Teleios. The Idea of Perfection in the New Testament* (Kampen, 1959); Karl Prümm, 'Das neutestamentliche Sprach-und Begriffsproblem der Vollkommenheit', *Biblica* 44 (1963) 76–92.
47. *Discourses* III.16.1, II.23.19.
48. *Sermo de legendis libris gentilium*; PG 31:581; Špidlík, *La sophiologie de S. Basile*, 101.
49. Gregory of Nazianzus, *Oratio* 2.16.; PG 35:425.
50. See Chapter IV, *Aphorisms on the Body*.
51. See Ephrem Boularand, 'Désintéressement', DS 3:550–91.
52. *Apophthegmata Patrum*, Antony 1; PG 65:76C [CS59:1].
53. See I. Hausherr, *Philautie*, OCA 137 (Rome, 1952) 17ff.
54. See Špidlík, *La sophiologie de S. Basile*, 149ff.
55. See Stanislas Giet, *Les idées et l'action sociales de saint Basile* (Paris, 1941); cf. Chapter VI, *The Practice of Charity in the Monasteries*.
56. See Ch. VI, *The Monks' Apostolate*.
57. Disc. 1.9; *Commentaire d'Abba Isaïe par Dadišo Quatraya*, French translation by René Draguet, CSCO 327 (*Scriptores syri*. 145) p. 10, 18ff.
58. See J. C. Huvé in DS 4/1:145.
59. See H. Crouzel, *Théologie de l'image de Dieu chez Origène*, 217ff.
60. See David Amand, *L'ascèse monastique de saint Basil* (Maredsous, 1948) 264ff.
61. See M. Spanneut, *Le stoïcisme des Pères de l'Église*, 242.
62. See I. Kologrivof, *Essai sur la sainteté en Russie* (Bruges, 1953) 12.
63. John Climacus, *Scala Paradisi* 1; PG 88:644A.
64. Evagrius, *Parainetikos*, p. 559, 156 a, ed. Frankenberg, *Evagrius Ponticus*, Abhandlungen der Gesellschaft der Wissenschaften zu Göttingen, N.F. 13,2 (Berlin, 1912).
65. Cassian, *Collatio* 14.2: PL 49:55A; SCh 54 (1958) 184.
66. Cassian, *De coenobiorum institutis* 4. 39; PL 50:198C–199B: ten degrees of humility must lead the soul to love of the good and to 'delight in the virtues'.
67. Isaac of Syria, *Sermones asceticae*; PG 86:854; Mark the Hermit, *De temperantia*; PG 65:1058–60.
68. See I. Hausherr, *Direction spirituelle en Orient autrefois*, OCA 144 (Rome, 1955) 322 [tr. forthcoming from Cistercian Publications—ed.]
69. See Hausherr, *ibid.*, 320.
70. PG 12:725B; see Walter Völker, *Das Vollkommenheitsideal des Origenes*, (Tübingen, 1931) 62–75; Jean Daniélou, 'Les sources bibliques de la mystique d'Origène', RAM 23 (1947) 131–37; *Origène* (Paris, 1948) 291–97.
71. *In Numeros* 27.3; PG 12:783C; GCS 7:259.
72. *In ep. ad Romanos* 5.8; PG 14:1042A.
73. See J. Daniélou, Introd. to the *Vie de Moïse*, SCh 1bis (1955) xviii–xix.
74. *Oratio* 24; PG 40:1174C.
75. *Homilia* 9; SCh 44 (1956) 263–66.
76. Roger le Déaut and Joseph Lécuyer, 'Exode', DS 4/2:1957–95.

The New Life 83

77. See Joseph Hazzayâ (7th century), ed. Alphonse Mingana, coll. *Woodbrooke Studies*, vol. 7 (Cambridge, 1934) 178–89, 255–61.
78. See Garcia M. Colombás, *Paradis et vie angélique*, 81ff., 92ff; E. Bertaud and A. Rayez, 'Echelle spirituelle', DS 4/1:62–86.
79. See Charles R. Morey, 'The Miniatures from a Manuscript of St. John Climacus, and their relation to Klimax Iconography', in *Studies in East Christian and Roman Art* (New York, 1918); J. P. Martin, *The Illustration of the Heavenly Ladder of John Climacus* (Princeton, 1954).
80. See Clement of Alexandria, *Stromata*. I.26; ed. Otto Stählin, GCS 2 (Leipzig, 1906) 107, 25ff.
81. *Stromata* IV.7; PG 8:1264C–1265A; see Basil, *Regula fusius tractata*, Prol. 3 (PG 31:896); Gregory of Nazianzen, *Homilia* 40.13; (PG 36:373); Gregory of Nyssa, *Homilia 1 in Cantica*. (PG 44:765).
82. *De oratione* 110; PG 79:1192; Hausherr, *Leçons d'un contemplatif*, (Paris, 1970), 142.
83. See I. Hausherr, *Jean Solitaire (Pseudo-Jean de Lycopolis). Dialogue sur l'âme et les passions des hommes* ... OCA 120 (Rome, 1939) 7ff., 37ff.
84. Isaac of Nineveh, *De perfectione religiosa* 12, ed. P. Bedjan, *Mar Isaacus Ninivita. De perfectione religiosa* (Paris-Leipzig, 1909) 122.
85. See A. J. Festugière, *Contemplation et vie contemplative selon Platon* (Paris, 1936) 82–249; René Arnou in DS 2/2:1730ff.
86. See R. Roques, *L'univers dionysien*, coll. Théologie 29 (Paris, 1954) 174–96; DS 2/2: 1785ff., 1890ff., DS 3:268ff.
87. *In Canticum Canticorum* II; PG 44:1000CD; see Chapter 13, *Ecstasy*. [Sermons from the Commentary on the Canticle may be read in *From Glory to Glory: Texts from Gregory of Nyssa's Mystical Writings*, trans. Herbert Musurillo, Introd. by Jean Daniélou (New York, 1979)].
88. See Plutarch as cited by Aetius, in H. Diel, *Doxographi graeci* (Berlin-Leipzig, 1929) 273; Arnim, SVF II, 15, where other texts are given.
89. See Hans von Balthasar. 'Die Hiera des Evagrius', in *Zeitschrift für katholische Theologie* 63 (1939) 96.
90. *Commentary on the Song of Songs*, Prol., GCS 8:75; see Jean Daniélou, *Origène* (Paris, 1948) 297ff; cf. DS 2/2:1769–72.
91. *Praktikos* 1; SC 171:499; [CS 4:15] see the Introduction by A. Guillaumont, SCh 170; p. 38ff.
92. Evagrius, *Praktikos*, Prologue 9, SCh 171:493 [CS 4:15, note 18].
93. Origen saw the distinction in the spiritual life between 'action' and 'contemplation' symbolized by Martha and Mary: *Commentary on the Gospel of John, fragments drawn from the catenae on John* 11.18, GCS 10: 547.
94. Ed. Jean Darrouzès, SCh 51 (1957) [English translation by Paul McGuckin, Cistercian Studies Series 41 (Kalamazoo, 1982)].
95. See Chapter 13, *The Degrees [of Contemplation]*.
96. See Albert Vanhoye, 'Accomplir', VTB, col. 8–11.
97. See I. Hausherr. *Penthos. La doctrine de la componction dans l'Orient chrétien* OCA 132 (Rome, 1944); 56. [English translation by Anselm Hufstader, *Penthos. The Doctrine of Compunction in the Christian East*, (Kalamazoo, 1982).]
98. John Climacus, *Scala* 29; PG 88:1148C; cf. step 26, col. 10688B.
99. Gregory of Nyssa, *Vie de Moïse* II.7.1. ed. Musurillo, *Gregorii Nysseni Opera*, VII (Leiden, 1964) 113, 4ff; SC la (1955), 104; see Cassian, *Conference* VI. 13ff, LNPF, vol 11, 359ff.

Chapter Three

100. Origen, *In Matthaeum Commentarium*, ser. 91; GCS 12: 207.
101. See W. Völker, *Das Vollkommenheitsideal des Origenes*, p. 110.
102. *De vita Moysis*; PG 44:405CD.
103. *Ibid.*; 977C.
104. See Placide Deseille, 'Épectase', DS 4/1: 785-88; T. Špidlík, 'L'eternità e il tempo, la zoē e il bios, problema dei Padri Cappadoci', *Augustinianum* 16 (1976) 107-16.
105. See Augustin Léonard, 'Expérience spirituelle', DS 4/2:2004-26.
106. M. Müller, *Expérience et histoire* (Paris-Louvain, 1959) 13.
107. See Réginald Grégoire, *L'intuition selon Bergson. Étude critique* (Louvain, 1947) 122-25.
108. Vladimir Lossky, *The Mystical Theology of the Eastern Church* (London, 1957) 8ff.
109. *Ibid.*, 230. In truth, can this experience be fully reconciled with the well-known 'kenosis (self-emptying) of the Holy Spirit ... who comes into the world, while his person is unrevealed in his very epiphany'?; see Evdokimov, *L'Esprit Saint et l'Église* (Paris: Fayard, 1969), 90; and Lossky, *The Mystical Theology*, 167.
110. See Hausherr, 'L'erreur fondamentale et la logique du Messalianisme', OCP 1 (1935) 328-60; *Études de spiritualité orientale* OCA 183 (Rome, 1969) 64-96.
111. Diadochus of Photice, 'On spiritual knowledge'; SCh 5ter (1966) 135; trans. *The Philokalia*, vol I, (London, 1979) p. 279; see Špidlík, *Théophane le Reclus*, p. 95.
112. *Théophane le Reclus*, p. 94ff.
113. *Catechesis* 38, ed. Athanasius Papadopoulos-Kerameus, *Megalē katechesis* (St Petersburg, 1904) p. 586.
114. Theophane the Recluse, *Načertanie christianskago nravoučenija* (*Christian Moral Teaching*) Moscow, 1895), 116ff., 318.
115. See *Théophane le Reclus*, 98ff.
116. Origen, *De principiis* I.8; GCS 5:104; See Hausherr, *Penthos*, OCA 132: 101f. [CS 53:88].
117. *Scala Paradisi* 13; PG 88:932.
118. Joseph Mac Avoy, 'Endurcissement', DS 4/1: 642-52.
119. Diadochus of Photice, *Hundred Chapters* 77; SCh 5ter (1966) 135; 'On Spiritual Knowledge', *The Philokalia*, vol. I (1979), 279.
120. See DS 4/1; 645; Symeon writes: 'Unless He [the Spirit] is present in a man and is known to dwell in him (*gnōstōs enoikesantos en autǫ*), it is in every way incongruous to call him spiritual'; tr. C. J. deCatanzara, *'The Catechetical Discourses*, X (1980) 163.
121. See above, Chapter I, *Spiritual Experience*.
122. Špidlík, *Théophane le Reclus, 102ff.*
123. *Pisma k raznym licam* (*Letters to various Persons*) n. 22 (Moscow, 1892) 108ff.
124. *Théophane le Reclus*, 101.
125. *Ibid.*, 95ff.; see Nicetas Stethatos, *On the Soul* 13ff.; *De l'âme* SCh 81 (1961) 76ff.
126. *On the Soul* 71, p. 132.
127. Paul Evergetinos, *Synagogē* II, Chapter 11 (Constantinople, 1861) 41.
128. See *Vitae Patrum* III, n. 181 (PL 73:799B); V, XVII, n. 19 (976BC); VII, XXVIII, n. 4 (1050C); I. Hausherr, *Direction spirituelle en Orient autrefois*, 51.

The New Life 85

129. *Vita Antonii* 38; PG 26:900A. [tr. *The Life of Antony*, Ch 15].
130. See I. Hausherr, *Direction spirituelle en Orient autrefois*, 51.
131. *Vie dans le Christ* 7; PG 150:685ff. [Trans. C. J. de Catanzaro *The Life in Christ*, Crestwood, New York, 1974).].
132. *Verba seniorum* XV, 68-71; PL 73:965C-966A; see J. Kirchmeyer in DS 6, col. 853.
133. Theodoret, *The Ecclesiastical History* IV (1C) 11; PG 82:1145A [Translation projected by Cistercian Publications — ed.].
134. PG 34:525D.
135. See Irénée Hausherr, 'Contemplation et sainteté', RAM 14 (1933) 192; *Hésychasme et prière*, OCA 176 (Rome, 1966) 34.
136. Published by François Nau in *Revue de l'Orient chrétien* 17 (1912) 206.
137. Hausherr, 'Contemplation et sainteté', 193, 35.
138. *Apophthegmata Patrum*, Titoes 6; PG 65:428 C [CS 59:237].
139. *Ibid.*, Colobos 22; 212D [CS 59:90].
140. See Chapter XI, CHARITY.
141. *Gnostic Chapters*, 90; SCh 5a (1966) 151; see *The Philokalia*, vol. 1:189.
142. 2 Macc 7:15; *Le quatrième livre des Maccabées*, ed. André Dupont-Sommer (Paris, 1939) 116.
143. *The Epistle to Diognetus* VII.9; tr. J. B. Lightfoot, *The Apostolic Fathers* (1978) 255.
144. See *To the Ephesians* 1.2; *Romans* 6.2; 4.2; 5.3; 6.1; *Trallians* 5.2; *Polycarp* 7.1.
145. *Adversus haereses* V.9.2; PG 7:1144C-1145A; ANF, vol. I:535; Harvey 2:342ff.
146. Eusebius, *Historia ecclesiastica* V.1.43; PG 20:425A; GCS 2/1:418.
147. *In Numeros* 10.2; PG 12:639a; *Exhortatio ad martyrium* 21; PG 11:589B. [English translation, *Exhortatio ad martyrium*, p.393ff., in *Alexandrian Christianity*, The Library of Christian Classics (Philadelphia, 1954.)]
148. See J. Kirchmeyer in DS 6; 862.
149. Athanasius *Vita Antonii* 47; PG 26, 912B; a formulation taken over by the *Vita Barlaam et Joasaph* 12 (103); PG 96:965b, ed. G. R. Woodward and Harold Mattingly, *St. John Damascene: Barlaam and Joasaph* (Loeb Classical Library 34, 1967) 172.
150. Edward Malone, *The Monk and the Martyr* (Washington, 1950).
151. *Parva Catechesis* 10, ed. E. Auvrey (Paris, 1891) 36.
152. *Adversus haereses* V.9.2; PG 7:1144, Harvey II, p. 342.
153. See Chapter XI, *Virtue-Likeness to God and Participation in Christ*.
154. *Scala Paradisi* 15; PG 88:88CD; virginity is always viewed as a gift of the Holy Spirit; see below, Chapter VIII, *Virginity*.
155. See Pierre Thomas Camelot, 'Gnose chrétienne', DS 6:509-24; Walter Völker, *Der wahre Gnostiker nach Klemens von Alexandrien*, TU 57 (Berlin, 1952).
156. Irenaeus, *Adversus haereses* II.39, Harvey I, 345; see Hausherr, *Direction spirituelle en Orient autrefois*, 40.
157. See T. Špidlík, '"Fous pour le Christ" en Orient', DS 5: 752-61; Guy Oury, 'Idiota', 7/2:1242-48.
158. See Chapter VIII, *Various Aspects of Flight from the World*.
159. See Hausherr, 'Contemplation et sainteté. Une remarquable mise au point par Philoxène de Mabboug (d. 523)', RAM 14 (1933) 171-95; *Hésychasme et prière*, OCA 176: 13-37.

160. *Adv. haer.* V.6.1; PG 7:1137B; ed. W. Harvey II. 334; ANF, I:531; see Antonio Orbe, 'La excelencia de los profetas según Origenes', *Estudios Biblicos* 14 (1955) 191–221; Spanneut, *Le stoïcisme*, 274, note. 35.
161. Pierre de Labriolle, *La crise montaniste* (Paris, 1913).
162. Eusebius, *Historia Ecclesiastica* V.16.4; PG 20:465A.
163. See the Syriac *Vita* of Peter the Iberian, ed. Richard Raabe (Leipzig, 1895) 47, 49ff.
164. *Vie de saint Dosithée* 1; SCh 92:123; [*The Life of St Dositheus* is summarized at length in *Dorotheos of Gaza: Discourses and Sayings*, CS 33 (1977) 33–44 — ed.] One reads in the Letters of Ammonas how the indwelling of the Spirit gives a *dioratikon charisma* (Greek text, ed. F. Nau (1915), PO 11:439), see J. Lemaitre (Hausherr) in DS 2/2:1856.
165. See Ivan Kologrivof, *Essai sur la sainteté en Russie* (Bruges, 1953) 398ff.
166. Evagrius, *On evil thoughts* 27; PG 79:1232BC; see *In Ps.* 32.15; PG 12:1305C; *Praktikos* 47, SCh 171, 607 [SC 4:29].
167. *Vita Antonii* 34; PG 26:893B; *Early Christian Biographies*, FC 15:166; Gregory of Nyssa, *De virginitate* 10; PG 46:360D.
168. See Chapter IX, *The Discernment of Spirits*; XI, *Obedience to the Spiritual Father*.
169. *In Numeros* 27:11; GCS 7:272; tr. A. A. Green, *Origen: an Exhortation to Martyrdom, Prayer and Selected Works* (New York, 1979) 261.

4

CHRISTIAN ANTHROPOLOGY

1. SELF-KNOWLEDGE

The Moral Aspect of Self-knowledge

IT IS INTRIGUING TO DISCOVER how much spiritual writers, even those who scarely dealt with philosophy, have been preoccupied with the problem of man. Lossky states that, 'It could not have been otherwise for a theological doctrine based upon the revelation of a living and personal God who created man "according to his image and likeness".'[1] Christian thought has extended the words carved on the temple at Delphi and transmitted by Socrates, *gnōthi seauton* (know thyself).[2] Basil's famous homily 'Give heed to thyself', based on a passage in Deuteronomy (15:6) is in the same tradition.[3]

What, then, is the exact meaning of self-knowledge in the thought of the spiritual writers? Philo had greatly insisted on the fact that self-knowledge should be moral, with a view to self-improvement, and anagogical, that is, the point of departure from which to arrive at the perfection of the Intellect guiding the world.[4] We shall find that several trends in christian literature correspond to these two points of view.

According to Origen, self-knowledge is a knowledge which has the virtues and the vices as its object and is not so much concerned with knowing the substance of the soul.[5] Hence, to know oneself means better to understand one's own capabilities, one's own power to grow in goodness and wisdom.[6]

But what was of interest to christian authors above all was its relationship to God, whether in connection with the origin of man, his concrete situation, or his relation to the world. Such knowledge, Basil says, 'will guide you to the memory of God'.[7] 'As the prophet says, "How wonderful is the knowledge drawn from myself", (Ps 138:6 [137:6]); that is, having carefully observed myself, I understood the superabundance of wisdom in you.'[8] In the same vein Gregory Nazianzus wrote, 'Know thyself, my friend. Understand your origin and your nature. The road to the beauty of the archetype is very straight.'[9]

Here man appears as he truly is, as God sees and wills him to be. But because of this, man also remains an insoluble riddle, a mystery, an *agnōstos* (unknown), as Philo had warned.[10] According to Lossky, 'The level on which the problem of the human person is posed goes beyond that of ontology as we normally understand it; it becomes a question of metaontology, only God can know....'[11] Paul Evdokimov adds, 'The deiform structure makes any autonomous solution to the destiny of man impossible. The soul is a place of encounters and presence; its nature is conjugal.'[12]

The language of the ascetics is simpler. The lowliness and the grandeur of man, his weakness and his strength, his ignorance of self and his self-knowledge are called by a single name, humility. This, according to Gregory of Nyssa's fine expression, is 'a descent toward the heights'.[13]

Humility

Augustine asserted that humility is a specifically christian virtue.[14] Clement of Alexandria, on the contrary, was convinced that Plato[15] had already taught humility.[16] Origen, in his commentary on the *Magnificat*, explained that what Scripture calls *tapeinōsis* (lowliness) is nothing but the *atyphia*, the absence of conceit, or the *metriotes*, the moderation, the modesty of which pagan sages spoke,[17] the middle road between vanity (*chaunotēs*) and small-mindedness (*mikropsychia*).[18]

The biblical tradition presents humility as a human experience lived sorrowfully in the midst of an unfriendly society, a poverty which slowly takes on a moral, religious, and eschatological shading.[19] In the New Testament humility is above all 'poverty in spirit'. Conscious of their need and deprived of self-sufficiency, the poor in spirit are in a privileged state of receptiveness to God's action (Lk 1:49). The child like spirit is after all but another way of expressing the same attitude.

The Fathers unanimously made Christ the model of humility.[20] The Russian authors called this virtue *christopodražatel'naïa*, 'the one that imitates Christ'.[21] Many texts have exalted this 'mother, root, nurse, foundation, and center of all the other virtues'.[22] Basil called humility *panaretos*, 'the all virtuous'.[23] It holds first place in the domain of good, just as pride does in that of evil. It is a general attitude of soul.

This is why humility, especially that of the saints, is something divine, mysterious, inexplicable.[24] According to John Climacus, 'Humility is like the sun. We cannot describe its power and essence, but from its properties and effects we can deduce its intrinsic nature.'[25] The spiritual masters nonetheless emphasized certain qualities or attitudes that help in discerning its essence.

Before all else humility is self-knowledge, a recognition of the limits of human weakness.[26] And because it is a sinner's knowledge it means a consciousness of one's misery, a self-accusation. 'The beginning of salvation for anyone is to condemn oneself.'[27]

Humility checks our impulse to judge, and to rule our neighbors.[28] With respect to the divinely established order, 'the practice of humility means silence, subordination, not contradicting one's superiors, despising rest, surrendering to work, and being vigilant,' in the words of Abba Isaiah.[29] Humility prevents the just man from attributing the gifts of God to himself.[30] In the teaching of Evagrius, the contemplative's humility consists above all in not forgetting to ascribe the entire merit of victories over his enemies to the grace of God.[31] It is at the same time the universal remedy which, according to Antony the Great, allows one to avoid 'all the nets of the enemy stretched out on earth'.[32]

The authors spoke about the degrees of this virtue[33] and frequently pointed out the road leading to it: bodily labors (*čornyje raboty*),[34] placing oneself below all others,[35] and obedience.[36]

Because the humble man sees God in everything, this virtue is the return to the pristine state, before the fall.[37] The humble are therefore great, filled with the gifts of God. Origen said that 'the humble walks in things great and wonderful, which are beyond his capacity'.[38] Humility requires that this greatness be recognized:

'Man is a great thing!' exclaimed Basil.[39] God himself, Clement of Alexandria said, will 'love man much more than the rest, and with reason; the living man, the noblest of all the beings he has made.'[40] 'For what other things on earth have been made according to the image of the Creator?' Basil wondered.[41] 'You have been given a mind capable of understanding.... All the animals on land... are subject to you.... For your sake, God dwelt among men, and the Holy Spirit spread out his gifts.'[42]

The Psychological Aspect of Self-knowlege

Origen warns us that in addition to the self-knowledge which develops a moral awareness, 'there is another self-knowledge which is more profound and more difficult.... The soul must know the nature of its constitution, whether corporeal or incorporeal, whether single or composed of two, three or more elements.'[43] This philosophical trend set man in the chain of being and viewed him within the confines of matter and spirit by, if one may say so, baptizing the anthropology of the ancient Greeks. Nemesius presented in the forty-four chapters of his book *On the Nature of Man*[44] a thorough, didactic, and in a word exact, precise, study of man and his place in the world; it shows throughout a great philosophical erudition and a detailed, minute knowlege of physiology.

The spiritual writers felt the need to describe the divine favors according to their psychological repercussions. It remains true, on the other hand, that when the authors spoke about human nature in these psychological terms they placed themselves on a level which had little to do with pure psychology. Hence the frequency of a certain confusion in the use and the meaning of the terms, even when the analysis of the human structure seems quite simple.

Inner Man-Outer Man

Within the perspective of Greek philosophy man was analyzed as a microcosm uniting two worlds, the spiritual and the material. The synthetic concept in Scripture was different: the entire man expresses himself in his various aspects. He is soul in so far as he is animated by the in-breathing of life; the flesh shows the perishable creature in him; the mind signifies his openness to God; the body is his way of expressing himself to the outside. In addition, the various attitudes shown by men over the centuries are synthesized in the two categories of sinner and new man, of carnal and heavenly man.[45]

A reconciliation with Greek terminology was therefore not easy, except for one concept which had been used from the beginning in a twofold spiritual and metaphysical sense, 'the inner man' and 'the outer man'. This distinction is part of St Paul's terminology (Rm 7:22, Eph 1:16, 2 Co 4:16), but it was open to the nuances imposed by hellenistic thought. Plato spoke of the *entos anthrōpos* (the man within) fighting against ferocious brutes, namely, the evil instincts.[46] The expression is found in Rabbinic literature, in Philo, in the hermetic texts, in the Stoics, and in Plotinus.[47]

Origen used it most often in the context of his theology of man created in the image of God: 'In the inner man are found the seat of the virtues and the totality of understanding and of knowledge; that is where the renewal of the image of God takes place.'[48] In Cassian, the inner man is 'he who devotes himself to the totally interior work of the struggle against thoughts'[49] that are evil. For Theophane the Recluse, the inner man is the heart, the center of the spiritual life, the seat of the Spirit.[50]

Body-Soul-Spirit

From the outset, then, christian anthropology distinguished two different levels of the human person. At the same time, especially among the Alexandrians, it began to be based on the Platonic doctrine of the soul so that its position could be defined with regard to philosophical problems. In this context the biblical contrast between the outer man and the inner man, earthly man and spiritual man, seemed to the Fathers to correspond well to the Greek distinction between the soul and the body.

It is true that orthodox writers have always insisted on the unity of body and soul. The whole person is surely a substance, but, on the other hand, the soul exists for itself and animates the body. One must admit that the Fathers's efforts to make this unity of body and soul understandable did not, from the speculative point of view, allow them to grasp this unity of essence. The problem would become easier later on for the scholastic authors who viewed the soul as the 'form' of a living, organic being.

The early Fathers had to overcome another great obstacle thrown up by Platonism. They readily defined man in Plato's own terms as *to ouranion phyton* (the celestial plant),[51] 'on account of the dignity of our soul'.[52] In Scripture the soul (*nepheš*) is 'the breath of life' which makes man into 'a living soul', although this term is often contrasted to the heavenly world of God and of the spirit (*ruah*).[53] This is why the philosophical *dichotomy* (body-soul) had to be completed by the theological *trichotomy* (body-soul-Spirit), which became traditional in the East.[54] Yet a certain confusion in the use and the meaning of terms may be noted.

Various Aspects of the 'Trichotomy'

We begin with the 'psychological trichotomy'. The tripartite division of man as *sōma, psychē, nous,* seems to go back to Posidonius, although it is common to Aristotle and the Peripatetics. A poem by Gregory Nazianzen[55] and one of his *Theological Orations*[56] present this idea as a generally accepted truth. Nonetheless, the first christian terminology depended rather more directly on Plotinus and the Neoplatonic world. There a different trichotomy is found: the soul itself is divided in three parts. Clement of Alexandria called the soul tripartite or threefold, and enumerated these three parts: *to noeron* (the intellectual), *to thymikon* (the irascible), *to epithymētikon* (the appetitive).[57]

A trichotomic formula is know to us from Scripture. In 1 Th 5:25, St Paul expressed the following wish in his prayer: 'May the God of peace make you perfect and holy; and may you all be kept safe and blameless, spirit (*pneuma*), soul (*psychē*), and body (*sōma*), for the coming of our Lord Jesus Christ'. Even if there is no evident trichotomy there in the Greek sense, there is no simple pleonasm either, because St Paul distinguishes between the phenomena that depend on the body, the soul, and the spirit. It may be noted that St Paul makes the *pneuma* not a physical element in the philosophic fashion, but a communication from God.[58] It is in connection with this meaning of the term *pneuma* that the distinction between the psychic (*psychikos*) and the spiritual (*pneumatikos*) man was established.[59]

Origen followed in this direction. He knew well that the soul becomes spiritual only when it puts itself under the influence of the Holy Spirit.[60] We find here an example of the transposition which the terminology had undergone in its christian context. The purest form of this is found in the famous definition of the spiritual man given by Irenaenus: 'The perfect man consists in the commingling and the union of the soul receiving the Spirit of the Father, [the whole] admixed to the flesh.'[61]

This spiritual trichotomy prevailed in the East. In his interpretation of the Epistle to the Romans, Theophane the Recluse wrote: 'Everything is brought about by the Holy Spirit.... Without the body the soul is lifeless, just as the soul has no spiritual life without the Spirit of God'.[62]

This spiritual trichotomy conformed nicely to the psychological dichotomy. Irenaenus could therefore say that 'man is by nature a composite, consisting of body and soul'.[63] Even in Clement of Alexandria, who from the psychological point of view is usually seen as a Platonizing trichotomist, there are numerous texts where he speaks only of body and soul.[64] Several others waver between one position or the other.[65]

The terms, however, were not always interchangable. This can easily be seen in Origen. On the one hand, he used the dichotomous formula,[66] which explains the presence of the human being on earth, and 'makes it possible for man to live upon the earth'.[67] However, he added a third element, and called it *pneuma* (spirit), *logos*, *dianoētikon* (intellectual), *kardia* (heart), and above all *hēgemonikon* (ruling).[68] To call it the Holy Spirit would be saying too much. It is, nonetheless, the best part of the human composite, that which is 'more divine' (*theiōteros*) than either the body or the soul,[69] and is man's 'main substance' (*proēgoumenē hypostasis*).[70] It has been defined as 'a certain self-transcendence of man'.[71]

Similar vacillations can be detected in Eastern spiritual writers until modern times. For Theophane the Recluse the third element of the human composite is the spirit, but even with him one does not always know exactly whether it should be written with an upper or lower case S.[72] This apparent confusion or variation is, nonetheless, very significant. We touch here upon the very difficult problem of the presence of the Holy Spirit: he comes 'from outside' and at the same time he belongs to the human 'self'. He is therefore man's 'spirit' and the Spirit.[73]

2. THE SPIRIT AND THE SOUL

Living According to the Spirit

Given the ambiguity of the term, describing what the spiritual writers called 'the spirit of man' is not easy. A good summary of the entire tradition can be found in Theophane the Recluse.[1] This 'superior part of the soul' unites man to God. He is the 'power that was breathed into the face of man at the moment of creation; the soul is an inferior power, or the part of the same power that is destined to perform the deeds of life on earth'.[2] 'The spirit ... contains in itself the feelings of the divine, the need of conscience, hope for the best, and at the same time the awareness of everything we do and know.'[3]

The practical consequences of this doctrine on the spirit are obvious. Since the spirit is the soul of our soul, the highest norm for the christian life will be to live according to the spirit and to obey his commands:

> If we satisfy the needs of the spirit they teach man how to bring the other demands into harmony with them, and this is why neither the satisfactions of the soul nor the demands of the body are contradictory to the spiritual life; on the contrary, they cooperate with its activity. What results from this is the perfect harmony of all movements and all attitudes: of thoughts, feelings, desires, intentions, impressions, and pleasures. This is Paradise![4]

The whole person is therefore under the influence of the Spirit. Nonetheless, Theophane affirms that the 'spiritual senses' and above all conscience are his truly personal voice, by which he makes himself 'felt'.

The Spiritual Sense

The doctrine of the 'spiritual senses' goes back to Origen.[5] Evagrius protested against those who wanted to exclude from the operations of the mind (*nous*) what everybody accords to the senses, that is the immediate apprehension of its object.[6] The most excellent of the senses, for a noetic like Evagrius, is spiritual sight, which becomes operative during prayer by the light of the Holy Trinity. The other senses play the role of substitutes to sight. That is, for want of the divine vision, they allow man to listen to the words of God[7] or to read them in creation.[8]

The followers of the 'school of feeling'[9] made subtle reflections about the peculiar functions of the other spiritual senses: the olfactory sense perceived the perfume of the virtues and the stench of evil and the Evil One;[10] taste discerns the goodness and sweetness of God;[11] the sense of touch gives 'certainty', as to Thomas (Jn 20:24).

It has been said clearly enough that this *aisthēsis* (perception) is 'fully in the intellect',[12] and that the spiritual sense awakens in proportion as the inferior senses are mortified. It is therefore not a revenge of sensualism against the excesses of spiritualism.[13] On the other hand, however, the graduated meaning of *nous* and its evolution into the term 'heart'[14] certainly averts any danger of intellectualism.

Conscience

Properly speaking, conscience is the functioning of a moral, personal decision. But the term has undergone so considerable an evolution that we cannot speak of it as a simple concept.[15] The ancient term to designate the conscience is the heart.[16] To the Greeks, *syneidēsis* expressed acts of a very different nature, such as perceiving, grasping, knowing, or being conscious of. On the other hand, the Greeks evaluated morality largely in terms of a sense of well-being and they expressed the sense of guilt very expressively (*aidōs, phobos, aisthēsis*). Seneca knew of a spirit dwelling within man, 'one who marks our good and bad deeds'.[17] According to Philo, the *syneidos* was placed in man by God.[18]

In early christian writings the term *syneidēsis* and *conscientia* were introduced sporadically at first but then became more numerous as time went on. The Latin West soon favored a moral interpretation[19] while in the Greek East the original meanings of the term were largely kept. Nonetheless, conscience in its proper sense is also mentioned frequently.

An excellent instruction on the subject can be read in Dorotheos. 'In creating man God implanted in him something divine — a certain faculty [*hōsper logismos*, perhaps 'like a *logismos*,' a thought coming from outside], warmer and more luminous than a spark — to illumine the mind and show what is good and what is bad. This is called conscience and it is the natural law.'[20] 'Conscience should be guarded towards God, towards one's neighbor and towards things.'[21] 'The Fathers said that a monk should never let his conscience torment him for any reason whatever....'[22]

The Nature of the Soul

From the moral point of view ('saving one's soul') the writings of the Fathers never lack resoluteness.[23] By contrast, from the speculative point of view many questions of interest to reason remained open. An inventory of these questions is found in Origen: 'Is the soul corporeal or incorporeal, simple or composite? Is it, as some believe, contained in the semen of the body and its germ passed on with the germ of the body, or does it come in a complete state from outside to clothe the already formed body?...'[24]

Not all these questions necessarily held the attention of spiritual writers. Nonetheless, they could not avoid sketching an ontological theory of the structure of the soul when they came to naming, describing, and ordering the divine gifts according to their psychological repercussion. Indeed, there are numerous texts 'on the soul' (*peri psychēs*) written *ex professo* by the Fathers and leaders of the Church.[25]

It is not easy to unravel the impact of the influences of the milieu in which they lived and then state with certainty the meaning of more than one term.[26] In general, we may distinguish two series of texts: some, less numerous, view the soul as the principle of 'the earthly life'[27] others speak of the 'spiritualized' soul united with 'the spirit',[28] and praise the beauty of the 'spiritual' soul, its divine origin, its freedom, and immortality.

The Divine Origin of the Soul, Its Spirituality

In the Middle Ages Thomas Aquinas worked out his theory of the soul[29] on the basis of Aristotle's psychology. Although it is the form of the body, the soul is 'spiritual' and simple, and has an activity independent of the body.

The early Fathers had no difficulty in recognizing a certain 'spirituality' of the soul. But on the other hand, if the soul was to be the principle of the earthly life, they had to create a close link between the body and the soul and give it some sort of subtle body. To Irenaeus, souls were incorporeal only 'when set in comparison to mortal bodies'.[30] Clement of Alexandria spoke of a 'corporeal soul', of a 'corporeal *pneuma*',[31] and of a 'carnal *pneuma*'.[32]

When they used these expressions, the Fathers were preoccupied with safeguarding the transcendence of the divine spirit, which was not clear in the Platonic concept. Among Christians, the term 'spiritual' took on a specific meaning.[33] Consequently, the soul may truly be called 'spiritual' in so far as it is 'permeated by the power of the Spirit'.[34] But it also must spiritualize itself through its free choice, Irenaeus says. It is 'between these two things', the body and the spirit. 'When it follows the spirit, it is raised up by it, but if it sympathizes with the flesh, it falls into carnal lusts.'[35] Consequently, only the souls of the just are 'spiritual'; the souls of the sinners become 'carnal' or 'earthly'.[36]

On the other hand, reminiscences of the Platonic doctrine remained commonplace. At the opening of *De anima*, a one-hundred-and twenty-nine line poem on the nature of the soul, Gregory Nazianzen stated a general thesis of the philosophy of his day: 'The soul is a breath of God, and it submits to the mixture with the earthly element even though it is of heavenly origin. It is a light hidden in a cave, but nonetheless divine and imperishable.'[37] As a Platonist, Gregory faulted the materialistic tendencies of the Stoics who had assimilated the soul to 'a burning fire', 'a breath of air', 'blood plasma', and even 'the harmony of the corporeal elements tending toward cohesion'.[38]

The Immortality of the Soul

It has been maintained that only the idea of the resurrection of the body is proper to Christianity, while the concept of the immortality of the soul was imported from outside under the influence of Greek philosophy.[39] It is, however, difficult to discover the convictions of antiquity on this matter.[40] Semitic anthropology was undoubtedly less apt than Greek philosophy (at least than that of Plato) to integrate the idea of immortality, to admit that there is in man an incorporeal element inaccessible to physical death.[41]

Scripture narrowly links sin and death (Rm 5:12–21), while Christ is for us the initiator of incorruptibility.[42] The theme of a 'medicine for immortality' in Ignatius of Antioch was perhaps borrowed from the mystery religions, but it was applied to the Lord's Supper and to the Bread of Life.[43] The importance which the ancient Church attached to the gift of *aphtharsia* (incorruptibility) is, moreover, a natural corollary to the role of the vivifying Spirit.[44] In this sense understand the opinion of a few ancient writers who went so far as to deny the incorruptiblity of the soul.[45] One should in any case take into account that the terms immortality and incorruptibility changed meaning with the christian authors. They express eschatological truths and the conviction that 'life does not arise from us, nor from our own nature; but it is bestowed according to the grace of God'.[46]

The Greek Concept of Freedom

By freedom, the Greek understood above all the 'freedom of choice' which was manifested first in the individual's social and public relationships (in the city-state, 'juridic' and social freedom was the opposite of slavery) and which later in Stoic anthropology became the inner, intangible freedom whereby an individual acquires self-sufficiency (*autarkeia*). It must be noted, moreover, that the Greeks did not speak of a special faculty of choice. For them the will was an aspect of knowledge.[47]

It is, incidentally, hard to understand how the Stoics, with their tendency toward fatalism, could have been viewed by history as the great champions of individual freedom. On the one hand, they saw the individual crushed by the necessity of cosmic laws, *fatum*;[48] on the other hand, they elaborated a mechanism of knowledge, characterized by Clement of Alexandria as 'the organization of the senses with a view to knowledge', which for all practical purposes resulted in psychological necessity. From sense perception (*aisthēsis*) one was led mechanically to a *typōsis en hēgemonikō* (an impression on the guiding faculty), then to a *phantasia* (image), and finally to a *katalēpsis* (comprehension).[49]

Philo was the great defender of freedom. It is his enduring merit to have linked man's freedom to the freedom of God who can perform miracles, that is, free, exceptional acts in a world ruled by cosmic laws.[50]

Christian Freedom

In the light of biblical revelation, the Fathers saw human freedom in the concrete relationship between man and God. Just as they defended the freedom of God in Providence,[51] so they insisted on man's free responsibility before God's call. Justin Martyr violently attacked the Stoics, insisting that free will is the condition and the basis of merit.[52] And Basil said: 'What a lack of sense it shows to assign good and evil without regard to personal merit!'[53]

The texts of Clement of Alexandria are of special interest. Against the gnostics he became the champion of human freewill; he certainly seems to have believed in the reality of a special faculty governing choice, and in that he went beyond the philosophers: 'Volition takes precedence over all else; for the intellectual powers are born to minister to the will'.[54] At any event, Clement of Alexandria denied that the process of knowing is mechanical: the image (*phantasia*) is common to man and animal. But man judges the images; approval (*synkatathesis*) is within our power and, without it, there is neither opinion nor judgment nor knowledge.[55]

This connection between freedom and knowledge is interesting.[56] There is no virtue without freedom and, to the Eastern mind, to arrive at truth without practicing the virtues is impossible. The union of truth and freedom already appears in St John, from a higher perspective: participation in the divine *gnōsis* and freedom. 'The truth shall make you free; ... if the Son of God makes you free, you will be free indeed' (Jn 8:32, 36). And St Paul says specifically that Christ who is the Truth makes man free through his Spirit: 'For where the Spirit of the Lord is, there is freedom' (2 Co 3:17).

In the West the problem of human freedom, like that of the spirituality and the immortality of the soul, was posed and studied by itself, and not in direct reference to the problem of truth and the divine life. Yet one should avoid 'confusion between the psychological term will and the metaphysical term freedom'. Paul Evdokimov writes,[57]

> The will is still bound to nature and is subject to necessity and to immediate goals. Freedom arises out of the spirit, out of the person. When it is raised to its highest level, it desires nothing but the true and the good.[58]

Indeed, the words of Gregory of Nyssa are characteristic of Greek Fathers: 'Freedom is resemblance to the One who is without master (*adespotos*) and is self-governed (*autokratēs*), a resemblance which we were granted by God at the beginning.'[59] 'It is through freedom, then, that man is deified and blessed.'[60] True freedom is therefore a 'spiritual' characteristic, a gift of the Holy Spirit.[61]

'Structural' Freedom and Freedom of Choice:
eleutheria *and* proairesis

Our fallen state is insufficient to define the condition of human freedom. When at the beginning God communicated his own freedom to man, it had several aspects: first, freedom from evil, from sin: 'Human life had but one character...; it had no contact with evil.'[62] By his incorruptibility and his immortality man surpassed cosmic and biological conditions. *Apatheia* meant the mind's freedom from and independence of the fleshly *pathos* (passion),[63] the victory over sexuality, and hence virginity with all its prerogatives.[64] The term *autokratēs*, self-ruling, indicates the royal character of independence with respect to 'other beings which are subject to the immutable laws of necessity'.[65] *Theōria* meant the freedom of the intelligence, the immediate grasp of truth, without illusions.[66] One term aptly summarizes all the main aspects of a human freedom elevated to the plane of divine freedom, *parrhēsia*, frankness with God, a trusting intimacy 'enjoying the vision of God, face to face'.[67]

But with the fall, everything was changed. Thereafter the situation of the sinner could be summarized by one word, bondage (cf Rm 5:12 ff.). Subject to biological and cosmic laws, man was condemned to physical suffering and to death; the passions awoke

Christian Anthropology

and darkened his mind; his strength was taken away. The annihilation of love led to social enslavement. *Theoria*, beholding God, became clouded through blindness, the trusting simplicity with God disappeared.[68]

Does freedom still exist if through Adam's transgression all have become 'slaves of sin' (Rm 6:20)? Scripture appeals constantly to the power of choice and stresses man's responsibility (cf Si 15:11–16). On the one hand, then, freedom has been lost but, on the other, it still exists. Gregory of Nyssa[69] explains this paradox through two terms: *eleutheria*, complete freedom, no longer exists in the sinner, but God in his goodness had kept for man a reminder, so to speak, of Paradise; *proairesis*, the freedom to choose between good and evil. It is by means of this *proairesis* that man is able to make a progressive return to his full, original freedom, *eleutheria*. If he chooses the good he uses his freedom to reinforce his freedom; if on the contrary, he chooses evil, he makes use of his freedom to annihilate true freedom. Therein lies the perverseness of sin.[70]

To Save Oneself, 'One Need Only Will It'[71]

In the Western Church Augustine was the one who especially treated grace as a separate theme, in order to combat the naturalistic moralism of the Pelagians. He coined the terms *gratia praeveniens* and *subsequens, gratia operans* and *cooperans*,[72] and he insisted on the weakness of man, on the impossibility of his doing good.[73]

The moralists and the preachers of the East, by contrast, frequently and strongly insisted on the role of the human will. Everyone has it in his power to observe all the commandments. In categorically rejecting every opinion to the contrary as 'slander' of the Lord and his light, sweet yoke,[74] Joseph of Volokolamsk is well within the tradition of the Greek Fathers.[75]

The charge of Pelagianism or Semi-pelagianism was early brought against them by Augustine.[76] Some of their expressions seemed scandalous, such as Chrysostom's saying that neither God nor the grace of the Spirit prevent our free choice.[77] These reproaches are unjust, however. In the East, the heart of the doctrine of grace is the deification of man, the image of God. *Theōsis* is identified with human nature itself.⁷⁸ We should therefore not be surprised if these authors did not confront the problem of the relationship between grace and free will, since this grace enters into the very structure of man, into the operation of his faculties, especially that of free will. In a balanced human being all the parts of which he is composed function in co-operation (*synergeia*).

A more explicit confrontation between 'the work of man' and 'the work of God' was the result of disputes in the East as in the West. The polemic against the Monothelites gave John of Damascus an opportunity to develop fully his doctrine of human freedom and God's help (*synergeia*). He explained clearly that man has received the capacity freely to choose the good, but that the accomplishment of the good depends on divine cooperation.⁷⁹

Theophane the Recluse recognized that the problem, even if complicated in theory, was not serious in practice:

> Theorists are greatly preoccupied with the question of the relationship between grace and free will. For anyone with grace within him, the question is resolved. Anyone who bears grace within himself offers and surrenders himself to its all-embracing action, and it is grace that acts in him. The truth of this is more evident to him, not only than any mathematical truth, but even than any outward experience....⁸⁰

Hence the famous maxim expressed by pseudo-Macarius, among others: we should act to the best of our ability,⁸¹ or, according to Theophane the Recluse, 'Exert all your strength, but rest your concern with success on God.'⁸²

The Parts and Faculties of the Soul

This question began to preoccupy philosophy, and later the spiritual writers, the moment a need was perceived of gathering into one psychic principle the power and the various forces manifest in man. Plato held a dualistic view of the soul or, at least, the patristic age interpreted his views on the matter this way.⁸³ There was the *nous*, the higher, rational part, and the *psychē*, the lower, animal part, called 'the passionate part of the soul' by Evagarius.⁸⁴ The *psychē* was subdivided into *thymikon* (the irascible) and *epi-*

thymētikon (the appetitive power). From this resulted a tripartition which was accepted by several Fathers. It is a key concept in Evagrius' anthropology.[85]

While tightening the unity of the soul, the Stoics generally noted eight parts: they are the five senses, the voice, the semen, and the *hēgemonikon*, that is, the modified Platonic *nous* which commands and unifies everything, as it is gifted with three faculties, the *phantastikon*, the *hormētikon*, and the *synkathetikon*.[86] This Stoic division was used, rather artificially, by Clement of Alexandria.[87]

In general, one can say that these divisions, and others like it, lack precision. Spiritual writers viewed the faculties of man as they related to the *pneuma*. They wondered about this privileged faculty which was in direct contact with the Spirit, with the divine.[88] We know that the Greek tradition played a considerable role in this matter. It was believed that only the *nous* gave access to the divine, and great efforts were expended to correct and christianize this concept they had inherited from philosophy. But in the end it was indeed necessary to give up the, often thankless, efforts. Christian writers then returned to the language of Scripture and of the people: it is the heart, with which the Spirit is linked, which is 'the seat of the Spirit'.

3. THE HEART

Its Importance to Eastern Spirituality

The concept of the heart, writes Boris Vyšeslavcev, occupies the central place in the mysticism, the religion, and the poetry of all peoples.[1] Many an Eastern author has taken the heart as an emblem to dissociate himself from the 'rationalist' West, which seemed often enough to forget that the heart is the foundation of the christian life.[2] Indeed, how often we come across the term heart in Eastern spirituality![3] They speak of custody of the heart, of attentiveness to the heart, of purity of the heart, of the thoughts, desires, and resolutions of the heart, of prayer of the heart, of the divine presence in the heart, and so on.

In Scripture the heart contains the fulness of the spiritual life, which involves the whole person, with all his faculties and all his activities:[4] in it resides fidelity to Jahweh (cf. Rm 11:3–4). To the Fathers and the medieval authors these biblical expression often sounded too Semitic. They felt obligated to paraphrase and add annotations which clearly reveal the tendencies of this spirituality.

Speculative by nature, the Greeks did certainly not by mere chance substitute *nous* (reason, mind) for the biblical *lev, levav* (heart). According to Gregory of Nazianzus the 'clean heart' of Ps 50:2 was the *dianoētikon* (mind).[5] On the contrary, Western medieval spiritual literature contrasted the *cordis affectus* to the *intellectus* and the *ratio*. Thomas Aquinas considered the evangelical counsel to love God wholeheartedly (cf. Lk 5:27) an *actus voluntatis quae hic significatur per cor* (an act of the will, which is indicated here by heart).[6] Sooner or later a reaction in favor of 'feelings' was bound to occur,[7] especially in popular piety. And for Theophane the Recluse, 'the part of the heart' or 'the part of feelings' are both one and the same.[8]

The heart is thus one of our most ambiguous concepts, and spiritual writers were conscious of the difficulty.[9] The psychological method to which people generally resort in discussions on this topic will never be able to clarify the question. There have been attempts above all to place the heart into a schematic presentation of man's psychological structure, and only then to ask which function such a 'heart' can have in the spiritual life. This procedure really needs to be reversed. The biblical concept of the heart poses religious questions. Once these have been more or less clarified, we can ask how they are reflected in man's psychological structure.[10]

The Point of Contact Between God and Man

As the pupil of the eye is, so to speak, the point of intersection between two worlds, the outer and the inner, so—the Fathers thought—there must be in man a mysterious point through which God enters the human heart with all his riches.[11] We know that for Plato, the *nous*, reason, is 'that which is best in the soul', 'the soul's pilot',[12] the faculty which is in contact with God. This tradition, corrected and christianized, persists in the classical definition of prayer, an ascent of the *nous* (mind) to God.[13]

Danger always lurks in this terminology, however, because it seems to imply a certain partialness in our relationships to God. This would only be *one* of the many relationships manifested in life because the *nous* is only *one*, although the highest of our faculties. The later mystics no longer spoke of an 'organ', or a 'faculty', but looked for the point of contact between God and man in 'the ground of the soul',[14] or in 'the essence of the soul',[15] in the 'center' or in 'the root' of life, where all the powers of man are concentrated. In popular parlance, this focal point is the heart. This being so, it is not surprising that the term *kardia* (heart) had to reclaim its place, even among the Greeks[16] but especially among the Russians.[17] The classical definition of prayer was then modified to an ascent of the mind and of the heart to God.[18]

The Heart — The Principle of Human Integration

'The heart sustains the energy of all the forces of soul and body', Theophane the Recluse wrote,[19] in conformity with the language of Scripture.[20] It is my 'I', it is the 'source' of human acts,[21] 'the focus of all the human forces, those of the mind, of the soul, of the animal and corporeal forces'.[22]

The heart, the principle of unity within a person, also gives stability to the multiplicity of successive moments of life. We cannot perform one act which continues forever. Bossuet detected here an error which wanted 'to put the perfection of this life in an act suited only to the life to come'.[23] For the Eastern Christian, however, the ideal has always been 'the state of prayer' (*katastatis tēs proseuchēs*), that is, an habitual disposition which somehow in itself deserves the name prayer, aside from the acts which it produces with greater or lesser frequency.[24] This state of prayer is at the same time the state of the entire spiritual life, a steadfast disposition of the heart.[25]

The definition of the spiritual man included the Holy Spirit.[26] Consequently, 'the limpid heart is the dwelling place of divinity':[27] 'Oh! the tiny, narrow heart which harbors spirituality in its bosom, as in a quiet abode, the one whom the heavens and the earth cannot contain!'[28] If virtue is by definition a steadfast disposition[29] and at the same time a participation in Christ, in the divine life,[30] it is therefore a disposition of the heart. This is why Russian authors are almost unanimous in viewing the christian life as an 'immediate disposition of the heart'.[31] The perfection of faith is true *gnōsis*,[32] loving contemplation: 'Oh! the limpid eye', Martyrius Sahdônâ cries, 'which owing to its purity sees unveiled the One at the sight of whom the Seraphim cover their face!... Where then shall God be loved, if not in the heart? and where does he show himself, if not there? Blessed are the pure in heart: they shall see God (Mt 5:8).'[33]

By the coming of the Spirit the kingdom of heaven is within us and the heart is therefore the field where the battle against the adversaries of God takes place, as we read in the beautiful pages of pseudo-Macarius.[34] By the same token, however, the heart is also called to unite the Creator to his entire creation: 'If the heart is at the center of man's being, then it is through the heart that man enters into relationship with everything that exists',[35] especially his neighbor. 'There is a certain road in particular which leads to the union of men; it is the heart.'[36]

The Feelings of the Heart

We are conscious of our acts and can evaluate their moral value. The heart, on the other hand, remains a mystery; it is the hidden part of man, known only to God.[37] To the repeated question, how man can know himself (and he is bound to do so),[38] the authors replied: by having the soul present to itself.[39] Depending on the degree of its transparency, it has a direct intuition of itself.[40]

According to Theophane the Recluse, the concept of the heart includes this total, intuitive understanding. This is 'the feelings of the heart'.

> The function of the heart consists in feeling everything that touches our being. Consequently, the heart always feels the condition of body and soul as well as the multiform impressions created by concrete activity, whether spiritual or physical, the things which surround us or cross our path and, in general, the course of life.[41]

Clearly, all these 'feelings' are not of equal value;[42] above all, the divisions of empirical psychology—the mind, the will, and the emotions—should not be accepted unthinkingly. In spite of certain superficial descriptions, the 'feelings of the heart' have assumed, among orthodox writers, a moral and theological meaning far wider than the usual psychological notion. Their infallibility and their usefulness in divine contemplation depend upon purity of the heart.[43]

Attention to the Heart

Attention to the heart is a well-known expression in Eastern spirituality. It assumes, first, a negative aspect: keeping away all evil thought coming from outside, healing the heart, educating it by means of watchfulness.[44] This attention is, nonetheless, 'the mother of prayer' (*prosochē-proseuchē*).[45] 'Attend to yourself so that you may be attentive to God,' said Basil.[46]

The natural desires of the heart are our tendencies toward the good, the just, the beautiful, God. Theophane the Recluse distinguished between feelings that are 'theoretical', 'practical', 'aesthetic', and 'spiritual'.[47] 'By the full renewal of God's grace, there is in the man who has abandoned sin and turned to God a sympathy with the spiritual world.'[48] It is dependent upon the degree of kinship between man and God (*srodstvo*, Theophane says).[49]

To be attentive to the voices of this 'connaturality' is to perceive the divine mysteries as they are within us, as they enter our lives. The heart then becomes a wellspring of revelation: 'The sensible air will perhaps become less present to the respiration of our outer senses than the Spirit of God will become intimate to our heart, ceaselessly insufflating his memory within, remaining longer in us....'.[50]

4. THE BODY

The Body in Antiquity and in Scripture

The cult of the body enjoyed great vogue in antiquity.[1] Beneath this euphoria for the body, however, lay a profound nostalgia.

No matter what school they belonged to, the philosophers arrived at the same conclusion: the body was despised as the 'enemy' of the soul, or it became a thing that was useful, like a 'slave'; one either used it at one's good pleasure or got rid of it. In the Platonic tradition, the union of the soul with the body was viewed as a fall.[2] The attitude of the Stoics toward the body was but an application of their general attitude toward things that did not depend on man's free will. They submitted to the body as they submitted to external events. 'In things pertaining to the body, do not go further than mere usefulness,' commanded Epictetus.[3]

In Scripture, on the contrary, the body is not just a collection of flesh and bones which man has for his lifetime on earth and which he is stripped of through death and will recover on the day of the resurrection. It has a much higher dignity, as Paul emphasized in his theology. He presents the person in major situations: the natural, sinful state; dedication to Christ; the life of glory.[4]

Whereas in the Old Testament flesh and body are designated by a single term (*basar*), they can be distinguished by two terms in New Testament Greek, *sarx* and *sōma*—a distinction which takes on its full force only in the light of faith. Unlike the perishable flesh (cf. Ph 3:19) which cannot inherit the kingdom of God (1 Co 15:50) the body will be raised like the Saviour (6:14), it is a member of the body of Christ (6:15), the temple of the Holy Spirit (6:19); man must therefore use his body to glorify God. (6:20)[5]

The Body in the Fathers and Spritual Writers

The confrontation of Scripture with philosophic thought was not easy in this area, and traces of dualism are more often found in anthropology than in cosmology. Platonism's hold on the Fathers is known. Mixed with the rugged asceticism of the early monks—in a proportion which is hard to determine—we find expressions which can mean on the one hand, the christian experience of the 'covetousness of the flesh' which struggles against the spirit and must be subdued, and, on the other, a mistrust of the body which seems very akin to Platonism. It is significant that Basil called upon the authority of Pythagoras and Plato[6] to justify his scorn for the body. But it is difficult to see that philosophy had

Christian Anthropology

any influence on the monks who were totally unlettered. Plato or Plotinus should therefore not be held responsible for the monks' severe asceticism.[7]

One thing is certain. On this subject expressions can never be taken out of context. Their merit must be judged in terms of the author and the circumstances in which they occur, the goal they wanted to reach, the persons to whom they were addressed, and whether they were an exposition of the christian faith or an exhortation to detachment.

The orthodox reaction against heretical dualism was decisive in the historical development of the concept of the body. At the same time, however, numerous problems in the spiritual life clearly reflect Greek thought, namely, the question of the relationship between soul and body, the ultimate foundation of which is the concept of a heteronomous being mysteriously united through the wisdom of God. After the fall, this constitution is characterized by an essentially dialectic opposition, which increases or decreases according to the degree of man's spiritualization.

The Orthodox Reaction Against Dualism

Against the gnostics, Irenaeus stated that, 'salvation was denied to the body, since it is taken from the earth'.[8] Yet, such a condemnation of the body implies a failure to recognize the totality of the christian mystery; creation, incarnation, and redemption. Even the Fathers who borrowed heavily from Plato clearly professed that the body is an integral part of human nature.[9]

According to the New Testament the body of Christ plays a crucial role in the mystery of redemption. The Apostle John anathematized those who denied that 'Jesus has come in the flesh' (1 Jn 4:2, 2 Jn 7). Ignatius of Antioch fought against Docetism because this doctrine undermined the very foundation of Christianity.[10]

The human body is 'capable of immortality', Irenaeus replied to the gnostics.[11] The resurrection of the body is an essential doctrine of christian teaching. On the basis of St Paul's words, 'flesh and blood cannot inherit the kingdom of God' (1 Co 15:50), the Origenists—Jerome thought—were denying the resurrection of the flesh.[12] In their eschatology, the *logikoi* (rational beings) would ascend gradually to the angelic state, characterized by the spiritual body. Such a reproach, however, is unjust. Although Evagrius considered the risen body no longer carnal, but 'spiritual', 'angelic', it is still composed of four elements and therefore material.[13] Meanwhile, one should not think that the tendencies which gave rise to Docetism have disappeared. Their influence continues in all periods of the history of the Church. The body is seen as a transitory element of which man must strip himself more and more completely as his deification becomes fully realized. Vladimir Soloviev saw an exaggerated 'spiritualism' as a permanent temptation for the Eastern Church. But the truly spiritual man never rejects corporeal reality, the 'external'; aspects of religion: 'it would not be a purely external aspect to him, for he would understand the fulness of the inner meaning inherent in it'.[14]

Theophane the Recluse also writes in this vein: 'Christianity is spiritual in its higher aspect since grace is of its essence, but it is not invisible. And so the true Christians are spiritual . . . but they are not disincarnate; although they are spiritual, and to the highest degree, they cannot not act bodily.'[15] To understand the contrast between flesh and spirit, one should properly evaluate the concept 'spirit'.

The Mysterious Union of Body and Soul

Descriptions of the wonderful constitution of the human body abound.[16] No one ever denied its beauty and its usefulness.[17] Yet 'man consisting of body and soul is dual,' Athenagoras said.[18]

The union of soul and body remains mysterious. 'On the one hand, the body is of carnal origin and, on the other, the soul is mingled with it in a manner unknown by incorporating itself from outside to a creature of dust.'[19] This strange association, *krasis, mixis*, a mingling of two diverse natures[20] remained an endless problem for Gregory Nazianzen. Why is the soul linked to the body, he asked himself. His reply: only God knows and understands all the reasons for this 'commingling'. Nonetheless, Gregory adds, two main reasons can be given: 'One, that we may inherit the glory above by means of a struggle and wrestling, being tried as gold in a fire. . . . The other reason is that the soul may draw the lower nature to itself and raise it to heaven, to the divine, in order that the soul may be for the body what God is for the soul.'[21]

Even though the theoretical doctrine of the human body remained complex, spiritual writers were, in practice, fully conscious of the twofold duty so emphasized by Gregory: one must constantly fight temptation, the demon within the body, and at the same time, the body and through it the entire visible cosmos must be spiritualized.

Aphorisms about the Body

Writers expressed their thoughts more frequently by maxims than in complete expositions. Often of non-christian origin, these maxims are one-sided, but they complete one another and, taken in context, are justified. Those most used were:

The body is a prison, a tomb of the soul. This is the ancient Orphic formula, *sōma-sēma*.[22]

To free the soul from the 'fetters of the flesh',[23] from its bond (*desmos*) with a corpse.[24]

The body is like a mire, where the soul can only befoul and defile itself.[25]

The body is a stranger to the soul, like a 'fleshly vestment', an 'ugly mask',[26] a 'skin of matter',[27] a 'garment of skin',[28]

The body is not myself, it is my first 'belonging',[29]

Take care of the soul, and never mind about the rest.[30]

To free oneself from the body, 'to lay down this burden',[31] 'he must not weigh down his soul with the thick heavy garments of a sensuous life, but he must make all the actions of his life as thin as a spider's web by the purity of his conduct.'[32]

To despise, to mistreat, to kill the body: 'It kills me, I kill it.'[33] 'It flays me, I flay it.'[34]

To weaken the body. The state of the soul, thought Antony the Great, is vigorous when the pleasures of the body are weakened.[35] 'As plumpness and a healthy color betoken the athlete, so dessication of the body marks the christian....'[36]

The body is 'an ungrateful and insidious friend',[37] of whom we should be suspicious.

Demons act through the intermediary of the body corrupted

by sin, whereas 'the grace of God dwells in the very depths of the soul'.[38]

'It is not the body which is the source of evil, it is free choice.'[39]
The body is the dwelling place of the soul.[40]
The body is 'the instrument of the spirit', as the flute is in the fingers of the flutist,[41] 'the working companion of the soul'.[42]
The oblation of the body in martyrdom[43] and in virginity.[44]
The body associated to prayer. The body is often represented as an opaque veil, 'the thickness of the body' prevents contemplation.[45] On the other hand, the body is linked to the prayer of the soul, especially in the liturgy.[46]
To spiritualize the body. 'The Word became flesh that he might change our flesh to spirit... and might sanctify the whole lump with himself, because in him its first-fruits have been sanctified.'[47]

Sex

The Fathers were of the opinion that before the fall there existed in Paradise neither marriage nor the begetting of children,[48] even if they did not all agree with Gregory of Nyssa's theory that sex was a consequence of the fall.[49] In actuality, sex will serve to bring about the pleroma of humanity.[50]

In itself the soul is undifferentiated, neither male nor female; it is incorporeal,[51] and the image of God is therefore equal in men and women. This Alexandrian teaching prevailed over the Antiochenes, who considered man alone the true image of God.[52] Through her deeds, St Melania 'clearly showed that with respect to virtue according to God, the female sex is not second in anything to the male'.[53]

Not taking much notice of psychology, the ancients imposed practically the same rule upon monasteries of monks and nuns. The ascetics' ideal was to go beyond sex in order to achieve the state of angels (Mt 22:30)[54] where, according to Origen's allegorical phrase, 'the wife becomes the man'.[55] Many women became 'spiritual mothers' (*ammas*), even though the expression 'womens' spirituality' is new in both East and West.[56]

Illnesses

The idea of healing became very popular in the second century: the gods became healers. The Christians made Christ into a healer of souls.[57] The Fathers' opinion about medicine that nurses the body, therefore, was not always high. To be preoccupied with the health of the body made no sense; being ill was worthy of a 'philosopher'[58]; 'when the body is sick, the soul is healthy'.[59]

To bring exhortations like this back into proportion, Clement of Alexandria reminded Christians that 'good health and an abundance of necessities keep the soul free and independent, and capable of making good use of what is at hand'.[60] And Basil, no doubt engaged in polemics with certain monks, warned that it is God himself who brought forth herbs and the medical art. Therefore, why should anyone refuse them?[61]

The tender care of the sick is certainly within the monastic tradition.[62] In the *Pechersky Paterik*, Agapit the Monk treated his sick by having recourse to prayer, giving them as 'medication' the same vegetables he ate himself. But this story intends to demonstrate that the monastic life was healthier than 'mundane' medicine.[63] In cenobitic monasteries, where there was lots of work, people knew that health of body and soul was a grace of God,[64] 'so as to be able to serve him'.[65]

Death

Ancient Eastern man saw life and death as two realms set over against one another. From the spatial point of view death was known as the realm of the dead; from the dynamic standpoint, as the power of death. Greek philosophy sought to master this primitive pessimism by emphasising the natural rewards of death: escape from the body, eternal becoming, reabsorption into the cosmos, and so on.[66]

In the Old Testament the abode of the dead is called *sheol*. It is described as a region, or an empire, holding sway over the nether world and making raids into the very heart of the land of the living. As a consequence, illness, captivity, and adversities were felt as a falling downward to the world of the dead.[67] On the other hand, the power of death or the angel of death did not act on their own authority: they could only operate where and when Jahweh allowed it. For it was Jahweh who stood behind the power of death and struck the sinner.

The necessity of human death is linked to human sinfulness (Gen 3), something expressly confirmed in the New Testament (Rm 5: 12). At the same time, the glorious Christ appears as the *Archēgos tēs zōēs* (the Prince of life) (Ac 3:15 and 5:31, Heb 2:10). Byzantine iconography has a long tradition of representing the mystery of Christ's descent into hell to free the dead detained there.[68]

From the christian perspective, death appears at a dual angle: a punishment for sin; and a sign of salvation, a form of likeness to Christ. To ponder the imminence of death was often recommended by the spiritual writers. A monk was to live 'as one who is daily at the point of death'.[69] Death was a favorite object of contemplation. 'If it inspires us with inexpressible terror', it also brings with it 'a depth and a greatness which shatter our everyday world and exceed the power we accumulated in this life which correspond only to the conditions of this world.'[70]

In order to exalt the positive aspect of christian death, the Fathers made good use of certain themes borrowed from platonic philosophy: the return of God, 'becoming spirit after having cast off the flesh',[71] liberation 'from this world',[72] 'purification from evil',[73] from the passions which end up disappearing when the garment of flesh is laid down,[74] the transition from ignorance to perfect *gnōsis*, 'from half-sleep' to 'super-consciousness'.[75] This way of presenting death has been severely criticized by Soloviev, who is convinced that this manner of speaking diminishes the importance of Christ's victory over death. For death in itself offers no positive value whatever. The so-called passage to the world of spirits is merely an illusion. Therefore, Soloviev exhorts, christian preaching on death must be focused on faith in the resurrection of the flesh.[76]

Notes

1. SELF-KNOWLEDGE

1. *In the Image and Likeness of God* (New York, 1974) 112ff.; see M. Spanneut, *Le stoïcisme*, 132.
2. Xenophon, *Memorabilia* 4.21.

Christian Anthropology 115

3. *Homilia* 3; PG 31:197-98; see Stanislas Giet, *Les idées et l'action sociales de saint Basile* (Paris, 1941) 21ff.; Špidlík, *La sophiologie de S. Basil*, 78. The saying of the Delphic temple meant that overstepping boundaries (*mega phronein*) was always castigated. In philosophic thought, however, the human limits are rather wide. Self-knowledge reveals the presence of a god. 'Why then are you ignorant of your own noble descent — Epictetus writes — '... know you not that you are nourishing a god, that you are exercising a god? Wretch, you are carrying about a god with you, and you know it not.' *The Discourses of Epictetus*, tr. G. Long (London, 1877) 119.
4. See A.J. Festugière, *La révélation d'Hermès Trismégiste*, vol. II (Paris, 1949) 575ff.
5. *In Canticum* 2; GCS 3: 142ff.
6. See Louis de Bazelaire in DS 2 2:1515ff.
7. *Homilia in illud, attende tibi ipsi* 7; PG 31:213D
8. Basil, *Homilia in hexaemeron* 9.6; PG 29:204bc; FC 46 (1963) 147.
9. *Carminum Liber* I.II.31, verse 7; PG 37:911.
10. *Legum allegoriae* I.91; *De mutatione nominum* 10; see Jean Daniélou, *Philon d'Alexandrie* (Paris, 1958), 174.
11. *In the Image and Likeness of God*, 122-23.
12. *La femme et le salut de monde* (Tournai-Paris, 1958) 67.
13. *Vita Moysis*; PG 44:416D.
14. *Enarrationes 2 in Psalmo* 31.18; PL 36:207B.
15. *Laws* IV, 715e-717a.
16. *Stromata* II.22.132-33; ANF 2:375-77.
17. *Homiliae in Lucam* VIII, 4-5; Sch 87: *Homélies sur S. Luc* (1962) 169-71.
18. See Aristotle, *Nicomachean Ethics* IV.7.1123b 1-24; 112a 12.
19. Pierre Adnès, in DS 7:1152
20. See, for example, *Homilia 20 de humilitate*. 6; PG 31:536-37.
21. See Staukc Janežič, *Imitazione de Cristo secondo Tihon Zahonskij* (Trieste, 1962) 133ff.
22. John Chrysostom, *In Acta apostolorum* 30.3; PG 60:225B.
23. *De renuciatione saeculi* 9; PG 31:645B; *constitutiones monasticae* 16; PG 31:1377C.
24. See Dorotheos, *Instructions* II.35 and 37; SCh 92 (1963) 200, 202 [trans. Eric P. Wheeler, *Dorotheos of Gaza: Discourses and Sayings*, CS 33 (Kalamazoo, 1977)].
25. *Scala Paradisi* 25; PG 88:989A. [English tr. by Lazarus Moore, The Ladder of Divine Ascent (Boston, 1978), and by Colm Luibhéid and Norman Russell (New York: Paulist, 1982)]
26. See John Chrysostom, *Ecloga de humilitate*; PG 63:618A.
27. Evagrius, *Capita paraenetica* 1; PG 79:1249C; see I. Hausherr, *Philautie. De la tendresse pour soi à la charité selon saint Maxime le Confesseur*, OCA 137 (Rome, 1952) 175ff.
28. John Climacus, *Scala* 25; PG 88:993B.
29. Abba Isaiah, *Oratio* 20, *de humilitate*; PG 40:1157A.
30. Basil, *Homilia* 20, 3-4; PG 31:529-33.
31. See I. Hausherr, *Les leçons d'un contemplatif* (Paris, 1960) 132.
32. *Apophthegmata patrum* Antonius 7; PG 65:77B [CS 59:2].
33. See Diadochus of Photice, *Gnostic Chapters* 95; SCh 5ter (1966) 157; 'On spiritual knowledge', *The Philokalia*, vol. I (1979) 292; Abba Dorotheus, *Instructions* II.33; SCh 92 (1963) 196; John Climacus, *Scala* 25; PG 88:1000A.

34. *Apophthegmata*, Sisoes 13; PG 65: 396B [CS 59:214]; G.P. Fedotov, *The Russian Religious Mind* (Cambridge, 1946) 387.
35. Abba Dorotheus, *Instructions* II.39 (Sch 92:204–6); XIV.152–53 (426– 30).
36. John Climacus, *Scala* 25; PG 88:1001B.
37. Basil, *Homilia* 20 *de humilitate* 1; PG 31:525B; Špidlík, *La sophiologie de S. Basile*, 73.
38. *Contra Celsum* VI.15; GCS 2:85.
39. *Homilia in Psalmum* 48.8; PG 29:449BC; Špidlík, *La sophiologie*, 12.
40. *Paedagogos* I.63.1; GCS 1:127.
41. *In psalmum* 48.8; PG 29:449BC.
42. *Homilia in illud, Attende* 6; PG 31:212B.
43. *In Canticum* 2; GCS 2:142–44 [annotated trans. by R.P. Lawson, *Origen. The Song of Songs: Commentary and Homilies*, ACW (1957)].
44. PG 40:483–818.
45. See Xavier Léon-Dufour, 'Chair', VTB, 146–52.
46. *Republic* IX. 589a.
47. The *Enneads* I.1.10 and V.1.10; see Aimé Solignac, 'Homme intérieur: 1. Saint Paul, 2. Age patristique', DS 7/1:650–58.
48. *Homilia in Numeros* 24.2; GCS 7:227–29; for other passages, see DS 7/1: 653ff.
49. See Julien Leroy, 'Le cénobitisme chez Cassien' RAM, 43 (1967) 155; on other usages, se DS 7/1:655.
50. See Špidlík, *Théophane le Reclus*, 43.
51. *Timaeus* 90ab.
52. *Homilia in Hexaemeron* 9.2; PG 29:192AB.
53. See Léon-Dufour, 'Ame', in VTB, 39–43.
54. See above, Chapter II, *Spiritual* [*Life*], *The Effects of the Spirit on the Soul*....
55. *Carminum liber* I.I.10; PG 37:464–67.
56. *Oratio* 30.21; PG 36:132B; see Špidlík, *Grégoire de Nazianze*, 101.
57. *Stromata* V.80.9, CGS 2, p. 379, 25.
58. See Viktor Warnach, EF II:253; Herrade Mehl-Koehlein, *L'homme selon l'Apôtre Paul*, Cahiers Théologiques 28 (Neuchâtel-Paris, 1950).
59. See Ferdinand Prat, *La théologie de Saint Paul* (Paris, 1923) vol. 2: 490ff.
60. *De oratione* 10; PG 11:445; see Josef Rius-Camps, *El dinamismo trinitario en la divinizacion de los seres racionales segun Origenes*, OCA 188 (Rome, 1970).
61. *Adversus haereses* V.6.1; PG 7:1142B; ANF 1:531; see Hausherr, *Direction spirituelle en Orient autrefois*, 39–55; see note 54 above.
62. Ed. Sergiev Posad (1910), 401ff.; Špidlík, *Théophane le Recluse*, 31.
63. *Adversus haereses* II.15.3, Harvey I, 282.
64. See Spanneut, *Le stoïcisme*, 167ff.
65. *Ibid.*, 138ff. Sergei Michel Zarin, a Russian author, states in his *Asketism* [*Handbook of Asceticism*] (St Petersburg, 1907) that one may or may not accept the trichotomy since it si not always recognized in patristic literature (vol. 2:228).
66. *De principiis* I.1.6 (GCS 5:22, 21–22) *In Matthaeum* 13.9, (GCS 10:203, 26 –27); see J. Dupuis, *'L'esprit de l'homme'. Étude sur l'anthropologie d'Origène* (Tournai: Desclée de Brouwer, 1967) 67.
67. *De principiis* I.1.6; GCS 5:22, 21–23.
68. See Dupuis, 70.
69. *In Joannem* 2.21 (15); GCS 4:78, 3–5.

Christian Anthropology

70. *Ibidem*, 20.22 (20); GCS 4:355, 9–10.
71. Henri de Lubac, *Histoire et Esprit. L'intelligence de l'Ecriture d'après Origène* (Paris, 1950), 157.
72. Špidlík, *Théophane le Reclus*, 35ff.
73. See above, Chapter II, *One Spirit with the Lord*.

2. THE SPIRIT AND THE SOUL

1. See Špidlík, *Théophane le Reclus*, 29ff.
2. *Sobranie pisem [Collected Letters]* (Moscow, 1898–), vol. I:162.
3. *Mysli na každyi deň ĝoda* [*Thought on Every Day of the Year*] Moscow, 1881) 394.
4. *Čto jest' duchovnaja žizň* [*What the Spiritual Life Is and How to Begin It*] 18 (Moscow, 1897) 65.
5. Karl Rahner, 'Le début d'une doctrine des cinq sens spirituels chez Origène', RAM 13 (1932) 113–45; Michel Olphe-Gailliard, 'Le sens spirituel dans l'histoire de la spiritualité;, in *Nos sens et Dieu', Etudes carmélitaines* (Tournai: Desclée de Brouwer, 1954) 179–93.
6. Among the letters of Basil, *Epistle* 8.12; PG 32:265.
7. See Symeon the New Theologian, *Ethics* II, 243ff.; SCh 122: *Traités théologiques et éthiques* (1966) 409. [English translation by Paul McGuckin *The Practical and Theological Chapters and the Three Theological Discourses*, CS 41 (1982)].
8. See I. Hausherr (Lemaitre), in DS 2/2:1843.
9. See above, Chapter I, *Spiritual Experience*....
10. *Vita Antonii* 63; PG 26:933A.
11. See Ps 33:9; Jozef G. Ziegler, *Dulcedo Dei. Ein Beitrag zur Theologie der greichischen und lateinischen Bibel* (Münster, 1937); P. Adnès, 'Goût spirituel', DS 6:626–44.
12. Symeon the New Theologian, *Ethics* III, 160ff.; SCh 122:403.
13. See Wilhelm Bousset, *Apophthegmata Patrum. Studien zur Geschichte des ältesten Mönchtums* (Tübingen, 1923) 318.
14. See below, 3. THE HEART, *Point of Contact*....
15. See J. Dupont, *Syneidesis. Aux origines de la notion chrétienne de la conscience morale*. Studia Hellenistica, fasc. 5 (1948), 119–93; J. Stelzenberger, 'Conscience', EF I, 255–66.
16. See below 3.THE HEART.
17. *Epistle* 41.1.
18. See Walter Völker, *Fortschritt und Vollendung bei Philo von Alexandrien* (Leipzig, 1938) 95–105.
19. See Johannes Stelzenberger, *Conscientia bei Augustinus* (Paderborn, 1959) 26–172.
20. *Instructions* 3.40; SCh 92: (1963), 209; *Discourses and Sayings*, CS 33: 104.
21. *Ibid.*, 3.44.45; 215–17.
22. *Ibid.*, 3.46; 219.
23. See Chapter III, *The Soul's Salvation* and IV *Aphorisms about the Body*.
24. *In Canticum* 1.2; PG 13:126–27.
25. See Jean-Vincent Bainvel, in DThC 1 (1909) 971ff.

26. See Leonce Reypens, 'Ame', DS 1:433–69; A.J. Festugière, *La révélation d'Hermès Trismégiste*, III. *Les doctrines de l'âme* (Paris,1953).
27. See Tatian, *Oratio ad Graecos* 13 and 15; PG 6:833ff., 837ff.
28. See Henri Crouzel, *Théologie de l'image de Dieu chez Origène* (Paris), 1956); M. Spanneut, *Le stoïcisme de Pères de l'Eglise*, 135ff.
29. Especially *Summa Theologiae*, I, q. 75–77.
30. *Adversus haereses* V.7.1; Harvey, II, p. 356ff.; see Spanneut, *Le stoïcisme*, 147.
31. *Stromata* VI.136.1; GCS 2:500.
32. *Stromata* VI.136.2 and 3; *ibidem*.
33. See above, Chapter II, 1. and IV, *Various Aspects of the Trichotomy*.
34. Irenaeus, *Fragmenta* VI; ed. François Graffin-Nau, PO 12:737–39.
35. *Adversus haereses* V.9.1; Harvey, II:342; ANF, 1:534.
36. See Crouzel, *Théologie de l'image*, 182ff.
37. *Carminum Liber* I.I.8, vv. 1–3; PG 37:446ff.; verses 66ff., col. 452; See Plato, *Republic* VII. 514a–518b.
38. *Carminum Liber* I.I.8, v. 7ff; Špidlík, *Grégoire de Nazianze*, 21.
39. See Oscar Cullmann, *Immortalité de l'âme our résurrection des corps?* (Neuchâtel-Paris, 1956); Franz Cumont, *Lux perpetua* (Paris, 1949); H. Cornélis, *La Résurrection de la chair* (Paris, 1962) pp. 21–133; Aimé Solignac, 'Immortalité', DS 7/2:1601–14.
40. See Augustin Mansion, L'immortalité de l'âme et de l'intellect d'après Aristote', *Revue Philosophique de Louvain* 31 (1953) 444–72; Justin Mossay, *La mort et l'au-delà dans saint Grégoire de Nazianze* (Louvain, 1966).
41. See Daniel Lys, *Nephesh. Histoire de l'âme dans la révélation d'Israel au sein des religions proche-orientales* (Paris, 1962); idem, *Ruach. Le souffle dans l'Ancient Testament. Enquête anthropologique à travers l'histoire théologique d'Israel* (Paris, 1962); R. Refoulé, 'Immortalité de l'âme et résurrection de la chair', *Revue de l'histoire des religions*, 163 (1963) 11–52.
42. See DS 7/2:1605.
43. *To the Ephesians*, 20.2.
44. See I. Hermann, *Kyrios und Pneuma. Studien zur Christologie der paulinischen Hauptbriefe* (Munich, 1961).
45. See Justin Martyr, *Dialogus cum Tryphone* 5.2–5; PG 6:488–89; see DS 6:829; [*The Dialogue with Trypho* is translated in FC 6 (1948) 147ff.].
46. Irenaeus, *Adversus haereses* II.52.2; Harvey, I:383; see Spanneut, *Le stoïcisme*, 148.
47. See Max Pohlenz, *Der hellenische Mensch* (Göttingen, 1974); idem, *Die Stoa. Geschichte einer geistigen Bewegung*, vol. I (Göttingen, 1974) 124–25.
48. See Simonides of Ceos, *Fragmenta* 27, cited by A.J. Festugière, *L'idéal religieux des Grecs et l'Evangile*, Etudes bibliques (Paris, 1932) 168.
49. See Spanneut, *Le stoïcisme*, 222ff.
50. See Harry Austyn Wolfson, *Philo. Foundations of Religious Philosophy in Judaism, Christianity, and Islam.* (Cambridge, Mass., 1948, 2d ed.).
51. See Chapter V. *The Unity of the Deified World*.
52. *Apologia* II.7.4; PG 6:456ff.; see Spanneut, *Le stoïcisme*, 236.
53. *The Hexaemeron, Homily VI*; (PG 23:133AC; LNPF 8:86); *homilia Quod Deus non est auctor malorum* 6 (PG 31:345B).
54. *Stromata* II.17.5; GCS 2:153.
55. *Stromata* II.54.5–55, 1; GCS 2:145; SCh 38:78; see Spanneut, *Le stoïcisme*, 225.

Christian Anthropology 119

56. See Špidlík, *La sophiologie de S. Basile*, 44.
57. *La femme et le salut du monde*, 48.
58. *Ibid.*
59. *De anima et resurrectione*; PG 46:101C; cf. Jerome Gaïth, *La conception de la liberté chez Grégoire de Nysse* (Paris, 1953) 17ff.
60. *De mortuis*, PG 46:524A.
61. See Špidlík, 'La libertà come riflesso del mistero trinitario nei Padri Greci', *Augustinianum* 13 (1973) 515–23.
62. Gregory of Nyssa, *De anima et resurrectione*; PG 46:81B.
63. See Gaïth, *La conception*, 62.
64. Gregory of Nyssa, *De hominis opificio* 18; PG 44:192AB.
65. See Gaïth, 73; Špidlík, *La sophiologie*, 40ff.
66. See Gaïth, 64.
67. *Ibid.*, p. 66; Evagrius, *Antirrheticos* VIII.10; ed. W, Frankenberg, *Evagrius Ponticus* AGG.NF 13/2:538, 12–13.
68. Gregory of Nyssa, *De anima et resurrectione*; PG 46:81B.
69. Gaïth, 77ff.
70. *Ibid.*, 103ff; *De hominis opificio* 18; PG 44:192AB.
71. John Chrysostom, *Les Lettres à Olympias*, X (III); SCh 13:242.
72. See Nicolas Merlin, *Saint Augustin et les dogmes du péché originel et de la grâce* (Paris, 1931).
73. See PL 46:35B, Index generalis: hominis crimen malum error et infirmitas.
74. Špidlík, *Joseph de Volokolamsk*, 32ff.
75. See Martin Jugie, *Theologia dogmatica christianorum orientalium* I-IV, (Paris, 1926–35) vol. 2:733.
76. St Prosper accused Cassian of it in his *De gratia Dei et de libero arbitrio contra collatorem*, PL 51:213–76.
77. See John Chrysostom, *Commentarium in Matthaeum homilia* 15.1; PG 58:471.
78. See above, Chapter III, 2.
79. See *De fide orthodoxa* [43–44] II.29–30; PG 94:968A, 972AB.
80. *Pisma o duchovnoj žizň* [*Letters on the Spiritual Life*] (Moscow, 1903) 121; *The Art of Prayer* (London, 1966) 142; Špidlík, *Théophane le Reclus*, 194.
81. *Homilia* 4.17; PG 34:493B.
82. *Cto jest' duchovnaja žizň* ... (IV, 2, note 4) 170; Špidlík, *Théophane le Reclus*, 195.
83. See Spannuet, *Le stoïcisme*, 133ff.
84. *The Praktikos* 84; SCh 171:674; CS 4:37.
85. See Antoine Guillaumont, *Le traité pratique*, SCh 171:104ff.
86. See M. Pohlenz, *Die Stoa*. (note 47 above) I:87–90; Arnim, SVF II:827-32, p. 226.
87. *Stromata* I.39, 1 (GCS 1:25; SCh 38); *Stromata* V.52.2 (GCS 5:362); *Stromata* IV.116, 1 (229); *Stromata* V.80, 9 (379, 25); see Spannuet, *Le stoïcisme*, 170.
88. See Špidlík, *Théophane le Reclus*, 296; cf., *The Point of Contact*, below.

3. THE HEART

1. *Serdce v christianskoj i indijsko mistike* [*The Heart in Christian and Indian Mysticism*] (Paris, 1929) 5; *Le Coeur. Etudes carmélitaines* (Tournai: Desclée de Brouwer, 1950).

2. See J.L. Shein, *Readings in Russian Philosophical Thought* (The Hague-Paris, 1969) 100ff.
3. See the Index of the Greek *Philokalia*, vol. 5 (Athens, 1963) 233–35.
4. See André Lefèvre, 'Cor et cordis affectus. Usage biblique' DS 2/2:2278–81; Johann B. Bauer, 'De "cordis" notione biblica et iudaica', *Verbum Domini* 40 (1962) 27–32.
5. *Orationes* 40.39; PG 36:416AB.
6. *Summa Theologiae* 2–II, 44.5; see Jean Chatillon, 'Cordis affectus au moyen âge', DS 2/2:2288–2300.
7. See above, Chapter I, *Spritual Experience*.
8. See *Théophane le Reclus*, 46ff.
9. The heart is, for example, the theme of an entire volume of the *Etudes carmélitaines* (see note 1) but it is surprising that after so many special studies no one has thought of creating or even outlining a synthesis.
10. See Špidlík, 'The Heart in Russian Spirituality', in *The Heritage of the Early Church . . . in Honour of G.V. Florovsky*, OCA 195 (Rome, 1973) 361–74.
11. See *Théophane le Reclus*, 292.
12. *Phaedrus* 247c; *Timaeus* 51d.
13. See Chapter XII, *The Ascent of the Spirit to God*.
14. See Fernand Jetté, 'Fond de l'âme chez Marie de l'Incarnation', DS 5:661–66.
15. See Héribert Fischer, 'Fond de l'âme chez Eckhart', DS 5:650–61.
16. See A. Guillaumont, 'Le 'coeur' chez les sprituels grecs à l'époque des anciens', DS 2/2:2281–88; *idem*, 'Le sens du coeur dans l'antiquité', in *Le coeur. Etudes carmélitaines*, 41–88.
17. See Špidlík, 'The Heart in Russian Spirituality.'
18. See Chapter XII, *The Ascent.* . . .
19. *Cto jest' duchovnaja žizň* . . . (IV, 2, note 4) 25ff.
20. See A. Lefèvre, DS 5:2279.
21. See Vyšeslavcev, *Serdce* (above, n. 1) 51; Sergei Verchovskoj, *Pravoslavie v žizni* [*Orthodoxy in Life*] (New York), 1953) 282.
22. Théophane le Reclus, *Načertanie christianskago nravoučenjia* [*Christian Moral Teaching*] (Moscow, 1895) 306.
23. *Instructions sur les estats d'oraison*, livre I.20 (Paris, 1697) 26.
24. F. Jetté, 'Etat', DS 4/2:1372–1388.
25. See above.
26. See above, Chapters II, 1 and IV, *Various Aspects*. . . .
27. Martyrius Sahdônâ, *Livre de la perfection* II.4 (9); CSCO 215, Syr.
28. *Ibid.*, 11.10ff.
29. See Chapter XI, 2.
30. See Chapter XI, *Virtue-Likeness to God and Participation in Christ*.
31. See Theophil Spáčil, *Doctrina theologiae Orientis separati de revelatione, fide, dogmate* (Rome, 1935), 106ff. Which does not necessarily lead them to 'Kantian irrationalism, to sentimentality and to the errors of modernism' (cf. *ibid.*).
32. See Chapter XIII, *From Faith to Gnosis*.
33. *Livre de la Perfection* II.12ff.
34. See, for example, *Homilia* 43.3; PG 34:772.
35. *Načertanie*, 306.
36. Théophane le Reclus, *Put' ko spaseniju* [*The Way to Salvation*] (Moscow, 1908) 27.

Christian Anthropology 121

37. See Origen, *Fragmenta in Joannem* 27, CGS 4, p. 504, 1.
38. See above, 1.
39. See Pseudo-Macarius, *Homilia* 7.5–6; PG 34:525–28.
40. See Chapter XIII, *Theologia*.
41. Theophane the Recluse, *Cto jest* . . . [*What is Spiritual Life*], 26.
42. *Id.*, *Načertanie* [*Christian Moral Teaching*], 313ff.
43. See *Théophane le Reclus*, 94ff.
44. See Chapter IX, 3.
45. See Irénée Hausherr, *La méthode d'oraison hésychaste* (Rome, 1927) 134ff., 118ff.
46. *Homilia in illud, Attende tibi ipsi* 7; PG 31:213D–216A.
47. *Načertainie*, 313.
48. *Ibid.*, 312.
49. *Ibid.*, 309. Cf. the *cognitio per connaturalitatem* of the scholastics; Thomas Aquinas, *Summa theologiae* 2–II. 45.2; Jacques Maritain, *Art et scolastique* (Paris, 1935) 3d ed.
50. Martyrius Sadhônâ, p. 16, lines 11ff.

4. THE BODY

1. See A.J. Festugière, *Contemplation et vie contemplative selon Platon* (2nd ed., Paris, 1950) 31.
2. *Phaedrus* 246c, 248ac.
3. *The Encheiridion*, 33.7.
4. See X. Léon-Dufour, 'Corps', VTB 210–13.
5. *Ibid.*
6. *De legendis libris gent.*, 7; PG 31:584B; see David Amand, *L'ascèse monastique de saint Basile* (Maredsous, 1949) 191–99.
7. See A.J. Festugière, *Antioche païenne et chrétienne* (Paris, 1959) 291ff. Pierre Thomas Camelot, 'Hellénisme', DS 7/2:151ff.; Špidlík, 'L'ascesi nella Chiesa Orientale', *Rivista di vita spir.* 31 (1977) 496–514; *Ascesi cristiana*, ed. Ermanno Ancilli (Rome, 1977) 163–81.
8. *Adversus haereses* V.9.2.
9. See, for example, E. Stephanou, 'La coexistence initiale du corps et de l'âme d'après saint Grégoire de Nysse', *Echos d'Orient* 31 (1932) 304–15; Gerhart B. Ladner, 'The Philosophical Anthropology of Saint Gregory of Nyssa', *Dumbarton Oak Papers* 11 (1959) 59–94.
10. *To the Smyrnians* 1.1–2.2; *Trallians* 9.1–2; see Gustave Bardy, 'Docétisme', DS 3:1461–68.
11. *Adv. haer.* V.12.4; PG 7:1154C.
12. *Contra Joannem* 25; PL 23:375B.
13. See Antoine Guillaumont, *Les* Kephalaia gnostica *d'Evagre le Pontique et l'histoire de l'Origénisme chez les Grecs et chez les Syriens* (Paris, 1962) 114.
14. *The Justification of the Good* (London, 1918) 175.
15. *Pisma k raznym licam* [*Letters to Various Persons*] (Moscow, 1892), 249; Špidlík, *Théophane le Reclus*, 181.
16. See Basil, *On The origin of man*; SCh 160 (1970) 169.
17. See above.
18. *De resurrectione* 18; PG 6:1008ff; see Spanneut, *Le stoïcisme*, 141.
19. Gregory of Nazianzus, *Carminum liber* I.I.8, vv. 79–80; PG 37:785.
20. See *Grégoire de Nazianze*, 100ff.

21. *Oratio* 2.17 (PG 35:425C–428A); See *Oratio* 7.23 (PG 35:785).
22. Plato, *Gorgias* 493a; *Cratylus* 300c; see Pierre Courcelle, 'Le corps-tombeau', *Revue des études anciennes* 68 (1966) 101–22; Gregory of Nazianzus, *Orationes* 26.13; PG 35:1245B.
23. Clement of Alexandria, *Stromata* VII.40.1; GCS 3:30, 19ff.
24. *Phaedo* 67d; Gregory of Nazianzus, *Ep.* 32; PG 37:72B.
25. See Michel Aubineau, 'Le theme du 'bourbier' dans la littérature grecque profane et chrétienne', *Recherches de science religieuse* 47 (1959) 185–214.
26. Gregory of Nyssa, *De oratione dominica* 5; PG 44:1165BD. [English translation by Hilda Graef, *The Lord's Payer, The Beautitudes*, ACW 18 (1954).]
27. Clement of Alexandria, *Stromata* V.67.4; GCS 2:371.
28. See Jean Daniélou, 'Les tuniques de peau chez Grégoire de Nysse', in *Glaube, Geist, Geschichte. Festschrift für Ernest Benz* (Leiden, 1967) 355–67.
29. Marcus Aurelius, *Meditations* 12.3; Basil, *Homilia in illud, Attende*; PG 31:197ff; Špidlík, *La Sophiologie*, 79.
30. *Phaedo* 64e; Basil, *De legendis libris gentilium* 6–7; PG 31:581.
31. Clement of Alexandria, *Stromata* V.83.1; CGS 2:381.
32. Gregory of Nyssa, *De vita Moysis*; PG 44:388D; H. Musurillo, *From Glory to Glory*, (New York, 1979) 139.
33. Palladius, *The Lausiac History* 2, Dorotheus [tr. Robert T. Meyer, ACW
34. *Ibid.*, 18, Macarius the Great.
35. *Vita Antonii* 7; PG 26:853A; Basil, *Homilia in illud, Attende* 3: PG 31:203CD.
36. Basil, *Regula fusius tractata* 17; PG 31:964C.
37. John Climacus, *Scala Paradisi* 9; PG 88:841.
38. Diadochus of Photice, 'On Spiritual Knowledge', *The Philokalia. The Complete Text*, (Chapter I, 2, note 4) vol. I (1979) 280.
39. Gregory of Nyssa, *De mortuis*; PG 46:529A.
40. Gregory of Nyssa, *De hominis opificio*; PG 44:237B.
41. *Ibid.*, 161AB.
42. Gregory of Nyssa, *In Christi resurrectionem* 3; PG 46:677A.
43. See Ignatius of Antioch, *Ad Smyrnaeas* 4.2.
44. Origen, *In epist. ad Romanos, homilia* 9.1; PG 14:1205A.
45. See *Grégoire de Nazianze*, 37.
46. See Boris Bobrinskij, 'Molitva i bogusluženie v pravoslavnoj Cerkvi', in Sergei Verchovskoj, *Pravoslavie v žizni* (New York, 1953) 252.
47. Gregory of Nyssa, *Contra Eunomium* 4; PG 45:637AB.
48. See, for example, John of Damascus, *De fide orthodoxa* 4.2; PG 94:1208.
49. *De virginitate* 14.4; PG 46:381AB; see Chapter VIII, *Virginity*.
50. Nyssa, *De hominis opificio* 22; PG 44:205AC.
51. See Clement of Alexandria, *Stromata* VI.52.1; GCS 2:458, 8.
52. See Hilda C. Graef, 'L'image de Dieu et la structure de l'âme', *La vie spirituelle*. Suppl. n. 22 (1952) 331–39.
53. *Life of Saint Melanie* 12 SCh 90 (1962) 151.
54. See Chapters VIII, *Virginity, Fasting*, and X, *Evagrius*.
55. See *Commentaire sur S. Jean*, Introd. by C. Blanc, SCH 157 (1970) 27ff.
56. See, for example, Paul Evdokimov, *La femme et le salut du monde, Etude d'anthropologie chrétienne sur les charismes de la femme* (Tournai-Paris, 1958).
57. A. Harnack, *Medicinisches aus der ältesten Kirche*, TU VIII, 4, part 2 (Leipzig, 1892).

Christian Anthropology 123

58. Gregory of Nazianzus, *Oratio* 25.1; PG 35:1197A.
59. *Id.*, *Oratio* 12.3; PG 35:840B.
60. *Stromata* IV.21.1; GCS 2:257.
61. *Long Rules* 55; PG 31:1044ff.
62. See Stanislas Giet, *Les idées et l'action sociales de saint Basile*, (Paris, 1941) 417ff.; Joan Sokolov, *Soctojanije monašestva v vizanijskoj cerkvi*... [*Monasticism in the Byzantine Church*] (Kazan, 1894).
63. *Paterik Pečerskij*, ed. Dmitri-Ivan Abramovič, reedited Dmitry Tschiževskij, in *Slavische Propyläen* 2 (Munich, 1964), chapter 28, pp. 128ff; see Ivan Kologrivof, *Essai sur la sainteté en Russie* (Bruges, 1953) 56.
64. Špidlík, *Joseph de Volokolamsk*, 27.
65. Theodore the Studite, *Letters* II.134; PG 99:1432B.
66. See A.J. Festugière, *Les moines d'Orient*, vol. 1: *Culture et sainteté* (Paris, 1961) 87ff.
67. See Paul Hoffmann, 'Mort. Etude biblique', EF 3:135.
68. Hans Joachim Schulz, 'Die "Höllenfahrt" als Anastasis', *Zeitschrift für katholische Theologie* 891 (1959) 1–66.
69. Cassian, *Institutiones monasticae* V. 41 (CSEL 17: 113, 4ff; SC 109 [1965] 256); *Vita Antonii* 19 (PG 26:872A); see the *meletē thanatou* (practice of dying) in *Phaedo* 67d; Seneca, *Letters to Lucilius* 12 and 16.
70. Nikolai Berdiaev, *The Destiny of Man* (London, 1937) 250.
71. Gregory of Nazianzus, *Carminum Liber* II.I.45 verses 11ff; PG 37:1354.
72. *Id., Ep.* 31:PG 37:68C.
73. Gregory of Nyssa, *In funere Pulcheriae oratio*; PG 46:876D.
74. Gregory of Nazianzus, *Carminum Liber* II.I.45, v. 20; PG 37:1355.
75. Nikolaj Berdiaev, *The Divine and the Human*, tr. R.M. French (London, 1949) 158.
76. Vladimir Soloviev, *Duchovnyje osnovy žizni* [*The Spiritual Foundations of Life*] (St. Petersburg, n. d., rpt. Brussels, 1966) vol 3; 356ff.

5

SPIRITUAL COSMOLOGY

1. THE WORLD AND DIVINE PROVIDENCE

The Problem of the World in Antiquity

IN ORDER TO UNDERSTAND ancient cosmologies, we should keep a basic distinction in mind. Speaking succinctly, we may say that in Greek philosophy there is one true reality—the world of Ideas, of the objects of thought (*noēta*)—, and there is the world of material objects (*aisthēta*) which is but a shadow of the first.[1] When we consider the relationship between them, the dualism of Plato's earlier dialogues emerges. There is, however, another Platonism where this radical opposition is overcome, where the concrete world is related to the Ideas through the intermediary of the soul.[2] For the Stoics, finally, the visible and the invisible were but the two senses of the same world-order: one is active and was called mind, the other is passive and was essentially material.[3] That the human soul belongs to the invisible world cannot be doubted. Its relationship to the visible order is expressed variously, depending on the author's views.

Some have spoken of a Greek optimism towards the world. N. Berdiaev has strongly denied it: 'The Greeks, who are accounted to have been enjoyers of life, say through their greatest creative achievement, in the voice of Greek tragedy, that it would have been better for man not to be born.'[4]

In an attempt to be more objective, we should perhaps distinguish two tendencies. For the radical Platonist, the material world could not be the place where unchanging truth is found. Therefore, the world was an obstacle to be overcome by flight.⁵ For the Stoics, by contrast, man was integrated into the cosmos as a part of the Whole.⁶ He has been invited to 'share with God in this great festival' (*sympanēgyrizein*).⁷ The Stoics even said that the world was beautiful only for man's enjoyment, well ordered only for his sake. Everything happens in function of man. Animals and plants are destined for him.⁸

The main concern of any religious spirit is seeking and finding God. The Stoic tendency gave rise to 'cosmic religion'.⁹ The universe is permeated by God: it is 'the temple of God'.¹⁰ The wisdom to which this view gave rise is found explicitly in Marcus Aurelius: the sage contemplates the order in the universe and forgets his misery at the sight of this beautiful order; he views himself only as part of the Whole; he serves this divine City.¹¹ Man has, therefore, a mission to fulfill in this world. According to the *Corpus Hermeticum* he was sent to earth to care for the things of this earth. He cooperates with God in governing the world.¹² This 'optimistic' tendency, however, created serious difficulties. The cosmos, with its laws, its beauty, its perenniality, and its eternal return of things, expresses in fact an order closed in on itself, containing man and the gods in its necessity.¹³

The World in Scripture

The world is usually designated by the expression 'the heavens and the earth' (Gn 1:1). But, the cosmological and cosmogonic representations are only secondary material to be of service to religious affirmations, the data of faith.

To begin with, there is the distinction between the world and the one God: there is an abyss between them, which is expressed by the verb *create* (Gn 1:1). On the other hand, however, the creative activity also explains the dependence of the world upon God, who 'spoke, and it came to be' (Ps 33:6–9).

Issuing from divine hands, the world manifests the goodness of God. For sinful man involved in his tragedy, however, the world signifies as well the anger of God, whose instrument it is (Gn 3:17). The world is linked to salvation history in this dual fashion, and from this is derived its true religious meaning. Each of the creatures who make up the world has some type of ambiv-

Spiritual Cosmology

alence, as is brought out in the Book of Wisdom: the same water that proved the ruin of Egypt also ensures the salvation of Israel (Ws 11:5-14).

Man is at the center of salvation history. The sacred cosmology shows the world as it relates to man in this fashion: he emerges from it in order to conquer it (Gn 1:28), and he takes it with him in his own destiny. Indeed, the world is unfinished: it is up to man to perfect the world by subduing it (1:28) through labor, and by putting his imprint on it.[14]

The Greek term *kosmos* is amply used in the New Testament. But the meaning which it carries there results from the entire elaboration wrought in the Old Testament. 'God loved the world so much that he gave his only-begotten son' (Jn 3:16). For the world, this is the beginning of a new victory by Jesus over a world delivered through sin into the hands of Satan. Christians therefore find themselves in the same complex relationship with the world as did Christ during his stay on earth. They are not of the world (Jn 15:19, 17:17) yet nevertheless are in the world (17:11). Their separation from the evil world leaves unimpaired their positve duty to a world which is to be redeemed (Cf. Co 5:10).

Christian tradition continued to preach this dual attitude, positive and negative, towards the world. The authors distinguished between, as it were, 'two worlds': one which is the natural sphere for human life and which must be loved and made to share in universal salvation; and the other which is the enemy of God and from which one must flee. The theme of the world must therefore be divided into two chapters which seem mutually exclusive: 1) cosmic spirituality and 2) flight from the world.[15] It is the first attitude to which we turn now.

The Goodness and the Beauty of the World Created for Man

The Fathers were reacting against Gnosticism, which looked upon matter with deep suspicion: the visible world is the work not of God but of a Demiurge; it served neither the glory of God nor the salvation of man. By contrast, the orthodox Church professed belief in God the Creator of 'the visible and the invisible'.

The *Epistle to Diognetus* early stated that 'things were created by God for men's use',[16] and that God 'made the world for their sake' and subjected to them all things that are on the earth.[17] This idea was often expressed by John Chrysostom: 'The earth is for him [man], for him are the heavens, the sun and the stars...':[18] hence the folly of idolatry should be clear.[19]

In dealing with the topic of the world, Western preachers loved to expand on what the world could offer human life: food of all kinds, the advantages of climate, of the sun's heat, and so forth. Those in the East believed that the world was first and foremost a school for souls[20] to lead man to the knowledge of God.[21]

This is how Origen rehabilitated matter: he discovered its place in the divine plan and noted its role in the education of man. It became the starting-point of the reascent to the knowledge of God.[22] The authors of *theōria physikē* (natural contemplation) spoke of an unmediated perception by the mind of the *logos* (reason) of created things.[23] But many others seemed to move in a sphere which was more aesthetic than intellectual and wanted to attain to the unutterable beauty of God through the beauty of the universe.[24] 'By the beauty of visible things let us raise ourselves to him who is above all beauty....'[25]

It should be noted, meanwhile, that just as intellectual contemplation is beyond the capacity of the merely human mind,[26] so is the beauty of God not perceived through man's aesthetic sense.[27] 'God saw that it was beautiful' (Gn 1:10) is explained by Basil: 'It is not with eyes that the Creator views the beauty of his works. He contemplates them in his ineffable wisdom.'[28] 'That which is truly beautiful exceeds all human apprehension and power and can be contemplated by the mind alone....'[29]

When they had to explain the beauty of the universe in human terms, the Fathers made ready use of the concept of the beautiful which they had inherited from Stoicism: the harmony which gives cohesion to a being composed of many parts.[30] The good arrangement of the universe (*diakosmēsis, eukosmia, eutaxia*, good order), became one of the main arguments in proving the existence of God.[31] This argument, borrowed from philosophy, took on a special character when viewed in the light of revelation.

The Unity of the Deified World

The early Fathers' deep admiration for the cosmos is one of the traits typical of the patristic period. Their reflections are tinged

Spiritual Cosmology

with Stoic terminology.[32] Zeno, who professed that one *logos* permeates the universe and causes all effects, viewed the noncomposite character of the world as dogma. This unity was presented from two aspects: the rigorous chain of events, and the hierarchy of beings 'sympathizing' through the power of the divine *pneuma* (breath) in them.[33]

The unity of the world is a familiar patristic theme. The universe is a Whole, *to pan*.[34] Clement of Alexandria saw 'things inanimate sympathizing with the animate creation in cosmic unity'.[35] The concept of *sympnoia* (breathing together)[36] brings to mind the theory of a *logos-pneuma* which penetrates everything like a common soul.[37] Clear traces of an animistic concept of the world can be found in the early Fathers.[38]

This 'animism,' however, was soon transposed into another register. In Stoicism, it was the 'eternal fire' that carried the logos and constituted the soul of the world.[39] In Irenaeus it is the Holy Spirit, who apparently received the function of being a cohesive force under the name Wisdom: 'He who made and formed . . . establishing all things by his Word, and binding them together by his Wisdom — this is he who is the only true God.'[40]

Clearly, the cosmic activity of God excludes neither the mysterious workings of grace in the human heart nor the redemptive action of Christ, sanctification within his Church. Such a total vision, which may be called 'sophiological' or 'sophianic' has dominated the recent theology of the Russians of Vladimir Soloviev, Pavel Florensky, Sergei Bulgakov, and B. Zeňkovsky.[41] According to Paul Evdokimov,

> sophiology, the glory of present orthodox theology, is alone in asking the immense cosmic question. It opposes all agnostic acosmism, all evolutionary materialism, and views the cosmos liturgically. The creation of God is interpreted through the inherent cosmism of the liturgy.[42] Man will recognize the beauty of the world in proportion to his communion with the Holy Spirit. . . .[43]

Recent sophiology has its roots in patristic reflections on the creative word of God. The visible cosmos is neither confused nor identified with God but emerges from its own nothingness to become beautiful in the eyes of God and man[44] through perfect obedience to the word of God, which becomes like a law of nature. Philaret of Moscow summarized this concept in one of his Sermons: 'All creatures are balanced upon the creative word of God, as if upon a diamond bridge; above them is the abyss of divine infinitude, below them that of their own nothingness.'[45]

Divine Providence or Fate?

The presence of the Spirit, of divine Wisdom, in the world, means freedom from enslavement to the gods, to 'the elemental principles of this world', to the princes and forces of fate (Ga 4:3, Col 2:8), and the conversion from 'idolatry to the living God' (1 Th 1:9, 1 Co 12:2). The image of God in Scripture is that of a father watching over his creation and providing for their needs (Pss 145–147). This is the aspect evoked by the term providence, a word for which there is no Hebrew equivalent and for which the Greek *pronoia* is used in Scripture only twice to indicate divine providence (Ws 14:3, 17:2).

In ancient philosophy, the defenders of providence were found among the Stoics. Their God was not a power removed from the world, but a rational force which penetrated everything.[46] For Epictetus there was not only a general but also a special providence: 'The first thing we must learn is this: that there is a God, and that he provides for the universe, and that it is impossible for man to conceal from him, not merely his actions, but even his intentions and his thoughts.'[47] Cicero's argument is valid even for a rather personal providence: 'The moment the gods are recognized, we must admit that they govern the world.'[48]

In keeping with their basic thought, the Stoics professed that providence was the law of the universe. It was essentially cosmic and not directly centered on man. Everything was perfectly logical because everything flowed from the *logos*, which was almost identified with *heimarmenē, moira*, fate.[49]

Some Stoics made a clever distinction between God and the order of the universe, but for most of them this order was God, Providence, Fate, and Nature. Seneca expressed this ideal very clearly:

Every name suits Jupiter. Do you want to call him Fate? You are not wrong.... Will you call him Providence? You are right again.... Would you rather call him Nature? There will be no error.... Do you see in him the World itself? You would not be wrong. He is everything you see; he penetrates each of the parts and sustains himself and all that belongs to him by his own power.[50]

The fatalistic trend became even more pronounced in the second century, when Stoicism encountered an astral fatalism originating in Chaldea. When Gregory of Nyssa wrote his *Tract Against Fate* astral fatalism seemed one of the most natural ways of presenting the inflexible fate to which all human beings are subject.[51] It goes without saying that this trend only aggravated the problem of free will, which posed difficulties the Stoics understood from the beginning.[52] The Fathers therefore had to defend the fatherly providence of God. Clement of Alexandria had already written his treatise *On Providence* (*peri pronoias*);[53] the Byzantines would deal with the subject at all periods.[54]

The Divine Oikonomia

In christian literature, providence is identified with the activity of God which is called *oikonomia* (literally 'household management'). By means of this term, John Chrysostom described the prudent conduct of someone who considers the circumstances before acting; it meant diplomacy or strategy, and how God adapts himself to man.[55] With the same term he also described the incarnation of Christ, which he qualified as an *oikonomia* according to the flesh. Generally, however, Chrysostom applied this term to God's plan or design for man. This plan (*oikonomia*) progresses towards the goal of salvation and glory and embraces two lives, the present life and the life to come. He enumerated the following events as belonging to the *oikonomia* of God: the activity of the wicked in the world, heresies, the devil, the demons, the Anti-Christ, difficulties, tempests, and suffering. Finally, the wise governance of the world in its cosmic and historic dimensions is also the 'economic' work of God.[56] It is presented to man as a strange event in whose presence he is 'filled with admiration and stupefaction'.[57]

Definitions and the Purpose of Providence. Distinctions

The definitions did not vary greatly after Maximus the Confessor. Two occur in succession in the *Ambigua*:[58] 'According to the God-bearing Fathers, providence is God's solicitude for that which exists,' and 'The will of God, thanks to which all beings are led to their appropriate end'.[59] For Maximus, the purpose of providence was 'the recapitulation in God of all the beings created by him';[60] its first and greatest mystery is Christ, and the Cross of Christ.[61] To say it differently, the aim of providence is not only the preservation of nature but its redemption and deification.[62] It therefore assumes three forms: it is *syntēretikē* (preserving), *epistreptikē* (directing towards God), and *paideutikē* (instructing or chastising).[63]

The early Fathers spoke of providence especially in formularies which bring to mind the cosmic *pneuma* of the Stoics. Clement of Rome wrote of God who 'embraces (*emperiechontos*) the universe'.[64] Aristides of Athens spoke of 'God, our Lord who, while being one, is present everywhere'.[65]

A question arose in relation to this cosmic providence: was it engaged with everything directly or indirectly?[66] Clement of Alexandria, who staunchly defended the universality of providence to the smallest detail, in no way claimed that God administers everything himself. He has established an uninterrupted series of intermediaries consisting, at the extreme end of the visible world, of the blessed angels arranged in ranks, but unified in the one Word.[67]

This 'distribution' of providence was traditional. Athenagoras seems early to have established a boundary line between direct and indirect providence.[68] The concept was part of the culture of the age.[69] The angels and the demons had received a thousand charges from the Fathers, yet they played a cosmic role. The angels, of course, are not the only servants of providence. Gregory Nazianzen stressed that through the creation of the visible world the power of God is still more apparent. It extends not only to the intellectual natures akin to himself but also 'to one altogether alien to him, of which sense can take cognizance; and in this category to natures furthest removed from him, all those which are destitute of soul and of the power of motion.'[70]

Spiritual Cosmology

This leads to another division of providence, the general and the particular. That providence is universal does not mean that it is the same for all beings. Alongside the universal providence which guides the world, Athenagoras perceived 'a particular providence' directed 'toward the deserving'.[71]

Personal Providence and the Law of the World

This particular providence directed 'toward the deserving' could refer to a special call in the biblical sense. However, the problem on Athenagoras' mind was different: how to reconcile human freedom with universal law. In the constitution of his body man simply depends on the immense cosmic order to which all physical nature is subject. By contrast, human activity, in so far as it is consonant with reason does not fall under this common law: it must be individualized.[72] An evasive answer, but it clearly indicates the problem.

In his *Discourses on Providence*,[73] Theodoret of Cyrus seemed to deny, or to cover over, this cosmic necessity; he compared God to a Pilot or a President of the games forever intervening in the course of events. It was impossible, however, not to see in the cosmos the normal concatenation of events (*akolouthia physikē*), the natural law (*anankē physikē*),[74] 'the physical necessity of the divine economy'.[75]

Following Philo and Clement of Alexandria, Basil took another tack to preserve the necessity of physical laws in the world and, at the same time, the freedom of God in governing the world. The cosmic law is nothing but the creative word of God,[76] 'the meaning implicit in the command' (*en tǫ prostagmati dianoia*).[77] Consequently, physical necessity does exist, but it originates in divine freedom.

Some more speculative Fathers saw the difficulty very clearly: how is such a mystery to be explained? Together with the problem, they also indicated from the beginning the right way of solving it. They recognized the explicit relationship which exists between the *logos*, the law of the universe, and the *Logos*, the Word, the Son, of the Father.[78] Progress in the spiritual life could therefore be presented as approaching Christ by observing the commandments, being united with him, and entering through him into a free dialogue with the Father. We can therefore say that the Fathers did not seek to solve the problem on the horizontal plane, as if it were a separation between two opposed domains, freedom and necessity. Their solution might instead be called vertical: they began from necessity and sought to transform it into the glorious freedom of the children of God in the Spirit.[79]

Surrender to Providence

The practical conclusions of this teaching are far-reaching. 'The surrender to providence' may be a new expression in modern treatises on asceticism, but, as doctrine, it is essential to all christian spirituality. The universe is the realm of God the Father: his work merits uninterrupted contemplation. To conclude the beautiful passages he selected from the writings of Basil, Symeon Metaphrastes, a Byzantine compiler, added an eloquent peroration:

> Nothing is excluded from divine providence. Nothing escapes his concern. His eye that never sleeps sees everything. He attends to everything and gives salvation to everyone. He deserves to have us say with the prophet: 'Yahweh, what variety you have created, arranging everything so wisely' (Ps 103:24).[80]

And Basil assures us that

> it is not possible to deviate from the straight road [as long as] the oblivion of God has brought no damage to the health of souls.[81]

The life of all humankind may, in addition, be compared to a grandiose liturgical service in the cosmic temple, with each human being performing, until death, the unique task assigned him by providence. Meanwhile, suffering and misfortunes will occur, and they swiftly put this beautiful faith in universal providence to the test. The christian's attitude towards suffering becomes a demonstration of virtue.

Spiritual Cosmology

2. EVIL AND PROVIDENCE

The Problem of Evil

'God saw all he had made, and indeed it was very good' (Gen 1:31). Nevertheless, to hasten the arrival of the eschatological kingdom, Christ has us ask in the Lord's Prayer: 'Deliver us from evil' (Mk 6:13). To the believer, the contradiction between these two formulas creates a problem to which Scripture itself offers elements of a solution: where does evil come from in a world that was made good? When, and how, will it be overcome?

In everyday life spiritual writers had to confront other circumstances than those which urged them simply to praise the world's beauty and the divine arrangements by virtue of which all unreasoning creatures were put at the service of man, the king of creation. If the waters flowed by virtue of the first divine command,[1] where do destructive inundations come from, or, by contrast, drought?[2] Where do public calamities come from, and earthquakes, shipwrecks, fires, military disasters, and all such events?[3] Certain things are subjectively good or bad to the person who has seen and experienced them. They create happiness and make life easier or, by contrast, lead to suffering in all its forms, and to death.

The ancients abhorred suffering. It was better not to be born than to suffer.[4] The religions of the East do not try to explain the problem of suffering: does it not depend on inexorable fate or the inscrutable will of the gods?[5]

In their writings, the Fathers viewed evil from various points of view. As apologists they refused to admit opinions that were contrary to the christian faith. But their works also show the compelling force of their lived experience. They had tragically felt the reality of human suffering and they tried to understand its meaning. Through his suffering, Christ has brought redemption and yet, as John Chrysostom notes, people reacted to this sight by being scandalized by it.[6] Offended by the daily experience of suffering, the spiritual man must nowadays still endeavor to 'suffer reasonably in the manner of the Fathers' (Paisius Velichkovsky).[7] Finally, as ascetics, the Fathers acknowledged their duty to fight the Evil One and, united to Christ, to free the world from evil.

Chapter Five

Refutation of False Opinions About the Origin of Evils

1. *There is no eternal principle of evil.* One rather widespread explanation for the existence of evil in antiquity arose out of a dualistic concept which became popular in the form of Manicheism.[8] In the opinion of the Fathers, to make the principle of Evil equal to God is blasphemy.[9]

2. *Matter is not evil.* The patristic argument was readily based on the positive judgment God has made of his work: 'and indeed it was very good' (Gn 1:31).[10] And when the body, along with all other matter, became the object of violent Manichaean attacks, John Chrysostom forcefully argued that the body is not evil and not in itself the seat of evil: 'The body is the handiwork of God'.[11]

3. *The absurdity of the fatalistic solution, as if evil were predetermined.* Chrysostom always observed that the doctrine of fate is the work of the demon, who introduced it among suffering people to remove them from God.[12]

4. *'That God is not the creator of evil.'*[13] If the origin of evil is not to be sought in created things, is it to be imputed to God? This is the temptation of man who in his suffering quarrels with the Creator. In a celebrated homily, Basil said that everything which comes from the hand of God is an expression of God's goodness.

Proairesis (Intention, Choice) — The Source of Evil

The goodness of man in the creation story, is a unique case. Goodness depended in part on man himself. God placed man before 'the tree of the knowledge of good and evil', leaving him with the capability of obeying, and enjoying the tree of life, or being taken away by death (Gn 2:9, 17) — the decisive test of freedom which is repeated in every person.

'Where does evil then come from?' Chrysostom inquired. 'Ask yourself... Is it not the result of your free will and your choice (*proairesis*)? Undeniably, and there is no one who would argue against this.'[14] This was the common teaching of all orthodox writers. By choosing evil, man becomes the agent of his own destruction and of the catastrophes that befall the world: 'Thence come the diseases in the cities and among the populations, and the dry weather, the barrenness of the soil..., the destruction of cities, the defeat of armies, shipwrecks...'.[15]

Divine Providence within Evil

The question is always asked about the part God has in all the disasters that beset man so frequently. Chrysostom uses the verb *synchōreō* (to acquiesce). He seems to have wanted to stress the noninterference of God, who permits or does not prevent.[16] Even more, he reacted strongly against those who were offended by the strange inertia of providence: the divine *oikonomia* radically surpasses human understanding.[17] The certainty that God directs all things is something for christians to fall back on in their trials.[18]

We could go back to Socrates to discover the origin of a clear distinction between physical and moral evil.[19] At any rate, the Fathers strongly insisted on this principle, that physical evils are not real evils but, on the contrary, instruments for good.[20] What is to be said about moral evil, sin? Origen did not hesitate to reply to Celsus that even though God has not created moral evil and and even though this evil always remains evil, no wicked event escapes the power of God: through divine providence even sin can become useful to the world, and to man.[21]

There is, of course, hardly any place for 'providential' sins in the exhortatory writings of spiritual writers, and for the speculative mind they constitute an all too impenetrable mystery. Attention was therefore centered on proving the usefulness of physical evils, suffering, and pain.

The Benefits of Suffering to the Sinner

The Fathers distinguished between the suffering of sinners and that of the just, while specifying that this distinction is not always fully adequate.[22] Berdiaev thinks that 'The idea that suffering is a punishment for sin was imported from outside'.[23] The idea is, nonetheless, in keeping with the demands of Antiquity.[24] Traces of the theory of the concordance of opposites (*concordia discors*) are found in patristic writings: the harmony of the world was composed of discordant elements which combine to create a unity as sounds do a melody.[25] Even more, the Fathers evoked the idea of the sacrifice of the part for the sake of the greater whole (*bonum universale — malum partiale*).[26] For Chrysostom, this *bonum universale* consisted above all in the salutary warning given to others: 'Punishment falls on those who have most to answer for, the others are saved so that they might profit by this example.'[27]

It was necessary, nonetheless, to arrive at a typically christian sense of the punitive action of God, through the concept of God the good physician. 'What the remedy applied by the physicians is, what fire and iron are in their hands, chastisements are in the hands of God.'[28] Punishments are like a new theophany appropriate to the sinner because they awaken the fear of God[29] and, at the same time, expiate sin: 'they amend our wrongs and work righteousness'.[30]

The Sufferings of the Just

'Those who cultivate virtue have misery as their life's companion; they are overcome by afflictions; they lack even necessities; they live in dust and squalor; they walk with bowed head; they suffer insults and abuse, and undergo untold sufferings.'[31]

Chrysostom cited innumerable examples of the sufferings of the just in the Old and the New Testament.[32] The most eloquent example is found in the First Homily *On the Statues* in which he clearly explains the reasons that give meaning to the tribulations of the saints.[33] The theme of the 'just sufferer' is known from religious Assyro-Babylonian texts.[34] In Book II of the *Republic*[35] Plato presents the 'just one impaled'; evil is seen there as an occasion for testing: 'the unexamined life (*anexestastos bios*) is not worth living.'[36] It is within the same framework of thought that the Fathers viewed suffering as a demonstration of the courage of the true christian.[37]

To this concept of examination was added that of reward. For pagans, the reward consisted in the glory of being remembered by the people; for christians, this glory 'transcends the earth after spreading throughout it, and is realized in heaven'.[38] Yet, it becomes theophanic even on earth: the sufferings of the just instruct the world and witness to divine truth.[39] Martyrdom is the classic example.[40]

Christlike Suffering

The crowning manifestations of the divine economy are the suffering of Christ and his death on the cross, 'the greatest of goods . . . by which the world is saved'.[41] 'That is why we travel the same road he traveled, that is, we become his brothers in this respect and, so to speak, other Christs.'[42]

A familiar theme in the age of the persecutions was that the martyrs were 'imitators of true charity', copies of the suffering Christ.[43] In hagiographic language, the Church intended to confine the title of martyr to its narrowest sense: the cause of violent death had to be hatred of the faith.[44] Russian piety, for its part, was less strict from the beginning. It has canonized *strastoterpsi*, that is, those who suffered a 'passion', a violent death for various reasons; these are very often little children 'decapitated for no reason at all'.[45] According to Berdiaev, 'we find here a very Russian theme — pity for those who suffer'.[46]

A text from Chrysostom may justify this attitude. There are benefits of persecution, 'so that, by taking another perspective, you might understand the profit gained from suffering, even when one does not suffer for God's sake'.[47]

Divine Paideia

Chrysostom stressed the analogy between the *paideia* (training) of athletes and the difficulty of the trials God sends to us.[48] A comparison with the *paideia* in the schools brings out the idea of progress in learning, in contemplation, in the understanding of suffering. An essentially Chrysostomian theme is found here: that an erroneous judgment, a false 'opinion' (*doxa*),[49] lies at the root of suffering. He took up a Stoic theme: 'There are many things which by ignorance alone cause us sorrow. If we come to understand them well, we banish our grief.'[50] The great challenge of the christian life consists therefore in correcting this error through a contemplation of the suffering Christ[51] or, as Berdiaev says, 'in turning the gloomy suffering which leads to perdition into a transfigured suffering which leads to salvation'.[52]

But what is to be said about the suffering of children? This problem may be countered by comparing baptism to dying for

Christ in martyrdom. Baptism cannot demand things from those who have not yet reached the age of reason, and Russian piety did not act differently when it venerated and canonized certain 'innocents', victims of some crime,[53] for the blood that was shed is 'like a purifying bath cleansing the victims of all sin and impurity'.[54] 'Everything is expiated through suffering', Dostoevsky said in turn.[55]

'No One Is Harmed Except By His Own Hand' (Chrysostom)

For his famous treatise *No One Is Harmed Except By His Own Hand* (*Nemo laeditur nisi a seipso*),[56] Chrysostom borrowed the content and form of his doctrine from Chrysippus and Epictetus, but he placed everything in the context of a lived experience of God's providence, for 'the effect of God's grace' is that no one can inflict misery on us.[57] The argument of the tract can be summarized as follows:

> 1) The wise man suffers neither injustice nor harm as long as he maintains his moral integrity through the rectitude of his will;
> 2) If the wise man is really harmed this is due to his own negligence, but then he ceases to be wise;
> 3) Far from suffering real harm, the truly wise man derives benefit and moral advantage from the injustice done to him;
> 4) Anyone who suffers harm is, in fact, the unjust and unrighteous man who commits injury to the wise man.

Briefly, we read here the strong conviction that there is only one real evil, which is sin, and that sin depends exclusively on our free choice.[58]

3. THE COSMIC VOCATION OF MAN

The Human Mission

'The religious sense innate in the human heart', Vladimir Soloviev wrote, 'induced people to leave the governance of the world to the gods, and because of this, the Roman emperors who believed that they ruled the *oikoumenē* (the habitable globe, the civilized world) claimed divine honors'.[1] But is man not lord and king over all things on earth? The question therefore arises: what room does God's activity leave man in the governance of infra-human nature?

To understand what the Fathers said about the human mission in the world, we must return not only to their cosmic perspectives but also to the anthropological question. Whatever they said about the mysterious union of the soul and the body, this union certainly must have had a special purpose in the intention of the Creator.[2] This strange association of body and soul caused an endless problem for Gregory Nazianzen. It revealed the wisdom of God in a very special way.[3]

Through the union of two such diverse elements — one visible, the other invisible — man somehow is a microcosm, a little universe (*ho mikros kosmos*).[4] The various theories of the ancients, frequently enhanced by the new context, are found again echoed in the Fathers.[5] We can find there a reflection of the theses of the Stoa insofar as they express the idea of a community of nature between man and the world.[6] The Fathers, however, following Philo,[7] attached greater importance to the microcosm than to the macrocosm.[8] Man shares his essence with all the categories of beings. He is therefore called, in Christ, to unite the entire creation.[9]

John Chrysostom often expressed man's responsibility towards nature in Semitic-sounding terms: 'The king has need of his subjects, and the subjects of the king; just as the head has need of the feet.'[10] God, who is the craftsman and worker of nature,[11] enjoined upon Adam, in paradise, the tillage of the soil.[12]

The Purification of the World and its Progressive Deification

According to the biblical concept, man, the sinner, dragged nature down with him in his fall. But the righteous prepare a profound renewal also for the world.[13] The Fathers frequently said that 'the world has been accursed because of [man's] wickedness'.[14] Chrysostom believed however, that if creation has suffered greatly because of man, 'it has not been treated unjustly, because it will be incorruptible again for our sake'.[15]

This is the aim of asceticism, and an idea cherished especially by the Russians. According to P. Florensky, for example, the ideal of christian asceticism is not contempt for the world but a joyful acceptance of it. This can enrich the world by raising it to a higher plane, even to the fullness of a transfigured life.[16]

The History of the World

In Scripture, God is not understood abstractly in his eternal essence, as in Plato or Aristotle, but by his interventions here below which transform history into sacred history. Spiritual writers were not concerned with solving the difficult problems of time and eternity. The eschatological character of Christianity[17] nonetheless appeared to them in the form of a question well formulated by Gregory of Nyssa: 'How to understand how someone comes when he is always present.'[18]

Christians could accept neither the idea of the eternal return of things professed by archaic cultures[19] nor the abstract immobility of the divine world which results from philosophic speculations about pure Being.[20] At the same time, the ascetics who yearned to leave 'this world' could not imagine eternity as an infinite continuation of 'this time'; they awaited the 'passing' of this world into the next (Cf Jn 13:1). Yet this passage not only occurs in death (called *exodos, transitus*): it characterizes the entire christian life.

Greek philosophy viewed time in opposition to eternity, as an illusion is contrasted to what is real. The *bios theōretikos* was therefore an attempt to escape the time-bound conditions of human life. Christian *praxis* is, by contrast, eminently 'historical', linked to the incarnation of Christ, and engaged in the present. It leads, however, to *theōria*;[21] it assigns a new value to time by tying it closely to eternity.[22] The 'economy' of salvation assumes therefore two inseparable aspects: it is historical in time, yet within a dimension of eternity. This is the mystery of Christ, of the Eucharist, of the liturgy, of the entire cosmos: it is the progressive realization of an 'uncreated reality, itself the Creator',[23]; and when the world looks towards its first Cause it is, in a certain sense, constantly being created.'[24]

The aim of the spiritual life therefore is to live in history and 'to transfigure time',[25] to grasp the eternal in the temporal, 'because eternity is not something; it is someone or, rather, the supreme love of the three persons'.[26]

The World of the Past Has Gone (Rv 21:4)

It would be impossible to review all the forms which the presentation of 'the things to come' (Judgment, Heaven, Hell . . .) has taken over the centuries, or still takes, in christian preaching. We know that ancient literature echoed extra-biblical traditions and that it used a terminology largely derived from Jewish apocalypticism.[27] Let us examine the aims which these meditations proposed for the spiritual life.

There is, first, the salutary fear capable of spurring the soul on to seek life eternal, to choose one of the 'two ways' offered to humankind, the way of light or the way of darkness, of life or of death.[28]

Fear, to be salutary, cannot be separated from hope in the coming of Christ, in Paradise, in the renewal of the world, in the kingdom of heaven. The works of Ephrem, for example, can be divided in two categories: exhortations to penance, and songs of the eternal hope which is enough for blessedness, the *Vae* (Woe!) and the *Beatus* (Blessed).[29] Even if the formidable menace of Judgment hangs only over the evil world, Judgment remains nonetheless a fearsome eventuality. Every person is a sinner. Who will escape the Judgment, if not through God's mercy? In Scripture, the eschatological judgment is presented as a fire (Is 66:15ff.). The Epistle to the Hebrews (10:27) shows the dreadful prospect of the fire which is supposed to burn the rebellious. But, the ambiguity of this symbol is also apparent in Scripture: whereas the godless are handed over to inner fire and worms, Jacob and Israel and all those who escaped the fire shall instead become fire (Obed 18), as if participating in the life of God. Christian tradition is convinced that, in union with Christ, the passage from this world to the next will be a purification and a deification[30] whereby mourning itself will be changed into hope because, as John Chrysostom says, 'it is possible to grieve for our own sins, and yet to rejoice in Christ'.[31]

Apokatastasis (Universal Salvation) or the Progressive Concept?

The theories about time and eternity had a repercussion in the thought of spiritual writers: how can one perceive progress in perfection?

The eschatology of the Greek Fathers is often strongly centered around a return to our original state of blessedness. The *apokatastasis*[32] appeared to be the normal outcome of the divine plan of salvation: 'Through this sequence of events, we, together with our first father, were excluded from paradise, and now, through the same sequence, it is possible for us to retrace our steps and return to our original blessedness.'[33] It soon became necessary to reject the Origenist *apokatastasis*, the theory of cyclical returns, and to admit but one single history, 'for those who hold this are only mixing and confusing good things and bad.'[34] It remains true, meanwhile, that human salvation will consist in finding again what we have lost. Adam, before the fall, was the type of the perfect man.[35]

It appears that Tatian, however opposed he was to the Greek philosophers, offered the first, albeit awkward, attempt to unite judaeo-christian speculations to Greek philosophy: 'Further, it is necessary for us now to seek what we once had, but have lost...'.[36] At the same time, Theophilus started another tradition which would be continued by Irenaeus, Clement of Alexandria, Tertullian, and Methodius of Olympus.[37] Methodius presented the first Adam as an imperfect sketch: 'In those days, man was not yet perfect.... Although he was born "in the image" of God he was still in need of receiving "the resemblance".'[38] 'Paradise was still halfway between heaven and earth.'[39] Likewise, for Irenaeus, perfection came not at the beginning but at the end. The first man was a child-man. Irenaeus defended this position by the very character of creation, which implies imperfection and temporality:

> If, however, anyone would say 'What then? Could God not have created man perfect from the very beginning?', let him know that all things are possible to God inasmuch as he is always the same. But created things must be inferior to him who created them, from the very fact of their later origin....

Spiritual Cosmology

As these things are of later date, they are children; and so they are unaccustomed to, and unexercised in, perfect discipline.[40]

Both views were developed and remained in force later on, occasionally in the same author.

Notes

1. THE WORLD AND DIVINE PROVIDENCE

1. See Plato, *Republic* VI.508c, VII.617bc; see Gregory Nazianzen, *Oratio* 28.30; PG 36:69A.
2. See A. J. Festugière, *La Révélation d'Hermès Trismégiste* (Paris, 1944–1954) vol. 2: xii.
3. See Michel Spanneut, *Le stoïcisme des Pères de l'Église*, 350.
4. *Dialectique existentielle du divin et de l'humain* (Paris, 1947) p. 92; trans. R. M. French, *The Divine and the Human* (London, 1949 p. 68.
5. See René Arnou, 'Platonisme des Pères', DThC 12/2 (1935) 2339.
6. Epictetus, *Discourses* II.5.13, II.10.3, IV.7.6–7.
7. *Ibid.*, III.5.10, IV.1.104–5; see Clement of Alexandria, *Paedogogos* I.5.22.1 (GCS 1;103); *Stromata* VII.7.49.3 (GCS 3:37) *Protrepticus* X.100.4 (GCS 1:72).
8. Von Arnim, SVF II, 1152–67.
9. See Festugière, *La révélation*, II: xivff.
10. *Ibid.*, 235ff, 538ff., 458ff; Spanneut, *Le stoïcisme*, 377.
11. Spanneut, 377.
12. *Ibid.*
13. See below. *Divine Providence or Fate?*
14. See Colomban Lesquivit and Pierre Grelot, 'Monde', VTB: col. 784–91.
15. See Chapter VIII,1.
16. *The Epistle to Diognetus IV.2*, trans. J. B. Lightfoot, *The Apostolic Fathers* (rpt Grand Rapids, 1978.) 253.
17. X.2,257 see E. H. Blakeney, 'A Note on the Epistle to Diognetus', X.1', *The Journal of Theological Studies 42 (1942)* 193–95; Spanneut, *Le stoïcisme*, 381.
18. *Expositio in Psalmum* 48.7; PG 55:233.
19. *Id., In Ephesios, homilia* 12.2 (PG 69:90) *In Genesim homilia* 6.6 PG 53:60) 7.6, (68).
20. Basil, *In hexaemeron homilia* 6.1; PG 29:117, trans. FC 46 (1963) 83ff.
21. See. Chapter XIII,4.
22. See Margherite Harl, *Origène et la fonction révélatrice du Verbe Incarné* (Paris, 1958) 372.
23. See Chapter XIII,2.
24. See *On the Holy Theophanies* (a text attributed to Hippolytus) I; GCS Hippolytus, I, part 2: p. 257, 2–6.

Chapter Five

25. Basil, *In hexaemeron homilia* 1.11; PG 29:28AB; LNPF series 2, vol. 8: 58ff.
26. See Špidlík, *La sophiologie de S. Basile*, 229.
27. See I. Hausherr (Lemaitre) in DS 2/2: 1818ff.
28. *In hexaemeron homilia* 4.6; PG 29:92B; LNPF[2] vol. 8:75.
29. Basil, *On psalm.* 44.5; PG 29:400; FC 46:285.
30. See Yves Courtonne, *S. Basile et L'Hellénisme* (Paris, 1954) 131ff.
31. See L. Spitzer, 'Classical and Christian Idea of World Harmony', *Traditio* 2 (1944) 408–64, 3 (1945) 307–64; Spanneut, *Le stoïcisme*, 372ff.
32. See Spanneut, 363ff.
33. See Victor Goldschmidt, *Le système stoïcien et l'idée du Temps* (Paris, 1953) 106; see above, Chapter III,2.
34. Irenaeus, *Adversus Haereses* I.4; Harvey I:94.
35. *Stromata* V.133.7; GCS 2:416,17; ANF 2:474.
36. See Jean Daniélou, *L'être et le temps chez Grégoire de Nysse* (Leiden, 1970) 51–74.
37. Spanneut, *Le Stoïcisme*, 390.
38. *Ibid.*, 344ff.
39. *Ibid.*, 87ff.
40. *Adversus haereses* III.24.2; Harvey II: 132–33; ANF 1:459.
41. See above, Chapter II *Equivalent Expressions*, and XIII,3.
42. *La femme et le salut du monde*, 65.
43. *Ibid.*
44. See *La sophiologie de S. Basile*, 6ff.
45. Quoted by G. Florovskij, *Puti russkago bogoslovija* [*The Ways of Russian Theology*] (Paris, 1937) 180.
46. Spanneut, *Le stoïcisme*, 269ff.
47. *Discourses* II.14.11.
48. *De natura deorum* 30.75; see A. J. Festugière, *Hermes* II:395.
49. The Latin *fatum* equally comes from a root that means 'to speak' (*fari, phēmi*). The parallel between *fatum, logos,* and *nomos* in the sense of destiny is therefore significant; see Brice Parain, *Essai sur le logos platonicien* (Paris, 1942) 20–21, n. 5; Pavel Ali Florenskij, *Stolp i utveržděnie istiny* [*The Pillar and Foundation of Truth*] (Moscow, 1914) 284ff. (a reflection on the Slavonic term).
50. *Questiones naturales* II.45.1–3; see W. Grundel, *Beiträge zur Entwicklungsgeschichte der Begriffe Ananke und Heimarmene* (Giessen, 1914).
51. See Jerome Gaïth, *La conception de la liberté chez Grégoire de Nysse* (Paris, 1953) 87ff.
52. See Emile Bréhier, *Chrysippe et l'ancien stoïcisme* (Paris, 1951) 187–97.
53. Now lost, but Maximus the Confessor still knew it. The last treatise of John Chrysostom, *Ad eos qui scandalizati sunt ob adversitates* (PG 52: 479–528: trans. *Sur la Providence de Dieu*, SCh 79 [1961]) takes on a special meaning because it was the result of a lived experience. Theodoret's *Ten Discourses on Providence* (trans. Y. Azéma, *Discours sur la Providence* [Paris, 1954]) are more theoretical and apologetic.
54. See Hans Georg Beck, *Vorsehung und Vorherbestimmung in der theologischen Literatur der Byzantiner*, OCA 114 (Rome, 1937).
55. See Edward Nowak, *Le chrétien devant la souffrance. Etude sur la pensée de Jean Chrysostome*, Théologie historique 19 (Paris, 1972), 97.
56. *In Ps.* 144.2; PG 55:466CD.
57. *Sur la Providence* 2.8.SCh 79:65.

Spiritual Cosmology 147

58. PG 91:1189B.
59. See Beck, Vorsehung, 189.
60. Quaestiones ad Thalassium 60; PG 90:621AB.
61. Ibid., q. 55; 545AB.
62. Ibid., 568B, scholion 28.
63. Quaestiones et dubia 79; PG 90:853D; for a long and subtle analysis of these distinctions, see Ambiguorum liber; PG 91:1133C–1136A.
64. The Letter to the Corinthians 28.4. F. X. Funk, Patres Apostolici vol. I (Tübingen, 1901) 136; see Theophilus of Antioch, Ad Autolycum I.5; SCh 20:66; ANF 2:90.
65. XIII.5, ed. A. Robinson in Texts and Studies I/1 (Cambridge, 1891) 108.
66. The question is asked by Justin, Legatio pro christianis 25; PG 6:949; see Spanneut, Le stoïcisme, 326.
67. Stromata VII.9.3; GCS 3:8, 17ff; trans. F. J. Hart, Miscellanies Book VII, (London, 1902) 17ff; cf. Spanneut, Le stoïcisme, 328.
68. The Resurrection of the Dead I.37; ed. G. N. Bonwetch, Methodius von Olympus (Erlangen, 1891) 329.
69. See Asclēpius 39, edd A. D. Nock–A. J. Festugière, Corpus Hermeticum, vol. 2 (Paris, 1945) 349, 17–18.
70. Oratio 45.6; PG 36:629C, LNPF ser. 2, vol. 7: 424–25.
71. A Plea for the Christians 25; SCh 3:135; ANF 2:142.
72. A Plea, 25; SCh 138; ANF 142–43.
73. Transl. with Introd. and notes, Yvan Azéma (Paris, 1954).
74. See Spanneut, Le stoïcisme, 401ff.
75. Ibid.
76. See Špidlík, La sophiologie de S. Basile, 16ff.
77. In hexaemeron homilia 7.1; PG 29:149A; SCh 26 (1950) 395.
78. See Spanneut, Le stoïcisme, 301ff.
79. See T. Špidlík, 'La libertà come riflesso del mistero trinitario nei Padri Greci', Augustinianum 13 (1973) 515–23.
80. Appendix-Symeonis Metaphrastae; PG 32:1372–1373A.
81. Quod Deus non est auctor malorum 1; PG 31:332A.
82. La sophiologie, 23; see Hans Urs von Balthasar, Kosmische Liturgie. Das Weltbild Maximus' des Bekenners (Einsiedeln, 1961; 1st ed., Freiburg-im-Breisgau, 1941); French translation, Liturgie cosmique, Maxime le Confesseur (Paris, 1947).

2. EVIL AND PROVIDENCE

1. See Špidlík, La sophiologie de S. Basile, 8ff.
2. Basil, Homilia dicta tempore famis et siccitatis; PG 31:304–28.
3. See Basil, Quod Deus non est auctor malorum; PG 31:337CD.
4. Pseudo-Plutarch, Consolatio ad Apollonium 27.
5. See Jozef Scharbert, 'Souffrance', EF 4: 248ff.
6. See Edward Nowak, Le chrétien devant la souffrance. Étude sur la pensée de Jean Chrysostome. Théologie historique 19 (Paris, 1972) 111ff.
7. In Žurnal moskovskoj patriarchii [The Journal of the Moscow Patriarchate] 10 (1910) 50.
8. See Henri-Charles Puech, Le manichéisme, son fondateur, sa doctrine (Paris, 1949).

9. Chrysostom, *In Acta Apostolorum homilia* 2.4; PG 60:31B.
10. See, for example, Chrysostom, *De providentia* 4.2, SCh 79: *Sur la Providence* (1961) 82.
11. *De resurrectione mortuorum* 6; PG 50:428A.
12. *In Epistolam ad Colossenses homilia* 2.6; PG 62:318B; see *Postquam presbyter Gothus* 6; PG 63:510D.
13. Basil, *Quod Deus non est auctor malorum* PG 31:329-53; see Nowak, *Le chrétien*, 39ff.
14. *In Matthaeum* 59.2; PG 58:576C.
15. Basil, *Quod Deus non est auctor malorum*; PG 31:337CD.
16. See *On the Statues* 65.5; PG 49:88A.
17. *De providentia* 12.1; SC 79:182.
18. *Id.*, *Lettres à Olympias* 14.1a; SCh13 (1947) 350.
19. See Anne-Marie Malingrey, Introduction to *Jean Chrysostome, Lettres d'exil*, SCh 103 (1964) 24.
20. See Špidlík, *La sophiologie de S. Basile*, 22ff.
21. See Hal Koch, *Pronoia und Paideusis. Studien über Origenes und sein Verhältnis zum Platonismus* (Berlin-Leipzig, 1932) 122-59.
22. See Nowak, *Le chrétien devant la souffrance*, 140.
23. *The Divine and the Human* (London, 1949) 78.
24. See Angelo Sodano, 'Premio e castigo ultraterreno', in *I beni terreni nella vita dei giusti secondo S. Giovanni Crisostomo* (Brescia, 1955) 20-24.
25. See Spanneut, *Le stoïcisme*, 379.
26. See Georges Soury, *Aperçus de Philosophie religieuse chez Maxime de Tyr, Platonicien éclectique* (Paris, 1942) 24-26, 68-71; Nikolaj Berdiaev, *The Divine and the Human*, p. 69.
27. *In Acta Apostolorum* 27.1; PG 60:205B; see *De Lazaro* 3.8; PG 48:1003BC.
28. John Chrysostom, *De Lazaro* 6.3; PG 48:1031B; cf. *In Acta Apostolorum* 54.3; PG 60:380A; see Nowak, 154.
29. See *La sophiologie de S. Basile*, 67ff.
30. John Chrysostom, *Letter* 4.64 from exile; SCh 103:81.
31. Theodoret of Cyrus, *Discours sur la Providence* (Paris, 1954) 200ff.
32. *In Epistolam ad Hebraeos* 28.1; PG 63:191B-192.
33. 1.6; PG 49:23C; see Nowak, 139ff.
34. See Edouard Dhorme, *Choix de textes religieux assyro-babyloniens*, Études bibliques (Paris, 1907) 372-79; H. Jaeger, 'Examinatio', DS 4/2:1851.
35. 360e-362a.
36. *The Apology* 38a; see Chapter IX, The Necessity of Warfare.
37. See Nowak, *Le chrétien devant la souffrance*, 185ff.
38. John Chrysostom, *Ep. 149: Cyriaco, Demetrio*; PG 52:700A.
39. Nowak, 173ff.
40. See above, Chapter III, 4: *The Outstanding Sign of the Spirit*.
41. John Chrysostom, *Sur la Providence* 15, SC 79 (1961), 214.
42. *Id., In Ep. ad Philip.* 11. 2; PG 62: 266CD.
43. See above, Chapter III, *The Outstanding Sign of the Spirit*.
44. See René Hedde, 'Martyre', DThC 10, 1 (1928) 221ff.
45. See Ivan Kologrivof, *Essai sur la sainteté en Russie* (Bruges, 1953) 27-34; T. Špidlík, 'Les 'Strastoterpsi' dans la spiritualité slave ou la valeur chrétienne de la souffrance', RAM 43 (1967) 453-61; *id., I grandi mistici russi* (Rome, 1977) 13ff.
46. Nikolaj Berdiaev, *The Divine and the Human*, trans. R. M. French (London, 1949) 68.

47. *Lettres à Olympias* 10.8a (SCh 13:268), 10.10a (278).
48. *In Epistolam ad Hebreos* 30.1; PG 63:209C; Nowak, *Le chrétien devant la souffrance*, 206ff.
49. A. M. Malingrey, *Lettre d'exil*, SCh 103 67, n. 3.
50. *Homily 7 on Thessalonians* 1; PG 62:435A; LNPF 13; 352; See Marcus Aurelius, *Meditations* VIII.40
51. It has been said that Eastern piety knows no devotion to the suffering Christ (see above, Chapter II, *Devotion to the Humanity of Christ.*). And yet, Berdiaev writes, 'Most of all perhaps suffering is vanquished by contemplation of the Cross' (*The Divine and the Human*, 81).
52. *The Divine and the Human*, 74–75; on the icon of St Paraskeva a red mantle covers a black tunic. This legendary saint personifies suffering, which is incomprehensible in itself but becomes an apotheosis of the redeeming and glorious cross once it is covered with the grace of God. [See Y. Smirnova and S. Yamshchikov, *Old Russian Painting:Latest Discoveries*, (Leningrad, 1974) pl. 37.]
53. See Kologrivof, *Essai sur la sainteté en Russie* (Bruges, 1953) 33ff.
54. *Ibid.*
55. *Ibid.*, p. 16.
56. *Liber Quod qui seipsum non laedit, nemo laedere possit*; PG 52:459–480.
57. *Ibid.*
58. *Ibid.*, 4; col. 464.

3. THE COSMIC VOCATION OF MAN

1. Vladimir Soloviev, *The Justification of the Good*, III.3.3 (London, 1918), 186ff.
2. See Špidlík, *Grégoire de Nazianze*, 104ff.
3. *Ibid.*, 102.
4. *Ibid.*, 105.
5. For example, in Maximus the Confessor, see Lars Thunberg, *Microcosm and Mediator. The Theological Anthropology of Maximus the Confessor* (Lund, 1965).
6. See Spanneut, *Le stoïcisme des pères de l'église*, 414.
7. See Jean Daniélou, *Philon d'Alexandrie* (Paris, 1958) 172ff.
8. See Walter Voelker, *Gregor von Nyssa als Mystiker* (Wiesbaden, 1955) 51ff.
9. See *Grégoire de Nazianze*, 107.
10. *Ad populum Antiochenum* 11.4; PG 49:125.
11. *In Epistolam I ad Timotheum homilia* 4.2; PG 62:523.
12. *Ad populum Antiochenum* 19.2; PG 49:189.
13. See Lesquivit and Grelot, 'Monde', VTB: col. 784–792.
14. John Chrysostom, *In Genesim homilia* 27.4; PG te:244.
15. *In Epistolam ad Romanos homilia* 14.5; PG 60:530.
16. See Nikolaj O. Losski, *Histoire de la philosophie russe* (Paris, 1954) 193.
17. See Chapter III, *Eternal Life*, VIII, *Various Aspects of Flight, Virginity*, and Conclusion.
18. *De pauperibus amandis*, oratio 2; PG 46:472C.
19. See M. Eliade, *Cosmos and History: The Myth of the Eternal Return* (New York, 1959).
20. See T. Špidlík, 'L'eternità e il tempo, la *zoē* e il *bios*, problema dei Padri Cappodoci', *Augustinianum* 16 (1976) 107–16.

21. See XIII, *Praxis Leads to Theoria.*
22. Špidlík, *Grégoire de Nazianze,* p. 128.
23. Gregory of Nyssa, *In Canticum Canticorum Homilia* 6; PG 44:885D.
24. *Ibid.,* ff.
25. See Olivier Clément, *Transfigurer le temps* (Neuchâtel-Paris, 1959).
26. *Ibid.,* 99.
27. See J. Kirchmeyer, in DS 6:812.
28. *The Didache* 19.1; *The Letter of Barnabas* 20; see J. H. Nicolas, 'Enfer', DS 4 1:729–49.
29. See Irenée Hausherr, *Penthos. The Doctrine of Compunction in the Christian East,* CS 53:139.
30. On how this purification and this deification may be explained, see the discussions on Purgatory.
31. *On Philippians, homily* 14; PG 62:282; LNPF 13:246.
32. See Henri Crouzel, 'Apokatastasis', *Sacramentum mundi,* I (Freiburg-im-Breisgau, 1967) col. 231–34.
33. Gregory of Nyssa, *On virginity* 12.4.15; SCh 119:418; trans. V. Callahan, FC 58:46.
34. *Id., De Anima et resurrectione;* PG 46:113C. [trans. by H. A. Wilson, *On the Soul and the Resurrection,* LNPF ser. 2, 430–68]
35. See I. Onings, 'Adam', DS 1:187–95.
36. *Oratio adversos Graecos* 15; PG 6:837A; see Jean Daniélou, *Message évangélique et culture hellénistique aux IIe et IIIe siècles,* Bibliothèque de théologie II (Tournai: Desclée de Brouwer, 1961), 359.
37. See Daniélou, 355.
38. *The Symposium. A Treatise on Chastity* 1.4 (23), trans. Herbert Musurillo in ACW 27:46.
39. *Ibid.*; it seems that these themes are of Jewish origin, see Robert M. Grant, 'Theophilus of Antioch to Autolycus', *The Harvard Theological Review* 40 (1947) 238–41.
40. *Adversus haereses* IV.38.1: SCh 100:942; ANF 1: 521ff; see J. Daniélou, *Message évangélique,* 369ff.

6

SPIRITUAL SOCIOLOGY

1. THE UNIVERSALITY OF CHRISTIAN LOVE

Man — a Social Being

THE UNIVERSE AND HUMAN SOCIETY were created as a totality, like a magnificent 'liturgy' celebrated together by all beings.[1] Being faithful to one's specific vocation does not authorize one to lose sight of this overall perspective. The men of the Old Testament understood their individual commitment inside the living community of the family and the clan, and, above all, of the chosen people; they were linked to others by their very being, in sin and in salvation. This human solidarity, however, is 'dialogical' in nature: his unique call from God constitutes the law of each person's being and personal development. The individual is singled out 'by name' in a unique, irrevocable utterance (Gn 35:10, Ex 31:2, Is 45:4).[2]

The ancient world also had a clear concept of mankind's 'social nature', but, at the same time, it loved freedom and independence, the necessary conditions for the development of one's own personality.[3]

The Fathers never denied these two natural requirements. They warned, however, that it was difficult to reconcile them 'in the company of people who hold the Lord's commandments in light regard', and that christians therefore should associate themselves with the lives of those 'who are of the same mind'.[4] If this unity in the same spirit seems to foster a certain exclusiveness, it transcends it on principle; for the union between christians gives rise to a love which is by nature universal, and is the surest road to the perfection of all humanity in union with God.

Love of God and Love of Neighbor

Our duty to love God and our neighbor has been affirmed too clearly ever to have been denied. 'Almighty God', wrote Dadišo Quatraya, 'has taught the people of Israel about the love of God and man separately, but not about their unity in the Spirit; the Son of God himself has revealed and make known to us, the christian people, how they are connected, are one, and resemble one another.'[5]

This connection may be illustrated by several considerations. We may apply here the doctrine of the image of God in man — Evagrius has said that 'Charity has the role of showing itself to every image of God as being as nearly like its prototype as possible, no matter how the demons ply their arts to defile them,'[6] and of adoptive sonship — one does not love the Father without likewise loving the Son beloved by the Father.[7] The *Sayings* report that 'If someone came to find [Abba Apollo] about doing a piece of work, he would set out joyfully, saying, "I am going to work with Christ today for the salvation of my soul, for that is the reward he gives."'[8] This union between the two loves may, nonetheless, be viewed differently, depending on one's perspective: charity towards our neighbor may be seen as the condition of our love for God or, by contrast, as its result. To Theodoret of Cyrus, the relationship between our love of God and love of neighbor is like the relationship between contemplation and action:[9] the first therefore precedes the other. And thus Basil said, 'He who loves his neighbor, fulfills the commandment to love God'.[10] On the other hand, the love of God gives form to our love of neighbor: it imparts vitality and authenticity to it. According to John Chrysostom, the love of God is like 'the soul' in respect to 'the body'.[11] To use a comparison made by Dorotheus, whoever comes near God moves toward the center of the circle, and the saints therefore come nearer to one another.[12]

This was not merely a theoretical question. It also concerns the practical application of each person's specific vocation, a problem discussed in the cenobitic tradition and by the solitaries.[13] Was it really necessary to live in society? The question of principle is one thing; the concrete applications quite another.

The General Principle: Love's Universality, Perpetuity, and Equality

As a participation in the love of God, charity ought to exclude no one. This was often repeated by Maximus the Confessor: 'Be eager to love everyone as much as you can. If you are unable to do this, at least hate no one.'[14] He also frequently reverted to the idea that when it comes to charity, variations in time are worth no more than variations of space. The unsteadiness of our feelings toward our neighbor denotes that passions are present; it indicates that our love is not yet spiritual: 'Those who are joined in love according to the principles of the world need each other's physical presence to keep this love; forgetfulness gradually consumes any love that has only a physical basis.'[15]

If *philautia* (self-love) were to disappear, all inequality would likewise vanish with it: 'If you hate some and some you neither love nor hate, while others you love, but only moderately, and others again you greatly love, learn from this inequality that you are far from perfect charity, which supposes that you love everyone equally.'[16]

The Difficulty of Application; The Order of Charity

Can this doctrine of equality of love be made real? Negatively, Evagrius thought: 'It is not possible to love all the brothers to the same degree. But it is possible to associate with all in a manner that is above passion, that is to say, free of resentment and hatred.'[17]

Maximus the Confessor taught that equal love would manifest itself in different ways depending only on the needs of the neighbor. If the needs are the same, any difference in the forms of charity ends.[18] By contrast, according to Origen, charity should take into account the neighbor's faith, his holiness, his relationship with God, and whether he possesses the quality of 'son' or only of 'servant'.[19] Maximus sought to soften this difference based on perfection: the motives of love may vary, but not its intensity;

following God's example, the man without passion 'loves all men alike — the virtuous because of his nature and good intention, the bad because of his nature and that fellow feeling which causes him to show mercy upon him as upon a fool who wanders in darkness'.[20]

What is to be said, meanwhile, about special affections based on nature? Maximus did not defend them, although he called them indifferent.[21] But in fact, these exhortations about the equality of love should be kept in mind as a shining ideal to correct the imperfections that so easily arise from natural, indestructible divisions.

There is, however, still another order of charity, the one concerned precisely with the needs of our neighbor. If the first commandment is to love God, then love of neighbor will consist first of all in bringing him also to the love of God. Spiritual charity normally precedes physical charity.

The Plurality of Nations

The plurality of languages gave rise to national divisions, and love of country easily changes into a love that is exclusive, hostile, and self-serving. Origen drew attention to two aspects of this deformation, one naïve, the other hateful. The Egyptians, 'because they were a selfish peole who honored those who were in any degree related to them far more than strangers of better lives',[22] could not bring themselves to recognize Moses' very evident superior qualities. They were moved by a systematic antipathy. Celsus, on the other hand, sinned through uncontrolled sympathy, being bewitched 'in favor of the Egyptians'.[23]

Christian preachers have endeavored to show that the love of God is essentially a love that unifies. The diversity of languages resulted from sin. This is why the return of the Spirit to earth is marked by an understanding of tongues.[24] In harmony with this Spirit all the languages on earth unite to sing an unequaled triumphal hymn to God.[25] From the outset, the Eastern liturgy has attested, in the language of the people, to the manifold wisdom of God (cf. Eph 3:10).

Christian Cosmopolitanism

The theme of the people of God, in whom all aspects of the life of Israel are synthesized, was as central to the Old Testament as that of the Church, the new people of God, would be to the New Testament. Nonetheless, a distinction was made between the people of God (*laos*, more rarely *dēmos*, in the Septuagint), and foreign nations (*ethnē*).[26] This specialized use of words is found still more clearly in the New Testament where a new term, the Church, took precedence over the others. The people of the Old Covenant, and then all nations, were invited to enter into it. This Church where 'there are no more distinctions between Jew and Greek' (Ga 3:28) constituted a *tertium genus* (third race), as the Christians of the early centuries said.[27]

In Scripture, the peoples are not equal in origin but are found to be equal in the Church. The cosmopolitanism of the ancient philosophers was somewhat different. The Stoics deserve real praise for having proclaimed the community of mankind on the basis of two ideas that they linked together: natural law, and the city of the world (*cosmopolis*).[28]

Stoic ideas proved very useful in christian thought.[29] The philosophic concept of a *communio naturae* crops up several times in Tertullian and others.[30] Clement of Alexandria was more theological. For him the unity of the peoples is based on the same divine vocation, on 'one symphony following one choir-master and teacher, the Word'.[31] Therefore not all, 'but those who put aside their carnal desires, are equal before God'.[32] Consequently, the christian brotherhood did not automatically coincide with biological solidarity or with the 'cosmopolitan' conscience.

The cosmopolitanism of the Stoics was positive. For Cicero, the world was 'like a city or state of which both men and gods are members'.[33] According to the *Apostolic Constitutions*,[34] the state of the world at the moment of creation was such that man was indeed the cosmopolite. But even now, Tertullian believed, we are 'fellow possessors of the world, though not of error'.[35]

Despite this, the 'negative cosmopolitanism' or the 'acosmism' of the early Christians is mentioned more frequently.[36] 'They dwell in their own countries', *The Epistle to Diognetus* states, 'but only as sojourners; ... Every foreign country is a fatherland to them, and every fatherland is foreign.'[37] It is added, however, that 'they bear their share of all their obligations as citizens'.[38] With the African Fathers, the concept of the human community was put to a special purpose: it was used to vindicate the suffering of christians. General adversities they shared with others. 'Our corporal condition must be common', wrote Cyprian. 'Meanwhile, we, good and evil, are contained within our house.'[39]

Russian Messianism

V. Soloviev has stated that 'The unity of tongues inspired by the Spirit of God permits communication and understanding between many, distinct languages.'[40] This does not mean 'a single nationality',[41] because, 'The multiplicity of languages is in itself something as positive and normal as the multiplicity of grammatical elements and forms in each of these languages'.[42]

Within this harmonious plurality of nations, every people has received its unique vocation from God, a special calling which, at the same time, serves the Church Universal.[43]

'Russian Messianism' is the conviction that divine providence has given the Russian people the very special mission to preserve, or proclaim, true Christianity to the world. A. Kartašev has stated that 'The Russian, conscious of having been sanctified for a holy service, has ascribed to himself and to his people, to his country, his government, and his church, the general name Holy Russia'.[44]

This concept is of rather remote origin. After the fall of Constantinople, Russia emerged as 'the third Rome', the center of orthodoxy.[45] Dostoevsky's messianic intuitions were more psychological.[46] Finally, on the basis of historical considerations, Soloviev arrived at the conclusion that his country had not yet had its say in universal history, and that one should await the plans of providence to reveal Russia's vocation on behalf of the universal Church.[47]

2. UNITY IN THE BODY OF CHRIST

The Church

Scripture refers to the Church as a mystery, at one time kept secret in God but unveiled and partly realized today (Eph 1:9 ff., Rm 16:25 ff.), the mystery of a people that is still sinful, yet possessing the earnest-money of salvation because it is the extension of the Body of Christ.

The ecclesiology of the Fathers was expressed largely through an interpretation of the terms in which Scripture spoke of the Church. Added to this was an entire typology worked out by means of the inexhaustible resources of symbolism.[1] The church of the Fathers, like that of the liturgy, encompasses a spiritual anthropology which is that of the image of God, of a deified human *plērōma* (fulness).[2] The Fathers viewed the community of baptized and anointed christians as all together consecrated, as performing the liturgical function all together and as a community; as together exercising spiritual motherhood through faith, love, prayer, and the testimony of faith.[3]

In order to understand what the faithful in the Eastern churches meant by a sense of the Church and how they lived by it, one might ask, for example, the Syrians and the Russians. Syrian spirituality is characterized by its enthusiasm for the 'Bride of Christ', the mother who gives life to the faithful, and by its very strong awareness of the need for church unity.[4] For the Russians,[5] the attitude which every christian is obliged to have toward the Church may be summed up in one word, which is hard to translate, *tserkovnost'*, a sense of Church, the desire and the will to live with and in her.[6] The celebrated axiom by Chomiakov expresses this attitude well: Everyone goes to hell on his own account, but no one can go to heaven except in the company of all the others.[7] 'In the Church, man finds nothing alien to him. There he finds himself again, no longer in the weakness of his spiritual isolation, but in the strength of an intimate spiritual union with his brothers and his Saviour.'[8]

Chapter Six

The Heavenly Church

The Church is the mystery of the whole Christ. Union in Christ makes the solidarity between all members of the Church Triumphant yet firmer. The blessedness of heaven keeps a communal, 'ecclesial' character. Far from being a stumbling block, the cooperation of the saints in the work of deifying the world is the very mortar between the 'living stones' of the Church.

Catholic theologians in the West have greatly insisted on the fact that the universal redemptive mediation of Christ is in no way impaired by the auxiliary intercession of the saints.[9] The idea which suggested itself to Eastern Christians was not so much a saint's intercession with Christ, *which may be helpful*, as the unity of all the saints in Christ, an 'ecclesial' union, the inseparability of God and his saints. Such a thought came very naturally to the Armenian Chosrov (Chosroès) when he spoke of the diptychs with the commemoration of the saints in his *Explanation of the Mass*: 'Because we are one in Christ the glorification of our brothers becomes our glory'.[10]

The Eastern liturgies invoke Christ '*with* the all pure and glorious Virgin Mary the Mother of Christ, *with* the angels, and *with* all the saints' (conclusion of prayers).[11] No matter which patron is invoked, there is always the awareness that the saints are 'one in Christ',[12] and that in the Church the individual prayer is always inserted into the common intercession of the angels, the apostles, the martyrs, the patriarchs, and especially the Mother of Christ,[13] and that 'this intercession by prayer is a participation in the destiny of the world'.[14]

Devotion to the Mother of God

Devotion to the Mother of God has always been held in high esteem among Eastern Christians: in fact, it constitutes one of the characteristics of their spirituality.[15] To explain this fact, we cannot simply make a superficial reference to the more 'sentimental' mentality of the East. The reason lies deeper, and is explained by the fact that devotion to the Theotokos agrees with the essential characteristics of Eastern spirituality.[16]

In the 'anthropological' aspect[17] of this spirituality, Mary appears as the *prepodobneïchaïa*, of all human beings the one who most resembles the Image of God, the incarnate Logos, and therefore the one in whom we may contemplate God as he has entered human life, and find a model to imitate.

In the 'eschatological' aspect,[18] Mary is the *eschaton*,[19] after Christ, the last and fullest deification of the human being. Because of this divinization, the Eastern church ascribes to Mary *theoprepēs doxa* (the glory appropriate to God), for she is 'the boundary between the created and the uncreated'.[20] In Eastern 'ecclesiological' spirituality,[21] the glorification of Mary can only be justified by Tradition and the feelings of the people of God.[22]

The East is 'contemplative'. As *prepodobneïchaïa*, 'the most resembling' Mary is presented to the people as an icon, an example to look to and to contemplate. Like John the Baptist she is, moreover, the first to be raised to the height of *theōria*: she has 'seen God',[23] the Logos, in his humble corporal appearance.[24] Through contemplation, the Logos born of her body rests forever in her heart, as is illustrated by the *Znamenye* icon, the praying Virgin with the divine Word on her heart. The prayer of Mary therefore shares in the power of God; she is a help and a sovereign power in the salvation of christians.

The Monastic Brotherhoods

The term 'brother', like 'brotherhood', was used in pre-christian Greek and Latin with multiple meanings which partially approached christian thought.[25] Whereas Stoicism was concerned with removing all barriers while affirming the brotherhood of man, the mystery religions, by contrast, laid stress on the individual and on the specific community where he found a new spiritual family.[26]

To call one's coreligionists 'brother' is common in the Old Testament (Ex 2:11, Lv 10:4, etc.). Christ designated his disciples by the name brothers (Lk 22:32, Mt 28:10), and he formally identified himself with 'the least of all his brothers' (Mt 25:31–46). Rm 8:11–17:19 brings out the common adoptive sonship of Christians in relation to God the Father, whose Spirit lets us cry out 'Abba'.

In the patristic period, 'brother' was used first as the natural term to designate Christians,[27] and 'brotherhood' to indicate the Church.[28] A little later, 'brother' tended to disappear as the name which christians gave one another and it was transferred to communities of monks.[29] After the third century, the concept of brotherhood narrowed even more. 'Brother' was the name clerics gave one another. A hierarchical and staggered system of spiritual parenthood was established: 'father', 'spiritual sons', 'brothers'.[30]

Above all, however, the 'brotherhoods' were the cenobitic communities which reproduced as closely as possible the life of the first community in Jerusalem, where everything was held in common, where distribution was made to all according to need, and where the gifts of the Holy Spirit given to individuals were used for the common good. On reading Basil's *Ascetica*, one is struck by his intentional repetition of three verses from the Acts of the Apostles (2:44, 4:32, 4:35).[31] At an age when the charity of the first centuries had cooled, the Bishop of Caesarea dreamed of reviving and perpetuating this lofty ideal of brotherly life in his monasteries.[32]

Praises of the Common Life

In christian spirituality, the classic text that inculcates the need of living in communion with others is still the seventh of Basil's *Long Rules*.[33] Let us briefly recall the supporting arguments. In the common life all assist each other in material and spiritual needs. Charity is practised on every occasion, help and guidance can be found with one's spiritual director. There Christians form one body of which Christ is the head. A charism privately bestowed becomes a common possession. The brotherhood observes all the commandments, which is not true at all in the case of some one living alone. Life in common offers better protection against the snares of the devil, for the other brothers are on guard. There will be the joy of dwelling in one habitation with brothers animated by the same ideal.[34] Basil's arguments applied to the monastic life. Yet we know that in Basil's view the life of his brotherhoods was a reproduction of the perfect ideal of the christian life.[35]

The question then arose: what was left of the practice of charity among the solitary monks? Under no circumstances were they to cherish solitude for its own sake. They chose this type of life because they saw in solitude, if not for everyone at least for themselves, an excellent way of arriving at union with God and hence with the children of God. 'The monk', Evagrius Ponticus wrote, 'is one who is separated from all and united to all.'[36] This is the principle expressed by Origen: 'Through contemplation, the saints are united with God and with one another.'[37]

The hesychasts considered this basic problem solved. They were neither bishops nor priests nor clerics, and they had not been charged with apostolic ministry. Their vocation was devoted exclusively to the pursuit of union with God through prayer. The question for them was merely to what degree external solitude was needed for such a goal: a psychological question. They did not consider other people evil; on the contrary, they had their own weakness, which prevented them from being at one and the same time with God and with man.[38]

Friendship

Universal charity, *agapē*, as it is presented in the teaching of Christ, differs from purely human friendship, *philia*, which is more or less exclusive. In the monastic Rules every particular friendship was banned as being contrary to the perfection of the common life.[39] It remains true, however, that even the monks did not always form a closed and uniform society. Here is what Cassian has said about it in his *Conferences*:

> True love set in order is that which, while it hates no one, yet loves some still more by virtue of the excellence of their virtues and merits . . . and loves these with a special affection; and which from this number makes a second choice through which are singled out some who are preferred to others in affection.[40]

The Russian Nil Sorsky (Nilus of Sora) even believed that the true monastic life is possible only with a small circle of friends.[41]

In antiquity, the great theoretician of friendship was Aristotle.[42] His distinction between the three objects of friendship — the useful, the pleasant, and the good — passed into patristic homilies, especially where the fathers commented on the primary example of friendship in the Old Testament, that between David and Jonathan (1 S 18–20, 2 S 1).[43] Based upon virtue, true friendship is found only among perfect Christians. That is why friendships with a heretic,[44] a beardless youth,[45] and women[46] were banned.

The Family

The ideal of the family is presented in innumerable patristic texts.[47] John Chrysostom placed the vocation of the spouses in the general context of the divine pedagogy whose aim is to educate the people to universal charity.[48] Sex differences and marriage are willed by God so that the ultimate foundation of mankind's unity would be not 'nature' (as with the Stoics) but love.[49] May the husband often express his love for his wife and say: 'I value your love above all things.... Though it should be my lot to lose all, to suffer any pain whatsoever, all will be tolerable so long as your feelings towards me are true.'[50]

Because Marriage is a school of love, its dignity was for John Chrysostom a necessary postulate for the demonstration of his thesis on virginity.[51] As an expression of perfect charity, virginity is rooted in the family environment.[52] To a greater extent than the Western Fathers, Chrysostom was sensitive to the role of the woman in the family setting.

The patriarchal society of ancient Russia stressed the importance of christian mothers even more.[53] The biography of Blessed Juliana of Lazarevskoe, written by her son in 1614,[54] is a remarkable document on the subject because of its simplicity and, at the same time, its lavish description of the christian family spirit of the day; it conforms as closely as possible to the regulations of the *Domostroj* (Instructions for Christian Families, attributed to Sylvester, the priest).[55]

On the other hand, the monks' break with their relatives was complete.[56]

The State Society

Around the years 177–80, Celsus upbraided Christians for not taking part in public affairs. Origen took over this objection word for word to show that Christians performed their duties better

Spiritual Sociology

than anyone else because their patriotism was not conditioned by personal ambition.[57] At the time the State was pagan, and occasionally hostile to the Church.

Later, the eschatological perspective that dominated Eastern thought made it difficult to divide human society into two 'perfect societies', the Church and the State. Present-day Orthodox theologians consider an equilibrium between the secular and the religious power as the ideal. As Evdokimov has it: 'Orthodoxy has put one of the two swords in the hand of the patriarch and the other in that of the emperor, their unity of aim creating the union of both powers. This is the famous "Byzantine symphony" of which Justinian spoke in his sixth *Novella*.'[58]

This union of the two powers made the differences between God's commandments and civil laws disappear very easily. In answering this difficulty, Joseph of Volokolamsk noted that the commandments of God and the canons of the councils inspired by the Holy Spirit have in fact since ancient times been mixed with civil legislation, and that this has been the work of the Church Fathers. He cited as examples the famous *Nomocanon* and Nikon of the Black Mountain.[59]

In such an ideal society the role of the sovereign was greatly exalted: 'The holy canons order us to reverence the emperor and not to quarrel with him. Neither the archpriests of old nor the four patriarchs nor the Roman pontiff, when he was in general council, would have dared act differently.'[60]

The important question, meanwhile, remained: would the authority of the State be competent in strictly Church affairs? Faced with such problems, which are still real, we may say that the East attempted not so much to solve the question of competence as, more properly, to determine whether a given order was in agreement with the commandments of God. After hailing the ruler as 'the lord of lords, to whom God has given all power', Joseph of Volokolamsk hastened to point out how the saints had opposed unjust orders, and how they did not hesitate to struggle to the death. This is how every good Christian must act.[61]

We can now understand why the *Skēdē Basilikē*, a hortatory little work addressed in the sixth century 'to our very divine and very pious emperor Justinian by Agapet, the humble deacon' became an unheard-of success.[62] Its author made the emperor

God's equal on one hand and, on the other, totally limited by God's commandments, and by the laws and traditions of the Fathers. Strictly speaking, it was therefore not a matter of 'attributing divine powers to the monarch,' but rather one of submissiveness to divine providence which has chosen certain peoples and their legitimate leaders to accomplish its historic plans in the service of the universal Church.

3. MAN'S CONCRETE OBLIGATIONS IN SOCIETY

Negative Principle and Positive Principle

Order demands that one begin by refraining from evil: 'Do to no one what you would not want done to yourself' (Tb 4:16). Indeed, no one wants to be injured by another. Therefore we should harm no one. When the damage done is spiritual, it is called a scandal, in the terminology of Scripture. A man is a stumbling block (*skandalon*) to another when he causes him to fall and drives him away from fidelity to God (Cf. Mt 18:6).[63]

The inner disposition which is diametrically opposed to charity is called hatred. The verb 'to hate' (*misein*) is found especially in the First Letter of John. It occasionally takes on an absolute sense: to will evil, to want to kill (Cf. 1 Jn 3:15). Early christian writers, in referring to hatred, adopted the same existential perspective as Scripture.[64] Hate is manifested through disdain (*exoudenōsis*): one abhors a neighbor like an abomination, one detests him utterly.[65] The long lists of injustices commited in society are rooted in this disdain. Yet, while speaking to monks, Dorotheus warned especially against two sins committed against a neighbor: to condemn (*katakrinai*) and to speak evil (*katalēsai*).[66]

The positive principle is taken from St Matthew (7:12): 'So always treat others as you would like them to treat you.'[67] Now, the primary good to desire for oneself is salvation. To love a neighbor therefore means first of all to seek his salvation.[68] Since salvation is a complex term covering all the gifts of divine philanthropy, man, by imitating the mercy of God in every endeavor, 'possesses nothing so much like God as generosity and beneficence'.[69]

The Example of the Christian Life

The obligation of setting a good example rests on all Christians: 'In the same way your light must shine in the sight of men, so that, seeing your good works, they may give the praise to your Father in heaven' (Mt 5:16). If all nature is a revelation of God,[70] the glory of God shines all the more brightly in the image of the perfect christians, images of Christ-the-Image.

Setting a good example is incumbent on everyone, but especially on those who have charge of a christian community.[71] The most effective preaching, moreover, is the example of the saints. This is one of the reasons explaining their cult; in the course of the liturgical year their procession around the exemplary person of Christ unfolds. It is therefore not surprising that the christian tradition has always considered meditation on or reading of saints' lives as a stimulant to the spiritual life.[72]

Brotherly Correction — An Act of Charity

The first form of brotherly love, John Chrysostom said, is 'to be concerned with one's brothers and to pay attention to their salvation'.[73] And 'because God has arranged it in this manner, that men be corrected by men',[74] the monks viewed the correction of those who had sinned as an act of charity.[75] Joseph of Volokolamsk defended this practice against all objections, for it seemed necessary to him in the common life in order to praise God with one heart and one voice.[76] He said: 'We kick the horse that deviates from the straight road; and to save our life does the physician not make us suffer?'[77]

When the common good, or the rule of the Fathers, is at stake, one should also admonish a superior, although Theodore the Studite thought this should be done 'by those who surpass the others in knowledge and prudence'.[78] Admonishing presupposes judging. Everyone agreed that only 'he that is spiritual judges all things' (1 Co 2.15).[79] It therefore remains to be decided who is 'spiritual' in a given case. Is it the popular prophets, these 'fools for Christ' who considered it their specific vocation to speak the truth before the powerful of the earth?[80] Following Basil, Joseph of Volokolamsk believed that this task should fall on those who know Scripture, the written commandments of God, better than the rest.[81]

At any rate, let the one who is admonished 'be convinced of the charity and the experience of the one who censures'.[82] 'If one is disturbed at being blamed for a passion, this is a sign that he obeyed the passion willingly. By contrast, to accept the censure or the correction without anger proves that one was overcome, or served this passion unknowingly.'[83]

The Service of the Word

Sergei Bulgakov has said that all the harmonies of creation find their resonance in man, the center of the universe.[84] The world teaches words to man. The gift of speech is one of the great prerogatives of our nature. It is true that the ascetics, depending on their point of view, centered their attention mainly on the abuses of language. Against them there is only one remedy, to practise silence. But the reason for this sacrifice is that we 'may learn to speak'.[85]

The lips are also in God's service, and this is in principle a universal mission. 'When you live in silence through asceticism' — we read in the *Life of Saint Cyril Phileotes*[86] — 'then silence is good. If this is not the case and you keep silent because you are afraid of trouble, then silence is harmful.'

Gregory Nazianzen believed he had received a personal mission to serve God through his words, to be 'the mouthpiece of Christ'.[87] In his opinion the gift of speech was 'the most valuable gift from heaven', an image of the Logos of God, for 'he who has many names rejoices above all when he is called the Word'.[88]

Meanwhile, not everyone will exercise this right in the same manner. The Church is a body, which presupposes a variety of functions: 'one instructs, the other learns'.[89] The right and the duty to discourse about divine truth are linked to the priestly function.[90] Monks, who were not priests, were in no hurry to converse with others. Before replying to a question, Pambo let his visitors, come from afar, wait for four days; finally he wrote his answer on the sand.[91]

The teaching preogative can also fall on someone who does

not belong to the priestly group. Origen's *didaskalos* (teacher) is the one who is perfect.[92] Progress in contemplation authorizes, even obliges, one to speak about God.[93] According to Barsanuphius,[94] the silence of a spiritual master who becomes disinterested in his disciples is a silence inspired by the devils (*siōpē para tou diabolou*).

A weak instrument in itself, the human word partakes of the power of God when it is united to the Word and 'guided by the Holy Spirit'.[95] The divine power then gives his servants a voice 'like a sharp sword'.[96] In the Spirit, Christians can be of one mind on the ineffable mysteries, can grasp the single meaning behind the multiplicity of words and concepts, and communicate in truth — in a spiritual *koinonia*.[97]

Almsgiving

Almost all the principal Church Fathers wrote on almsgiving, either directly and expressly or indirectly in connection with other themes.[98] They affirmed that the giving of alms was a matter of strict justice to the poor. According to Basil, the superfluity of the rich was the possession of the poor, and anyone who kept this overabundance was a thief: 'Are you then not covetous and avaricious when you keep for yourself what you have received to give to several?'[99]

According to Nikon of the Black Mountain, 'even monks must give alms when they themselves receive work from others; and while giving alms, one should not distinguish between believer and unbeliever, but help everyone'.[100] Joseph of Volokolamsk enumerated the purposes for which the goods of the monastery were used. They were destined first of all to provide for the monastery itself: to buy icons, sacred vessels, books, sustenance for the monks, and then to distribute alms to the poor. Each day, six to seven hundred poor received bread at Volokolamsk. 'As much as God has sent us, so much has been distributed'. Joseph concluded.[101]

John Chrysostom never ceased to praise the spiritual benefits secured by *elemosynē* (charitable giving) which is, among men, an image of the compassion of God.[102]

Chapter Six

The Obligation to Work

For the Christian, there is no clearer invitation to work than the saying of St Paul: 'If anyone will not work, let him not eat' (2 Th 3:10).[103] It is known that the Messalians[104] excluded manual labor from the activity of the perfect, who were fully given over to 'spiritual work', prayer. After they arrived in Byzantium they were accused of 'teaching laziness with all its results, under the pretense of unceasing prayer'.[105]

Such a view of the spiritual life was opposed by John Chrysostom, among others.[106] Work is a law of nature. Chrysostom did not hesitate to draw a parallel between the activity of God and the works of man. In the hexahemeron, the six-days' work, God showed himself an artisan (*technitēs*), and a workman (*dēmiourgos*).[107] Through his work, man finds himself in a certain relationship with God. He cooperates with creation, with the action of divine providence in this world.[108] Of course, man must work in conformity with the will of God, if not, his hard labor changes into *mataioponia* (fruitless toil) and becomes a 'stumbling block'.[109] Moreover, if the greatness of man consists in thought, he must understand the divine idea included in the command and grasp it consciously (in this he differs from unreasoning creatures).[110] This is the primary idea of Basilian asceticism: the wisdom of God is the continued presence of God's thought in the world; human wisdom is the continued presence of God's thought in the work of man, the unceasing remembrance of God.[111]

The aim of work is spiritual, for this is the goal of providence and of human life. John Chrysostom enumerated the various aspects of this universal vocation to labor: it creates a bond between people,[112] it is the clearest manifestation of charity, helping the poor.[113] As a natural activity unrelated to sin, work was an *ergasia* (occupation); it has now become *ponos*, toil, weariness.[114] But even this punishment attached to work is a remedy, *pharmakon*,[115] that appeases the passions.[116]

The ideal model would be the work of monks. It is performed in an atmosphere conducive to prayer. Accompanied by explicit prayers, it becomes in itself a prayer, because its motivation is charity.[117]

Spiritual Sociology 169

The Practice of Charity in the Monasteries

In a series of *Short Rules*, Basil enumerated the dispositions of soul needed to practice brotherly love in an effective and sincere manner.[118] As a man of action, he was practical in his teaching. Neighborly love becomes externalized, on the one hand, through good example and prayer and, on the other, through manual labor, teaching, or hospitable work. All the details of the *Rules* concerning the making and selling of articles made in the monastery,[119] service to the sick and travelers at the hospice,[120] the care of orphans, the instruction and education of the young accepted at the monastery school,[121] sufficiently prove that Basil wanted his monks to practise active charity.

When it is claimed that the principal aim of the monastic life is *theoria* (contemplation),[122] one should not, on the pretext of this term taken in isolation, eliminate all charitable and apostolic activity from Eastern monasteries. The directives of the legislators and the reforms, and the general practice over the centuries, have never done that.[123]

The Monks' Apostolate

The Council of Chalcedon ordered monks to remain in their cells and to devote themselves to *hesychia* (quietness) and prayer.[124] It is in this line that Russian monks of the past century replied to a visitor from the West who had asked them about their apostolate and preaching the word of God: 'The vocation of the monks consists neither in studying nor in any other type of work; they have been called to sing the Office, to work for the salvation of their own soul, and to do penance for everyone.'[125]

On the other hand, it has been proved that the first cenobites, and frequently also the hermits, took a hand in the affairs of Church and State.[126] Numerous monks were ordained priests and bishops by John Chrysostom, who defended this action.[127] Syrian monks were active in the lives of their countrymen,[128] the Byzantine directed schools,[129] and among the Armenians *vartapeds* were monks who had been ordained priests and had received special privileges for preaching,[130] and finally, the Moscow Synod of 1917–18 exhorted monks to all forms of apostolate.[131]

It is true that the problem is posed differently in the East where no distinction exists between 'active' and 'contemplative' orders, as in the West. At the beginning of his vocation, every monk is obligated to practise meditation and flight from the world. Only monks who had reached perfection and possessed the gift of speaking were then charged with an apostolic mission.[132] It is easy to understand, then, why the monks on their part avoided the priesthood[133] and why, on the other hand, the Eastern Church sought candidates for the episcopacy only among them.[134]

Educating the Young

The Fathers quite rightly esteemed the benefits of the ancient *paideia* (training) which fashioned the cultivated man — eloquent, trained in rhetoric, and subtle.[135] They impressed upon parents their duty to bring up 'athletes for Christ'.[136] Even though the monks did not accept young people and took steps to prevent the brothers from 'laughing in the midst of children',[137] monastery schools were not unknown in the East.[138]

The fifteenth of Basil's *Long Rules*[139] is of special interest here because it deals with a problem that is still current: is it really possible to rear someone to a life of perfection and virginity? Firmly convinced that it was, Basil argued that the religious life should be nothing but the result of 'one's own decision and of the maturing of reason'. But then, what good was education? Instruction would contain three valuable elements: 1) the child would receive 'the first elements of discipline from the beginning'; 2) he would be armed with 'the traditional forms of piety he had been taught'; 3) and finally, 'the acquired habit would impart facility in right action', for 'the mind of a child is still easy to mold; soft and pliable as wax it easily takes the form of what is impressed upon it.'[140] Once this program was finished, the educator yielded to the authority of the impartial Judge who would thenceforth mete out eternal reward or punishment.

Notes

1. THE UNIVERSALITY OF CHRISTIAN LOVE

1. Špidlík, *La sophiologie de S. Basile*, 237.
2. See Viktor Warnach, 'Homme', EF II:249.

Spiritual Sociology 171

3. See Plato, *Republic*, especially 617e.
4. Basil, *The Long Rules* 7, *interrogatio*; PG 31:928BC [trans. FC 9:223-337.
5. *Comm. d'Abba Isaïe*, Disc. 1.17, French trans. R. Draguët, *Scr. Syri* 145, CSCO 327:18, 33-34.
6. *Praktikos* 89; SCh 171:678; CS 4:38.
7. John Chrysostom, *Homilia* 32 *in I. ad Corinthios*; PG 61:272.
8. *Apophthegmata Patrum*, Apollo 1; PG 65:133C; [CS 59:36].
9. *Interpretatio Epistolae ad Romanos, cap.* 13.10; PG 82:196D-197A.
10. *Regula fusius tractata* 3; PG 31:917B.
11. *De caritate*; PG 60:773-774.
12. *Instruction* VI.78, SCh 92 (1963) 284-86; CS 33:138-39; cf. 'Directions on spiritual training.42', *Early Fathers from the Philokalia* (London, 1963) 165.
13. See Chapter VIII, *Various Forms of the Eremetic Life*.
14. *Century IV on Charity* 82; SCH 9:170; trans. P. Sherwood, St. Maximus the Confessor: *The Ascetic Life, The Four Centuries on Charity*, ACW 21 (1955) 205; see I. Hausherr, *De la tendresse pour soi à la charité selon saint Maxime le Confesseur*, OCA 137 (Rome, 1952) 113ff.
15. *Epistola* 27; PG 91:617C.
16. *Century* II, 10; SCh 9:96; ACW 21:154.
17. *Praktikos* 100; SCh 171:711; CS 4:41.
18. *Century* I.24; SCh 9:73ff; ACW 21:140ff.
19. *Homilia* 2 *in Cant.* 7 (PG 13:54), *Liber 3 in Cant.* (PG 13:155-60).
20. *Century* I.24; SCh 9:77; ACW 21:140.
21. See Hausherr, *Philautie*, 117.
22. *Contra Celsum* III.5; GCS 1:207; ANF 4:467.
23. *Ibid.*, 6:467.
24. Gregory Nazianzen, *Oratio* 41.16; PG 36:449C.
25. *Oratio* 4.12; PG 35:541B.
26. See Pierre Grelot, 'Peuple, VTB, 969ff.
27. *Ibid.*, 991.
28. See Spanneut, *Le stoïcisme des Pères*, 252.
29. *Ibid.*, 256ff.
30. *Ibidem.*
31. *Protrepticos* 88.3; GCS 1:65, 31 [trans. *Exhortation to the Greeks*, ANF 2:171-206].
32. *Paedagogos* I.32, 2ff.; GCS 1:109. [trans. by S. Wood, *Christ the Educator*, FC 23 (1954)].
33. *De finibus* III.64.
34. VII.34.6; ed. F. X. Funk, *Didascalia et Constitutiones Apostolorum* (Paderborn, 1905) p. 428.
35. *De idolatria* 14 (CSEL 47:306, 5), IV.6 (P. 471, 19); ANF 3:70.
36. See Étienne Gilson, 'Le christianisme et la tradition philosophique', *Revue des sciences philosophiques et théologiques*, 2 (1941-42) 249-66; A. J. Festugière, *Hermès* II:270, n. 2.
37. V.5; SCh 33:255; J. B. Lightfoot, *The Apostolic Fathers* (1978, rept) 254.
38. *Ibidem.*
39. *Ad Demetrianum* 19; CSEL 3/1:364, 17-24.
40. *The Justification of the Good* III.10.6 (London, 1918) 426ff.
41. *Ibid.*
42. *Ibid.*, 425.
43. *Ibid.*, III.5.4, 286ff.

44. See Sergei Verchovskoj, *Pravoslavie v žizni* [*Orthodoxy in Life*] (New York, 1953) 181.
45. See Hans Schaeder, *Moskau, das dritte Rom* (Hamburg, 1929, rpt Darmstadt, 1957); Wilhelm Lettenbauer, *Moskau, das dritte Rom. Die Geschichte einer politischen Theorie* (Munich, 1961).
46. See Bernhard Schultze, 'Profetismo e messianisme russo religioso. Essenza, origini e rappresentanti principali', OCP 22 (1956):172–97.
47. Vladimir S. Soloviev, *L'idée russe* (Paris, 1888) 6.

2. UNITY OF THE BODY IN CHRIST

1. See, for example, Ph. Rancillac, *L'Église de l'Esprit chez saint Jean Chrysostome*. Preface by P. André Scrima (Lebanon, Dar Al-Kalima, 1970).
2. See Jerome Gaïth, *La conception de la liberté chez Grégoire de Nysse* (Paris, 1953) 120ff.
3. Yves Congar, 'Eglise. Histoire dogmatique', EF 1:421ff.
4. Gulielmus [Wilhelm] de Vries, 'Le sens ecclésial . . . chez les Syriens (jacobites et nestoriens)', DS 4/1:432–42.
5. Stanislas Tyskiewicz, Le sens ecclésial . . . chez les Russes séparés, DS 4/1: 442–50.
6. Špidlík, *Théophane le Reclus*, 173.
7. See *Cerkov odna* [*The One Church*] (Prague, 1967) 18.
8. *L'Église latine et le protestantisme* (Lausanne, 1872) 116.
9. See B. Köttig, 'Saints (culte des)', EF 4:186ff.
10. See Sévérien Salaville, '"L'Explication de la messe" de l'Arménien Chosrov (950)', *Théologie et liturgie*, Etudes d'Orient 39 (1940–42) 349–82.
11. The idea was developed early by Origen, *De oratione* 11; PG 11:448ff.
12. Joseph de Volokolamsk, *Prosvětitěl* [*Illuminator*] (Kazaň, 1857) 306ff.
13. Alexij Step. Chomiakov, *Cerkov odna* (Prague, 1867) 18.
14. S. Bulgakov, *L'Orthodoxie* (Paris, 1932) 169; see T. Špidlík, 'La preghiera presso i popolo slavi', in R. Boccassino *La Preghiera* (Rome, 1967) vol. 2:787–817.
15. Mauricio Gordillo, *Mariologia orientalis*, OCS 141 (Rome, 1954) 250ff.
16. See T. Špidlík, 'La pietà mariana nella Chiesa orientale', in *Maria, mistero di grazia*, ed. Ermanno Ancilla (Rome: Teresianum, 1974), 270–86.
17. See above, Chapter IV, 1, and below, Conclusion.
18. See above, III, *Eternal Life*.
19. Vladimir Lossky, *In the Image and Likeness of God* (Crestwood, New York, 1974) 208.
20. *Ibid.*, 196 and 208.
21. See above, I, *Cosmic Spirituality*, and VI, 2.
22. Lossky, *Image and Likeness*, 209.
23. See below, Chapter XIII, 1.
24. T. Špidlík, 'La pietà mariana' 279ff.
25. See J. Ratzinger, 'Fraternité', DS 5:1141–67.
26. See the prayer in Nock-Festugière, *Hermès Trismégiste. Corpus Hermeticum* (Paris, 1945–54) I.31–32.
27. See, for example, Origen, *De oratione* 15.4; GCS 2:335.
28. Irenaeus, *Adversus haereses* II.31.2; PG 7:825A.
29. See Basil, *Regula fusius tractata* 104; PG 31:1153C; Gregory Nazianzen, *Ep.* 238; PG 37:380C; Pseudo-Macarius, *Homilia* 3.1; PG 34:468C.

Spiritual Sociology 173

30. See Franz Jozef Dölger, 'Brüderlichkeit der Fürsten', *Reallexicon für Antike und Christentum*, 2:col. 641–46.
31. Acts 2:44: the *Long Rules* 7.4 (PG 31:933C), 35.3 (1008A). Acts 4:32; *On the Judgment of God* 4 (660C), *Moralia* 60.1 (793C), LR 7.4 (933C), 32.1 (996A), 35.3 (1008A); the *Short Rules* 85 (1144A), 183 (1205A). Acts 4:35: *LR* 19.1 (968B), 34.1 (1000B), *Short Rules* 93 (1148B), 131 (1169C), 135 (1172C), 148 (1180C) 252 (1252B).
32. David Amand, *L'ascèse monastique de saint Basile* (Maredsous, 1948) 129.
33. PG 31:928C–933B.
34. See Špidlík, *La sophiologie de S. Basile*, 233ff.
35. See Stanislas Giet, *Les idées et l'action sociales de saint Basile* (Paris, 1941).
36. Evagrius, *De oratione* 124; PG 79:1193; [CS 4:76]; Irénée Hausherr, *Les Leçons d'un contemplatif. Le traité de l'Oraison d'Evagre le Pontique* (Paris, 1960) 158.
37. *In Proverbia* XVI; PG 17:196D.
38. See *Apopthegmata*, Arsenius 13; PG 65:92A; CS 59:11.
39. See the *Constitutiones monasticae* attributed to Basil (chapter 29; PG 31: 1417–20).
40. *Collationes* 16.14; SCh 54:234; LNPF, series 2, vol. 11:454–55.
41. *Predanie i Ustav, Pam. drev. piśm. i isk*, CLXXIX (1912); see Ivan Kologrivof, *Essai sur la sainteté en Russie* (Bruges, 1953) 187ff.
42. He devotes a long chapter to this subject in his *Nicomachean Ethics* (Bk. VIII); the Western Fathers knew the ideas of Aristotle through Cicero's *De amicitia*.
43. See John Chrysostom, *De Davide et Saule, homilia* 1; PG 54:680.
44. See John Moschus, *Pratum spirituale* 12; SCh 12 (1946) 55. According to John Chrysostom, heretics belong to the Body of Christ since they received the dignity of baptism, but it falls to Christ, to the Apostles, and to their successors to remove them from the Church as diseased members which one cuts out to save the rest of the body (*Homilia de anathemate* 3–4; PG 48:948ff). However, there are other texts that express a more lenient attitude. Speaking of those have lapsed into heresy, Irenaeus exclaims, 'Wherefore it shall not weary us, to endeavor with all our might to stretch out the hand to unto them' (*Adv. haer.* III.25.7; PG 7:972A; ANF 1:460). As for anger against heretics, see Chapter IX, *Anger*.
45. See Špidlík, *Joseph de Volokolamsk*, 114ff; Theodore the Studite, *Testamentum spirituale* 18 (PG 99:1821), *Apophthegmata*, Isaac 8 (PG 65:226BC; CS 59:85, = Isaac 5) Ephrem, *Paraenesis* (Rome, 1732–) vol. II:77.
46. See DS 1:525ff.
47. See DS 5:66–67. Some texts on the spirituality of the family may be found in R. Flacelière, *Amour humain, Parole divine* (Paris, 1947).
48. *In Epistolam ad Ephesios* 20.1; PG 62:135ff; LNPF 13:151.
49. T. Špidlík, 'Il matrimonio, sacramento di unità nel pensiero di Crisostomo', *Augustinianum* 17 (1977) 221–26.
50. *In Epistolam ad Ephesios* 20.1; PG 62:135, LNPF 13:151.
51. *De virginitate* 10.1; SC 125 (1966) 122.
52. *Ibid.*
53. See N. von Arseniew, 'Die Spiritualität der Ostkirche' in *Handbuch der Ostkirchenkunde* (Düsseldorf, 1971), 539ff [cf. Nicholas Arseniev, *Russian Piety* (Crestwood, N.Y.)]; T. Špidlík, *I grandi mistici russi* (Rome, 1977) 311ff.

Chapter Six

54. A Tolstoj, *Pravednaja Juliana Lazarevskaja* (Paris, n. d.); see Kologrivof, *Essai sur la sainteté en Russie* 280–88.
55. Ed. St. Petersburg, 1911; see Alexandr Serg Orlov, *Domostroj. Izsledovanije* [*Research on the D.*] (Moscow, 1917). Russian Reprint Series 53, (The Hague, 1967).
56. See Chapter VIII, *Parents*.
57. *Contra Celsum* 8.73; GCS 2:290ff.
58. *La femme et le salut du monde*, 111.
59. *Prosvětitěl* [*Illuminator*] (Kazaň, 1857) 537ff.
60. See Špidlík, *Joseph de Volokolamsk*, 140.
61. *Ibid.*, 141.
62. Marie-Théophane Disdier, 'Agapet', DS 1:246–247; J. Ševčenko, *A Neglected Byzantine Source of Muscovite Political Ideology*. Essay Dedicated to Francis Dvornik on the Occasion of his Sixtieth Birthday (Harvard Univers. Press, 1954) 141–80.
63. See Antiochus Monachus, *Homilia 50*; PG 89:1588–1589.
64. See André de Bovis, 'Haine', DS 7/a:29–50.
65. Dorotheus, *Instructiones* 6; SCh 92:271ff; CS 33:131ff.
66. *Ibid.*
67. See Gregory the Great, *Homilia 38 in Evangelio* 11; PL 76:1288.
68. *Martyrium Polycarpi* 1.2; F. X. Funk, *Patres Apostolici* I (Tübingen, 1901) 315.
69. Gregory Nazianzen, *Oratio 17 ad cives nazianzenos* 9; PG 35:976C.
70. See Chapter V, 1, and XIII, *The Glory of God*.
71. See Gregory the Great, *Regula Pastoralis* 2.3; PG 77:28B.
72. See Pierre Adnès, 'Exemple', DS 4/2:1878–1885.
73. *De beato Philogonio* VI; PG 48:752A.
74. *Pratum spirituale* 199; SCh 12:271ff.
75. See Basil, *Short Rules* 176; PG 31:1200AB; Étienne Sargologos, *La vie de saint Cyrille le Philéote* (Bruxelles, 1964) chap. 39, 14, pp. 402ff; Dadišo Quatraya, *Commentaire d'Abba Isaïe*, Disc. 1.3, CSCO 327 (*Scriptores Syri* 145) 5, 3–7.
76. Špidlík, *Joseph de Volokolamsk*, 76ff.
77. *Ibid.*
78. *Letters* I.4; PG 99:324B.
79. See John the Solitary (Pseudo-John of Lycopolis), *Dialogue sur l'âme et les passions des hommes*, trans. I. Hausherr, OCA 120 (Rome, 1939) 32.
80. See T. Špidlík, '"Fous pour le Christ"—en Orient', DS 5:756.
81. See Jean Gribomont, 'Obéissance et évangile selon saint Basile le Grand', *La vie spirituelle*, Suppl. VI (1952) 207.
82. Basil, *Short Rules* 158; PG 31:1185C.
83. Dorotheus, *Doctrina* XIX (PG 88:1809D–1812A), *Sentences* 18, (SCh 92:531).
84. *Filosofia imeni* [*The Philosophy of the Name*] (Paris, 1953) 33.
85. Gregory Nazianzen, *Ep. 108*; PG 37:208A.
86. Ed. Étienne Sargologos, *Vie de saint Cyrille le Philéote* (Brussels, 1964) p. 398; see Gregory Nazianzen, *Oratio 30.1*; PG 36:176A.
87. It is Basil (?) who gave this beautiful title to his friend, *Ep. 8.1*; PG 32:248; see Špidlík, *Grégoire de Nazianze*, 138ff.
88. *Carminum liber* II.II.5, vv. 1–4; PG 37:1521A.
89. Gregory Nazianzen, *Oratio 32.12*; PG 36:188B.

Spiritual Sociology 175

90. See Jean Plagnieux, *Saint Grégoire de Nazianze, Théologien*. (Paris, 1952) 433.
91. *Apophthegmata*, Pambo 2; PG 65:368; CS 59:164–5; see *Vie de sainte Mélanie* 36; SCh 90 (1962) 195.
92. See Walter Völker, *Das Vollkommenheitsideal des Origenes* (Tübingen, 1931) 169ff.
93. Gregory Nazianzen, *Oratio* 27.3; PG 36:13A
94. *Letter* 187, ed. Nicodemus the Hagiorite (Venice, 1816) p. 99. see *Letter* 478 (p. 235); *Letter* 650 (p. 269).
95. Gregory Nazianzen, *Oratio* 32.1; PG 36:176A.
96. *Id., Ep.* 171; PG 37:280C–281A.
97. See T. Špidlík, 'La parola della lingua nativa nel servizio del mistero inesprimibile: problema di Gregorio Nazianzeno', *Augustinianum* 14 (1974) 541–48.
98. See Clement of Alexandria, *Paedagogos* III.6 (PG 8:603–607), *Stromata* II.8 (PG 8:1015–1039), Cyril of Jerusalem, *Catecheses* 15.26 (PG 33:907), Basil, *Sermo de eleemosyna* (PG 31:1154–1167, Gregory of Nyssa, *Oratio* I.2, *De pauperibus amandis (PG 46:454–490)*; See E. Cavalcanti, in OCP 44 (1978) 170–80.
99. Basil. *De eleemosyna*; PG 31:1158.
100. *Pandectes* 21, cf. Charles de Clercq, *Les textes juridiques dans les Pandectes de Nicon de la Montagne Noire* (Venice, 1942) 40.
101. See *Joseph de Volokolamsk*, 117.
102. See John Chrysostom, *Homilia de paenitentia seu de eleemosyna*; PG 49:291–300.
103. Its influence can already be felt in the *Didache* XII.3–5; F. X. Funk, *Patres Apostolici* I (2d ed. Tübingen, 1901) 30 [English translation by R. A. Kraft in *The Apostolic Fathers*, ed. J. Sparks (Nashville, 1978) 308ff.]
104. See Chapter XII, 3, note 4.
105. See *Epistolae S. Nili, De voluntaria paupertate ad Magnam* 31, *Patr. Syr.* III (Paris, 1926) p. CLXXXII–CLXXXIII and PG 79:997A.
106. See Lucien Daloz, 'Le travail selon saint Jean Chrysostome, Théologie Pastorale et Spirituelle 4 (Paris, 1959).
107. *In Genesim homilia* 5.3 (PG 53:51), 3.3 (35).
108. See *La sophiologie de S. Basile*, 36ff.
109. *Expositio in Psalmum*, 48.8; PG 55:234.
110. See *La sophiologie de S. Basile*, 11ff.
111. *Ibid.*, p. 45.
112. John Chrysostom, *In Epistolam I ad Cor. homilia* 4; PG 61:210ff.
113. See Daloz, 111ff.
114. John Chrysostom, *In Joannem homilia* 3; PG 59:206.
115. *Id., Adversus Judaeos* 8.2; PG 48:929 [trans. by P. W. Harkins in FC 68 (1977).] *In Priscillam et Aquilam* 1.5; PG 51:194.
116. See Theodoret of Cyrus, *Discours sur la Providence* (Paris, 1954) 205.
117. See Daloz, 108ff.
118. See David Amand, *L'ascèse monastique de saint Basile* (Maredsous, 1948) 307.
119. See the *Long Rules* 38, 39, and 40; PG 31:1016C–1021A.
120. *Short Rules* 15; PG 31:1184BC.
121. The *Long Rules* 155, 1–4 (952A–957A); *Short Rules* 292 (1288B).
122. Justinian, *Novella* 133.

Chapter Six

123. See T. Špidlík, 'Das östliche Mönchtum und das östliche Frömmigkeitsleben', in *Handbuch der Ostkirchenkunde*, 551ff; *id.*, 'Bizantino monachesimo', DIP 1 (1974) 1466-74.
124. Canon 4; F. B. Pitra, *Iuris ecclesiastici Graecorum historia et monumenta* (Rome, 1864-68) I, p. 524.
125. William Palmer, *Notes of a Visit to the Russian Church* (London, 1882) 524.
126. Leo Ueding, 'Die Kanones von Chalkedon in ihrer Bedeutung für Mönchtum und Klerus', in A. Grillmeier and H. Bacht, *Das Konzil von Chalkedon, Geschichte und Gegenwart*, 3 vols., (Würzburg, 1951-1954) vol. II:569-676; H. Bacht, 'Die Rolle des orientalischen Mönchtum in den kirchenpolitischen Auseinandersetzungen um Chalkedon', *Ibid.*, vol. 2:193-314.
127. See Ivo auf der Maur, *Mönchtum und Glaubensverkündigung in den Schriften des heiligen Johannes Chrysostomus* (Freiburg, Switz., 1959).
128. After his arrival in Mesopotamis, Mar Eugene 'understood that he had to travel over the land with his children to convert the people to the true faith', *Patrologia Orientalis* 4:235 (25).
129. See Špidlík, 'Bizantino monachesimo', in DIP 1 (1974) col. 1466-74.
130. G. Amadouni, 'Le rôle des hiéromoines arméniens', in *Il monachesimo orientale*, OCA 153 (Rome, 1958) 279-305.
131. See J. Rezáč, *De monachismo secundum recentiorem legislationem russicam*, OCA 138 (Rome, 1952) 211ff.
132. See *La sophiologie de S. Basile*, 251ff.
133. See John Chrysostom, *De sacerdotio*; PG 48:623-692; [trans. by G. Neville, *Six Books on the Priesthood* (London: SPCK, 1964)]. Gregory Nazianzen, *Oratio apologetica, de sacerdotio*; PG 35:395-402.
134. See Špidlík, 'Das östliche Mönchtum und das östliche Frömmigkeitsleben', in *Handbuch der Ostkirche*, 543-68.
135. See Henri I. Marrou, *A History of Education in Antiquity*, trans. G. Lamb (New York, 1956).
136. John Chrysostom, *Sur la vaine gloire et l'éducation* 19, SCh 188 (1972), 103; [*Address on Vainglory and the Right Way of Parents to Bring up their Children* may be found in M. L. Laistner, *Christianity and Pagan Culture in the Later Roman Empire* (Ithaca, 1951).]
137. Amand Boon, *Pachomiana latina* (Louvain, 1932) 60.
138. T. Špidlík, 'Educazione nei monasteri orientali', DIP 3 (1976) col. 1065-1067; J. Rezáč, *De monachismo secundum recentiorem legislationem russicam*, OCA 138 (Rome, 1952) 218-253.
139. PG 31:952-957; tr. M. Wagner, *Saint Basil. Ascetical Works*, FC 9 (1950) 264ff.
140. The comparison of the human soul to soft wax is found in Plato (*Thaetetus* 191c), Aristotle (*De anim.* III, 424a), Chrysostom, *In Ep. II ad Thess.* 2.4 (PG 62:476); *Sur la vaine gloire et l'éducation* 20 (SCh 188:105).

7

NEGATIVE PRAXIS

1. PRAXIS

The Spiritual Life – The Work of God

THE BOOK OF GENESIS (2:2) tells of 'the great work of God', creation. The work or works of God, *ergon* or *erga*,[1] is Christ's entire life, everything that filled his life. When his listeners asked him a question of immediate concern to them, 'What must we do if we are to do the work God wants?' he replied: 'This is the work of God: to believe in the one whom he has sent' (Jn 6:28–29). The 'work of God' is therefore the life of faith; it is following Christ.

The expression 'work of God' has a wide scope and includes a great deal in monastic literature. In Greek texts, *to ergon tou theou* (the work of God) does not refer to the liturgy (in Latin, *opus divinum*) but to asceticism in general.[2] According to Athanasius, a virgin's 'work of God' includes all that is necessary to safeguard virginity.[3] Abba Isaiah returned again and again to this thought: 'Ah! What a hard *kopos* (occupation) the way of God is'.[4] *Ergon* (task) is contrasted to *parergon*, a subordinate work that is not 'the work of the soul'.[5]

The monks were convinced that the spiritual life is laborious: 'It is necessary to take great pains (*kopos*), and without *kopos* one cannot come to his God.'[6] John the Dwarf even went so far as to define the monk laconically in one word, *kopos*. 'The monk toils at all he does (*eis pan ergon kopią*). That is what a monk is'.[7] According to Basil, spiritual goods are acquired 'through toil and sweat' (*ponois kai hidrōsi*).⁸ 'One must wrestle and do battle' (*poiein agōna kai polemon*), Pseudo-Macarius said.⁹ The Slav would describe this laborious work by the terms *trud* and *podvig*.¹⁰ The word *podvižnik* means the ascetic.

The Term Praxis

It has been said that *theōria* was the ideal of the Greeks, and this is undoubtedly correct. No statement, however, should be too sweeping. After predominating at the beginning, as is normal, the ancient 'practical' tendency always remained alive.¹¹ At the close of antiquity, the contrast between the active and the contemplative life had become so classic that to discuss the relative merits of each came to be a school exercise.¹²

Nonetheless, the accepted meaning of the terms is often hard to determine in specific texts.¹³ The vocabulary played a role in this. Greek has two specific terms to designate an action, *poiēsis* (a making) and *praxis* (a doing). The element of weariness, of human effort, of toil, remains associated with the evolution of the second term.¹⁴ For Plotinus, *praxis* meant an 'impure', a 'mixed' action, one tainted by the matter toward which it tended; it was the activity of man in the flesh. The activity of God was *poiēsis*.¹⁵

In christian terminology, *praxis* in its widest sense could refer to any work of salvation. The use of the word *praktikos* to designate the monk who distinguished himself by his spiritual life became frequent after Evagrius.¹⁶ And since there was complete agreement about the primacy of prayer in the spiritual life, contemplation of the truth and exegesis were, for Origen, 'the most excellent work of God'.¹⁷

Yet, following the ancient Greeks who restricted *praxis* to man's physical activity in the world and *theōria* to the activity of the mind, Christians, too, began to make a careful distinction between *praxis* and *theōria*.¹⁸ *Theōria* became spiritual and was used to refer to the 'true *gnōsis*'.¹⁹ *Praxis*, too, acquired the specific meaning given to it by Evagrius; hence, 'knowledge of God is divided in two parts, *praxis* and *theōria*'.²⁰ Evagrius gave the following definition: 'The practical life is the spiritual method for cleansing the affective part of the soul'.²¹

This definition, however famous, was still negative. The explanation given by Gregory Nazianzen is more general and hence more inclusive: 'Understand by *theōria* an examining of the intelligibles (*skepsis noetōn*) and by *praxis* the sphere of action'.[22] The aim of such an activity was of course not vice, but a virtuous act. And since from the christian point of view practice of the virtues consisted in observing the commandments, the first of which was charity, *praxis* would be nothing but the life of faith in Christ and in imitation of the Saviour. Its first aspect was purification from sin. We can therefore speak of a negative *praxis* when it is aimed at overcoming obstacles (sins, the passions) and evil thoughts, and of a positive *praxis* when it is directed at cultivating the virtues.[23]

Asceticism

The etymology of the Greek terms *askeō* (to exercise), *askēsis* (training), and *askētēs* (one who practises) remains obscure. Homer used the term to express the idea of an artistic[24] or technical work.[25] The term became highly successful when it was applied to 1) physical exercise (that of athletes and soldiers); 2) exercising the mind and will (here it was used alternately with *meletē*, meditation, and particularly its attentive and progressive application); and 3) the cultic and religious life (Isokrates calls the 'pious practices' instituted in Egypt *askēseis*).[26]

St Paul used the term *askeō* once (Ac 24:16), though what it describes is found frequently in his thought; he calls the practice of the godly life exercise (1 Tm 4:6–7).[27] In the Apostolic Fathers and the second century apologists, the Christian was called not *askētēs* but *athlētēs*.[28] With Clement of Alexandria and Origen the term took on current and precise meanings in christian parlance, especially through the intermediary of Philo.[29] In comparison with the Pythagoreans, Origen called those who lived the life of perfection *askētai*.[30] Derivatives were coined: *asketeria* (nun), *askētērion* (monastery; the Latin form is *asceterium*), and *askētikon* (works dealing with the spiritual, especially the monastic, life).[31]

Asceticism entails a training that is both reflective and persevering. For Athanasius, the ascetic effort meant a tension which knew no rest and tolerated no inattention. It is in this sense that he had Antony begin his great discourse to the Egyptian monks.[32] Yet there is also the less organized form of asceticism which counts mainly on the difficulties of daily life and which patiently overcomes the hardships of each day. It is in this sense that one may speak of the 'moderate asceticism' of the Russian monks who endured hard manual labor and inclement weather.[33]

Christian asceticism is undoubtedly different from mere gymnastics. It is a quest for a life with God. On the other hand, there has always been a strong belief in the effectiveness of cooperation between God and man. This means not only a reordering of the various elements of human psychology but also, and above all, the growth of Christ in the soul. We can therefore say that the union of asceticism and mysticism is the doctrinal foundation of all forms of monasticism.[34]

Self-denial, Renunciation

The negative aspect of *praxis* is indicated in the New Testament by several terms: self-denial, renunciation, detachment, 'being crucified' with Christ. Each term expresses a special nuance of a common root. The verb *apotassesthai* (to renounce) is found in Lk 14:33. Elsewhere in the New Testament, this term is used several times in the sense of saying farewell, taking leave (Lk 9:61, Ac 18:8, 2 Co 2:13). In ascetic texts, the direct object of the verb is *tǫ kosmǫ toutǫ* (the entire world), or *pasin* (everything), or *chrēmaton* (property). The more ancient noun is *apotaxis*, the more recent one *apotagē*.[35]

For Justin, the detachment from all things, even life itself, which christians practised in martyrdom was enough to prove their innocence and their virtue.[36] For monks, *apotagē* meant a true renunciation of all property, of being without possessions (*aktēmosynē*). To renounce things inwardly was necessary for all Christians.[37]

John the Solitary drew a distinction between three degrees of detachment:

> physical detachment, the abandonment of possessions; psychic detachment, the removal of passions; and spiritual detachment, the surrender of one's opinions. Detachment from

possessions and from the passions can be practised on earth, but being detached from one's opinions belongs to the life following the resurrection.[38]

The Gospel writers also used the verb *aparneisthai*, to deny oneself, as if to cut someone one no longer wants to recognize (Mt 16:24-26, Mk 8:34-36, Lk 9:23-25).

The Stripping of Self

Ekduō simply means to get away from (Cf. Lk 10:10). The composite *apekduō* had a stronger meaning and was used in the metaphoric sense: 'You have stripped off the old man' (Col 3:9). The concept of stripping is clarified by the nature of what is being put on: christian armor (Rm 13:12, 1 Th 5:8, Eph 6:11, 14), or certain feelings (Col 3:12), more generally a new life (2 Co 5:4), or, more deeply, Christ (Ga 3:17, Rm 6:11, 6:5, Col 3:5, 3:3). Generations of christians have meditated and reflected on these texts.[39]

The stripping off of the sinful life was expressed very early and strongly in the liturgy of baptism: before descending into the baptismal font, the catechumen took off his garment and, after baptism, was covered with a new vestment. In order to show their decision of having nothing in common with the world, the ascetics adopted the dress and the way of living of the poor. Their garb, which was often blessed, marked their consecration to a new life. This is the meaning of the religious habit and, in a sense, also of the liturgical vestments.[40]

Mortification

In Lk 14:33, a text which speaks of renunciation, the formula 'carrying one's cross' is also found. In the proper sense, this means 'to walk to the infamous punishment' of the cross.[41] 'To lose one's soul' recurs several times in the Gospels.[42] The soul one must lose is *psychē*, a synonym for life; one must therefore be ready to sacrifice the present life to insure life eternal. 'To hate his soul' (Jn 12:25, Lk 14:26) has the same meaning: to die in order to live. We 'mortify', 'put to death' the deeds of the body (Rm 8:13), our passionate nature that belongs to earthly life. (Col 3:5).

The term 'mortification' is used frequently in the West. It is said to be foreign to Eastern spirituality which preaches 'the joy of Pascha'.[43] And yet, this paschal joy cannot be separated from death because it is the fruit of the Cross. This is why the term 'mortification', which is indeed rare in the East, receives a beautiful epithet in Symeon the New Theologian: *zōopoios nekrōsis*, 'a life-giving mortification'.[44]

Chastity

The term *enkrateia*[45] is not scriptural. St Paul uses the verb *enkrateuesthai* (to exercise self-control) (1 Co 9:25, 7:9), and in Ga 5:23 chastity appears in the list of virtues; for him, however, it was not an ideal of life.[46] By contrast, 'mastery of self' is found very frequently in Greek and Hellenistic literature.[47] For Philo, continence was the opposite of the love of pleasure (*philēdonia*)[48]; it leads to heaven and to immortality.[49]

Christian literature had to wait for Clement of Alexandria to develop a somewhat full and coherent theory of continence. In the *Miscellanies* he gave the Stoic definition: 'Self-restraint is that quality which does not overstep what appears in accordance with right reason.'[50]

Basil devoted two chapters of the *Long Rules*,[51] to chastity, and he was careful to find references to it in St Paul. The term occurs rather frequently in the great doctors of monasticism. John Climacus distinguished bodily chastity (*aisthētē*) from spiritual chastity (*noētē*).[52] Nonetheless, one should note the tendency, especially among the Western Fathers, to restrict the word to bodily chastity and even to complete, absolute continence. In the *encratic* sects this trend went so far as to deprecate the value of the body and of creation.[53]

2. PURIFICATION FROM SIN

Purification

Purity, a common concept in ancient religions, meant the disposition that was required to approach sacred things. According

Negative Praxis

to this primitive concept, which usually tended to become more and more profound, purification was acquired not by moral actions but by ritual, and was lost through contact with matter. In Scripture, the notion of purity tends to become interior and moral.[1]

Greek philosophy insisted on purification for the sake of *theōria* (contemplation): only the pure could attain the Pure.[2] This theme was taken over by the Fathers,[3] but was put into a wider context. They frequently presented perfection as the restoration of the original, primitive condition.[4] From this perspective, perfection coincided with *katharsis* (purging),[5] but it included the fulness of life eternal: the 'all pure' Mother of God is fully deified.[6] Usually, however, the term was reserved for the first degree of the spiritual life, *praxis*, 'the spiritual method of cleansing the affective part of the soul'.[7]

In order to determine the essential elements of this purification, we must first know what was considered evil: was it the body, the senses, or the passions? For Christians, the one real evil was sin. It therefore became the main object of purification. Later, however, the term purification was extended to everything that was an allurement to, or a consequence of, sin.

The State of Sin

Sin belongs to the realm of faith and has not often been introduced as a common concept in the history of human thought. Even in christian teaching the term can be understood in a strict or in a broad sense. After reading the texts of the Eastern ascetics, Theophane the Recluse concluded that sin could mean 1) the guilty deed, 2) a passion, 3) a state of soul, an inner disposition.[8]

The theology of sin as it has been elaborated by Western moralists refers to sin as an act; on this ground it is distinguished from vice, which refers to a disposition.[9] For St John, by contrast, sin is a state, an abiding inner disposition. Not only the individual person, but 'the world', is in sin (Jn 1:29). With St Paul, sin becomes personified: it has 'entered the world'.

The same expressions are often found in the spiritual literature of the East. The *Spiritual Homilies* of Pseudo-Macarius, with their Messalian tendencies, contain innumerable traces of the doctrine that the human heart, even brought to deliverance by Christ, is an abyss where good and evil, sin and grace, are mixed.[10]

The orthodox, of course, had to impugn the consubstantiality of evil, a concept denounced as a Messalian error by John of Damascus.[11] They all knew that 'Evil does not exist by nature (*en physei*), nor is any man naturally evil, for God made nothing that is not good'.[12] Following the Platonic principle which identifies the good with being, Gregory of Nyssa defined evil as the negation of being.[13] However paradoxical it may seem, he said that evil 'has its being in non-being' (*en tǫ mē einai to einai echei*).[14] And yet, he too described evil as a dynamic force which is born, germinates, and develops.[15]

Eastern writers in general are known to have viewed *katastasis* (the state of prayer, of perfection, and so forth) as having greater importance than an isolated act.[16] Sin, too, was therefore readily viewed from this angle — one which westerners would call 'less strict', but which has the advantage nonetheless of being closer to scriptural and liturgical ways of speaking. This concept also saved these writers from complex speculations about original sin.

Full Responsibility for Sin

That the saints considered themselves great sinners is a commonplace in saints' lives.[17] In the pages of the Old Testament there was already a consciousness of man's radical impurity before God (Pr 20:9, Jb 9:30ff.). As sin marked the beginnings of human history, so it also marked the beginning of the history of Israel and of every individual life. Better to underline the character of the inner experience which leads to this awareness, Theophane the Recluse intentionally chose a vague expression: 'You have become aware of something new in yourself, and your conscience tells you that this newness is of your doing, an evil work which has already begun to reproach you.'[18]

Are such movements involuntary or culpable? Theophane said that it is always praiseworthy to repent, even when there was no consent. Disordered movements are always impure. They are in the heart, and can therefore 'not be viewed as being entirely alien'. One feels obliged to judge oneself according to one's proclivities.[19]

Moral teaching in the West carefully established criteria to

Negative Praxis

distinguish between what was voluntary and involuntary. The Eastern *catanyctic* prayers (*catanyxis* = compunction) ask forgiveness for 'voluntary and involuntary' faults.[20] Sins of 'weakness' are hardly mentioned in the exhortations of the Greek Fathers.[21] Theophane, it is true, recognized that there are also 'sins of weakness', but he hastened to add that anyone who knows his weakness would not dream of justifying himself.[22]

Inordinate voluntary and involuntary movements should not be confused with this,[23] for there is a world of difference between one sin and another. Nonetheless, one should never seek to absolve oneself from the involuntary, for we are responsible for the state of our heart, and the ascetic effort of the converted sinner is characterized by a purification of feelings.[24]

As for individual responsibility for an evil deed, we know how often and how vehemently the Fathers repeated that neither the devil nor the world, neither evil thoughts nor strong passions were sufficient reasons to explain sin.[25] With John Chrysostom, Theophane insisted that guilt lies neither in the eye nor in any other part of the body, but only in the perverse will.[26] 'Sin is always the activity of our free will. Resist and you will not fall.'[27]

Sin as Ignorance

It comes as no surprise that the Fathers applied the philosophic concept of their day, especially those concerning 'ignorance', to sin. Greek morality had a decidedly intellectual bent: it considered virtue as knowledge and vice as ignorance.[28] This ignorance is caused by the 'heaviness' of the body, by the 'veil of the senses'.[29]

This terminology was to be perpetuated in ascetic language for centuries. When Origen spoke of *hamartēma* (transgression), he often meant a doctrinal error.[30] Gregory of Nyssa attributed the choice of evil to an error of intelligene, which allows itself to be led astray by deceitful appearances. If evil were to expose itself in its nakedness, man would not be taken by it.[31] The word *agnōsia* (ignorance) linked to *kakia* (wickedness) occurs frequently in Evagrius. In attacking the monks, the demons have as their main goal depriving them of knowledge.[32]

Higher knowledge in the christian sense, *gnōsis alēthinē*

(true knowledge), differs in essence from the 'mere knowledge' of the philosophers.[33] 'True knowledge' presupposes observance of the commandments. And thus, the lack of knowledge which manifests itself in sin goes hand in hand with disobedience, with revolt against the law of God.[34] It is therefore the failure to practise the virtues which causes 'ignorance'.[35] When *praxis* is lacking, Evagrius says, the mind is dulled by passions and 'takes flight': it abandons its duty, contemplation, [36] and the sinner is plunged into a deep sleep.[37]

Other related terms that help explain the cause of sin occur in this context, for example, *aboulia* (thoughtlessness),[38] and especially *koros*, 'satiety'.[39] For Origen, the Word of God is 'the bread of life', the 'true drink', and life eternal is preserved by this nourishment. *Koron labein tēs theōrias* means to stop contemplating because of a lack of love and vigilance, according to Origen's development of the concept. But by the end of the fourth century this was no longer accepted because Neo-Platonic influences had brought the risk of seeing in it the idea that the good itself could bring about an effect of 'satiety'.[40]

Transgressing the Commandments, Offending God

St John identifies sin as *he anomia*, lawlessness, (1 Jn 3:4), the root of which is *nomos*, the law. The term was usually translated as a 'violation of the law', a transgression of the law. The word became practically synonymous with *hamartia* (sin).[41]

The Pharisees viewed the Law as being outside the realm of personal relationships between man and God. In the Old Testament, however, violating a commandment was interpreted as commiting a misdeed against Yahweh. The Prophets and the entire New Testament invariably based the Law on the love of God and of neighbor, and on the person of Christ.[42]

Clearly, there were numerous christian authors who viewed sin primarily as a transgression of any of Christ's commandments. This is the foundation of Basil's moral teaching. Still, he is far removed from mere legalism. The fatherly providence of God, he said, is manifest in this world as 'a thought included in the command'.[43] For man, true wisdom therefore consists in recognizing this divine voice in all creation, and in obeying it.[44] Transgressing a commandment therefore means resisting a Person, God, out of perversion of heart.[45]

Since observance of the commandments constitutes *praxis*,[46] every sin is, from a certain point of view, an omission: according to the strange expression of Gregory of Nyssa, the Law was given in Paradise as 'material (*hylē*) for the free will to act upon'.[47] Sin is not the use of one's freedom but, on the contrary, a refusal to use its natural function: to respond to the love of God.

The Distinction Between Sins

Western manuals on morality traditionally list several categories of sin, and these are occasionally found as well in the East.[48] The main problem, however, remains the distinction between grave sins and 'venial' sins. It was as the result of its debate with Pelagianism that the Western Church developed its doctrine on venial sin,[49] which found its most precise formulation at the Council of Trent.[50]

The ascetic authors of all times insist instead on the need to understand and to sense the ugliness of each sin as much as possible. As Theophane the Recluse notes: 'Every sin is serious because it saddens God.... Nonetheless, there are degrees of seriousness, even degrees so different that certain sins seem light when compared to others.'[51] Still according to Theophane, a sin can be considered light for four reasons: 1) ignorance; 2) inadvertency; 3) comparison with other more serious sins; 4) the easier conversion of the sinner.[52] Point three indicates that the 'matter' is serious or less serious (*materia gravis* or *levis*).

On the other hand, Eastern writers have almost always remained under the influence of Basil, in whose eyes every transgression of the law of God is, in its matter, 'one and the same' transgression.[53] A schematic classification of grave sins was therefore very difficult for Eastern moralists.[54] They, and still more the ascetics, centered their attention not so much on the external result of the evil deed but rather on the inner perversion of the heart,[55] which could be 'serious' even when unimportant, external things were involved.

Chapter Seven

The Consequences of Sin

Sin obscures the image of God in man.[56] Depending on the tendencies and the various facets of this image,[57] attention may be centered on one or another anomaly of the state of sin. If human perfection is viewed mainly as the capacity of the mind to contemplate God, then sin is an obscuring, a beclouding, darkness.[58] When compared to the great gifts of free will and the governance of the world, sin is slavery.[59] Virtue imparts strength, love means constancy, sin is weakness and instability.[60] 'Eternal life' is succeeded by death,[61] the 'spiritual life' by 'suffocation of the spirit'.[62]

An expression borrowed from Greek secular literature became very popular with the Fathers: the sinner is like a person who has fallen into the mire (*borboros*), into 'the land of unlikeness'.[63] Because of Adam's disobedience, disorder and a lack of harmony have become evident throughout the world and in the natural structure of our being, but especially in the suffering heart which pleads for healing.[64]

The Social and Cosmic Dimensions of Sin

In the early popular mentality of the Russians there existed a mysterious relationship between the earth and man's diseased conscience. The earth, man's common mother, is sacred; but man can injure, profane, and hurt it. The sinner therefore confessed to the earth (by means of a ritual related to that of confession).[65] The Russians asked God for mercy and 'the Earth darkened by sin and dishonesty' for forgiveness and, like Alyosha in Dostoevsky's *The Brothers Karamazov*, they kissed it and promised to love it 'for all eternity'.[66]

Such rituals are an archaic survival of pagan beliefs mixed with a form of christian religiosity often called 'sophianic', which creates an unbreakable bond between the divine world, the perfection of man, and creation,[67] and insists on 'the responsibility of all for all', as Dostoevsky said.[68] In such a piety there is no room for any 'private', 'merely individual' sin. Every breach carries with it a social and cosmic disturbance and 'darkens the earth'.

3. REPENTANCE

Exhortations to Repentance

That repentance is absolutely necessary for everyone was commonly held. In the *Spiritual Meadow*, Abba Menas declares: 'Every age group, the young as well as the old, is in need of repentance if a person is to enjoy the eternal life of praise and glory; the young by bowing their head under the yoke when passions arise, the old by being able to change the wicked propensities to which they have so long inured themselves.'[1]

Repentance is called a second baptism: 'Repentance is the renewal of baptism and a contract with God for a second life.'[2] A good many spiritual writers (James of Sarug,[3] Theodore the Studite[4]) have echoed and commented on the expression of Gregory Nazianzen, 'the baptism of tears'.[5] The repentance of the Ninevites has inspired many preachers. When Ephrem spoke of it he was carried away by enthusiasm:[6] 'The soul is dead because of sin. . . . Tears falling on a corpse cannot bring it back to life; but if they fall on a soul they do revive and bring it back to life again.'[7]

One need only add that no sin is so serious that it cannot be forgiven through repentance and, on the other hand, that a relapse into sin should be no reason for the guilty person to despair. Depending on their temperament, some authors have stressed this consoling aspect more (John Chrysostom insisted on it to a surprising degree), while others at the same time have spoken about the danger of trying God's patience. It remains true, however, that no one has taught that it is impossible to come back to one's senses after failing repeatedly. Basil's teaching, for example, has been compared to a diptych; on the first panel one reads the words, 'all sins are extremely serious', and on the second, 'God forgives all sins if we repent suitably'.[8]

John Chrysostom seemed above all to fear the sinner's despair. *Monon me apognos*, 'only do not despair', are the closing words of his *Exhortation to the Lapsed Theodore*.[9] In his homilies he tried to show how easy forgiveness was: 'You have sinned? Say to God, "I have sinned." How much trouble is that? . . .'[10]

Chapter Seven

Essential Elements of Repentance

Repentance, a virtue in the Old Testament, a sacrament in the new, — P. N. Trembelas explains in his *Dogmatic Theology of the Orthodox Catholic Church*[11] — is defined by various names: penance, conversion, confession or opening up, second baptism, baptism of tears, absolution or reconciliation, and tablet of salvation.[12] He adds that Roman Catholics, not without reason, view penance as a virtue in the general sense of the term and as a sacrament instituted by Christ which strengthens and quickens the virtue of repentance and makes it fruitful indeed. Such a distinction, we would add, is manifestly useful. Yet a certain confusion which we come across in the spiritual writings of the East, a lack of precision between one type of repentance and the other, suggests that we consider the mystery of the forgiveness of sins within the total richness of salvation.

Repentance, then, contains several elements. The first one is 'to recognize the sins, to condemn the faults, and to blame oneself'.[13] It is an *automatokritos logismos* (a self-condemning thought).[14] According to a recent Russian author, repentance manifests our capacity to be human, to reflect on our actions.[15] This attitude is surely required of all Christians.[16] In the wake of Western handbooks of morality, the *Dictionnaire de la théologie catholique*[17] states that the soul renders this judgment 'about a certain past action which has pleased him [the person] at least momentarily'. Those in the East are less interested in the 'act' than in the 'state' of man.[18] Thus, for Theophane the Recluse, the feeling 'I am a sinner' is more important than 'I have sinned'.[19] And since the state of the heart is shown through feelings,[20] Eastern monks have always viewed as important such emotional signs as sorrow and tears, which accompany this evaluation of the past.[21]

This self-condemnation is woven into the entire context of the Gospel, into the preaching of the Kingdom (Mk 6:12). Progress in faith is therefore linked to the spirit of repentance.[22] For Symeon the New Theologian the baptism of tears was the true baptism of the Spirit, the great *phōtismos* (illumination) by which a man becomes all light.[23] It stands to reason that faith implies a resolution for the future. The Septuagint uses the verb *metanoein* (to repent), which aims at inner conversion, together with the verb *epistrephein* (to turn around), which connotes a practical change in attitude. For John Climacus, repentance 'is a contract with God for a second life',[24] a decision for the good, the *prothesis agathē*.[25]

If one were to inquire about the reasons for such a change in perception, one would have to study first the history of 'conversions' in the lives of the saints. Origen saw in the 'satiety' of sin the crucial moment that conditions the return to God,[26] and most authors believe in the efficacy of the fear of God, 'the beginning of knowledge' (Pr 1:7).[27] For John Climacus, repentance is 'the daughter of hope',[28] the assurance that all sins are forgiven.[29]

Sacramental Repentance

The Fathers insisted strongly on the conversion of the sinners: the decision to cleave to the good is essential.[30] To limit repentance to a personal conversion alone was not enough, however.[31] Indeed, sin is an act which affects the entire dimension of the person, including his essential relationship with the community of the Church.[32] From the third century onwards we have information about the ritual of repentance: the reconciliation, the prayer, and the laying on of hands; in the Eastern Church, unction was associated with it.[33] One of the oldest and clearest allusions to sacramental absolution is found in Origen.[34]

As to the prayer of reconciliation, with the development of the theology of the sacrament of confession, the deprecatory (impetratory) form was replaced in the West during the thirteenth century by the indicative form of absolution. In the East, however, the deprecatory form continued to be considered valid. P. N. Trembelas writes that 'It is almost superfluous to mention a statement by John Chrysostom[35] which confirms that priests have the authority not to pronounce the sin removed, but actually and absolutely to take it away.'[36]

At one point, meanwhile, Origen's personal views did shine through, namely in the connection he established between holiness and the power to remit sins.[37] Much later, Symeon the New Theologian explained and explicitly defended this thesis.[38]

There have undoubtedly been people in the East, especially

the Byzantines, who claimed for spiritual persons as such the power 'to bind and loose' whether they were priests or not. Before drawing any conclusions from this, however, one should carefully avoid a twofold confusion. First, two types of confession must be clearly distinguished: the accusation of sins with a view to receiving absolution for them, and the 'manifestation of thoughts', the aim of which was to receive guidance — a distinction which the documents do not always adequately make. To determine the meaning, one should read the entire context.[39] The exercise of power through the sacrament remained subject to the granting of a personal authorization, of an *entalma* (injunction) or an *enaltēria grammata*.[40]

But another confusion is possible. One cannot prevent nonpriests, both men and women, from becoming spiritual fathers and mothers.[41] Such spiritual direction brings with it a confession of faults and ends logically with a prayer by the spiritual father. And among the demands which God hears most readily, John Chrysostom specifically counted the prayer for the forgiveness of sins.[42] Besides, let us keep in mind that sacramental absolution in the Eastern rites is in the 'deprecatory' form.[43]

Disciplines and Acts of Repentance

There are manuals called *Exomologētaria*, corresponding to the Latin penitentials, in which are enumerated the various categories of sins and the penances or punishments which could be appropriately imposed for each of them.[44] The *Symbolic Books* of the Orthodox Church also mention penances, but they greatly stress their pedagogic character; consequently, the one who imposes them 'should not equally smite both the pious and the indifferent'.[45]

This insistence on the educational character of the canonical punishments was often motivated by the polemic against the 'expiatory' values given to them in the West.[46] One thing, however, cannot be denied: that penalties imposed by the confessor are works of christian praxis. Now, doing good is undoubtedly a true penance that wipes out sin and purifies the soul by fulfilling the commandments of God.[47] An Ethopian document entitled *The Mysteries of Heaven and Earth*[48] assures us that, 'In cases where the sins of the believer would be numerous and as big as mountains, if his righteousness resembles a spark, this remnant of righteousness will prevail and wipe out all his sins.'

Since christian practice varies widely, there were several ways to obtain remission of sins. In a curious Greek treatise entitled *From Saint Athanasius and Saint John, on the Different Ways of Finding Salvation, and on Repentance*,[49] the author enumerates ten ways of obtaining forgiveness of sin: 1) not condemning others, 2) forgiving trespasses, 3) being humble, 4) tears, 5) prayer, 6) alms and deeds of mercy, 7) conversion to the true faith, 8) illnesses and tribulations, 9) unceasing prayer, 10) declaring one's faith in Christ before a pagan emperor.

Among various deeds, almsgiving, an imitation of the mercy of God, is mentioned often and by preference.[50] James of Sarug explained its efficacy by means of an ingenious scheme: 'You have no tears? Buy tears from the poor. You have no sadness? Call the poor to moan with you. If your heart is hard and has neither sadness nor tears, with alms invite the needy to weep with you....'.[51]

A strange custom of having penances performed by another in exchange for giving him an alms is attested to in Ethiopia.[52] But it shows perhaps the great danger of attributing an 'expiatory' value to the deed itself, materially considered, whereas it ought to be an expression, a sign, of charity. Charity, by its very essence, destroys all sins.[53]

4. PENTHOS

Perpetual Compunction[1]

The Desert Fathers firmly believed in the rapid effect of repentance. Abba Poemen reassured a brother: 'At the moment when a man goes astray, if he says, I have sinned, immediately the sin ceases.'[2] And yet, among the ascetics, forgiveness never made the fountain of tears run dry. Chrysostom affirms how the promptness of remission is reconciled with perpetual compunction: 'Once purified from our faults, we must yet have the same faults before our eyes.'[3] Compunction (*penthos*) goes therefore much further than repentance (*metanoia*). John Climacus deals with them in two different chapters.[4] Lasting compunction has been justified by Origen's doctrine of the traces of sin in the soul[5] and by the second beatitude in the gospel (Mt 5:4).[6]

There is another difference: repentance is personal. To mourn for others is a sign of charity.[7] Secondly, penance in the strict sense must be tied to specific sins. Once they have been forgiven, it is no longer appropriate to recall them one by one. According to Mark the Ascetic, 'When sins are remembered in detail, they harm a man of good hope.'[8] *Penthos* is general, without specifics; psychologically, it is not conceived without tears. Repentance has no need of the emotions; compunction, by contrast, was to become the name for all the saintly emotions.

Penthos (from the same root as *pathos*) — *dolor, luctus,* mourning[9] obviously comes from Mt 5:4. Etymologically different, *katanyxis* (compunction) became practically synonymous with *penthos*. It is the latter term which has prevailed among the Greeks. The liturgy knows 'catanyctic' prayer whose aim it is to cause compunction, 'tears'.

The Eastern documents dealing with compunction are numerous.[10] The doctrine of *penthos* was so deeply engrained in the Syriac-speaking Christians that *penthountes* (mourners), *'abîlā*, became the name for monks. The habit of the hermit was the habit of repentance, of mourning.[11] Among the Armenians, the ninety-two *Sacred Elegies* by Gregory of Nareg[12] might deservedly be called 'catanyctic prayers'.

Examples abound in the Lives of the saints. Abba Taleleus, for example, had spent sixty years of his monastic life without ever ceasing to weep, and he always said: 'God has given us the present time to repent; let us therefore do our utmost to use it as well as we can'.[13]

Causes of Compunction

Gregory of Nyssa writes: *Penthos* [in general] is a sorrowful disposition of the soul, which arises from being deprived of something desirable.'[14] Now, in christian thought there is one word which includes everything desirable: salvation. Christian compunction is therefore mourning for a salvation lost by oneself or through others.

Consequently, the ascetics viewed mourning for relatives or friends, or for any occurrence whatever, as unreasonable. Barsanuphius wrote: 'One must absolutely not be saddened by anything in this world, but only by sin'.[15] John the Solitary arrived 'at the distinction of shedding tears . . . according to the three classes', that is to say, according to the three degrees of christian perfection.[16]

> The tears of the bodily man, even when he weeps before God in prayer, are provoked by the following thoughts: anxiety about his poverty, remembrance of his misfortunes, concern for his children, suffering coming from his oppressors, care for his house, remembrance of his dead relatives, and other such things. The continual harassament of these thoughts augments his sadness, and from sadness tears are born.
>
> At the mental stage, tears in prayer are provoked by the following thoughts: fear of judgement, a conscience burdened by sins, remembrance of God's goodness to himself, meditation on death, the promise of things to come. . . .
>
> The tears of the spiritual man are determined by these thoughts: admiration of God's majesty, awe before the depth of his wisdom, and other such things. . . . Moreover, these tears come not from sadness, but from an intense joy.[17]

The cause of *penthos* is thereby indicated. It takes different forms. First, there is 'the loss of our salvation'.[18] In the remembrance of past sins compunction finds its stimulant. The intensity of tears must correspond to the gravity of faults.[19] The possibility of future sins, the uncertainty of final victory make us fear judgement[20] and, according to Peter of Damascus, the origin of *penthos* is fear.[21] Numerous examples illustrate how saintly persons took daily faults tragically, because 'it is characteristic of the humble to blame and disparage himself'.[22]

Finally, concern for the eternal destiny of others should lead us to mourn when they are lost: 'One should weep with those who weep . . .'.[23] From neighborly love one undoubtedly moves to the love of God. We must admit that at first sight this appears only rarely as a source of compunction. One does not find ascetic *penthos* linked to the death of Christ.[24] Later, however, a different spirit would be seen in the mystics. For Symeon the New Theologian, it was indeed the love of God which caused him to shed many tears.[25]

The Effects of Penthos and Ways of Obtaining It

According to John Chrysostom a single tear extinguishes a brazier of faults and washes away the venom of sin.[26] In one sentence Ammonas summed up the doctrine of the Fathers on the curative power of *penthos*: 'Undisturbed, *penthos* drives away all wickedness'.[27]

Cleansed of their passions, those who weep will enjoy true peace. Mourning will be tantamount to consolation, *charopoion penthos* (joy-making mourning).[28] We learn from Athanasius that Antony sighed daily over himself.[29] And because of that, 'his countenance was extraordinarily beautiful...; he was never troubled because his soul was calm.'[30] 'A face bathed with tears has an undying beauty', Ephrem says.[31]

Compunction is a grace from God, occasionally given 'without effort, naturally'.[32] Yet, one should pray to obtain it.[33] Grace often makes use of external events, calamities, and punishments, to shake the hardness of the human heart. This is the aim of 'physical ill'.[34]

On our part, there are two great means for awakening and maintaining compunction: examination of conscience and meditation on the last things. Ephrem says, 'The beginning of *penthos* is to know oneself'.[35] And according to Chrysostom, 'When tears come from the fear of God they last forever'.[36]

It stands to reason that in order to maintain compunction one should remove the obstacles: frivolity and laughter;[37] and create a favorable atmosphere: poverty, solitude, and the practice of exterior penances.

Notes

1. PRAXIS

1. See Irénée Hausherr, 'Opus Dei', OCP 13 (1947) 195–218; *Etudes de spiritualité orientale*, OCA 183 (Rome, 1969) 121–44.

Negative Praxis

2. See *Apophthegmata*, Antonius 13; PG 65:80A; CS 59:3.
3. *De virginitate*; PG 28:253B.
4. *Logos* 23.7 ed. Augostinos Monachos, *Logos* 29 (Jerusalem, 1911) 132.
5. *Apophthegmata*, Theodore of Pherme 10; PG 65:189B: CS 59:75.
6. *Apophthegmata*, Elias 7; PG 65:185A; CS 59:72; see Karl Heussi, *Der Ursprung des Mönchtums* (Tübingen, 1936) 218–66.
7. *Apophthegmata*, John Colobos 37; PG 65:216CD; CS 59:93; see Adolf Harnack's article, '"*kopos (kopian, hoi kopiōntes)* dans le vocabulaire chrétien primitif', *Zeitschrift für neutestamentliche Wissenschaft* 27 (1928) 1–11.
8. *Homilia in principium Proverbiorum* 16; PG 31:421A.
9. *Homilia* 3.4; PG 34:469B.
10. See Špidlík, *Joseph de Volokolamsk*, 27.
11. See A. J. Festugière, *Contemplation et vie contemplative selon Platon* (Paris, 1936) 18ff; Špidlík, *Grégoire de Nazianze*, 50ff.
12. See René Arnou, 'Platonisme des Pères', DThC 12/2 (1935) col. 2366.
13. See *Grégoire de Nazianze*, 113ff.
14. See Kittel, 6:633.
15. Arnou, *Praxis et Theōria. Etude de détail sur le vocabulaire et la pensée des Ennéades de Plotin* (Paris, 1921, 2d ed., Rome, 1972).
16. See, for example, the *Apophthegmata Patrum* (PG 65:1560) where mention is made of a monk of Scete who was 'a great *praktikos*'. See S. Marsili, Giovanni Cassiano e Evagrio Pontico', *Studia Anselmiana* 5 (Rome, 1956) 90, n. 1.
17. *Commentarium in Joannem* 6.1; GCS 4:106; cf St Benedict's *Rule*, 43: the liturgy is the *opus Dei*.
18. See above, Chapter III, *Praktikē, Physikē, Theologikē*.
19. See below, *Transgressing the Commandments*.
20. *In psalmos* 5.13; PG 12:1173B; see A. Guillaumont, introd. to the *Traité pratique*, SCh 170 (1971) 50.
21. *Praktikos* 78; see SCh 170: 38ff; CS 4:36.
22. *Carminum liber* I.II.34, v. 130; PG 37:955.
23. See Chapter XI, 1.
24. The *Iliad*, X, 438; XXIII, 743; *Odyssey*, XXIII, 198.
25. *Iliad* III, 388; IV, 110.
26. *Busiris* 26.
27. See M. Gaucheron, 'Ascèse', *Catholicisme* I:890.
28. Ignatius of Antioch, *To Polycarp* 1.3, 2.3, 3.1.
29. See Marcel Viller and Michel Olphe-Galliard, 'Ascèse, Ascétisme, DS 1:941.
30. *Homilia 20 in Ieremiam*; ed. Klostermann, GCS 3:188, 25.
31. The Council of Ephesus (431) condemned the *asceticon* of the Messalians (Joseph de Guibert, *Documenta ecclesiastica christianae perfectionis studium spectantia* [Rome, 1931], n. 178.)
32. See J. Roldanus, *Le Christ et l'homme dans la théologie d'Athanase d'Alexandrie* (Leiden, 1968) 294ff.
33. See Ivan Kologrivof, *Essai sur la sainteté en Russie* (Bruges, 1953) 108ff.
34. See David Amand, *L'ascèse monastique de saint Basile* (Maredsous, 1949) 251ff.
35. See J. de Guibert, 'Abnégation (dépouillement, renoncement). Fondements scripturaires de l'abnégation chrétienne'. DS 1:67–73; I. Hausherr, 'Abnégation, renoncement, mortification: trois épouvantails et un peu de lumière', *Regina Mundi*, 6 (1957) 2–16; *id.*, *Etudes de spiritualité orientale* OCA 183 (Rome, 1969) 301–13.

36. *II. Apologia* 11.8–11.1; PG 6:463.
37. See I. Hausherr, 'Vocation chrétienne et vocation monastique selon les Pères', *Laïcs et vie chrétienne parfaite* (Rome, 1963) 33–115; *Études de spiritualité orientale*, 403–85, especially 466ff.
38. *Dialogue on the Soul and Human Passions* ed. Sven Dedering, *Joannes von Lykopolis. Ein Dialog über die Seele und die Affekte des Menschen* (Upsala, 1936) p. 85, trans. I. Hausherr, OCS 120 (Rome, 1939) 99.
39. See Gustave Bardy, 'Dépouillement chez les Peres', DS 3:458ff.
40. See Nikolaj Gogol, *The Divine Liturgy*, trans. R. Edmunds (London, 1960) 1ff.
41. See Hausherr, 'Abnégation, renoncement, mortification', *Christus* 20 (1959) 182–94.
42. Mt 16:25ff, Mt 10:39, Lk 14:26, 17:33, Jn 12:25.
43. See Chapter I, *Cosmic Spirituality*, and VIII, *A Double Spirituality*.
44. *Oratio* 57, cf. PG 120:297BC; in the title of Step 18 of *The Ladder* of John Climacus, the term *nekrōsis* simply means death.
45. See P. Th. Camelot, '*Enkrateia (continentia)*;, DS 4/1:357–70.
46. See Walter Grundmann, in Kittel, vol. 2 (1935) col. 340.
47. See Ottman Dittrich, *Geschichte der Ethik*, vol. 1 and 2, (Leipzig, 1926) *passim*.
48. *De Abrahamo* 24.
49. *De specialibus legibus* IV.112.
50. *Stromata* II.18.80–81; GCS 2:154ff; ANF 2:365.
51. 16–17; PG 31:957–965.
52. *Scholion 7 ad gradum 15*; PG 88:905B.
53. See Augustine, *De continentia*; PL 40:348–373, small work against the Manicheans and their 'deceptive continence'.

2. PURIFICATION FROM SIN

1. See Ladislas Szabó, 'Pur', VTB, 1068–74.
2. Plato, *Phaedo* 66d, 67bc, 70a; see René Arnou, *Le désir de Dieu dans la philosophie de Plotin* (2d ed. Rome, 1967) 139ff.
3. See Špidlík, *Grégoire de Nazianze*, 73.
4. See Chapters II, *Devotion to Christ*, and V, *Apokatastasis*.
5. See, for example, Gregory of Nazianzus, *Oratio*, 2.20; PG 35:812C: the entire life of his sister Gorgonia was nothing but a cleansing and a perfecting (*katharsis . . . kai teleiōsis*).
6. See Mauricio Gordillo, *Mariologia orientalis*, OCA 141 (Rome, 1954) 111ff.
7. Evagrius, *Praktikos* 78; SCh 171:667; CS 4:36.
8. *Načertanie christianskago nravoučenija* [*Christian Moral Teaching*] (Moscow, 1895) 145; Špidlík, *Théophane le Reclus*, 163.
9. See Thomas Aquinas, *Summa Theologiae* I-II.21.1.
10. *Homiliae* 47.9 (PG 34:801C); 7.2 (524D), 16.5 (616D–617A).
11. See I, *Spiritual Experience*, III, *The Happy Life, Orthodox Opposition, The Indirect Experience*, X, *The Messalians*, and XII.3.
12. Diadochus of Photice, *On Spiritual Knowledge and Discrimination: One Hundred Texts*; SCh 5:86; *The Philokalia*, Vol. 1 (1979) 253.
13. *De anima et resurrectione*; PG 46:93B.

Negative Praxis 199

14. *Ibid.*
15. *De oratione dominica* 5; PG 44:1192ff.
16. See Špidlík, *Théophane le Reclus*, XIII.
17. See *Apophthegmata* Arsenius 40; PG 65:105C; CS 59:15.4, Hausherr, *Penthos* CS 53:41.
18. *Čto jest' duchovnaja žizn* [*What is Spiritual Life*] (Moscow, 1897) 66ff; *Théophane le Reclus*, 153.
19. *Pis'ma k raznym licam* [*Letters to Various Persons*] (Moscow, 1892) 304, n: 37, *Théophane le Reclus*, 147.
20. See André Méhat, "Pénitence seconde' et 'péché involontaire' chez Clément d'Alexandrie', *Vigiliae Christianae*, 8 (1954) 225–33.
21. See Walter Völker, *Das Vollkommenheitsideal des Origenes* (Tübingen, 1931) 34ff.
22. *Pis'ma* [*Letters*] 3:24ff; *Théophane le Reclus*, 161.
23. See *Čto jest duchovnaja žizn*, Chapter 57, 203ff.
24. See *Théophane le Reclus*, 89ff.
25. See Völker, *Das Vollkommenheitsideal*, 31ff.
26. *Théophane le Reclus*, 161; John Chrysostom, *Homilia in Genesim* 22.1; PG 53:197.
27. *Mysli na každyj deň goda* [*Thoughts on Every Day of the Year*] (Moscow, 1881) 70.
28. See *Grégoire de Nazianze*, 75; M. Spanneut, *Le stoïcisme des Pères de l'Eglise*, 246; A. Jagu, 'Les philosophes grecs et le sens du péché', in *Théologie du péché* (Tournai, 1960) 189–240; Aimé Legrand, 'Aveuglement spirituel', DS 1:1175–85.
29. See Kittel 6 (1959) 634; Plato, *Protagoras* 357e, *Gorgias* 488a.
30. See Margherite Harl, *Origène et la fonction révélatrice du Verbe Incarné* (Paris, 1958) 357; Spannuet, *Le stoïcisme*, 246ff; J. Kirchmeyer, DS 6:825.
31. *De hominis opificio* 20; PG 44:200A.
32. See I. Hausherr, 'Ignorance Infinie', OCP 2 (1936) 352ff.
33. See below, p.331.
34. See J. Kirchmeyer, DS 6:825.
35. See *Grégoire de Nazianze*, 79.
36. *Praktikos* 41; SCh 171:595; CS 4:27.
37. Theophane the Recluse, *Put' ko spaseniju* [*The Way to Salvation*] (Moscow, 1908) 74.
38. Basil, *Homilia, Quod Deus non est auctor malorum* 7; PG 31:345; Špidlík, *La sophiologie de S. Basile*, 54.
39. M. Harl, *Recherches sur l'origénisme d'Origène: La "satiété" (koros) de la contemplation comme motif de la chute des âmes*, Studia Patristica VIII, TU 93 (Berlin, 1966) 373–405.
40. *Ibid.*, 374.
41. See Ignace de la Potterie, '" Le péché c'est l'iniquité (1 Jn 3:4)"' in *La vie selon l'Esprit*, Unam Sanctam, 55 (Paris, 1965) 65–83.
42. See Piet Schoonenberg, *L'homme et le péché* (Paris, 1967) 9ff.
43. *Homilia VII in hexaemeron*, 1; PG 29:149A; SCh 26:392 [trans. by A. C. Way, *Saint Basil, Exegetic Homilies*, 46:106].
44. See Špidlík, *La sophiologie de S. Basile*, 12ff.
45. *Ibid.*, 51ff.
46. See Chapter XI, *Obedience to Divine Commandments*.
47. Gregory Nazianzen, *Oratio* 38.12; PG 36:324B.

48. See Theophane the Recluse, *Načertanie christianskago nravoučenija* [*Christian Moral Teaching*] 19ff., 150, 162; Špidlík, *Théophane le Reclus*, 167ff.
49. See Denziger, *Enchiridion symbolorum*, 107ff: in the 1963 ed., p. 229.
50. See Leo Scheffczyk, 'Péché', EF III:391.
51. *Načertanie*, 163; Špidlík, *Théophane le Reclus*, 167.
52. *Nastavlenie o preuspěvanii v christianskoj žizni* [*Instruction on How to Make Progress in the Christian Life*] (Moscow, 1911) 20ff; Špidlík, *Théophane le Reclus*, 167.
53. D. Amand, *L'ascèse monastique de saint Basile*, 152ff; Špidlík, *La sophiologie*, 58ff.
54. See Stanislas Tyszkiewicz, *Moralistes de Russie* (Rome, 1951) *passim*.
55. See IV, *Aphorisms*, and IX,3.
56. See above, III, 2.
57. See above, III, *The Place of the Image*.
58. See, for example, Maximus the Confessor, *Quaestiones ad Thalassium*, Prol.; PG 90:253CD: 'Man is burdened by ignorance about his own cause'; see H. Crouzel, *Théologie de l'image*, 197–206.
59. Gregory of Nyssa, *De beatitudinibus Oratio* 3: PG 44:1228B [trans. by H. C. Graef, *St Gregory of Nyssa. The Lord's Prayer. The Beatitudes*, ACW 18 (1954)]; Gregory of Nazianzus, *Oratio* 19.13; PG 35:1060B.
60. See Špidlík, *Théophane le Reclus*, 164ff.
61. See Ephrem, *Sermones exegetici*, in *Is. 26:10*, edd. J. Assemani and P. Benedetti, (Rome, *Ephraem Syri, Opera omnia quae exstant graece, syriace, latine*, II,1740) 346: "The soul is dead through sin..."
62. See Špidlík, *Théophane le Reclus*, 164ff.
63. Michel Aubineau, 'Le thème du "bourbier" dans la littérature grecque profane et chrétienne', RSR 47 (1959) 185–214.
64. See *Théophane le Reclus*, 151.
65. I. Kologrivof, *Essai sur la sainteté en Russie*, 165ff.
66. *Ibid.*, 169.
67. See above, II *Equivalent Expressions*, V, *The Unity*..., and below, XIII.3.
68. See Špidlík, *I grandi mistici russi*, 354ff.

3. REPENTANCE

1. SCh 12 (1946) 213.
2. John Climacus, *Scala Paradisi* 5; PG 88:764B; [Luibheid and Russell, p. 121].
3. Paul Bedjan, *Mar Jacobi Sarugensis homiliae* (Paris-Leipzig, 1905–10) vol. 2:224.
4. *Great Catechesis* 27 ed. A. Papadopoulos-Kerameus, *Megalē katechechesis* (St Petersburg, 1904) 191; see Hausherr, *Penthos*, 144ff. [ET 130ff.].
5. *Oratio* 39.17, *In sancta Lumina*; PG 36:356 [*The Oration on the Holy Lights*, LNPF, series 2, vol. 7:352–59].
6. *Ephraem Syri Opera omnia quae extant graece*, ed. J. S. Assemani (Rome, 1732–46) vol. 5:359–86: 'Surge, vade in Ninive'.
7. *Sermones exegetici*, *In Is. 26:10*, *Ibid.*, vol. 2:346ff.
8. See Amand, *L'ascèse monastique de saint Basile*, 173.
9. PG 47:308; LNPF, series 1, vol. 9:111.
10. *De paenitentia* 2.2; PG 49:285.

Negative Praxis 201

11. *Dogmatique de l'Englise orthodox catholique*, Vol. 3 (Chevetogne-Tournai: Desclée de Brouwer, 1969) 255.
12. *Ibid.*, 259.
13. *Ibid.*, 275.
14. John Climacus, *Scala Paradisi* 5; PG 88:765B.
15. Vjačeslav Ivanov, *Smirenie vo Christě* [*Humility in Christ*] (Paris, 1925) 212.
16. See I. Hausherr, *Philautie. De la tendresse pour soi à la charité selon Maxime le Confesseur*, OCA 137 (Rome, 1952) 175: "The beginning of salvation for everyone is to condemn oneself'.
17. DThC 12: col. 733.
18. See above, Chapter IV, *The Heart*.
19. See Špidlík, *Théophane le Reclus*, 146ff.
20. See above, IV, *The Feelings of the Heart*.
21. See below, VII, 4.
22. See Theophane the Recluse, *Mysli* [*Thought for Every Day of the Year*], 9; V. Lossky, *The Mystical Theology of the Eastern Church*, 49.
23. See *Practical and Theological Chapters*, nn. 68, 69, 74, 75, etc:, SCh 51: 59ff.; CS 41:54ff.
24. *Scala Paradisi* 5; PG 88:764B.
25. *Ibid.*, 26; 1069D.
26. See Hal Koch, *Pronoia und Paideusis. Studien über Origenes und sein Verhältnis zum Platonismus* (Berlin-Leipzig, 1932) 112–59; Špidlík, *La sophiologie de saint Basile*, 21f.
27. See above, V, *The World of the Past*.
28. *Scala Paradisi* 5; PG 88:764B.
29. See *The Letter of Bishop Ammon*; Halkin, *Sancti Pachomii Vitae Graecae* (Brussels, 1932) 115, n. 28 [translated by A. Veilleux, *Pachomian Koinonia*, vol. 2 *Pachomian Chronicles and Rules*, CS 46 (Kalamazoo, 1981) 71–109].
30. See Bernhard Poschmann, *Paenitentia secunda. Die kirchliche Busse im ältesten Christentum bis Cyprian und Origenes* (Bonn, 1940).
31. See Paul Galtier, *L'Énglise et la rémission des péchés aux premiers siècles* (Paris, 1932).
32. See V. Vorgrimler, 'Pénitence', EF 3:411ff.
33. See *ibid.*, 424–25 (bibliogr.).
34. See Jean Daniélou, *Origène* (Paris, 1948) 81.
35. See *De sacerdotio* 3.6; PG 48:644.
36. Panagiotis N. Trembelas, *Dogmatique de l'Église Orthodoxe Catholique*, 3 vols., (Chevetogne-Tournai: Desclée de Brouwer, 1966–68) vol. 3:270.
37. *Commentarium in Matthaeum* 12.14; GCS 10:73; PG 13:981.
38. Especially in a letter sometimes attributed to John of Damascus; Michel Lequien, *S. Joannis Damasceni opera*, vol. 1 (Paris, 1712) 598–610; PG 95:283–304; see I. Hausherr, *Direction spirituelle en Orient autrefois*, 107ff.
39. Thus, at a time when the discussions about the minister of the sacrament were closed, St Germanus the Hagiorite († about 1336) chose for himself several spiritual fathers in succession, but went to Pezos the hieromonk to receive absolution (Philotheus Coccinos, *Life of Saint Germain the Hagiorite*, n. 11, 14, 24, ed. P. Ioannou in *Analecta Bollandiana* 70 (1952) 47; See I. Hausherr, *Direction spirituelle*, 106.
40. Examples may be found in Leunclavius, *Jus Graeco-Romanum* (Frankfurt, 1596) vol. 1:437; *entalma eis to genesthai patera pneumatikon*; cf. Hausherr, *Direction Spirituelle*, 108ff.

41. See Hausherr, *Direction*, 105ff.
42. See *De Anna sermo* 4.6; PG 54:667.
43. See Alfred Vacant, 'Absolution: sous forme déprécative' DThC 1 (1909) 244–52.
44. See the *Exomologetarion* of Nicodemus the Hagiorite (Venice, 1794); Sergei Smirnov, *Drevněrusskij duchovnik* [*The Spiritual Father in Old Russia*] (Moscow, 1914) 32ff.
45. See Trembelas, 295ff.
46. *Ibid.*; on the meaning of the term 'expiation', see Louis Moraldi, 'Expiation', DS 4/2:2026–45.
47. See the Preface to Basil's *Long Rules*, PG 31:900B.
48. A fifteenth-century work, edited by Jules Perruchon and Ignazio Guidi, PO 1:86; see John Climacus, *Scala Paradisi* 26; PG 88:1069.
49. Published by N. Suvorov in *Vizantijskij Vremennik* 10 (1903) 55–61.
50. See Hausherr, *Penthos*, 144 (ET 130].
51. Paul Bedjan, *Mar Jacobi Sarugensis Homiliae* (Paris-Leipzig, 1905–10) vol. 2:226.
52. See S. Cobat, *Journal of a Three Years Residence in Abyssinia* (London, 1834) 346.
53. See Edmondo Dublanchy, 'Charité: Effets de l'acte de charité parfaite', DThC 2 (1910) 2236ff.

4. PENTHOS

1. Myrrha Lot-Borodine, 'Le mystère des larmes', *Vie spirituelle* 48 (1936) [65] –[110]; I. Hausherr, *Penthos. La doctrine de la componction dans l'Orient chrétien*, OCA 132 (Rome, 1944) [Translated by Anselm Hofstader, *Penthos. The Doctrine of Compunction in the Christian East*, CS 53 (Kalamazoo, 1982)].
2. *Apophthegmata patrum*, Poemen 99: PG 65:345C; CS 59:181.
3. *Homilia 7 de paenitentia* 4; PG 49:328.
4. *Scala Paradisi* 5 (on repentance); PG 88:764–81; step 7 (on *penthos*), col. 801ff.
5. *In Matthaeum Commentarium series* 30; GCS 11:56.22.
6. See Theophanes Cerameus, *Homilia* 51; PG 132:913.
7. See Mark the Ascetic, *De paenitentia* 11; PG 65:981A.
8. *De his qui putant se ex operibus iustificari*, PG 65:952C, n. 139; see also n. 140; (Selections from 'To Those who Think to be Justified by Deeds' are found in *Early Fathers from the Philokalia*, tr. E. Kadloubovsky and G. E. H. Palmer (London: Faber and Faber, 1954), 86–93; n. 139 in the PG is n. 151 in *Early Fathers*.]
9. See Anastasio Gomez, 'Compunctio lacrymarum. Doctrina de la compunción en el monacato latino de los siglos IV-VI', *Collectanea* OCR 23 (1961) 232–53.
10. *Verba Seniorum*, liber 3: *De compunctione* (PL 73:1029ff); John Climacus, *Scala*, gradus 7 (PG 88:801–16); Antiochus, *Homilia* 90, (PG:1709–12); Manuel Paleologus put 'catanyctic prayers' into verse, PG 156:576; see Hausherr, *Penthos*, 18ff. [ET 14ff.].
11. See Ephrem, *Hymns to Abraham Kidunaya and Julian Saba*, ed. T. J. Lamy, *S. Ephraem Syri hymni et sermones*, 3 vols. (Mechlin, 1889) vol. 3, col. 843, 14ff.

Negative Praxis 203

12. *Grégoire de Narek: Le livre de Prières*, trans. (into French) by I. Kéchichian SCh 78 (1961).
13. John Moschus, *Pratum spirituale* 59; SCh (1946) 102; PG 87:2911.
14. *De beatitudinibus* 3; PG 44:1244A.
15. *Letter* 682, ed. Nicodemus the Hagiorite (Venice, 1816) 327; French translation from Greek by Lucien Regnault and Philippe Lemaire, and from Georgian by Bernard Outtier *Barsanuphe et Jean de Gaza, Correspondance* (Solesmes, 1971), Letter 674, 437. [English translation projected by Cistercian Publications —ed.]
16. Translated by I. Hausherr, *Jean Solitaire (Pseudo-Jean de Lycopolis). Dialogue sur l'âme et les passions des hommes*, OCA 120 (Rome, 1939) 40ff.
17. *Ibid.*
18. John Chrysostom, *De compunctione* 1.10; PG 47:409.
19. See Paul Evergetinos, *Synagogē* II.32 (Constantinople, 1861) 103.
20. *Ibid.*, III.9 (Constantinople, 1861) 22–27.
21. *Philokalia*, vol. III (Athens, 1960) 132 cf. *The Philokalia, The Complete Text*, vol. 3 (London, 1984) 88, 199.
22. See Paul Evergetinos, *Synagogē* I, 40 (Constantinople, 1861), 142.
23. *Homilia in martyrem Julittam* 9; PG 31:257D.
24. The *Apostolic Constitutions* V, 19–20 (Funk, 295) positively forbid mourning for Christ.
25. See I. Hausherr, *Vie de Syméon le Nouveau Theologien*, OC 12/45 (Rome, 1928), Introd. xxxiff.
26. *De paenitentia* 7.5; PG 49:334.
27. *Instruction* 4.14; PO 11:476; *to penthos ekdiokei pasas tas kakias atarachos.*
28. John Climacus, *Scala Paradisi* 7; PG 88:801C.
29. *Vita Antonii* 45; PG 26:908C.
30. *Ibid.*, 67; col. 840.
31. *Sermo asceticus*, ed Assemani, *Ephraem Syri opera omnia quae extant graece* (Rome, 1732–46) vol. I: p. 60.
32. Basil, *Regulae brevius tractatae* 16; PG 31:1092.
33. Ephrem, *Sermo asceticus*; Assemani, I: p. 60.
34. See above, Chapter V, *Divine Providence within Evil.*
35. Assemani (n. 31), vol. I:254f: *Quod non oportet ridere et extolli sed plangere potius et nos ipsos deflere.*
36. *Homilia 3 in Epistolam ad Philemonem*, 4; PG 62:204.
37. Basil, *Reg. Brev.* 31; PG 31:1104B.

8

FLIGHT FROM THE WORLD AND THE RENUNCIATION OF THE FLESH

1. THE CHRISTIAN IS NOT OF THIS WORLD

Flight from the World in Greek Thought

SPONTANEOUS RENUNCIATION of the world seems not to have been attractive to the Greek mind. For the word *kosmos* alone already spoke of order, of beauty, of value.¹ Nonetheless, the ancients certainly knew of an eudaimonistic *fuga mundi* (flight from the world) which tended to prove that a life detached from earthly things, and solitary, was not without happiness; on the contrary, that it was the best way.²

In Pythagoreanism the renunciation of material possessions was motivated by religious among other, considerations.³ The starting point of Plato's metaphysic was a yearning for the Absolute. 'This is the effort to be undertaken: to take flight from this world to the other as quickly as possible (*pheugein hoti tachista*). To escape is to become like God as far as this is possible (*phygē de homoiōsis theǫ kata ton dynaton*).'⁴ This observation leads one to think that the 'flight' of which Plato speaks is nothing other than a concentration of the mind on spiritual values; it does not therefore necessarily imply an actual separation from earthly things. Plotinus, too, thought above all of inner detachment: the flight of the one to the One (*phygē monou pros monon*).⁵ Porphyrius, his biographer, nonetheless describes the master's asceticism and the usefulness of a concrete separation.⁶

Chapter Eight

Flight from the World in Christianity

Israel was deeply convinced that the created world was very good (Gen 1:31). Nevertheless, the Jews did not totally ignore the idea of 'flight from the world', as we see in Abraham (Gn 12:1), the experience of the Exodus (Ex 16:3), and other passages. In the time of Christ, people were convinced that the encounter between Israel and the Messiah would take place 'in the desert', that is, far from the world of sin.[7] St Paul and St John have contributed to the theology of flight from the world by deepening the concept of 'this world' which does not know Christ (Jn 1:10) but hates him and his word (7:7, 15:18, 17:14–16). The spirit of the world does not come from God (1 Co 2:12); its wisdom is 'foolishness to God' (1 Co 3:19). All this shows that the world is subjected to Satan: 'The entire world lies in the power of the Evil One' (1 Jn 5:19, Cf 1 Co 2:6, 2 Co 4:4). In this situation, leaving the world seemed to Christians a necessary outcome of the love of God.[8]

'To leave the world', Philoxenes of Mabbug said, is the path whereby one becomes 'an imitator of Christ, a companion of Jesus, and adorned with Christ'.[9] The flight from the world is explained by the fact that two loves cannot develop in the same person.[10] For Theophane the Recluse, nostalgia for the spiritual life is shown 'in a general discontent with every creature';[11] the first temptation is to fall under 'the stultifying power' of this world and thereby to become insensitive to the spirit of Christ.[12]

Various Aspects of Flight from the World

Flight from the world, in the christian sense, presupposes a moral situation caused by sin. It does not imply a dualistic structure of reality.[13] And yet authors tried to state precisely how one could actually flee this world which is opposed to Christ. In this attempt it has never been easy to indicate the boundaries between the moral and physical meanings of flight. On several concrete points, the Gospel, ancient dualism, and common psychological experience agree. In the fervor of their exhortations, ascetics were not always concerned with precision of concepts. All this should be taken into account when one is faced with the radical opposition between the 'two worlds' so frequently found in the ascetic writings and expressed in various terms.

The present world — the world to come. The dualism in Eastern religions is chiefly temporal and opposes the present world to that in which the good divinity destroys the adversary powers.[14] Nothing is easier than to express christian eschatological hope in the same terms. 'Knowing the good they were to receive, the saints hated this world for that reason.'[15] It is said especially that 'this expectation, this search for the City to come always lives somehow in the depths of the Russian mind'.[16] But it has been evident since the beginnings of Christianity in the christians' readiness to accept martyrdom,[17] and in the ascetics' laments about this life which is 'short, ephemeral, filled with suffering and snares'.[18] On the other hand, christian eschatologism is essentially different from Eastern religions in that the eternal life (*zoē*) is being realized within this ephemeral life (*bios*).[19].

The visible — invisible world. Platonic dualism is ontological and is expressed according to a spatial scheme: in the present world there is the superior, spiritual sphere and the material sphere. True life is found in the spiritual. Christian authors naturally did not forget these speculations and they drew their inspiration largely from philosophic texts to prove that the ideal of the ascetic is 'to become spirit after being divested of the flesh and the fettering mass' and to contemplate God.[20] The real meaning of this 'Platonism of the Fathers'[21] is apparent:[22] Christians did not identify the Platonic 'invisible' with the 'spiritual' as they conceived it.[23]

The public life — the solitary life. Euthymia, tranquility, personal blessedness, invited the pagan sage to renounce the business of the world and of public society.[24] The society which the Christian avoids is that of 'vain and thoughtless men'.[25] It remains true that for certain monks flight from people took on a rather fierce significance.[26]

The opinions of the world — the domain of truth. More than philosophers,[27] the Christian is separated from the world because he cannot accept its ways of thinking. 'Accomplishments for seculars are faults for monks; accomplishments for monks are faults for seculars,' wrote Maximus the Confessor.[28] Flight is *metanoia*, the conversion to faith.

Forgetting God — the true gnosis. The knowledge which the monks sought through 'flight' was not philosophic theory but the unceasing remembrance of God, contemplation.[29] In order to hear the sweet voice of God[30] they willingly sacrificed all the solicitudes and conversations of man, every obstacle to continual prayer.[31]

Sin — virtue. The world to be avoided can indeed be defined by the Platonic term 'land of unlikeness', by taking this expression in the christian sense as everything that darkens the perfection of the divine image and likeness in man.[32] According to Abba Isaiah, the world is 'the attraction of the soul to sin'.[33] There is therefore an *anachoresis* which is indispensable and possible to all, the withdrawal from sin (*tēs hamartias he anachōrēsis*)[34] the concern with freeing oneself from every impediment to salvation.[35]

Poverty

Those who possess the goods of this earth in abundance are of 'the world'. The Old Testament reveals the spiritual riches of poverty, and the New Testament recognizes the privileged heirs of the Kingdom of God among the true poor.[36] In order to translate *anaw*, the afflicted man 'brought low', the Septuagint also used — besides *ptōchos* (poor) and *penēs* (needy) — *prays* (humble) which evokes the idea of the meek man, 'at peace', even in affliction. But it always is someone who suffers and is 'indigent'.

Patristic reflections, especially in the homilies 'against the rich',[37] but also in Basil's monastic *Rules*, start from a different point of view. In an unreasoning nature which automatically carries out the creative world of God, there are neither rich nor poor, because for all 'God has created nothing unnecessarily and has omitted nothing that is necessary'.[38] Human wisdom consists in understanding this relationship and the just measure of one's own 'need', and in avoiding thereby either overabundance or indigence.[39]

But is the person who satisfies all his needs still poor in the biblical sense? Only if he does not forget that the first of his 'needs' is the spiritual welfare of souls. This calls for an assimilation to the poor Christ (*christopodražatel'naja nisčeta*, as the Russians say) which often presupposes a lack of things necessary to this life.⁴⁰

Because material poverty facilitates *penthos*,⁴¹ John of Pitra, a monk in the *Spiritual Meadow*, gave the following testimony to Egyptian monks:

> Love poverty and abstinence. Believe me when I tell you that when I was in Scetis as a youth, one of the Fathers suffered from spleen, and they looked for a little vinegar in the four lauras at Scetis without finding any, so great was the poverty and the abstinence. Now there were about three thousand five hundred Fathers over there.⁴²

True poverty is of course spiritual; it is the poverty of the person 'who, in severing his attachment to his body, has entrusted himself to the care of God and spiritual men'.⁴³ Scorn for money⁴⁴ is a possibility for someone who has tasted the things on high.⁴⁵ The result of this attitude is *amerimnia* (freedom from care) or *phrontidōn apothesis* (putting away anxiety), the freedom necessary for prayer.⁴⁶ On the other hand, poverty is troubled by 'anxiety about the future,'⁴⁷ by sadness over material loss, because the person 'who worries about something, has not yet become non-possessive'.⁴⁸ The miraculous stories in the biographies of monks are often used to instill faith in providence in those who practise true poverty, for 'according to Scripture, those who seek the Lord lack no good thing'.⁴⁹

Pure trust in providence, then, seemed threatened by the fact that monasteries owned common possessions. At the Council of Moscow in 1503 two clearly opposed tendencies confronted one another: on the one side stood Nilus of Sora and his hermits, advocates of absolute poverty (*nest'ažatele*, from the word *nest'ažanie*, *aktēmosynē*, contempt for material possessions); on the other, the cenobites, followers of Joseph of Volokolamsk, who wanted to combine the monk's individual poverty with ecclesiastic possessions.⁵⁰ It was Joseph's opinion which prevailed at the Council.

The teaching of Joseph of Volokolamsk was perfectly in keeping with that of Basil or Theodore the Studite: 'No personal property, everything in common'. To keep this rule, the monk must retain for his private use only what is strictly necessary; he can neither buy nor sell nor receive anything without the permission of his superior.[51]

The situation of the monks we know from the *Sayings of the Fathers* was different. The solitary had to provide for his own needs by the work of his hands. To accept alms was considered a shameful thing.[52] Likewise, Abba Mark testified in the *Spiritual Meadow*: 'I accept nothing, for the work of my hands feeds me and those who come to me because of God.'"[53]

A Double Spirituality?

Everything that is exists to evoke in the human mind the thought of the Creator;[54] at the same time every created thing can, because of sin, lead us away from the remembrance of God. In the second case, renunciation of the world takes on a general meaning: 'The mind of the Christian ought not to be distracted', said Basil 'nor by anything drawn from the recollection of God.'[55] Evagrius' contemplative bent was characterized by such a total forgetting of the things of this world.[56] For Basil, the first case would be more characteristic: a 'paradisal' state where man nourishes the remembrance of God through a contemplation of the universe.[57]

We seem therefore to be in the presence of two different and radically opposed trends. One would find its place in the desert or behind the closed windows of a cell; the other would open its windows wide because God has created wonderful things in heaven and on earth. Some tell us that Eastern spirituality belongs to the first, while others maintain that it is, by contrast, the people of the East who, in their paschal joy try to see God in nature, in animals, and in their neighbor.

In fact, however, Christianity does not admit of two opposing tendencies in dealing with the problem of the world. It is certainly possible to stress one aspect, one phase of the redemptive activity, more than the other. In the *Hexaemeron*, for example, Basil stood on the first plane of creation.[58] In the *Asceticon*, by contrast, he presented radical renunciation as necessary for contemplation.[59] But one always presupposes that the perfect will arrive at the third phase and will then open their eyes to rediscover the wonders of the visible world.

Flight from the World 211

The 'Paschal Joy of the Eastern Church' is woven into a pattern.[60] Exhortations and monastic rules have been written not for the perfect but rather for *eisagomenoi*, novices,[61] for those to whom 'the whole world is crucified for the sake of Christ'.[62] Hence this frequent insistence on radical flight from all things created.

2. THE SOLITARY LIFE

Affective and Effective Flight from the World

It is sometimes said that the New Testament mentions only an affective detachment from the world (Cf. 1 Co 7:29-31). Yet St Paul recognized that contact with earthly realities could endanger one's inner sense of justice: the married man is 'divided' (1 Co 7:33-34); 'people who long to be rich are a prey to temptation' (1 Tm 6:9).

Renunciation, of course, means above all an inner disposition: taking no interest in the doings of the world.[1] A more active view of flight from the world is found in the African Fathers of the second and third centuries.[2] For their point of view, the instructions of Clement of Alexandria are very important. He taught in a masterful way that to make use of the things of this world and to renounce them (the flight) are complementary manifestations of temperance.[3]

Origen may be considered the forerunner of flight from the world in the monastic sense. He believed that inner detachment from the things of this world is indispensable to the service of God: 'I say, we must flee it [the world] not in place, but in thought.'[4] But anyone progressing in the ascent to God seeks a separation that is ever more intense. Such a man is found 'in no worldly deed, in no fleshly thing, in vain conversation'.[5]

Flight from the World in the Hesychast Tradition

By vocation, the monk is devoted exclusively to the pursuit of union with God through prayer, which presupposes total detachment, a renunciation of everything that could slow down the spiritual ascent. The one question that is asked of him is to know how far exterior solitude is necessary or useful for inner quietude.

A voice from heaven told Arsenius: 'Flee, be silent, remain quiet (*hesychaxe*)',[6] and this has impressed the hesychasts of all ages.[7] A person is alone when he runs no risk of meeting another human being in his habitual living area. This is flight in the material sense. He is still alone as long as he does not converse with anyone. This is the solitude of silence. Finally, he is alone when his mind at its inmost depth has no interlocutor, when *logismoi* (thoughts) do not trouble his mind. This is the solitude of the heart.[8]

Morally speaking, the most profound solitude is the third, silence of the heart. In the opinion of the hesychasts, however, it could not be separated from material solitude, the flight from human society, and silence. In the language of the Eastern ascetics, *hesychia* (stillness) is the equivalent of *erēmia*, the solitary life.

In Praise of the Eremitic Life

The origin of the eremitic life likely coincides with the very beginnings of philosophy.[9] The flight from men has as its aim the good of the intellect, instruction, or contemplation. Christian hermits love solitude only to find God, there to do 'the work of God', prayer.

Ammonas, the disciple of Antony, represented the best tradition of the Egyptian solitaries when he wrote: 'First, solitude; solitude begets asceticism and tears; tears engender fear; fear brings forth humility and [the gift of] foresight; foresight engenders charity. Charity makes the soul free of disease, dispassionate; after all these things, man then understands that he is not far from God.'[10]

Contrary to Basil's criticism of them,[11] the hermits did not believe they were slighting the first and second commandment of the Gospel, and they viewed their obstinacy in remaining alone as the best way of loving their neighbor, in God.[12]

If this charity seems too negative, the cenobites often provided a balance to the solitaries. Encounters between the advocates of each tradition occasionally took on a polemic tone.[13] A calm and very judicious confrontation can be found in Cassian's Nineteenth Conference, of Abba John. His conclusion has become common teaching in the East: either of the two ways of life is partial (*merikē*). There are advantages on both sides. Yet the solitary life is more perfect. No one, however, should be allowed to choose it before he has learned discretion and obedience, before he is able to guide himself without any danger of illusions.[14]

Various Forms of the Eremitic Life

The hermit Monks (*erēmitai*), also called *anchorites* (*anachore tai*)[15] often practised their withdrawal from the world in an eccentric manner. Evagrius the Scholastic[16] mentions *grazing* or 'browsing' monks (*boskoi*),[17] who had no fixed abode. The *dendrites* lived in trees;[18] the *statics* remained standing in open air.[19] An equally rugged way of defending solitude was *stylitism*[20] When, over the centuries, places conducive to the eremitic life became more and more scarce, *recluses*[21] locked themselves in a cell. *Xeniteia*[22] was life as a stranger, to which an individual condemned himself by going away to live alone in a land not his own.

The *lavras* (*laura, vicus*), hermit colonies around a church, softened the inconveniences of this life of isolation.[23] On Mount Athos, the *sketes* (*sketai*) form a group of isolated houses or cottages. The *kalyves* (*askētikai kalybai*) are inhabited either by a small group of anchorites or by a single hermit (*hesychastēria*, hermitages). In the *kellia* (cells), rustic houses, monks live under the direction of an elder. The *kathismata* are hermitages rented to a monk, who is sometimes a bishop who has resigned. Furthermore, there are the *gyrovagi* (roving monks), called *kaviotes* (*kabiōtai*), who belong to no monastic foundation.[24]

Finally, one saying applies, like a verse from Scripture, to the ascetics of all ages: 'Keep to your cell, and your cell will teach you everything!'[25] Only in his cell is a monk in his element, like a fish in water.[26]

3. FLIGHT FROM THE WORLD IN CENOBITISM

Life in Common, Separated from the World

Through his unrelenting criticism of the hermits,[1] Basil restored the flight from the world to its moral sense. Renunciation of the world remains an ascetic principle for everyone, even those who live, as we say, 'in the world'.[2] By imposing the form of cenobitism on the *fuga mundi* Basil succeeded in assigning a special place within the community of the Church to christian ascetism.

On the other hand, the brothers became conscious of their uniqueness and, as the years pass, we hear them speak about 'outsiders', 'seculars', 'laity', the 'people of the world'. As the Basilian *Asceticon* progressed, an increasing hostility appeared in it towards public life, towards 'this ordinary life' which removes one from the remembrance of God.[3] The Basilian monk therefore broke off relations with the world and its human friendships.[4] He came to wear a special habit, a distinctive mark, a uniform vestment, symbolizing his separation from the world.[5] He made journeys only rarely and his superiors authorized them only cautiously.[6] Trades and labor which could cause detriment to the recollected life were gradually excluded from the monastery.[7] Works of charity and assistance do, of course, bring the monk into contact with the world, but it was taken for granted that he was not thereby contaminated by the world.

Guests

Hospitality is an ancient monastic virtue. Abba Isaiah wanted the charity for guests to be exquisite, but he added: 'The greetings you extend [to a brother come from afar] will have to keep the measure dictated by the fear of God.... Refrain from asking him questions about things of no profit to yourself; have him pray...'[8] Barsanuphius advised that words be as brief as possible: 'Receive your guest; after you greet him ask "How are you?" Then remain seated with him in silence.'[9]

Monasteries did, however, receive outside guests. The general principle for these cases is found in Basil's *Long Rules*, 32: 'In general, neither relatives nor any other extern should be allowed to talk with the brethren, unless we are certain that their conversation will bring about the edification and perfection of the soul. If, however, it be necessary to hold discourse with those who have been once admitted, it should be done by those who have the gift of speaking...'.[10] The guestmaster therefore exercised a type of apostolate.

Relatives

The ancient monks called for a complete break with their relatives. They were reminded of the words of the Gospel: 'If anyone comes to me without hating his father, mother, ..., he cannot be my disciple' (Lk 14:26).[11] Symeon the Studite, the spiritual father of Symeon the New Theologian, summarized this entire monastic tradition by saying: 'Upon entering the cenobium, engrave on your mind the true idea that all your relatives and friends are dead.'[12]

Basil, meanwhile, distinguished three different attitudes to be adopted towards relatives, depending on their spiritual condition. If they, too, live in the monastery, they are united equally to all the brothers; their care devolves upon the superior. If they remained in the world, remembering them causes nothing but distraction; we can be of no assistance to them in the area of virtue. Finally, if they hold the commandments of God in light esteem, they are for us no more than publicans, and we should not receive them when they come to see us.[13] The Basilian monk can say no more special prayers for his relatives than for anyone else, believer or unbeliever.[14]

Following this principle, Joseph of Volokolamsk took care of his father who had entered the monastery. But when his mother visited him once, he repeated to her the words which we read in the *Sayings of the Fathers*: 'You will see me no longer in this life!'[15]

Silence

The flight from men will never be total, even if one wants it to be. Solitude must therefore be completed or intensified by silence. Silence is the portable cell which the man of prayer does not leave easily. 'If you are silent, you will have peace wherever you live', Abba Poemen said.[16]

In antiquity, Pythagoras is reputed to have understood the value of silence best of all. The Pythagorean type of life (*pythagoreos tropos tou biou*),[17] was held in high esteem by Christians. One of the most famous maxims, which the *Sayings of the Fathers* put into the mouth of Arsenius,[18] 'I have often repented of having spoken, but never of having been silent', can be traced back to Simonides († 467 BC).[19]

Among Eastern monks there were 'the silent ones';[20] Sabas the Younger († 1349), for example, kept perfect silence during twenty years of wanderings.[21]

The rule given by Basil was ordinarily valid for all: 'In general, every word which adds nothing to the proposed goal in the service of God is idle; even if what is said would be good in itself, the danger of that kind of word is so great that if it is not directed toward the edification of faith, the one who has uttered it cannot escape this danger, not even through the goodness of the word; it will sadden the Holy Spirit in so far as it would have contributed nothing to edifying faith.'[22]

Abstaining from Laughter

According to Aristotle, 'those who joke in a tasteful way are called *eutrapeloi* (of graceful wit)'.[23] Thomas Aquinas therefore counted *eutrapelia* among the virtues.[24] In Eph 5:4, however, the term is understood in a pejorative sense.

Eastern, especially monastic, literature almost unanimously condemned fits of laughter, jesting, idle talk, and frequently even a smile:[25] 'Since Christ condemns those who laugh', Basil said, 'it is clear that no time for laughter is allowed the believer.'[26] If the Coptic theologian Ibn Saba (at the end of the thirteenth century) may be trusted, laughter was mentioned, in Egypt, along with other works of Satan during the ceremony of baptism.[27]

All this rigorism may be explained by a concern for perpetual compunction. However, this absolute prohibition of laughter was softened by the theory of moderation so dear to Clement of Alexandria,[28] and by a distinction Basil made between laughter as an uncontrolled impulse and 'a cheerful smile which gives evidence of merriment of soul'.[29]

Flight from Divisions, Unanimity

With perfect simplicity, Abba Arsenius explained the stern intransigence of the solitaries: 'Abba Mark said to Abba Arsenius, "Why do you avoid us?" The old man said to him, "God knows that I love you, but I cannot live with God and with men. The thousand and ten thousands of the heavenly hosts have but one will, while men have many. So I cannot leave God to be with men."'[30]

What the solitaries considered incompatible, Basil resolutely wanted to harmonize: to live among men, to obey men and, in intention, to remain with God alone. In the early church in Jerusalem, 'the multitude of believers had but one heart and one mind' (Ac 4:32). 'There was very evidently no dwelling apart for any of them', Basil commented.[31] The legislator of cenobitism, then, frequently emphasized 'that one should live with the brothers united in spirit (*sympsychoi*).'[32] For those living together, to flee the world is to flee from everything that divides: envy, wounding words, discussions (even theological), heresies, schisms — all of which stem from one source, 'a great lack of charity towards God and towards one another'.[33]

4. RENUNCIATION OF THE FLESH

Temperance — the Broad and Narrow Meanings

In commenting on the famous line from Deuteronomy (15:9) 'Give heed to thyself', Basil pointed out a gradation. There is 1) 'myself', and this 'I' is identified with 'the soul and the mind' (*he psychē kai ho nous*); 2) what is 'ours', that is, our body and our senses; 3) what is 'extraneous to us, that is, objects and other appurtenances of life'. To give heed to oneself means 'to attend neither to the goods you possess nor to the objects that are round about you, but to yourself alone.'[1] Attention to oneself therefore includes the renunciation of everything in the second and the third categories. With this easy scheme, Basil justified the necessity of flight from the world and of the struggle against the flesh, or temperance 'which betokens the man who has died with Christ and mortifies his members that are upon the earth' (Cf. Col 3:3-5); this temperance is 'the mother of chastity, the protector of health, the effective remover of obstacles to the fruitfulness of good works in Christ'.[2]

Yet, if we keep in mind that in ascetics' teaching the concepts 'world' and 'flesh' carry the moral meaning of what is in revolt against man's true nature (my 'I'), the philosophic scheme loses a good deal of its apparent precision. Still, it is to be observed because of its practical utility, for certain temptations do indeed seem to be associated with the body, and others with external objects.

One can say with John Climacus that temperance is 'the name common to all the virtues',[3] or, in a stricter sense, that its function is 'to control man's irrational part',[4] and to subjugate the covetousness of the flesh.

The Pauline Basis of the Doctrine of Renunciation of the Flesh

'If you are guided by the Spirit you will be in no danger of yielding to self-indulgence...' (Ga 5:16). Basil compared the spirit and the flesh to two armies arrayed for battle. To bring aid to the one means to assure its victory. Anyone who joins the flesh fights against the spirit, and anyone who crosses over to the camp of the spirit brings the flesh into subjection.[5]

Philosophic views were often mixed with biblical convictions[6] to prove that temperance,[7] or the renunciation of the pleasure of the flesh, is the pre-eminent monastic virtue. 'The Apostle says, "and make no provisions for the flesh and its concupiscences" (Rm 13:14).... The Apostle also showed how much intemperance is to be dreaded.... All the saints, on the contrary, were renowned for temperance. The entire life of the saints and of the blessed, the example of the Lord himself while he was with us in the flesh, are aids to us in this matter.'[8]

This temperance has many forms,[9] the most important is the one which concerns physical desires and food.

Chastity

The purity of bodies is called chastity. 'For the other sins', Gregory of Nyssa writes, 'seem to spare the body of those who commit them, while unchastity ruins both [body and soul] at the same time' (Cf. 1 Co 6:18).[10]

It is the duty of all Christians to preserve the innocence of baptism, which constitutes the essence of this virtue. The appearance of monasticism did not reserve it to monks. 'Intercourse of a man with his lawful wife is chastity.'[11] Clement of Alexandria formulated this same principle in more than one place.[12]

A lawful marriage protects chastity. Joseph of Volokolamsk pointed this out to a noble man, one of his spiritual sons whom he had urged to marry off his children as early as the age of fifteen, or to direct them to a monastery. 'Otherwise you will be responsible', he concludes, 'if the young man or the young girl falls into impurity.' 'Alas!' he added, 'this custom does not exist in our Russia.'[13]

Marriage

In patristic literature, a theology of marriage was constructed on the basis of Eph 5:25: 'Husbands should love their wives as Christ loved the Church...'. Meanwhile, we should recognize that although the link between christian marriage and its main biblical model (Christ-the Church) has an universal application, it was generally not presented in depth or developed into a complete theology of marriage, except perhaps in Chrysostom and Augustine. In this connection, liturgies have a much broader didactic character, and pay a delicate and well-balanced attention to the whole mystery of man and woman.[14]

The Fathers defended the lawfulness of marriage against every form of heresy which denied the body and the realities of marriage. Gregory of Nyssa, who in a certain sense is the most enthusiastic defender of virginity, said that 'the one who is issued from marriage should not despise his origin.'[15] In their interpretation of the laws of marriage, however, the Fathers were under the influence of Stoic argument (*diatribē*): they insisted more on the morality of marriage than on its sacramental aspect.[16]

Furthermore, according to the teaching of the New Testament, marriage is a temporary state of life; it will not exist in the world to come (Mk 12:25), and even in this life it is better not to marry (1 Co 7:1 ff.). For the contemplative mind of the East, St Paul could not have given a more convincing reason than this, that marital relations impede prayer (v. 5). Anything that prevented prayer was inevitably considered impure. Marital relations could not therefore be an 'indifferent matter'.[17] Origen prohibited sexual relations before receiving the Eucharist.[18] The stain of intercourse, however licit, contaminated the child because concupiscence had somehow entered into it. Original sin is therefore linked to the manner of human generation.[19]

'We marry, in the first place, in order to raise children', Justin wrote.[20] Within such a limited perspective, marriage and virginity are opposed to one another as 'two ways' that are different.[21] Perhaps only John Chrysostom understood that the essence of marriage is love and that its primary aim is to unify mankind. Even if this love is carnal at the outset, it should progressively become spiritualized. In this context, virginity, and celibacy, appear as the natural improvement of marriage.[22] This idea was to be developed much later by Soloviev in *The Meaning of Love*.[23]

Virginity

The high esteem given virginity from the outset assumed an important place in the christian literature of Cyprian, Methodius of Olympus, Gregory of Nyssa, John Chrysostom, Ephrem the Syrian, and others. An important literature on the subject arose in the fourth century.[24] When the Fathers speak of virginity, their positions, which are frequently antithetical and complementary, are not so simple that one can reduce them to a single insight. It is evident that even dualistic ideas on the stain resulting from sexual intercourse and practical considerations made their influence felt in the ascetic treatises. The impact of any one writer depends less on isolated expressions than on the depth of the spiritual vision this author had of life. What follows are the most frequently used 'arguments' and images.

Virginity — martyrdom. Even before the end of the persecutions, virginity and monasticism were viewed as equivalent to martyrdom. The hundred and forty-four thousand who have kept their virginity (Rv 14:3 ff.) are the first fruits of the spiritual Israel, the most excellent gift offered to God.[25]

'Circumcision', spiritual 'castration'. The circumcised man of the Old Testament symbolizes the chaste person who has rejected concern for the body.[26] The Christian 'amputates the passions of the soul without touching the body'.[27]

The angelic life. Virginity is an 'escape (*ekbasis*) from the body.'[28] Like fasting, it was, for Ephrem, a *jejunare a natura* (a fasting from nature) which will receive a special reward in paradise.[29] The angel's level of virginity is surpassed by the chaste man: 'The angels have received this gift without effort, but you' — Ephrem is speaking of John the Apostle — 'by means of combat.'[30]

An *anticipation of the eschatological realities* (Cf. Mt 19:12: 'for the sake of the kingdom of heaven'), of the paradisiacal state (therefore also a renewal of the primitive and natural state of man) where sexuality will disappear.[31]

An *image of the most holy Trinity* (purely spiritual relationships), of Christ, of Mary, of John the Baptist, and so forth.[32]

Betrothal to Christ,[33] imitation of the union of Christ with the Church, spouse and virgin.[34]

Spiritual fruitfulness. The fecundity of the chaste person imitates that of Mary, virgin and mother: 'every uncorrupted virgin soul, having conceived by the Holy Spirit to engender the will of the Father, is a mother of Christ.'[35]

Restoration of Freedom, of *parrhēsia* (frankness), free access to God,[36] not to belong to anyone in order to belong to God.[37] Continence has no value if the love of God is not joined to it:[38] 'To others I leave the perfect mastery of the body, which they practise without love of God. This is not what I call chastity.'[39]

Unceasing prayer, 'the interior sense constantly attached to God'.[40]

Widowhood and Second Marriage

In the ancient Church the problem of widowhood was as acute as that of virginity. Second marriages were severely judged. With regard to remarriage, Athenagoras early spoke of 'adultery in disguise', 'decorous adultery'.[41] In two pieces, *Letter to a Young*

Widow and *On the Single Marriage*, John Chrysostom praised the christian value of widowhood accepted out of love for God without, however, condemning a second marriage.[42] On third and fourth marriages, the position of the Eastern moralists was generally much more severe.[43]

The Preservation of Chastity

There was general agreement that the passion of the flesh is very dangerous.[44] 'Can a man, Solomon says, hug fire to his breast without setting his clothes alight?' (Pr 6:27).[45]

Virginity and chastity are a gift from God. 'God therefore will give the good gift, perfect purity in celibacy and chastity, to those who ask him with their whole soul, and with faith, and in prayers without ceasing.'[46]

At the same time, virginity is retained only with great effort. St Paul's crucifixion to the world presupposes the rejection of all fleshly pleasure.[47] The custody of the heart, fleeing from opportunities, resisting temptations, and fasting were all linked to chastity.[48] In several places the writers enumerated practices which tend to reduce and radically weaken the 'shameful passions'. Fasting occupied a place of honor, but they also cited vigils, psalmody, prolonged prayer, manual labor, silence, and the patient bearing of humiliations.[49] John Climacus praised the medical effects of a peaceful religious life spent in obedience.[50] But the golden rule remained, 'He is pure who expels love with love and who has extinguished the material fire with the immaterial fire'.[51]

Flight from Women and 'Beardless Youths'

The monk who has renounced marriage must wage war against all forms of physical love, whether the love of a woman, the 'instrument of the devil',[52] or the love of a man. This saying has become famous: 'A certain elder said, "My children, salt comes from the water, and when it comes into contact with water it dissolves and disappears. The monk likewise comes from a woman; and when he approaches a woman he dissolves and ends by being a monk no more."'[53]

There were monks who practised flight from women very rigorously.⁵⁴ Basil, by contrast, believed that in monasteries there was a need to converse with women for the sake of personal edification or to take care of business matters. In such cases the superiors were to choose with care the persons, the time, and the place of conversation.⁵⁵

Another danger which the ascetics wanted removed from the monasteries at all cost was homosexual love; hence their severity towards the 'beardless'. St Sabas 'absolutely did not allow any beardless youth to live with his community before he had a full beard on his chin, because of the Enemy'.⁵⁶ In Basil's *Exhortation to Renounce the World* we read: 'Avoid all intimacy with young companions your own age. Flee from them as from fire.'⁵⁷

Bodily mortification

'It is neither customary nor possible', Hesychius wrote, 'to befriend a snake and carry it about in your shirt, or to attain holiness while pampering, serving, and cherishing the body above what is necessary and indispensable.'⁵⁸ When left to their own fancy, the monks translated their asceticism into rather unexpected exhibitions. An almost complete enumeration of ascetic mortifications practised among Eastern monks has been given us by Eusthatius, Metropolitan of Thessalonika toward the end of the twelfth century:⁵⁹ the naked (*gymnitai, gymnoi*), the unkempt (*hoi tōn trichōn anepistrophoi*), those who slept on the bare ground (*chamaieunai*), walked barefoot (*gymnopodes*), covered themselves with mire (*rypōntes*), those who never washed (*aniptoi*) or never washed their feet (*aniptoi*), those who lived in caves (*spēlaiōtai*), wore iron chains (*sidērophoroi, sidēroumenoi tou Theou*, 'God's armoured soldiers'), lived under trees (*dendritoi*), in a shelter on top of pillars (*kiones*), stood on top of a column (*stylitai*), were buried alive (*en askēsei tethamenoi*), were partly covered with earth (*chōstoi*), recluses (*enkleistoi*), 'and those who in a thousand other ways had renounced the world'.

Fasting

The canonical authors of the East distinguished between *monophagy*, that is, eating only once a day, preferably at a late hour (cf. the Latin *ieiunium*), and *xerophagy* (eating 'dry food'), which consisted in abstaining from certain more nourishing or tasty foods (cf. *abstinentia*).[60] With spiritual writers the term *fast* can cover all the various forms of ascetic dietary restrictions.

In archaic cultures, fasting was almost always associated with rites of mourning or rejunvenation or initiation.[61] Among Christians the only reason for mourning is the loss of Christ's grace,[62] and since renewal is in Christ, fasting assumes meaning from its relationship to the mystery of Christ. This is why fasting did not disappear with the end of the Old Testament, even if Christians felt themselves free of the law.[63]

The prophets greatly stressed the need to accompany fasting with the corresponding inner dispositions (cf. Is 58:6-7). The book of Tobit echoes this teaching: 'Prayer with fasting, and alms with right conduct are better than riches with iniquity' (Tb 12:8). This became the foundation of the triad fasting-prayer-alms inherited by the christian tradition.[64] Soloviev has indicated the union of the three by means of an ingenious reflection: Prayer unites us to God, almsgiving is the extension of this grace to others, and fasting sanctifies the earthly creation through the sanctification of the body.[65]

The Greek philosophers frequently praised sobriety for reasons of hygiene[66] and recommended fasting for the sake of philosophy.[67] Prayer is the pre-eminently christian philosophy. Fasting 'transmits prayer to heaven; like a wing it causes it to ascend'.[68] Fasting may be considered nowadays as a sacrifice added to prayer, but for the Fathers, bodily abstinence was the necessary preparation for one's real prayer.[69] Fasting is also the outer manifestation of prayer; it is, so to speak, the prayer of the body. 'By its beauty, fasting etches the image of eternal life into the body; the conduct which it [implies] suggests the condition of the new age; it teaches us which spiritual food we shall receive at the resurrection.'[70] Because of this eschatological perspective and its intimate connection with prayer, fasting seems essentially linked to the 'angelic life' of the monks.[71]

Flight from the World

Notes

1. THE CHRISTIAN IS NOT OF THIS WORLD

1. See above, Chapter V, *The Goodness and Beauty of the World.*
2. See Epictetus, *Discourses* III.22.47–48.
3. Philostratus, *Vita Apollonii* 8.7.
4. *Theaetetus* 176ab.
5. *Enneads* VI.9.11, ed. Émile Bréhier, *Ennéades* vol. 6 (Paris, 1938) p. 188.
6. *Life* 1.2–8, Bréhier, vol. I:1–3 and vol. II.
7. See J. Schmitt, 'Les écrits du nouveau Testament et les textes de Qumran', in RSR 29 (1955) 396–98.
8. Theodoret of Cyrus, *Philotheos historia* 2; PG 82:1308, 3; 1324–25. [Translation projected in the Cistercian Studies Series. —ed.]
9. *Homilia* 9; SCh 44 (1956) 245–311.
10. See Pseudo-Macarius, *Homilia* 5.6; PG 34:500Bff. [For the most recent translation, see George Maloney, *Intoxicated with God: The Fifty Spiritual Homilies of Macarius* (Denville: Dimension Books, 1978.]
11. Špidlík, *Théophane le Reclus*, 143ff.
12. *Ibid.*, 146.
13. See above, Chapter V, 1.
14. See Maurice Goguel, *Les premiers temps de l'Église* (Neuchâtel, 1949) 40ff.
15. Pseudo-Athanasius, *De virginitate* 18; PG 28;273A.
16. Ivan Kologrivof, *Essai sur la sainteté en Russie* (Bruges, 1953) 14; T. Špidlík, *I grandi mistici russi* (Rome, 1977) 350ff.
17. See Ignatius of Antioch, *To the Romans* 6.1; SCh 10:102 J. B. Lightfoot, *The Apostolic Fathers* (rept. Grand Rapids, 1978) 77.
18. See Špidlík, *Joseph de Volokolamsk*, 68ff.
19. See above, Chapter III, *Eternal Life.*
20. Gregory Nazianzen, *Carminum liber* II, sectio I, (*poemata de seipso*), 45, 11–23; PG 37:1354ff.
21. See René Arnou, 'Platonisme des Pères', DThC 12/2 (1935) 2258–2392.
22. See above, Chapter I, *Hellenism*, IV, *Aphorisms.*
23. See above, IV, *The Divine Origin of the Soul.*
24. See Albert Grilli, *Il problema della vita contemplativa nel mondo greco-romano* (Milan-Rome, 1953).
25. Basil, *Sermo de renuntiatione saeculi* 5; PG 31:636B.
26. See Irénée Hausherr, *L'Hésychasme. Étude de spiritualité*, OCP 22 (1956) 20ff.; *Étude de spiritualité orientale*, OCA 176 (1966) 177ff.
27. See A. J. Festugière, *Contemplation et vie contemplative selon Platon* (Paris, 1936) 28; Grilli, 54ff.
28. *Century* III.85, SCh 9:147; trans. P. Sherwood, *St Maximus the Confessor. The Ascetic Life and the Four Centuries on Charity*, ACW 21 (New York, 1955) 189.
29. See Chapter XIII, 5.
30. Theodoret of Cyrus, *Religiosa historia* 3; PG 82:1324–25.
31. See Chapter XIII, 3.
32. See Michel Aubineau, 'Le thème du "bourbier" dans la littérature profane et chrétienne', RSR 47 (1959) 185–214.

33. *De paenitentia*; PG 40:1159B.
34. Basil, *Long Rules* 7; PG 31:932C.
35. See Ludwig von Hertling, *Antonius der Einsiedler* (Innsbruck, 1929) 30.
36. Léon Roy, 'Pauvres', VTB, col. 927-32.
37. See, for example, Yves Courtonne, *S. Basile, Homilies sur la richesse*, éd. critique et éxégétique (Paris, 1935).
38. Basil, *Homilia in Hexaemeron*, 8.7; PG 29:184AB; LNPF series 2, vol. 8:100.
39. See Špidlík *La sophiologie de S. Basile*, 91ff.
40. See Basil, *Moralia* 48.3 (PG 31:770A), *Short Rules* 205 (1218C); Jesus, the Son, was the great Poor Man, see DS 4:692ff. [For the *Short Rules*, see Saint Basil Ascetical Works FC 9, trans. M. Monica Wagner (New York, 1950.]
41. See Hausherr, *Penthos*, CS 53:88.
42. *Pratum spirituale* 113; PG 87:2978C.
43. Maximus the Confessor, *Century on Charity* II.88; SCh 90:199; ACW 21 (1975) 171.
44. See *Vie de sainte Mélanie* 38; SCh 90:199.
45. John Climacus, *Scala Paradisi* 17; PG 88:927D.
46. *Ibid.*, gradus 27; col. 1096ff.
47. Basil, *Short Rules* 206; PG 31:1220A; Evagrius, *Praktikos* 9; SCh 171:513 4:17.
48. John Climacus, *Scala Paradisi* 17; PG 88:928C. The *Verba Seniorum* has a chapter (III, PL 73:1029ff) entitled, 'The monk should not be saddened in the least if he happens to suffer a loss'; see I. Hausherr, *Penthos*, CS 53:4ff.
49. *Vie d' Hypatios*, ed. A. J. Festugière, *Les moines d'Orient*, vol. II (Paris, 1961) 32.
50. Špidlík, *Joseph de Volokolamsk*, 137ff; Cassian had already made a distinction between these two tendencies, *Collationes* 19.9; PL 49:1139; SCh 64:46ff; LNPF series 2, 11:493ff.
51. Špidlík, *Joseph de Volokolamsk*. 116.
52. See Pambo 8; PG 65:369CD; CS 59:197.
53. *Pratum spirituale* 13; SCh 12:56; PG 87:2861B.
54. See above, Chapter V, *The Goodness and Beauty of the World*.
55. Epistle 22; PG 32:288B; [For the most recent translation of Basil's Letters, see vol. 13 (1951) and vol. 28 (1955) of *The Fathers of the Church*.]
56. See Chapter XIII, *Ecstasy*.
57. See Špidlík, *La sophiologie de S. Basile*, 97.
58. *Ibid.*, 6ff.
59. See, for example, *Homilia de fide*; PG 31:465AB.
60. See above, Chapters I, *Cosmic Spirituality*, and VIII, *Continence*.
61. *Long Rules* 13; PG 31:94B.
62. *Ibid.*, 8.1; 936B.

2. THE SOLITARY LIFE

1. See *The Epistle to Diognetus* 5.5; SCh 33:63; Lightfoot, *The Apostolic Fathers*, 254.
2. See Cyprian, *De habitu virginum* 13; 3: p. 196.
3. See Walter Voelker, *Der wahre Gnostiker nach Clemens Alexandrinus*, TU 57 (Berlin, 1952) 188-219.
4. *Homilia 3 in Exodum*, GCS 6:165; SCh 16:108.

5. *Homily 27 on Numbers 12;* SCh 29:554; tr. R. Greer, *Origen: An Exhortation to Martyrdom, First Principles* (Bk IV), ...*Homily XXVII on Numbers* (New York, 1979) 268.
6. *Apophthegmata,* Arsenius 1; PG 65:88B; CS 59:9; Cf. René Basset, –ed., *Synaxaire arabe jacobite,* PO 16 (Paris, 1922) 13, *mois de Bachons,* [1022].
7. I. Hausherr, 'L'hésychasme. Etude de spiritualité,' OCP 22 (1956), 5–40, 247–85; *Hésychasme et priere,* OCA 176 (Rome, 1966), 163–237; see above, p. 225.
8. See below, IX, 3.
9. See I. Hausherr, 'L'hésychasme. Etude de spiritualité' OCP 22:19ff; *Hésychasme et prière,* OCA 176:177ff.
10. Ed. François Nau, *Ammonas, successeur de saint Antoine. Textes grecs et syriaques,* PO 11 (Paris, 1915) 480ff; Hausherr, *L'hésychasme,* 31; 191.
11. See above, Chapter VI, *Praises of the Common Life.*
12. See I. Hausherr, L'hésychasme, 26ff; 184ff.
13. See J. Meyendorff, 'Partisans et ennemis des biens ecclésiastiques au sein du monachisme russe au XVe et XVIe siècles', *Irénikon* 29 (1956) 28–46, 151–64.
14. PL 49:1125ff.
15. J. Gribomont, 'Anacoreta', DIP 1 (1973) col. 539–40.
16. *Historia ecclesiastica,* 1.21; PG 86:2419; T. Špidlík 'Dendriti', DIP 3 (1976) 442.
17. Špidlík, 'Boskoi', DIP I:1538; Jean Martial Besse, 'Anachorètes', DThC 1 (1909) 1141.
18. See Bibliography, *Hesychasm.*
19. See Theodoret of Cyrus, *Religiosa historia* 17; PG 82:1420; *ibid.,* 21, col. 1432ff.
20. See T. Špidlík, 'Stylites', in *New Catholic Encyclopedia* 13 (1967) 750–51.
21. Henri Leclercq, 'Reclus', DACL 14/2 (1948) 2149–59.
22. See T. Špidlík, 'Xeniteia', DIP (in progress).
23. H. Leclercq, 'Laures Palestiniennes', DACL 8/2 (1929) col. 1961–86; Igino Cechetti, 'Laura', *Enciclopedia cattolica* 7 (Vatican City, 1951) col. 958–60.
24. T. Špidlík, 'Ermites. En Orient', *Dictionnaire d'histoire et de géographie ecclésiastique* 15 (1963) 766–71.
25. Barsanuphius, *Letter* 458, ed. Nicodemus the Hagiorite, Biblos psychophelestate... (Venice, 1816) 227; French trans. by L Régnault, *La correspondance de Barsanuphe et Jean* (Solesmes, 1971) 526, Index: *cellule;* Hausherr, *Penthos,* CS 53:81.
26. *Apophthegmata Patrum,* Antonius 10: PG 77BC; SC 59:3.

3. FLIGHT FROM THE WORLD IN CENOBITISM

1. See above, Chapter VI, *Praises of the Common Life.*
2. For example, those who held a government office, like Macarius and John under Julian the Apostate (*Ep.* 18; PG 32:281; ed., Yves Courtonne, *Saint Basile. Lettres,* texte établi et traduit [Paris, 1857–66] 48).
3. Jean Gribomont, 'Le renoncement au monde dans l'idéal ascétique de saint Basile', *Irénikon* 31 (1958) 283–307, 460–75.
4. *Long Rules* 8.1; PG 31:936C.
5. *Ibid.,* 22.2–3; 980AC.
6. *Ibid.,* 44.1–2; 1029B–1032A.

7. *Ibid.*, 38; 1017A; see David Amand, *L'ascèse monastique de saint Basile* (Maredsous, 1948) 248ff.
8. *Logos* 3, ed. Augoustinos Iordanites, To;y]os?ioy patr,ow]hm;vn $abb;a [Hsa?ion l?ogoi kd (Jerusalem, 1911), 11; French trans. by the monks of Solesmes, *Abbé Isaïe. Réveil ascétique* Spiritualité orientale, (Etoilles, 1970) 50.
9. See the correspondence of Barsanuphius and John, ed. Nicodemus the Hagiorite (Venice, 1816) n. 208; Régnault trans., *Lettre* 311, p. 230.
10. PG 31:996; FC 9:296; see Amand, *L'ascèse monastique de saint Basile*, 254.
11. Basil, *Long Rules* 8.2; PG 31:937A.
12. Chapter 130, *Philokalia*, vol. 3 (Athens 1960) 262; English, *The Philokalia* 3.
13. *Long Rules* 32.1-2; PG 31:993D-997A; see Amand, *L'ascèse monastique de saint Basile*, 251f.
14. *Short Rules* 190; PG 31:1209D.
15. See Špidlík, *Joseph de Volokolamsk*, 125ff; *Apophthegmata*, Poemen 76 (PG 65:341A; CS 59:149) where Abba Poemen asks his mother: 'Would you rather see us here or in the age to come'?
16. *Apophthegmata*, Poemen 84; PG 65:321ff; CS 59:178.
17. Jamblichus Chalcidensis, *De vita Pythagoreica* XVII.72, ed. Augustus Nauck, (Petersburg, 1884) 51ff.
18. *Apophthegmata*, Arsenius 40; PG 65:103C; CS 59:18.
19. Plutarch, *De garrulitate*, n. 23, end.
20. T. Špidlík, 'Silenziari' DIP (in progress).
21. Life by Philotheus Coccinus, ed. Papadopoulos-Kerameus, *Hierosolym. Stachyologia* V, p. 190-359.
22. *Short Rules* 23; PG 31:1098D-1099A.
23. *Nichomachean Ethics* IV.8.1128a.
24. *Summa theologiae* I-II.60.5; II-II.72.2. *diff.* 1; II-II, 160.2; see Hugo Rahner, 'Eutrapélie', DS 4/2:1726-29.
25. For the strong evidence in support of this prohibition, see Hausherr, *Penthos*, CS 53:95ff.
26. *Short Rules* 31; PG 31:1104B.
27. *La perle précieuse, traitant des sciences écclesiastique, par Jean, fils d'Abou–Zakariyâ surnommé Ibn-Sabâ*, Chap. 31; ed. Jean Périer, PO 16 (Paris, 1922) 674.
28. *Paedagogos* II, 5, ed. O. Stählin, GCS 1:184-87. Trans. S. Wood, FC 23:135: 'It is true that man is an animal who can laugh, but it is not true that he therefore should laugh at everything. The horse is an animal that neighs, yet it does not neigh at everything.'
29. *Long Rules* 17.1; PG 31:961AB; see Špidlík, *La sophiologie de S. Basile*, 90.
30. *Apopthegmata Patrum*, Arsenius 13; PG 65:92A; CS 59:11.
31. Basil, *Long Rules* 35.3; PG 31:1008AB; FC 9:304.
32. *La sophiologie de S. Basile*, 233ff.
33. John Moschus, *Pratum spirituale* 74; PG 87:2925D, SCh 12:115.

4. THE RENUNCIATION OF THE FLESH

1. *Homilia in illud, Attende tibi ipsi* 3; PG 31:204A; *St. Basil: Ascetical Works*, FC 9:431ff.

Flight from the World

2. *Long Rules* 18; PG 31:975C; FC 9:274.
3. *Scala paradisi* 15; PG 88:880D.
4. See Maximus the Confessor, *Century on Charity* II.83: SCh 9:118; ACW 21:169.
5. *Homilia* I *de ieiunio* 9; PG 31:180A; see Amand, *L'ascèse monastique de saint Basile*, 199ff.
6. On the doctrine of the Eastern authors on the body, see above, Chapter IV, 4.
7. See above, IV, 4, *Aphorisms*.
8. *Long Rules* 16.1ff.; PG 31:957; FC 9:269.
9. *Ibid.*, ff.
10. *In illud: Qui fornicatur in proprium corpus peccat*; PG 46:492BC.
11. Socrates, *Historia ecclesiastica* 1.11; PG 67:104AB.
12. See, for example, *Stromata* VII.12; PG 9:497C; Irénée Hausherr, 'Vocation chrétienne et vocation monastique selon les Pères', in *Laïcs et vie chrétienne parfaite* (Rome, 1963) 33–115, reprinted in *Etudes de spiritualité orientale*, OCA 183 (Rome, 1969) 403–85, especially 464ff.
13. Špidlík, *Joseph de Volokolamsk*, 113.
14. See Alphonse Raes, *Le mariage, sa célébration et sa spiritualité dans les Églises d'Orient* (Chevetogne, 1958).
15. *On virginity* 7.2; SCh 119:355f.; FC 58:31ff.
16. See M. Spanneut, *Le stoïcisme des Pères de l'Eglise*, 259ff., bibliography, 259.
17. See Henri Crouzel, *Virginité et mariage selon Origène* (Paris, 1962), 60ff.
18. *Selecta in Ezechielem* 7.22; PG 13:793B; see J. B. Pitra, *Juris ecclesiastici Graeci historia et monumenta* (Rome, 1864) 544, and the commentators on these canonical texts, Theodore Balsamon and John Zonaras, PG 10:1287–90.
19. Origen, *Homilia in Lucam* 14; GCS 9 (2d ed.) pp. 87, 21.
20. *I Apologia* 29.1; PG 6:373.
21. Athanasius, *Epistola ad Amunem*; PG 26:1175C.
22. See T. Špidlík, 'Il matrimonio-sacramento di unita nel pensiero di Crisostomo', *Augustinianum* 17 (1977) 221–26.
23. *Smysl ljubvi*, Oeuvres, 2nd, edn. (rpt. Brussels, 1966) 3–60; tr. J. Marshall, (New York: International Universities Press, 1945) 5–64.
24. See Pierre Thomas Camelot, *Les traités De virginitate au IVᵉ siècle*, Etudes carmélitaines (1952) 273–92; M. Aubineau, in SCh 119 (1966) 23ff.
25. Origen, *Commentarium in Joannem* 1.1; GCS 4:35.
26. *Id., Comm. in Ep. ad Romanos* 2.13; PG 14:907C.
27. *Id., Comm. in Matthaeum* 15.4; GCS 10:358, 18.
28. Gregory Nazianzen, 'Summary Definitions', *Carminum liber* 1.II.34, v. 175; PG 37:958.
29. *De paradiso* 7.18; ed J. S. Assemani, *Opera omnia . . . graece* vol. 3:548c; Beck, *Des hl. Ephraem des Syrers Hymnen De Paradiso und Contra Julianum*, CSCO Scr. Syr. 7 (Louvain, 1957) p. 70.
30. *De virginitate* 15.4; ed I. E. Rahmani, *Hymni de virginitate* (Scarfea, 1906–08) p. 46' see Gregory of Naziánzus, *Oratio* 37.11; PG 36:296B; John Climacus, *Scala Paradisi* 15; PG 88:880D.
31. Ephrem, *De paradiso* 7.5; Assemani, vol. 3: 582b, Beck, p. 64ff; see also Garcia M. Colombás, *Paradis et vie angélique* (Paris, 1961) 149ff.
32. See W. Völker, *Gregor von Nyssa als Mystiker* (Wiesbaden, 1955) 257; Gregory Nazianzen, *In laudem virginitatis*, *Carminum Liber* I.II, v. 20; PG 37:523.

33. Ephrem, *De virginitate* 25.26 (Rahmani, p. 73); Gregory Nazianzen, *Carminum Liber* I.II.2, vv. 255ff; PG 37:598.
34. Origen, *Homilia in Genesim* 3.6; GCS 6:47, 6.
35. Origen, *Fragmenta in Matthaeum* 281 (GCS 12:126, 11); see Ephrem, *De virginitate* 25.10 (Rahmani, p. 72); *Carmina Nisibena* 46.1 (ed. Gustavus Bickel, [Leipzig, 1866] pp. 90 and 175); Špidlík, *Joseph de Volokolamsk*, 85ff.
36. See Chapters VII, *Full Responsibility*, and IX, *Vainglory*.
37. Garcia M. Colombás, 152.
38. Origen, *Fragmenta in I Cor* 37, JTS 9, p. 507, 38; Clement of Alexandria says the same thing about the Valentinians, *Stromata* III.7.60.1; GCS 2: p. 223, 21.
39. Gregory Nazianzen, *Carminum liber* I.II.2, v. 567; PG 37:564.
40. Diadochus, *One Hundred Gnostic Chapters* in E. Des Places, ed., *Oeuvres spirituelles*, SCh 5 (1966) 84.
41. *A Plea for Christians* 33; PG 6:968A; see M. Spanneut, *Le stoïcisme des Pères*, 259.
42. Ed. SCh 138 (1963). [Orthodox practice, however, has allowed second marriages more freely than has the western Church.]
43. See Louis Godefroy, 'Le mariage au temps des Pères', DThC 9 (1927) 2077-2113, and 2096 (second marriages).
44. See Chapters VI, *The Family*, and IX, *Fornication*.
45. *Monastic Constitutions*, attributed to Basil, 3; PG 31:1344C; see John Climacus, *Scala paradisi* 15; PG 88:880D.
46. Origen, *Commentarium in Matthaeum* 14.25; GCS 10:348ff; ANF 10: 512; see John Climacus, *Scala paradisi* 15; PG 88:880D, 882A.
47. Origen, *Comm. in Matth.* 12.24; GCS p. 123.
48. See Crouzel, *La virginité et le mariage selon Origène*, 122.
49. Basil, *Sermo de renuntiatione saeculi* 9; PG 31:648A; *Long Rules* 51: PG 31:1040ff.
50. Climacus, *Scala paradisi* 880D; *The Ladder of Divine Ascent* (Boston: Holy Transfiguration Monastery, 1978) 104.
51. *Ibid*.
52. Špidlík, *Joseph de Volokolamsk*, 114.
53. *Pratum spirituale* 217; SCh 12:291; PG 87:3107.
54. *Ibid*., 3 (SCh p. 48), 88 (134ff.).
55. *Long Rules* 33 (PG 31:997ff); *Short Rules* 220 (1228D); see Amand, *L'ascèse monastique de saint Basile* 243ff.
56. *Vie de saint Sabas*, ed. A. J. Festugière, *Les moines d'Orient* (Paris, 1961-65) vol. 3:40; see *Vie de Kyriakos, ibid.*, vol. 3 3: p. 41.
57. 5; PG 31:637B; see Amand, 246ff.
58. *Century I on Temperance* 33; PG 93:1492C; *The Philokalia*, vol. 1 (London, 1979) 168.
59. *Ad stylitam quendam* 48; PG 136:241.
60. See the articles by Marie Albert Michel, N. Tolstoy and Thomas Joseph Lamy on abstinence among the Greeks, the Russians, the Syrians, in DThC 1 (1909) 262-69; T. Špidlík, 'Xerophagia' in DIP (in progress).
61. See J. Claudian, 'Le jeûne dans les civilisations "primitives" et dans les religions du passé, in *Redécouverte du jeûne. Sagesse du corps* (Paris, 1959) (German translation, *Wiederentdeckung des Fastens* (Vienna-Munich, 1963) 153-84.
62. See above, *Causes of Compunction*.

63. See Pie Raymond Régamey, in *Redécouverte du jeûne*, 42.
64. See, for example, Pseudo-Athanasius, *De virginitate* 6; PG 28:257B.
65. *Duchovnyja osnovy žizni* [*The Spiritual Foundations*], *Oeuvres* (St. Petersburg, n. d. rpt Brussels, 1966), vol. 3:315ff. English translation by Donald Attwater, *God, Man and the Church: The Spiritual Foundations of Life* (London, 1937) 87ff.
66. Basil follows them in the *De ieiunio* 7–9; PG 31:176A–177B; *Long Rules* 19; PG 31:968C.
67. Porphyry, *Treatise on Abstinence*, 37–38, trans. in D. Amand, *L'ascèse monastique de saint Basile* (Maredsous, 1948) 262ff.
68. Basil, *De ieiunio* (col. 1730); Nilus, *De octo spiritibus malitiae* 1; PG 79:1145B.
69. John CLimacus, *Scala paradisi* 26; PG 88:1085B.
70. Martyrius Sahdônâ, *Livre de la perfection* 2.7; CSCO 215 (*Scriptores Syri* 91) p. 91.
71. Garcia M. Colombás, *Paradis et vie angélique* (Paris, 1961) 167ff.

9

SPIRITUAL WARFARE

1. THE STRUGGLE AGAINST DEMONS

The Visible and Invisible War

THE SPIRITUAL TRADITION, entering upon the road opened by Scripture[1] and incorporating, in addition the Stoic ideal,[2] has often compared the ascetic life to a struggle, to a war against the enemies of the soul. Texts abound everywhere.[3] The *Praktikos* by Evagrius contains repeated expression and metaphors which refer to war and struggle: *agōn* (contest), *palē* (wrestling), *polemos* (strife); above all the monk must struggle, *agōnizesthai, polemein, machesthai*, against the enemies, *polemoi*, or the adversaries, *antikeimenoi*.[4]

Spiritual warfare also occupies an important place in Cassian's spirituality.[5] This war is universal, on all sides: 'Just as shadows follow bodies', Dorotheos writes, 'so temptations follow the commandments.'[6] There are outer and inner struggles: we must fight night and day, Gregory Nazianzen believed, openly and secretly, within ourselves and without.[7] Evagrius speaks of the 'material and immaterial conflict' (*ahylos polemos*).[8] Those who live in communities are opposed by 'the more careless brethren. Now this ... form of combat is much lighter' than the one waged by the 'naked' demons, openly.[9] Dadišo Quatraya quotes the *Great Letter* of Macarius 'where he has enumerated all the wars which are against the love of God and against prayer.'[10]

The enemies who incite this war have already been unmasked in Scripture: Satan, the world, and the flesh.[11]

233

Chapter Nine

The Necessity of Warfare

We read in *The Apology* of Socrates that, 'The unexamined life (*anexestastos bios*) is not worth living'.[12] That trials are a narrow strait through which we must pass to come near God, is an ancient idea. But the discourses of the 'suffering just' in Assyro-Babylonian literature are only monotonous lamentations;[13] Plato's 'impaled just' man bears witness to his justice.[14]

By contrast, the trials undergone by Job elucidate his humility and his faith. Along the same line, the Fathers called up examples of the *probatio fidei* (the testing of faith) among the just in the Old Testament as prefigurations of the demands of the Gospel.[15]

Clement of Alexandria's true 'gnostic' must ask God for afflictions: 'O Lord, put me to the test'.[16] The pre-eminently proven man is the monk: *dokimos monachos* (the tried monk).[17] Because 'wisdom is not won except by battle',[18] the ascetics are called *agōnizomenoi, agōnistai* (strugglers), *podvižniki* in Slavic.[19]

For Cassian, the struggle is a providential means of acquiring spiritual perfection,[20] it is a testimony of steadfastness,[21] it perfects our free will.[22] According to Dorotheos, the ascetic does not even have to be afraid of 'occasionally falling into the mud, to find the road again,'[23] because 'those who must swim in the sea and know the art of swimming dive when the wave comes upon them, and let themselves go under; after this, they continue to swim without difficulty.'[24]

The struggle cannot be avoided, whether one is perfect or not.[25] If there is a tendency toward quietism in the *apatheia* (dispassion) of the Messalians,[26] Evagrius, by contrast, believed that temptations grow with progress in the spiritual life. The soul's progress in impassibility can be measured according to the quality and the strength of the attacking demons.[27] When we pray, 'Lead us not into temptation', we are not asking not to be tempted, for that is impossible, but not to be swallowed up by doing what is displeasing to God.' This is a traditional explanation we read in the *Spiritual Meadow*.[28]

The Enemy

Chapter twelve of the Apocalypse, rehearsing and completing the story of Genesis, synthesizes the biblical doctrine on the devil and his role in salvation history.[29] It is a personal confrontation between the Man-God and the 'deceiver' (Rv 12:9), 'the prince of this world' (Jn 12:31).

It was from this perspective that the Fathers interpreted various events in the life of Christ, for example, the adoration of the Magi, the temptation in the wilderness, baptism, but especially the cross: why was Christ crucified? That he might crucify the demon, Theodore the Studite replied.[30]

And thus, for Christians, the spiritual life is essentially warfare against demons (Eph 6:12). This traditional concept took on a new dimension in the monastic spirituality of the desert. The desert is the demons' very favorite domain, and the monk who withdraws there will confront them in face-to-face combat.[31] The demonology expressed in the *Life of Antony*,[32] in the work of Evagrius[33] and Cassian[34] became classical of the desert and was integrated as an important element into traditional ascetic doctrine.

It is true that demons misuse, but still keep, their cosmic function; they are then *kosmokratores* (world-rulers),[35] associated with false gods,[36] linked to animals and plants. The concepts christian authors used to explain the activity of the demons in the world came from the influence of Greek philosophy on the one hand and, on the other, certain Jewish tendencies.[37] But their practical conclusions were always the same: to purify the places of the power of evil through faith in God and through asceticism.[38] The hermits chose to fix their abode where they believed they would find many demons.[39]

The Power of Demons

Origen asked himself the question, 'If it is true that the devil and his legions have been destroyed, how is it we believe him still so powerful against the servants of God?' Origen's answer consisted in affirming that the demon's malignant activity is inflicted only on the wicked, because he no longer has any power over those who are in Christ.[40]

Subordinated to divine providence, the activity of demons is an instrument of the trials that preceed victory. It was said about St Melania that: 'The enemy, realizing that he had arrived at nothing by fighting against her, even when, being defeated, he gave her crowns that were still more beautiful, no longer dared to harass her, being in utter confusion.'[41] St Sabas was not afraid of Satan, who appeared to him in the shape of a fearsome lion. As a reward, 'God set under him every poisonous and carnivorous beast.'[42]

There is also the fact that the demon is not the cause of sin, as was said 'among the more simple', against whom Origen wrote.[43] Evagrius points out that the demon does not directly reach our intellect,[44] and is powerless to raise knowledge in the mind, powerless to inform us about the 'inner purpose' of things.[45] He can only present images to us (*phantasiai, eidōlon*).[46] Through the 'composition' of the body, demons cause a certain 'phantasm' to rise in the mind.[47] The *logismos* is only an image.[48] The struggle against demons therefore takes place especially in the *logismoi*, in the imaginary world of illusions, false consolations, and ruses of all kinds. One fights them through discernment and by maintaining custody of the heart.[49]

But one should also use bodily means: fasting, putting on sackcloth, and so on,[50] because the demons make use of the body. The body, Evagrius believed, is not evil in itself; it is, by itself, a protection against demons. This is why they attack us in our sleep, when we are defenseless.[51]

'To observe', to be on watch, *epitērein* (to look out), is the demons' constant occupation in their war against monks. 'The demons do not know our hearts, as some people think...'[52] Only through observation do the demons learn to know us. But in this 'art', Evagrius assures us, they have great skill.[53]

Knowing all this, the ascetic is convinced, as Cassian says, 'that the demons cannot prevail against men...'[54] The contest is one of equal forces; the soul emerges victorious if it wills to win, and is forced into submission if it does not will to win.[55] To be defeated, then, means to fall into the slavery of the Evil One, with all the disastrous results that follow.

Exorcism

The casting out of demons was considered by the christian writers of the second and third centuries as one of the proofs of the divine nature of Christianity.[56] Beginning with the first half of the third century, the practice of exorcism began to be regulated.[57] It eventually survived in the Church in two different forms: exorcisms performed over the sick who were considered possessed; and exorcisms that were part of the liturgy preparatory to baptism.[58]

But these practices are but one special application of a general faith in the power of God's word, of prayer, and of christian asceticism. In addressing pagans, Origen stressed a special feature of the Scriptures: they bring about what they say, they have power.[59] Evagrius explained that the word of God is not only special nourishment, it is also a 'weapon'.[60] 'In the words of Scripture is the Lord, whose presence the demons cannot endure', said Athanasius.[61]

The same was said of the name of Jesus,[62] the sign of the cross,[63] and all prayer, especially psalmody.[64] Finally, if the virtues are a participation in Christ,[65] it is by means of the works of God that the enemies are scattered. The entire spiritual life purifies the world and destroys the power of evil.[66]

2. LOGISMOI

The Struggle Against Evil Thoughts

'A man's whole effort should be employed upon his thoughts', Pseudo-Macarius said, 'he must cut away the bush of evil thoughts which besets him'[1] From the fifteenth chapter of St Matthew Origen drew his statement: 'The spring and source of every sin then are evil thoughts.'[2] This is the 'invisible struggle'.

According to Evagrius' explanation, 'With laymen the demons fight rather by means of present things, . . .'.[3] The 'visible struggle' concerns *pragmata* (objects). Contact with them gives rise to passions. To resist the demon in this arena, the principal means is abstinence, the renunciation of things.[4]

'But with monks, [the demons fight] mostly by means of thoughts; for in the wilderness they have not things.'[5] The visible struggle was considered easier, the beginners' strife.[6] But from a theological and psychological point of view, the struggle with thoughts, 'inner warfare', 'the inner practice' (*vnutrennoe delanie* in Slavic) is more basic; it touches on the root of sin. And thus sin and warfare *kat'energeian* (in deed), waged by means of 'things', are contrasted to the inner, 'immaterial' war *kata dianoian* (in thought).⁷ In this connection, there is an admonition of Maximus the Confessor which expresses the entire tradition: 'Do not misuse thoughts, lest you be forced to misuse things too. For unless a man first sin in thought, he will never sin in deed.'⁸

The Term Logismos

The noun *logismos* (thought, from the verb *logizomai*, to reflect) can mean the thinking faculty, the *logos* (intellect), reason, the *hēgemonikon* (ruling faculty), the spirit.⁹ But most frequently, *logismos* is the product of intellectual activity, a thought (*ennoia*).¹⁰ We should note here that it is especially the *dianoia*, discursive reason, which produces thoughts, not the *nous*, the intuitive faculty.¹¹

Not all thoughts are evil, certainly because not all constitute obstacles to the knowledge of God; only those are 'which attack [the mind] from the irascible power and from [the soul's] appetitive power, and which are against nature'.¹² An evil thought is 'a seed of sin'.¹³ but the origin of the virtues is attributed to the good thought.¹⁴ One must therefore cultivate good thoughts in the heart.¹⁵ Even the voice of conscience is like a *logismos*.¹⁶ To distinguish between them, Origen called the ones pure (*logismos katharos*), the other impure (*logismos akatharos*).¹⁷ But there are many other qualifiers for good thoughts: *logismos theios*, divine thought,¹⁸ *pneumatikos*, spiritual,¹⁹ *eusebēs*, devout,²⁰ *agathos*, good,²¹ *emphytos*, natural,²² *gnōstikos*, 'gnostic', appropriate for contemplation,²³ *hagios*, holy,²⁴ and so on.

But the attention of the spiritual authors dwelt far more on evil thought, the *logismos ponēros*.²⁵ Such a thought may be *daimonikos*, demonic,²⁶ *empathēs*, passionate,²⁷ *anthropinos*, human (in the pejorative sense),²⁸ *idios*, 'one's own' (Cf. *voluntas propria*, one's own will).²⁹

Very frequently the world *logismos* (usually in the plural, *logismoi*) in itself is adequate to designate evil thoughts.³⁰ The New Testament offers a single, but remarkable, example of *logismos* (in the plural) used without adjective in the pejorative sense (2 Co

10:4), and numerous examples of the word *dialogismos* (thought), in the singular and the plural, used pejoratively.³¹

The Definition of Logismos

Evagrius has given a very long, descriptive definition of *logismos:*

> *logismos daimoniōdēs estin eikōn tou aisthētou anthrōpou synistamenē kata dianoian meth' he ho nous kinoumenos empathōs legei ti hē prattei anomōs en tǫ kryptǫ pros to parempeson eidōlon ekdiōchtheis hyp' autou.*
>
> A *demonic logismos* is an image belonging to the sensitive life of a man which has been composed in the understanding, with which the mind, when moving in an impassioned way, says something or does somethig secretly against the law in accordance with the image which has effected an entrance because the mind has been overpowered by it.³²

This text, however difficult to translate, contains important elements. The *logismos* is not a 'thought' in the true sense of the word; it is a mental 'image' which arises in a person endowed with sensibility. This image appears not in the *nous*, the mind, but in the inferior part of the human cognitive faculty, the *dianoia*, where reasoning for and against something takes place. This image, meanwhile, proves attractive; it stirs the mind; a passionate movement then arises which incites the person to a secret decision against God's law, or at least to some sort of dialogue with this image, which presents itself as some sort of idol, and should instead be driven away.

'Passionate' thoughts

Evagrius' definition is too complicated. In practice, it was easier to learn how to differentiate between a 'simple' and a 'passionate' thought. Here is a characteristic text from Maximus the Confessor: 'Thing, representation, passion—all differ. A thing is, for instance, a man, a woman, gold, and so on; a representation is a mere recollection of one of these things; passion is an unreasonable affection or senseless hate for one of the foregoing.'[33]

Dorotheus spoke of an inclination, a *prospatheia*, a self-will which accompanies a thought which could, in itself, be pure.[34] The entire program of purification was proposed, then, in these terms: 'The monk's whole war is against demons, that he may separate the passions from the representations. Otherwise he will not be able to look on things with detachment.'[35]

The Origin of Evil Thoughts

Origen frequently posited a correlation between *logismos* and *pneuma* or, also, *daimon*.[36] Behind the term *logismos*, as Evagrius used it in Origen's wake, we should recognize an important concept of Jewish ethics, one formulated by the word *yeser*, 'thought',[37] which in man is understood as something concrete, almost personal, and which the Greek text translated as *diaboulion* (counsel).[38]

In the *Life of Antony* we already find the doctrine that evil thoughts are the demons' weapon against solitaries.[39] Evagrius made no distinction between 'the demon' and the 'thought' or the 'mind' of a given vice.[40]

This identification clearly indicates that the *logismoi* do not belong to human nature, and do not come directly from the things created by God, where there is no evil. But since the demons act on the human mind by 'altering the condition of the body',[41] Maximus the Confessor noted specifically that, 'The mind receives impassioned thoughts from three sources—from the senses, from the body's condition and temperament, and from the memory.'[42]

Let us add that the tyranny of the demon over men is exercised especially through the passions: passionate memories supply the raw material for evil thoughts. Ancient philosophers discussed the question from a psychological point of view: 'It is worth considering whether thought brings passions into motion, or passion thought.'[43] Evagrius correctly warned that from the moral point of view the causality is mutual: 'Those memories, colored by passion, that we find in ourselves come from former experiences we underwent while subject to some passion. Any experience we now undergo while under the influence of passion will in the future persist in us in the form of passionate memories.'[44]

The passions upset the state of the heart. One can therefore say with the Gospel that 'from the heart come evil intentions' (Mt 15:19). But in what sense? We know that Messalianism subverted all of orthodox spirituality. Evil thoughts did not come 'from outside', on the contrary, the human heart is an abyss where divine inspirations and 'serpents' mix.[45] But Theophane the Recluse was fond of specifying in what sense this proposition could be accepted: once corrupted, once wounded from the outside, the heart becomes a source of passionate movements. But this is not in its 'nature'; it is a perversion which asceticism seeks to heal.[46]

All the orthodox therefore agree in principle with Evagrius: an evil thought cannot be engendered either by God or by the angels or by man's natural being, but only by the demons and man's free will.[47]

The Degrees of Penetration by an Evil Thought into the Heart

The mechanism of temptation, the various moments of which are interlinked, has been analyzed very well by Eastern spiritual writers, especially those of the Sinaite tradition (Nilus, John Climacus, Hesychius, Philotheus).[48] They often spoke of the successive moments which unfold before consent to sin is given and of the psychological changes which follow this decision of the will.

First comes the *prosbolē*, the suggestion, which is 'a simple idea or image suggested to the mind or the heart by "the enemy"'.[49] In Evagrius, the verb *hypoballein* is the proper term to indicate suggestions of demonic (occasionally angelic) origin.[50]

Next comes the *syndiasmos*, the drawing near, the coupling, which is 'parleying' with the suggested object (to do it or not?).

Synkatathesis is 'giving mental consent to some forbidden pleasure'.[51] This constitutes sin. The term itself is Stoic.[52]

Palē, the inner struggle, is often mentioned. It is decisive to consent and is therefore placed before or after it.[53]

The last term in this progression is captivity, *aichmalosia*, the forcible carrying away of the heart, passion, *pathos*, a vicious habit become like a second nature, the result of a long series of assents.[54]

This order is common in the East. Some minor variations may be noted, for example, in John Climacus: assault (*prosbolē*), converse (*syndiasmos*), consent (*synkatathesis*), captivity (*aichmalōsia*), struggle (*palē*), passion (*pathos*).[55] Philotheus of Sinai mentions only four steps: impact, coupling, captivity, passion.[56] Theophane the Recluse distinguished between *prilog* (suggestion), *vnimanie* (attention), *slažděnie* (delight), *želanie* (desire), *rešimost'* (the resolution), and *dělo* (deed).[57] In the West, in Augustine, we read *suggestus, delectatio, consensus*,[58] but he, too, speaks of struggle, of the sinful work, of *consuetudo*, the habit of evil.

3. CUSTODY OF THE HEART

'The Elimination of Thoughts'

Avoiding consent to sin, *synkatathesis*, is already a great thing, but it is not perfection. Christians must tend towards perfection, towards peace of heart, *hesychia, amerimnia*, stillness, freedom from blameworthy desires;[1] and this freedom consists in 'the elimination of [evil] thoughts' (*apothesis noēmatōn*).

Can one avoid the first 'suggestions'? According to Origen, it is impossible to be entirely free of them; souls who have turned to God must 'experience conflicts of thought';[2] all one can do is not to dwell upon them,[3] not to 'converse' with them (as Eve did with the serpent). Prudence demands 'that one slaughter at once these children of Babylon',[4] that one 'crush the serpent's head',[5] and not let it enter the paradise of the heart. To express this idea, Eastern spiritual writers came to adopt and explain several expressions which are more or less synonymous.

The heart is the seat of the intelligence, of the mind. Some authors therefore speak of *phylakē kardias*, guarding the heart, of *tērēsis noos*, guarding the intellect, of *phylakē tōn endon*, guarding inward being. One will even find 'to guard' (*phylassein*), used absolutely,[6] or 'to watch oneself' ('Watch yourself with care'; *tērei seauton akribōs*—the leitmotif of a small work attributed to Ammonas).[7]

To watch oneself, one should be sober and vigilant, 'neptic' (cf. 1 P 5:8).[8] Antony opposed alertness (*gregorsis*) and watchfulness (*nēpsis*) to the demons' assaults.[9] For Hesychius of Sinai, 'Watchfulness is the spiritual method which, if sedulously practised over a long period, completely frees us, with God's help, from impassioned thoughts, impassioned words, and evil actions.'[10]

One sentence of Evagrius came to be quoted frequently because it contains a suggestive alliteration of the two words *prosochē* and *proseuchē*, attentiveness and prayer: 'When attention seeks prayer it finds it. For if there is anything that marches in attention's train it is prayer; and so it must be cultivated.'[11] It will be said that attention (*prosochē*) is the mother of prayer (*proseuchē*).[12]

Guarding the 'entrance to the heart' is above all a method of defense to repel intruding thoughts immediately. It is the theme of several sayings: 'Be the doorkeeper of your heart, so that the stranger does not enter; say "Are you one of ours, or one of our enemies?"'[13]

The Method of Fighting Hostile Thoughts

'We should not believe these demons, but strive all the more to do the opposite.'[14] Generally speaking the method is *praxis* in all its fulness, because it purifies the heart. Abstinence, (*enkrateia*) especially, had already been called by Philo[15] 'the destroyer of serpents' (*ophiomachēs*: Lv 11:12). But Evagrius notes that most of the exercises that allow one to struggle against the demon[16] cannot be done all the time; prayer alone must be constant.

The outstanding method against evil thought is called *antirrhesis* ('counter-speaking'). When tempted by the devil, Christ replied to his suggestions with texts from Scripture, and did not enter into discussion with the Evil One (Mt 4:3–11). We read about certain ascetics that they knew 'the entire Scriptures' by heart,[17] that is, they were able to answer every question put to them with sacred texts, but, more than that, they knew a good quotation from Scripture against each demonic suggestion. The classical manual of this art is the *Antirrheticus* of Evagrius,[18] divided into eight chapters according to the number of the eight vices. He cited scriptural texts pertinent to each thought, texts

which help drive it away (taken from Genesis to the Book of Revelation, there are 487 altogether).
What a job for an uneducated monk to learn these! But practice modified the proposed principle. The invocation of Christ came to be enough to 'drive away all the demons.'[19] and the Jesus prayer[20] replaced the complicated catalogues.

The Discernment of Spirits

Scripture presents a series of choices man must take part in (Gn 2:17, 12:4, and others). The choice has special features. Over against the mysterious voice of God another, also mysterious, voice is raised, that of sin, of Satan. What criterion can be used to distinguish one from the other? To bear witness to the voice of God was the role of the prophets. The Wisdom Books were written only to learn how to distinguish the voice of wisdom from that of folly, that of the just from that of the ungodly. The expression 'to distinguish between spirits' is found even in the New Testament Epistles (1 Co 12:10, 1 Jn 4:1).[21]

The problem did not cease to occupy a very important place in spiritual literature.[22] Origen carefully discussed the various sources from which human thoughts proceed, and indicated the different sorts of spirits capable of acting on us.[23] The tendency of Antony and the simple monks in Egypt was more descriptive and concrete;[24] The teaching of Evagrius was, by contrast, systematic. The basic rules formulated by Cassian were the most complete of his time.[25] After him, Diadochus of Photice, who had to fight against Messalian doctrines, indicated the problems involved in discriminating between true and false consolations and desolations.[26] It is within this tradition that in more recent times, Theophane the Recluse interpreted the rules adopted from Lorenzo Scupoli.[27]

Discernment as a Gift of God, a Spiritual Art, and the Fruit of Experience

For St John, spiritual experience is an 'anointing', a state of light (1 Jn 2:20, 27).[28] According to Diadochus of Photice, the Holy Spirit is the 'lamp' of this knowledge.[29] For Paisius Velichkovsky, discernment is 'the spiritual understanding given by God'.[30]

Consequently, this experience cannot be separated from the observance of the commandments on charity (Cf 1 Jn 2:3, Ph 1:9). Antony said: 'Thus there is need of much prayer and of discipline, that when a man has received through the Spirit the gift of discerning spirits, he may have the power to recognize their characteristics...'.[31]

Finally, the recognition of spirits is given as the result of long observation: 'We have learnt, after much observation (*meta pollēs katatērēseōs*)', Evagrius said, 'to recognize the difference between angelic thoughts, human thoughts, and thoughts that come from demons.'[32] Demons betray themselves through their conduct, through the frequency and the manner of their assaults, but especially through the thoughts they inspire.[33] Thus one acquires a special 'sense', a spiritual intuition, and one identifies an evil thought 'by the demons' evil smell'.[34]

The 'Psychological' Rules: How Spirits Act

More than others, Evagrius singled out the thoughts which demons suggest,[35] and Antony observed the states created in the soul by the spirits. Antony's great discourse lays down the golden rule of this discernment: good visions give rise to 'joy unspeakable, cheerfulness, courage, renewed strength, calmness of thought, boldness and love of God'; the others, by contrast, bring with them 'apprehension of soul, confusion and disorder of thought, dejection, hatred toward ascetics, spiritual sloth, affliction, the memory of one's family, and fear of death; presently, there is craving for evil, a contempt for virtue, and instability of character'.[36]

This rule was later simplified into an axiom: *Quidquid inquietat est a diabolo* (Anything disquieting comes from the devil). Evagrius speaks of a 'peaceful state' and 'turbulence of mind'.[37] After them, authors realized very well that it was not only a matter of 'consolation' or 'desolation', for these are by themselves not sufficient to make their origin known.[38] The demon is a deceiver. 'When our intellect begins to perceive the grace of the Holy Spirit', Diadochus of Photice remarks, 'then Satan, too, importunes the soul with a sense of deceptive sweetness in the quiet times of the night, when we fall into a light kind of sleep.'[39]

But in his teaching, Antony does not speak of a mere feeling of joy or, by contrast, of a mere sadness. He comments rather that at one time there is a *katastasis* (settled state), at another time an *akatastasia* (state of disorder) introduced into the soul.[40] One could therefore say that angelic manifestations are 'according to nature', whereas demonic ones disturb the good natural order.

Even if the demon assumes the form of an angel of light (2 Co 11:14), with a 'fraudulent adornment of light',[41] if he 'gently wags his tail',[42] one recognizes him by his works, according to the effect he produces in the image of God within the soul, for there dwells the most decisive criterion of discernment. This is how the 'peaceable state' or the 'state of turbulence' ought to be explained.[43]

The monks were especially warned to pay attention to the weak points in their virtues or, by contrast, to immoderation in their asceticism: 'When the demons become exhausted in their struggle with monks, they withdraw a little and watch which virtue will be neglected during that interval; then, suddenly attacking this side they pillage the poor soul'.[44] Pushing the ascetic to exaggeration, the demons seek to 'prevent our fulfilling what is possible and constrain us to undertake things that are impossible for us.'[45]

The Manifestation of Thoughts

The discernment of thoughts is the art of arts. How can it be assumed to be in a beginner, someone who ought therefore to manifest his thoughts to a 'discerning' (*diacritic*) Father, a practice called *exagoreusis*.[46] In cenobitic monasteries everyone came to be obliged to make this accounting of conscience. Theodore the Studite called it 'a great means of salvation' and he was not at all pleased if his monks appealed infrequently to their abba.[47]

The principle was laid down by Antony himself: 'If he is able to, a monk ought to tell his elders confidently how many steps he takes and how many drops of water he drinks in his cell.'[48] Above this necessity, no love of silence obtains; on the contrary, what is appropriate is the *asiōpēton*, that is, 'never to keep silent about one's own thoughts', as Barsanuphius explained.[49]

Exagoreusis is a confession not of sins—at least this is not its primary and exclusive aim—but of 'thoughts', to know whether they are good or bad. Many of the apophthegmata are the detailed recital of a question and an answer. Everything was done in a few words. Letters of direction replied with the same conciseness.[50]

Among the Studite monks,[51] manifestation of thoughts was made daily to the *hegoumen*.[52] Many *typika* allowed other 'spirituals' than the *hegoumen* to receive intimate secrets. Dorotheos, who held this practice indispensable to salvation, gave this reason: 'Being passionate, we should absolutely not entrust ourselves to our own heart; for a crooked rule makes crooked even that which is straight'.[53] His fifth *Instruction* is entitled, 'That One Should Not Follow One's Own Judgment.'[54]

Examination of Conscience

In order to reveal his thoughts, one ought to examine what goes on in his soul. The practice of daily self-examination was recommended first in pastoral literature. The Father who most frequently expressed his opinion on the subject was John Chrysostom.[55] But it is to fourth-century Syro-Palestinian literature that we must turn to discover the most thorough prescriptions on the method to be followed. The writer who gave the most explicit instruction on this subject was Dorotheos of Gaza.[56] The psychological practice seems very close to the examination of conscience familiar to Neo-Stoicism,[57] but its aim was different. For Dorotheos, a mere 'return to self' was not the purpose; one scrutinized oneself with a view to *exagoreusis*. This examination was an element of spiritual direction.

John Climacus informs us that he had seen many monks carrying a small book in which they wrote down their faults and thoughts each day.[58] And, he says: 'Anyone who sees that some passion is getting the better of him, should first of all take up arms against this passion, . . . ; because until this passion is destroyed, we shall not derive any profit from the conquest of other passions'.[59] The general examination practised faithfully was in itself to become a 'special examination' (and organized into a method, later, in the West).[60]

4. THE EIGHT EVIL THOUGHTS

The Theory of the Eight Evil or 'Generic' Thoughts

'All demonic thoughts carry into the soul notions of sensible things.'[1] 'We shall know [the demons] from our thoughts, and our thoughts we know from objects).'[2] This reflection led Evagrius to base the discernment of spirits on a new, schematic foundation.

His teaching is condensed in Chapter Six of the *Praktikos*:

> There are eight principal thoughts, from which all other thoughts stem (*hoi genikōtatoi logismoi*).[3] The first thought is of gluttony (*gastrimargia*); the second, of fornication (*porneia*); the third, of love of money (*philargyria*); the fourth, of discontent (*lypē*); the fifth, of anger (*orgē*); the sixth, of despondency (*akēdia*); the seventh, of vainglory (*kenodoxia*); the eighth, of pride (*hyperēphania*).[4]

The chapters that follow analyze each of these eight thoughts and expound the remedies to them. The theory of the eight thoughts (*logismoi*) holds a key position in Evagrian doctrine. Beginning with him, it has had a great influence in the history of spirituality.

Was Evagrius the first to teach this doctrine? At the end of the fifth century Gennadius of Marseilles was already asking himself this question.[5] Origen had given lists of vices which are not without resemblance to that of Evagrius,[6] who had borrowed from Origen the symbolism of the conquest of Canaan under the leadership of Joshua-Jesus[7]: according to Dt 7:1, there are 'seven nations opposed to the people of Israel'; why therefore eight vices? 'It is because the Hebrews had already left Egypt.'[8] It appears, however, that Evagrius' list is linked to a much broader tradition. The various literatures of the Hellenistic epoch present a great number of catalogues of vice; the New Testament presents several examples of them.[9] Among the eight vices, the one in which Evagrius' originality is most evident is the sixth in the list, *acēdia*, the pre-eminent temptation of the solitary.

The Sequence of Logismoi *and the Latin List*

Transferred to the work of John of Damascus, the list of Evagrius has become an integral part of the common teaching,[10] with one slight variation: the order of sadness and of anger is sometimes reversed.[11] What were the reasons for this sequence?

Evagrius specified that the three temptations undergone by Christ were, in succession, gluttony, greed, and vainglory.[12] These three *logismoi* therefore constituted the framework of the list; all the others were connected to one or another of them.[13] But the order corresponds above all to an empirical sequence; it follows a spiritual progression.

We know how successful this classification of vices has been in the West, after Cassian. A decisive role in its evolution was played by Gregory the Great, author of the *Moralia in Job*.[14] He kept Cassian's terms, with the exception of *acēdia*; instead of it he introduced envy (*invidia*), and left out *superbia* (pride — like *philautia* [self-love] in the East, considered to be the queen of vices[15]) — thereby reducing the list to seven. He also changed the order, taking his inspiration from the Vulgate rendition of Sirach 10:15: *Initium omnis peccati est superbia* (Pride is the beginning of all sin). Later, vainglory and pride came to be combined, and thus we arrived at the definitive classification of the seven deadly sins which has been standard in the West since the thirteenth century.[16]

The differences between the Eastern list and the Western are negligible. Envy, which takes the place of sadness, is indeed a special sadness, for the good of another. If *acedia* is viewed mainly as laziness, this is again nothing but a more specific point of view. We can say that the Latin sequence proceeds from a dogmatic perspective, while the Eastern is more psychological; this is why it was used more often in the practical teaching of spiritual writers.

Gluttony[17]

Christian authors have preferred to use the living examples of gluttony given to them by Scripture: Eve, Esau, Holophernes. Gluttony is the beginning of the passions, just as Amalek is the first of the nations.[18]

Clement of Alexandria discerned three manifestations of this vice: *opsophagia*, the immoderate use of delicacies; *gastrimargia*, 'belly-madness' or gluttony; and *laimargia*, 'madness of the throat'.[19] Cassian distinguished between the sort of gluttony which drives a monk to eat before the appointed times, that which incites to over eat, and that which leads him to be on the lookout for dainties and delicacies.[20] Evagrius understood by gluttony the temptation which impels a monk to soften the rigors of his fast under the pretexts that asceticism is bad for his health.[21] John Climacus mentions also the desires, imaginations, dreams and such things as prove that covetousness has not yet been suppressed completely.[22] A special fault among monks was *latrophagia*, eating in secret.[23]

They enumerate bodily means to overcome this vice,[24] but Cassian adds that 'We cannot possibly scorn the gratification of the food presented to us, unless the mind finds a greater joy in the contemplation of divine things.'[25]

Fornication

The connection between gluttony and fornication has been noted frequently.[26] Contrarily, this demon is incompatible with the demon of vainglory.[27] Evagrius defined fornication as 'lusting after bodies'.[28] Three 'movements of the body' are differentiated in the *Sayings*:[29] the natural movement (*physikē kinēsis*, Cassian's *naturalis carnis motus*[30]); one caused by too much eating and drinking; and a third which comes from the demons. 'If the thoughts which the demon stirs up are not accompanied by passions, then,' Evagrius believed, 'they will not stand in the way of our contemplation of God.'[31]

Avarice

According to Maximus the Confessor, 'There are three reasons for love of money: love of pleasure, vainglory, and lack of faith and confidence. Lack of faith is worse than the other two.'[32] It was this last reason which Evagrius especially had in mind when he wrote that the demon of avarice suggests the feeling of insecurity;[33] John Climacus called this vice 'the worship of idols'.[34]

Solitary or idiorrhythmic monks were especially vulnerable to the danger of avarice,[35] tempted to distribute alms under the pretext of doing good to others,[36] whereas in fact 'it is an impossibility for charity to exist in anyone along with money'.[37]

Melancholy

Melancholy is defined by Evagrius as *stērēsis hēdonēs*, a deprivation of sensible pleasure,[38] and a result of anger.[39] According to the object of this frustration, one ought to distinguish sadness 'according to God', *penthos*,[40] from melancholy as a vice, when it bears upon 'worldly objects, when it is bodily', as John the Solitary says.[41]

There is no evil worse than melancholy; it breaks the will. John Chrysostom said: 'It attacks not only the flesh but also the very soul ... [It is] an unceasing executioner who saps the strength of the soul.'[42] He encouraged Olympias, a virtuous woman, to overcome *athymia*, 'the tyranny of discouragement'.[43] Abba Isaiah said that the spirit of melancholy 'puts many hunting devices to work until it has removed all strength from you'.[44] Against it, John Chrysostom set christian patience,[45] Abba Isaiah *penthos*, sadness according to God.[46] Before him, Evagrius had written, 'The man who flees from all worldly pleasures is an impregnable tower before the assaults of the demon of melancholy'.[47]

The Russian authors talk much about melancholy.[48] Theophane the Recluse knew that consolations and desolations are stages on the road of the inner life and laid down rules of conduct on how to draw spiritual profit from them.[49]

Anger[50]

The definition of anger as 'a boiling of our irascible part' (*zesis thymou*) is attributed by Seneca to certain Stoics,[51] and was borrowed by Evagrius.[52] It is 'a stirring up against one who has given injury — or is thought to have done so.'[53] As with sadness, one can distinguish here between the natural activity of irascibility and an activity 'contrary to our nature'.[54]

'The role of anger', John Climacus says, 'is to fight against the demons.'[55] Evagrius viewed *thymos* (the irascible power) as a great force 'that destroys the [evil] thoughts'.[56]

Anger should therefore not be directed against human beings. Nikon of the Black Mountain, however, advised that we distinguish between cases: 'One should act according to his spiritual understanding and the sense of Holy Scripture, with a merciful and free heart; to be angry on account of any fleshly object whatever is contrary to piety, but one should reprimand the lack of spiritual gifts.'[57]

According to Joseph of Volokolamsk anger should also be directed against heretics, and he commented in a curious way on the word of the psalmist, 'Be angry, but sin not' (Ps 4:4). 'Be angry' against the heretic, 'but sin not' by the sin of negligence.[58]

The effect of anger is to increase anger (*thymos*), which leads us towards the demonic state, according to Evagrius.[59] He enumerated four signs that accompany resentment: it irritates the soul all day long, especially during prayer; it brings before one's eyes the face of the offender; it stirs up alarming dreams and terrors in the night.[60] Most importantly, anger disturbs the normal activity of the mind, which is contemplation.[61] This is why *mnesi kakia*, the remembrance of slights, is an obstacle to prayer.[62]

Linked to hatred,[63] anger gives rise to a false desire for the solitary life.[64] Hospitality, by contrast, the means of reconciliation, calms excited minds.[65] Antony counseled his monks 'to heed constantly the Apostle's word' in Eph 4:25: 'Do not let the sun go down upon your anger'.[66] Dorotheos believed that we should first cut the root of this vice, that is, considering ourselves superior to our neighbor.[67]

Evagrius has summed up the cures in one sentence: 'Turbid anger is calmed by the singing of psalms, by patience, and by almsgiving.'[68]

Acedia

In the *Life of Antony*[69] and from the pen of Origen, the term *acēdia* still kept the meaning given it by classical usage: negligence, lack of interest (Cf. Ps 118:28, Is 61:3). But it was surrounded by terms that were already directing it towards its Evagrian sense: cowardice (*deilia*), dejection (*katēpheia*), sadness (*lypē*), and others. Evagrius seems to have been the first to identify the demon of *acēdia* with the 'noonday demon' of Psalm 90:6.[70] Coptic translators rendered the word by *pehloped*, weariness (of heart), the Syrians by *qûtâ, re^yânâ*, depression of spirit,[71] the Slavs by *unynie*, breaking. Later, the Latin *taedium* was used, but Cassian kept the Greek word *acidia*.[72]

Evagrius has drawn a very picturesque scene of the monk prey to despondency:

> The demon of *acedia* — also called *the noonday demon* — is the one that causes the most serious trouble of all. He presses his attack upon the monk about the fourth hour[73] and besieges the soul until the eighth hour.[74] First of all he makes it seem that the sun barely moves, if at all, and that the day is fifty hours long. Then he constrains the monk to look constantly out the windows, to walk outside the cell, to gaze carefully at the sun to determine how far it stands from the ninth hour,[75] to look now this way and now that ... Then too he instills in the heart of the monk a hatred for the place, a hatred for his very life itself, a hatred for manual labor. He leads him to reflect that charity has departed from among the brethren, that there is no one to give encouragement. Should there be someone at this period who happens to offend him in some way or the other, this too the demon uses to contribute further to his hatred. This demon drives him along to desire other sites where he can more easily procure life's necessities, more readily find work and make a real success of himself. He goes on to suggest that, after all, it is not the place that is the basis of pleasing the Lord. God is to be adored everywhere.[76] He joins to these reflections the memory of his dear ones and of his former way of life. He depicts life stretching out for a long period of time, and brings before the mind's eye the toil of the ascetic struggle and, as the saying has it, leaves no leaf unturned to induce the monk to forsake his cell and drop out of the fight. No other demon follows close upon the heels of this one (when he is defeated) but only a state of deep peace and inexpressible joy arise out of this struggle.[77]

It is not easy to be specific about the difference between despondency and sadness; the Eastern monastic tradition makes a distinction between them to underline a special circumstance: despondency, as defined by Evagrius, is linked to the anchoretic way of life and is opposed to perseverance in the cell and the solitary life. For John Climacus, the most efficient cure for despondency is the cure for sadness, *penthos*.[78]

Vainglory[79]

Scripture linked glory to moral and religious values. The one solid foundation for it is God (Ps 62:6, 8). Glory is therefore 'vain' when it seeks a reward for virtue in the admiration of men. Vainglory increases with progress in the virtues,[80] but it dissipates their value.[81]

> The spirit of vainglory is most subtle and it readily grows up in the souls of those who practise virtue. It leads them to desire to make their struggles known publicly, to hunt after the praise of men.[82] This in turn leads to their illusory healing of women, or to their hearing fancied sounds as the cries of the demons — crowds of people who touch their clothes. This demon predicts besides that they will attain to the priesthood. It has men knocking at the door, seeking audience with them. If the monk does not willingly yield to their request, he is bound and led away.[83]

Parrhēsia (frank speech, in the pejorative sense)[84] is a manifestation of vanity, as is exaggerated pertness, being rude with people.[85] Against vanity one should set *to apsēphiston*, an untranslatable term comprising many aspects: neither to award to oneself, nor to claim from others, a vote for any precedence or distinction whatever, to consent to be nothing, 'to deny oneself,[86] which presupposes that one has arrived at 'knowledge',[87] at the contemplation of true values.

Pride

In Scripture, pride is above all the vice of pagans tempted to oppose God; Holophernes expressed it by asking 'Who is God except Nebuchadnezzar?' (Jdt 6:2).[88] Forgetfulness of God manifests itself in vainglory. Some saw in it a less serious form of pride,[89] but most Eastern authors kept the Evagrian distinction. At its base is the difference between the things for which one seeks esteem: are they 'vanities' (beautiful hair, a good voice, and so on) which have no value; or, by contrast, are they divine gifts of grace and holiness, and in such cases one denies 'that God is his helper'.[90]

Spiritual Warfare 255

'The demon of pride has a twofold wickedness', Maximus the Confessor said. 'Either he persuades the monk to ascribe his virtuous deeds to himself... or,... he suggests scorn for the brothers still imperfect.'[91] This, then, is the danger for the perfect. The *Sayings* speak of monks who fell after long asceticism, and went out of their mind (*ekstasis phrenōn*) as a result of pride.[92]

Pride is the greatest of all sins, Origen explained; it is the devil's chief sin,[93] According to John Chrysostom, it is 'the root, the source, the mother of sin'.[94] But it comes at the end, 'when passions are inactive',[95] when one has somehow overcome the seven preceding vices.

Pride is removed 'when we ascribe our right actions to God,'[96] and, in general, by humility: 'The demon can actually imitate all the good actions which we seem to perform, but he is genuinely vanquished in the realm of love and humility.'[97]

The pre-eminent sign of pride is blasphemy (*blasphēmia*) because this is the antithesis of the praise which man owes God.[98] The violence and suddenness of this demon has been indicated;[99] he is opposed to prayer.

The Root of All Evil Thoughts: Love of Self

Gregory the Great spoke of pride as the root of the vices.[100] For Evagrius, 'the first of all the [evil] thoughts is that of self-love (*philautia*); the eight others derive from it'.[101] This is the common teaching of the Eastern Fathers.[102]

Etymologically, *philautia* means love of self. 'Man is by nature his own friend: it is legitimate', said Plato.[103] He notes, meanwhile, that 'in fact,... this great friendship for oneself becomes for each the cause of all missteps'.[104] For Aristotle, there are two types of self-love: a noble man desires virtue for himself; the base man material goods and sensual pleasures.[105]

For Philo, self-love was tantamount to impiety;[106] more and more the word took on a pejorative meaning (Cf. 1 Tm 3:2). Maximus the Confessor is really the great doctor of self-love,[107] which he defined as 'the passion of attachment for the body',[108] and 'unreasonable affection for one's body'.[109] The basic choice between the spirit and the pleasures of the senses is, in his moral system, the choice between happiness and pleasure. The self-lover (*philautos*) is 'a lover of self against self'.[110] One moves from self-love to the quest for sensuous pleasure and thus through all the vices to pride.

Self-will

Like self-love, self-will (*voluntas propria*) — the *thelēma idion* (one's own will), the fleshly will, to *thelēma sarkikon, kakon, ponēron, idia synesis, idia kardia* — is a desire contrary to the true nature of man.[111] Few authors in the history of Christianity have pointed out the dangers of man's self-will so insistently as Dorotheos of Gaza.[112] He insisted on the need to bring down this 'brass wall between man and God', this 'rock of repulsion',[113] and he provided a description of it. Self-will is neither the faculty of will nor, properly speaking, an act of will opposed, as in Clement of Alexandria, to concupiscence;[114] it is the passionate movement that follows the *logismos*, the evil thought. It is an inclination, the *prospatheia*, which arises immediately after its representation.[115]

To the prime mover, one's own will, is joined the *dikaiōma*, a 'pretense at justice', 'self-justification'. Instead of cutting off this attraction after a passionate thought, the person who 'does his own will' finds confirmation and support in some passage from Scripture, some aphorism of the Fathers, which gives him the appearance of being on the right road. The *dikaiōma* is then escorted by *monotonia*, obstinacy.[116] 'If the pretense of justice lends support to the will, it turns out badly for man.'[117]

Notes

1. THE STRUGGLE AGAINST THE DEMONS

1. See Jb 7:1, Lk 11:21, Jn 16:33, 1 Co 9:24–27.
2. See Seneca, *Letter* 51: 'nobis quoque militandum est...'.
3. See Pierre Bourguignon and Francis Wenner, 'Combat spirituel', DS 2/1:1135–42; Adalbert de Vogüé, *La Règle du Maître*, vol. 1 (Paris, 1964) 89 [cf. *The Rule of the Master*, CS6 (1977) Introduction, pp 44–5]; Garcia M. Colombás, *Paradis et vie angélique* (Paris, 1961) 118ff; Edward Malone, *The Monk and the Martyr* (Washington, 1950) 91ff.
4. See Antoine Guillaumont, SC 170 (1971), 95.
5. See Michel Olphe-Galliard, 'Cassien', DS 2/1:214ff; Owen Chadwick, *John Cassian: A Study in Primitive Monasticism* (Cambridge, 1950) 95ff.

Spiritual Warfare 257

6. *Letter* 14; SCh 92:521; PG 88:1840D.
7. *Oratio* 2.91; PG 35:493B.
8. *Praktikos* 34; SCh 171:579; CS 4:25. Cf. 48, 609; CS 4:48, 29.
9. *Ibid.*, 5; SCh 171:505; CS 4:16.
10. *Commentaire d'Abba Isaïe*, Disc. 1.16; French trans. René Draguet, CSCO 327 (*Scriptores Syri* 145) p. 17, 22–27.
11. Cf. Rom 7–8, 12:31, 14:30, 16:11.
12. 38a.
13. See Edouard Dhorme, *Choix de textes religieux assyro-babyloniens*, Études bibliques (Paris, 1907) 372–79.
14. *Republic* II, 360e–362e.
15. See H. Jaeger, 'Examinatio', DS 4/2:1849ff.
16. *Stromata* IV.7.55.1; PG:1268A, ed. O. Stählin, GCS 2 (1906) 273.
17. See Jean-Claude Guy, 'Remarques sur le texte des Apophthegmata Patrum', RSR 43 (1955) 254; *The Lausiac History*, Chapter 18: Pachomius *andra dokimōtaton* (a most tried man), ed. C. Butler (Cambridge, 1904) 52 [*Pachomian Koinonia* 2: *Pachomian Chronicles and Rules*, CS 46: p. 124]; likewise Dorotheos, chapter 18; SCh 92:86.
18. Evagrius, *Praktikos*, 73; SCh 171:661; CS 4:35.
19. Diadochus of Photice, *Cent Chapitres gnostiques* 82 and 90; SCh 5a (1966) 141 and 151; see Introd., 31ff; ['On Spiritual knowledge and Discrimination: One Hundred Texts', *The Philokalia. The Complete Text*, vol. 1:253ff]; Spidlík, *Joseph de Volokolamsk*, 27.
20. *Collationes* 18.13; CSEL 13:520; PG 49:1113; SCh 64 (1959) 26.
21. *Ibid.*, 4.6–7; CSEL 101; PG 590; SCh 42:170ff.
22. *Institutiones* 12.4; ed. Michael Petschenig, CSEL 17 (1888) p. 208; PL 49:429, SCh 109 (1965) 454ff.
23. *Letter* 12; SCh 92:519; PG 88:1840D.
24. *Instructions* 13.140; SCh 92:407.
25. Origen, *Homilia in Librum Jesu Nave*; PG 12:885A.
26. In the opinion of Pseudo-Macarius the warfare ceases only for those who have reached perfect charity and are bound by grace, *Homilia* 26.16; PG 34:684.
27. *Antirrheticos* IV.3, ed. Frankenberg, 502; *Praktikos* 59; SCh 171: 639; CS 4:33.
28. 209; SCh 12:284.
29. See Stanislas Lyonnet, 'Le démon dans l'Écriture', DS 3:142–52.
30. *Oratio 4 in sanctum Pascha* 6; PG 99:717A; see J. Kirchmeyer, in DS 6:8333.
31. Evagrius, *Praktikos* 5; SCh 171:505; CS 4:16.
32. See Louis Bouyer, *La vie de saint Antoine* (Abbaye de Wandrille, 1950) 103ff.
33. See A. and C. Guillaumont, Introduction to *Le Traité pratique* of Evagrius, SCh 170:94ff.
34. See M. Olphe-Galliard, in DS 2/1:242.
35. See Louis Bouyer, 'Le problème du mal dans le christianisme antique', *Dieu vivant* 6 (1946) 31.
36. See Spanneut, *Le stoïcisme des Pères de l'Église*, 329, n. 32.
37. See Jean Daniélou, 'Démon dans la littérature ecclésiastique jusqu'à Origène', DS 3:152–89.
38. See John Moschus, *Pratum spirituale* 115; SCh 12:167.
39. Thus, for example, Daniel the Stylite; see A. J. Festugière, *Les moines d'Orient*, II:101ff.

40. *In Librum Jesu Nave homilia* VIII.4; GCS 7:339.
41. *Vie de sainte Mélanie* 18; SCh 90:163.
42. *Vie de S. Sabas*, ed. A. J. Festugière, *Les moines d'Orient* (Paris, 1961-1965), vol. III:2, 24.
43. *De principiis* III.21; GCS 5:246.
44. *De oratione* 63 (PG 79:1180D); cf. *Praktikos* 46 (SCh 171:620ff; CS 4:28ff).
45. *De diversis cogitationibus malis* 7; PG 79:1209B.
46. *Praktikos* 48 (SCh 171:608ff; CS 4:29, 26 (560ff; 23).
47. *De oratione* 68; PG 79:1181B; CS 4:66.
48. *Centuriae Supplementum* 14; the Greek is in J. Muyldermans, *Evagriana* (Paris, 1931), 39.
49. See below, section 3.
50. Evagrius, *Antirrheticos* II.55; Frankenberg, 492.
51. See A. and C. Guillaumont, 'Démon dans la plus ancienne littérature monastique', DS 3:203ff.
52. Evagrius, *De diversis cogitationibus malis* 27; PG 79:1232BC; [Selections from 'On Various Evil Thoughts' are found in *Early Fathers from the Philokalia*, ed. E. Kadloubovsky (London, 1963) 117ff.]; *Praktikos* 47; SCh 171:607; CS 4:29.
53. *Praktikos* 50; SCh 171:614; CS 4:29-30.
54. *Collationes* 7.19ff.; SCh 54:25ff. [LNPF series 2, vol. 11:368ff.]
55. Pseudo-Macarius, *Homilia* 3.6 (PG 34:472B; John Climacus, *Scala Paradisi* PG 88:896ff).
56. See Jean Daniélou, 'Exorcisme', DS 4/2:1995-2004.
57. Jean Michel Hanssens, *La liturgie d'Hippolyte* OCA 155 (Rome, 1959) 372.
58. See André Benoît, *Le baptême chrétien au second siècle* (Paris, 1953) 39.
59. *Contra Celsum* 3.14; ed. Paul Koetschau, GCS 1 (Leipzig, 1899) 213.
60. This is an aspect brought out in the famous *Antirrheticos*.
61. *Epistola ad Marcellinum* 33; PG 27:45A.
62. See T. Špidlík, 'Gesù nella pietà dei Cristiani orientali', in E. Ancilli, *Gesù Cristo — mistero e presenza*, Teresianum (Rome, 1971) 398ff.
63. See Gregory Nazianzen, *Oratio* 4.55; PG 35:580A.
64. See John Moschus, *Pratum spirituale* 152; PG 87/3:3017; SCh 12:205.
65. See Chapter XI, *Virtue, Likeness to God*.
66. A. and C. Guillaumont, 'Démon', DS 3:189-211.

2. LOGISMOI

1. *Homilia* 6.3; PG 34:520B, ed. Hermann Dörries, E. Klostermann, M. Kröger, *Die 50 geistliche Homilien des Makarios*, Patristische Texte und Studien (Berlin, 1964) 66; trans. A. J. Mason, *St Macarius the Great. Fifty Spiritual Homilies* (London, rpt. Willits, 1974) 58.
2. *Commentarium in Matthaeum* 21, edd. Ernst Benz and Erich Klostermann, CGS 40:48.
3. *Praktikos* 48; SCh 171:609; DS 4:29).
4. See above, Chapter VII, *Chastity*.
5. *Praktikos*, 48.
6. *Ibid*.
7. *Ibid*.
8. *Century II on Charity* 78; SCh 9:117; ACW 21:168.

9. Dorotheus, *Letter* 4.189 (SCh 92:507); *Instruction* 14.162 (p. 453); Philo, *De congressu* 98; G. Lampe, *A Patristic Greek Lexicon* (Oxford, 1961) 806.
10. See A. Guillaumont in SCh 170 (1971) 63.
11. See Dorotheus, *Instruction* 13.147; SCh 92:417: *kata dianoian logismous*.
12. Evagrius, *Kephalaia gnostika* VI.83, ed. A. Guillaumont, *Les 'Kephalaia gnostica' d'Evagre le Pontique*, Patristica Sorbonensia (Paris, 1962) 253.
13. Athanasius, *Expositio in Psalmo* 20.11; PG 27:129.
14. Gregory of Nyssa, *De vita Moysis*; PG 44:328 [Trans. Everett Ferguson and A. J. Malherbe, *The Life of Moses* (Kalamazoo: Cistercian; New York: Paulist, 1978)].
15. See Dorotheus, *Instruction* 12.129; SCh 92:389.
16. See above, IV, *The Nature of The Soul*.
17. *In Proverbia* 7; PG 17:181B.
18. Maximus the Confessor, *Ad Thalassium, quaestio* 22; PG 90:808B.
19. *Ibid*.
20. *Ad Thalassium, quaestiones* 49–50; col. 4520–468BC.
21. *Ibid*.; col. 452D.
22. *Ibid*.
23. *Ibid*.; col. 460D.
24. *Ibid*.; col. 461C.
25. Dorotheus, *Instruction* 11.116; SCh 92:363; CS 33:171ff.
26. Dorotheus, *Letter* 8.139; SCh 92:516.
27. Dorotheus, *Instruction* 3.43 (215); 5.54 (237); 11.120 (371) and others.
28. *Ibid*., 19.111 (353); 12.137 (401); 14.155 (436), etc.
29. *Ibid*., 6.65 (255); 5.65 (257) etc.; Cf. below, *Self-will*.
30. See Stephanus Bettencourt, 'Doctrina ascetica Origenis', *Studia Anselmiana* 16 (Rome, 1945) 77ff; Jean Daniélou, 'Démon', DS 3:187ff. A. Guillaumont in SCh 170:58.
31. Lk 2:35, 5:22, 6:8, 9:46–47, 24:28; with an adjective, Mt 15:9; Mk 7:21.
32. J. Muyldermans, *Evagriana*. Extrait de la revue *Museon*, tome XLIV, augmenté de nouveaux fragments grecs inédits, 1 fasc. (Paris, 1931) 54, 59; translation by Norman Russell, *The Lives of the Desert Fathers*. [*The historia monachorum in Aegypto*] CS 34 (London-Kalamazoo, 1981) 127.
33. *Century III on Charity* 42; SCh 9:136; ACW 21:180.
34. See *Self-will*, below.
35. Maximus the Confessor, *Century III*.41; SCh 9:136; 21:180.
36. *Homilia 15 in Numeros* 5; CGS 33:389; ed. A. Jaubert, SCh 71 (1960) 348–50.
37. S. Bettencourt, 'Doctrina ascetica Origenis', 77ff.; J. Daniélou, DS 3:187.
38. Cf Si 15:14.
39. Chapter 5 (PG 26:848B); Chapter 23 (877A).
40. See the treatise *De octo spiritibus malitiae*, PG 79:1145ff. *Spiritus* is the usual term in Cassian, see *Institutiones* 5–12; SCh 109 [NPNF 11].
41. Maximus the Confessor, *Century II on Charity* 92; SCh 9:121; 21:171–72.
42. *Century II on Charity* 74; SCh p. 115; ACW p. 167.
43. *Praktikos* 37; SCh 171:685; CS 4:61. See also Abba Evagrius the Monk, *To Anatolius: Texts on Active Life*, 26. *Early Fathers from the Philokalia* (London, 1963) 100.
44. The *Praktikos* 34; SCh 171:579; CS 4:25.
45. Spidlík, *Théophane le Reclus*, 14.ff.; see Pseudo-Macarius, *Homily* 16.6; PG 34:617AB.

46. *Théophane le Reclus*, 88.
47. *Praktikos* 55; SCh 171:628; PG 40:1240A; CS 4:31.
48. See I. Hausherr, 'La méthode d'oraison hésychaste', OC 9/2 (Rome, 1927) 119ff.
49. John of Damascus, *De virtutibus et vitio*, PG 95:93 ['On the Virtues and the Vices', *The Philokalia. The Complete Text*, vol. 2:334ff.).
50. *Praktikos*, 9 and 22; SCh 171:513, 553; CS 4:17, 22.
51. *Ibid.*, 75 (663; 35).
52. Arnim, SVF III, p. 42, n. 117.
53. *Praktikos*, 72; SCh p. 660, note; CS 4, p. 35.
54. See Chapter X, 1.
55. *Scala Paradisi* 15; PG 88:896.
56. *Philokalia*, chapter 34; vol 2 (Athens, 1968) 285.
57. *Načertanie christianskago nravoučenija* [*Christian Moral Teaching*] (Moscow, 1895) 156ff.; Špidlík, *Théophane le Reclus*, 163.
58. *Enarratio in Ps.* 145.6; PL 37:1859ff.

3. CUSTODY OF THE HEART

1. See I. Hausherr, 'L'hésychasme. Etude de spiritualité, OCP 22 (1956) 5–40, 247–85; *Hésychasme et prière*, OCA 176 (Rome, 1966) 163–237, especially 214ff.
2. *Commentarium In Canticum* II; GCS 8:133, 16ff. [trans. by R. P. Lawson, *Origen. The Song of Songs: Commentary and Homilies*, ACW 26 (London, 1957)].
3. *In Proverbia* 5; PG 17:176CD.
4. *In librum Jesu Nave, Homilia* 13.1 (GCS 7:373); *Homilia* 15.3, (p. 387); Dorotheus, *Instruction* 11.117 (SCh 92:363; CS 33:174).
5. Hesychius, *De temperantia et virtute, Centuria* II.76; PG 93:1537A; Severus of Antioch, *Homilia* 57; PO 4:93.
6. See *Apophthegmata Patrum*, Poemen 35 and 39; PG 65:332B; CS 59:172.
7. This is the subject and the title of numerous patristic homilies, the best known of which are Basil's *Homilia in illud: Attende tibi ipsi*, PG 31:197–217 [English translation in *The Fathers of the Church*, vol. 9:431–46], or the one by Abba Isaiah *Logos* 27 (ed. Augoustinos monachos. *Logoi 29* [Jerusalem, 1911], re-ed. S. Schoinas [Volos, 1962] 172–75). Of the latter, there is a Latin translation in PG 40:1194D–1197B; a French translation in *Abbé Isaïe, Recueil ascétique*, Spiritualité orientale 7 (Etoilles, 1970) 247ff; and extracts in English in *The Philokalia. The Complete Text*, vol. 1:23–28.
8. Notice the title-page of the *Philokalia: tōn hierōn neptikōn*.
9. See I. Hausherr, 'L'hésychasme', OCP 22 (1956) 273ff.; *idem*. OCA 176 (1966) 225ff.
10. Hesychius, *Century* I.1; PG 93:1490D; [trans. by E. Kadloubovsky and G. E. H. Palmer, 'Texts on Sobriety and Prayer', *Writings from the Philokalia on Prayer of the Heart*, 279–321].
11. *De oratione* 149; PG 79:1200A; CS 4:79.
12. See I. Hausherr, 'La méthode d'oraison hésychaste', (Rome, 1927) 134ff., 118ff.
13. See Josh 5:13; Evagrius, *Antirrheticos*, 'Pride' 17. (Frankenberg, 539); *Letter* 11 (Frankenberg, 675); Nicetas Stetathos, *Century* I.89 (PG 120:893A).

Spiritual Warfare 261

14. Evagrius, *Praktikos* 22; SCh 171:553; CS 4:22. See also 'Texts on Active Life' 13, in *Early Fathers from the Philokalia* (London, 1963) 99.
15. *De opificio mundi* 164.
16. *Praktikos* 49; SCh 171:610ff.; CS 4:29ff.
17. See Špidlík, 'L'autorità del libro per il monachesimo russo', in *Monachesimo orientale*, OCA 153 (Rome, 1958) 172.
18. Edited in Syriac by Wilhelm Frankenberg, *Evagrius Ponticus* (Berlin, 1912) 46-544.
19. See T. Špidlík, 'Gesu nella pieta dei Cristiani orientali', in E. Ancilli, *Gesu Cristo – mistero e presenza*, Teresianum (Rome, 1971) 398.
20. See Chapter VII, *The Jesus Prayer*.
21. See Jacques Guillet, 'Discernement des esprits dans l'Ecriture', DS 3:1222 –47.
22. See Gustave Bardy, 'Discernement des esprits chez les Pères', DS 3:1247 –54.
23. Marcel Viller, *La spiritualité des premiers siècles chrétiens* (Paris, 1930) 46.
24. Louis Bouyer, *La vie de saint Antoine* (Saint Wandrille, 1955) 15-30, 119-52; see DS 3:190-96.
25. See J. C. Guy, *Jean Cassien. Vie et doctrine spirituelle* (Paris, 1961).
26. See Edouard des Places, 'Diadoque de Photicé', DS 3, col. 817-34.
27. See *Théophane le Reclus*, 116ff.
28. See Guillet, DS 3:1246.
29. *Cent chapitres gnostiques* 28; SCh 5a:99; ['On Spiritual Knowledge and Discrimination', *The Philokalia*, vol. 1 (London, 1979) 253ff.]
30. *Letter to the Monastery of Poljamerulskij. Life and Works* (in Russian) (Moscow, 1947) 235.
31. *Vita Antonii* 22; PG 26:876B; LNPF series 2, 4:202.
32. *Praktikos* 57; SCh 171:617; CS 4:32; 'Texts on Discrimination in Respect of Passions and Thoughts 7, *The Philokalia. The Complete Text*, vol. 1:42.
33. *Praktikos* 43; SCh p. 599; CS 4:28.
34. *Ibid.*, 39; SCh 591; CS 4:26.
35. *Ibid.*, 51; SCh p. 617; CS 4:30.
36. *Vita Antonii* 36; PG 26:896.
37. *Praktikos* 80; SCh 171:669; CS 4:36; *On Prayer* 30 (PG 79:1173B; CS 4:59); 74-75 (1184B; 67-8).
38. See *Théophane le Reclus*, 193ff.
39. *Cent chapitres gnostiques* 31; SCh 5a:101; *On Spiritual Knowledge and Discrimination: One Hundred Texts*, The Philokalia, vol. 1 (London, 1979) 261.
40. *Vita Antonii* 35.36; PG 26:896BC [NPNF series 2, 11].
41. Gregory Nazianzen, *Carminum liber* II, sectio I.83, vv. 7ff. (PG 37:1429); cf. *Carm.* I.II.2, vv. 114-115 (PG 37:588).
42. Gregory Nazianzen, *Oratio* 40.10; PG 36:396B.
43. See below, X, 2.
44. *Praktikos* 44; SCh 171:601; CS 4:28; *Early Fathers from the Philokalia*; see *On Prayer* 47 (PG 49:1176D–1177A; CS 4:62); *Ibid.*, 134 (1196B; 77).
45. *Praktikos* 40: SCh 171:593; CS 4:27.
46. See I. Hausherr, *Direction spirituelle en Orient Autrefois*, OCA 144 (Rome, 1955) 212ff.
47. *Parva catechesis* 133, ed. Emmanuel Auvray and A. Tougard (Paris, 1891) 464.

48. *Apophthegmata*, Antonius 38; PG 65:88B; CS 59:9.
49. *Letter* 417, ed. Nicodemus the Hagiorite (Venice, 1916) 175; see SCh 92, Introduction, 53ff.
50. See the *Letters of St Barsanuphius and St John*, ed. Nicodemus the Hagiorite (Venice, 1816); French trans. by Lucien Regnault, Ph. Lemaire, and B. Outtier, *Barsanuphe et Jean de Gaza. Correspondance. Recueil complet* (Solesmes, 1971). [A translation is projected in Cistercian Studies Series—ed.]
51. See *Vita S. Euthymii* 15; ed. Jean Baptiste Cotelier, *Ecclesiae Graecae Monumenta* (Paris, 1677–1689), vol. II:213–14.
52. *Constitutiones Studitae* 22, PG 99:1712B; Julien Leroy, 'La vie quotidienne du moine studite', *Irénikon* 27 (1954) 33.
53. *Instruction* 5.66: SCh 92:259; CS 33:122ff.
54. *Ibid.*; 251; 122.
55. See *Catéchèses baptismales* 4.2 (ed. Antoine Wegner, SCh 50:198–9); 5.27 (213); 8.25 (260); *In Genesim* 11.2 (PG 53:93), see 4.6–7 and 23.6 (PG 53; 45 and 206).
56. See *Instruction* 11.5 (PG 88:1740B; SCh 92:362ff; CS 3:172–81); 10.7 (1733BC; SCh 352, CS 163–71).
57. See H. Jaeger, 'L'examen de conscience dans les religions non-chrétiennes et avant le christianisme', in *Numen*, 6 (1959) 175–233; see DS 4/2:1790–99.
58. *Scala paradisi* 4; PG 88:702D.
59. *Ibidem*, 15; col. 887D.
60. See Atanas Liuma and André Derville, 'Examen particulier', DS 4/2: 1838–48

4. THE EIGHT EVIL THOUGHTS

1. Evagrius, *De malignis cogitationibus* 2; PG 79:1201B [Excerpts from 'On Various Evil Thoughts' are translated in *Early Fathers from the Philokalia* 117ff.]
2. *Praktikos*, 43; SCh 171:599; CS 4:28.
3. The term means that these thoughts are 'the most general' and also that they 'generate' others; it was used by the Stoics in their classification of the passions: see Arnim, SVF III, p. 94, n. 386, and the testimony of Clement of Alexandria in *Pedagogos* I.101.1; SCh 70:290.
4. *Praktikos* 6; SCh 506; CS 4:16–17; 'To Anatolius: On Eight Thoughts', *Early Fathers from the Philokalia*, 110.
5. Gennadius of Marseille, *De viris illustribus* II; ed. Ernest C. Richardson, TU 14 (Leipzig, 1896) 65.
6. See Irénée Hausherr, 'L'origine de la théorie orientale des huits péchés capitaux', *OC* 30/3 (1933) 164–75, reprinted in *Études de spiritualité orientale*, OCA 183 (Rome, 1969) 11–22.
7. *In librum Jesu Nave homilia* 15.5, ed., Baehrens, CGS 30:385; SCh 71:348ff; Evagrius, *Kephalaia gnostica* 30.36.68.71; ed. Guillaumont, PO 28/1 (1958) pp. 189, 191, 207.
8. See Cassian, *Collationes* 5.17–18; CSEL 13:143ff; SCh 42:210 [NPNF[2], 11]
9. See A. Guillaumont in SCh 170 (1971) 75ff (with other bibliographic information).
10. See *De octo spiritibus nequitiae*; PG 95:80; see *On the Virtues and the Vices* where chapter 6 of the *Praktikos* of Evagrius is taken over almost literally

Spiritual Warfare 263

(PG 95:92C–93A); see also the Pseudo-Athanasian treatise *Syntagma ad quemdam Politicum*, PG 28:1397D–1400A.
11. See *De octo spiritibus malitiae* (PG 49:1145–1164) and *De virtutibus et vitio* by John of Damascus (PG 95:92C–93A).
12. *De diversis malignis cogitationibus* 1 (PG 79:1200D–1201B); John Climacus, *Scala paradisi* 26 (PG 88:1013).
13. See A. Guillaumont, in SCh 170:91.
14. See the Introduction by Louis Gillet, SCh 32:89ff, where the parallel texts of Cassian and Gregory are studied.
15. See below, *Pride*.
16. See Morton W. Bloomfield, *The Seven Deadly Sins* (Ann Arbor, Michigan, 1952).
17. See William Yeomans and André Derville, 'Gourmandise et Gourmandise spirituelle', DS 6:612–626.
18. Evagrius,*De octo spiritibus malitiae* 1; PG 79:1145A.
19. See Aristotle, *Nicomachean Ethics* III.13.1118 a 38, and elsewhere; Clement of Alexandria, *Paedagogos* II.1 and 2; PG 8:377–432.
20. *Conferences* 5.11; SCh 42:199; NPNF[2] 11:343–4.
21. *Praktikos* 7; SCh 171:508ff.; CS 4:17.
22. *Scala paradisi* 14; PG 88:872CD.
23. See Dorotheos, *Instruction* 11.121; SCh 92:370ff.; CS 33:172ff.
24. Cassian, *Conferences* 5.11; SCh 42:199; NPNF[2] 11:343–4.
25. *Institutes* 5.14; SCh 109:212ff; NPNF[2] 11:238.
26. See Evagrius, *De octo spiritibus malitiae* 4; PG 79:1149CD.
27. *Praktikos*, 58; SCh 171:637, note; CS 4:32.
28. *Ibid.* 8; 511ff; 17ff.
29. Antony 22; PG 65:84AB; CS 59:6.
30. *Conferences* 12.7; SCh 54:133.
31. *Praktikos*, 51; SCh 171:617; CS 4:30. For discussions about the sinful character of nocturnal pollutions in the ancient Church, see F. Refoulé, 'Rêves et vie spirituelle d'après Evagre le Pontique', *Vie spirituelle*, *Suppl.* 59 (1961) 470–516, 488–93.
32. *Century III on Charity* 17; SCh 9:128; ACW 21:175.
33. *Praktikos* 9; SCh 171:513; CS 4:17; *Antirrheticos* II.2, Frankenberg, 494, 12–14.
34. *Scala paradisi* 16; PG 88:924CD.
35. See the examples in Chapter 33 of the *Pečersk Patericon*, ed. D. Abramovič, reprinted by D. Tschižewskij, *Slavische Propyläen* 2 (Munich, 1964) 161ff.
36. See John Climacus, *Scala paradisi* 16; PG 88:924D.
37. Evagrius, *Praktikos* 18; SCh 171; 547; CS 4:21.
38. *Ibid.*, 19; SCh 547; CS 21.
39. *Ibid.*, 10; 515; 17.
40. See above, Chapter VII, 4, *Penthos*.
41. *Dialogue sur l'âme et les passions* IV, trans. I. Hausherr, OCA 120 (Rome, 1938) 99.
42. *Lettres à Olympias* 10.2; SCh 13bis:246ff.
43. *Ibid.*, Index, 459, and Introduction, 49ff.
44. *Logos* 16; ed. Augoustinos (Jerusalem, 1911) 90.
45. *Lettres à Olympias* 13.4; p. 346.
46. *Logos* 16.
47. *Praktikos* 19; SCh 171; 547; CS 4:21.

48. See Nilus of Sora, *Predanie i Ustav*, ed. in *Pamiatniki drevnej pis̆mennosti i iskusstva*, 179 (St. Petersburg, 1912) 49ff; in German in Fairy von Lilienfield, *Nil Sorskij und seine Schriften* (Berlin, 1963) 228ff; see T. Špidlík, *I grandi mistici russi* (Rome, 1977) 132–34.
49. See *Théophane le Reclus*, 109ff.
50. H. D. Noble and Marcel Viller, 'Colère', DS 2/1:1053–77; André-Ignace Mennesier, 'Douceur', DS 3:1674–85.
51. *De ira* II.19; ed. Bourgery, p. 516.
52. *Praktikos* 11; SCh 171:516; CS 4:18.
53. *Ibid.*, 519; 18; see Chrysippus, Arnim, SVF III, p. 96, 37, n. 397; n. 395, 396.
54. *Praktikos* 24; SCh p. 557; CS p. 23.
55. *Scala paradisi* 26; PG 88:985B (*Scholion Evagrii*).
56. *Skemmata* 8. Muyldermans ed., *Evagriana* (Paris, 1931) 38.
57. *Pandecta* 9, ed. Charles de Clercq, *Les textes juridiques dans les Pandectes de Nicon de la Montagne Noire* (Venice, 1912) 29ff.
58. See Špidlík, *Joseph de Volokolamsk*, 133ff.
59. *Letter* 56; ed. Frankenberg, *Evagrius Ponticus* (Berlin, 1912) 604, 14–16; see the note by Guillaumont to *Le Traité pratique* 20, SCh 171:549.
60. Evagrius, *Praktikos* 11; SCh 171:519; see the notes by Guillaumont, and the note by Bamberger, *Praktikos*, CS 4:18.
61. *Ibid.*, 63; p. 647; CS p. 33.
62. *Ibid.*, 26; p. 561; CS p. 23; See John Climacus, *Scala paradisi* 9; PG 88:840D.
63. Evagrius, *Praktikos* 20 (SCh p. 76; CS p. 21); 76 (p. 664; p. 36).
64. *Ibid.* 22 (p. 553, and the note there; CS, p. 22, and note.
65. *Ibid.* 26; 561; 23.
66. *Vita Antonii* 55; PG 26:921B–924A.
67. *Sentences* 17; SCh 92:531; PG 88:1809D.
68. *Praktikos* 15; SCh 171:537; CS 4:20.
69. Chapter 36; PG 26:896.
70. See Guillaumont in SCh 170:86ff.
71. *Ibid.*, 85ff.
72. See Cassian, *Institutes* 10.1; CSEL 17:173, 20–21; SCh 109:384; *Verba Seniorum*, Pelagius VII.1; PL 73:893A (Antony 1; PG 65:76A; CS 59:1); Pseudo-Rufinus 105; PL 73:780C.
73. That is, about ten in the morning.
74. Two o'clock in the afternoon.
75. The ninth hour (3 PM) was the usual hour for dinner; see *Apophthegmata patrum*, Antonius 34; PG 65:85D–88A; CS 59:8; and *Apo* Macariu; 276C 1; 151–2.
76. See Jn 4:21–24.
77. *Praktikos* 12; SCh 171:521ff; CS 4:18–19.
78. *Scala paradisi* 13; PG 88:860D; cf. Evagrius, *Praktikos* 27; SCh 563; CS 23.
79. Pierre Miquel, 'Gloire (vaine gloire), Tradition monastique orientale', DS 6:494–502; Jean Kirchmeyer, 'Vaine gloire. Littérature occidentale', *Ibid.*, DS 6:502–8.
80. Evagrius, *Praktikos* 31; SCh 171; 573; CS 4:24.
81. John Climacus, *Scala paradisi* 22; PG 88:949A.
82. See 1 Th 2:6, Jn 5:44.
83. Evagrius, *Praktikos* 13; SCh 529ff; CS p. 19. Abba Isaac (PG 65:224BC)

Spiritual Warfare 265

had run away, refusing the priesthood, and gave in only when he was about to be bound.
84. See above, Chapter IV, *Structural Freedom*, and VIII, *Widowhood*.
85. See Dorotheus, *Expositiones et doctrinae diversae* IV.5–6; PG 88:1665; SCh 93:232.
86. See Barsanuphius, *Letter* 255; ed. Nicodemus the Hagiorite, (Venice, 1816) 140.
87. Evagrius, *Praktikos* 30; SCh 171; 571; SC 4:32.
88. See M. F. Lacan, 'Orgueil', VTB, 872–74.
89. See Theophrastus, *Characters* 21.23.24 (Paris, 1840): he distinguishes between *mikrophilotimia* (petty ambition), *alazoneia* (vain boasting), and *hyperephania*, arrogance which consists in showing disdain for everyone, except self.
90. Evagrius, *Praktikos* 14; SCh 171:533; CS 4:20; see Cassian, *Institutes* 12.9–11; CSEL 17:213, 10–18; SCh 109:464ff.
91. *Century II on Charity* 38; SCh 9:106; ACW 21:160. [The most recent English translation of the *Four Centuries on Love* is in *The Philokalia. The Complete Text*, vol. 2:52ff.]
92. Antony 37; PG 65:88B; CS 59:8.
93. *In Ezechielem* 9.2; PG 13:734CD.
94. *In Joannem* 9.2; PG 59:72C.
95. Maximus the Confessor, *Second Century on Love* 40; SCh 9:107; *Early Fathers from the Philokalia*, 306; ACW 21.
96. *Idem, Century III on Charity* 62:142; ACW 21:184.
97. *Life of Saint Melanie* 43; SCh 90:211.
98. See R. Deville, 'Blasphème', VTB, 136–38; Dorotheus, *Instruction* II.39; SCh 92:206ff.
99. Evagrius, *Praktikos* 46 (SCh 171:603ff; CS 4:28ff); 51 (SCh, 617; CS, 30; Climacus, *Scala paradisi* 23 (PG 88:976).
100. *Moralia in Hiob* 45.87; PL 76:621A; See above, *Pride*.
101. J. Muyldermans, 'Note additionnelle à Evagriana', *Le Muséon* 44 (1931) 382.
102. See Irénée Hausherr, 'L'origine de la théorie des huit péchés capitaux' *OC* 30 (1933), 164–74; *Etudes de spiritualité orientale*, OCA 183 (Rome, 1969) 11–22; *Philautie. De la tendresse pour soi à la charité selon saint Maxime le Confesseur*, OCA 137 (Rome, 1952); René Daeschler, 'Amour-propre', DS 1:533–44.
103. *Cratylus* 428d.
104. *Ibidem*.
105. *Nicomachean Ethics* IX.8.
106. *Legum allegoriae* III.28.
107. See I. Hausherr, *Philautie* (n. 102).
108. *Century* II.8; SCh 9:126; ACW 21:153.
109. *Century* III.8; SCh, 126; ACW, 174.
110. *Preface to Quaestiones ad Thalassium*; PG 90:257B.
111. See Dorotheus, *Instruction* 3.41 (SCh 92:211); 13.142 (409); 16.168 (463); 3.41 (211); 7.85 (299); 1.8 (159). *Sententiae* 1–2, (2/2). [English translation of *The Instructions*, CS 33]
112. See T. Špidlík, 'L'obéissance et la conscience selon Dorothée de Gaza', *Studia Patristica* XI, TU 108 (1972) 72–78; Italian trans. in *Vita consecrata* 13 (1977) 105–12.

113. *Instruction* 5.63; SCh 92:253ff; see *Apophthegmata patrum*, Poemen 54; PG 65:333–336; CS 59:174; Mark the Ascetic, *De lege spirituali* 3a; PG 65: 909B.
114. *Stromata* III.7; Staehlin, 222, 29 PG 8:1161B.
115. *Instruction* 1.14 (169); 1.17 (175); 1.19 (177) etc.
116. *Instr.* 4.60 (249); 7.85 (299).
117. *Ibid.* 5.63 (255).

10

PURIFICATION OF THE PASSIONS

1. 'DISEASES OF THE SOUL'

Philosophic Theories about the Passions

IN CLASSICAL GREEK the word *pathos* (from the verb *paschein*, to suffer) can mean, on the one hand, an accident, an illness, and, on the other, a feeling, an inner disposition (good or bad), an appetite, a passion and, finally, changes, transformations.[1] The Platonic theory of the passions is linked to the tripartite division of the soul: the rational power (*logistikon*), the irascible power (*thymikon, thymos*), and the concupiscible power (*epithymētikon, epithymia*). The last two depend on the joining of the fallen mind to a body, are of accidental origin, and constitute the 'passionate part of the soul' (*to pathētikon meros tēs psychēs*).[2]

In the eyes of the Stoics, the moral life was a struggle between free reason and the passions, the soul's diseases.[3] Of these there were essentially four: *hēdonē* (pleasure) and *lypē* (pain) in the present; *epithymia* (desire) and *phobos* (fear) concerning the future.[4] Their variations created ups and downs in the mind, moments of tension and rest.[5] Even passions which seem praiseworthy to us, like mercy, the Stoics banned as discordant to reason. To be *logikos* (reasonable) and *apathēs* (dispassionate) was the same thing.[6]

Western scholastics, by contrast, distinguished between the metaphysical meaning of passion (receptivity)[7] and the psychological meaning (the sensitive appetite, the irascible, and the concupiscible). From the moral point of view, a passion is neither good nor bad in itself; its virtuous use makes it morally good, sin makes it evil.[8] Passion is not necessarily discordant with reason; it can be provoked deliberately.[9]

Christian Writers of the East

For the Eastern Fathers, the passions could be neither good nor indifferent. The soul is by nature the image of God. As the result of sin, it has been cloaked with various passions. The aim of *praxis* is to strip the soul of these *pathē*. In using these concepts, christian writers created more and more new meanings, unknown in Platonism and Stoic philosophy, and made many subtle distinctions.

In Ignatius of Antioch, the word *pathos* refers to the suffering and death of Christ.[10] Starting with the third century, however, we find among the Fathers the profound and varied influence of Stoicism in this area.[11] Clement of Alexandria enumerated the four classical pasions: pleasure and lust, grief and fear.[12] Like the Stoics, the Fathers called the passions 'diseases of the soul'[13] opposed to the virtues. It is the demons who 'rule over the passions',[14] which are intimately linked to sin. Theophane the Recluse, a faithful reader of the Fathers' writings, gave this definition: 'The disposition to sin or the propensity to sin or passion is the strong and constant desire to sin in a certain way; it is a love for guilty actions.'[15]

The passions, then, are desires. But Clement of Alexandria was already able to distinguish between two tendencies of desire: one unreasonable and bringing intemperance with it; the other linked to natural needs. Following Chrysippus, he called the latter appetites: 'Appetite is then the movement of the mind to or from something. Passion is an excessive appetite exceeding the measures of reason, or appetite unbridled and disobedient to the Word.'[16]

Gregory of Nyssa spoke of the 'powers' (*dynameis*) fashioned by God in the soul and intended to serve as 'instruments and vessels' for it.[17] Sin introduced alien elements into human nature, elements inherent in brute, irrational nature. These are the same powers that have become dangerous because the mind has lost control over them.[18] It is then that Gregory calls them passions (*pathē*).[19]

Purification of the Passions

Theophane decided to make a psychological analysis to explain the birth of desires. The 'needs' (for example, the need for food) come from nature. Once someone has frequently satisfied this need by means of some object, the 'desire' for this object overwhelms him. Consequently, the 'desires' are the fruit of earlier free choices, frequently guilty choices, and are therefore passions.[20]

Passions, Feelings, and Human Corruptibility

Maximus the Confessor defined self-love, the root of the passions, as attachment to the body.[21] But he, too, knew that not all the passions are derived from man's bodily nature.[22] Like Aristotle, Evagrius distinguished the 'passions of the body' which come from the natural needs of the body, from the 'passions of the soul' which arise from human relationships.[23] John the Solitary outlined another subdivision: 'If you want to distinguish between passions, we find three varieties of them in man: one comes from the nature of the soul, another from the activity it carries on through the body, and [another] from the body itself.'[24] This 'animal nature,' then, which Gregory of Nyssa usually symbolized by the 'garments of skin' (Gen 3:21) with which Adam was said to be clothed after the fall, is not only the sensory nature of man: it is the fact that we are subject to the laws of a new existence due to sin, and this existence involves corruptibility, 'the transmutation ...of nature from its state of incorruptibility to that of corruptibility'.[25]

Transformation of the Passions

At the Incarnation, the Word assumed human nature, passible and corruptible, but without the propensity to evil. This new nature—a fusion of human nature before the fall with that after the fall—was to serve as the instrument of Christ's struggle against the powers of evil.[26]

In accordance with the example of Christ, man cannot ascend to God except through his transformed passions. Then, Maximus the Confessor says, 'even the passions become useful to studious and virtuous men each time they make use of them to acquire spiritual goods.... As I said, the passions become good by reason of their use for the one whose thought and will are in captive obedience to Christ'[27]

Is this still a matter of the 'passions,' as was indicated earlier? The terminology is not always easy, but the teaching is unvarying: every passion is curable 'through abstinence and love'.[28]

2. APATHEIA

Biblical Zeal

In most mythologies the gods conceived by man share his passions. They seem jealous of human happiness, anxious to defend their privileges. The name of the God of Israel is 'the Jealous One; he is a jealous God' (Ex 20:5, 34:14, Dt 4:24, 5:9, 6:15). Yet the jealousy of Yahweh has nothing to do with human little-mindedness. God is not jealous of some 'other' who would be equal to him; he wants an exclusive adoration from man; he is holy and does not want anyone to injure his honor (Josh 24:19 ff.).

This intransigence is tantamount to 'a consuming fire' (Dt 4:24). The Greek word *zēlos* comes from a root which means to be hot, to boil up. It renders well the Hebrew word *quin'ah* the root of which designates the heightened color in the face of an impassioned man. This passion, which often resembles wrath (Dt 29:19), makes one think of fire (Is 26:11). Yahweh's zeal, then, is a reaction of his holiness, in the service of which he uses all his power (Ez 16:38-42). Usually God communicates his own ardor to one elect or another. The psalmist is able to say: 'Zeal for thy house devours me' (Ps 69:10, 119:139).

There is also a christian zeal which unfolds itself in various ways as a race in Christ's service (Ph 3:12 ff.), because the salvation obtained by Christ has raised up a 'people zealous for good deeds' (Tt 2:14, cf.1P 3:13).[1]

The Peaceful State — The Greek Philosophic Ideal

The God of the great philosophers is absolutely free of passions. There is nothing that could provoke him, because he is utterly disinterested in the world and its human concerns.² And because the ideal of the philosophic life was to imitate God,³ must the perfect man not arrive at dispassion if this is divine perfection? Especially if his most noble faculty, the *nous*, is *apathēs* (dispassionate) by nature, as Anaxagoras had early declared?⁴

The term *apatheia* (dispassion) belongs principally to the terminology of the Stoics. Their sage must free himself from the passions (especially the four main ones), remain calm in the face of the attractions and adversities of the world. It is the doctrine of Seneca: '*Quid enim prohibet nos beatam vitam dicere, liberum animum et erectum et interritum ac stabilem, extra metum, extra cupiditatem positum?*' (For what prevents us from saying that the happy life is having a mind that is free, lofty, fearless, and steadfast — a mind that is placed beyond the reach of fear, beyond the reach of desire).⁵

Philo of Alexandria, who owed much to the Stoics, saw in dispassion the symbol of the perfect life taught by Scripture. Moses in his Song praises God for having cast into the sea both horse and rider, that is, the four passions and the wretched intellect which they carried, toward the bottomless abyss.⁶

The Christian Adaptation of the Ideal

Athanasius described the dispassion which asceticism and the struggle against demons created in Antony:

> His body was unchanged.... The temper of his soul, too, was faultless, for it was neither straitened as if from grief, nor dissipated by pleasure, nor was it strained by laughter or melancholy. He was not disturbed when he saw the crowd, nor elated at being welcomed by such numbers; he was perfectly calm as befits a man who is guided by reason and who has remained in his natural state.⁷

On the basis of this passage some have concluded that Athanasius copied the portrait of his monk from an Hellenistic model.⁸ But one can draw an entirely different conclusion: Athanasius could knowingly have wanted his hero, an uneducated Copt, to parallel the Hellenistic ideal, to bear witness to Christ, who had wrought this miracle. One thing is sure. Toward the end of the patristic age we find *apatheia* being taught and defended again in the East by the great masters of the spiritual life: Hesychius, Diadochus of Photike, Abba Isaiah, Issac of Syria, John Climacus, Maximus the Confessor, Nicetas Stethatos, Ignatius and Callistus of Xantopoulos, and others. To form some idea of this, we need only glance at the six columns of references in the Index of the recent Greek edition of the *Philokalia*.[9]

The Impassibility of God

In the history of *apatheia* among christians, one ought to distinguish between the ideal of inner peace on the one hand and, on the other, the philosophic concepts and terms in conformity with the Gospel used to express this ideal.[10] Among the authors who preceded Evagrius, it was common usage to apply the words *apathēs* (impassible) and *apatheia* to God, of whom impassibility is an attribute, just like incorruption and immortality. If, in the language of Scripture, the Fathers, like Theophilus,[11] occasionally admitted the wrath of God, they all removed from God any necessity.[12] True enough, certain texts in which Origen expresses the educational character of scriptural anthropomorphisms seem to dissipate the mystery (the anger of God is compared to the feints of an educator),[13] but elsewhere the passions are shown as the sign of certain divine powers (*virtutes*) or realities.[14]

The Quality of the Risen Body

There is among orthodox authors a certain hesitancy to attribute impassibility to man. According to Justin,[15] man passible (*empathēs*) is contrasted to God impassible (*apathēs*): man can participate in this perfection, but only after the Resurrection, just as the glorious Christ became impassible.[16] If impassibility exists in man, John Climacus believed, it is a foretaste of the incorruptibility to come.[17]

But this eternal life begins already on earth,[18] and from now on we must become like God.[19] This is why Clement of Alexandria sought to propose *apatheia* as the ideal of the christian ascetic. This divine virtue is also the virtue of the gnostic, and Clement devoted a long chapter to him.[20] The basis of *apatheia* is *enkrateia,* mastery over the body.²¹ On the other hand, however, Clement made a radical innovation with respect to Stoicism by linking *apatheia* closely to *gnosis* and charity.²²

Nonetheless, a certain reservation about the Stoic term remained, even after Clement. The *Life of Antony* used the word *ataraxia* (calmness), a synonym,²³ probably for the same reason Basil always preferred equivalent terms, using *apatheia* to designate a divine attribute.²⁴

Evagrius: Men Like Angels

After Clement, Evagrius is the great doctor of *apatheia*: it was he who introduced the term and the concept it carried, into monastic literature. He defined in a systematic way the connections between *apatheia,* charity, and *gnosis.* He says: '*Apatheia* has a child called *agape* who keeps the door to deep knowledge of the created universe'.²⁵ *Apatheia* makes man resemble the angels, rather than God. It is even possible to say more: man becomes an angel when he has reached perfect dispassion.²⁶

It is interesting to note, at the same time, that Cassian, who otherwise readily kept the Greek terms of Evagrius' technical language, never used the word *apatheia* or the corresponding Latin *impassibilitas,* but resorted to equivalent expressions such as *puritas mentis* and *tranquillitas mentis.*²⁷

The Messalians

Dispassion, according to the Messalians, may be defined as a state of the soul consisting of the absence of confusions, of delights, of sensory agitations. The *Book of Degrees* comments: 'When we have mounted these steps and have eradicated sin and its fruits from our heart, we will be filled with the Spirit Paraclete: Christ will live in us perfectly and we will freely eat of the tree of life of which we were deprived at the transgression of the commandment.'²⁸ But to the simplistic Messalians, the Spirit expelled all possibility of sinning. To them, these words were identical: *apatheia,* perfection, sinlessness.²⁹

Jerome, together with many others, was wrong when he lumped Origen, Evagrius, and the Messalians into the same category.³⁰ It was precisely during the reaction against the Messalians that the terms *pathos* and *apatheia* received their distinct moral meaning. The term *apatheia* became fully orthodox then.

Apatheia: *Not the Absence of Suffering or Feeling*

St Paul rejoiced 'in [his] sufferings', in the hope of completing in his 'flesh what is lacking in Christ's afflictions' (Col 1:24). Bodily man suffers, then, because of his natural sensibility. It is true that Clement of Alexandria and Origen, in the wake of Philo,[31] spoke of a complete cutting off of the concupiscible and the irascible power, of the need to eradicate completely the affective part of the soul through reason' (*ektemein logǫ to pathētikon tēs psychēs*).[32] But there are incoherencies in these expressions. How can they be harmonized with mercy and pity for the neighbor?[33]

Evagrius correctly stated that *apatheia* does not imply the suppression of either the *thymos* (irascible power) or the *epithymia* (concupiscible power), but that it purifies them; *praktike* (the practice of virtue) is therefore called 'the spiritual method for cleansing the affective part of the soul',[34] for the soul must operate according to its nature: concupiscible while desiring virtue, and irascible while struggling against the demons.[35]

There is nothing wrong with these movements of feeling in themselves. Gregory of Nyssa, for whom virginity was an angelic, 'immaterial' life, admitted nevertheless that the irrational *eros* which draws bodies together by physical attraction is a symbol of the irresistible attraction which draws the soul towards God by a 'passionless passion' (*pathos apathes*).[36] In spite of the etymology which could make them synonymous, dispassion and insensibility are diametrically opposed.

Apatheia: *Not the Absence of Passionate Thoughts*

Evil thoughts come to mind whether we are perfect or not; they do not depend on us. 'It is not in our power', Evagrius says, to determine whether we are disturbed by these thoughts, but it is up to us to decide if they are to linger within us or not and whether or not they are to stir up (*kinein*) our passions.'[37] *Kinein* is a word typical of Evagrius' psychological vocabulary. It is of Stoic origin: passion is a disordered movement (*kinēsis*) of the soul.[38]

Apatheia: *An Inner Force Capable of Resisting the Passions*

We owe this remarkable definition to Isaac of Syria: 'What is human dispassion? It consists, not in not feeling the passions, but in not welcoming them; (*ou to mē aisthēthēnai ... alla to mē dexasthai ta pathē*).[39] Or, according to the usual expression of Maximus the Confessor, in the inner freedom capable of separating passions from representations.[40] On the level of asceticism, this freedom is often shown by a certain ability to make a 'royal road' between two opposite passions, in order to keep, as Gregory of Nyssa expressed it, 'the golden mean of passionlessness' (*epi tou mesou tēs apatheias*).[41] It is this idea which Lossky correctly sees in the Virgin Mary: 'Here was the highest point of holiness.... She was without sin under the universal sovereignty of sin.'[42] 'Sin could never have become actual in her person.'[43]

Apatheia *and Love*

Far from being a dead insensitivity, christian dispassion is rather the 'consuming fire' of which Scripture speaks, the divine fire.[44] There is therefore an intimate connection and a reciprocal relationship between dispassion and love. '*Agapē* is the progeny of *apatheia*', Evagrius says.[45] The struggle against passionate thought is called by Dadišo Quatraya, 'struggle for the love of God'.[46]

On the other hand, if we can sometimes drive away one passion through another,[47] no other virtue is able to procure perfect dispassion for the soul except love,[48] which is the fullness of divine freedom: 'If we genuinely love God, we cast out the passions by this very love', Maximus the Confessor said.[49] Love assembles all man's powers under the direction of the Spirit.

Apatheia *and* Gnosis

Among the Fathers, as with the Stoics, right reason is linked to dispassion.[50] But since christian dispassion is different, the ensuing knowledge will also differ from purely human knowledge.

According to Evagrius, 'this *apatheia* has a child called *agape* who keeps the door to deep knowledge of the universe. Finally, to this knowledge succeed theology and the supreme beatitude.'[51]

Dispassion is not an end in itself. It is the restoration of the image of God after one has removed that which has darkened its beauty, the 'alien' element, the passions.[52] At that moment one sees 'the place of God'.[53]

Apatheia *and Sinlessness*

According to the Stoics, virtue once acquired can never be lost.[54] In his description of the gnostic, Clement of Alexandria stressed absolute stability in the good: 'he will not hold virtue as a thing to be lost in any case, either awake or in dream, or in any vision.'[55] Dispassion imparts a special strength to all the virtues. On the other hand, however, the orthodox never identified dispassion with sinlessness, the state of one who cannot commit sin.[56] They never confused sin with the passions, as did the Messalians.[57] Even Pseudo-Macarius opposed this error: in the 'spirituals' the temptation to pride remains.[58]

The very fact of relying on one's *apatheia* constitutes a very dangerous temptation which leads to regrettable falls.[59] Does perfect *apatheia* exist anywhere? At first, Mark the Ascetic, writing against the Messalians, seemed to allow for the existence of perfect souls, but later he clearly showed that he did not believe in it.[60] The danger of illusion is too great here: one easily mistakes the 'inactivity' of the passions (*tōn pathōn anergēsia*) for their absence.[61] 'Men are often freed from [evil] thoughts' — Maximus the Confessor says — 'when the objects of their passion are not before their eyes.'[62]

The Signs of Apatheia

The signs of *apatheia* are studied in Chapters 54–70 of the *Praktikos* of Evagrius.[63] Because there is a false 'peaceful state of the soul' provoked by demons,[64] Evagrius insisted on 'proofs' (*tekmēria*), signs telling the monk when he was standing 'near the confines of *apatheia*', or when he moved from a relative to a 'very deep' *apatheia*,[65] from an 'imperfect' to 'perfect apatheia'.[66]

The pre-eminent indication of passionlessness consists in no longer being agitated by thoughts, in being unmoved 'at the memory of them as well'.[67]

The soul is master of its thoughts at the point where it can use one of them to drive out another, as one drives out 'a nail with a nail'.[68]

But even more than thoughts, dreams reveal the deep state of the soul — and Evagrius saw this long before modern psychology.[69] The proof of passionlessness comes when the mind 'remains in a state of tranquillity in the presence of the images it has during sleep.'[70]

Finally, because one's state of prayer is like a 'barometer of the spiritual life',[71] there is proof of dispassion when one prays 'without distractions', when 'the spirit begins to see its own light'.[72]

The Condemnation of Apatheia by the West

Jerome showered vehement reproach on the term:[73] 'it is impossible for man to free himself from the passions (then he is either a stone or God — *vel saxum vel deus est*); in reality, no one can say that he is without sin ... *haeresis Pythagorae et Zenonis apatheias et anamartēsias, id est impassibilitatis et impeccantiae* — the heresy of Pythagoras and Zeno concerning *apatheia* and *anamartēsias*, that is Impassibility and Sinlessness'. Jerome saw in *apatheia* a pagan concept which the Pelagians were using as a synonym for sinlessness. These Pelagian theses on dispassion were refuted primarily by St Augustine.[74]

Moreover, the West had in view certain scandalous deeds, real or rumored, from the Lives of the Saints. The 'fools for Christ'[75] wanted to create the impression that they enjoyed the sinlessness of Adam in earthly Paradise; they refused all clothing,[76] seemed untouched by the elements, by bad weather, hunger, or burning coals, and so forth.[77]

Among those in the West, the term *apatheia* was doomed to failure in advance, for Western Christians never understood how it is possible to struggle against 'all the passions'. The ideal represented by *apatheia* was expressed there by another vocabulary: peace of soul, detachment, and other terms like these.

Chapter Ten

Notes

1. DISEASES OF THE SOUL

1. In the Septuagint, *pathos* in the sense of disease is found only once (Pr 25:20). To translate the dispositions and the evil desires which induce man to transgress the law of God, the Greek Scriptures use the words *epithymia, epithymein* (Si 5:2, 18:30-31, 23:5, Ws 2:12). In the New Testament, the term *pathos* is found only in St Paul (Rom 1:26, Col 3:5, 1 Th 4:5) in a rather restricted sense, as erotic passion, and hence a form of *epithymai* (see Michaelis, in Kittel 5:926).
2. See A Guillaumont, *Les Képhalaia gnostica d'Evagre le Pontique et l'histoire de l'origénisme chez les Grecs et les Syriens* (Paris, 1962) 37ff; Evagrius, *Praktikos* 84; SCh 171:674; CS 4:37.
3. M.Pohlenz, *Die Stoa. Geschichte einer geistigen Bewegung* (Göttingen, 1948–49) vol. 1 412ff.
4. M. Spanneut, *Le stoïcisme des Pères de l'Église*, 232.
5. See Arnim, SVF III, 463, p. 116.
6. Spanneut, 242.
7. Thomas Aquinas, *Summa Theologiae* I.77.2.
8. *De veritate* 24.7.
9. *Summa Theologiae* I-II, 59.2 ad 3; *De ver.* 26.7
10. *Ephesians* 20.1; *Magnesians* 11.1,.
11. See Spanneut, *Le stoïcisme*, 232ff.
12. *Paedagogos* I.101.1; GCS 1: 151, 21.
13. See John the Solitary (Pseudo-John of Lycopolis), *Dialogue sur l'âme et les passions des hommes*, trans. I. Hausherr, OCA 120 (Rome, 1939) 51.
14. Evagrius, *Praktikos* 36; SCh 171:583; CS 4:25.
15. *Načertanie christianskago nravoučenija* [*Christian Moral Teaching*] (Moscow, 1895) 167; Spidlik, *Théophane le reclus*, 149.
16. *Stromata* II.59.6 (GCS 2:145, 3; SCh 38:82; ANG 2:361); 11.61.2 (GCS 2:146; SCh 38:84); cf. Arnim, SVF III, 278-384, p. 92ff.
17. *De virginitate* 12.2.16-17 (SCh 119:402); 13.3.44 (416) [trans. in FC 58 (1966) 6ff.].
18. *De hominis opificio* 18; PG 44:192AB, 193AD; *De anima et resurrectione*, PG 46:148A, 61BC. [trans. *On the Making of Man*, in LNPF, series 2, vol. 5: 387ff., *On the Soul and the Resurrection, ibid.*, 430ff.]
19. *De virginitate* 3.4.14-20 (SCh 119:419ff.); 4.5.25-34 (320); *De hominis opificio*, 18 (PG 44:192C).
20. *Put' ko spaseniju* [*The Way to Salvation*] (Moscow, 1908) 30; *Théophane le Reclus*, 13ff.
21. See above, *Self-will*.
22. *Century* I *on Charity* 64; PG 90:973C.
23. *Praktikos* 35-36 (SCh 171:581; CS 4:25); *Tractatus ad Eulogium* 23 (PG 79:1124C); Aristotle, *Nicomachean Ethics* X.2.1173b.7-9.
24. John the Solitary, *Dialogue sur l'âme*, OCA 120: 67.
25. See Jean Daniélou, *Platonisme et théologie mystique. Essai sur la doctrine spirituelle de saint Grégoire de Nysse*. Théologie 2 (Paris, 1944) 52ff.
26. Maximus the Confessor, *Quaestiones ad Thalassium* 21; PG 90:317.
27. *Ibid.* 1; PG 90:269 [First Century on Various Texts 65, in *The Philokalia. The Complete Text*, vol. 2: 178-79].

28. See Irénée Hausherr, *Philautie. De la tendresse pour soi à la charité selon saint Maxime le Confesseur*, OCA 137 (Rome, 1952) 141ff.

2. APATHEIA

1. See Bernard Renaud and Xavier Léon-Dufour, 'Zèle', VTB, 1391-94.
2. See above, Chapter III, *The Body*.
3. See above, II, 3.
4. See Aristotle, *Physica* IX.5.256b 24.
5. *De vita beata* 4.
6. *Legum allegoriae* II.25.102. See Emile Bréhier, *Les idées philosophiques et religieuses de Philon d'Alexandrie* (Paris, 1908) 254.
7. *Vita Antonii* 14; PG 26:864C-865A, trans. FC 15:148.
8. Richard Reitzenstein, *Des Athanasius Werk über das Leben des Antonius*, in *Sitzungen der Heidelberger Akademie der Wissenschaften* 1914, Kleine Abhandlungen 8, p. 32; J. Roldanus, *Le Christ et l'homme dans la théologie d'Athanase d'Alexandrie. Etude de conjonction de sa conception de l'homme avec sa christologie* (Leiden, 1968), 308.
9. See the Greek *Philokalia*, Athens ed. (1957-1963) vol. 5: 140-41, Index.
10. See above, Chapter IX, 3.
11. *To Autolycus* 1.3.
12. See Spanneut, *Le stoïcisme des Pères*, 292; J. K. Mozley, *The Impassibility of God* (Cambridge, 1926).
13. *Homilia 18 in Jeremiam* 6; GCS 3:157, 17.
14. *Homilia 3 in Genesin* 2; GCS 6: 41, 1.
15. See Theodor Rüther, *Die sittliche Forderung der Apatheia in den beiden ersten christlichen Jahrhunderten und bei Klemens von Alexandrien* (Freiburg-im-Breisgau, 1949) 39-42.
16. See Ignatius of Antioch, *Polycarp* 3.2; *To the Ephesians* 7.2.
17. *Scala Paradisi* 29; PG 88:1148A.
18. See above, Chapter III, *Eternal life*.
19. See above, II, *The God of Christian Revelation*.
20. *Stromata* VI.71-79; GCS 2:467ff.; ANF 2:496ff.; see Rüther, *Die sittliche Forderung* 50ff. Walter Völker, *Der wahre Gnostiker nach Clemens Alexandrinus*, TU 57 (Berlin, 1952) 542ff.
21. *Stromata* IV.22.138.1; ed. W. Stählin, GCS 15: 309, 11-12; see Evagrius, *Praktikos* 68; SCh 171: 652; CS 4:34.
22. *Stromata* III.5.43.1; GCS 15: 215, 26-27.
23. See Epictetus, *Enchiridion* 12.2.
24. See Augustinus Dirking, 'Die Bedeutung des Wortes Apathie beim heiligen Basilius dem Grossen', *Theologische Quartalschrift* 134 (1954) 202-12.
25. *Praktikos*, Introductory Letter to Anatolius (Sch 171:492; CS 4:14 and note); 81 (670; 36).
26. See Antoine Guillaumont, *Les Kephalaia gnostika* (Paris, 1962) 249-52.
27. *Ibid.*, 79.
28. *Liber graduum* XX.7, as quoted in I. Hausherr, OCA 183: 85 [trans. projected by Cistercian Publications— ed.] See also note 29 below.
29. See Irénée Hausherr, 'L'erreur fondamentale et la logique du Messalianisme', OCP I (1935) 348ff; *Études de spiritualité orientale*, OCA 183 (Rome, 1969) 84ff.

30. See above, Chapter III, *The Happy Life, Orthodox Opposition*.
31. *Legum allegoriae* III.129.
32. Clement of Alexandria, *Stromata* VI.9.74,1 (GCS 15:30ff); Origen, *Commentary on the Gospel of Matthew* 15.4 (PG 13:1264A; ed. Klostermann, GCS 40:358, 32–33).
33. See D. D. Pirre, *Pitié ou insensibilité? Le témoignage de Clément d'Alexandrie* (Thuillies, 1939).
34. *Praktikos* 78; SC 171:666; CS 4:36.
35. *Ibid.* 24 and 86 (556 and 676; 23 and 37).
36. *In Canticum*; PG 44:772A; see above. IX. *The Degrees of Penetration*....
37. *Praktikos* 6; SCh 171:509; CS 4:17.
38. Arnim, SVF, I, p. 50, n. 508.
39. *Sermon* 81, ed. Joachim Spetsieri, *Ta eurethenta Asketika* (Athens, 1895) 310.
40. *Century* III. 41; SCh 9:136; 21: 180.
41. *De virginitate* 17.2; SCh 119:460.
42. *In the Image and Likeness of God* (Crestwood, New York, 1974) 204.
43. *Ibid.*
44. See above, APATHEIA.
45. *Praktikos* 81; SCh 171:670; CS 4; 36.
46. *Commentaire d'Abba Isaïe*, Disc. 1, 16, trans. Draguet, CSCO 327 (Scriptores Syri 145) p. 17, 28.
47. See Evagrius, *Praktikos* 45, 58; SCh pp. 603, 637; CS 4, pp. 28, 32.
48. Diadochus of Photice, *Capita centum* 89; SCh 5a:150.
49. *Century III. 50*; SCh 9:138; ACW 21:182.
50. See Spanneut, *Le stoïcisme*, 246.
51. *Praktikos*, Introductory Letter to Anatolius; SCh 171:492; CS 4:14.
52. See Gregory of Nyssa, *De virginitate* 12.2.63–66; SCh 119:408; cf. *ibid.*, Introduction, p. 166.
53. See below, XIII, Theologia.
54. See Spanneut, 244.
55. *Stromata* IV.139.2; GCS 2:309, 25; cf. Th. Rüther, *Die sittliche Forderung*..., 78–81.
56. See Pierre Adnès, 'Impeccabilité', DS 7/2:1614–20.
57. See I. Hausherr, 'L'erreur fondamentale...'.
58. See *Homilia* 15.28 (PG 34:601); *Homilia* 27.9 (700ff.) [translation by George A. Maloney, *Intoxicated with God. The Fifty Spiritual Homilies of Macarius* (Denville, 1978)].
59. Nilus, *Liber de monastica exercitatione* 37; PG 79:765Bff. [translation in *The Philokalia. The Complete Text*, 1:200ff.].
60. *De paenitentia*, n. 8; PG 65:977.
61. Maximus the Confessor, *Century II on Charity* 40 (SCh 9:107; ACW 21:161); Hesychius, *De temperantia et virtute* I.74; PG 93:1504B ['On Watchfulness and Holiness', 74, *The Philokalia*, 1 (1979) 175.]
62. *Century* III.78; SCh 9:146; trans. *Early Fathers from the Philokalia*, 329.
63. SCh 171:624–56; CS 4; 31–34.
64. *Prakticos* 57; SCh p. 634; CS 4, p. 32.
65. *Ibid.*, 58; 636; 32.
66. *Ibid.*, 60; 640; 33.
67. *Ibid.*, 67; 653; 34.
68. *Ibid.*, 58; 636; 32; cf. SCh 170:109.

69. *Ibid.*, 54–56; 624ff.; 31ff.
70. *Ibid.*, 64; 648; 33–34.
71. Theophane the Recluse, *Čto jest' duchovnaja žizň* [*What The Spiritual Life Is and How to Begin It*] (Moscow, 1897) 165; see Špidlík, *Théophane le Reclus*, 240.
72. Evagrius, *Praktikos* 63 (SCh 171:646; CS 4:33); 65 (648; 33).
73. *Letter 133, To Ctesiphon* (CSEL 56: 246); *Against the Pelagians*, Prologue (Pl 23:496A); *Commentary on Jeremiah 4.1 (CSEL 59: 220*–21); see A. Guillaumont in SCh 170:98ff.
74. *De gestis Pelagii* VI (16); PL 44:329; cf. *De civitate Dei* 14.9.5; PL 41:415.
75. See T. Špidlík, '"Fous pour le Christ" en Orient', DS 5: 752–61.
76. See *idem*, '*Boskoi (pastori)*', DIP 1 (1974) 1538.
77. See *Vie de Daniel le Stylite*, in A. J. Festugière, *Les moines d'Orient* II (Paris, 1961) 127.

11

POSITIVE PRAXIS

1. THE WILL OF GOD

Obedience to the Will of God

TO OBEY, IN THE CONTEXT OF SCRIPTURE, means to lend an ear to the expression of another's will, and to respond to it. Obedience, then, is being subject to (*hypotassesthai*) and acting (*poiein*). No creature can shy away from submission to the will of God; even the pagans have sometimes recognized this splendidly.[1]

The diligent search for the will of God is therefore the ground rule of spiritual practice.[2] The ascetics took the love of God's will so far that in the one area where they could have escaped it, that of personal initiative, they wanted to make sure that they would never deceive themselves. The great problem for them was, where is the will of God manifest?

Everywhere in the ancient Near East lived men judged to be capable of receiving a message from the divinity through direct inspiration. 'As for prophecies, they will pass away', St Paul explained (1 Co 13:18). But this will be at the end of time. In the present Church, Evergetinos believed, the 'leaders among the Fathers had as their master not a man, but God and their conscience, and they became enlighteners of the world'.[3] He could have mentioned here echoes of the struggle of Symeon the New Theologian in favor of the privileges of spiritual men: 'They are rare, but they are found nevertheless, these men who were led by the Holy Spirit from the beginning, who personally did not need human guidance, and still became leaders of men later. Something to be admired but not imitated, considering our human weakness.'[4]

Obedience to the Spiritual Father

'If only the whole people of Yahweh were prophets', Moses sighed (Nb 11:29). St Paul was not so convinced of this. He held that the gift of prophecy should be exercised in good order and for the good of others (1 Co 14:29-33). The great renown of the 'spiritual fathers', the abbas, and the *startzy* (elders) in monasticism rests on the assumption that no one is any longer worthy to be enlightened directly by the Holy Spirit—although this would be in conformity with human nature—and especially, that not everyone is able to discern whether thoughts come from the Holy Spirit or not. The advice of Barsanuphius is traditional: 'Brother, do not rush headlong into the discernment of thoughts that come to you. You are not up to it... But mention to your abba the thought that lingers with you and makes war upon you, and he will heal you through God.'[5] A true spiritual father is not easily found; one must hunt for him, even if one has to change monasteries to do this.[6] Once he has been found, one remains faithful to him.[7]

Spiritual direction is an obligation of the gnostic, 'the one who knows'.[8] It is simply the discernment of spirits put into practice. Consequently, the gift of *diakrisis* (discernment) governs all others in the area of guidance. The *diakritikos* (discerning person) can at the same time be *dioratikos*, with the gift of 'clairvoyance' or even *kardiognosis* (the reading of hearts).[9] The gift of discernment joined to that of 'prophecy,' being able to speak in the name of God, makes the perfect spiritual father.[10]

Should he be a priest? Should he be a *hegoumenos* (superior)? There were varying views and controversies about each of these questions.[11] This is because a theological question, the value of the sacrament of penance,[12] had entered the discussion, along with an eternal practical problem: is there to be a centralized government in the monasteries or freedom for the monks to choose their spiritual fathers? The ideal solution would be the combination of the three: an holy *hegoumen* who is a priest and *diakritikos* in charge of spiritual direction. In itself, however, the *diakritikos* is neither an hierarchical nor a juridical function. It is a readiness to take upon oneself the task and the difficulties which the care of a soul desirous of salvation brings with it.

Hierarchical Obedience

There are numerous examples in monastic literature in which the authority of a superior seems to assume the character of divine absolutism. One has the impression that the superior is a *Pantokrator* (Ruler of All) with a reduced territory and image, fully responsible for everyone and everything that occurs under his never-sleeping eye.[13]

How did men pass so easily from obedience to the god-bearing spiritual father, the prophet, to the juridical chief? This passage 'from charism to the law' is only justified to the extent that one believes in the great charism of the Church itself, in the presence of the Spirit within human structures. If this is the case, then, it becomes a matter not of replacing charism by law but rather of submitting the individual gift to the universal charism of the Church.[14]

Obedience to a Person or to the Written Law?

An eleventh-century Muslim was struck by the esteem Christians had for their 'fathers' and he explained it to himself this way: Christianity was originally not 'codified'.[15] Indeed, the title 'father' was the greatest honor which could be awarded among Christians, whether it meant the 'spiritual father' or the 'abba' of a monastery, the 'Fathers' in council, or the 'fathers'—priests.[16]

One naturally supposes therefore that they are all 'fatherly'. Spiritual guidance demands great patience and gentleness,[17] which does not work without strict discipline: it is not afraid of speaking strongly and clearly[18] while at the same time it brings help through prayer. 'Father, pray for me', is the formula which often introduces the request of a disciple.[19] And when he speaks of the good he has done, he never fails to add, 'Through the prayers of my spiritual father'.[20]

The main virtue characterizing the abbot of a community is

the responsibility either for his subjects or for the observance of God's law.[21] If he were to neglect this serious obligation, he would incur his own damnation along with that of his subjects, no matter how perfect his own life had been.[22] 'The one who seeks counsel from the fathers is detached from worldly cares and remains in tranquillity.'[23] By contrast, superiors have obligations: to instruct,[24] to watch over and correct sinners,[25] to oversee the work.[26] In short, nothing must be done without the superior's blessing. This blessing—Joseph of Volokolamsk assures us—draws the grace of God upon us, whereas every deed done without permission is already cursed.[27]

On this subject, however, opinions were not unanimous. It seems that for Basil the function of the superior consisted only in discerning whether the deed to be done was according to or against God's commandment. The *hegoumen* was not invested with an authority that allowed him to change a deed indifferent in itself into a good deed by giving it the value of an express desire of God.[28]

Thereafter the monastic tradition would waver between two forms of obedience: the more 'personal', where the superior actually holds the place of God, and the more 'scriptural', where the written law is the real 'superior'. In the second case, there is a danger of reducing the 'father' to a rabbi who applies the Torah; in the first case, there is the opposite danger: that the 'father' may feel himself above God's commandments.[29]

Obedience to Divine Commandments

God's will, transmitted by the lips of the spiritual father, was expresssed by means of a *logion*, a *dictum*, a saying. What strikes us in the *Sayings* is their variety and their apparent contradictions. Spiritual direction left some room for personal initiative in the choice of what is called a *politeia*, a 'diligence', the means used to reflect the virtuous life.[30]

Was it this individualism which offended Basil during his travels in Egypt? Or was it instead his sad experience with his own spiritual father, Eustathius of Sebaste?[31] What is certain is that he did not recommend to his monks any *logion* coming from the mouth of a charismatic. The divinely-inspired Scriptures contain enough for everyone. They are 'like a remedy within everyone's reach', and each will take from it 'a suitable remedy for his infirmity'.³²

The christian has no need of proofs to know that the will of God is manifest in the commandments of Scripture. When, in his perplexity, the Syriac translator of Evagrius translated the unfamiliar word *praktikē* by *pulhâma d⁰puqddânê*, the 'practice of the commandments', he was not entirely wrong, because Evagrius himself stated that *praktikē* 'rests on the observance of the commandments'.³³

By contrast, 'everything that is disorderly and evil in the world derives from the fact that one does not accept the divine Scriptures as one should'.³⁴ The opusculum *On the Judgment of God* among Basil's works developed this doctrine with passionate eloquence.³⁵ To Basil, a basic demand of the Gospel was to fulfill all God's commandments.³⁶ The violation of one single precept brought with it a violation of all the others.³⁷ To the question, 'If one thing is remiss from all our virtuous actions, will we fail to obtain salvation for that reason?' he replied affirmatively.³⁸ Joseph of Volokolamsk replied in the same sense: 'Ordained for our salvation, all the commandments are admirable and useful'. One should therefore observe everything which the Lord has commanded.³⁹ Moreover, man has the ability, 'the power and the necessary inclination to fulfill all the commandments given us by Him'.⁴⁰

The observance of divine precepts installs order in the world, a unity through divine Providence which is no different from 'a thought included in the command',⁴¹ a 'wise and orderly arrangement' (*sophē kai eutaktos diakosmēsis*).⁴² Within a community, the faithful observance of the commandments creates harmony among the members; they become unanimous (*homopsychoi adelphoi*).⁴³

Precepts and Counsels, Christian and Monastic Spirituality

Nowadays, we have separated 'salvation of soul' too much from 'perfection', and divided into categories those who want to work at salvation: one speaks of monastic spirituality, of the spirituality of secular clergy, of the laity, and so on. The great masters of the East believed that it was wrong and damaging to everyone, monks and non-monks, to insist more on the differences than on their almost perfect equality. 'The Scriptures knew nothing of such a division, but they want all [Christians] to lead the monastic life, even if they are married', wrote John Chrysostom.[44]

In the East, people did not speak of the 'evangelical counsels'. They preferred to use an old and traditional distinction between the virtues of the soul and those of the body, psychic and somatic.[45] The evangelical counsels are the 'somatic virtues', tools of virtue, means of acquiring virtues. As a consequence, the monks, who are virgins and poor, found themselves in the best condition for leading the life of salvation necessary for all Christians.[46]

2. THE 'PATH OF VIRTUE'

The Virtuous Life

In pagan antiquity, virtue was recommended by various but always enthusiastic systems. For Christians, doctrine on the virtues is a basic part of moral and ascetic teaching. The Eastern authors were here less systematic than the *Summa Theologiae* of Thomas Aquinas, even though they, too, frequently treated of the virtues. On several occasions in the *Life of Anthony*, Athanasius qualifies the ascetic life as 'virtue' or the 'path of virtue'.[1] For Cassian, virtue was 'that through which we give the kingdom of our heart ... to Christ'.[2] For Symeon the New Theologian, the virtues were like the members of the human spiritual body.[3]

In its original sense, however, the word *aretē* did not have a well-defined moral meaning. It simply expressed any admirable quality in a man, or the consciousness this man had of his value. It was physical strength, which above all, called for admiration: *andreia, virtus,* courage, the excellence of the male.[4] A society organized as a *polis* was bound to admire any service rendered to the community and to the citizens' public morals: the civic and moral virtues. Lastly, the Socratic *aretē* was knowledge, understanding, wisdom.

Plato did not forget, however, that human dignity is not shown only through knowledge.[5] The Aristotelian distinction between intellectual and moral virtues sought the correct balance to transcend a moral intellectualism.[6] Finally, with the Stoics the concept of virtue began to be clearly distinguished from knowledge and to be identified only with 'the moral virtues'. Cleanthes defined virtue as *tonos,* strength of soul, the strength needed to live according to the *logos.*[7]

In Philo, we find the formulas of Aristotle and the Stoics and the heritage of Scripture side by side. The virtues are implanted in the soul and brought to fruition by God's power.[8] Indeed, neither the Old nor the New Testament exalt the superiority and strength of man, but the power of God. St Paul used the word *aretē* only once (Ph 4:8: *ei tis aretē kai ei tis epainos*; let us note the terms: virtue, praise, a quality worthy of praise). In the Epistles of St Peter the word is found three times. On two occasions it deals with the power of God (1 P 2:9, 2 P 1:3). In 2 P 1:5 it concerns human virtue, but set within evangelical trust: *pistis kai aretē* ('add virtue to your faith').

Axioms on the Virtues

When the Fathers defined the virtues, they did so without expressing their full significance in the christian sense. Besides, they readily took over certain popular axioms, mostly inherited from the Stoic teaching on virtue. We will cite the most important ones.[9]

Virtue is the Only Good, Vice the Only Evil;
Everything Else is Indifferent
This maxim, adopted wholeheartedly by the christian authors, goes back to Socrates.[10] Gregory Nazianzus added an explanation which echoes St Paul (Rm 8:28): 'For the good, all things turn to the good, but for the wicked everything becomes altogether wicked.'[11]

Virtue: The Mean between Two Extremes
The *metron* (measure) required by physical health became for Aristotle the *mesotēs* (mean) demanded by moral health;[12] thus, for example, courage is placed between cowardice and foolhardiness.[13] The Fathers sought to base this principle on texts of Scripture, developing it in reference to Qoheleth: to everything there

is a season (Qo 3:1ff.),[14] and to the 'narrow path' of the Gospel (Mt 7:13), the one which parts neither to evil on the left or to a supposed goodness on the right.[15]

Yet a problem arises: if the virtues are a participation in the divine life, how can one say that perfection consists in not exaggerating? To avoid this difficulty, medieval scholastics distinguished between two types of virtue: the theological virtues which grow indefinitely, and the moral virtues, the perfection of which is found *in medietate*.[16] Let us stipulate, however, that this objection arises from a misunderstanding only if virtue is practised in a mediocre way. It is a matter not of limiting the impulse to do good but of differentiating and separating what is good from what is not, of practising virtue, according to Cassian's admonition, without disturbing the marvelous order of creation where each being has its place and each action is subject to the discretion without which good changes into evil. Such is the judgment 'of Saint Anthony and all the Fathers'.[17]

Virtue is its Own Reward (*Virtus sibi ipsi premium*)

In the opinion of the ancients, this maxim marked the height of moral nobility. The Apologists praised highly the self-sufficiency (*autarkeia*) of virtue, especially in the face of martyrdom. Does it not lead to perfect happiness, (*eudaimonia*), Justin wrote.[18] 'Virtue, that it may remain virtue, is without reward', said Gregory Nazianzen.[19]

Thus understood and accepted, virtue ran the risk of remaining a sheer disinterestedness separated from higher values. One had to deepen the concept of this axiom in order to raise it to the christian level to show its true reality as a participation in the divine life.

Virtue: Likeness to God and Participation in Christ

Plato realized that the virtuous life also had to have some aim, and he assigned to it becoming like God,[20] the desire to be 'a friend of God'.[21] For Philo, only the souls who recognized their aim in *exomoiōsis* (assimilation) to the Creator walked the path of virtue.[22] The Fathers were very conscious of the intimate relationship which exists between man's moral conduct and man's participation in the divine life present in him, the celestial image.

Gregory Nazianzen said that, 'God is called love and peace, and by these names he urges us to become transformed according to the virtues that qualify him'.[23] The virtues are therefore the measure of our deification.[24]

And because we were created as 'Image' according to Christ,[25] the virtues, in Origen, become one with Christ: he *is* the virtues, whereas we *possess* them. Christ 'is not different from the virtues that fill him'.[26] He is at the same time Justice, Wisdom, and Truth. This is why the practice of these virtues is a true participation in the essence of Christ.[27]

The Difficulty and Ease of the Virtuous Life

Ancient wisdom recognized that the path of virtue is a difficult road and demands much sweat; that of vice, by contrast, is an easy road.[28] Christian authors taught, likewise, that virtue is acquired 'at the price of toil and hard labor'.[29] Yet Anthony's great discourse celebrates an affirmation diametrically opposed to this: 'Virtue is not far from us, nor is it without ourselves, but it is within us, and is easy if only we are willing.'[30] For Ammonas, virtue was repose (*anapausis*).[31]

A profound reason that solves the apparent contradiction between the two positions is the theandric character of the salvific works: the human activity of sinful man brings with it exhaustion, grace gives more and more lightness (*elaphrotēs*), towards this is directed the work of those who valiantly undertake 'spiritual cultivation'.[32] The great struggle for virtue is 'first exhaustion, and then ineffable joy'.[33]

Let us further note that this apparent contradiction is often found in monastic legislators. When they make exhortations about the diligent practice of virtue, they lay stress on the 'hard labor'. But when they compare cenobitic life to anchoretic they proclaim loudly that the common life is easy, makes few demands, and that everyone is able to submit to it.[34]

The Oneness of the Virtues

Virtue is one. Its single reality was affirmed by Plato when he compared the cardinal virtues to the parts of a face.[35] Aristotle touched upon the question when he said that without *phronēsis* (prudence) all the other virtues are also missing.[36] For the Stoic all the virtues were but different species or forms of one single virtue.[37] In this sense Philo wrote that 'virtue is the whole and is seen as a genus, and then it is divided into its species.'[38]

This thesis became very popular among Christians. A Greek *Ascetic Sermon* attributed to Ephrem exhorts:

> Strive to acquire perfect virtue, adorned with all that is pleasing to God. This is called the one virtue which includes within itself the beauty and the variety of all the virtues. As a diadem cannot be made without jewels and pearls, so the single (*monoeidēs*) virtue cannot subsist without the beauty of various virtues.[39]

Gregory Nazianzen sought to affirm the oneness of the virtues with the authority of St Paul: 'Is one member afflicted? All the other members suffer with it'.[40]

Others admitted that the virtues are different, distinct from one another, but still connected. There is an *anakolouthia* (reciprocal implication) among the virtues;[41] they are linked to one another,[42] like the commandments of God.[43] From this premise various practical conclusions could be drawn. The first is that of the Stoics: there is no middle ground between the perfect virtue of the sage and the ignorance of the wicked. One should cultivate all the virtues without exception. 'Any form of virtue, divorced from the others, could never by itself be a perfect virtue', said Gregory of Nyssa.[44] Softened, this maxim would state more correctly that one virtue cannot reach perfection without the others, but that it is already a good.[45]

In the view of Gregory of Nazianzus, pure virtue is hard to find here below.[46] Moreover, one would be wrong in wanting to embrace all the virtues at once: 'Be careful not to lose everything by trying to embrace everything at once.'[47] 'We should perfect certain virtues, reserve others, and desire still some others until we reach our goal.'[48]

But this slow progress in the virtues does not contradict the basic unity of all the virtues, for 'the person who possesses one virtue, possesses all of them in the manner of the gnostic because of their mutual concatenation'; — Clement of Alexandria drew this different conclusion from the Stoic *anakolouthia*.[49] Let everyone therefore cultivate his own virtue, Gregory Nazianzen said;[50] 'By honoring one virtue, you open the road to many, and you will receive from God the reward of many'.[51]

The Division Between the Virtues

One finds in the spiritual writers abundant instruction on the practice of the virtues. But while the catalogue of vices soon became traditional, the classification and the division of the virtues were mentioned only occasionally. The Aristotelian distinction between the intellectual and the moral virtues, the contemplative and the practical, is found only rarely. It was said rather that true virtue includes both knowledge and righteousness, practice and contemplation inseparably.[52]

Scholasticism has carefully distinguished the 'natural' virtues, 'acquired' as the result of effort, from the 'infused', 'supernatural' virtues which are gifts of grace. This 'supernatural' character is seen above all in the three 'theological' virtues: faith, hope, and charity.[53] This distinction is hard to apply to the concept of 'nature' generally accepted in the East.[54] Moreover, all the virtues are viewed as participation in God,[55] and all demand a certain 'effort' on man's part. That does not prevent faith, hope, and charity from being viewed as privileges, as a special gift from God. John Chrysostom declared that 'through baptism we received remission of sins, sanctification, participation in the Spirit, adoption, eternal life, faith, hope, and charity, the abiding things'.[56]

In Plato's day, the four basic (or cardinal) virtues were so well structured that they were used as the outline for an eloquence contest. For Plato, virtue was above all knowledge, wisdom, and prudence (*phronēsis*). It was therefore the first basic virtue, residing in the *logistikon* (the rational power). But Plato became ever more conscious that the mind can be influenced positively or negatively by the other parts of the soul. The dignity of man therefore expresses itself also in the power of the *thymoeides* (the irascible): this is fortitude, courage. Then there is temperance, in the capacity to resist the *epithymētikon* (appetitive power). If we add justice, which brings the right proportion and cooperation between the three preceding powers, we arrive at the four cardinal virtues.[57]

An anonymous treatise *On the Virtues and the Vices* by a first century Peripatetic,[58] served as the source for Chapter 89 of Evagrius' *Praktikos*, where we read the following explanation:

> According to our master, that man of wisdom,[59] the rational soul is composed of three parts.[60] When virtue comes to birth in the rational part (*en tọ logistikọ*), it is called prudence (*phronēsis*), understanding (*synesis*), and wisdom (*sophia*). When it is developed in the concupiscible part (*en tọ epithymētikọ*) it receives the name of temperance (*sophrosynē*), charity (*agapē*), and continence (*enkrateia*). The virtue of the irascible part (*to thymikon*) is termed courage (*andreia*) and patience (*hypomenē*). Justice (*diakosynē*), however, is located in the whole of the soul.[61]

Philo and Clement of Alexandria wanted to find the basis of this Greek division in the Old Testament (Ws 8:7). In the West it was raised into a principle by Thomas Aquinas to structure his entire philosophic-theological doctrine of the virtues.[62] In the East, a very schematic exposition of the four virtues can be read, for example, in Gregory Plethon.[63]

There was a division of the virtues which was very appropriate for the spiritual writers, between the virtues 'of the soul' and the virtues 'of the body', between the psychic and the somatic.[64] The virtues of the body should not properly be called virtues, but *ergaleia aretōn*,[65] instruments of virtue, exterior means of acquiring the virtues.[66] Thus, for example, 'the first virtue' consisted for Cassian in 'purity of heart', and 'it is for the sake of this that we must seek for solitude, and ought to submit to fastings, vigils, and so on'.[67]

The Genealogy of the Virtues

That the virtues are born from one another (*antakolouthein allēlais*) was an idea dear to the Stoics.[68] Among the Christians, we frequently find lists of virtues appropriate to various situations, analogous to the lists made by St Paul in his pastoral epistles, or by Clement of Rome,[69] or in the Letter of Polycarp.[70] A list of concatenated virtues is found in Hermas,[71] and in the Gospel according to Philip.[72]

A traditional outline seems to come from Clement of Alexandria: 'Thus faith appears to us as the first movement which leads us to salvation; after that, fear, hope, and repentance, developing together with abstinence and perseverance, lead us to charity and *gnōsis*.'[73] For this teaching, Clement himself refers back to 'the apostle Barnabas'.[74] The Evagrian outline, which is similar, is found in the Prologue to, and in Chapter 81 of, the *Praktikos*[75] but in a different order.[76] This scheme is found again in Maximus the Confessor.[77] Abba Isaiah marked out an ascending series of virtues, beginning with rest and ending with charity, which gives rise to the dispassionate soul.[78] Others worked out other series. But in general they all had a common basis already explained by Ignatius of Antioch: 'Faith and love are the beginning and end of life. Faith is the beginning and love is the end.'[79] For Evagrius, the goal of *praktikē* (the ascetic life) is charity; the goal of contemplative knowledge is 'theology'.

3. CHARITY

Perfection in Charity

Explicit testimony to the link between charity and perfection comes to us from the best commentaries on Lk 10:25–38, Mt 25: 31–46, 1 Co 13, and on the Song of Songs. Charity introduces us into the mystery of God (1 Jn 4:16).

Any Church Father could have signed the definition given by Thomas Aquinas: 'The perfection of the christian life resides in charity'.[1] According to the Epistle of Barnabas, we were created to love, because we are 'children of love'.[2] The same view, but more considered, stands out in Irenaeus' polemic against the gnostics: 'Apart from the love of God, neither knowledge, nor the understanding of mysteries, nor faith, nor prophecy avails anything—without love all are hollow and vain.'[3] Eusebius of Alexandria wrote that 'Man cannot do anything good without charity'.[4] For Chrysostom, charity is the summit of the spiritual mountain of the virtues;[5] John of Damascus says the same thing;[6] For Symeon the New Theologian charity is the head of the spiritual man's body and the other virtues are its members.[7]

Three Objections

1. *The ascetic monks accentuated asceticism.* While speaking of temperance, Basil concluded 'Do you see how all the other precepts cluster about this one...?'[8] By way of answer, we need only read the *Treatise on Charity* which concludes Theodoret of Cyrus' *Religious History*. He wants to show that the real reason for the ascetic exploits he has just narrated is charity,[9] which replaces martyrdom. This can be applied especially to christian virginity.[10]

2. *The ancient ascetics said little of charity.* Actually, they admitted that they were weeping for a salvation they had squandered. The writings 'On Charity' are a late phenomenon without any pretensions to systematization. Paul Evergetinos, who searched through the whole ascetic literature prior to his time, has only one chapter on the love of God and there only half a column, taken from the *Geronticon*.[11] But on this great 'mystery'[12] there is silence through humility and for fear of self-deception.[13] We could say that the ascetics showed their love by the earnestness with which they applied it in practice.

3. *For contemplatives charity seems to be a means*, 'the door to *gnosis*',[14] whereas 'our aim is to do everything for the sake of knowledge of God'.[15] Here is a remarkable explanation of this statement by Philoxenes of Mabbug:

> Although the spiritual life of the mind is divine contemplation, Blessed Paul exclaims: I do not aspire to it outside of charity. And if I cannot approach it through the lawful door of charity, I do not desire it either. And if it were given to me as a gift while I have not yet acquired charity, I do not want it, unless I approach it through the natural door which is charity.[16]

'True knowledge' and charity are intimately and inseparably connected.[17]

Greek Terms[18]

To express the idea of loving, the Hebrews only had the verb *aheb* and the substantive derived from it, *ahabah*. The Greeks had four verbs at their disposal: *stergein* (which designates the love parents have for their children), *eran* (from which is derived *erōs*, tainted by association with impure ideas), *philein* (friendly relationships), and *agapan* (the term chosen in Scripture to preserve in its newness a reality unknown by the pagan world). In Homer the verb *agapao* means to receive a person, to treat him amicably, or to approve of something.

The substantive *agapē* is not found in pagan writings; the Jews evidently borrowed it from Scripture. Among the Fathers it is the usual term to designate christian charity. Theodoret, Diadochus, Pseudo-Macarius, and the Areopagite use *erōs* to indicate a more ardent *agapē*. In Hesychius, the two terms are almost synonymous. One could further add the terms *pothos* and *eunoia* (benevolence) used by some as synonyms of charity.

'Love' in Greek Philosophy, Summarized in Three Points:

1. *God loves neither the world nor men.* Philosophy offers us the concept of a highest good which is supremely desirable, but unable to love anyone beside himself, confined to indifference, and a blessed solitude which excludes the need for, and the possibility of, making friends.[19]

2. *Man tends toward God and desires him through a natural need.*[20] Love, Socrates says in *Phaedrus*, makes the soul grow wings to make it possible for her to return to Full Truth, Justice, Wisdom, Beauty, Knowledge.[21] Aristotle's first mover 'produces motion as being loved, *kinei hōs erōmenon*.[22]

3. *Felicity does not consist in love.* To love means to seek one's perfection. But God possesses perfection in his self-sufficiency (*autarkeia*).[23]

Christian Teaching

1. *Love, the divine reality. God is love.* It is the secret (1 Jn 4:8, 16) to which we have access through Jesus Christ, by 'rec-

ognizing' in him 'the love that God has for us' (4:16). Love therefore expresses the very mystery of God.[24] This explains why the spiritual authors were afraid of dealing with this subject.[25]

2. *If man loves God, this 'love is of God'* (1 Jn 4:7). John teaches the divine origin and character of love, and the powerlessness of man to attain it under his own steam.[26]

3. *Felicity, salvation, consists in love.* According to John, eternal life consists in the relationship which God wants to establish with man through the revelation of his love by the mediation of his Son (Jn 17:3).

Eros *and* Agape, Amor Concupiscentiae *and* Amor Benevolentiae

God's love cannot be 'a desire for his own perfection', the Platonic *erōs*. Divine *agapē* is a super-abundance.[27] The Father in heaven does not seek a *more* that would fill him; on the contrary, he wants to open his own treasures. Gregory of Nyssa wrote: 'The Maker of man's nature was not driven to frame him by any necessity. Man is called into being in order to be a partaker of the good things in God.'[28] This is the *proagapan*[29] (love prevenient) which has manifested itself all through the history of salvation; it is *philanthrōpia* (love towards men), according to the term preferred by the Greek Fathers.[30]

Do the two 'loves' contradict one another?[31] God is *agapē*; it is his definition. But at the root of our activity as children of God lie two tendencies: *erōs*, the specifically human way of loving, by which we seek to fulfill our destiny; and *agapē*, the divine way of loving, our participation in the generous love of the three Persons of the Trinity, the source of giving, of sacrifice.[32] *Erōs* is the insatiable desire of the human heart, *agapē* is the gift of the Spirit residing in that heart through grace. This is why the two loves are united in their duality. Whereas with the philosophers desire was a one-way movement, God the Father plants a desire only to fulfill it; *eros* is realized and satisfied beforehand.[33] In Gregory of Nyssa, *eros* is compared to the intoxication and ecstasy which are experienced when God-Love is near.[34]

The 'First Commandment'

The love of God is 'innate in our souls and implanted by nature'.[35] Basil was among the first to embark on the subject of the love of God. In the second of *The Long Rules*, he says, 'Love of God is not something that is taught,'[36] it is within us as a basic desire, a predisposition, a seed.[37] The Stoic and Philonian theme of the 'seeds of virtue' had already been applied to love by Origen.[38] All progress in love thereby creates life.[39]

The love of God is at the same time the greatest commandment (Mt 22:37). 'This germ', Basil continues, 'is then received into the school of God's commandments, where it is carefully cultivated.'[40] For Basil, the practice of the commandments consists specifically in discovering the voice of God who creates and orders the universe.[41] Love is 'the queen of virtues'. We are 'not impelled to it automatically',[42] but it is of our 'free choice,'[43] which is the foundation of every virtue.

The Love of God: Eros or Agape?

Platonic doctrine allowed no doubt that the love of God (*erōs*) consists of a certain desire (*epithymia*).[44] Likewise, according to Basil, the love of God as 'seminal reason', shows itself in the psychological order first as a great desire for God's magnificence, a 'passionate, poignant, eager, intolerably keen desire.'[45]

But toward the end of the second *Long Rule*, Basil still speaks of his 'own feeling'[46] about the love of God: 'In the presence of the Lord he [the devil] will present to our Judge our falling away from God's love as a reproach to Christ. . . . This reproach to the Lord and this triumph of our Enemy whom we have provided with matter for boasting appear to me more dreadful than the punishments of hell.'[47] This 'personal feeling' is inspired no longer by self-interest but by a love which seems to ignore its reward, at least in so far as a limited being can achieve this, by the grace of God. But this *agapē* is his reward already, for God is love: 'God is truly God only to those who are united with him through love.'[48]

Such love is 'spiritual' because it either confers or presupposes our resemblance to God-Love. We understand that it is therefore rare. For Maximus the Confessor, it exists only in those who have eliminated every trace of self-love.[49] But when it is achieved it purifies the soul of every stain and of the passions that dull the soul, and it persuades us 'to disregard not only sensible things, but even our transient life.'[50]

To love God for God's sake also means to choose the entire work of God, to love all of creation and the marvelous order that reigns in it, that is, to observe the commandments, especially the second, which consists in loving one's neighbor. It is impossible, Maximus the Confessor says, really to love God without loving our neighbor, or really to love our neighbor without loving God.[51] And it is this inseparable union of the two loves which makes it possible for us to love with an *agapē* that expects no reward, with a love that goes out to another: 'For I was hungry and you gave me food.... Lord, when did we see you hungry and feed you? I tell you solemnly, in so far as you did this to one of the least of these brothers of mine, you did it to me' (Mt 25:35-40). Therefore, 'The task of love is to behave towards every person bearing God's image, almost as it does towards the Prototype.'[52]

Notes

1. THE WILL OF GOD

1. See, among others, Epictetus, *Discourses* 4.1,79ff. (trans. W. A. Oldfather, Loeb Classical Library [1952] 271ff.); *The Encheiridion* 53 (ibid., 537ff.); A. Jagu, 'Epictète', DS 4/1:825ff.
2. See the commentaries on the Lord's Prayer, for example, by Origen (*De oratione* 261; PG 11:439) by Gregory of Nyssa (PG 44:1161ff) [translation by Hilda Graef, *The Lord's Prayer, The Beatitudes*, ACW 18 (1954)]; see Albert Hamman, *Le Pater expliqué par les Pères* (Paris, 1951).
3. *Synagogē* (Constantinople, 1861) IV, chapter 38, p. 126; see Irénée Hausherr, 'Paul Evergetinos a-t-il connu Syméon le Nouveau Théologien?, OCP 23 (1957) 73; *idem. Études de spiritualité orientale*, OCA 183 (Rome, 1969) 276ff.
4. *Synagogē*, p. 126.
5. Ed. by Nicodemus the Hagiorite n. 69 (see above, IX, 3, n. 7); see SCh 92:54.
6. See Emil Herman, 'La "stabilitas loci" nel Monachismo Bizantino', OCP 21 (1955) 115-42.
7. See I. Hausherr, *Direction spirituelle en Orient autrefois*, OCA 144 (Rome, 1955) 186; *idem*, DS 3:1047ff.

Positive Praxis 301

8. See above p. Chapter III, *The 'True Gnostic'*.
9. Hausherr, *Direction spirituelle*, 97ff; OCA 144: col. 1016ff, 1033ff.
10. *Ibid.*, 103; col. 1024ff., 1032ff.
11. *Ibid.*, 105; 1017ff.
12. See above, Chapter VII, *Sacramental Repentance*.
13. See T. Špidlík, 'Le concept de l'obéissance et de la conscience selon Dorothée de Gaza,' *Studia Patristica XI*, TU 108 (Berlin, 1972) 72–78; Italian trans. in *Vita consacrata* 13 (1977) 105–12.
14. See T. Špidlík, 'L'obbedienza tra carisma e istituzione', *Vita Monastica* 24 (1974) 36–49.
15. Mohamed al-Birouni, 'Les fêtes des Melchites', ed. R. Griveau, *Kânoun I*, (*Décembre*) PO 10:298.
16. *Ibid.*; cf. Hausherr, *Direction spirituelle*, 17.
17. See Hausherr, *ibid.*, 68ff; 1028ff.
18. *Ibid.*; 76ff; col. 1030ff.
19. *Ibid.*; 130, col. 1024ff.
20. See, for example, Dorotheus, *Instruction* 1.23; SCh 92:181; CS 33:90.
21. Basil, *Short Rules* 98; PG 31:1150D–1151A.
22. See Špidlík, *Joseph de Volokolamsk*, 41.
23. See Dorotheus, *Instruction* 1.25; PG 88:1640D; SCh 92: 184, CS 33:83.
24. See Johannes Řezáč, *De monachismo orientali secundum recentiorem legislationem Russicam*, OCA 138 (Rome, 1968) 79ff.
25. See Špidlík, *Joseph de Volokolamsk*, 42.
26. See Julien Leroy, 'La réforme studite', in *Monachesimo orientale*, OCA 153 (Rome, 1958) 195ff.
27. Špidlík, *Joseph de Volokolamsk*, 43 [see *The Monastic Rule of Josif Volotsky*, CS 36, trans. D. M. Goldfrank (Kalamazoo, 1983) p. 107.]
28. Jean Gribomont, 'Obéissance et evangile selon saint Basile le Grand', *La Vie spirituelle*, Suppl. VI (1952) 192–215.
29. T. Špidlík, L'obbedienza tra carisma e istituzione', *Vita monastica* 24 (1970) 36–49; id., '"Fous pour le Christ" en Orient', DS 5: 752–761.
30. See Irénée Hausherr, *Noms du Christ et voies d'oraison*, OCA 157 (Rome, 1960) 162ff. [translation by Charles Cummings, *The Name of Jesus*, CS 44 (Kalamazoo, 1978)].
31. See J. Gribomont, 'Eustathe le Philosophe et les voyages du jeune Basile de Césarée', *Revue d'histoire écclesiastique* 54 (1959) 115–24; *idem.*, 'Le monachisme au IVᵉ siècle en Asie Mineure', *Studia Patristica* II, TU 64 (Berlin, 1957) 400–15
32. Basil, *Epistola* 2,3; PG 32:22BC; see J. Gribomont, 'Les Règles Morales de saint Basile et le nouveau Testament', *Studia Patristica* II: 416–26.
33. See Antoine and Claire Guillaumont, Introduction to the *Traité pratique d'Évagre*, SCh 170 (1971) 51.
34. Joseph of Volokolamsk, *Prosvětitel* [*The Englightener*] (Kazań, 1857) 412; see Basil, *Homilia Quod Deus non est auctor malorum* 4; PG 31:337CD.
35. *De judicio Dei* (PG 31:653–676); see D. Amand, *L'ascèse monastique de saint Basile* (Maredsous, 1948) 152ff.
36. Amand, 271ff.
37. *Ibid.*, 275ff.
38. *Short Rules* 233; PG 31:1237D–1240A.
39. Špidlík, *Joseph de Volokolamsk*, 30ff.
40. *Long Rules* 2; PG 31:908C–909B; Amand, 284ff.

41. Basil, *Homilia 7 in Hexaemeron* 1; PG 29:149A; SCh 26:295.
42. *Ibid.*, 7.4. (col. 156A; p. 409); Špidlík, *La sophiologie de S. Basile*, 17.
43. See above, VIII, *Flight from Divisions*.
44. *Adversus oppugnatores vitae monasticae* 3.15; PG 47:373A.
45. See John Damascene, *De virtute et vitio;* PG 95:85–98; [*On the Virtues and the Vices*, in *The Philokalia: The Complete Text*, 2 (London, 1981) 334–42]; cf. below, *The Division between the Virtues*.
46. See Irénée Hausherr, 'Vocation chrétienne et vocation monastique selon les Pères', In *Laïcs et vie chrétienne parfaite* (Rome, 1963) 33–115; and *Etudes de spiritualité orientale*, OCA 183 (1969) 403–85.

2. THE 'PATH OF VIRTUE'

1. *Vita Antonii* 17; PG 26:869A.
2. *Collationes* 1.13; SCh 42:91; NPNF² 11:300.
3. *Ethical Treatises* IV.369ff; SCh 129:35ff.
4. See A. J. Festugière, *Contemplation et vie contemplative selon Platon* (Paris, 1936) 19ff.
5. See Wilhelm Michaelis, *Die Entwicklungsstufen in Platos Tugendlehre* (Barmen, 1893); Evangeles G. Konstantinou, *Die Tugendlehre Gregors von Nyssa* (Würzburg, 1966), 37ff.
6. *Nicomachean Ethics*, 1102–3.
7. Arnim, SVF I, 563.
8. *Legum allegoriae* I.52; 48; 49.
9. See Špidlík, *Grégoire de Nazianze*, 60ff.
10. W. Kutschbach, *Das Verhältnis der stoischen Ethik zur Ethik Platons* (Halle, 1912) 20.
11. Gregory Nazianzen, *Carminum Liber* II.II.7, vv. 1210–1231; PG 37:1567.
12. *Nicomachean Ethics* 1106b–1107a, 1–3; see H. Kalchreuter, *'Die Mēsotes bei und vor Aristoteles'* (Dissertation, Tübingen, 1911).
13. *Nicomachean Ethics* 1107b, 4–8.
14. Gregory of Nyssa, *In Ecclesiasten homilia*, ed. P. Alexander, *Gregorii Nysseni Opera*, 5, (Leiden, 1962) 374.
15. *Id.*, *De vita Moysis*, ed. Werner Jaeger, *Gregorii Nysseni Opera* 5: 132, 8–10.
16. See A. Michel, 'Vertu', DThC 15/2:2791ff.
17. Cassian, *Collationes* 2.4; PL 49:528; SCh 42:116:NPNF² 11:310.
18. 2 *Apology* 11.2; PG 6:461C; FC 6:119–135.
19. *Oratio* 42.12; PG 36:472C.
20. *Theaetetus* 176ab; *Politics* X.613a.
21. *Laws* IV.716d.
22. *De opificio mundi* 144.
23. Gregory Nazianzen, *Carminum Liber* I.II.9, vv. 19ff; PG 37:668.
24. *Oratio* 6.12; PG 35:737C; cf. *Oratio* 11.7; 841C.
25. See above, III, *After the Image of God*.
26. Origen, *Fragmenta in Joannem* IX; GCS 4:490, 24.
27. See Henri Crouzel, *Théologie de l'image de Dieu chez Origène* (Paris, 1956) 239ff.
28. See Plato, *Laws* 718d–719a; Walter Voelker, *Fortschritt und Vollendung bei Philo von Alexandrien*, TU 49 (Leipzig, 1938) 299.
29. Origen, *In Lucam homilia* 39; GCS 9:239.

Positive Praxis

30. *Vitae Antonii* 20; PG 26:873A; LNPF 4: (1891 rpt 1978) 201; see J. Roldanus, *Le Christ et l'homme dans la théologie d'Athanase d'Alexandrie* (Leiden, 1968).
31. *Letter* 7.3; PO 11:453.
32. *Ibid.*
33. *Life of St Syncletica* 40; ed., Jean Baptiste Cotelier, *Ecclesiae Graecae monumenta* (Paris, 1677–1886) vol. I:240; see I. Hausherr, *Penthos. La doctrine de la componction dans l'Orient Chretien*, 56 [*Penthos. The Doctrine of Compunction in the Christian East*, CS 53:47].
34. See Špidlík, *Joseph de Volokolamsk*, 27ff.
35. *Protagoras* 349b.
36. *Nicomachean Ethics* 1145a. 1–2.
37. Arnim, SVF I, 201; see Johannes Stelzenberger, *Die Beziehungen der frühchristlichen Sittenlehre zur Ethik der Stoa* (Munich, 1933) 317ff.
38. *De sacrificiis Abelis et Caini*, 84.
39. Ed. rom., I, P. 61; see Clement of Alexandria, *Stromata* I.20.97.3; SCh 30:122.
40. *De virginitate*, ed. F. P. Cavarnos, *Gregorii Nysseni Opera*, 8 (Leiden, 1952) p. 311, 3–13.
41. Arnim, SVF III, 295, p. 72; 299, p. 73; 302, p. 74.
42. See John Climacus, *Scala paradisi* 9 (PG 88:839D–841A; Luibheid-Russell translation, 152–3); Pseudo-Macarius, *Homily* 40.1; PG 34:764A.
43. See above, *Obedience to Divine Commandments.*
44. *De beatitutinibus* 4; PG 44:1241C [ACW 18 *(1954)*].
45. *Idem, Oratio catechetica magna;* PG 45:56D–57A.
46. *Carminum liber* I.II, vv. 4ff; PG 37:667.
47. *Ibid.*, I. II. 33, vv. 37–39; PG 37:931.
48. *Oratio* 5.124; PG 35:664C.
49. *Stromata* II.80.3; GCS 2:155, 4; SCh 38:97.
50. *Oratio* 14.5; PG 35:864B.
51. *Carminum liber* II.II.1, vv. 313ff; PG 37:1473.
52. See Philo, *Legum allegoriae* I. XVII. 57; Origen, *Expositio in Proverbia* 17 (PG 17:197ff.).
53. See A. Michel, in DThC 15/2:2757ff.
54. See above, Chapter III,2.
55. See above, *Virtue-Resemblance to God.*
56. *In Acta apostolorum homilia* 40.2; PG 60:285; LNPF 11:248; see Gregory of Nazianzus, *Oratio* 2 (PG 35:860B).
57. *Republic* 439aff.
58. Ed. Franz Susemihl, *Aristotelis Ethica Eudemia* (Leipzig, 1884) 181ff.
59. See above III. *Various Aspects of the Trichotomy.*
60. This expression, which Evagrius substituted for Plato's name, refers to Gregory Nazianzen.
61. *Praktikos* 89; SCh 171:681ff (see also the note); CS 4:38.
62. *Summa Theologiae*, II–II.
63. *Quatuor virtutum justa explicatio*, PG 160:880–81.
64. John of Damascus, *De virtute et vitio;* PG 95:85–98; see *Apophthegmata*, Poemen 60; PG 65:336C: CS 59:147.
65. John of Damascus, *op. cit.*; col. 85C.
66. See Irénée Hausherr, 'Vocation chrétienne et vocation monastique selon les Pères', in *Études de spiritualité orientale*, OCS 183 (Rome, 1969) 408.

67. *Collationes* 1.7: SCh 42: 84, LNPF² 11:297.
68. Diogenes Laertius VII.125; Arnim, SVF III, p. 72.
69. See *To the Corinthians* 13-15.
70. 4-6.
71. 16.7, and *Vision* III.8.7; SCh 53:120ff.
72. *L'Evangile selon Philippe*, ed. Jacques E. Ménard (Strassburg, 1967) 102-103; 22-25.
73. *Stromata* II.31.2; GCS 2:129.
74. *Ibid.*, I.II.31 (GCS 2:129); *Epistle of Pseudo-Barnabas* I. 5-6; F X. Funk, *Patres Apostolici* I (Tübingen, 1901) 36ff.
75. *Prologue* 8: SCh 171:493; CS 4:14.
76. *Ibid.*; 671; 36.
77. *Century I on Charity* 2; PG 90:961AB; SCh 9:69; ACW 21:137; *Ad Thalassium*, PG 91:1464D.
78. *Oratio* 17.8; PG 40:1150CD.
79. *To the Ephesians* 14.1 [trans. J. B. Lightfoot, *The Apostolic Fathers* (rpt 1978) p. 66].
80. *Praktikos* 84; SCh 171: 675; CS 4:37.

3. CHARITY

1. *Summa theologiae* II-II.184.1; *De caritate* a.3; *De perfectione vitae spiritualis*, c. 1.
2. *Ep.* 9.7, ed. F. X. Funk, *Patres Apostolici*, I (Tübingen, 1901) 66; SCh 172 (1971) 146.
3. Irenaeus, *Adversus haereses* IV.12.2; PG 7:1005A; ANF 1:476.
4. *Sermo 2 de caritate*; PG 86:354D.
5. *Homilia de perfecta caritate*; PG 56:279-290.
6. *Sermo de transfiguratione*, 10; PG 96:561A.
7. *Ethical Treatises* IV. 485ff; SCh 129: 43.
8. *Long Rules* 16.3; PG 31:961A.
9. *Oratio de divina et sancta caritate*; PG 82:1497-1522.
10. See Garcia M. Colombás, *Paradis et vie angélique* (Constantinople, 1961) 152ff.
11. Paul Evergetinos, *Synagogē*, IV, chapter 4 (Constantinople, 1861) 12-19.
12. See John Climacus, *Scala paradisi* 30; PG 88:1156BC.
13. See Hausherr, *Penthos*, pp. 55f (French), 51f (English).
14. Evagrius, *Praktikos*, SCh 171:492; CS 4:14, and note.
15. *Ibid.* 32; 574; 24-25.
16. See Irénée Hausherr, 'Contemplation et sainteté. Une remarquable mise au point par Philoxène de Mabboug (d. 523)', RAM 14 (1933) 189; *idem.*, *Hésychasme et prière*, OCA 176 (Rome, 1966) 31.
17. See below, XIII, *No True Knowledge Without Love*.
18. See F. Prat, 'La charité dans la Bible', DS 2/1:508ff.
19. The First Unmoved Mover who 'causes motion but in itself is unmoved', Aristotle, *Physica* VIII.5.256a 4-6, 260a 19.
20. See Léon Robin, *La théorie platonicienne de l'amour* (Paris, 1908) 228.
21. 252a-252c.
22. *Metaphysics* XII.7.1072a 26- b 4.

Positive Praxis 305

23. See Aristotle, *Eudemian Ethics* VII.12.16, ed. Franz Susemihl, (Leipzig, 1884) 107: *autos autou to eu estin*, (he is in himself his own well-being).
24. See Claude Wiener, 'Amour', VTB, col. 45–56.
25. See Hausherr, *Penthos*, pp. 55ff. (French), 51ff. (English).
26. See C. Wiener, 'Amour', VTB col. 54ff.
27. John Chrysostom, *De statuis* 10.4; PG 49:116ff; see Anders Nygren, *Eros et Agape, la notion chrétienne de l'amour et ses transformations*, French trans. by Pierre Jundt, vol. 1 (Paris, 1944) vols. 2 and 3 (Paris, 1952), English translation by Philip S. Watson, *Agape and Eros, A Study of the Christian Idea of Love* (New York, 1953) and reviewed by I. Hausherr, OCP 3 (1937) 314: 'the ideal geometry of the two concepts'.
28. Gregory of Nyssa, *Oratio catechetica* 5.3–4; PG 45:22C; cf. Irenaeus, *Adversus haereses* 4.13.4–14.1; SCh 100:534–40; cf. DS 6:459.
29. *Epistola ad Diognetum* 10.3; PG 2:1181B; SCh 33bis:76; see 1 Jn 4:10.
30. See, for example, G. Müller, *Lexicon Athanasianum* (Berlin, 1952) 1537.
31. From his study, A. Nygren draws the conclusion that Eros and Agape cannot coexist.
32. Marguerite-Marie Laurent, *Réalisme et richesse de l'amour chrétien Essai sur Eros et Agapē* (Rome, 1962) 71ff.
33. See Špidlík, *Théophane le Reclus*, 298.
34. See Gregory of Nyssa, *Commentarium in Canticum*; PG 44:878CD: 'For this reason the Word says once again to His awakened bride: *Arise*, and, when she has come, *Come*. For he who is rising can always rise further; and for him who runs to the Lord the open field of the divine course is never exhausted. We must therefore constantly arouse ourselves and never stop drawing closer in our course. For as often as He says, *Arise*, and *Come*, He gives us the power to rise and make progress.' Translation by Herbert Musurillo, *From Glory to Glory. Texts from Gregory of Nyssa's Mystical Writings* (New York, 1979) 191.
35. Basil, *Long Rules* 2; PG 31:908; ACW 9:283. David Amand, *L'ascèse monastique de saint Basil* (Maredsous, 1948) 296.
36. Basil, *loc cit.*
37. See Špidlík, *La sophiologie de S. Basile*, 151.
38. *In Canticum homilia* 2.9; PG 13:55C; GCS 8:55; see DS 6:866.
39. See Georges Dejaifve, 'Vers une théologie de l'Agape', NRT 74 (1952) 1076.
40. Basil, *loc cit.* (n. 35).
41. See Špidlík, *La Sophiologie de S. Basile*, 12ff.
42. *Ibid.*, 151.
43. Basil, *Long Rules* 2.1; PG 31:908C.
44. *Phaedrus* 237d; see Evagrius, *Praktikos* 4 SCh 171:503; CS 4:16; René Arnou, in DS 2/2:1722; Léon Robin, *La théorie platonicienne de l'amour* (Paris, 1908).
45. *Long Rules*, 2.1; PG 31:909C.
46. This 'personal feeling' is found in other saints; cf. *La sophiologie de S. Basile*, 153ff.
47. *Long Rules* 2; PG 31:916 [FC 9:239].
48. Basil, *In Psalmum* 29.3; PG 29:309C.
49. See Irénée Hausherr, *Philautie. De la tendresse pour soi à la charité selon saint Maxime le Confesseur*, OCA 137 (Rome, 1952) 128.
50. Maximus the Confessor, *Century* II.3; SCh 9:94; ACW 21:128.
51. *Ibid.*, I.13.23; SCh p. 72; ACW pp. 139ff; PG 90:964ff.
52. Evagrius, *Praktikos* 89; SCh 171:687; CS 4:38, this translation is taken from *Early Fathers from the Philokalia* (London, 1963) 104.

12
PRAYER

1. THE ESSENCE OF PRAYER

The Excellence and Necessity of Prayer

NOTHING EQUALS PRAYER,' wrote John Chrysostom. 'It makes possible what is impossible, easy what is difficult. It is not possible for the person who prays to fall into sin.'[1]

Theophane the Recluse explained why the fathers wrote so many treatises on prayer: 'Prayer is everything, it is the summary of everything: the faith, life according to the faith, salvation . . . . Let us hope that someone will collect the prayers written by the holy Fathers, for they would make a veritable handbook of salvation.'[2] For prayer is the expression of the life of the Holy Spirit within us, the 'breath of the spirit',[3] the 'barometer of the spiritual life'.[4] The entire Church 'breathes through prayer'.[5]

The monks of old called prayer the divine philosophy, 'the science of sciences'.[6] Philosophy has always searched out first principles, the reason for things that are. For Christians this is the Father, to whom the Spirit leads us through the Son.[7] Because he is a Person (and not a 'cosmic law'), the approach to him presupposes a dialogue, that is, prayer.

To Whom do We Pray?

According to the ancient liturgical rule, prayer is addressed to the Father through the Son in the Holy Spirit. Origen believed that one ought to pray not *to* Christ but *through* Christ.[8] Only later would the direct invocations to 'the intermediaries' become more frequent.

During prayer, the soul is guided by the Spirit of God (*hodēgoumenos hypo theou pneumatos*);[9] it prays 'in the Spirit'. It is therefore a sort of 'inspiration', because the Spirit prays in us; only in this way do we know what to ask and does our voice reach God.[10]

Our prayer is, furthermore, a participation in the prayer of the Word[11] who, in Origen's beautiful expression, is not alone in his prayer.[12] In the modern idiom we would say that we participate in the prayer of the 'mystical Christ'. Here is how Khomiakov expresses the ecclesial character of prayer:

> No one can rely on his private prayer. Anyone who prays asks for the intercession of the entire Church. Let the angels pray for us, the apostles, the martyrs, the patriarchs, and the one who is the greatest of all, the Mother of our Saviour. This holy union constitutes the true life of the Church.[13]

It is to underline this 'help, full of love, an intercession through prayer, a participation in the destiny of the world' that the Orthodox do not like the expression, 'the reversibility of the merits of the saints'.[14]

Definitions of Prayer

Before proposing their own definitions of prayer, the medieval theologians collected those inherited from the Fathers.[15] Most frequently these have no claim to being definitions in the true sense of the term; they describe one or another aspect of this life-giving act which is prayer. Thus, for example, prayer is called 'a state of the mind which destroys all earthly thoughts'.[16] or 'the manifestation of God's glory',[17] and so on.

Meanwhile, three definitions have become famous in all of christian tradition:
1. asking God for what is fitting;[18]
2. an ascent of the spirit to God;[19]
3. the spirit's colloquy with God.[20]

John of Damascus unified the first and the second definition:

'Prayer is an ascent of the mind to God, or the asking God for things which are fitting',[21] a formula borrowed by many others.[22]

The Prayer of Supplication

As human communication with God, prayer assumes this aspect first: a humble asking for the gifts of heaven and the disposition to receive them.[23]

Prayer in the true sense of the word, according to Theophane the Recluse, is always done for everyone, for the whole Church: the Fathers demonstrated this many times in interpreting the words of the Lord's Prayer.[24] It is useful nonetheless for a person to pray to obtain everything he especially needs,[25] although it is more perfect to ask for heavenly things rather than earthly and temporal things.[26]

To the question why our prayers are not always answered, the spiritual masters frequently replied that this is because we pray too little and because we are sinners.[27] The following advice is given to the person who prays: 'Do not be over-anxious and strain yourself to gain an immediate hearing for your request. The Lord wants to confer greater favors than those you ask, in reward for your perseverance in praying to him. For what greater thing is there than to converse intimately with God and to be preoccupied with his company?'[28]

And why does God not answer sinners (cf. Jn 9:31)? The Fathers knew well that sinners need to pray with confidence.[29] How can we say, meanwhile, that someone prays 'with faith' when the request is formulated in 'ignorance'?[30] Shadows of this ignorance of the true good, caused by sin, frequently remain even in the prayers of the just. In this case, the Holy Spirit who prays in our heart formulates, so to speak, a higher request than the one coming from human consciousness; the prayer of the Spirit, which is also our prayer in the secret of our heart, is always answered.[31]

Praying in the Spirit, the Church is not afraid of presenting in its liturgy 'all the needs' of the faithful to God. Yet frequently and insistently one request is repeated: the remission of sins. For here, John Chrysostom says, we accomplish the will of God, and as a consequence we are sure of being heard.[32]

Thanksgiving is our response for gifts received. Through the

Septuagint, christian hymnographers inherited the Semitic language of thanksgiving to God expressed by such verbs as *homologeō* (to acknowledge), *aineō* (to praise), *doxazō* (to glorify), and *eulogeō* (to bless). But a new term, *eucharisteō* (to give thanks), *eucharistia*, made inroads in the New Testament, showing the originality and importance of christian thanksgiving, the response to grace given by God through Christ. The Fathers speak of it when they comment on the four types of prayer known through St Paul (1 Tm 2:1): *deēsis* (supplication), *proseuchē* (prayer), *enteuxis* (intercession), *eucharistia* (thanksgiving). A close look at the explanation provided by Origen[33] tells us that these four were in practice reduced to two, inseparably united: supplication and thanksgiving; the latter becoming more and more the very soul of the spiritual life. For St Paul (1 Th 3:9ff., 5:17ff., Rm 1:8ff.), the entire christian life is carried and surrounded by a constant combination of supplication and thanksgiving.[34]

The Ascent of the Spirit to God

The ancients had spoken of the ascent of the soul to God. Plato described 'the ascent (*anabasis*) to and the contemplation of the things above, that is, the soul's ascent to the intelligible region.'[35] An equivalent expression is found on many pages of Scripture.[36] It is the *Sursum corda* ('Lift up your hearts') of the liturgy.

In order to avoid the danger of platonic intellectualism, it became necessary to explain and adapt the *nous*, the pre-eminent organ of this ascent,[37] or replace it with the heart (*kardia*),[38] or even unite the two terms[39] and thereby profess that all of man's faculties move and direct themselves toward God in prayer.[40] Because man raises himself to God who is Father, this ascent is not limited to a single 'vision' (in the platonic sense), but becomes 'a colloquy of the spirit with God'.[41] 'The monk is called monk on this account: day and night he converses with God.'[42]

From the outset, a practical question arose for Christians: how and to what degree the body shares in this ascent toward the invisible God and in spiritual conversation with him. Against the formalism of pagan rituals, the Fathers frequently offered assurances that the position of the body is of no importance: Saint Paul prayed while lying in prison, the good thief while extended on the cross.[43] For normal situations, however, the following exhortation by Basil is much more typical: 'Consider, also, what this power is which the soul imparts to the body and what sympathy the body renders the soul in return.'[44] Joseph of Volokolamsk summarized the opinion of cenobitic monks on this matter: a devout deportment of the body facilitates inner attention, and inward recollection shows itself on the outside through a serious and thoughtful attitude.[45] Even the solitaries practised 'bodily prayer', especially in the form of prostrations and profound bows;[46] the psychosomatic technique of the hesychasts was intended to make the body participate in deep contemplation.[47] Let us not forget the liturgy. To its external rituals can be applied Origen's statement that the one who prays 'bears in his body, as it were, the image of the characteristics befitting the soul during prayer'.[48]

2. THE DEGREES AND THE TYPES OF PRAYER

The Degrees of Prayer

During prayer all man's powers and faculties enter into action. One may speak of different degrees of prayer depending on which element is stressed.[1] Theophane the Recluse has drawn a traditional picture of these various degrees, one which corresponds to the structure of the human composite:[2]
1. bodily or oral prayer (*telesnaja, molitvoslovnaja*);
2. mental prayer (*umnaja*);
3. prayer of the intellect and of the heart or only of the heart, of feeling (*umnoserdečnaja, serdečnaja, čustva*);
4. spiritual or contemplative prayer (*duchovnaja, sozercatel' naja*).

By way of contrast to the first, the last three forms of prayer are also called interior prayer.

Oral prayer consists in reading or reciting texts, making inclinations, and so on.[3] The spiritual masters view this prayer mainly as a necessary preparation for higher prayer, a step, the 'leaf' that comes before the flower and the fruit,[4] the first contact with 'the flesh of Christ',[5] and also the participation of the human word in the creative word of God and in its effective power in the world.[6]

Yet this prayer is not free from distractions. Those who view it only as a stepping stone to higher prayer severely condemn the mere recitation of formulas without application and without feeling. Martyrius Sahdônâ, for example, said: 'They are vain and profit nothing . . . the office and the prayer during which one does not converse with the Lord of the universe in vigilance, fear, and attention. [Let us rather say] that instead of being disrespectful, our office and our prayer will turn to our own condemnation.'[7] Origen, on the contrary, valued this first merely 'corporal', contact with Christ.[8] There are even those who believe that if we understand nothing of the prayers we are saying, 'the devil, he understands!' and he is chased away.[9]

The second type of prayer calls upon the activity of discursive thinking. This is what would be called *consideratio* reflection, or meditation in the West. We cannot say that these forms of prayer were unknown in the East.[10] Theophane, however, voiced the fear that we might forget the relative value of these exercises.[11] Intellectual reflection serves as a preparation for the prayer of the heart; one 'meditates' the words recited in order to 'taste' them.[12] When the feelings slowly begin to warm the heart, the prayer will become 'the heart's sighing after God.'[13]

The prayer which has become a 'state of the heart',[14] already contains all the elements desired in prayer. A yet higher contemplation is reserved for the elect: when the spiritual element outstrips the corporal, and even human thoughts and feelings, when prayer is achieved in the depths of the spirit,[15] in the silence of what is human ('prayer of silence'), in ecstasy.[16]

Liturgical Prayer

In the East one finds beautiful pages on the ecclesiastical character of public prayer. It is the Church which celebrates these rites and ceremonies, Theophane the Recluse wrote, and when we are present we unite ourselves with the Church and share in its grace:[17] 'The person who withdraws from external ceremonies withdraws from the prayers of the Church, and the person who withdraws from the prayer of the Church deprives himself of the Lord's great promise, "where two or three are gathered together in my name, there am I in the midst of them"'(Mt 18:2).[18]

The sacramental character is derived from this ecclesiastical character, because the sacraments are framed as it were by the whole life of the Church and its liturgy.[19] Sergei Bulgakov has spoken 'of the realism of the Eastern rites',[20] Boris Bobrinsky of their 'eucharistic character', so that in the churches Christ is truly born at Christmas and really dies at Easter and is risen.[21]

The instructive and educational character of public prayer has been brought out especially by Nikolaj Gogol in his *The Divine Liturgy*.[22] The ceremonies act as a school in training the taste of the Christian, in disciplining and guiding him.[23] One must recognize, however, that a real danger lurks in the offices of the Church: formalism.[24] Their very variety can impede the simplicity of 'pure prayer'.[25]

Icons

Icons occupy a special place in Eastern spirituality: they make up the *iconostasis*, they are carried in procession, and the assistants are blessed with them; private houses have a little sanctuary called 'the corner of beauty' (*krasnyi ugol*). 'Family icons' are painted.[26] Intimately linked to the economy of salvation, the sacred images bring out in full the two major aspects of the redemptive work of Christ: the preaching of the truth; and the communication of God's grace.

'The icon is one of the manifestations of the holy Tradition of the Church, just the same as the written and oral traditions.'[27] Following Basil, the Seventh Ecumenical Council (787) compared painting to the proclamation of the faith.[28] Iconographic art resembles the priestly ministry.[29] Traditional instructions for painters were gathered in several manuals, the most famous of which is the *Hermēnia tēs zōgraphikōs technēs* by Dionysius of Phourna (1745). In Russia, these books of instruction were called 'podlinniks',[30]

As a preaching of the divine truth, the icon possesses the 'dynamic' power of the words of God:[31] grace is given to the people by means of the sacred image.[32] 'The liturgical and sacramental life of the Church is inseparable from the image', Ouspensky says,[33] an icon is a symbol 'which expresses and in a certain way embodies and makes present a higher reality'.[34] It is not a mere painting.[35]

Consequently, one venerates and contemplates icons. The aim of the art of iconography is to give witness to the presence of God in his visible image, to decipher the meaning of what strikes the eye, which is nothing else than contemplation.[36] The iconographer shows the mysterious and divine meaning of the world he paints. Hence the dense symbolism of the icon: the composition and the perspective, the colors and the light, the decorative elements: everything takes on a spiritual meaning. On the other hand, the person who looks at an icon must make himself ready to receive the mystery which it reveals and 'approach icons with dignity, with a pure conscience'.[37]

The Symbolism of the Church Building

From the fourth century on, the symbolism of the churches began to be explained and commented on.[38] But it was particularly in the seventh and eighth centuries that it acquired its most complete theoretical expression in the *Mystagogy* of Maximus the Confessor, in the writings of Sophronius, Patriarch of Jerusalem, in those of Germanus, Patriarch of Constantinople, and, later, with Symeon of Thessalonica in the fifteenth century.

The church building is first of all a symbol of the church-assembly of the faithful, where 'the souls are but one, because the Holy Spirit unites them'.[39] Christians have been conscious from the beginning that they themselves are the new temple, the extension of the body of Christ.[40]

By means of the liturgical sacrifice the presence of God inside the church is sacramental.[41] But those in the East seem to insist instead on 'the other essential truth which is the goal and the result of this sacrifice: the transfiguration of man, and with him, of the whole visible world.'[42] The church is 'heaven on earth',[43] where the presence of God becomes somehow visible in the beauty of the rituals and the symbolism of the building.[44] 'In a church,' writes Patriarch Alexis of Moscow, 'everything is different from what we constantly see around us in our homes....; everything shines brightly, everything raises the spirit and removes it from its usual thoughts and impressions of this world.'[45]

3. UNCEASING PRAYER

Pray Without Ceasing (1 Th 5:17)

'We are not commanded', Evagrius says, 'to work, keep vigil and fast unceasingly; but we are commanded to pray without ceasing,'[1] because the mind 'was created to pray'.[2] Maximus the Confessor added, in full agreement with all the other Eastern spiritual writers, 'that Scripture commands nothing that is impossible',[3] Still, the spiritual writers went their separate ways over the interpretation of two words, *to pray* and *always*.

The *Messalians* took the command quite literally: *to pray* means to say prayers, and *always*, meant to refuse all secular work, especially manual labor.[4]

The *Acoemeti* (non-sleepers) believed they could achieve continual prayer by team work, by rotating within the community, by having the various groups of monks pray their offices in succession in such a way that prayer was never interrupted inside the walls of the monastery.[5] This is why their neighbors called them *acoemeti*, those who do not sleep.[6]

The classical solution of the problem is found in Origen:

> Since virtuous deeds and the carrying out of what is enjoined are parts of prayer, he prays without ceasing who adds prayer to works that are of obligation, and good works to his prayer. For thus alone can we accept 'pray without ceasing' as a possible command, namely, if we speak of the entire life of a saint as one continual prayer, of which what is customarily called prayer is a part.[7]

This teaching of the greatest of the Greek exegetes was to become that of the greatest of the Latin, Augustine,[8] and of the foremost among the Syrians, Aphrahat.[9]

A problem then arose: what should be the relationship between explicit prayer and works? Origen believed that it was enough to 'pray' not less than three times a day.[10] Alexander, the founder of the *acoemeti*, created twenty-four daily exercises to correspond to the twenty-four hours of the day.[11] Later, the discipline of the seven canonical hours was developed. But almost every saint organized the times for prayer to suit himself.[12]

Why this wavering? The 'classical' solution makes a 'prayer' out of 'work'. But it presupposes that the work is done with a good inward disposition, a *diathesis agathē*.[13] This good disposition is born and nourished through contemplation, through explicit prayers. This is why the monks always sought to increase their practice of prayer. But their aim is summed up in Cassian's expression *orationis status*,[14] the state of prayer. The continuity of the acts of prayer soon leads to weariness and distractions. Life, by contrast, is a state, a *katastasis*, an habitual disposition of the heart.[15] We should therefore give our heart this habitual disposition which somehow by itself deserves the name prayer, outside of the acts which it makes with greater or lesser frequency.

Ejaculatory Prayers

It is impossible to arrive at continual prayer right away. One should begin by being faithful to vocal prayers and recite them well. Theophane the Recluse frequently spoke of the 'rule of prayer' which every good Christian establishes with his spiritual father; to this he will also add other prayers suggested by special needs or the inspiration of his heart.[16]

One reads in the Russian translation of *Spiritual Warfare*[17] that the Fathers invented ejaculatory prayers to avoid distractions. Cassian mentions them and says that they were used in Egypt. They were also used in the Sinai, in Syria, and throughout the christian world.[18] The usual distinguishing mark of these prayers is their brevity and simplicity, their continued rumination (*meletan*, 'to meditate').[19] At first we find a great variety of these prayers among the ascetics. But as time went on preference was given to certain ones (for example, verse 1 of Ps 69, 'O God, make speed to deliver me; make haste to help me, O Lord'),[20] and, in the end, the monks began to exclude other free formulas in favor of a single one, the 'Jesus prayer'.[21]

The Jesus Prayer

This is generally called the Jesus 'prayer', which is a literal translation of the Russian *molitva Jisusova*, in itself the equivalent of the Greek *euchē Jesou* (where the name *Jesou* is an objective genitive). For centuries it has been expressed in the following way: 'Lord Jesus Christ, Son of God, have mercy upon me' ('a sinner,' the Russians add). This prayer has been called the 'heart of orthodoxy',[22] 'a practice which, while going back to remotest antiquity, remains very much alive today in the christian East'.[23] Byzantine and Russian monks associate the Jesus prayer with the use of a rosary (*kombologion, komboskoinon, lestovka, vervitsa, tchotki*), which helps to count the invocations and the bows that accompany them.[24]

Until the middle of the eleventh century, this prayer was not as widespread as it came to be in the fourteenth; various authors, contained or not contained in the *Philokalia*, have outdone each other in celebrating its excellence.[25] Theophane the Recluse, like others, borrowed the teaching of Abba Philemon:[26]

> Call to him with fervor: 'Lord Jesus Christ, Son of God, have mercy upon me a sinner'. Do this constantly in church and at home, travelling, working, at table, and in bed: in a word from the time you open your eyes till the time you shut them. This will be exactly like holding an object in the sun, because this is to hold yourself before the face of the Lord, who is the Sun of the spiritual world.[27]

Three Stages in the Jesus Prayer

In keeping with what has been said about prayer in general,[28] there are three distinct degrees to this prayer: oral, mental, and of the heart.[29] Oral recitation possesses an unquestionable value, as does the practice of short, frequent prayers.[30] But Theophane the Recluse was right in opposing those who wanted to give this prayer an almost sacramental character and who believed they had discovered a 'talisman' in it.[31]

With regard to content, several authors, beginning in the fourteenth century, have highly praised the superiority of the formula and have indicated its many virtues.[32] But it is possible to stress the first or the second element of the prayer. In the latter case, the Jesus prayer is one of the numerous catanyctic prayers that were popular in the monastic circles that cultivated *penthos*.[33]

The more recent authors give preference instead to the first element: the special power of the name of Jesus. But it is better not to separate one element from the other: adoration from compunction, an awareness of the abyss between the divine and the human from what surpasses them, the mercy of the God-Man.[34]

Lastly, the stage of the heart: 'Make it your habit' Theophane the Recluse wrote, 'to pray these words with your mind in your heart: "Lord Jesus Christ, Son of God, have mercy on me". And this prayer, when you have learnt to use it properly, or rather, when it becomes grafted to your heart, will lead you to the end which you desire: it will unite your mind with your heart, it will quell the turbulence of your thoughts, and it will give you power to govern the movements of your soul.'[35]

The 'Psychosomatic', 'Scientific Method'

The aim of this prayer is to create and reinforce a certain state of heart. The Athonite hesychasts wanted to help this process of interior assimilation by means of a psychosomatic method. Its oldest known theoretician was Nicephorus the Monk in the second half of the thirteenth century.[36] This presupposed a moral preparation: a pure conscience, *amerimnia* (tranquillity).[37] External conditions were required next: a closed cell, a seated position on a low bench, with one's beard resting on one's chest, 'one turned the eye of the body with the whole mind on the middle of the abdomen, also called the navel'.[38]

The exercise even contained a regulated slowing down of the breathing (later, it was said that the repetition of the formula should be synchronized with the slowed-down breathing rhythm), a mental exploration of the visceral 'me' in search of the place of the heart, and the unceasing invocation of the name of Jesus.

Painful and filled with darkness at the beginning, the unification of the mind joined to prayer soon led to joy, ineffable delights, invincibility against the attacks of the Enemy, a growing love of God, and a great light (later called 'Taboric').[39]

The Russian Pilgrim

Through *The Way of a Pilgrim*,[40] translated into several languages, readers in the West have come to know the Jesus Prayer.[41]

According to the story, the pilgrim, a simple peasant, is seeking an answer to the traditional question: how to pray without ceasing? The *staretz*-spiritual father suggests a simplified method to him. He begins with the repeated invocation of Jesus and goes from 300 to 6,000 and 12,000 aspirations a day. After that he no longer counts them because his lips and tongue pronounce the words by themselves, without any urging, even during sleep.

After some time he enters the second stage: the movement is transferred from his lips, which must not move, to his tongue. Then the prayer passes from his tongue to his heart. The pilgrim is aware that his prayer is now recited within the beating of his heart, as if the heart somehow began to say, *one*, 'Lord', *two*, 'Jesus', *three*, 'Christ', and so on.

The conclusion which bears in upon the reader is that the person who unites prayer to the beating of his heart will never be able to stop praying, because prayer becomes like a vital function of his existence. Is this already perfect prayer? The pilgrim does not want to say it, but he believes that he is on the right road to arrive at it, with the grace of God.

Reflections on the Jesus Prayer

Recent commentators have carefully distinguished the prayer itself from the psycho-physical method, which is only an 'auxiliary means'.[42]

Devotion to the name of Jesus is the result of a slow awakening of christian sentiment.[43] One can follow the Eastern tradition from the fifth century to the Russian spiritual masters of the eighteenth century.[44] The shadings of this devotion are numerous. For Hesychius the invocation of Jesus is linked to *nepsis* (vigilance),[45] it is therefore an effective *antirrhesis* (counter-argument) against demons.[46] Beginning with the fourteenth century certain authors saw in it a brief summary of the christian faith.[47]

An extreme veneration of the name of Jesus led certain Russian monks at the end of the nineteenth century, called 'idolaters of the name', to a doctrine which was to rock the Russian church, especially in 1912–1913.[48] Without identifying the name with the person Sergei Bulgakov developed a theory of the dynamic and quasi-sacramental power of the name of God.[49] Ivan Kologrivof, in line with the Eastern tradition, tied the pronunciation of the name of Jesus by the lips to the presence of the Lord 'in a blessed icon'.[50]

For all that, one should not belittle the interest which the psychophysical method offers from the point of view of religious psychology.[51] Several elements can be found in it. Already in antiquity, physicians always considered the problem of how the breath in respiration combined with the elements of the organism.[52] The Fathers, perceived an encounter between the *pneuma* and the blood, the soul, and the voice.[53] In our day the breathing technique of the hesychasts has been compared to the breathing in Hindu yoga, the *pranayama*, which aims at unifying consciousness and preparing for meditation,[54] or likewise to the 'third manner of praying' of Ignatius Loyola.[55]

The authors of the *Conferences on the Jesus Prayer*[56] and of *The Way of a Pilgrim* saw no problem with the warmth and the feelings of consolation that follow the diligent practice of the method. Yet they warn against mistaking a 'natural effect' for the grace of the Spirit, which certainly would be a serious deviation. One could say the same of the other effects produced by the 'localization' of the attention of the heart (understood in a physical and not a symbolic sense),[57] of the kinesthetic sensations coming from the region of the heart, all of which favors a movement of introversion.[58]

A quiet setting, darkness, a seated position, muscle tension, can all be reduced to the general experience in which the attention of the soul depends on the position of the body, which, in prayer, is 'like the foundation of a building'.[59]

But on the other hand, the real spiritual writers all agree that the method cannot be viewed as a 'short cut' to contemplation without the normal means of christian *praxis*. Moreover, 'all this does not suit everyone and can often be dangerous without personal guidance'.[60]

Notes

1. THE ESSENCE OF PRAYER

1. *De Anna sermo* IV; PG 54:666.
2. Načertanije christianskago nravoučenija [*Christian Moral Teaching*] (Moscow, 1895) 122.

3. *Ibid.*, 406.
4. See Špidlík, *Théophane le Reclus*, 240.
5. *Ibid.*, 241.
6. *Ibid.*, 240.
7. See above, II The 'Super-essential' Unity.
8. *De oratione* 10ff.; PG 11:445ff.
9. *Contra Celsum* VII.4; GCS 2:196, 3.
10. *De oratione* 2; PG 11:421CD.
11. *Ibid.* 10; PG 11:445–48.
12. *Ibid.* 11; 448–49.
13. *Cerkov odna* [*The One Church*] (Prague, 1967) 18.
14. Sergei Bulgakov, *L'Orthodoxie* (Paris, 1962) 169.
15. See, for example, Thomas Aquinas, *Summa theologiae* 2–II.83.1; Suarez, *Opera omnia, tract.* IV, liber I. c. 1 (Paris, 1859) pp. 4ff; A. Vermeersch, *Quaestiones de virtutibus religionis et pietatis* (Bruges, 1912) 57.
16. Evagrius, *Centuriae Supplementum* 29; ed. W. Frankenberg, *Evagrius Ponticus*, AGG, Neue Folge 13, 2 (Berlin, 1912) 453.
17. John of Damascus, *Sermo de transfiguratione* 10; PG 96:561A.
18. Basil, *Homilia in martyrem Julittam* 3; PG 31:244A.
19. Evagrius, *De oratione* 35; PG 79:1173; CS 4:60; see I. Hausherr, *Les leçons d'un contemplatif. Le traité de l'oraison d'Évagre le Pontique* (Paris, 1960) 53ff.
20. *De oratione* 3; P679:1168; CS 4:56; Hausherr, 16ff.
21. *De fide orthodoxa* 3.24; PG 94:1089C; FC 37:378.
22. Thomas Aquinas, *Summa Theologiae* II–II.83. lc; *Expositio in epistolam beati Pauli ad Colossenses* 1.3.
23. Theophane the Recluse, *Piśma k raznym licam* . . . [*Letters to Various Persons*] (Moscow, 1895), Letter 151, 460ff.
24. *Id.*, *Istolkovanije Molitvy Gospodnej* . . . [*Commentary on the Lord's Prayer*] (Moscow, 1889) 454ff.
25. *Id.*, *Commentary on the Letter to Timothy*, in *Dušepoleznje čtenije* 22/2 (1881) 365ff.
26. Origen, *De oratione* 8 (PG 11:441); 14 (460BC); Ambrose, *Expositio in Psalmo 118, sermo 19*.11 (PL 15:1471); Evagrius, *De oratione* 37–38 (PG 79: 1176; CS 4:61; Hausherr, *Leçons d'un contemplatif*, 55ff); Theophane the Recluse (who quotes especially Isaac the Syrian), *O molitvě i trezvenii* [*On Prayer and Vigilance*] (Moscow, 1889) 307.
27. See John Chrysostom, *In dimissionem Chananaeae* 10; PG 52:457.
28. *De oratione* 34; PG 59:1173; CS 4:60; Hausherr, 51f.
29. See above, Chapter VII, 3.
30. Origen, *De oratione* 21; PG 11:481B.
31. *Ibid.*, 2; 421.
32. See *Expositio in Psalmo* 4.4; PG 55:44ff.
33. *De oratione* 14; PG 11:460; See Cassian, *Collationes* 9.9; PL 49:780; SCh 54:48ff; NPNF² 11:391.
34. See André Ridouard and Jacques Guillet, 'Action de grâces', VTB, col. 12–15.
35. *Republic* VII.517b, ed. Émile Chambry, coll. Budé (Paris, 1933) 149.
36. Ps 123:1, 141:2.
37. See Cyprian, *De oratione dominica* 31; PL 4:539B.
38. See below, XIII, 3.
39. See above, Chapter IV, 3.

40. See Špidlík, *Théophane le Reclus*, 24.
41. Evagrius, *De oratione* 3 (PG 79:1168; CS 4:56; Hausherr, 16ff); John Chrysostom, *Homilia 6 de precatione* (PG 64:464ff); John of Damascus, *In Sabbatum* 25 (PG 96:640CD).
42. Paul Evergetinos, *Synagogē* I, chapter 12 (Constantinople, 1861) 75.
43. John Chrysostom, *De Anna sermo* 4.6; PG 54:668.
44. *Homilia in illud, Attende tibi ipsi* 7; PG 31:261B; FC 9:444.
45. *Duchovnaja gramota* [Monastic Rule], in Makarij, *Velikija Minej Cetij*, September vol, (St Peterburg, 1868) col. 506. [See D. M. Goldfrank, trans. *The Monastic Rule of Josif Volotsky*, CS 36 (Kalamazoo, 1983)].
46. See E. Bertaud, 'Génuflexions et métanies', DS 6:213–26.
47. See below, *The 'Psychosomatic', 'Scientific' Method*.
48. *De oratione* 31.2; PG 11:552A.

2. THE DEGREES AND THE TYPES OF PRAYER

1. See Hal Koch, 'Kennt Origenes Gebetsstufen?', *Theologische Quartalschrift* 87 (1905) 592–96.
2. *Pis'ma o duchovno žizni* [*Letters on the Spiritual Life*] (Moscow, 1903) 112, 170ff.
3. See Špidlík, *Théophane le Reclus*, 245.
4. *Ibid.*, 409.
5. *In Librum Jesu homilia* 20.1; GCS 7:415ff; see Henri de Lubac, *Histoire et Esprit* (Paris, 1950) 323ff.
6. Nikolai Gogol, *The Divine Liturgy of the Eastern Orthodox Church*, trans Rosemary Edmonds (London: Darton, Longman, 1960) 62ff.
7. *Livre de la perfection* II.8 (22); CSCO 253, Syr. 111, p. 7, 10–14.
8. See above, n. 5.
9. See *Otkrovennyje rasskazy strannika* (The Way of A Pilgrim), (Paris, 1948) 38 [translation by R. M. French, *The Way of a Pilgrim* (New York: Seabury, 1965)].
10. See the *Pachomian Rule*, A. Boon, *Pachomiana Latina, Sancti Pachomii Praecepta*, n. 36 (Louvain, 1932) [trans. Armand Veilleux, *Pachomian Koinonia*, 2(1981) 148]; S. Salaville, 'Formes de prière d'après un byzantin du XIVe siècle', *Echos d'Orient* 39 (1940–42) 1–25.
11. See Špidlík, *Théophane le Reclus*, 249ff.
12. *Pis'ma k raznym licam* . . . [*Letters to Various Persons*] (Moscow, 1892), Letter 66, 333ff.; see Jacques Serr, *La prière du coeur*, Spiritualité orientale 6 (Etoilles, 1970).
13. *Théophane le Reclus*, 249ff.
14. See above, IV, *The Heart, Principle of Human Integration*.
15. See *Théophane le Reclus*, 251ff.
16. On 'the prayer of silence' in the West, see DThC 13/1 (1936) col. 174.
17. Theophane the Recluse, *Pis'ma k raznym licam* [*Letters to Various Persons*] (Moscow, 1892) 249ff. Let us note, however, that it is not easy to fix the limits between public prayer and private prayer; see A. Fonck, 'Prière', DThC 13/1: 192.
18. *Pis'ma.*, p. 283.
19. *Ibid.*, p. 282.
20. *The Orthodox Church* (London, 1935) 150.

Prayer 323

21. In Sergei Verchovskoj, *Pravoslavie v žizni* [*Orthodoxy in Life*] (New York, 1953) 244ff.
22. *The Divine Liturgy of the Eastern Orthodox Church* (London, 1960) 14ff; *Razmyšlenija o Božestvennoj liturgii* (St. Petersburg, 1902), 70.
23. See *Théophane le Reclus*, 182.
24. *Ibid.*
25. See Cassian, *Collationes* 10.13 (SCh 54:94; NPNF² 11:409) Irénée Hausherr, *Noms du Christ et voies d'oraison*, OCA 157 (Rome, 1960) 138. *The Name of Jesus*, CS 44 (1978).
26. See T. Špidlík, 'La preghiera presso i popoli slavi', in *La preghiera*, ed. Renato Boccassino, vol. 2, (Milan, 1967) 787–817.
27. Leonid Ouspensky, *Essai sur la théologie de l'icône dans l'Eglise orthodoxe*, vol. 1 (Paris, 1960) 10 [*Theology of the Icon* (New York: St Vladimir's Seminary Press, 1978)].
28. See J. D. Mansi, *Sacrorum conciliorum noua et amplissima collectio* (Florence, 1759–) 13:300c; 268c; Basil, *Homilia in quadraginta martyres* 2; PG 31: 509A.
29. See *Podlinnik* [*Manual of Sacred Iconography*], ed. T. Bolšakov, (Moscow, 1903) 3.
30. For the editions, see DS 7/2:1227.
31. See above, IX, *Exorcism*.
32. See Sergei Nikol Bulgakov, *L'Orthodoxie* (Paris, 1932) 206.
33. Ouspensky, *Theology of the Icon*, 1:10.
34. *Ibid.*
35. Bugakov, *loc. cit.*
36. See below, XIII, 4.
37. *Domostroj* [Instructions on family life attibuted to Sylvester the Priest] chap. 11–12, ed. V. Jakovlev (St Petersburg, 1867) 27ff.
38. See Ouspensky, *Theology of the Icon*, 1:25ff.
39. John Chrysostom, *De incomprehensibili Dei natura* 3; PG 48:725.
40. See 1 Co 3:10–17, 2 Co 6:16ff, Eph 2:20ff, 1 Co 6:15, 12:27; See *Joseph de Volokolamsk*, 104.
41. See Symeon of Salonica, *De sacro templo*; PG 155:305.
42. Ouspensky, 26.
43. The title of a work by Sergei Bulgakov, published at Munich in 1928.
44. See Symeon of Salonica, *De sacro templo*, 131; PG 155:337D: the church as the shadow of the Trinity.
45. Paschal message to the rectors of the churches in Moscow, *Calendar of the Patriarchate of Moscow 1947* (in Russian), quoted in Ouspensky, 36.

3. UNCEASING PRAYER

1. Evagrius, *Praktikos* 49; SCh 171:611; CS 4:29; *Early Fathers from the Philokalia* 106.
2. *Ibidem*; SCh 613.
3. *Liber asceticus* 25; PG 90:929D, 932A.
4. Augustine, too, wrote *On the Work of Monks* (PL 4:547–82); see G. Folliet, 'Des moines euchites à Carthage en 400–401', *Studia Patristica* 2, TU 64 (Berlin, 1957) 386–99.
5. This is the principle of 'perpetual adoration' and the 'perpetual rosary' known in the West in recent times.

324   Chapter Twelve

6. See Venance Grumel, 'Acémètes', DS 1:169–75; T. Špidlík, 'Acemeti', DIP 1 (1974) 88.
7. *De oratione* 12; PG 11:452 [trans. by J. O'Meara, *Origen. Prayer. Exhortation to Martyrdom*, ACW 19 (1954) 47].
8. *De haeresibus* 57; PL 42:40.
9. *Demonstrationes* IV.14–17.
10. *De oratione* 12; PG 11:452CD.
11. See V. Grumel, in DS 1:172.
12. Pierre Maraval, Introduction to *Vie de S. Macrine*, SCh 178 (1971) 68ff.
13. See Špidlík, *La sophiologie de S. Basil*, 49; see below, XIII, 5.
14. *Collationes* 10.14; SCh 54:95; NPNF² 11:409.
15. See above, IV, *The Principle of Human Introspection*.
16. See *Théophane le Reclus*, 276ff.
17. By Lorenzo Scupoli, adapted by Nicodemus the Hagiorite in Greek. [English translation by E. Kadloubovsky and G. E. H. Palmer, *Unseen Warfare* (Crestwood, New York, 1978).]
18. *Nevidimaja braň* [*Unseen Warfare*] (Moscow, 1892) 198ff.
19. See Heinrich Bacht, '"Meditari" in den ältesten Monchsquellen', *Geist und Leben* 28 (1955) 360–73.
20. See Cassian, *Collationes* 10 (PL 49:832D; SCh 54:87); I. Hausherr, *Noms du Christ et voies d'oraison*, 187ff.); Špidlík, *Théophane le Reclus*, 278.
21. See Hausherr, *Noms du Christ*, 209.
22. N. Crainic, 'Das Jesusgebet', an article translated from the Rumanian by W. Biemel, *Zeitschrift für Kirchengeschichte* 60 (1941) 341–53.
23. A Monk of the Eastern Church, *La prière de Jesus. Sa genèse et son développement dans la tradition religieuse byzantino-slave*, 3d ed., (Chevetogne, 1963) 7.
24. *Ibid.*, 68ff.
25. Hausherr, *Noms du Christ*, 276.
26. *Ibid.*, 239ff. [*The Name of Jesus*, 274ff.].
27. *Pis'ma o duchovnoj žizni* [*Letters on the Spiritual Life*] (Moscow, 1892) 63; trans. E. Kadloubovsky and A. M. Palmer, *The Art of Prayer* (London, 1966) 154.
28. See above, part 2.
29. See Sergei Boulgakov, *L'Orthodoxie* (Paris, 1932) 206ff.
30. See above, *The Jesus Prayer*.
31. See *Théophane le Reclus*, 289ff.
32. See Hausherr, *Noms du Christ*, 276ff.
33. *Ibid.*, 216; see above, VII, 4.
34. 'God, sin', see *The Cloud of Unknowing and Other Works*, trans. Clifton Wolters (New York: Penguin, 1978); cf. P. Dubourg in RAM 7 (1926) 188–99; [William Johnston, *The Mysticism of the Cloud of Unkowing: A Modern Interpretation* (St Meinrad, Indiana, 1975).]
35. *Pis'ma o duchovnoj žizni* [*Letters on the Spiritual Life*] (Moscow, 1903) 54, *The Art of Prayer*, p. 195; Špidlík, *Théophane le Reclus*, 291.
36. Ed. Irénée Hausherr, 'La méthode d'oraison hésychaste', OC 9/2 (Rome, 1927).
37. See above, Chapter VIII, *Poverty*.
38. Hausherr, (n. 36) 161.
39. *Ibid.*, 164ff.
40. *Otkrovennyjie rasskazy strannika duchovnomu svojemu otcu* (Kazan, 1870,

reedited 1881 and 1884). The origins of the work remain mysterious; see Pierre Pascal, in *Dieu vivant*, 147-49.
41. Among the translations are those published in *Irénikon* 4/5-7 (1928); by J. Gauvain in *Cahiers du Rhône* 12 (Neuchâtel, 1945); the German translation edited by E. Jungclaussen (Freiburg-im-Breisgau, 1975), the Italian translations by Carlo Carretto (Assisi, 1970, 3d ed.) and M. Marinelli (Milan, 1973); and the English translation by R. M. French, *The Way of a Pilgrim* (New York: Seabury, 1965).
42. See Basile Krivochéine in *Seminarium Kondakovianum*, 8 (Prague, 1936) 111; Špidlík, *Théophane le Reclus*, 285ff.
43. Irénée Noye, 'Jésus (nom de)', DS 8:1109-26 (bibliography).
44. See Pierre Adnès, in DS 8:1129ff.
45. *Philokalia*, vol. I (Athens, 1967) 143.
46. See above, IX, *The Discernment of Spirits*.
47. See Hausherr, *Noms du Christ*, 276ff.
48. See Bernhard Schultze, 'Der Streit um die Gottlichkeit des Names Jeus in der russischen Theologie', OCP 17 (1951) 321-94; *id.*, 'Untersuchungen über das Jesus-Gebet', OCP 18 (1952) 319-43; *id.*, 'Auf den Bergen des Kaukasus', *Geist und Leben* 32 (1959) 116-27.
49. See Bibliography, DS 8:1145.
50. *Essai sur la sainteté en Russie* (Bruges, 1953) 393.
51. See Adnès, in DS 8:1146.
52. See Franz Ruesche, *Blut, Leben und Seele. Ihr Verhältnis nach Auffassung der griechischen und hellenistischen Antike* (Paderborn, 1930) 209-65.
53. M. Spanneut, *Le stoïcisme des Pères de l'Église*, 202.
54. Bibliography: see DS 8:1147.
55. I. Hausherr, 'Les Exercices spirituels de saint Ignace et la méthode d'oraison hésychastique', OCP 20 (1954) 7-26; *idem.*, 'Hésychasme et prière', OCA 176 (Rome, 1966) 134-53.
55. See *Besedy o molitvě Jisusovoj [Conferences on the Jesus Prayer]* (Serdobol, 1938) 243.
56. See Adnès, DS 8:1147.
57. We know, however, that Russian authors have severely condemned navel-gazing as 'stupid and gross' (see *Théophane le Reclus*, 287) and something which could even produce sexual feelings; they wish attention to be centered on the chest 'a little to the left', see *Besedy o molitvě Jisusovoj [Conferences on the Jesus Prayer]* (Serdobol, 1938) 441ff.
59. Theophane the Recluse, *Pišma o duchovnoj žizni [Letters on the Spiritual Life]* (Moscow, 1903) 271.
60. *Ibidem*, 289.

--- 13 ---

CONTEMPLATION

1. THE NATURE OF CONTEMPLATION

Definition and Terms

THE TERM CONTEMPLATION was early given widely different meanings, depending on the progress of reflection.[1] But with the spiritual masters of the Christian East, the meaning was soon crystallized in a definition based on a false etymology: *theōria* meant *theon oran*, to see God in everything.[2]

Should one say that contemplation is identical with prayer? What remains true is that *gnosis* grows in proportion as prayer increases. Evagrius assimilated the superior contemplation (*theologia*)[3] to the highest degree of prayer; hence this remarkable sentence: 'If you are a theologian you will pray truly. And if you pray truly, you are a theologian.'[4]

Theoria *and* Gnosis

The word *theōria* is supposed to be derived from *thea*, vision, and as a consequence it expresses in an intensified form the idea of seeing:[5] looking, seeing a spectacle; by extension, reflecting, meditating, philosophizing. Accordingly, mere seeing can be accompanied more and more by reflective reasoning. When this reasoning becomes scientific, we have what is called *theory* as contrasted to practice or putting into effect. In the religious sense, among the christian spiritual writers, *theoria* means vision, apparition, but above all 'true contemplation', of the object of our consideration.[6] Still one should not forget that this word had a certain ambiguity among the early Fathers.[7] The Gospel used the word *theoria* once: in connection with the *spectacle* of Christ on the cross (Lk 23:48).[8] Properly speaking, the term is absent from the vocabulary of the Apostolic Fathers. It appears only with Clement of Alexandria and Origen, but was used frequently thereafter.[9] Its Greek origin is so apparent that the Syrians attempted to translate it only rarely.

At the same time another term made its appearance in christian circles, *gnōsis*.[10] For Clement of Alexandria, *gnōsis* is 'that light which is kindled in the soul as the result of obedience to the commandments'.[11] We know that *gnōsis* was the salient characteristic of certain Eastern religions. From the etymological point of view, the *gnōmai* makes appeal to no particular organ of sensory knowlege. But the will may be involved, and thus *gnōsis* means at the same time judgement, decision, and resolution.[12]

'The Contemplative East'

The Eastern church has frequently been compared to Mary and the Western church to Martha.[13] More than one spiritual writer has exalted the delights of contemplation. The entire spiritual life has often been structured with a view to contemplation, which according to Justinian's legislation,[14] is the only aim of the monastic life.

Contemplation seems to blend with perfection. It is said to be a foretaste of heaven, a return to Paradise.[15] 'A man gains the kingdom of God through knowledge of the things of the spirit.'[16] Charity itself has been defined as 'the higher state of the reasonable soul in which it is impossible to love something on earth more than the knowledge of God'.[17] Impurity of mind, sin, is an erroneous knowledge, ignorance of God.[18]

The East has been blamed for 'being numbed by a lazy passivity under the guise of contemplation'.[19] What is more, some have even asked themselves whether the Eastern ideal of contemplation is nothing but 'adaptation to the Hellenistic context and environment'.[20] 'visual' in its outlook, whereas Scripture promises happiness based on obedience to the commandments, and not on a quest for the vision of God.[21]

The Incomprehensibility of God

Since 'all men by nature desire to know', as Aristotle wrote,[22] chief among the faculties of soul for the Greeks could only be the faculty of knowing. And if blessedness depends on the object, then certainly the most magnificent object imaginable is 'the beautiful subsisting on itself',[23] God. The Hellenistic era was dominated by the desire to reach God.[24]

In christian circles, the gnostics excluded faith and charity for the sake of knowledge alone.[25] But their condemnation by the orthodox does not mean that in the opinion of many Fathers, rationality would not be a mark of the divine nature.[26] The Fathers declared that everything has been created for the sake of the knowledge of God.[27] 'The one who says and does everything in view of the knowledge of God has the eyes of his soul always turned towards the Lord.'[28]

But when they were faced with the error of Eunomius, the late fourth-century Fathers were led to lay their stress again on the opposite: on the absolutely unknowability of the divine essence.[29] This anti-Eunomian reaction gave rise to polemical writings, but beyond that it led to a deeper sense of the mystery of God, which came to be expressed especially in the mystical writings of Gregory of Nyssa.[30]

This evolution endowed the Greek term *theōria* with new perspectives and brought it closer to the Hebrew *yd'*. For a Semite, 'to know' surpasses abstract knowledge and expresses an existential relationship.[31] One knows God when one enters into his covenant (Jr 31:34) and is introduced little by little into intimacy with him.[32] In the New Testament Christ is the Truth (Jn 14:6). This supreme mystery is not an idea, but a Person, the Son, the image of another Person, the Father. When the Greek Fathers desired 'to know God', perhaps the greatest difference from their Platonic sources lay here, in spite of the similarities.

2. THE OBJECT OF CONTEMPLATION

Not the 'Surface' of Things

In their search for the truth, the Greek *sophoi* quickly experienced that the senses only yield an opinion (*doxa*). If man has ever apprehended something beautiful or good, he has perceived it, Plato states, 'through a non-bodily sense'.[1] It is true that the Greek Fathers were sensitive to the beauty of the sensible world,[2] but this beauty was different from aesthetic contemplation.[3] Ancient monasteries are frequently found on impressive sites, and yet the monks cultivated little 'feeling for nature' in the modern sense.[4]

Not the Philosophic Logos

Cicero summarized the tradition of the ancient philosophers by saying: to contemplate is to consider things with the mind in order to search for their nature; it is to philosophize.[5] Plato said that contemplation sees 'what is best among realities', the 'divine beautiful' (*to theion kalon*), and this is the pure intelligible.[6] The christian spiritual writers were strongly convinced that such a knowledge was not true *gnosis*, contemplation. They differentiated between, and contrasted, 'mere' (*psilē*) knowledge and 'spiritual' (*pneumatikē*) knowledge.[7] 'There is a double knowledge of the world: the pragmatic which even the impious obtain, and the spiritual which is reserved for the saints.'[8] Mere knowledge is 'sterile', unable to subordinate itself to the kingdom of God.[9]

The Theoteles Logos

Contemplation must understand beings in their ultimate truth, which is neither the Platonic Idea nor the definition of Aristotle nor the Stoic 'seminal reasons'—in spite of clear analogies. Things should be seen 'as they relate to God', in their providential function. The ultimate foundation of created beings is the *logos* (reason) which is hidden in them and 'which tends toward God', the *theotelēs logos*.[10] It is the divine intention (*theia thelēmata*) which brings about and explains beings.[11] It is hard to express this with words because one touches here upon the mystery which is found only 'gropingly'.[12]

In the area of Scripture, the *theotelēs logos* is the search for the spiritual, pneumatic meaning. Scripture, Origen said, is like a great living body announcing the Word, this 'one Word composed of the many sentences, each of which is a part of the Word in its entirety'.[13] In this search for the spiritual meaning of Scripture there are obviously differences between the schools (of typological, allegorical, or moral exegesis)[14] but no one method by itself is adequate for finding in this reading the spiritual food appropriate to every person.

When it comes to deciphering the mystery of the visible world, this *theotelēs logos* can be expressed in a manner which is, let us say, christological or sophianic. The secret of the creative act, this *ratio mundi*, is revealed progressively in the Son, who, according to Origen, is the receptacle of all the *logoi* of creation; he is the knowledge of their relationships.[15] Contemplation is therefore the understanding of the various 'incarnations' of the *Logos-Christ*[16] (it is therefore not fruitless that the famous Jesus prayer seeks to unite the memory of Christ to everything that exists).

The 'sophianic' tradition is more in line with Basil. This common, original meaning in all creatures is *sophia tou kosmou*, wisdom of the world, conceived before creation, inserted, living within, and leading to God. Its equivalent in man is *anthropinē sophia*, human wisdom, a virtue which brings to light the divine truth hidden under the phenomena of the world, to lead to God.[17]

3. THE ORGAN OF CONTEMPLATION

Beginning with the Senses

The distance which the Platonists set between knowledge and sensation was greatly reduced with the Fathers.[1] They knew very well that it is not the senses which yield a true knowledge of God. Nonetheless, this knowledge begins with an apperception of sensible things, which are the mirror of God's goodness, of his power, and his wisdom.'[2] 'Just as those who teach letters to children trace them on tablets, so also has Christ, while teaching his wisdom to reasonable beings, traced it in physical nature.'[3] This is how one learns to know the 'hand of God', the 'names of God'.[4]

To explain this function of the senses, the Fathers were able to profit from the Stoic concept of knowledge, according to which there is no apprehension except through the senses.[5] But texts of Platonic origin were frequently used, too. After Plato[6] and Proclus,[7] Celsus borrowed this commonly accepted principle: 'Instead of exercising your senses, look upward with the soul . . . open the eye of your mind; thus and only thus will you be able to see God.'[8] In turn, Gregory Nazianzen professed: 'Nothing seemed to me as desirable as to close the door to my senses . . .';[9] what falls under the senses is alien to God.[10] These expressions and others like them are justified if one takes the term 'sense' in a moral way (as passion, the flesh, and so on): anything that turns us away from the knowledge of God.[11] At all events the texts are more correct which, instead of 'getting rid of the senses' advise us instead 'to transcend the senses', 'not to stop with the senses'.[12]

The Nous — *the Divine Faculty*

It is hardly necessary to show how much Greek antiquity stressed the excellence of the mind which ascends to a knowledge of heavenly things thanks to an affinity (*kata to xyngenes*) with the higher world.[13] The Fathers viewed the rationality of God as his basic characteristic.[14] In consequence, the *nous* (mind) is the place of God; it is 'able to see' by creation,[15] 'Godlike and divine'.[16]

They normally made a distinction, however, between the *nous* and *dianoia* (reason). Reasoning, the *diatribē*,[17] is not contemplation according to Plato[18] or according to the christian mystics. The Stoics spoke of a *prolēpsis*, an inborn intuition.[19] Evagrius protested against anyone who would not allow to the *nous* what everyone accorded to the senses: the direct intuition of its object. The *nous* is a 'sense', the spiritual sense.[20] Only *seeing* spiritual realities gives one the power to speak about them: 'Someone who has not seen God cannot speak of him'.[21] In this context one can say that the organ of contemplation is 'the spiritual sense',[22] or the 'heart' with its integral intuition.[23]

The Deified and Purified Nous

For Christians it is self-evident that an understanding of the reason of things is a gift of God, and that divine mystery is known through revelation.[24] If men are *logikoi* (rational) by nature,[25] if their *nous* is the natural image of God[26] this is because they partake of the divine *logos* and possess its revelation in their heart.

On the other hand, the indispensable condition for such a revelation is purity of the *nous*, of the spiritual eye, of the heart. They all—Platonists, Stoics, and Christians—insisted on the need of purification before *theoria*; the difference appears only on the question of determining in what such a purification consists: purification of the flesh, the senses, from evil thoughts, the passions, sin.

In the christian tradition the Evagrian purification is the most demanding: it requires perfect nakedness of mind, stripped not only of all passionate movements but also of all imagination (because this is corporal) and all multiplicity of rational concepts (because they are incomplete), to be a vision of pure light.[27]

Unlike Alexandrian intellectualism, the Antiochene Theodoret was not embarassed by the generous use of such constructions as this: *tēn theian theōrian phantazomenos* (imagining the divine *theoria*).[28] Popular devotion was attached to images[29] and even Origen clearly admitted that to reach the mystery we must first pass through the mediation of the image.[30]

If there is some purification of the natural senses, this must be understood as a continued progress which passes 'from the shadow to the image and finally to the truth'.[31] Continuing along this line, one should evidently also move beyond rational concepts, and avoid 'the idolatry of concepts',[32] so as not to recognize as God something that is only a product of the activity of our intellect.

What, then, is sin if not the refusal of the process of ascending to God? In this context the Evagrian purification itself becomes moral. This is how his faithful disciple Isaac of Nineveh understood it, and he has described its three principal modes: a) the corporal step (*dûboro pagronô*), struggling with bodily passions; b) the psychic step (*napšono*), waging war with alien thoughts; c) the spiritual step (*ruhomûtô*), to be entirely submitted to the Spirit.[33] In simple terms, the entire purification is summarized by the word *praxis*,[34] which is therefore the indispensable precondition for *theoria*.

Praxis *Leads to* Theoria

The formulations that had become classic as early as Origen's day are of two kinds:[35]

1) *oute gar praxis oute theōria aneu thaterou*: no *praxis* without *theoria* and no *theoria* without *praxis*;[36]

2) *praxis gar theōrias anabasis*: it is through *praxis* that one ascends to *theoria*.[37] This latter axiom came to be proposed as a kind of maxim by the spiritual masters.[38]

One also finds equivalent expressions in great number: the virtues lead to knowledge;[39] the road to knowledge passes through the observance of the commandments;[40] 'when we begin to act out of the fear of God, the action of this fear gives birth to spiritual knowledge';[41] 'mystical contemplation is revealed to the mind after the soul has recovered its health';[42] and still others like these.

According to the traditional definition, prayer is the ascent of the mind to God.[43] But after they had moved beyond Greek rationalism, Christians became well aware that 'the mind will make no progress, will not safely complete this way of trials and will not enter the realm of the incorporeal, unless it sets right what is within'.[44] It is therefore in need of a radical purification, which is christian repentance and life in Christ, who embodies all the virtues, above all charity. Consequently, the effects of this maxim are far-reaching for the entire concept of the christian life.[45]

No True Knowledge Without Love

The christian East has always remained faithful to the idea of the intimate link between love and knowledge.[46] Boris Vyšeslavcev stated that 'this expression by Leonardo da Vinci, "a great love is the child of a great knowledge", is prophetic of all recent intellectualism. We, the Christians of the East, can say the contrary, "a great knowledge is the daughter of a great love".'[47] Everyone, including Evagrius, has assigned love of neighbor and of God enough of a role to safeguard his orthodoxy. 'The first and the greatest of the commandments is charity, thanks to which the mind sees the first love, that is, God.'[48] It is clear that without love the knowledge of God through 'connaturality' is impossible, because 'God is love' (1 Jn 4:8,16). The exclamation which preceeds the recitation of the Creed in the byzantine rite states, 'Let us love one another that with one accord we may confess, "I believe in God the Father..."'.

Clearly, one should avoid the danger of seeing in charity only a preliminary condition, of making it inferior to *gnosis*.⁴⁹ But this danger is only theoretical, because in reality contemplation and charity, truth and love are, according to Ephrem, inseparable wings.⁵⁰

From Faith to Gnosis

In St Paul the term faith refers to the christian life.⁵¹ When Clement of Alexandria spoke of the faith, he was thinking instead of *praxis*. Those who have faith, the faithful, are those who keep the commandments, especially charity: and so they can understand God-Charity.⁵²

If *praxis* leads to *theōria*, it is, then, the door to knowledge.⁵³ Indeed, of itself it constitutes a purification of the mind which allows the mind to contemplate God.⁵⁴ Knowledge, the realization then, of faith, is—in the words of Paul Evdokimov⁵⁵—'the only thing capable of breaking the seals of the Book of Life,' of deciphering the mysteries of the cosmos.

The two aspects of faith—trust, the most biblical, and the truths of orthodoxy, after the councils the most 'Greek',—are clearly distinguished from one another by Martirius Sadhônâ: 'But faith [in God] is presented under a double aspect: we [must] believe that he exists, and trust his promises ... Indeed, the two are intimately connected: the one brings the other along with it; they are interconnected.'⁵⁶ 'The true faith', the same author says, 'is the source of life and the light of knowledge, the junction in the road of salvation.'⁵⁷

Clearly, this means a living faith which freely clings to the good⁵⁸ and excludes sin: 'The one who dies in his sin, Origen states, 'does not really believe in Christ even if he says he does; if what he calls faith is not accompanied by works, it is dead.'⁵⁹

4. PROGRESS IN CONTEMPLATION

The Degrees

According to Origen, the mysteries of the sensible world will be revealed first to souls, and afterwards man will ascend to the vision of the realities of heaven.¹ Evagrius later codified this distinction and imposed his own terminology. Accordingly, he saw two levels of contemplation:

> 1) the contemplation of nature (*theōria physikē*): *theōria deutera* (the second contemplation),² *tōn somatōn* (of bodies),³ *ton aisthēton* (of the senses),⁴ *tou kosmou toutou tou oratou* (of the entire visible world).⁵
> 2) theology (*theologia*): *theōria protē* (the first contemplation), *tōn asōmatōn* (of the incorporeal beings), *tōn pneumatikōn* (of spiritual realities),⁶ *tōn noēmaton* (of the intelligibles).⁷

Here is a still longer list:

> There are five basic types of knowledge which contain all the others: the first, according to the Fathers, is knowledge of the adorable Trinity; the second and the third are knowledge of incorporeal and corporeal beings; the fourth and the fifth are knowledge of the judgment and knowledge of divine providence.⁸

This distinction is of no great historical importance; except in Evagrius and Maximus the Confessor,⁹ it represents nothing that is essential to byzantine mysticism.¹⁰

The following tripartite division was generally used by Gregory of Nyssa: 'the apparition of God to Moses began in light (*dia phōtos*); afterwards God spoke to him in a cloud (*dia nephelēs*); and finally in the darkness (*en gnophō*)'.¹¹

Natural Contemplation

Natural contemplation includes the ancient idea of *physis* (physical science), but it does so in order to go beyond it. This is why it is also called *theōria physikē* (the contemplation of nature), *theōria tōn ontōn* (the contemplation of beings) or *gegonotōn* (of the created), *gnōsis tōn ontōn* (knowledge of beings). That God can be known from his works was proclaimed by all the Fathers.¹² And thus, 'every one is able to arrive at the knowledge of God through creation'.¹³ For the friends of God the universe therefore becomes an open book,[14] a school for souls.[15] God saw that it was very good (Gn 1:9): this is because he saw the *logoi* (reasons) of the things which are 'already white for the harvest' (Jn 4:35).[16]

How was the contemplation of nature lived by the spiritual writers? Basil's reflections on the Hexaemeron simply follow the line drawn by the Gospel: 'consider the birds of the air, . . . the lilies of the field' (Mt 6:26 ff.). Beings were considered; they were compared to the qualities of man, and moral statements from Scripture were cited.[17] One often comes across a strange mixture of secular erudition and scriptural echoes.[18] The work of Tikhon of Zadonsk, *Spiritual Treasure Gathered in the World*,[19] has a gospel-like simplicity. But there is always the danger that this method be reduced to speculation or to pleasant phantasies.[20] The most orginal contemplation of nature occurs in the mystagogic tradition.[21] By contrast, the simplified contemplation of nature came to be the direct experience of beauty, a quality found everywhere and in everything; by directly nourishing the remembrance of the divine Craftsman, it fills the soul with love and gratitude.[22]

The Contemplation of Invisible Beings

For Origen, knowledge of the invisible beings, of angels and demons, is 'the mystery of the Resurrection to come'. But 'the Son is preparing our knowledge of this day and this hour even now'.[23] This becomes a matter of seeing how, behind the surface of world events, the angelic forces, good and bad, struggle above us and in us,[24] and of arriving at a consideration of the *logoi*, the 'reasons for this warfare'.[25] In practice, then, this is the wisdom of the discernment of spirits.[26]

The Contemplation of Providence and of Judgment

The contemplation of providence is one aspect of the consideration of nature which recovers divine wisdom in beings; it discovers, so to speak, its most paternal, most 'historical' side, either in the evolution of salvation-history or in the history of day-to-day life.[27]

Providence becomes judgment, reprimand, chastisement of the sinner, without ceasing to be providence for him.[28]

Theologia

The word *theologia* seems to have appeard for the first time in Plato[29] and was applied to discourse dealing with the gods.[30] In the Eastern tradition, John the Evangelist is called the theologian (*theologos*) because at the opening of his Gospel he witnesses to the divinity of the *Logos*[31] and thereby introduces us into the mystery of the Holy Trinity. For Evagrius, theology was the higher degree of the spiritual life, where this sublime mystery is lived and contemplated: 'contemplation of the Holy Trinity'.[32] But, it is not easy to explain of what this contemplation consisted.

It is certain that theology was not the direct intuition of the essence of God.[33] With greater reason it cannot be compared to visions of a sensible nature[34] or to be the end product, a rational dialectic.

Nonetheless, the expressions 'to see God', and 'vision of God' were used very frequently.[35] It was a vision 'in a mirror', certainly, not a vision into the lower creatures but an indirect vision of God in the soul itself, in the deified mind which is the image of God.[36] All the Eastern mystics spoke at length of this vision of God through the vision of self. This tradition was passed on to the Muslim mystics undoubtedly through the Syrians.[37]

This vision of God in the soul became fused with the vision of 'the place of God' (*locus Dei*). Evagrius used the text of Ex 24:9–11 (according to the Septuagint); there was for all practical purposes an identification between 'the vision of one's appropriate state' and the vision of the Holy Trinity.[38] Although for Evagrius this 'appropriate state' is 'the state appropriate to the mind', for most Eastern spiritual writers man's state is his heart.[39] The height of contemplation is therefore the contemplation of God in one's heart.[40]

The concept of the vision of God in an image could imply a distance between the Creator and the creature; the expression 'place of God' encourages movement toward a more direct encounter, but all this is, so to speak, on the level of the soul and never 'face to face'. To become the object of human contemplation, God must somehow go out of himself, manifest his 'glory',[41] and transfigure the soul and the entire universe through his 'energy', his light (the 'light of Tabor' is the most typical effulgence of this divine energy). These considerations lie at the heart of the Palamite synthesis. We know that it was to defend the hesychast method of prayer, the vision of God in the soul, that Gregory Palamas was led to become the doctor of the transfiguration of man and of the world through the glory of God.[42] But the problem which arose for deeply religious souls was this: does man, in turn, not also somehow go out of himself in order to meet God? This brings up the problem of ecstasy, 'going out of oneself'.

Ecstasy

It is very difficult to make statements about all the phenomena of ecstatic appearances we find among non-christians.[43] Even among the great philosophers, enthusiasm occupied an important place.[44] For a scriptural study of ecstasy we have only meager information at our disposal. On the other hand, the epithet of certain exegetes is well known: 'ecstasy is the basic experience of all prophecy'.[45] In the first christian communities the Spirit awakened ecstatic enthusiasm; later, Montanus brought into prominence the passivity of man in such states.[46]

In the lives of the first monks, the 'enthusiastic' elements occupy less space than one might be led to believe.[47] Their ecstasies had the character of 'vision' (*orasis*),[48] not of going beyond the understanding. Nonetheless, if the term has entered the vocabulary of the contemplatives, this is because it expresses a certain spiritual reality.

Here is how Theophane the Recluse explains it. Perfection consists in the harmonious cooperation of all the parts of the human composite: the body, the soul, and the Spirit.[49] It is unnatural if a lower part, for example, the body, prevails while the higher parts are silent; on the contrary, the opposite is praiseworthy. This is what happens in the highest contemplation, in ecstasy. The natural faculties of the soul are suspended; but there is no suspension of the Spirit.[50] This 'suspension' is realized in various degrees. The first ecstasy, according to the definition of prayer given by Nilus, is a 'rapture (*harpagē*) of the mind and a total ecstasy out of the sensible'[51]; one puts off 'all ignorance that comes from the senses'.[52] A relationship was frequently set up between such an ecstasy and the prophetic dream.[53]

The understanding can, in ecstasy, forget everything that is not God. The Syrian authors seem to have understood ecstasy as the attitude of a soul which is perfectly detached from distractions; it was a reward for moral purity, for victory over the passions.[54]

The Evagrian ecstasy was more radical. The result of apophatic theology, it was an 'infinite ignorance' of all partial concepts of notions; state of 'pure intellectuality'. On this intellectual summit the *nous* which is the image of God becomes pure light and 'reflects the light of the Holy Trinity', but does not go out of itself: it is not 'ecstatic' but 'catastatic'. Entry into the gnostic life is called both *apodēmia* (departure) and *endēmia* (sojourning).[55] This is the 'mysticism of light'.[56]

The 'mysticism of darkness'[57] adds another degree. It was treated by Gregory of Nyssa[58] who distinguished between three degrees in the ascent to God: 1) in the light (*dia phōtos*)—this is the time of purification; 2) in the cloud (*dia nephelēs*)—the entry into the contemplation of the intelligibles; 3) in the darkness (*en gnophǫ*)—the last step of intellectual knowledge is mounted and the soul then takes another road, that of love, 'the wings of love'. This therefore is a true *ek-stasis*, a 'going out' of the intellectual state. While experiencing a burning desire for God, one acquires a new knowledge of God-Love. Love thereby becomes knowledge.[59]

In the scheme of Theophane the Recluse we must presuppose still another degree of ecstasy: the suspension of all the soul's faculties and the activity of the power of the Spirit alone. But to what psychological state does this correspond? It is perhaps the state which is called 'wakeful sleep'.[60] In ordinary sleep the soul is carried away from itself and is subject to dreams. The mystical sleep subjects the soul to the sublime presence of the Holy Spirit. This is at the same time like an awakening because the soul finds itself in the presence of the one true reality.[61]

5. THE EFFECTS OF CONTEMPLATION

Unceasing Remembrance of God

In a world marked by forgetfulness (*lēthē*)[1] of God, contemplation strives to promote an unceasing union with the Lord, to 'see' God in everything.² The expression *mnēmē theou* (memory of God) is Philonian and Stoic,³ but the idea is biblical. The monks who searched for it saw in it an angelic liturgy.⁴

It is evident that the authors did not all envisage this 'attention to God' and the means of promoting it in the same way. Evagrius understood this remembrance as a movement of the 'immaterial spirit drawing near Immaterial Being'.⁵ But such a 'remembrance' will never become 'unceasing' because this is psychologically impossible for a being intimately linked to matter and earthly concerns. And yet, thinking of God should be more habitual for man than breathing.⁶

The spirituality of the continual remembrance of God can therefore not be indentified with the highest degrees of Evagrian 'true *gnōsis*'. It is not afraid of images or of daily life. It is not always a 'science'; but it is always a 'con-science', a stable disposition toward good (*diathesis agathē*), and 'this vehement desire to please God,'⁷ an incentive which is always present and always at work in every human activity. This disposition, then, is born and nourished by contemplation, an explicit remembrance.

Transformation and Holiness

Contemplation transforms.⁸ Man becomes more and more like that which he contemplates. 'By an assiduous remembrance, we keep God dwelling in us' (*enoikon echontes heautōn ton theon*).⁹ But these expressions, which occur very frequently, could be understood in a platonic or gnostic sense: one could forget that holiness must be measured by the charity which informs and animates contemplation. This is why Philoxenes of Mabbug, one of the few authors to deal with this question deliberately, generally considered that the two, contemplation and holiness, can be separated: one can exist without the other.¹⁰

Clearly, he saw the danger of an imbalance, of a lack of proportion between knowledge and love, or of extraordinary illuminations, or of the 'unbridled' *theōria* of enthusiasts. By contrast, if one takes the 'knowledge of God', and contemplation in their vital and total christian sense, the formulas of Origen, and of many others, present no problem: knowledge of the mystery becomes a loving exchange between the *Logos* and the believer.¹¹

This is a knowledge similar to that of the Son of God,[12] and a foretaste of the bliss of heaven, where 'knowledge becomes love'.[13] In such a context, the approximation between contemplation and holiness is legitimate.

The Glory of God

Contemplation is the rediscovery of the true transparency of the mind;[14] it is a *diorasis* (insight).[15] The clear-sighted person recognizes divine Wisdom operating in the world, and 'glorifies God'.[16] From Origen the Eastern spiritual writers learned that the deification of the Christian is his participation in the glory of Christ; it culminates in an experience analogous to that of the Apostles on Tabor, an experience which corresponds to the highest form of the spiritual exegesis of Scripture.[17]

Man becomes conscious of God's gifts and of the greatness of the Giver, and becomes a being of praise like the angels. Summarizing the contemplative tradition, Gregory Palamas stated that, 'Enlightened, man reaches the eternal heights ... And even without being in heaven, he cooperates with the heavenly powers in their unceasing song; while on earth, he, like an angel, leads every creature to God.'[18]

Philaret of Moscow shows that the entire economy of salvation has no other aim than to remind us of the glory of God. And this glory is 'the revelation, the reflection, the garment of the inner perfection' of the Holy Trinity; 'God gives it, those whom he causes to participate in it receive it; the glory comes back to him, and in this, so to speak, eternal circumvolution of the divine glory does the blessed life of creatures consist'.[19]

Notes

1. THE NATURE OF CONTEMPLATION

1. See René Arnou, in DS 2/2::1916ff; for the various Greek terms, see Henri Crouzel, *Origène et 'la connaissance mystique'* (Paris-Bruges, 1961) 395ff; M. Spanneut, *Le stoïcisme des Pères de l'Eglise*, 266ff.
2. Pseudo-Plutarch (*De musica* 27) makes of *Theos, theōrein* as well as *theatron*, the theater having originally been intended to honor the gods. This false ety-

Contemplation 343

mology was still exploited in the fourteenth century by Callistus Cataphygiotes (*De vita contemplativa* 2 and 19; PG 147:836B and 859B).
3. See below, *Theologia*.
4. *De oratione* 60; PG 79:1180B.
5. See Arnou, DS 2/2:1717. The highest justification which Dionysius brings to his theory of the *thea* or *theōria* seems to lie in the etymology he proposes of *theos*, and *theotēs: theotēs de hē panta theōmenē pronoia kai ... panta peritheousa* (*De divinis nominibus*, PG 3:969C) [for a translation, see C. E. Rolt, *The Divine Names and The Mystical Theology* (London: SPCK, 1977)].
6. See I. Hausherr (J. Lemaitre), in DS 2/2:1764.
7. See Špidlík, *Grégoire de Nazianze*, 113ff.
8. See Irénée Hausherr, 'Tēn theōrian tautēn', Bolletino Regina Mundi 11 (Rome) 10ff; and 'Hésychasme et prière', OCA 176 (Rome, 1966) 247ff.
9. See Hausherr DS 2/2:1762.
10. See Jacques Dupont, *Gnosis. La connaissance religieuse dans les Épîtres de saint Paul*, 2d ed. (Louvain-Paris, 1960); and Pierre Thomas Camelot, 'Gnose chrétienne', DS 6:509–23.
11. *Stromata* III.5.44; Stählin II:216, 20; trans. by Owen Chadwick in *Alexandrian Christianity* (Philadelphia, 1954) 60; see André Méhat, *Étude sur les 'Stromates' de Clément d'Alexandrie* (Paris, 1966) 421–88.
12. See Hausherr, DS 2/2:1765.
13. See Ernst Benz, *Die Ostkirche im Lichte der protestantischen Geschichtsschreibung von der Reformation bis zur Gegenwart* (Munich, 1952) 181.
14. *Novella* 133.
15. See John of Damascus, *Sermo de transfiguratione* 20 (PG 96:567A, 585D); 10, (561B); Gregory of Nazianzus, *Oratio* 16.9 (PG 35:945C); Maximus the Confessor, *Ambigua* (PG 91:1088A).
16. Cassian, *Collationes* 1.14; SCh 42:93; NPNF[2] 11:301.
17. Evagrius, *Centuriae* I.86; ed. W. Frankenberg, *Evagrius Ponticus*, 123.
18. Maximus the Confessor, *Century III on Charity* 34; SCh 9:135; ACW 21 (1955) 179 (cf. SCh p. 183).
19. Vladimir S. Soloviev, *The Great Schism and Christian Politics*, in Russian (St Petersburg, n. d.), vol. 4:1–5.
20. Patricius van der Aalst, 'Contemplation et Hellénisme', *Proche-Orient Chrétien* 14 (1964) 151–68.
21. On the two mentalities, the visual type of the Greeks and the accoustic type of the Jews, see my *Grégoire de Nazianze*, 1ff.
22. *Metaphysics* I.1.980a.
23. Plato, *Symposium* 211.
24. See M. Spanneut, *Le stoïcisme des Pères de l'Église*, 41ff.
25. See above, XI, 3. By contrast, John of Damascus (*De haeresibus* 88; PG 94:757A) and Theodore the Studite (*Epistle* I.48, PG 99:1080D) allude to obscure partisans of a faith without knowledge (*gnosimachoi*).
26. See Spanneut, 343.
27. See Špidlík, *La sophiologie de S. Basile*, 11ff.
28. Evagrius, *In Psalmum* 24:16; PG 12:1272C.
29. See below, *Ecstasy*.
30. See Jean Daniélou, Introduction to John Chrysostom's homily on the incomprehensibility of God, *Sur l'incomprehensibilité de Dieu*, SCh 29 bis (1968) 16ff.

31. In this way one 'knows' suffering (Is 53:3), sin (Ws 3:13), war (Jg 3:1), peace (Is 59:8), good and evil (Gn 2:9, 17).
32. See Léon-Dufour, in VTB, 199ff.

2. THE OBJECT OF CONTEMPLATION

1. *Phaedo* 65d; see A. J. Festugière, *Contemplation et vie contemplative selon Platon* (Paris, 1936) 28.
2. See M. Spanneut, *Les stoïcisme des Pères de l'Eglise*, 283.
3. See above, V *The Goodness and the Beauty of the World*.
4. See J. Lemaitre (Hausherr), DS 2/2:283.
5. *Tusculan Disputations* V.III.8-9.
6. *Republic* VII.532c; *Symposium* 210e-212a; see R. Arnou, DS 2/2:1818ff.
7. See J. Lemaitre, DS 2/2:1802ff; Jean Kirchmeyer, DS 6:847.
8. Evagrius, *Kephalaia gnostika* 6.2; ed. A. Guillaumont, PO 28:216.
9. See Clement of Alexandria, *Stromata* III.5.44; ed. Stählin, GCS 2:126; PG 8:1148B.
10. Maximus the Confessor, *Quaestiones ad Thalassium* 32; PG 90:372BC; see Dionysius the Pseudo-Areopagite, *De divinis nominibus* 2, PG 3:637C; J. Lemaitre, in DS 2/2:1818ff.
11. Maximus the Confessor, *Ambigua* (PG 91:1085A); see the icon of the Wisdom of God on the throne of the world (Novgorod School).
12. *Quaestiones ad Thalassium* 32; PG 90:372BC.
13. *Commentary on the Gospel of John* 5.5; ed. Erwin Preuschen GCS 4 (Leipzig, 1963) 102.
14. See Jean Daniélou, 'Ecriture et vie spirituelle dans la Tradition. Epoque patristique', DS 4/1:132-38 (see also the articles that follow).
15. See Henri Crouzel, *Origène et la 'connaissance mystique'*, (Bruges, 1960) 54ff: 'Christ, the Intelligible World of the ideas and of the reasons of the sensible world.'
16. See Henri de Lubac, *Histoire et Esprit* (Paris, 1950).
17. See Špidlík, *La sophiologie de S. Basile*, 27ff.

3. THE ORGAN OF CONTEMPLATION

1. See Clement of Alexandria, *Stromata* VI.136.5; GCS 2:500; Spanneut, *Le stoïcisme des Pères de l'Eglise*, 225.
2. Evagrius, *Kephalaia gnostika* I.14 (ed. Guillaumont, p. 23); II.2 (61).
3. *Ibid.*, III.57 (121).
4. See E. von Ivánka, 'Vom Platonismus zur Theologie der Mystik (Zur Erkenntnislehre Gregors von Nyssa)', *Scholastik* 11 (1936) 163-95.
5. See Victor Goldschmidt, *Le système stoïcien et l'idée de temps* (Paris, 1953) 163ff; Spanneut, 205ff.
6. *Politicus* 273d.
7. *Alcibiades* II.90.
8. Origen, *Contra Celsum* VII,36; PG 11:1472A; ANF 4:625.
9. *Oratio* II.7 (PG 35:413C); Špidlík, *Grégoire de Nazianze*, 30.
10. *Grégoire*, 31.
11. *Ibid.*, 30ff.

12. See Crouzel, *Origène et la 'connaissance mystique'*, 273ff.
13. Plato, *Phaedo* 79a–81a; 84b; *Republic* VI, 490b; *Symposium* 212a.
14. See M. Spanneut, *Le stoïcisme des Pères de l'Église*, 293ff; E. von Ivánka, *Plato christianus* (Einsiedeln, 1964).
15. Pseudo-Macarius, *Homilia* 25.10 (PG 34:673C; edd. Hermann Dörries, E. Klostermann, M. Kroeger, *Die 50 geistliche Homilien des Makarios*, PTS 4 [Berlin, 1964] 205; see A. Schneider, *Der Gedanke der Erkenntnis des Gleichen durch Gleiches in antiker und patristischer Zeit*, Beiträge zur Geschichte der Philosophie des Mittelalters, Supplementband 2 (1923) 65ff.
16. Gregory of Nazianzus, *Oratio* 28.17; PG 36:48C.
17. See the diatribes of Epictetus, collected by Arrian; ed. H. Schenkl, *Epicteti dissertationes ab Arriano digestae* (Leipzig, 1898).
18. *Symposium* 210e; Letter VII.341cd: the light bursts forth suddenly (*exaiphnēs*); see R. Arnou in DS 2/2:1720.
19. See Spanneut, *Le stoïcisme des Pères*, 206ff.
20. *Letter* VIII.12 (among Basil's Letters): PG 32:266Dff.
21. *Kephalaia* 5.26; ed Frankenberg, 329; see J. Lemaitre (Hausherr), DS 2/2:1822ff.
22. See above, Chapter IV, 2.
23. See above, IV, *The Feelings of the Heart*.
24. See J. Lemaitre, DS 2/2:1821ff.
25. See *Grégoire de Nazianze*, 144ff.
26. See above, III, *Is the Image of God the Soul Alone...?*
27. See I. Hausherr, 'Ignorance infinie', OCP 2 (1936) 351–62; reprinted in *Hésychasme et prière*, OCA 176 (Rome, 1966) 38–49; G. Békés, 'Pura oratio apud Clementem Alexandrinum', in *Studia Benedictina in memoriam gloriosi ante saecula XIV transitus S. P. Benedicti* (Vatican City, 1947) 157–72.
28. *Historia religiosa* 12 (PG 82:139C); 18(1425D); 24(1460A); see J. Lemaitre, DS 2/2:1859.
29. See above, I, *Cosmic Spirituality*, and XII, *Icons*.
30. *Homilia 1 in Psalmum* 38.2.2 (PG 12:1402B); see H. Crouzel, *Origène et la 'connaissance mystique'*, 262ff.
31. See Margherite Harl, *Origène et la fonction révélatrice du Verbe Incarné* (Paris, 1958) 144f.
32. Gregory of Nyssa, *The Life of Moses*, PG 44:377; in the Malherbe-Ferguson translation, 94ff; see Špidlík, *Grégoire de Nazianze*, 40.
33. See Elie Khalifé-Hachem, in DS 7/2:2043ff.
34. See above, VII, 1.
35. See J. Lemaitre DS 2/2:1802.
36. *In Lucam fragmenta* 39 (ed. Rauer, GCS 9:9–10). See Plotinus, *Enneads* 3.8, (*Ennéades*, ed É. Bréhier [Paris, 1924–38], and the note by Bréhier, 1952). See René Arnou, *Le désir de Dieu dans la philosophie de Plotin* (Rome, 1967²) 87.
37. *In Lucam fragmenta* 39 (Rauer, GCS 9:252, 2); cf. the same idea in *In Psalmo* 5.13; PG 12:1173.
38. Gregory Nazianzen, *Oratio* 20.12 (PG 35:1080); Cassian, *Collationes* 14.9 (SCh 54:192ff; PL 49:969ff; NPNF² 11:439): from *scientia actualis* (practical knowledge) one should proceed to *scientia theoretica* (spiritual knowledge); Nicephorus the Monk, *De sobrietate et cordis custodia* (PG 147:948A); Abba Philemon in the *Philokalia* (Athens, 1958) vol. II: p. 250, 39.

39. Origen, *Commentarium in Matthaeum* 12.14 (GCS 10:96, 30); Evagrius, *Praktikos* 90 (SCh 171:643; CS 4:38–39).
40. John the Solitary (Pseudo-John of Lycopolis), *Dialogue sur l'âme et les passions des hommes*, trans. I. Hausherr, OCA 120 (Rome, 1939) 32ff.
41. Isaac of Nineveh, *De perfectione religiosa* (Syriac edition of Paul Bedjan, *Mar Isaacus Ninivita. De perfectione religiosa* (Paris-Leipzig, 1909) 320: *Early Fathers from the Philokalia*, 267–68.
42. Philoxenes of Mabbug, text cited by I. Hausherr, *Hésychasme et priere*, OCA 176 (Rome, 1966) 28ff.
43. See above, VII, *Sin As Ignorance*, and XIII, 2.
44. Evagrius, *Praktikos* 61; SCh 171:643; CS 4:33; *Early Fathers from the Philokalia*, 108.
45. The formula can be adapted to various levels depending on the meaning one wants to give these terms; see my *Grégoire de Nazianze*, 119ff.
46. See Pavel Al. Florenskij, *Stolp i utverždĕvije istiny* [*The Pillar and Foundation of Truth*] (Moscow, 1914) 70ff.
47. *Serdce v christianskoj i indijskoj mistikĕ* [*The Heart in Christian and Indian Mysticism*] (Paris, 1929) 26.
48. Evagrius, *Letter* 56; Frankenberg, 605.
49. See above, XI, *Greek Terms*.
50. *De fide* 20.12; Assemani, 3:37d; Beck, 59–60.
51. See, for example, RM 3:24 to 4:16.
52. *Stromata* V.13 (GCS 2:334, 17); see *Grégoire de Nazianze*, 122ff.
53. See W. Völker, *Das Vollkommenheitsideal des Origenes* (Tübingen, 1931) 777ff; H. Crouzel, *Origène et la 'connaissance mystique'*, 448.
54. See John of Damascus, *Dialogus* 1 PG 94:529A–532D; ed. B. Kotter, *Die Schriften des Iohannes von Damaskos* 1, PTS 7 [Berlin, 1969] 53–55; *De virtutibus* (PG 95:92AB).
55. *La femme et le salut du monde* (Tournai-Paris, 1958) 14.
56. *Livre de la perfection* II.1 (4) (CSCO 215, Syr. 91, p. 9); see Cyril of Jerusalem, *De fide et symbolo* 10–11 (PG 33:517ff. LNPF[2] 7:57–71).
57. *Livre de la perfection* II.2 (8ff.)
58. See Clement of Alexandria, e.g. GCS 4:645 (indexes).
59. Origen, *Commentarium in Joannem* 19.23 (6); GCS 4:325, 5.

4. PROGRESS IN CONTEMPLATION

1. *Peri Archon* II.11.6-7 (GCS 5:189-192); see *In Canticum prologue* (PG 13:73A–77A; GCS 8:75–76); see Clement of Alexandria, *Stromata* I. 28.176.1–2, (PG 8:921–924; GCS 2:108).
2. *Centuriae* 3.19.21: ed. W. Frankenberg, *Evagrius Ponticus* (Berlin, 1912) 201, 203.
3. *Selecta in Psalmos*, *Psalm*. IV; PG 12:1661C (under Origen's name).
4. *Kephalaia* 2.47; Frankenberg, 161.
5. *Ibid.*, 2.88; 187.
6. *Ibid.*, 2.72; 179.
7. *Ibid.*, 2.47; 161.
8. *Ibid.*, 1.27; 73. See also *Letter* 7 (Frankenberg, 571); *Selecta in Psalmos* (PG 12:1661c).
9. *Century on Charity* I.99; SCh 9:91.

10. See Lemaitre, DS 2/2:1824.
11. *Homilia XI in Canticum*; PG 44:1000CD; see above, Chapter III, *Praktikē*...
12. See M. Spanneut, *Le stoïcisme des Pères de l'Eglise*, 286ff.
13. Evagrius, *Centuriae* 3.53; ed. Frankenberg, 225.
14. See *Vita Antonii* 72-80 (PG 26:944B-856A); Evagrius, *Praktikos* 92 (SCh 171:695, CS 4:39).
15. Basil, *Homilia VI in Hexaemeron*. 1; PG 29:117, SCh 26:324.
16. Origen, *Commentarium in Joannem* 13.42; GCS 4:268, 17.
17. See Špidlík, *La sophiologie de S. Basile*, 225ff.
18. The *Physiologus* was to contribute to the extraordinary development of this method during the Middle Ages.
19. *Sokroviščé duchovnoje v mire sobiramoje* [*The Spiritual Treasure Collected in the World*], *Works* vol. IV (Moscow, 1899).
20. Just as in the area of scripture studies there was a propensity for scientific rigor in the learned exegesis of the Syrians there were, on the other hand, among Alexandrians rather imaginative exercises.
21. See René Bornet, *Les commentaires byzantins de la divine liturgie du VIIe siècle* (Paris, 1966).
22. See Špidlík, *La sophiologie de S. Basile*, 227ff.
23. *Sermo in Matthaeum* 55; GCS 11:128, 1.
24. *In Librum Judicum homilia* 7.2; GCS 7:500, 9.
25. Evagrius, *Praktikos* 50; SCh 171:615; CS 4:29-30.
26. See above, III, *The True Gnostic*, IX, *Discernment of Spirits*, and XI, *Obedience to the Spiritual Father*.
27. In this sense, contemplation coincides more or less with the examination of conscience.
28. The meaning of this entire doctrine varies considerably from Origen to Evagrius, and especially from Evagrius to Maximus the Confessor; see Hans Urs von Balthasar, 'Die gnostische Centurien des Maximus Confessor', Freiburger theologische Studien 61 (Freiburg, 1941) 46ff.
29. See A. J. Festugière, *La révélation d' Hermès Trismégiste* (Paris, 1944-54) vol. 2:598.
30. *Republic* II.379a 5.
31. See Pierre Battifol, 'Théologia, Théologie', in *Ephemerides Theologicae Lovanienses* 5 (1928) 275; Špidlík, *Grégoire de Nazianze*, 127.
32. See The Prologue to *Le Traité pratique*, SCh 171:501; and *Praktikos* 84 (674; CS 4:37).
33. See, for example, John of Damascus, *De spiritibus* (PG 95:84B); *Homilia in transfigurationem* 15 (PG 96:569A) and the entire treatise of John Chrysostom, *On the incomprehensibility of God* (SCh 28bis).
34. See above, III, *The Indirect Experience*.
35. See, for example, Evagrius, *Kephalaia* 5.26; Frankenberg, 329.
36. See J. Lemaitre DS 2/2:1836ff.
37. *Ibid.*
38. *Letter* 39; Frankenberg, 587. Cf. J. Lemaitre, DS 2/2:1830ff.
39. See above, Chapter IV, 4.
40. See the entire spiritual doctrine of Theophane the Recluse.
41. See Donatien Mollat, 'Gloire', VTB, 504-11; P. Adnès, 'Gloire de Dieu', DS 6:421-87.
42. See Jean Meyendorff, *Introduction à l'étude de Gregoire Palamas* (Paris, 1959), [*A Study of Gregory Palamas* (London, 1964)].

43. See the series of articles in DS 4/2:2045ff.
44. See Armand Delatte, 'Les conceptions de l'enthousiasme chez les philosophes présocratiques', in *L'antiquité classique* 3 (1934) 5–75; (off-print, Paris, 1935); Edouard des Places, 'L'extase dans la Grèce classique', DS 4/2:2059–67.
45. Herman Gunkel, *Die Schriften des Alten Testaments in Auswahl. Die grossen Propheten*, part 2, vol. 2 (Göttingen, 1923) XVIII; cf. DS 4:2078.
46. See Epiphanius, *Panarion* 48.4.1; ed. Karl Holl, GCS 2:224ff.
47. Monasticism has known 'men of God', 'Spirit-bearers' (*pneumatophoroi*), 'clear-sighted' (*dioratics*); it does not know 'ecstatics' except in the case of fools (*Vita S. Pachomii*, I^a, ed. François Halkin, *Sancti Pachomii Vitae Graecae*, Subsidia Hagiographica 19 (Brussels, 1932) 64, 26.
48. See Antony's ecstasy, PG 26:9333C–936B; DS 4/2:2104.
49. See above, II, 1 *Spiritual*, and *The Effects of the Spirit*, and IV *Inner Man-Outer Man*.
50. Pisma o dochovnoi žizni [*Letters on the Spiritual Life*] (Moscow, 1903) 251; see *Théophane le Reclus*, 253.
51. *Ad Magnum* 27; PG 79:1004A.
52. Origen, *Exhortatio ad Martyrium* 13; GCS 1:13, 14.
53. See Palladius, *The Lausiac History* 29; ed. Cuthbert Butler, *The Lausiac History of Palladius*, Texts and Studies 6/2 (Cambridge, 1904) 85.
54. See Philoxenes of Mabbug, *Exhortation à un juif converti*, trans. Micheline Albert, in *Orient Syrien*, 6 (Paris, 1961) 44, 5.
55. See I. Hausherr, 'Ignorance infinie', OCP 2 (1936) 351–62; *Hésychasme et prière*, OCA 176 (Rome, 1966) 38–49, 238–46; 'Ignorance infinie ou science infinie?, OCP 25 (1959) 44–52.
56. See J. Lemaitre, DS 2/2:1830ff.
57. *Ibid.*, 1862ff.
58. Gregory of Nyssa discloses his division in *Homilia* 11 *in Canticum* (PG 44:1000CD) and develops it in *The Life of Moses*; see Jean Daniélou, 'Mystique de la ténèbre chez Grégoire de Nysse', DS 2/2: 1872ff. [See also Daniélou's Introduction to *From Glory to Glory*, H. Musurillo ed., (New York, 1979) 23ff.]
59. Daniélou, DS 2/2:1881ff.
60. *Ibid.*, 1879; H. Lewy, *Sobria ebrietas* (Giessen, 1929).
61. See Gregory of Nyssa, *Homilia 11 in Canticum*; PG 44:996AD.

5. THE EFFECTS OF CONTEMPLATION

1. The word *alētheia*, truth, means therefore, by contrast, that which is no longer hidden, that which has not been forgotten; cf. Spidlík, *Grégoire de Nazianze*, 1ff.
2. See above, XIII, 1.
3. Philo describes the retreat of the Therapeutae who keep the memory of God alive (*De vita contemplativa* 26, edd. Leopold Cohn and P. Wendland, *Philo Alexandrinus*, vol. 6 [Berlin, 1915] 52–53). Zeno the Stoic considered memory the 'treasure house of images' (Arnim, SVF 1, p. 19, n. 64).
4. See Ephrem, *Beatitudines* 10; ed. J. S. Assemani, *Ephraem Syri opera omnia . . . graece* vol. 1 (Rome, 1732) 283.
5. *De oratione* 5 (PG 79:1181A); I. Hausherr, 'Les leçons d'un contemplatif', 93.
6. Gregory of Nazianzus, *Oratio* 27.4; PG 36:16BC.

Contemplation

7. Basil; see Špidlík, *La sophiologie de S. Basile*, 45ff.
8. See Henri Crouzel, *Théologie de l'image de Dieu chez Origène* (Paris, 1956) 232ff.
9. Basil, *Homilia in Hexaemeron* 3.10; PG 29:77C.
10. See I. Hausherr, 'Contemplation et sainteté. Une remarquable mise au point par Philoxène de Mabboug († 523)', RAM 14 (1933) 171-95; *Hésychasme et prière*, OCA 176:13-37.
11. Origen, *Commentarium in Canticum* I; GCS 8:100, 21.
12. *Id.*, *Commentarium in Joannem* 1.16; GCS 4:20, 15; see Odo Casel, 'Glaube, Gnosis, Mysterium', in *Jahrbuch für Liturgiewissenschaft* 15 (1941), off-print (Münster/W, 1941) 28: 'For Origen, theological knowledge is "becoming embodied" (*sicheinverleiben*) in the substance of the divine Truth.'
13. Gregory of Nyssa, *De anima et resurrectione*; PG 46:96C.
14. See Athanasius, *Vita Antonii* 73; PG 26:946A; Socrates, *Historia ecclesiastica* 4.23; PG 67:516C.
15. See above, III, *The True Gnostic*.
16. See Basil, *Homilia 3 in Hexaemeron*, 10; PG 29:77BC; SCh 26:243.
17. See *Homilia in Genesim* 1.7; SC 7:72-73; Margherite Harl, *Origène et la fonction révélatrice du Verbe Incarné* (Paris, 1958) 205ff.
18. *De passionibus;* PG 150:1081AB; see Gregory of Nazianzus, *Hymnus ad Christum*, PG 37:1327.
19. *Choix de sermons et discours*, trans. A. Serpinet (Paris, 1898) 1:3-10; see Placide Deseille, 'Glorie de Dieu, Dans l'Ecriture et chez les Pères de l'Eglise jusqu'à saint Bernard', DS 6:422-63.

CONCLUSION

BEFORE WE SUMMARIZE the chararacteristic traits of Eastern spirituality, we must stress one principle and stress it hard, that the Latin church originated from the Greek church as a branch grows from a tree trunk. The Church was implanted by the Greeks and expressed itself in the greek language until the end of the fourth century. As early as the beginning of the fourth century centrifugal forces came into play which brought about the breakup of the political and cultural unity of the two halves of the Roman Empire, not without repercussions on the life of the Church, and on the mentality of those who devoted themselves to the spiritual life.[1] This principle will place a relative value upon specific key features among Eastern Christians. From it comes the nature of Eastern spirituality.

The Ideal of Deification

'For it was for this end that the Word of God was made man, and he who was the Son of God became the Son of Man, that man, having been taken into the Word, and receiving adoption, might become the son of God.'[2] This summary of sacred history, borrowed with variations at all periods, lies at the base of the spiritual teaching of the East. The aim of this instruction is the deification of man.

Trinitarian

The God of Christians is the Father who reveals himself through the Son in the Holy Spirit. The 'royal road' of our sanctification is nothing but the ascending movement which goes from the Son to the Father in the Spirit. For those in the East, this principle is not a *theologoumenon*, an object of speculative discussion. On the contrary, it has applications which lead one to qualify Eastern spirituality by these three characteristics: it is pneumatological, Christological, and Trinitarian. The contemplation of the Trinity is the summit of 'theology'. Theology is defined as the unremitting effort to discover, behind the cosmos and its laws, the personal relationships of man in God and with God.

Contemplative

Freed from cosmic laws and enslavement to fate, man converses with the Father in his presence. Upon this dialogue with God depend man's relationships with beings and things. Consequently, he can even now neither live nor organize anything without praying; and the intensity of his prayer is the 'barometer of his spiritual life'.

Anthropological

Eastern spirituality starts with the 'image of God' according to which man was created and arrives at the 'likeness' to the Creator. It is an entirely spiritual (supernatural, the West would say) anthropology. It encompasses all of man, the faculties of his soul and of his body according to the possibility they possess of submitting themselves to the Spirit, of being spiritualized. All the problems which secular 'philosophy' and secular science and culture try to solve on the purely human level ('natural', in the sense of *natura pura*) — knowledge, freedom, the spiritual character of man, the desires of the soul, the appetites of the body, hygiene in the physical life — are thereby transposed to a higher level. If the ideal of humanism is the perfection of man, that of christian anthropology is the ideal of the Man-God.

Ecclesiological

The *tserkovnost'*, this sense of Church so familiar to the Russians, amounts to the consciousness that salvation is universal and

Conclusion

that no one may believe he is saved unless he is saved together with others. The unity of 'human nature', presupposed in the moral reflections of the Ancients, is seen and lived to a surprising degree by Christians. Because man's true nature includes the Holy Spirit, he is 'like a soul' common to all men, and the 'spirituality' of one person can progress only in a divinized human *pleroma*, the Church.

Cosmic

The Jews found God in history; the Greeks searched for him in the beauty and harmony of the cosmos. Having become Christians, Hellenized peoples were deeply conscious of their cosmic vocation. It was not a matter of inserting oneself into the universal harmony, but rather of actively cooperating to re-establish this beauty, spoiled by sin. By vocation, the Christian must work at the perfection and the deification of the world, of the universe in whose midst humankind was placed at the moment of creation and from which we may not separate ourselves, except for the ascetic purification which preceeds 'cosmic joy'.

Monastic

Monks and monasteries have played a decisive role in the Eastern concept of the christian life. From the beginning, the monastic life was the image of the authentic christian life. The monks were those who wanted to observe the commandments, all the commandments; they were therefore the only true Christians. Their tenacious flight from the world, their rigorous asceticism, and their toil were all aimed at the very goal of baptism: to purify the image of God in man, which has been tarnished, and to give back to it its full splendor.

With Eremitic Tendencies

Although contemplation gave the monks a deep awareness of the spiritual link between themselves and all humankind, they frequently thought it more useful to live this union while isolated from human beings and from things. They saw in the eremitic life the means of intensifying their relationship with God through prayer.

Catanyctic

The Eastern rites abound with insistent repetitions of the *Kyrie Eleison*, with requests for the remission of sins. They unfold in an atmosphere of *penthos*. Far from being sad or pessimistic, however, the Eastern ascetics proclaimed a joyous faith: sin is the only evil, and it can always be wiped out by repentance.

Ascetic

One of the foundations of monasticism was the belief in the union of asceticism and mysticism — a belief which may be expressed by saying: *praxis* leads to *theoria*. The Eastern ascetics never doubted the value of their mortifications, which were frequently rather harsh; and they strongly believed that this 'replacement for martyrdom of blood' was an authentic exercise of love for God, a return to 'nature' created by God, a purification of the world, and a testimony to the power of the Spirit.

Spirit of Freedom

The ascetic practices of the monks were their way of moving from 'slavery to freedom'.[3] It is true that this practice often manifested itself to the outside as a desire to free oneself from social 'structures', from the so-called laws of convention. Inwardly, however, asceticism kept its authentic aim: to arrive at *apatheia*, to make the human heart inaccessible to sin, to the passions, to everything that could disturb *parrhēsia*, free access to God. This objective is not 'passive' at all, but presupposes, on the contrary, a continual combat to achieve and retain purity of heart.

The Spirituality of the Heart

Eastern Christians have accused those in the West of 'rationalism', while Westerners have charged them with 'sentimentalism'. Could this not be a misunderstanding? One thing is certain: the contemplatives, more than men of action, were conscious of being in the presence of a mystery which one can only penetrate 'gropingly'.[4] Furthermore, what most interests the man of action is the perfection of *acts*, of doing things. Books on morality attract his interest and cry out for his research. Those in the East, by contrast, were preoccupied with the *state* (*katastasis*) of the heart, with its permanent disposition.

Eschatological

The West has been compared to Martha and the East to Mary. There are those who reproach monks for their lack of an apostolic spirit, and their passivity. In fact, the contemplative spirit of the Eastern church goes hand in hand with its eschatology. The perfection of man in the cosmos is the 'glory of God', the penetrating insight, the clearsightedness, the vision of God's presence in everything. This is where man's ultimate perfection lies, and this is also the aim of contemplation: to see God in everything.

By the richness of their ceremonies and their chants, Eastern liturgies seek to unveil to human gaze the presence of God within creation. They invite us to enter their churches with their magnificent icons to see 'heaven on earth'.

> To him, the God who did appear
> And did descend into this world,
> To him who transfigured creation,
> Be glory and praise for ever.

(Matins of the Feast of Epiphany in the Byzantine Church)

Notes

1. See Aimé Solignac, 'Latine (Eglise), DS 9:329–38.
2. Irenaeus, *Adversus haereses* III.19.1 (PG 7:939C; ANF 1:448) III.16.3 (922B; 440).
3. A favorite expression of Nikolaj Berdiaeff, see his book *Slavery and Freedom* (*De l'esclavage et de la liberté de l'homme* [Paris, 1946]).
4. See above, XIII, 3.

TABLE OF ABBREVIATIONS

ACW	Ancient Christian Writers series. Westminister, Maryland, 1946–.
AGG	Abhandlung der Gesellschaft der Wissenschaften zu Göttingen. Göttingen, 1843–.
ANF	Ante-Nicene Fathers. Rpt. Grand Rapids, 1978.
CIS	*Centrum Ignatianum Spiritualitatis*. Rome, 1979–.
CS	Cistercian Studies Series. Spencer, Washington, Kalamazoo, 1969–.
CSCO	*Corpus Scriptorum Christianorum Orientalium*. Paris, 1913–.
CSEL	*Corpus Scriptorum Ecclesiasticorum Latinorum*. Vienna, 1866–.
DACL	*Dictionnaire d'Archéologie chrétienne et de Liturgie*. Paris, 1907–.
DESp	*Dizionario Enciclopedico di Spiritualità*, ed. Emmanuel Ancilla. Volumes 1–2, Rome, 1975.
DHGE	*Dictionnaire d'Histoire et de Géographie Ecclésiastique*. Paris, 1912–.
DIP	*Dizionario degli Istituti di Perfezione*. Rome, 1973–.
DS	*Dictionnaire de Spiritualité*. Paris, 1937–.
EF	H. Fries, *Encyclopédie de la Foi*, 1–4. Paris, 1965–67.
FC	Fathers of the Church series. New York-Washington, 1948–.
Grégoire de Nazianze	T. Špidlík, *Grégoire de Nazianze. Introduction à l'étude de sa doctrine spirituelle*, OCA 189. Rome, 1971.
GCS	Die griechischen christlichen Schriftsteller, Berlin-Leipzig, 1897–.

Handbuch der Ostkirchenkunde	E. von Ivánka, J. Tyciak, P. Wiertz, editors. Düsseldorf, 1971.
Joseph de Volokolamsk	T. Špidlík, *Joseph de Volokolamsk. Un chapitre de la spiritualité russe*, OCA 146. Rome, 1956.
JTS	*The Journal of Theological Studies*. London, 1899–.
Kittel	Gerhard Kittel, *Theologisches Wörterbuch zum Neuen Testament*. Stuttgart, 1933. English translation by Geoffrey W. Bromiley, *Theological Dictionary of the New Testament*. Grand Rapids, 1964–74.
La sophiologie de S. Basile	T. Špidlík, *La sophiologie de S. Basile*, OCA 162. Rome, 1961.
LNPF	*A Select Library of the Nicene and Post-Nicene Fathers*. Rpt. Grand Rapids, 1979.
LThK²	*Lexikon für Theologie und Kirche*, Second edition, Freiburg im Breisgau, 1957–.
OC	*Orientalia Christiana*. Rome, 1923–34.
OCA	*Orientalia Christiana Analecta*. Rome, 1935–.
OCP	*Orientalia Christiana Periodica*. Rome, 1935–.
PO	*Patrologia Orientalis*. Paris, 1907–.
PTS	Patristische Texte und Studien. Berlin, 1964–.
Pusey	Philip Edward Pusey, ed., *Sancti Patris Nostri Cyrilli archiepiscopi Alexandrini . . . Opera*. Two volumes. Second edition, Brussels, 1965.
RAM	*Revue d'Ascétique et de Mystique*. Toulouse, 1920–.
RHR	*Revue de l'Histoire des Religions*. Paris, 1880–.
RSR	*Recherches de Science Religieuse*. Paris, 1910–.
SCh	Sources Chrétiennes. Paris, 1941–.
M. Spanneut *Le stoïcisme des Peres...*	Michel Spanneut, *Le stoïcisme des Peres de l'Eglise de Clément de Rome à Clément d'Alexandrie*, Patristica Sorbonensia. Paris, 1957.
SVF	Hans von Arnim, *Stoicorum Veterum Fragmenta*. 1–4. Leipzig, 1921–24.
Théophane le Reclus	T. Špidlík, *La doctrine spirituelle de Théophane le Reclus*, OCA 172. Rome, 1965.

A SELECTED BIBLIOGRAPHY

ARRANGED IN TOPICAL ORDER

EASTERN SPIRITUALITY IN GENERAL, p. 1

Marcel Viller. *La spiritualité des premiers siècles chrétiens.* Paris, 1930.
Vladimir Lossky. *Essai sur la théologie mystique de l'Église d'Orient.* Paris, 1944. English translation by the Fellowship of St Alban and St Sergius, *The Mystical Theology of the Eastern Church.* London, 1957.
A Monk of the Eastern Church [Lev Gillet]. *Orthodox Spirituality: An Outline of the Orthodox and Mystical Tradition.* London, 1945.
Georg Wunderle. *Das geistliche Antlitz der Ostkirche.* Würzburg, 1949.
Hans von Campenhausen. *Griechische Kirchenväter.* Stuttgart, 1955. Translated by S. Godman, *The Fathers of the Greek Church.* New York, 1959.
G. A. Stogogliou and G. I. Mantzarides. 'Pneumatikotes, Orthodoxos' in *Threskeutikē kai ethikē enkyklopaideia,* vol. 10, col. 467–75. Athens, 1960.
Gustave Bardy. *La vie spirituelle d'après les Pères des trois premiers siècles.* Revised by A. Hamman. Tournai, 1968.
Louis Bouyer. *La spiritualité orthodoxe et la spiritualité protestante et anglicane. Histoire de la spiritualité,* III 1. Paris, 1965. English translation by Barbara Wall, *Orthodox Spirituality and Protestant and Anglican Spirituality.* A History of Spirituality, III. New York, 1969.
Tomaš Špidlík. 'Moral Theology and Spirituality, Greek Orthodox', in *The New Catholic Encyclopedia,* vol. 9: 1126–28. 1967.
―――――. 'Spiritualität des östlichen Christentums', in *Handbuch der Ostkirchenkunde,* 483–502.
―――――. 'L'Orient chrétien dans la patristique et la spiritualité, *Seminarium* 27 (1975) 431–44.
―――――. 'Oriente christiano (spiritualità dell')', *DESp* II (1975) 1329–40.
Paul Evdokimov. *La nouveauté de l'Esprit. Etudes de spiritualité,* Spiritualité orientale 20. Abbaye de Bellefontaine, 1977.
Tomaš Špidlík. 'Oriente cristiano', in S. de Fiores and T. Goffi, *Nuovo Dizionario di Spiritualità,* 1091–1105. Rome, 1979.
―――――. 'Orthodoxe (Spiritualité), *DS* 11 (1982) 972–1001.
Tomaš Špidlík and I. Gargano. *La spiritualità dei Padri greci e orientali.* Storia della spiritualità, vol. 3a. Rome, 1983.
―――――. 'Esperienza ortodossa', in T. Goffi-B. Secondin, *Problemi e prospettive di spiritualità.* Brecia, 1983, 113–26.

HOLY SCRIPTURE, p. 5

D. Kastolskij. *O domašněm upotreblenii slova božija u christian pervych věkov* [The Use of the Word of God in the Christian Families of the First Centuries]. *Dušepolenznoje čtěnie* 17 (1876) vol. II: 320–50, 412–43.
Hermann Dörries. 'Die Bibel im ältesten Monchtum', *Theologische Literaturzeitung* 72 (1946) 215–22.
Jean Daniélou. *Sacrementum futuri, Etudes sur les origines de la typologie biblique*. Paris, 1950. English translation by W. Hibbard, *From Shadows to Reality: Studies in the Biblical Typology of the Fathers*. London, 1960.
Henri de Lubac. *Histoire et Esprit, L'intelligence de l'Ecriture d'après Origène*, Théologie 16. Paris, 1950.
Georgij Florovsky. 'La Bible et l'Eglise', *Dieu Vivant* 21: 95–105. Paris, 1952.
Jean Gribomont. *Les Règles Morales de saint Basile et le Nouveau Testament. Studia Patristica* 2, TU 64. Berlin, 1957. 416–26.
Rolf Goegler. *Zur Theologie des biblischen Wortes bei Origenes*. Düsseldorf, 1963.
Garcia m. Colombás. 'La Biblia en la espritualidad del monacato primitivo', *Yermo* 2 (1964) 113–29.
La Bible et les Pères. Colloque de Strasbourg (1–3 Oct. 1969). Paris. 1971.

THE TRADITION OF THE CHURCH, p. 6

R.P.C. Hanson. *Origen's Doctrine of Tradition*. London, 1954.
Joseph Pieper. *Ueber den Begriff der Tradition*. Cologne, 1958.
Yves Congar. *La tradition et les traditions*, I–II. Paris. 1960–1963. English translation by M. Naseby and T. Rainborough, *Tradition and Traditions: An Historical and Theological Essay*. London, 1966.
J. R. Geiselmann. *Die Heilige Schrift und die Tradition*. Freiburg, 1962.
_____. 'Tradition', *EF* 4 (1967) 337–347 (bibliography).
Vladimir Lossky. *A l'image et à la ressemblance de Dieu*, ch. VIII: 'La tradition' et les traditions', 139–66. Paris, 1967. Translated by Ge. E. H. Palmer and E. Kadloubovsky, 'Tradition and Traditions', in *In the Image and Likeness of God*. Crestwood, New York (1974) 141–68.
G.I. Mantzarides. *Tradition and Renewal in the Theology of Gregory Palamas* (in Greek). Thessalonica. 1974.

THE JUDAEO-CHRISTIAN ENVIRONMENT, p. 8

H. J. Schoeps. *Urgemeinde, Judenchristentum, Gnosis*. Tübingen, 1956.
Jean Daniélou. *Histoire des doctrines chrétiennes avant Nicée, Théologie du judéo-christianisme*, 1. Tournai, 1958. English translation by J. A. Baker, *A History of Early Christian Doctrine before the Council of Nicea*, vol. 1, *The Theology of Jewish Christianity*. London, 1977.
_____. *Études d'exégèse judéo-chrétienne*, Théologie historique 5. Paris, 1966.
Roger Le Déaut, Annie Jaubert, and Kurt Hruby. 'Judaïsme', DS 8 (1974) 1487–1564.

Bibliography 361

Judéo-christianisme. Recherches historiques offertes en hommage au cardinal J. Daniélou. RSR 60 (1972) 1-320.

HELLENISM, p. 9

The problem of the relationships between Hellenism and Christianity has been studied from various angles (for a list of works studying the relationship of Hellenism to Christianity, see Michel Spanneut, *Le stoïcisme*, 55ff.); for studies that show the continuity between Hellenism and Christianity, *ibid.*, 57, n. 9; the history of dogma and patristics have frequently taken the philosophy of the Fathers as their object, cf. *ibid.*, 60ff. Many other studies give preference to a particular doctrine or to an author's philosophy. Here are a few works of a more general interest.

Michel Spanneut, *Le stoïcisme des Pères de l'Église*.
A. J. Festugière. *L'idéal religieux des Grecs et l'Evangile*. Paris, 1932.
_____. *L'enfant d'Agrigente*, 2nd ed., Paris, 1950.
René Arnou. 'Platonisme des Pères', DThC 12 (1935) 2258-2395.
E. von Ivánka. *Hellenistisches und Christliches im frühbyzantinischen Geistesleben*. Vienna, 1948.
_____. *Plato Christianus, Uebernahme und Umgestaltung des Platonismus durch die Väter*. Einsiedeln, 1964.
H. A. Wolfson. *The Philosophy of the Church Fathers*, I. *Faith, Trinity, Incarnation*. Cambridge (Mass.), 1956.
P. Th. Camelot. 'Hellénisme et pensée chrétienne', in *Catholicisme* 5 (1958) 588-95.
_____. 'Hellénisme (et spiritualité patristique)', DS 7 (1968) 145-64.
Jean Daniélou. *Message evangélique et culture hellénistique aux IIe et IIIe siècles. Histoire des doctrines chrétiennes avant Nicée*, II, Bibliothèque de Théologie. Paris-Tournai, 1961. English translation by J. A. Baker, *Gospel Message and Hellenistic Culture, A History of Early Christian Doctrine before the Council of Nicea*, II. London, 1973.
_____. *Humanisme et spiritualité*, I. *Le christianisme et le monde gréco-romain*, DS 7 (1969) 947-59.
Henri Crouzel. *Origène et la philosophie*. Théologie 52. Paris, 1961.
Werner Jaeger. *Das frühe Christentum und die griechische Bildung*. Berlin, 1973. English translation, *Early Christianity and Greek Paideia*. Boston, 1961.
Owen Chadwick. *Early Christian Thought and Classical Tradition: Studies in Justin, Clement and Origen*. Oxford, 1966.
Albert Warkotsch. *Antike Philosophie im Urteil der Kirchenväter*. Munich-Paderborn-Vienna, 1973.

BYZANTINE, p. 11

Karl Krumbacher. *Geschichte der byzantinischen Literatur*, 2d ed. Munich, 1897.
Franz-Josef Dölger and A. M. Schneider. *Byzanz*. Bern, 1952.
Irénée Hausherr. *Contemplation chez les Orientaux chrétiens*. 2. *Exposé historique*. 'Principaux auteurs', DS 2/2 (1953) 1787-1801.
Hans Georg Beck. *Kirche und theologische Literatur im byzantinischen Reich*. Munich, 1959.

Byzantine Christian Heritage. Lectures at the John XXIII Institute. New York, 1966.
Tomaš Špidlík. 'Bizantino, monachesimo', DIP 1 (1973) 1466–74.
John Meyendorff. *Byzantine Theology: Historical Trends and Doctrinal Themes.* Crestwood, New York, 1974.
Tomaš Špidlík. 'Constantinopoli', DIP 3 (1976) 173–77.
The Philokalia. The Complete Text. Edited by G. E. H. Palmer, Philip Sherrard, and Kallistos Ware. London and Boston, 1979– .
La Filocalia. Translated by E. Artioli and F. Lovato. Turin, 1982– .
Aimé Solignac. 'Nicon de la Montagne-Noire', DS 11 (1982) 319–20.
D. Stiernon. 'Nicodème l'hagiorite', *ibid.*, col. 234–50.
John Meyendorff. *The Byzantine Legacy in the Orthodox Church.* Crestwood, New York, 1982.

COPTIC, p. 13

Paul van Cauwenbergh. *Étude sur les moines d'Egypte depuis le Concile de Chalcédoine (451) jusqu'à l'invasion arabe (640).* Louvain, 1914.
Antoine Guillaumont. 'Copte (littérature spirituelle)', DS 2/2 (1953) 2266–78.
O. Meinardus. *Monks, and Monasteries of the Egyptian Deserts.* Cairo, 1961.
_____. *Christian Egypt, Ancient and Modern.* Cairo, 1965.
Pierre du Bourguet. *Die Kopten.* Baden-Baden, 1967.
_____. *Handbuch der Ostkirchenkunde,* 811ff., 778 (bibliography).
O. Meinardus. 'Recent Developments in Egyptian Monasticism', OCP 49 (1965) 79–89.
H. Malak. 'Copto, monachesimo', DIP 3 (1976) 132–47.

ETHIOPIAN, p. 14

August Dillmann. *Chrestomatia aethiopica* (excerpts from texts). Leipzig, 1866. Rev. ed., 1941.
Camillo Beccari. *Rerum aethiopicarum scriptores occidentales inediti a saeculo XVI ad XIX.* 15 vols. Rome, 1903–17.
J. M. Harden. *An Introduction to Ethiopic Christian Literature.* London, 1926.
E. A. Wallis Budge. *The Book of the Saints of the Ethiopian Church.* Cambridge, 1928.
S. Zanutto. *Bibliografia etiopica,* 3 fasc., Rome, 1929–36; a continuation of G. Fumagalli. *Bibliografia etiopica.* Milan, 1893.
Ignazio Guidi. *Storia della litteratura etiopica.* Rome, 1932.
Enrico Cerulli. *Il libro etiopico dei Miracoli di Maria.* Rome, 1943.
_____. 'La littérature éthiopienne dans l'histoire de la culture médiévale', in *Annuaire de l'Institut de philologie et d'histoire orientales,* vol. 14. Brussels (1954–57) 17–35.
_____. *Storia della letteratura etiopica.* Milan, 1956.
_____. 'Il monachesimo in Etiopia', in *Monachesimo orientale,* OCA 152: 259–78. Rome, 1958.
Enno Littmann. 'Die äthiopische Literatur', in *Handbuch der Orientalistik,* vol. 3: 375–85. Leiden, 1954.

Bibliography 363

Bernard Velat. 'Ethiopie', DS 4/2 (1961) 1453-77.
Jean Doresse. *L'empire du Prêtre Jean*, I-II. Paris, 1957.
J. Doresse. *La vie quotidienne des Ethiopiens chrétiens (aux XVIIe et XVIIIe siècles)*. Paris, 1972.
M. da Abiy-Addi. 'Etiopico, monachesimo', DIP 3 (1976) 1330-39.

SYRIAN, p. 14

Rubens-Duval. *La littérature syriaque*. Paris, 1907.
Anton Baumstark. *Geschichte der syrischen literatur*. Bonn, 1922.
Jean-Baptiste Chabot. *Littérature syriaque*. Paris, 1934.
Ignace Ziadé. 'Syrienne (Église)', DThC 14/2 (1941) 3017-88.
Eugène Tisserant. 'Syro-malabare (Église)', *ibid.*, 3089-3162.
'Syrienne (Église)', DThC, Tables générales III: col. 4108-11.
Ignazio Ortiz de Urbina. *Patrologia syriaca*. Rome, 1965.
A. Vööbus. *History of Asceticism in the Syrian Orient, A Contribution to the History of Culture in the Near East*. CSC 184, 197, Subsidia 14, 17. Louvain, 1958-60.
──────── . *Syriac and Arabic Documents regarding Legislation relative to Syrian Asceticism. Edited, Translated and Furnished with Literary Historical Data*. Stockholm 1960.
Placid I. Podipara. 'Die Thomas-Christen', *Das östliche Christentum*, NF 18. Würzburg, 1967.
Louis Leloir. 'Martyrius (Sahdônâ)', DS (1980) 737-42.
M. Hayek. 'Maronite (Église)', *ibid., 631-44.*

ARMENIAN, p. 15

Edouard Dulaurier. *Histoire, dogmes, traductions et liturgie de l'Église Arménienne*. Paris, 1857.
L. A. Boettinger. *Armenian Legends and Festivals*. Minneapolis, 1920.
Irénée Hausherr. 'Arménienne (spiritualité), DS 1 (1937) 862-76 (bibliography).
Malachy Ormanian and T. Poladian. *The Church of Armenia*. 2nd ed. London, 1955.
Garabed Amadouni. 'Le rôle historique des hiéromoines arméniens', in *Monachesimo orientale*, OCA 153: 279-305. Rome, 1958.
J. Mécérian. *Histoire et institution de l'Église arménienne*. Coll. Recherches 30. Beirut, 1975.
Handbuch der Ostkirchenkunde. Düsseldorf, 1971. p. 778 (bibliography).

GEORGIAN, p. 15

The original, general work on the history of Georgian religious literature is Korneli Kekelidze, *K'art'uli literaturis istoria* [History of Georgian Literature], vol. 1. Tiflis, 1923, 1941, 1951, 1960; there is a shortened version of the first edition by Joseph Karst, *Littérature géorgienne chrétienne*, Bibliothèque catholique des sciences religieuses 62, Paris, 1934; and a German adaptation of the second edition by Michele Tarchnišvili, *Geschichte der kirchlichen georgischen Literatur*, Studi e Testi 185, Vatican City, 1955.

David Marshall Lang. *Lives and Legends of the Georgian Saints*. London, 1956.
Michele Tarchnišvili. 'il monachesimo georgiano nelle sue origini e sviluppi', in *Monachesimo orientale*, OCA 153: 307–19. Rome, 1958.
Gérard Garitte. 'Géorgienne (littérature spirituelle)', DS 6 (1967) 244–56.

RUSSIAN, p.17

E. Poseljanin. *Russkije podvižniki 19go věka* [The Nineteenth Century Russian Ascetics]. St Petersburg, 1910 (3rd ed.).
Georgij P. Fedotov. *Svjatyie drevnei Rusi* [The Saints of Old Russia.]. Paris, 1931.
———. *The Russian Religious Mind*. Cambridge, 1946.
———. *A Treasury of Russian Spirituality*. London, 1950.
Igor Smolitsch. *Das altrussische Mönchtum (11–16 Jahrhundert)*, Das Ostliche Christentum, Heft 11, Würzburg, 1940.
———. *Russisches Mönchtum, Entstehung, Entwicklung und Wesen* (988–1917). Würzburg, 1953.
Elisabeth Behr-Sigel. *Prière et sainteté dans l'Église russe*. Paris, 1950.
Stanislas Tyszkiewicz. *Moralistes de Russie*. Rome, 1951.
———. 'La spiritualité orthodoxe russe', in A. Ravier, *La mystique et les mystiques*, 463–518. Desclée de Brouwer, 1965.
Ivan Kologrivof. *Essai sur la sainteté en Russie*. Bruges, 1953.
Ernst Benz. *Russische Heiligenlegenden*. Zürich, 1953.
Stanislas Tyszkiewicz and Théodore Belpaire. *Écrits d'ascètes russes*. Namur, 1957.
M. J. Rouët de Journel. *Monachisme et monastères russes*. Paris, 1952.
Constantin de Grunwald. *Quand la Russie avait des saints*. Paris, 1958.
Serge Bolshakoff. *I mistici russi*. Turin, 1962. Translated by the author, *Russian Mystics*. Cistercian Studies Series 26. Kalamazoo, 1977. See The Bibliography.
N. Arseniev. *La pieté russe*. Neuchâtel, 1963. English translation by A. Moorhouse, *Russian Piety*. London, 1964.
Tomaš Špidlík. 'Slavi orientali (spiritualità degli)', DESp 2 (1975) 1738–41.
———. *I grandi mistici russi*. Rome, 1977.
———. 'Influsso dei mistici russi nella letteratura russa moderna', in *Mistica e misticismo oggi...*, Rome (1979) 135–50.
Saint Nil Sorsky. Textes traduits par Sr. Sophia M. Jacamon. Bellefontaine, 1980.
S. Chetverikov. *Starets Paisii Velichkovskii: His Life, Teachings, and Influence on Orthodox Monasticism*. Translated from the Russian by V. Lickwar and A. Lisenko. Belmont, 1980. (ed.)
M. Klimenko, transl. *The 'Vita' of St. Sergii of Radonezh*. Boston, 1980. (ed.)
Tomaš Špidlík. *La spiritualità russa*, La spiritualità cristiana. Storia e testi, 16, Rome, 1981.
———. 'Tratti salienti della spiritualita slava', in *The Common Roots of the European Nations*, 102–5. Florence, 1982.
Elisabeth Behr-Sigel. 'Nil Sorskij (Saint)', DS 11 (1982) 356–67.

Bibliography 365

WISDOM, p.22

Johannes Stelzenberger. *Die Beziehung der frühchristlichen Sittenlehre zur Ethik der Stoa*, 277–306: Das Ideal des Weisen. Munich, 1932.
A. J. Festugière. 'Le sage et le saint', in *La Vie intellectuelle* 27 (1934) 390–408.
Sergei Bulgakov. *The Wisdom of God*. London, 1937.
Henri Crouzel. *Origène et la 'connaissance mystique'*, 451ff. Paris-Tournai: Desclée de Brouwer, 1961.
H. Jaeger. *The Patristic Conception of Wisdom in the Light of Biblical Research*, 90–106: Studia Patristica IV, TU 79. Berlin, 1961.
Ulrich Wilckens and Georg Fohrer. '*Sophia, sophos, sophidzo*', in Kittel 7 (1962) 465–528.
Burghard Gladigow. *Sophia und Kosmos, Untersuchungen zur Frühgeschichte von sophos und sophië*. Hildesheim, 1965.
Vincenz Hamps. 'Sagesse, Étude biblique', EF 4 (1967) 141–47.
Johann Baptist Metz. 'Sagesse, Étude théologique', *ibid.*, 147–56.
André Barlucq and Pierre Grelot. 'Sagesse', VTB (1971), col. 1170–78.

PHILOSOPHY, p. 22

Werner Jaeger. 'Ueber Ursprung und Kreislauf des philosophischen Lebensideal', in *Sitzungsbericht der preussischen Akademie der Wissenschaften* 25 (1928) 290–421.
A. Chroust. 'Philosophy: Its Essence and Meaning in the Ancient World', *Philosophy Review* 56 (1947) 19–58.
Franz-Josef Dölger. 'Zur Bedeutung von 'philosophos' und 'philosophia' in byzantinischer Zeit', in *Byzanz und die europäische Staatenwelt*. Ettal, 1953.
G. J. M. Bartelinck. '"Philosophie" et "philosophe" dans quelques oeuvres de Jean Chrysostome', RAM 36 (1960) 486–92.
Gregorio Penco. 'La vita ascetica come "Philosophia" nell'antica tradizione monastica', in *Studia monastica*, 2. Montserrat, 1960.

SPIRITUAL, p. 29

J. D. Frangoulis. 'Der Begriff des Geistes. 'Pneuma bei Clemens von Alexandrien'. Dissertation, Jena, 1936.
Fairy von Lilienfeld. 'Anthropos Pneumatikos-Pater Pneumatophoros: Neues Testament und Apophthegmata Patrum', *Studia Patristica* 5, TU 80 (1962) 382–92.
Stanislas Lyonnet. 'Perfection du chrétien "animé par l'Esprit" et action dans le monde selon saint Paul', in *Vie selon l'Esprit*, Unam Sanctam 55: 239–62. Paris, 1965.
Jacques Dupuis. *"L'Esprit de l'homme," Étude sur l'anthropologie religieuse d'Origène*. Desclée de Brouwer, 1967.

THE HOLY SPIRIT, p. 30

Pavel Florenskij. *Stolp i utverždēnije istiny* [*The Pillar and Foundation of Truth*] 109–42. Moscow, 1914.

'*Pneuma*', in Kittel VI: 330–453.
Pneuma, in G. W. H. Lampe, *A Patristic Greek Lexicon*, 1097–1104. Oxford, 1961.
Gervais Aeby. 'Les missions divines, de saint Justin à Origène', *Paradosis* 12, Friburg (Switzerland), 1958.
Benjamin Drewery, *Origen on the Doctrine of Grace*. London, 1960.
A. M. Bermejo. *The Indwelling of the Holy Spirit according to Saint Cyril of Alexandria*. Ona, 1963.
Ignace de la Potterie and Stanislas Lyonnet. 'La vie selon l'Esprit, condition du chrétien', *Unam Sanctam* 55. Paris, 1965.
Antonio Orbe. 'La Teologia del Espiritu Santo', in *Estudios Valentinianos* 4. Rome, 1966.
Paul Evdokimov. *L'Esprit Saint dans la tradition orthodoxe*. Bibliothèque oecuménique 10. Paris, 1969.
Jean-Pierre Martin. *El Espiritu Santo en los origenes del cristianismo, Estudio sobre I Clemente, Ignacio, II Clemente y Justino Mártir*. Zürich, 1971.
Charles Graves. 'The Holy Spirit in the Theology of Sergius Bulgakov.' Dissertation, Geneva, 1972.
Wolf-Dieter Hauschild. *Gottes Geist und der Mensch, Studien zur frühchristlichen Pneumatologie. Beiträge zur evangelischen Theologie* 63. Munich, 1972.
Boris Bobrinskoy. 'L'Esprit du Christ dans les sacrements chez Jean Chrysostome et Augustin', in Charles Kannengieser, ed., *Jean Chrysostome et Augustin*, Théologie historique 35: 247–79. Paris, 1975.
Mélanges Schillebeeckx. L'expérience de l'Ésprit. Le point théologique 18. Paris, 1976.
Tomaš Špidlík. 'Lo Spirito Santo nella catechesi di S. Basilio. La docilità allo Spirito Santo', in S. Felici, *Spirito Santo e Catechesi patristica*, 33–46. Rome, 1983.
———. 'Lo Spirito nell' antropologia della Chiesa Orientale', in *Credo in Spiritum Sanctum*. Atti del Congresso teologico internazionale di pneumatologia, Roma, 22–26 marzo 1982: 409–21. Città del Vaticano (?).

THE MYSTERY OF CHRIST, p. 34

Aloys Grillmeier. *Mit ihm und in ihm, Christologische Forschungen und Perspektiven*. Freiburg-Basel-Vienna, 1975. *Christ in Christian Tradition. From the Apostolic Age to Chalcedon (451)*. London-Oxford, 1975 (bibliography).

CHRIST SAVIOUR, p. 35

I. Orfanickij. *Istoričeskoe izloženie dogmata ob iskupitěl'noj žertvě Gospoda Jisusa Christa* [Historical Exposition of the Dogma of the Redeeming Sacrifice of Jesus Christ]. Moscow, 1904.
Metropolitan Antonij. *Dogmat iskuplenija* [The Dogma of the Redemption]. Stremski Karlovci, 1926.
Jean Rivière. *Le dogme de la rédemption. Études critiques et documents*, 3rd ed. Louvain, 1931.
Nicolas Ladomersky. *Une histoire orthodoxe du dogme de la Rédemption*. Paris, 1937.

Emmeran Scharl. *Recapitulatio mundi. Der Rekapitulationsbegriff des hl. Irenäus.* Freiburg-im-Breisgau, 1941.
Bernhard Schultze. *La nuova soteriologia russa.* OCP 9 (1943) 406–30; 11 (1945) 165–215; 12 (1946) 130–76.
──────. *Probleme der orthodoxen Theologie,* in E. von Ivánka, J. Tyciak, and P. Wiertz, *Handbuch der Ostkirchenkunde,* 97–186; especially 156ff. Düsseldorf, 1971.
Gustav Aulén. 'Die drei Haupttypen des christlichen Versöhnungsgedanken', Zeitschrift für systematische Theologie 1930: 501–38. Translated into English by A. G. Hebert, *Christus Victor: An Historical Study of the Three Main Types of the Idea of the Atonement.* London, 1931.
P. Gnedič. 'Mysl' of iskuplenii v propovedach Mitropolita Filareta' [The Doctrine of Redemption in the Sermons of Metropolitan Filaret], *Zurnal' Moskovskogo Patriarchy* 4 (1954) 31–5.
Russkaja bogoslovnaja literatura o dogmatĕ iskuplenija v period s 1893 po 1944 god [Russian Theological Literature on the Dogma of the Redemption from the year 1893 to the year 1944], *ibid.,* 8:68–72.
H. E. W. Turner. *The Patristic Doctrine of Redemption. A Study of the Development of the Doctrine during the First Five Centuries.* London, 1965.
Vladimir Lossky. *In the Image and Likeness of God.* ch. V, 96–110. Crestwood, New York, 1974.
Julius Tyciak. *Gegenwart des Heils in den östlichen Liturgien.* Sophia 9. Frieburg-im-Br., 1968.
Heinz Althaus. *Die Heilslehre des heiligen Gregor von Nazianz,* Münsterische Beiträge zur Theologie 34. Münster, 1972.
Norbert Brox. 'Soteria und Salus. Heilsvorstellungen in der Alten Kirche', *Evangelische Theologie* 33 (1973) 253–79.
José Antonio Alcain. *Cautiverio y redención del hombre en Origenes.* Bilbao, 1973.
Reinhard M. Huebner. *Die Einheit des Leibes Christi bei Gregor von Nyssa. Untersuchungen zum Ursprung der 'physischen' Erlösungslehre.* Philosophia Patrum 2. Leiden, 1974.
Georgij Florovsky. *Creation and Redemption.* Belmont, Mass., 1976.

CHRIST-LIGHT, p. 35

Margherite Harl. *Origène et la fonction révélatrice du Verbe Incarné,* Pattistica Sorbonensia 2. Paris, 1958.
Erich Fascher. 'Der Logos-Christus als göttlicher Lehrer bei Clemens von Alexandrien', in *Studien zum Neuen Testament und Patristik,* TU 77:193–207. Berlin, 1961.
M. Costanza. 'Christus, het licht der wereld, gezien in de Byzantijnse liturgie', *Het Christelijke Oosten* 14 (1961–62) 51–82.
Friedrich Normann. *Christos Didaskalos.* Münster, 1967.
Jean Kirchmeyer. 'Grecque (Église)', DS 6 (1967) 824–27: Libération de l'ignorance.
Charles Traets. *Voir Jesus et le Père en lui selon l'évangile de saint Jean.* Rome, 1967.
Carlo Skalicky. *La gloria nel vangelo di Giovanni.* Rome, 1970.

CHRIST-UNIFIER, p. 36

F. Wagner. *Der Christ und die Welt nach Clemens von Alexandrien, Ein noch unveraltetes Problem in der altchristlichen Beleuchtung.* Göttingen, 1903.
Wladimir Szylkarski. *Solowjews Philosophie der All-Einheit.* Kauna, 1932.
Franz Mussner. *Christus, das All und die Kirche.* Trier, 1955.
Karl Vladimir Truhlar. *Teilhard und Solowjew, Dichtung und religiöse Erfahrung.* Freiburg-im-Br., 1966.
Tomaš Špidlík. 'Il Christo nel pensiero di Basilio Magno', *Bessarione* 3 (Rome, 1982) 91–103.

CHRIST-MEDIATOR, p. 36

Franz Josef Schierse. 'Médiateur', EF 3: 46–9.
Karl Theodor Schaefer and Joseph Ratzinger. 'Mittler', LThK² (1962) LThK² 7:489–502.
Grégoire de Nazianze, 83ff.

DEVOTION TO CHRIST, p. 37

P. J. Madosz. 'El amor a Jesuchristo en la Iglesia de los Mártires', *Estudios Eclesiasticos* 12 (1933) 313–44.
E. Grébaut. 'La prière "'Eqabani" ou les litanies du Christ', *Orientalia* 4 (1935) 426–40.
Sévérien Salaville. 'Christus in Orientalium pietate', *Ephemerides liturgicae* 52 (1938) 221–36.
──────────. 'Office du Très Doux Jésus, antérieur au *Jubilus* de saint Bernard', RAM 25 (1949) 247–59.
Aloysius Lieske. *Die Theologie der Logosmystik bei Origenes.* Münster, 1938.
──────────. 'Die Theologie der Christusmystik Gregors von Nyssa', *Zeitschrift für katholische Theologie* 70 (1948) 49–93, 129–68, 315–40.
Sergei Bulgakov. *Du verbe incarné.* Paris, 1943.
Léon Cristiani. 'Saint Ignace d'Antioche, Sa vie d'intimité avec Jésus-Christ', RAM 25 (1949) 109–16.
Bernhard Schultze. *Russische Denker, ihre Stellung zu Christus, Kirche und Papsttum.* Vienna, 1950. *Pensatori russi di fronte a Cristo.* 2 vols., Florence, 1947–49.
Frédéric Bertrand. *Mystique de Jésus chez Origène.* Théologie 23. Paris, 1951.
Irénée Hausherr. *Noms du Christ et voies d'oraison.* OCA 157. Rome, 1960. Translated by Charles Cummings, *The Name of Jesus,* CS 44, Kalamazoo, 1978.
Jean [John] Meyendorff. *Le Christ dans la théologie byzantine.* Paris, 1969. Translated by Yves Dubois, *Christ in Eastern Christian Thought.* Crestwood, New York, 1975.
Paul Evdokimov. *Le Christ dans la pensée russe.* Théologie sans frontières 14. Paris, 1970.
Tomaš Špidlík. 'Gesu nella pietà dei Cristiani Orientali', in E. Ancilli, *Gesu Cristo — mistero e presenza:* 385–408. Roma: Teresianum, 1971.

Bibliography

THE DEVOTION TO THE HUMANITY OF CHRIST, p. 38

Irénée Noye. 'Humanité du Christ, au temps des Pères de l'Église', DS 7/1 (1969) 1033–43.
Paul Agaësse. 'La contemplation de l'humanité du Christ', *ibid.*, col. 1043–53.
Tomaš Špidlík. 'Gesu Cristo "Uomo dei dolori" nell'arte iconografica orientale e occidentale', *Asprenas* 25 (1978), 431–36.

THE IMITATION OF CHRIST, p. 39

Irénée Hausherr. 'L'imitation de Jésus-Christ dans la spiritualité byzantine', in *Mélanges ... F. Cavallera:* 231–59. Toulouse, 1948, OCA 183 (1969) 217–45.
S. Agouris. 'The Imitation of Christ' [in Greek], *Ecclesia* 41 (1964), 168–72, 200–204.
Grégoire de Nazianze, 107ff.
Edouard Cothenet. 'Imitation du Christ, dans L'Écriture', DS 7/2 (1971) 1536–62 (bibliography).
Étienne Ledeur. 'Imitation du Christ, Tradition spirituelle', DS 7/2:1562–87 (bibliography).
Pierre Adnès. 'Imitation du Christ, Réflexions théologiques', DS 7/2:1587–97.

GOD, p. 42

G. L. Prestige. *God in Patristic Thought.* London, 1952.
A. J. Festugière. *La révélation d'Hermès Trismégiste,* vol. II: *Le Dieu cosmique.* Paris, 1949.
Peter Nemeshegui. 'Le Dieu d'Origène et le Dieu de L'Ancient Testament', *Nouvelle Revue Théologique* 80 (1958) 495–509.
―――――. *La Paternité de Dieu chez Origène,* Bibliothèque de théologie, Histoire de la théologie, 2. Tournai, 1960.
Juan Alfaro. 'Dieu-Père', EF 1:355–64.
Bernhard Schultze. *Das Gottesproblem in der Osttheologie.* Aevum Christianum. Münster, 1967.
Wilhelm Maas. *Unveränderlichkeit Gottes. Zum Verhältnis griechisch-philosophischer und christlicher Gotteslehre.* Munich―Paderborn-Vienna, 1974.
W. Marchel and J. Ansaldi. 'Paternité de Dieu', DS 12: 413–37.

THE MOST HOLY TRINITY, p. 44

Pavel Al. Florenskij. *Stolp i utverždĕnie istny* [*The Pillar and Foundation of Truth*], 593ff. Moscow, 1914.
Irénée Chevalier. 'La présence de la Trinité par la sanctification, d'après les Pères grecs', *La vie spirituelle* 55 (1938) 153–86.
Paul Galtier. *L'habitation en nous des trois Personnes.* Rome, 1928.
―――――. *De SS Trinitate in se et in nobis.* Rome, 1953.
Gervais Aeby. *Les missions divines de saint Justin à Origène.* Freiburg, Switz., 1958.

Jean Daniélou. *La Trinité et le mystère de l'existence*. Brussels, 1968.
Philippe Ferlay. *Prêcher la Trinité, Affirmation trinitaire et prédication du salut*. Lyon, 1973.
Josef Rius-Camps. *El dinamismo trinitario en la divinización de los seres racionales según Origenes*, OCA 188. Rome, 1970.
Bertrand de Margerie. *La Trinité chrétienne dans l'histoire*, Théologie historique 31 Paris, 1975.

DEIFICATION, p. 45

Jules Gross. *La divinisation du chrétien d'après les Pères grecs. Contribution à la doctrine de la grâce*. Paris, 1938.
_____. 'Die Vergöttlichung des Christen nach den griechischen Vätern', ZAM 14 (1939) 79-94.
Ephraem Hendrikx. 'De leer van de vergoddelijking in het oud-christelijk geloofsbewustzijn', *Genade en Kerk, Studies ten dienste van het gesprek Rome-Reformatie*: 101-54. Utrecht, 1953.
Archimandrite Cyprien [Kern]. '"Homotheos" et ses synonymes dans la littérature byzantine', in *Église et les Églises* (1054-1954), vol. II:15-28. Chevetogne, 1955.
M. Aubineau. 'Incorruptiblité et divinisation selon saint Irénée', *Recherches de science religieuse* 44 (1956) 25-52.
I. H. Dalmais and Gustave Bardy. 'Divinisation', DS 3 (1957) 1376-98.
J.G. Remmers. *De vergoddelijkte mens in de spiritualiteit van het christelijk oosten*, Theologische week over Mens. Nijmegen, 1958.
Panagiotis Bratsiotis. *Die Lehre der orthodoxen Kirche über die Theosis des Menschen*. Brussels, 1961.
G. I. Mantzarides. *The Doctrine of Man's Deification in Gregory Palamas* [in Greek]. Thessalonica, 1963.
Lars Thunberg. *Microcosm and Mediator. The Theological Anthropology of Maximus the Confessor*. Lund, 1965.
Elias D. Moutsoulas. *The Incarnation of the Word and the Deification of Man According to the Doctrine of Gregory of Nyssa* [in Greek]. Athens, 1965.
David L. Balas. '"*Metousía Theou.*" *Man's Participation in God's Perfections According to Saint Gregory of Nyssa*', Studia Anselmiana 55. Rome, 1966.
Jean Kirchmeyer. 'Grecque (Église)', DS 6 (1967) 840-41 (bibliography).
Myrrha Lot-Borodine. *La déification de l'homme selon la doctrine des Pères grecs*. Paris, 1970 (articles published in *Revue de l'histoire des religions*, 1932-33).
Antonio Orbe. 'Los valentinianos y el matrimonio espiritual', *Gregorianum* 58 (1977) 5-53.

ADOPTIVE SONSHIP, p. 47

Adolf Harnack. *Die Terminologie der Wiedergeburt und verwandter Erlebnisse in der ältesten Kirche*, TU 42.3. Leipzig, 1918.
Karl Rahner. 'Die Gottesgeburt, Die Lehre der Kirchenväter von der Geburt Christi im Herzen des Gläubigen', *Zeitschrift für katholische Theologie* 59 (1935) 333-418.

Louis Janssens. 'Notre filiation divine d'après saint Cyrille d'Alexandrie', *Ephemerides Theologicae Lovanienses* 15 (1938) 233-78.
S. Zedda. *L'adozione a figli di Dio e lo Spirito Santo*. Rome, 1952.
Edouard des Places. *Syngeneia, La parenté de l'homme avec Dieu d'Homère à la Patristique*. Paris, 1964.
Charles Baumgartner. 'Grâce', DS 6 (1967) 715-21.

THE IMAGE OF GOD, p. 55

Augustin Mayer. *Das Gottesbild im Menschen nach Clemens von Alexandrien*, Studia Anselmiana 15, Rome, 1942.
Roger Leys. *L'image de Dieu chez saint Grégoire de Nysse. Esquisse d'une doctrine*, Museum Lessianum, Section théologique 49. Brussels, 1951.
Panagiotis Bratsiotis. 'Genesis 1.26 in der orthodoxen Theologie', in *Evangelische Theologie* 11 (1951-52) 289-97 (in Greek in *Orthodoxia* 27 [1952] 359-72.
Hilda C. Graef. 'L'image de Dieu et la structure de l'âme', in *La vie spirituelle*, Suppl., 22 (1952) 331-39.
R. Bernhard. *L'image de Dieu d'après S. Athanase*, Théologie 25. Paris 1952.
Hubert Merki. *Homoiosis Theo. Von der platonischen Angleichung an Gott zur Gottähnlichkeit bei Gregor von Nyssa*, Paradosis 7. Freiburg, Switz., 1952.
J. Lemaitre (I. Hausherr). 'Contemplation', DS 2/2 (1953 1828-30.
James J. Meany. *The Image of God in Man according to the Doctrine of Saint John Damascene*. Manila, 1954.
Pierre-Thomas Camelot. 'La théologie de l'image de Dieu', *Revue des sciences philosophiques et théologiques* 40 (1956) 443-71.
N. Vornicescu. 'The Teaching of St. Gregory of Nyssa About Image and Resemblance' [in Rumanian]. *Studii teologice* (Bucharest) 8 (1956) 595-602.
Henri Crouzel. *Théologie de l'image de Dieu chez Origène*, Théologie 34. Paris, 1956.
Walter Burghardt. *The Image of God in Man according to Cyril of Alexandria*. Maryland, 1957.
Michele Pellegrino. 'La spiritualità dell'immagine nei Padri della Chiesa', *Asprenas* 5 (1958) 324-47.
I. Turcu. 'The Notion of Image and Its Soteriological Import' (in Rumanian), *Orthodoxia* 3 (1959) 414-29.
W. R. Jenkinson. 'The Image and the Likeness of God in Man in the Eighteen Lectures on Credo of Cyril of Jerusalem (c. 315-87)', *Ephemerides Theologicae Lovanienses* 40 (1964) 48-71.
Jean Kirchmeyer. 'Grecque (Église): L'image et la ressemblance', DS 6 (1967) 813-22.
Vladimir Lossky. *In the Image and Likeness of God*, 125-39. New York, 1974.
Peter Schwanz. *Imago Dei as christologisch-anthropologisches Problem in der Geschichte der alten Kirche von Paulus bis Clemens von Alexandrien*. Halle: Saale, 1970.

THE NATURAL LIFE, p. 62

Joannes Stelzenberger. *Die Beziehungen der frühchristilichen Sittenlehre zur Ethik der Stoa*. ch. IV, pp. 158ff. Munich, 1932.
Henri de Lubac. *Surnaturel*. Paris, 1946.

———. *Le mystère du surnaturel*. Paris, 1965. English translation by R. Sheed, *The Mystery of the Supernatural*. New York, 1967.
A. J. Festugière. *L'enfant d'Agrigente*. Paris, 1960.
Irénée Hausherr. *Philautie: De la tendresse pour soi à la charité selon Saint Maxime le Confesseur*. OCA 137: pp. 135ff. Rome, 1952.
Lars Thunberg. *Microcosm and Mediator; The Theological Anthropology of Maximus the Confessor*, pp. 92ff. Lund, 1965.
Théophane le Reclus, OCA 172, pp. 156ff. Rome, 1965.
H. Kuhn and S. Otto. 'Nature', EF 3 (1967) 189–200.

THE HAPPY LIFE, p. 64

C. H. Turner. 'Makarios as a Technical Term'. *The Journal of Theological Studies* 23 (1922) 31–5.
Jozef Ziegler. *Dulcedo Dei. Ein Beitrag zur Theologie der griechischen und lateinischen Bibel*. Münster, 1937.
R. A. Gauthier. 'Eudémonisme', DS 2/2 (1961) 1660–74.
Aimé Solignac. 'Jubilation', DS 8 (1972) 1471–78.
François Bussini. 'Joie', DS 8:1236–56.
Riccardo Terzoli. *Il tema della beatitudine nei Padri siri, Presente e futuro della salvezza*. Rome, 1972.

ETERNAL LIFE, p. 65

Rudolf Bultmann. 'Zaō, Zoē', in Kittel 2 (1935 and 1957):833–44, 850–53, 856–74.
Gerhard Gruber. 'Zoē. Wesen, Stufen, und Mitteilung des wahren Lebens bei Origenes', *Münchener Theologische Studien, Systematische Abteilung*, 23. 1962.

ESCHATOLOGY, p. 65

Nikolaj [Nicolas] S. Arseniev. *Duša pravoslavija. Radost' voskresenija i preobraženije tvari* [The Soul of Orthodoxy. The Joy of the Resurrection and the Transfiguration of the Creatures]. Novyi Sad, 1927.
———. *Ostkirche und Mystik*. (2nd ed.), Munich, 1943. Translated into English by A. Chambers, *Mysticism and the Eastern Church*. Crestwood, New York, 1979.
S. Zankow. *Das orthodoxe Christentum des Ostens, sein Wesen und seine Gestalt*. Berlin, 1928.
Louis Bouyer. *Christianisme et eschatologie*. Paris, 1948.
———. *Humain ou chrétien?* Paris, 1958.
Hermegild Biedermann. *Der eschatologische Zug in der östkirchlichen Frömmigkeit*, Das östliche Christentum, N.F. 8. Würzburg, 1949.
Franz Jozef Schierse. 'Eschatologismus', LThk² 3 (1959) 1098–99.
Garcia M. Colombás. *Paradis et vie angélique*. Paris, 1961.
C. Berset. *Incarnation ou Eschatologie?* Paris, 1964.

Jean Leclercq. *Le défi de la contemplation*. Paris, 1970. [*The Challenge of the Contemplative Life*, forthcoming – ed.]
T. Alvares. 'Escatologismo', DESp I:696–98.

THE SALVATION OF THE SOUL, p. 66

Wilhelm Koester and Joseph Ratzinger. 'Heil', LThK² 5 (1960) 76–80.
Ghislain Lafon. *Essai sur la signification du salut*. Paris, 1964.
Wolfgang Trilling and Otto Semmelroth. 'Salut', EF 4 (1967) 175–86.
Colomban Lesquivit and Pierre Grelot. 'Salut', VTB, col. 1187–92.
Augustin George. 'Luc (saint)', DS 9 (1976) 1106–08: Le salut de Dieu: 1108–20: La voie du salut.

PROGRESS IN THE SPIRITUAL LIFE, p. 68

Walther Völker. *Das Vollkommenheitsideal des Origenes*. Tübingen, 1931, p.110ff.
_____. *Fortschritt und Vollendung bei Philo von Alexandrien. Eine Studie zur Geschichte der Frömmigkeit*. Leipzig, 1938.
Emile Bertraud and André Rayez. 'Echelle spirituelle', DS 4/1 (1960) 62–86.
Paul Evdokimov. *Les âges de la vie spirituelle, des Pères du desert à nos jours*. Paris, 1965. Translated into English by Sister Gertrude, *The Struggle with God*. New Jersey, 1966.
Jean Daniélou. *L'être et le temps chez Grégoire de Nysse*, pp. 154ff. Leiden, 1970.

PERFECTION, p. 69

Nicolas Fonck. 'Perfection chrétienne', DThC 12/1 (1933) 1219–51.
R. Newton Flew. *The Idea of Perfection in Christian Theology*. London, 1934.
P. J. du Plessis. *Teleios. The Idea of Perfection in the New Testament*. Kampen, 1959.
Karl Prümm. 'Das neutestamentliche Sprach-und Begriffsproblem der Vollkommenheit', *Biblica* 44 (1963) 86–92.
Albert Vanhoye. 'Accomplir', VTB (1970) 8–11.

THE CONSCIOUSNESS OF GRACE, p. 71

William James. *The Varieties of Religious Experience*. London, 1902.
Jean Mouroux. *L'expérience chrétienne, Introduction à une théologie*, Théologie, 26. Paris, 1952.
Irénée Hausherr. *Direction spirituelle en Orient autrefois*, OCA 144: pp. 39ff Rome, 1955.
Johannes B. Lotz. 'Metaphysische und religiöse Erfahrung', *Archivio di filosofia* 25 (1956) 79–121.
Augustin Léonard. 'Expérience spirituelle', DS 4/2 (1961) 2004–26.

J. Kalogirou. 'Christianity as an Objective and Subjective Confirmation of Human Religious Sentiment' (In Greek), *He Athonikē Politeia:* 256-79. Thessalonica, 1963.
Thomas̆ Špidlík. *La doctrine spirituelle de Théophane le Reclus. Le Coeur et l'esprit,* OCA 172: pp. 94ff. Rome, 1965.
J. A. Cuttat. 'Expérience chrétienne et spiritualité orientale', in A. Ravier, ed., *La Mystique et les mystiques:* pp. 825-1020. Paris-Tournai: Desclée de Brouwer, 1965.
D. P. Miquel. 'Les caractères de l'expérience spirituelle selon le Pseudo-Macaire', *Irēnikon* 39 (1966) 497-513.

THE MESSALIANS, p. 72

Theodoretus. *Historia Ecclesiastica,* IV. 11. PG. 82:1142-46.
Epiphanius. *Panarion* 80. PG 42:755-62.
Georges Bareille. 'Euchites', DThC 5/2 (1913) 1454-65.
Irénée Hausherr. 'L'erreur fondamentale et la logique du Messalianisme', OCP 1 (1935) 238-60. Rpt. in *Études de spiritualité orientale,* OCA 183. (Rome, 1969) 64-96.
Friedrich Doerr. *Diadochus von Photike und die Messalianer.* Munich, 1937.
Hermann Dörries. *Symeon von Mesopotamien. Die Ueberlieferung der messalianischen 'Makarios' Schriften,* TU 55/1. Leipzig, 1941.
Werner Jaeger. *Gregory of Nyssa and Macarius.* Leiden, 1954.
Alfons Kemmer. 'Gregor von Nyssa und Ps. Makarius. Der Messalianismus im Licht östlicher Herzensmystik', in Basilius Steidle, ed., *Antonius Magnus Eremita, Studia Anselmiana* 38:268-82. Rome, 1956.
_____. 'Messalianismus bei Gregor von Nyssa und Pseudo-Makarius'. *Revue bénédictine* 72 (1962) 278-306.
G. Folliet. 'Des moines euchites à Carthage en 400-401', *Studia Patristica* 2, TU 64:386-99.
Hugo Rahner. 'Messalianismus', LThK² 7 (1962) 319-20.
Jean Gribomont. 'Le *De instituto christiano* et le Messalianisme de Grégoire de Nysse'. *Studia Patristica* 5, TU 80:312-22. Berlin, 1962.
_____. 'Le monachisme au IVᵉ s. en Asie Mineure: de Gangre au Messalianisme', *Studia Patristica* 2, TU 64:400-26.
Reinhart Staats. *Gregor von Nyssa und die Messalianer.* Berlin, 1968.
Antoine Guillaumont. 'Messaliens', DS 10 (1980) 1074-83.

VISIONS, p. 73

Louis Monden. 'Erscheinungen', LThK² 3 (1959) 1047-50.
Elpidius Pax. 'Vision. In der Bibel', LThK² 10 (1965) 811-12.
Ernst Benz. *Die Vision.* Stuttgart, 1969.
Ermanno Ancilli. 'Visioni a rivelazioni', DESp 2 (1975) 2008-12.

MARTYRDOM, p. 75

Marcel Viller. 'Martyre et perfection', RAM 6 (1925) 3-25, 105-42.
_____. *La spiritualité des premiers siècles chrétiens:* 15-24. Paris, 1930.

Marcel Viller and Karl Rahner. *Aszese und Mystik in der Väterzeit:* 29–40. Freiburg-im-Breisgau, 1939.
Hans von Campenhausen. *Die Idee des Martyriums in der alten Kirche.* Göttingen, 1936.
Edward Malone. *The Monk and the Martyr.* Washington, 1950.
_____ . 'The Monk and Martyr', *Studia Anselmiana* 38:201–28. Rome, 1956.
François Bourassa. 'Excellence de la virginité., *Sciences ecclésiastiques* 5 (1933) 29–41 (martyrdom of conscience).
Michele Pellegrino. *La spiritualità del martirio. Il Martire e Cristo.* Turin, 1957.
Marc Lods. *Confesseurs et martyrs, successeurs des prophètes dans l'Église des trois premiers siècles,* Cahiers théologiques 41. Neuchâtel-Paris, 1958.
Prosper Hartmann. 'Origène et la théologie du martyre d'après le Protreptikos de 235', *Ephemerides Theologicae Lovanienses* 34 (1958) 774–824.
Uta Ranke-Heinemann. *Das frühe Mönchtum. Seine Motive nach Selbstzeugnissen.* Essen, 1964.
Jean Kirchmeyer. 'Grecque (Église)', DS 6 (1967) 859ff. (bibliography).
W. Rordorf and Aimé Solignac. 'Martyre', DS 10 (1980) 718–37.

THE GNOSTIC, p. 76

Rudolf Bultmann. *'Gignōskō, gnōsis'.* Kittel 1 (1953) 688–719. English transl., 'Gnosis', *Bible Key Words,* vol. 5. London, 1952.
Walter Völker. *Der wahre Gnostiker nach Clemens Alexandrinus,* TU 57. Berlin-Leipzig, 1952.
Louis Bouyer. 'Gnosis. Le sens orthodoxe de l'expression jusqu'aux Pères alexandrins', *The Journal of Theological Studies,* New Series 4 (1953) 188–203.
J. Lemaitre, R. Roques, M. Viller. 'Contemplation: Étude de vocabulaire,' DS 2/2 (1953) 1762–87.
John E. Steely. *Gnosis. The Doctrine of Christian Perfection in the Writings of Clemens of Alexandria.* Louisville, 1954.
Henri Crouzel. 'Le vrai gnostique de Clément d'Alexandrie d'après W.Völker.' RAM 31 (1955) 77–83.
Carstein Colpe, Ernst Haenchen, Georg Kretchmar. 'Gnosis', *Die Religion in Geschichte der Gegenwart:* col. 1648–61. Tübingen, 1958.
R. M. Grant. *Gnosticism and Early Christianity.* London, 1959.
Karl Rahner. 'Gnosis', LThK² 4 (1960) 1019–21.
Henri Crouzel. *Origène et la 'connaissance mystique'.* Bruges-Paris, 1961.
G. W. H. Lampe. *A Patristic Greek Lexicon.* Fasc. 2: col. 315: *gignōskō;* col. 318–20: *gnōsis-gnōstos.* Oxford, 1962.
Étienne Cornélis. 'Le gnosticisme', DS 6 (1967) 523–41.
P. Th. Camelot. 'Gnose chrétienne'. DS 6:509–23.
_____ . *Foi et Gnose: Introduction à l'étude de la connaissance mystique chez Clément d'Alexandrie.* Paris, 1945.
Reinhard Wagner. *Die Gnosis von Alexandria. Eine Frage des frühen Christentums an die Gegenwart.* Stuttgart, 1968.
Manlio Simonetti. *Testi gnostici cristiani.* Bari, 1970.

CHRISTIAN ANTHROPOLOGY, p. 87

A. Hermegild M. Biedermann. 'Das Menschenbild bei Symeon dem Jüngeren, dem Theologen (949–1022)', *Das Oestliche Christentum*, Neue Folge 9. Würzburg, 1949.
H. Karpp. 'Probleme altchristlicher Anthropologie, biblische Anthropologie und philosophische Psychologie bei den Kirchenvätern des dritten Jahrhunderts', *Beiträge zur Forderung christlicher Theologie* 44/3. Gütersloh, 1950.
Archimandrite Kiprian [Kern]. *Antropologija sv. Grigoria Palamy* [The Anthropology of Gregory Palamas]. Paris, 1950.
B. Zeňkovsky. *Das Bild vom Menschen in der Ostkirche*. Stuttgart, 1951.
Nikolaj Berdiaev. *Le sens de la création. Un essai de justification de l'homme*, Textes et Études philosophiques. Bruges, 1955. English translation by D. A. Lowrie, *The Meaning of the Creative Act*. London, 1955.
Hermann M. Diepen. *Aux origines de l'anthropologie de saint Cyrille d'Alexandrie*. Bruges, 1957.
Antonio Orbe. 'El hombre ideal en la teología de S. Ireneo', *Gregorianum* 43 (1962) 449–91.
Paul Krüger. *Der erlöste Mensch in der Welt. Grundzüge einer Anthropologie im Lichte der morgenländischen Theologie*, Sophia 2. Freiburg-im-Breisgau, 1962.
Jacques Dupuis. *'L'esprit de l'homme'. Étude sur L'anthropologie religieuse d'Origène*. Desclée de Brouwer, 1967.
E.A. Davids. *Das Bild vom neuen Menschen*. Salzburg-Munich, 1968.
S. De Boer. *De antropologie van Gregorius van Nyssa*. Assen, 1968.
J. Roldanus. *Le Christ et l'homme dans la théologie d'Athanase d'Alexandrie*. Leiden, 1968.
Antonio Orbe. *Antropologia de san Ireneo*. Madrid, 1969.
B. Zeňkovsky and H. Perzold. 'Das Bild des Menschen im Lichte der orthodoxen Anthropologie', *Orthodoxe Beiträge* 4. Marburg, 1969.
Bernhard Schultze. 'Byzantinisch-patristische ostkirchliche Anthropologie (Photius und Joannes von Damaskus)', OCP 38 (1972) 172–94.
Théologie de l'homme. Essais d'anthropologie orthodoxe (J. Coman, P. Nellas, D. Staniloe, Ch. Yannaras). *Contacts*, n. 84, vol. 25 (1973).
Tomaš Špidlík. 'Antropologia dell' Oriente cristiano', E. Ancilla, ed., in *Temi di antropologia teologica*: 377–402. Rome, 1981.

SELF-KNOWLEDGE, p. 87

Pavel Al. Florenskij. *Voprosy religioznago samopoznanija* [Problems of Self-knowledge from the Religious Point of View]. Sergiev Posad, 1907.
Stanislas Giet. *Les idées et l'action sociales de saint Basile*: pp. 21ff. Paris, 1941.
A. J. Festugière. *La révélation d'Hermès Trismégiste*, Vol. II, pp. 575ff. (Philo). Paris, 1944–54.
Louis de Bazelaire. 'Connaissance de soi'. DS 2/2 (1953) 1511–43.
Jean Meyendorff. 'Le thème du "retour en soi" dans la doctrine palamite du XIVe siècle'. *Revue d'histoire des religions* 145 (1954) 188–206.
Henri Charles Puech. 'Les thèmes gnostiques se rassembler en soi, se concentrer sur soi'. *Annuaire de l'École pratique des Hautes-Études*, Section des Sciences religieuses. (1962–63) 84–86.

Pierre Courcelle. *Connais-toi toi-même, de Socrate à saint Bernard*, Études augustiniennes. Paris. 1975.

HUMILITY, p. 88

Pierre Adnès. 'Humilité', DS 7/1 (1969) 1136-87 (bibliography, 1186ff.)

TRICHOTOMY, p. 91

A. J. Festugière. 'La trichotomie de 1 Thess. 5.23 et la philosophie grecque', RSR 20 (1930) 385-415.
_____. *L'idéal des Grecs et l'Évangile:* 196-220. Paris, 1932.
Gerard Verbeke. *L'évolution de la doctrine du Pneuma du stoicisme à saint Augustin.* Paris-Louvain, 1945.
Edward Schweizer. 'Pneuma', Kittel 6 (1959) 394-449.
Cornelis A. Van Peursen. *Leib, Seele, Geist.* Gütersloh, 1959.
Jean Gribomont. 'Ésprit saint chez les pères grecs', DS 4/2 (1961) 1264ff.
Lars Thunberg. *Microcosm and Mediator. The Theological Anthropology of Maximus the Confessor.* Lund, 1965.
Tomaš Špidlík. *La doctrine spirituelle de Théophane le Reclus. Le coeur et l'Ésprit,* OCA 172: pp. 3ff. Rome, 1965.

THE SPIRITUAL SENSE, p. 94

Karl Rahner. 'Le début d'une doctrine des cinq sens spirituels chez Origène', RAM 13 (1932) 113-45.
J. Lemaitre. 'Contemplation', DS 21 (1953) 1843-45.
Nos sens et Dieu. Les Études Carmelitaines. Desclée de Brouwer, 1954.
Jean Châtillon. 'Dulcedo, dulcedo Dei', DS 3 (1957) 1777-95.
Pierre Adnès. 'Goût spirituel', DS 6 (1967) 626-44.
Donatien Mollat. 'S. Jean Evangéliste', DS 8:192-248: col. 217ff. : L'éveil des sens spirituels.

CONSCIENCE, p. 95

M. Waldmann. 'Synteresis oder Syneidesis?', *Theologische Quartalschrift* 119 (1938) 332-71.
Jacques Dupont. 'Aux origines de la notion chrétienne de conscience morale', *Studia Hellenistica* 5 (1948) 119-53.
René Carpentier. 'Conscience', DS 2/2 (1953) 1548-75.
L. Brunschwigg. *Le progrès de la conscience dans la philosophie occidentale.* 2 vols. 2nd edn., Paris, 1953.
C. A. Pierce. *Conscience in the New Testament.* London, 1955.
Philippe Delhaye. *La conscience morale du chrétien.* Tournai, 1964. (with bibliography).
Johannes Stelzenberger. 'Ueber Syneidesis bei Klemens von Alexandria', *Festgabe für Seppelt*, 27-33. Munich, 1953.

———. 'Conscientia bei Tertullianus', *Vitae et Veritati. Festgabe für Karl Adam.* 28–43. Düsseldorf, 1956.
———. *Conscientia bei Augustinus.* Paderborn, 1959.
———. *Syneidesis im Neuen Testament.* Paderborn, 1961.
———. *Syneidesis bei Origenes. Abhandlungen zur Moraltheologie.* Paderborn, 1963.
———. 'Conscience', *Encyclopédie de la foi* I (1967) 255–66.

THE SOUL, p. 96

Erwin Rohde. *Psyche, Seelenkult und Unsterblichkeitsglaube der Griechen.* Freiburg-im-Breisgau, 1890–94. English translation by W. B. Hillis, *Psyche: The Cult of Souls and Belief in Immortality among the Greeks.* New York, 1925.
Vasilij V. Zeňkovskii. *Ob ierarchičeskoj stroje duši* [The Hierarchical Structure of the Soul], in *Naučn. Trudy Russk. Nar. Universiteta v Prage.* Vol. II. 1929.
Franz Rüsche. *Blut, Leben und Seele, Ihr Verhältnis nach Auffassung der griechischen und hellenistischen Antike, der Bibel und der alten Alexandrinischen Theologen*, Studien zur Geschichte und Kultur des Altertums. Ergänzungsband. Paderborn, 1930.
———. *Seelenpneuma. Seine Entwickelung von der Hauchseele zur Geistseele.* The same collection, 18/3. 1933.
———. 'Pneuma, Seele und Geist', *Theologie und Glaube* 23 (1932) 606–25.
Leonce Reypens. 'Ame', DS 1 (1937) 433–63.
Gaston Rotureau. 'Ame', *Catholicisme* 1 (1948) 422–34.
A. J. Festugière. *La révélation d'Hermès Trismégiste* III: *Les doctrines de l'âme.* Paris, 1953.
Antonio Orbe. 'Homo nuper factus', *Gregorianum* 46 (1965) 481–544.
Jacques Dupuis. *'L'Ésprit de l'homme' Étude sur l'anthropologie religieuse d'Origène.* Desclée de Brouwer, 1967.

IMMORTALITY, p. 97

Michel Aubineau. 'Incorruptibilité et divinisation selon saint Irénée', RSR 46 (1956) 25–52.
G. Langevin. 'Le thème de l'incorruptibilité dans le commentaire de saint Cyrille d'Alexandrie sur l'Évangile selon saint Jean', *Sciences ecclésiastiques* 8 (1956) 295–316.
Walter J. Burghardt. *The Image of God in Man according to Cyril of Alexandria:* 84–104. Woodstock, 1957.
José M. Arroniz. 'La immortalidad como deificación del hombre en S. Ireneo', *Scriptorium victoriense* 8 (1961) 262–87.
———. 'La salvación de la carne en S. Ireneo', *Ibid.*, 12 (1965) 7–29.
Gerhard Gruber. *Zoē. Wesen, Stufen und Mitteilung des wahren Lebens bei Origenes.* Munich, 1962.
Jaroslav Pelikan. *The Shape of Death: Life, Death and Immortality in the Early Fathers.* London, 1962.
La Résurrection de la chair (a collective work): 165–262: patristic doctrine. Paris, 1962.

F. Refoulé. 'Immortalité de l'âme et résurrection de la chair', *Revue de l'histoire des religions* 163 (1963) 11–52.
Jean Kirchmeyer. 'Grecque (Église)', DS 6 (1967) 827ff.

FREEDOM, p. 98

M. Müller. 'Freiheit, Ueber Autonomie und Gnade von Paulus bis Clemens von Alexandrien', *Zeitschrift für die neutestamentische Wissenschaft* 25 (1926) 177–236.
Heinrich Schlier. 'Eleutheros', in Kittel 2 (1935) 484–500 (bibliography).
Nikolaj Berdiaev. *De l'esclavage et de la liberté de l'homme*. Paris, 1946, 1963 (in Russian 1939). Translated into English by R. M. French, *Slavery and Freedom*. London, 1944.
Jérome Gaïth. *La conception de la liberté chez Grégoire de Nysse*, Études de philosophie médievale 43. Paris, 1953.
A. Zeoli. 'Libero arbitrio, grazia e predestinazione nel pensiero di Clemente Alessandrino', *Humanitas* 9 (1954) 851–54.
H. Jaeger. 'Parrhesia et fiducia', *Studia Patristica* I, TU 63 (1967) 221–39.
Michel Spanneut. *Le stoïcisme des Pères de l'Église;* 236–41. Paris, 1957.
Johannes Baptist Metz. 'Freiheit als philosophisch-theologisches Grenzproblem', *Gott in Welt* (*Festgabe für Karl Rahner*) 1:287–319. Freiburg-im-Br., 1964.
Peter Bläser. 'Freiheit', LThK² 4 (2nd ed. 1960) 329–31.
Heinrich Schlier. 'La loi parfaite de liberté', in *Le Temps de l'Église:* 201–11. Tournai, 1961.
René Schaerer. *L'homme devant ses choix dans la tradition grecque*. Louvain, 1965.
Gustav Siewerth, G. Richter, J. B. Metz. 'Liberté', in *Encyclopédia de la foi* 2 Paris, 1967 (bibliography).
Tomaš Špidlík. 'La libertà come riflesso del mistero trinitario nei Padri greci', *Augustinianum* 13 (1973) 515–23.
Edouard Pousset, Jacques Guillet, Aimé Solignac, and Paul Agaësse. 'Liberté', libération', DS 9 (1976) 780–838.

THE HEART, p. 103

Pavel Florenskij. *Stolp i utverždĕnie istiny* [*The Pillar and Foundation of Truth*]: pp. 267ff. Moscow, 1914.
Boris Petr Vyšeslavcev. *Serdce v christianskoj i indijskoj mistikĕ* [The Heart in Christian and Indian Mysticism). Paris, 1929.
Vasilij V. Zeňkovskij. *Ob ierarchičeskom stroje duši* [The Hierarchical Structure of the Heart], in *Naučn. Trudy Russk. Nar. Universiteta v Prage* II. 1929.
Friedrich Baumgärtel and Johann Behm. '*Kardia*', in Kittel 3 (1938, 1957) 611–16.
Myrrha Lot-Borodine. 'La doctrine du coeur théandrique et son symbolisme dans l'oeuvre de Nicolas Cabasilas', *Irēnikon* 13 (1936) 652–73.
Pierre Pourrat. 'Affective (spiritualité)' DS 1 (1937) 240–46.
Alfonso Čuk. *La Chiesa russa e il culto del S. Cuore*. Gorizia, 1941.
E. Von Ivánka. 'Apex mentis', *Zeitschrift für Theologie und Kirche* 72 (1950) 129–76.

Le coeur. Études carmélitaines. Desclée de Brouwer, 1950.
Auguste Hamon. 'Coeur (Sacré)', DS 2/1 (1953) 1023–46.
A. Lefèvre. 'Cor et cordis affectus. Usage biblique', DS 2/1:2278–81.
A. Guillaumont. 'Le coeur chez les spirituels grecs à l'époque ancienne', DS 2/1 2281–88.
Tomaš Špidlík. *La doctrine spirituelle de Théophane le Reclus. Le Coeur et l'Ésprit*, OCA 172. Rome, 1965.
——————. 'The heart in Russian Spirituality'. *The Heritage of the Early Church . . . in honour of V. Florovsky*, OCA 195:361–74. Rome, 1973.
A. Maxsein. *Philosophia cordis. Das Wesen der Personalität bei Augustinus.* Salzburg, 1966.
Tomaš Špidlík. 'Il Cuore, simbolo di unione', *Vita consecrata* 13 (1977) 329–44.
Tomaš Špidlík. 'El corazón en la spiritualidad del oriente cristiano', *Cor Christi*: 145–57. Bogota, 1980.
——————. Il cuore nella spiritualità russa', in R. Faricy and E. Malatesta, *Cuore del Cristo: cuore dell' uomo*: 48–73. Naples, 1982.

THE BODY, p. 107

A. Deckers. *Kenntnis und Pflege des Körpers bei Clemens von Alexandreia.* Innsbruck, 1936.
Alphonsus de Castro Albarrán. *Concepto pagano y concepto cristiano de nuestro cuerpo.* Madrid, 1942.
André de Bovis. *La sagesse de Sénèque*, Théologie 13. Paris, 1948.
Henri Irénée Marrou. *Histoire de l'éducation dans l'antiquité.* Paris, 1948. Translated by G. Lamb, *A History of Education in Antiquity.* New York, 1956.
A. J. Festugière. *L'enfant d'Agrigente.* Paris, 1950.
D. Gorce. 'Corps (spiritualité et hygiène du)', DS 2/2 (1953) 2338–78.
W. Stählin. *Vom Sinn des Leibes.* 2d ed. Stuttgart, 1953.
Michel Aubineau. 'Incorruptibilité et divinisation selon saint Irénée', *Recherches de science religieuse* 46 (1956) 25–52.
Edouard Schweizer. 'Sarx', in Kittel 7 (1964) 98–151.
Pierre Courcelle. 'Tradition platonicienne et tradition chrétienne du corps-prison *(Phédon* 62b; *Cratyle* 400c)', *Revue des études latines* 43 (1965) 406–43.
Johannes Baptist Metz. 'Corporalité', EF 1 (1967) 273–80.
Jacques Dupuis. *'L'Ésprit de l'homme'. Étude sur l'anthropologie religieuse d'Origène*: pp. 42–44: the antagonism between flesh and spirit. Desclée de Brouwer, 1967.

SEX, p. 112

Johannes Stelzenberger. *Die Beziehung der frühchristlichen Sittenlehre zur Ethik der Stoa*, ch. 12: sexual morality, 403–47. Munich, 1932.
Paul Evdokimov. *La femme et le salut de monde. Étude d'anthropologie chrétienne sur les charismes de la femme.* Tournai-Paris, 1958.
D. S. Bailey. *The Man-Woman Relation in Christian Thought.* London, 1959.
Robert Tamisier. 'La femme dans l'Écriture', DS 5 (1964) 132–39 (bibliography).

Bibliography 381

René d'Ouince. 'La vocation chrétienne de la femme', *Ibid.*, col. 139-51 (bibliography).
Lars Thunberg. *Microcosm and Mediator. The Theological Anthropology of Maximus the Confessor*: 396ff. Lund, 1965.
Raniero Cantalamessa. 'Etica sessuale e matrimonio nel cristianesimo delle origini', *Studia Patristica Mediolanensia*. Milan, 1976.
Jean Leclercq. 'Femminile, monachesimo', DIP 3 (1976) 1445-51.

DEATH, p. 113

Rudolf Bultmann. 'Thanatos', in Kittel 3 (1938) 7-21.
Franz W. M. Cumont. *Recherches sur le symbolisme funéraire des Romains, Bibliographie archéologique et historique*. Paris, 1942.
_____ . *Lux perpetua*. Paris, 1949.
Nikolaj Berdiaev. *Dialectique existentielle du divin et de l'humain*. Paris, 1947. Translated from the Russian by R. M. French, *The Divine and the Human*. London, 1949.
Jean Daniélou. 'La doctrine de la mort chez les Pères de l'Église'. *Le mystère de la mort et sa célébration*. Paris, 1949.
_____ . *L'être et le temps chez Grégoire de Nysse*: 154-85. Leiden, 1970.
J. A. Fischer. *Studien zum Todesgedanken in der alten Kirche. Die Beurteilung des natürlichen Todes in der kirchlichen Literatur der ersten drei Jahrhunderte*. Munich, 1954.
Jaroslav Pelikan. *The Shape of Death: Life, Death and Immortality in the Early Fathers*. London, 1962.
Justin Mossay. *La mort et l'au-delà dans saint Grégoire de Nazianze*. Louvain, 1966.
Jean Kirchmeyer. 'Grecque (Église), DS 6 (1967) 831ff. (bibliography).
Tomaš Špidlík. 'Il mistero della morte nel pensiero dei cristiani dell' Oriente', in E. Ancilli, *La morte incontro con la vita*: 73-81. Rome: Teresianum, 1972.
_____ . 'Les strastoterpsi dans la spiritualité slave ou la valeur chrétienne de la souffrance', RAM 43 (1967) 453-61.
_____ . 'Il problema della sofferenza nella spiritualità russa'. *La Sapienza della croce oggi*. Atti del Congresso internazionale, Roma, 13-18 ottobre 1975. Vol. 2:479-85. Turin, 1976.
Charles Kannengieser. 'Le mystère pascal du Christ mort et ressuscité selon Jean Chrysostome', in Ch. Kannengieser, ed., *Jean Chrysostome et Augustin*, Théologie historique 35:221-46. Paris, 1975.

SPIRITUAL COSMOLOGY, p. 125

Edmond W. Moeller. *Geschichte de Kosmologie in der griechischen Kirche bis auf Origenes*. Halle, 1860.
Pierre Duhem. *Le système du monde. Histore des doctrines cosmologiques de Platon à Copernic*. Paris, 1914.
Pavel Al. Florenskij. *Stolp i utveržděnie istiny* [*The Pillar and Foundation of Truth*]:260-318. Moscow, 1914.
V. Monod. *Dieu dans l'univers. Essai sur l'action exercée sur la pensée chré-

tienne par les grands systèmes cosmologiques depuis Aristote jusqu'à nos jours. Paris, 1933.
A. J. Festugière. *La Révélation d'Hermès Trismégiste*, Vol. 2: *Le Dieu cosmique*. Paris, 1949.
J. F. Callahan. 'Greek Philosophy and the Cappadocian Cosmology', *Dumbarton Oak Papers* 12 (1958) 29–57.
Jean Pépin. *Théologie cosmique et théologie chrétienne* (*Ambroise, Exam.* I, 1–4). Paris, 1964.
Richard A. Norris. *God and World in Early Christian Theology. A Study in Justin Martyr, Irenaeus, Tertullian, and Origen*. London, 1965.
L. Scheffczyk and Hermann Volk. 'Création', EF 1:281–305 (bibliography).
Ursula Fruchtel. *Die Kosmologischen Vorstellungen bei Philo von Alexandrien*. Leiden, 1968.
A. P. Orban. *Les dénominations du monde chez les premiers auteurs chrétiens*. Nijmegen, 1970.
Th. N. Zissis. *Man and the Word in God's Economy According to Chrysostom, Analecta Vlatadon* 9. (in Greek). Thessalonica, 1971.

THE WORLD IN SCRIPTURE, p. 126

Werner Foerster. 'Ktizo' in Kittel 3:999–1034.
Colomban Lesquivit and Pierre Grelot. 'Monde', VTB, 784–92.
Evode Beaucamp. *La Bible et le sens religieux de l'univers*. Paris, 1959.
John L. McKenzie. 'God and Nature in the Old Testament', *Catholic Biblical Quarterly* 14 (1952) 18–39.
Anton Vögtle. *Das Neue Testament und die Zukunft des Kosmos*. Düsseldorf, 1971.
Norbert Brox. 'Monde—Étude biblique', EF 3, 105–14 (bibliography).

THE BEAUTY OF THE WORLD, p. 127

La sophiologie de saint Basile. pp. 227ff.
Hans Urs von Balthasar. *Herrlichkeit, Eine theologische Aesthetik*. 3 vols. Einsiedeln, 1965.
Paul Evdokimov. *L'art de l'icône. Théologie de la beauté*. Desclée de Brouwer, 1972.

SOPHIOLOGY, p. 129

Nikolaj Serg. von Arseniew. *Fürst Eugen N. Trubetzkoy. Die religiöse Weltanschauung der altrussischen Ikonenmalerei*. Paderborn, 1927.
Georgij Vas. Florovskij. 'O počitanii Sofii-Premudrosti Božiej, v Vizantii i na Rusi [On the Cult of Sophia-Divine Wisdom in Byzantium and Russia], *Travaux du Ve congrès des organisations académiques russes à l'etranger*, vol. I:489–90, 492.
Archbishop Seraphim [Sobolev]. *Novoe učenie o Sofii Premudrosti Božiej* [New Teaching on Sophia, the Wisdom of God]. Sofia, 1935.
C. Lialine. 'Le débat sophiologique', *Irénikon* 13 (1936) 168–205.

Sergei Bulgakov. *The Wisdom of God. A Brief Summary of Sophiology*. New York-London, 1937.
Serge Obolenskij. 'La sophiologie et la mariologie de Paul Florensky', *Unitas* 1 (1946) n. 3:63–70; n. 4:31–49.
Alojz Litva. 'La "sophia" dans la création selon la doctrine de Serge Boulgakof', OCP 16 (1950) 39–74.
Bernhard Schultze. 'Zur Sophiafrage', OCP 3 (1937) 655–61.
_____. 'Ein Beitrag zur Sophiafrage', OCP 5 (1939) 223–29.
_____. 'Der gegenwärtige Streit um die Sophia, die göttliche Weisheit, in der Orthodoxie', *Stimmen der Zeit* 70 (1940) 318–24.
_____. 'Maria und Kirche in der russischen Sophia-Theologie'. *Maria et Ecclesia, Acta congr. Mar.* —*Lourdes 1958*, vol. 10:51–141. Rome, 1960.
_____. *La mariologie sophianique russe*. Paris, 1961. (excerpted from H. du Manoir, ed., *Maria*, vol. VI.)
Léon A. Zander. *Bog i mir, mirosozercanie otca Sergia Bulgakova* [God and the World. The World View of Father Sergius Bulgakov). 2 vols. Paris, 1948.
_____. 'Die Weisheit Gottes im russischen Glauben und Denken', *Kerygma und Dogma* 2 (1956) 29–53.
Tomaš Špidlík. *La sophiologie de saint Basile*, OCA 162. Rome, 1961.

DIVINE PROVIDENCE, p. 130

Pavel Florenskij. *Stolp i utveržděnie istiny* [*The Pillar and Foundation of Truth*]: pp. 284ff. Moscow, 1914.
Hal Koch. *Pronoia und Paideusis. Studien über Origenes und sein Verhältnis zum Platonismus*. Berlin-Leipzig, 1932.
C. Cioffari. *Fortune and Fate from Democritus to St. Thomas Aquinas*. New York, 1935.
Henri-Dominique Simonin. 'La Providence selon les Pères grecs, DThC 13/1 (1936) 941–60.
Hans-Georg Beck. *Vorsehung und Vorherbestimmung in der theologischen Literatur der Byzantiner*, OCA 114. Rome, 1937.
William Chase Greene. *Moira, Fate, Good and Evil in Greek Thought*. Cambridge (Mass.), 1944.
David Amand. *Fatalisme et liberté dans l'antiquité grecque*. Brussels, 1945.
A. J. Festugière. *La révélation d'Hermès Trismégiste*, Vol. I. *L'astrologie et les sciences occultes*. 2nd ed., Paris, 1950.
J. Wytzes. 'Paideia and Pronoia in the works of Clemens Alexandrinus', *Vigiliae Christianae* 9 (1959) 146–58.
Michel Spanneut. *Le stoïcisme des Pères de l'Église*: 326ff. Paris, 1957.
Leo Scheffczyk. *Création et providence*, (tr. P. Prévot) Histoire des dogmes 2, Paris, 1967.
V. Schubert. *Pronoia und Logos. Die Rechtfertigung der Weltordnung*. Munich-Salzburg, 1968.
Tomaš Špidlík. 'La Trinità nella spiritualità della Chiesa Orientale', in E. Ancilli, *Il mistero del Dio vivente*: 230–45. Rome: Teresianum, 1968.

THE DIVINE OIKONOMIA, p. 131

Wilhelm Gass. 'Das patristische Wort oikonomia', *Zeitschrift für wissenschaftliche Theologie* 17 (1874) 465–504.

K. Duchatelez. 'La notion d'économie et ses richesses théologiques', NRTh 92 (1970) 267–92.
J. Reumann. 'Oikonomia as ethical accommodation in the Fathers, and its pagan backgrounds'. *Studia Patristica* 3, TU 78:370–79. Berlin, 1961.
R. Girod. Introduction to *Commentaire sur l'évangile selon Matthieu d'Origène*, SCh 162 (1970) 28–47.

THE PROBLEM OF EVIL, p. 135

Paul Siwek. *Le Problème du mal*. Rio de Janeiro, 1942.
Louis Bouyer. 'Le problème du mal dans le christianisme antique', *Dieu vivant* 6 (1946) 17–42.
Henri-Charles Puech. *Le manichéisme, son fondateur, sa doctrine*. Paris, 1949.
Françoise Petit. *Le problème du mal*, Je sais, je crois, Paris, 1958.
J. Wytzes. 'The twofold way', *Vigiliae Christianae* 11 (1957) 226–45; 14 (1960) 129–52.
Charles Journet. *Le mal. Essai théologique*. 2nd ed. Bruges, 1962.
F. P. Hager. *Die Materie und das Böse im antiken Platonismus. Museum Helveticum* 19 (1962) 73–103.
Joseph Bernhart. 'Mal', EF 3:9–23 (bibliography).
E. Borne. *Le problème du mal.* Initiation philosophique 33. 4th ed. Paris, 1967.
W. E. G. Floyd. *Clement of Alexandria's Treatment of the Problem of Evil*. Oxford, 1971.
Étienne Borne. 'Mal', DS 10:122–36.

SUFFERINGS, p. 137

J. Paulus. 'Le thème du Juste souffrant dans la pensée grecque et hébraïque', *Revue de l'histoire des Religions* 121 (1940) 18–66.
Gabriele M. Roschini. *Il problema del dolore*. Rome, 1949.
Ernst Benz. *Der gekreuzigte Gerechte bei Plato, im Neuen Testament und in der alten Kirche.* Akademie der Wissenschaften und der Literatur in Mainz, Geistes- und Sozialwiss. Klasse 1950, 12. Mainz, 1950.
Jean Mouroux. 'Théologie de la croix, théologie de la gloire', in De Flore and P. Horay, eds., *L'humanisme et la grâce*. 1950.
R. Brancati. *Il problema del dolore nel mondo pagano e nel mondo cristiano*. Catania, 1952.
Jean Coste. 'Notion grecque et notion biblique de la souffrance éducatrice', RSR 43 (1955) 481–523.
Philippe de la Trinité. 'Epreuves spirituelles', DS 4/1 (1960) 911–25.
L. Moraldi. 'Expiation', DS 4/2 (1961) 2026–45.
Jeanne Russier. *La souffrance*, Initiation philosophique 61. Paris, 1963.
Edouard des Places. 'Un thème platonicien dans la tradition patristique: Le juste crucifié (Platon, *République* 361 e 4–362 a 2), *Studia Patristica* 9, TU 94: 36–40. Berlin, 1966.
P. Stockmeier. *Theologie und Kult des Kreuzes bei Johannes Chrysostomus, Ein Beitrag zum Verständnis des Kreuzes im IV. Jahrhundert,* Trierer Theologische Studien 18. Trier, 1966.
Pie-Raymond Régamay. *La croix du Christ et celle du chrétien*. Foi vivante 112. Paris, 1969.

Edward Nowak. *Le chrétien devant la souffrance. Étude sur la pensée de Jean Chrysostome.* Théologie historique 19. Paris, 1972.

THE COSMIC VOCATION OF MAN, p. 140

Pavel Florenskij. *Stolp i utveržděnie istiny* [*The Pillar and Foundation of Truth*]: 540ff. Moscow, 1914.
Konrad Onasch. *Die Idee der Metamorphosis (Verklärung in der östlichen Liturgien, in der russischen Frömmigkeit und in der russischen Religionsphilosophie).* Danzig, 1945.
Albert Frank-Duquesne. *Cosmos et Gloire. Dans quelle mesure l'univers physique a-t-il part à la chute, à la redemption et à la gloire finale?* Paris, 1947.
Robert Gillet. 'L'homme divinisateur cosmique dans la pensée de S. Grégoire de Nysse', *Studia Patristica* 6, TU 81:62–83. Berlin, 1962.
Placide Deseille. 'Gloire de Dieu: dans l'Écriture, des Pères de l'Église à saint Bernard', DS 6 (1967) 422–63.
M. Girad. *Louange cosmique. Bible et animisme.* Montréal-Paris, 1975.

THE MICROCOSM, p. 141

A. Meyer. *Wesen und Geschichte der Theorie von Mikro- und Makrokosmos.* Bern, 1901.
G. P. Conger. *Theories of Macrocosms and Microcosms in the History of Philosophy.* New York, 1922.
R. Allers. 'Microcosmos, from Anaximandros to Paracelsus', *Traditio 2 (1944) 319–407.*
A. Olerud. *L'idée de macrocosmos et de microcosmos dans le Timée de Platon.* Upsala, 1951.
Cyrill Korvin-Krasinski. *Mikrokosmos und Makrokosmos in religions-geschichtlicher Sicht.* Düsseldorf, 1960.
Lars Thunberg. *Microcosm and Mediator. The Theological Anthropology of Maximus the Confessor.* Lund, 1965.
Grégoire de Nazianze, OCA 189:104ff Rome, 1971.

THE JOY OF PASCHA, p. 141

Nikolaj von Arseniew. *Ostkirche und Mystik*: 71–91: the transfiguration of the world and life in the Eucharist. Munich, 1925.
——————. *Prosvětlenije mira i žizni v christianskoj miskike Vostoka i Zapada* [The Illumination of the World and of life in Mysticism East and West]. Varšava, 1934.
——————. *Preobraženije mira i žizni* [The Transfiguration of the World and of Life]. New York, 1959.
Placide Deseille. 'Gloire de Dieu: dans l'Écriture, des Pères de l'Église à saint Bernard', DS 6 (1967) 422–63 (bibliography).
M. Girad. *Louange cosmique. Bible et animisme.* Montréal-Paris, 1975.
Alexander Schmemann and Olivier Clément. *Le Mystère pascal. Commentaires liturgiques*, Spiritualité orientale 16. Abbaye de Bellefontaine, 1975.

Bibliography

THE HISTORY OF THE WORLD, p. 142

Jean Daniélou. *Essai sur le mystère de l'histoire*. Paris, 1953.
Michel Spanneut. *Le stoïcisme des Pères de l'Eglise:* p. 360, n. 73 (bibliography). Paris 1957.
Olivier Clément. *Transfigurer le temps. Notes sur le temps à la lumière de la tradition orthodoxe*. Neuchatel-Paris, 1959.
R. Weil. *Aristote et l'histoire*. (Diss.) Paris, 1960.
S. G. F. Brandon. *History, Time and Deity*. Manchester-New York, 1965.
Giorgio Jossa. *La teologia della storia nel pensiero cristiano del secondo secolo*. Pompeii, 1965.
Theological Seminary of Thessalonica. *God and History according to the Orthodox tradition* (in Greek). Thessalonica, 1966.
Lloyd G. Patterson. *God and History in Early Christian Thought. A Study of Themes from Justin Martyr to Gregory the Great*. London, 1967.
Hans Urs von Balthasar. *Theologie der Geschichte*. Einsiedeln, 1950.
Tomaš Špidlík. 'L'eternità e il tempo, la zoé e il biós, problema di Padri Cappadoci', *Augustinianum* 16 (1976) 107–16.

APOKATASTASIS, p. 144

D. Riemann. *Die Lehre von der Apokatastasis*. Magdeburg, 1889.
Eugène Michaud. 'S. Grégoire de Nysse et l'apocatastase', *Revue Internationale de Théologie* 10 (1902) 37–52.
L. Onings. 'Adam', DS 1 (1937) 187–95.
Jean Daniélou. 'L'apocatastase chez saint Grégoire de Nysse', RSR 30 (1940) 328–47.
_____ . 'Notes sur trois textes eschatologiques de saint Grégoire de Nysse', *Ibid.*, 348–96.
P. Sherwood. *The Earlier Ambigua of St. Maximus the Confessor*: 205–22. Rome, 1953.
André Méhat. 'Apocatastase, Origène, Clément d'Alexandrie, Act. 3.21', *Vigiliae Christianae* 10 (1956) 196–214.
G. Müller. 'Origenes und die Apokatastasis', *Theologische Zeitschrift* 14 (1958) 174–90.
Paolo Siniscalco. '*Apokathistēmi* et *apokatastasis* nella tradizione della Grande Chiesa fino ad Ireneo', *Studia Patristica 3, TU* 76: 380–96. Berlin, 1961.
Henri Crouzel. 'Apokatastasis', in *Sacramentum Mundi* 1:231–34. Freiburg-Basel-Vienna, 1967.
Augustin Mouhanna. *La doctrine de l'Apocatastase d'après saint Grégoire de Nysse*. Diss., Pontifical Oriental Institute. Rome, 1973.

ESCHATOLOGY, p. 144

Martin Jugie, 'La doctrine des fins dernières dans l'Église gréco-russe.' *Echos d'Orient* 17 (1914) 5–22, 209–28, 402–21.
Georgij Florovsky. 'Eschatology in the Patristic Age', *The Greek Orthodox Theological Review* 2 (1956) 27–40. Rpt *Studia Patristica* 2, TU 64 (1967) 235–50.

Bibliography 387

H. Cornélis. 'Les fondaments cosmologiques de l'eschatologie d'Origène', *Revue des sciences philosophiques et théologiques* 43 (1959) 32–80.
Lars Thunberg. *Microcosm and Mediator. The Theological Anthropology of Maximus the Confessor.* Lund, 1965.
Vladimir Lossky. *In the Image and Likeness of God*: 211–27. Crestwood, New York, 1974.
Ricardo Terzoli. *Il tema della beatitudine nei Padri siri. Presente e futuro della salvezza.* Rome, 1972.
Hans Urs von Balthasar. *Eschatologie im Umriss. Pneuma und Institution,* Skizzen zur Theologie 4:410–55. Einsiedeln, 1974.
Job Ghebreyesus. *L'escatologia intermedia nella tradizione della Chiesa ortodossa d'Etiopia.* Diss., Pontifical Oriental Institute. Rome, 1975.
Boris Bobrinskij. 'L'Ésprit du Christ dans les sacrements chez Jean Chrysostome et Augustin', in Ch. Kannengieser, ed., *Jean Chrysostome et Augustin,* Théologie historique 35:247–75. Paris, 1975.

THE CHURCH, p. 157

F. Gössmann. *Der Kirchenbegriff bei Wladimir Solovjeff.* Das östliche Christentum 1. Wurzburg, 1936.
Emile Mersch *Le corps mystique du Christ.* Brussels-Paris, 1936. Translated into English by J. R. Kelly, *The Whole Christ: The Historical Development of the Doctrine of the Mystical Body in Scripture and Tradition.* Milwaukee, 1938.
Louis Bouyer. *L'incarnation et l'Église Corps du Christ dans la théologie de saint Athanase,* Unam Sanctam 11. Paris, 1943.
J. C. Plumpe. *Mater Ecclesia. An Inquiry into the Concept of Church as Mother in Early Christianity.* Washington, 1943.
Henri de Lubac. *Méditation sur l'Eglise,* Théologie 27. Paris, 1953. Translated into English by M. Mason, *The Splendour of the Church.* New York, 1956.
'*Église*' (several authors), DS 4/1 (1960) 370–479.
Hugo Rahner. *Symbole der Kirche. Die Ekklesiologie der Väter.* Salzburg, 1964.
Jacques Chênevert. 'L'Église et les parfaits chez Origène', *Sciences ecclésiastiques 18 (1966) 253*–82.
Michel Dupuy. 'Hiérarchie', DS 7/1 (1969) 440–51.
Ph. Rancillac. *L'Église, manifestation de l'Ésprit chez Jean Chrysostome.* Dar Al-Kalima, Lebanon, 1970.
Ernst-Christoph Suttner. *Offenbarung, Gnade und Kirche bei A. St. Chomjakov,* Das östliche Christentum. Neue Folge 20. Würzburg, 1967.
Paul Evdokimov. 'L'Ésprit saint et l'Église d'après la tradition liturgique', *L'Esprit saint et l'Église:85*–123. Paris, 1969.
'*Koinonia*' (several authors). DS 8 (1972) 1743–69.
Alain Riou. *Le monde et l'Église selon Maxime le Confesseur,* Théologie historique 22. Paris, 1973.
Jean Rupp. *Message Ecclésial de Solowiev. Présage et illustration de Vatican II.* Paris, 1975
Tomaš Špidlík. 'L'ecclesiologia di una icona russa', *Asprenas* 27 (1980) 239–45.
_____ . '"Sentirsi Chiesa" nella catechesi di Basilio Magno', in S. Felici, ed. *Ecclesiologia e catechesi patristica*: 113–22. Rome, 1982.

THE SAINTS, p. 158

Paul Séjourné. 'Saints (Culte des)', DThC 14 (1939) 870–978.
B. Köttig. 'Heiligkeit und Heiligentypen in den ersten christlichen Jahrhunderten', *Diözesanpriester* 1:12–27, Münster, 1949.
Sergei Bulgakow. 'Grundsätzliches über die Heiligenverehrung in der orthodoxen Kirche des Ostens', E. Benz and L. Zander, eds., *Evangelisches und orthodoxes Christentum in Begegnung und Auseinandersetzung*: 219–27. Hamburg, 1952.
B. Köttig. 'Saints (Culte des)', EF 4:166–75.
Articles in *Oikonomia*, vol. 6. Erlangen, 1977.

THE MOTHER OF GOD, p. 158

Mauricio Gordillo. *Mariologia Orientalis*, OCA 141. Rome, 1954.
Antonio Koreň. 'La Russia e la Madonna', *Maria e la Chiesa del silenzio*: 87ff. Rome, 1957.
Paul Evdokimov. *La femme et le salut du monde*. Tournai-Paris, 1958.
Tomaš Špidlík. 'La pietà mariana nella Chiesa Orientale', in E. Ancilli, *Maria—mistero di grazia*. Rome: Teresianum, 1974.
Pierre Grelot, Domiciano Fernandez, Theodor Koehler, Stefano De Fiores, and René Laurentin. 'Marie (Sainte vierge)', DS 10:409–89.
Tomaš Špidlík. 'Per una mariologia antropologica (utilizzando le analisi di L. S. Frank'), *Marianum* 41 (1979) 491–506.
————. 'La devozione alla Madre di Dio nelle Chiese Orientali', *Scripta de Maria*: 123–57. Saragossa, 1981.

THE COMMON LIFE, p. 160

Henri Leclercq. 'Cénobitisme', DACL 2/2 (1910) 3047–3248.
Michel Olphe-Galliard. 'Cénobitisme', DS 2/1 (1953) 404–16.
Jean Gribomont. 'Cenobio. Cenobita. Cenobitismo', DIP 2 (1975) 761–64.
Gregorio Penco. 'Cenobitismo', DESp 1 (1975) 260–63.

FRIENDSHIP, p. 161

Aristotle. *Nicomachean Ethics*, Bks VIII and IX.
Cicero. *Laelius* or *De amicitia*.
A. Gazet. 'Commentaire de la Règle de Cassien', PL 49:1011–44.
Ludovic Dugas. *L'amitié antique*. 2nd ed. Paris, 1914.
Pavel Florenskij. *Stolp i utverždĕnie istiny* [*The Pillar and Foundation of Truth*]: 393–463. Moscow, 1914.
Friedrich Hauck. *Die Freundschaft bei den Griechen und im Neuen Testament*. Leipzig, 1928.
Joseph de Guibert. 'Amitié', DS 1 (1937) 500–30.
Lukas Vischer. 'Das Problem der Freundschaft bei den Kirchenvätern', *Theologische Zeitschrift* 9 (1953) 173–200.

Bibliography 389

THE FAMILY, p. 162

F. X. Funck. *Klemens von Alexandrien über Familie und Eigentum*. Paderborn, 1899.
Nikolaj Arseniew. 'Duchovnyje tradicii russkoj semji' [The Spiritual Traditions of the Russian Family], in S. Verchovskoj, *Pravoslavie v žizni*: 211-39. New York, 1953.
_____. *Die geistigen Schicksale des russischen Volkes*. Graz, 1966.
_____. 'Die Spiritualität der Ostkirche', in E. von Ivánka, J. Tyciak, and P. Wiertz, eds., *Handbuch der Ostkirchenkunde*: 503-42. Düsseldorf, 1971
Joseph Mac Avoy. 'Famille', DS 5 (1964) 61-74.

THE STATE, p. 162

Ivan Kologrivof. 'Royaume de Dieu et royaume de César (d'après la pensée d'un philosophe orthodoxe russe)', OC 24, vol. 6/3 (1926) 139-60.
Kirche, Staat und Mensch. Russisch-Orthodoxe Studien, ed. by the Forschungsabteilung des Oekumenischen Rates für Praktisches Christentum. Geneva, 1937- .
Stanislas Giet. *Les Idées et l'action sociales de saint Basile*: 152ff. Paris, 1941.
Anton Michel. *Die Kaisermacht in der Ostkirche* (843-1204). Darmstadt, 1959.
Francis Dvornik. *Byzanz und der romische Primat*. Stuttgart, 1966.
K. Alland. 'Kirche und Staat in der alten Christenheit', *Kirche und Staat. Festschrift für H. Kunst*: 19-49. Berlin, 1967.
_____. 'The Relation between Church and State in Early Times: A Reinterpretation', *The Journal of Theological Studies*, NS 19 (1968) 115-27.
Adolf Wilhelm Ziegler. *Religion, Kirche und Staat in Geschichte und Gegenwart. Ein Handbuch*. Munich, 1969.
H. Hunger. *Das byzantinische Herrscherbild*. Darmstadt, 1975 (bibliography).
Claude Lepelley. 'Saint Augustin et la cité romano-africaine', in Ch. Kannengieser, ed., *Jean Chrysostome et Augustin*, Théologie historique 35 (1975) 13-39.
Alain Natali. 'Christianisme et cité à Antioche à la fin du IVe siècle d'après Jean Chrysostome', *Ibid.*, 41-59.

BROTHERLY LOVE, p. 164

Georg Wunderle. *Das Ideal der Brüderlichkeit in ostkirchlicher Sicht*. Dülmen i.W., 1949.
Ruggero Balducelli. *Il concetto teologico di carità attraverso le maggiori interpretazioni patristiche di I ad Cor. XIII*. Washington, 1951.
T. Barrosse. 'The Unity of the Two Charities in Greek Patristic Exegesis', *Theological Studies* 15 (1954) 355-88.
Hélène Pétré. 'Ordinata caritas. Un enseignement d'Origène sur la charité', *Recherches de science religieuse* 42 (1954) 40-57.
Mario Serra. *La virtù della carità verso il prossimo in S. Gregorio Nazianzeno*. Rome, 1956.

Giovanni M. Cossu. 'L'amore naturale verso Dio a verso il prossimo sell'insegnamento di S. Basilio Magno.' *Bolletino della Badia greca di Grotta-ferrata* 14 (1960) 87–107.
Iréneé Hausherr. 'La charité fraternelle', *Christus* 8, n. 31 (1961) 291–305.
Michel Aubineau. 'Exégèse patristique de Mt. 24.12: *Quoniam abundavit iniquitas refrigescet charitas multorum*', TU 79:3–19. Berlin, 1961.
Richard Völkl. *Frühchristliche Zeugnisse zu Wesen und Gestalt der christlichen Liebe*. Freiburg-im-Breisgau, 1963.
H. C. Baldry. *The Unity of Mankind in Greek Thought*. Cambridge, 1965.

ALMSGIVING, p. 167

Auguste Beugnet. 'Aumône', DThC 1/2 (1923) 2561–71.
Charles Antoine. 'Aumône', DAFC 1 (1925) 319–28.
R. Brouillard. 'Aumône', *Catholicisme* 1 (1948) 1050–56
Gottfried Dümpelmann. 'Almosen', LThK² 1 (1957) 359–62.

WORK, p. 168

Irénée Hausherr. 'Opus Dei', OCP 13 (1947) 195–218. Rpt. in OCA 183 (1969) 121–44.
Henri Rondet. *Die Theologie der Arbeit. Ein Entwurf*. Würzburg, 1956.
Lucien Daloz. *Le Travail selon Saint Jean Chrysostome*, Théologie, Pastorale et Spiritualité, Recherches et Synthèses 4. Paris, 1959.
G. E. Kaiser. *Theology of Work*. Westminster, Maryland, 1966.
Tomaš Špidlík. 'Das östliche Mönchtum und das östliche Frömmigkeitsleben', in *Handbuch der Ostkirchenkunde*, 551ff.

THE APOSTOLATE OF THE MONKS, p. 169

Sergei Smirnov. *Kak služili miru podvižniki drevnej Rusi* [How the Ascetics of Old Russia Served the People]. Sergiev Posad, 1903.
Armand Delatte. 'Le sage-témoin dans la philosophie stoïco-cynique', *Bulletin de la Classe des Lettres et des Sciences morales et politiques, Académie Royale de Belgique* 39,4:166–86.
Heinrich Bacht. 'Die Rolle des orientalischen Mönchtums in der kirchenpolitischen Auseinandersetzungen um Chalkedon', in Aloys Grillmeier and Heinrich Bacht, *Das Konzil von Chalkedon*, Vol. 2:193–314. Würzburg, 1951–54.
Leo Ueding. 'Die Kanones von Chalkedon und ihre Bedeutung für Mönchtum und Klerus', *Ibid.*, 569–676.
Philip Hofmeister. 'Mönchtum und Seelsorge bis zum 13. Jahrhundert', *Studien und Mitteilungen aus dem Benediktiner- und Zisterzienserorden* 65 (1953-1954) 209–73.
Remigius Rudmann. *Mönchtum und kirchlicher Dienst in den Schriften Gregors des Grossen*. St Otilien, 1956 (bibliography).
O. Rousseau. *Religion et apostolat dans l'Eglise orientale. Apostolat*, Problèmes de la religion d'aujourd'hui: 77–96. Paris, 1957.

Garabed Amadodouni. 'Le role des hiéromoines arméniens', *Monachesimo orientale*, OCA 153:279-305. Rome, 1958.
Ivo Auf der Maur. *Mönchtum und Glaubensverkundigung in den Schriften des heiligen Johannes Chrysostomus*. Frieburg, Switz., 1959.
Adalbert de Vogüé. 'Monachisme et Église dans la pensée de Cassien', *Théologie de la vie monastique: 219*-40. Paris, 1961.
A. Yannoulatos. 'Spiritualité orthodoxe et mission', *Contacts* 16 (1964) 38-41.
Jean Bernardi. *La prédication des Pères Cappadociens*. Paris, 1966.
Tomaš Spidlík. 'Das östliche Mönchtum und das östliche Frömmigkeitsleben', in *Handbuch der Ostkirchenkunde*, 543-68, especially 556ff.
J. M. Leroux. 'Saint Jean Chrysostome et le monachisme', in Ch. Kannengieser, ed., *Jean Chrysostome et Augustin*, Théologie historique 35 (1975) 125-44.

EDUCATION, p. 170

Skabalanovič. *Vizantijskaja nauka i školy v XI veke* [Knowledge and the Byzantine schools in the Eleventh century]. *Christianskoe čtenie 1884, ns. 3-4.*
J. Sokolov. *Sostojanie monašestva v Vizantijskoj Cerkvi poloviny IX do načala XIII veka* (842-1204) [Monasticism in the Byzantine Church from the Middle of the Ninth Century to the Beginning of the Thirteenth]. Kazan, 1894.
L'Abbé Marin. *Les moines de Constantinople (330-898)*:373-522 (the monks' intellectual activity). Paris, 1897.
Karl Weiss. *Die Erziehungslehre der drei Kappadokier*. Freiburg-im-Breisgau, 1903.
Gustave Bardy. *Greek Literature in the Early Church*. English translation by M. Reginald. London, 1929.
———. 'L'Église et l'enseignement pendant les trois premiers siècles', *Recherches de science religieuse* 12 (1932) 1-28.
———. 'L'Église et l'enseignement au IVᵉ siècle', *Ibid., 14 (1934) 525*-49.
Damien Van den Eynde. *Les normes de l'enseignement chrétien dans la littérature patristique des trois premiers siècles*. Gembloux-Paris, 1933.
Mauricio Gordillo. 'La pensée religieuse et la théologie en Russie depuis l'etablissement du Saint Synode', DThC 14 (1939) 333-71.
L. Millar. *Christian Education in the First Four Centuries*. London, 1946.
Henri I. Marrou. *Histoire de l'éducation dans l'Antiquité*. Paris, 1948, 1956. English translation by G. Lamb, *A History of Education in Antiquity*. London, 1956.
Joannes Rezáč. *De monachismo secundum recentiorem legislationem russicam*, OCA 138:218-233. Rome, 1952.
A. J. Festugière. *Les Moines d'Orient*, I. *Culture ou sainteté*. Paris, 1961.
Werner Jaeger. *Early Christianity and Greek Paideia*. Cambridge (Mass.). 1961.
Antonios Danassis. *Johannes Chrysostomos. Pädagogisch-psychologische Ideen in seinem Werk*. Bonn, 1971.
W. Barclay. *Educational Ideals in the Ancient World*. Twin Brooks Series. Grand Rapids, 1974. Especially 192-262.
Tomaš Spidlík 'Educazione nei monasteri orientali', DIP 3 (1976) 1065-68.
E. Matsagouras. *The Early Church Fathers as Educators*. Minneapolis, 1977.

PRAXIS, p. 177

Christian Maurer. 'Prassō', in *Kittel* 6 *(1959) 632–45*.
René Arnou. *Praxis et Theōria. Étude de detail sur le vocabulaire et la pensée des Ennéades de Plotin.* Paris, 1921. Rpt Rome, 1972.
R. Joly. *Le thème philosophique des genres de vie dans l'antiquité classique* Mémoires de l'Académie royale de Belgique. Classe Lettres 51, 3. Brussels, 1956
Tomaš Špidlík. *Grégoire de Nazianze. Introduction à l'étude de sa doctrine spirituelle,* OCA 189: especially pp. 49ff. Rome, 1971.
————. 'la theoria et la praxis chez Grégoire de Nazianze', *Studia Patristica* 14, TU 117:358–64. Berlin, 1976.

THE WORK OF GOD, p. 177

Jean Rivière. 'Mérite', DThC 10/1 (1928) 574–685: col. 612ff.: the patristic tradition.
Georg Bertram. 'Ergon', in Kittel 2 (1935) 631–53.
Irénée Hausherr. 'Opus Dei', OCP 13 (1947) 195–218. *Études de spiritualité orientale,* OCA 183:121–44. Rome 1969.
Karl Rahner. 'Werke', *Sacramentum mundi* 4 (1969) 1343–47.

ASCETICISM, p. 179

H. Strathmann. *Geschichte der frühchristlichen Askese,* I. Leipzig, 1914.
Edmondo Dublanchy. 'Ascétique, Ascétisme', DThC 1/2 (1923) 2037–77.
Irénée Hausherr. *S. Theodore Studite. L'homme et l'ascète (d'après ses Catéchèses), Orientalia Christiana* VI, 1. Rome, 1926.
E. Bonaiuti. *Le origini dell'ascetismo cristiano.* Pignerol, 1928.
Hans Windisch. 'Askeō', in *Kittel* 1 *(1933 and 1957) 492–94*.
Joseph de Guibert, Michel Olphe-Galliard, Alexander Willwoll. 'Ascèse, ascétisme, ascétique (théologie)', DS 1 (1937) 936–1017.
M. Gaucheron. 'Ascèse', Catholicisme 1 (1948) 890–92.
David Amand. *Ascèse monastique de saint Basile.* Maredsous, 1948.
Hermann Strathmann and P. Keseling. 'Ascèse', RAC 1 (1950) 749–95.
Giuseppe Turbessi. *Ascetismo e monachesimo prebenedettino.* Rome, 1961.
Georg Kretchmar. 'Ein Beitrag zur Frage nach dem Ursprung frühchristlicher Askese', *Zeitschrift für Theologie und Kirche* 61 (1960), Heft 1, 27–67.
Louis Cognet. *L'ascèse chrétienne.* Paris, 1967.
J. Roldanus. *Le Christ et l'homme dans la théologie d'Athanase d'Alexandrie.* Leiden, 1968.
Friedrich Wulf. 'Ascèse', EF 1 (1967) 128–37.
Bernhard Lohse. *Askese und Mönchtum in der Antike und in der alten Kirche.* Munich, 1969. (Review by T. Špidlík, OCP 38 (1972) p. 488).

THE STRIPPING OF SELF, p. 181

R. L. Oechslin. 'Dépouillement dans l'Écriture', DS 3 (1957) 456–58.
Gustave Bardy. 'Dépouillement-chez les Pères', DS 3:458–68.

CHASTITY, p. 182

Pierre Thomas Camelot. 'Enkrateia (continentia)', DS 4/1 (1960) 357-70.
George Blond. 'Encratisme', Ibid., col. 628-42.
Cf. Temperance

PURIFICATION, 182

L. E. Toombs. 'Clean and unclean', *The Interpreter's Dictionary of the Bible*, vol. 1:642-48. Nashville, 1962.
Friedrich Hauck and R. Meyer. 'Katharos, katharidzo, etc', in Kittel 3, 416-34.
René Arnou. *Le désir de Dieu dans la philosophie de Plotin*: 153ff. 2nd ed. Paris, 1967.
M. Simon. 'Souillure morale et souillure rituelle dans le christianisme primitif', *Studi e materiali di storia delle religioni* 38 (1967) 498-511.
Wilfried Paschen. *Rein und Unrein. Untersuchungen zur biblischen Wortgeschichte*. Munich, 1970.
Jean Trouillard. 'Katharsis dans la philosophie antique', DS 8 (1974) 1664-70.
Juana Raasch. 'Katharsis—de l'ancien Testament aux Pères de l'Eglise', DS 8: 1670-1883.

SIN, p. 183

Pavel Florenskij. *Stolp i utveržděnie istiny* [*The Pillar and Foundation of Truth*]: 166-204. Moscow, 1944.
Henri Rondet. 'Aux origines de la théologie du péché', NRT 79 (1957) 16-32.
_____. *Notes sur la théologie du péché*. Paris, 1957.
Georg Teichtweier. *Die Sündenlehre des Origenes. Studien zur Geschichte der katholischen Moraltheologie* 7. Regensburg, 1958.
Ambrosius Ruf. *Sünde und Sündenvergebung nach der Lehre des hl. Johannes Chrysostomus*. Freiburg-im-Breisgau, 1959.
A. Jagu. 'Les philosophes grecs et le sens du péché', *Théologie du péché*: 189-240. Tournai, 1960.
Louis Ligier. *Péché et connaissance. Essai de théologie biblique sur le péché d'Adam et le péché du monde*. Paris, 1960.
_____. *Péché d'Adam et péché du monde*. Théologie 43 and 48. Paris 1960-1961.
Lars Thunberg. *Microcosm and Mediator. The Theological Anthropology of Maximus the Confessor*. Lund (1965) p. 152 ff.
Panagiotis N. Trembelas. *Dogmatique de l'Église orthodoxe catholique*, vol. 1: 580ff. Chevetogne-Desclée, 1966.

ORIGINAL SIN, p. 183

Jules Gross. *Enstehungsgeschichte der Erbsündendogma. Von der Bibel bis Augustinus. Geschichte des Erbsündendogmas, Ein Beitrag des Erbsündendogmas, Ein Beitrag zur Geschichte des Problems vom Ursprung des Uebels* I. Basel, 1960.

Henri Rondet. *Le péché originel dans la tradition patristique*. Paris, 1967.
Leo Scheffczyk. *Urstand, Fall und Erbsünde. Von der Schrift bis Augustinus*. Freiburg-Basel-Vienna, 1981.

REPENTANCE, p. 189

Karl Holl. *Enthusiasmus und Bußgewalt beim griechischen Mönchtum*. Leipzig, 1898.
Sergei Smirnov. *Duchovnyi otec v drevnej Vostočnoj cerkvi* [The Spiritual Father in the Ancient Eastern Church]. Sergiev Posad, 1906.
_____. *Drevne-russkij duchovnik* [The Spiritual Father in Old Russia]. Moscow, 1914.
Alfred Vacant. 'Absolution sous forme déprécatoire', DThC 1 (1909) 244–52.
Paul Galtier. *L'Église et la rémission des péchés aux premiers siècles*. Paris, 1932.
Emile Amann. 'Pénitence-sacrement. La pénitence primitive', DThC 12.1 (1933) col. 748–845.
B. Poschmann. *Paenitentia secunda. Die Kirchliche Buße im ältesten Christentum bis Cyprian und Origenes*. Bonn, 1940.
Karl Rahner. 'La doctrine d'Origène sur la pénitence', *Recherches de science religieuse* 37 (1950) 54–97, 252–86; 422–56.
Bernard Poschmann. 'Buße und letzte Oelung', in Michael Schmaus, *Handbuch der Dogmengeschichte* IV, 3. Freiburg-im-Breisgau, 1951.
André Méhat. 'Pénitence seconde et péché involontaire chez Clément d'Alexandrie', *Vigiliae Christianae* 8 (1954) 225–33.
Jozef Grotz. *Die Entwicklung des Bußtufenwesens in der vornicäischen Kirche*. Freiburg-im-Breisgau, 1955.
Paul Galtier. *Aux origines du sacrement de pénitence*. Rome, 1951. *Liturgie et rémission des péchés*. Conférences Saint-Serge, XXe semaine d'études liturgiques, 2–5 juillet 1973. Rome, 1975.
Jean Gribomont. 'Epitimia', DIP 3 (1976) 1141–42.

PENTHOS, p. 193

Irénée Hausherr. *Penthos. La doctrine de la componction dans l'Orient chré tian* OCA 132. Rome, 1944. English translation by Anselm Hufstader, *Penthos. The Doctrine of Compunction in the Christian East*. Kalamazoo, 1982.
Joseph Pegon. 'Componction', DS 2/2 (1953) 1312–21.
Myrrha Lot-Borodine. 'Le mystère des larmes', *Vie spirituelle* 48 (1936) (65)–(110).
_____. 'Le mystère du "don des larmes" dans l'Orient chrétien', *La douloureuse joie*, Spiritualité orientale 14:131–95, Abbaye de Bellefontaine, 1974.
Alexander Schmemann. *Le grand carême*, Spiritualité orientale 13. Bellefontaine, 1974. English version *Great Lent*, pp. 31ff.: 'bright sadness'. New York, 1969

Bibliography 395

THE FLIGHT FROM THE WORLD, p. 205

Irénée Hausherr. *L'hésychasme. Étude de spiritualité*, OCP 22 (1956) 5-40, 247-85. OCA 176 (1966) 162-237, especially 19-40 (= 177-198).
Jean Gribomont. 'Le renoncement au monde dans l'idéal ascétique de saint Basile', *Irēnikon* 31 (1958) 282-307, 460-75.
Demosthenes Savramis. 'Max Webers Beitrag zum besseren Verständnis der östkirchlichen 'aussenweltlichen' Askese', *Kölner Zeitschrift für Soziologie und Sozialpsychologie* 15. Sonderheft 7 (1963) 334-58.
Zoltan Alezeghy. 'Fuite du monde *(Fuga mundi)*', DS 5 (1964) 1575-1605.
René Antoine Gauthier. 'Corrispondenza', DIP 3 (1976) 166-68.
Tomas̆ S̆pidlík. 'Stare nel mondo o fuggire il mondo?' *Vita consecrata* 13 (1977) 170-77.

POVERTY, p. 208

M. von Dmitrewski. *Die christliche freiwillige Armut*. Berlin, 1913.
Stanislas Giet. *Les idées et l'action sociales de saint Basile*. Paris, 1941.
Charles Journet. *Propriété chrétienne et pauvreté chrétienne*. Freiburg, 1951.
A. Sodano. *I beni terreni nella vita dei gusti secondo san Giovanni Crisostomo*. Brescia, 1955.
René Carpentier. 'États de vie', DS 4/2 (1961) 1406-28.
Irénée Hausherr. 'Vocation chrétienne et vocation monastique selon les Pères', in *Laïcs et vie chrétienne parfaite*. Rome, 1963, 33-115. *Études de spiritualité orientale*, OCA 183 (Rome, 1969) 403-85.
Elie Melia. 'Aspects de la pauvreté', *Le Messager Orthodoxe* (Paris), 21-22 (1963) 19-29.
Wolfgang Trilling. 'Pauvreté-étude biblique', EF 3 (1966) 371-75.
Lothar Hardick. 'Pauvreté-étude théologique', *Ibid.*, 376-82.
S. Zincone. *Richezza e povertà nelle omelie di Giovanni Crisostomo*. L'Aquila, 1973.
M. Hengel. *Eigentum und Reichtum in der frühen Kirche*. Stuttgart, 1973. English translation by J. Bowden, *Property and Riches in the Early Church*, Especially 1-11, 74-83. Philadelphia, 1974.
H. M. Biedermann. 'Economia monastica orientale', DIP 3 (1976) 1011-20.
A. Solignac. 'Pauvreté chrétienne-Pères de l'Église et moines des origines', DS 12: 634-47.

HESYCHASM, p. 211

Irénée Hausherr. *La méthode d'oraison hésychaste*. Oriens Christiana 36. Rome, 1927.

_____. L'hésychasme. Étude de spiritualité, OCP 22 (1956) 5-40, 247-85. Rpt in *Hésychasme et prière* (where other articles on the same subject are found), OCA 176 (1966) 163-237, and slightly modified in *Solitude et vie contemplative dans l'hésychasme*. Etoilles, 1962 (mimeograph).

_____. *Noms du Christ et voies d'oraison*, OCA 157. Rome, 1960. English translation by Charles Cummings, *The Name of Jesus*. Kalamazoo, 1978.

George Wunderle. *Zur Psychologie des hesychastichen Gebetes*. Würzburg, 1949.
Jean Meyendorff. *St. Grégoire Palamas et la mystique orthodoxe*. Paris, 1959.
—————. English translation by A. Fiske, *St. Gregory Palamas and Orthodox Spirituality*. New York, 1974.
—————. *Byzantine Hesychasm: historical, theological, and social problems*. Articles in English, French, Russian. Rpt 1974.
—————. *Introduction à l'étude de Grégoire Palamas*. Paris, 1959. English translation by G. Lawrence, *A Study of Gregory Palamas: 'Theological Integration of Hesychasm: the Life in Christ'*, 134–56. [ed.] London, 1964.
Gerhard Podskalsky. 'Zur Gestalt und Geschichte des Hesychasmus', *Ostkirchliche Studien* 16 (1967) 15–32.
Walther Völker. *Scala Paradisi. Eine Studie zu Johannes Climacus und zugleich eine Vorstudie zu Symeon dem neuen Theologen*: 278ff.: the hesychast as the culmination of the monastic life. Wiesbaden, 1968.
Pierre Adnès. 'Hésychasme', DS 7/1 (1969) 381–99.
Bernhard Schultze. 'Esicasmo e esicasti', in *Enciclopedia delle religioni*, vol. 2: col. 1207–09. Florence 1970.
Tomaš Špidlík. 'Esicasmo'. DESp I: 707–9.
—————. 'Esicasta', DIP 3 (1976) 1306–13.
—————. 'Il metodo esicastico', in E. Ancilli, *Alla ricerca di Dio. La tecniche della preghiera:* 197–215. Rome, 1978.
M. Paparozzi. *La spiritualita dell' Oriente cristiano*. Rome, 1981.
D. Stiernon. 'Nicéphore l'hésychaste', DS 11 (1982) col. 198–203.
Jean Meyendorff. 'Palamas (Grégoire)', DS 12: 81–107.

THE EREMITIC LIFE, p. 212

Hugo Rahner. 'Einsiedler', LThK², 3 (1959) 767–69.
Clément Lianine. 'Erémitisme en Orient'. DS 4/1 (1960) 936–53.
Tomaš Špidlík. 'Ermites en Orient', *Dictionnaire d'Histoire et Géographie ecclesiastique* 15 (1963) 766–71.
Giuseppe Cacciamani. 'Eremitismo', DESp 1 (1975) 683–87.
Jean Gribomont. 'Eremita. Filologia', DIP 3 (1976) 1153.
—————. 'Eremitismo in Oriente'. *Ibid.* 1228–30 (bibliography).
Johannes Rezáč. 'Eremita. In Oriente', *Ibid.*, 1153–54.

DENDRITES, p. 213

Henri Leclercq. 'Dendrites', DACL IV, I (1920) 582–83.
Germano Giovanelli. 'Dendriti', in *Enc. Catt.* IV (1950) 1430.
Tomaš Špidlík. 'Dendriti', DIP 3 (1976) 442.

STYLITES, p. 213

Hieromonk Alexij [Kuznecov]. *Jurodstvo i stolpničestvo. Religiozno-psichologičeskoe izledovanie* [Foolishness for Christ and Stylitism. Religious and Psychological Investigation]. St. Petersburg, 1913.

Hippolyte Delehaye. *Les saints stylites*. Brussels, 1923, 1962.
Henri Leclercq. 'Stylites', DACL 15/2 (1953) 1697-1718.
B. Köttig. 'Styliten', LThK² 9 (1964) 1128-29.
Tomaš Spidlík. 'Stylites', *New Catholic Encyclopedia* 13 (1967) 750-51.
I. Peña, P. Castellana, R. Fernandez. *Les stylites syriens*. Milan, 1975.

XENITEIA, p. 213

Hans von Campenhausen. *Die asketische Heimatlosigkeit im altkirchlichen und frühmittelalterichen Mönchtum*. Tübingen, 1930.
B. Köttig. 'Peregrinatio religiosa', *Forschungen zur Volkskunde* 33-35 (1950) 302-7.
G. Zoras. *Xeniteia in Greek Poetry* (in Greek). Athens, 1953.
Georg Kretschmar. 'Ein Beitrag zur Frage nach dem Ursprung frühchristlicher Askese', *Zeitschrift für Theologie und Kirche* 64 (1964) 27-64.
A. Guillaumont. 'Le dépaysement comme forme d'ascèse dans le monachisme ancien', *Annales de l'École pratique des hautes études* 76 (1968-69) 31-58.
Juan V. Catret. 'Para una espiritualidad del camino: "La búsqueda de una persona," nota común en la peregrinación de los monjes cristianos y budistas en la Edad Media', *Manresa* (1972) 349-60.
J. Sumption. *Pilgrimage. An image of medieval religion*. London, 1975.
Tomaš Spidlík. 'Girovaghi (in Oriente)', DIP 4 (1974) col. 1302-3.

LAVRAS, p. 213

Siméon Vailhé. 'Les premières monastères de Palestine', *Bessarione* 3 (1897) 39-59, 4 (1898) 25, 334-56.
Henri Leclercq. 'Laures palestiniennes', DACL 8/2 (1929) 1961-88.
R. Janin. 'Laura', LTHK² 6 (1961) 828-29.

SILENCE, p. 215

Odo Casel. *De philosophorum graecorum silentio mystico*. Giessen, 1919.
Friedrich Heiler. *Das Gebet*. 5th ed. Munich-Basel, 1969. English translation by S. McComb and J. E. Park, *Prayer: A Study in the History and Psychology of Religion*. London, 1932.
Louis Bouyer. *Le sens de la vie monastique*, especially 215-220. Paris, 1950. English translation by K. Pond, *The Meaning of the Monastic Life*. New York, 1955.
Irénée Hausherr. *L'hesychasme. Étude de spiritualité*, OCP 22 (1956) 247ff *Hésychasme et prière*, OCA 176: 199ff. Rome, 1966.
Gustav Mensching and E. Hertzsch. 'Schweigen', *Die Religion in Geschichte und Gegenwart* 5 (1961) 1605-6.
A. Kemmer. 'Schweigen', LThK² (1964) 540-41.

TEMPERANCE, 217

Francis Mugnier. 'Abstinence', DS (1937) 112-33.
Joseph de Guibert and René Daeschler. 'Abnégation (dépouillement, renoncement), DSI: 67-110.

Anton Michel. 'Tempérance', DS 15/1 (1946) 94–9.
P. Laféteur. 'La temperanza', in *Iniziazione teologica* 3: 825–889. Brescia, 1955.
Pierre Thomas Camelot. *'Enkrateia (Continentia)'*, DS 4/1 (1960) 357–70.
George Blond. 'Encratisme', DS 4/1: 628–42.
Archimandrite Sophrony. 'De la nécessité des trois renoncements chez St. Cassien le Romain et St. Jean Climaque', *Studia Patristica* 5 TU 80 (1962) 393–400.
Evangelos G. Konstantinou. *Die Tugendlehre Gregors von Nyssa:* 136ff. Würzburg, 1966.
U. Rocco. 'Temperanza', DESp 2 (1975) 1840–41.

CHASTITY, p. 219

Johannes Stelzenberger. *Die Beziehung der frühchristlichen Sittenlehre zur Ethik der Stoa:* 403–438: Die Sexualethik. Munich, 1932.
Raoul Plus and A. Rayez. 'Chasteté et perfection', DS 2/1 (1953) 777–97.

MARRIAGE, p. 219

Anatole Moulard. *Saint Jean Chrysostome, le défenseur du mariage et l'apôtre de la virginité.* Paris, 1923.
Herbert Preisker. *Christentum und Ehe in den ersten drei Jahrhunderten.* Berlin, 1927.
Louis Godefroy. 'Le mariage aux temps des Pères', DThC 9/2 (1927) 2077–2113, col. 2096 (second marriages).
Robert Flacelière. *Amour humain, parole divine. Recueil de textes des Pères de l'Église sur le mariage.* Paris, 1947.
Denys Gorce. *Mariage et perfection chrétienne chez Jean Chrysostome.* Études carmélitaines, 1936.
J. Durmontier. 'Le mariage dans les milieux d'Antioche et de Byzance d'après saint Jean Chrysostome', *Lettres d'humanité* 6 (1947) 102–66.
Henri Rondet. *Introduction à l'étude de la théologie du mariage.* Paris, 1960.
Henri Crouzel. *Virginité et mariage selon Origène.* Paris, 1962.
_____. *L'Église primitive face au divorce.* Théologie historique 13. Paris, 1971.
J. P. Broudehoux. *Mariage et famille chez Clément d'Alexandrie.* Paris, 1970.
John Meyendorff. *Marriage: An Orthodox Perspective.* New York, 1971.
Tomaš Špidlík. 'La consezione cristologica del matrimonio nelle liturgie orientali', *Bessarione*, 1: 139–52. Rome, 1979.
Pierre Adnès. 'Mariage et vie chrétienne', DS 10 (1980) 355–88.
_____. 'Mariage spirituel', DS10; 388–408.

VIRGINITY, p. 220

Pierre Thomas Camelot. *Virgines Christi.* Paris, 1944.
_____. 'Les traités *De Virginitate* au IVe siècle', *Études Carmélitaines* 31 (1952) 273–292: Mystique et continence.

Francisco de B. Vizmanos. *Las Virgenes cristianas de la Iglesia primitiva.* Madrid, 1949
D. Amand de Mendieta. 'La virginité chez Eusèbe et l'ascétisme familial dans la première moitié du IVe siècle', *Revue d'histoire ecclésiastique* 56 (1955) 777–820.
Garcia M. Colombás. *Paradis et vie angélique:* 145ff. Paris, 1961.
Henri Crouzel. *Virginité et mariage selon Origène*, Museum Lessianum Section théologique 58. Paris-Bruges, 1963.
Aimé Legrand. *Mariage et célibat.* Paris, 1965
Michel Aubineau. Introduction au *Traité de la virginité* de Grégoire de Nysse, SCh119 (1966).
Bernard Grillet. Introduction au traité *La virginité* de Jean Chrysostome. SCh125 (1966).
John Bugge. *Virginitas. An Essay in the History of a Medieval Ideal.* Archives Internationales d'Histoires des Idées. Series Minor 17. The Hague, 1975.
Tomaš Špidlík. 'Il matrimonio, sacramento di unita nel pensiero di Chrisostomo', *Augustinianum* 17 (1977) 221–26.
Pierre Adnès. 'Mariage spirituel', DS 10: 388–408.

BODILY MORTIFICATIONS, p. 233

Jean Bremond. *Les Pères du desert:* Ch. IV, rigueurs corporelles, pp. 155–202 Paris, 1927.
Irénée Hausherr. 'Abnégation, renoncement, mortification'. *Christus* 20 (1959) 182–195. Cf. *Études de spiritualité orientale.* OCA 183: 301–13. Rome, 1969.
Bernard Lohse. *Askese und Mönchtum in der Antike und in der alten Kirche.* Vienna, 1969.

FASTING, p. 233

S. Congregazione per la Chiesa orientale. Codificazione canonica orientale, Città del Vaticano: fasc. 1 (1936) pp. 56–8 (Egyptians); fasc. 7 (1937) pp. 234–48 (Syro-Malabarese); fasc. 10 (1949); Byzantines (Cf. Index: *ieiunium*); fasc. 12 (1940) pp. 61ff (Armenians); fasc. 15 (1940) Chaldeans (Cf. Index: *ieiumium*); fasc. 28 (1943) Syro-Antiochians (Cf. Index: ieiunium).
Friedrich Heiler. *Die katholische Kirche des Ostens und Westens.* Vol. I. Munich, 1937.
Maria-Albert Michel, Joseph Lamy, N. Tolstoy. 'Abstinence: chez les Grecs, Syriens, Arméniens, Coptes, Russes ...', DThC I (1909) 262–71.
P. Ioannou. 'Fastentage der byzantinischen Kirche', LThK^2 4: 38.
T. Pichler. *Das Fasten bei Basilius dem Grossen und im antiken Heidentum.* Innsbruck, 1955.
Herbert Musurillo. 'The Problem of Ascetical Fasting in the Greek Patristic Writers', *Traditio* 12 (1956) 1–64.
J. F. Perridon. 'De vasten in de Byzantijnse Kerk', *Het Christelijk Oosten en Hereeniging* 11 (1958–59) 79–96.
S. Vukovič. 'Comment on a résolu la discussion sur le jeûne au Mont Athos dans le XIe siècle' (in Serbian), *Bogoslovie* 6 (1962) 13–15.

Placide Deseille. 'Jeûne, Écriture, La tradition de l'Église', DS 8: 1164–75 (bibliography).
H. J. Sieben. Dossier patristique sur le jeûne, DS: 1175–79. J. Řezáč. 'Digiuno (nella Chiesa bizantina)' DIP 3 (1976) 498–500.
Garcia M. Colombás. 'Dietetica monastica', Ibid. 492–495.

SPIRITUAL WARFARE, p. 233

J. A. Sawhill. *The Use of Athletic Metaphors in the Biblical Homilies of St. John Chrysostom.* (Diss.) Princeton, 1928.
Pierre Bourguignon and F. Werner. 'Combat spirituel', DS 2/1 (1953) 1135–42.
Adalbert de Vogüé. Introduction to *Règle du Maître*, SCh 105 (1964) 89ff.
Henri Crouzel. 'L'anthropologie d'Origène dans la perspective du combat spirituel', RAM 31 (1955) 364–85.

THE DEMON, p. 234

Joseph Eugène Mangenot. 'Démon', DThC 4/1 (1939) 339–76.
Edward Langton. *Good and Evil Spirits. A Study of Jewish and Christian Doctrine, its Origin and Development.* London, 1942.
Stephanus Bettencourt. *Doctrine ascetica Origenis seu quid docuerit de ratione animae humanae cum daemonibus*, Studia Anselmiana 16. Rome, 1945.
Satan, Études carmélitaines. Paris: Desclée de Brouwer, 1948.
Uta Ranke-Heinemann. 'Die ersten Mönche und Demonen', *Geist und Leben* 29 (1956) 165–70.
H. Wey. *Die Funktionen der bösen Geister bei den griechischen Apologeten des zweiten Jahrhunderts nach Christus.* Winterthur, 1957.
Jean Daniélou. 'Démon – dans la littérature ecclésiastique jusqu'à Origène, DS 3 (1957) 152–89.
———. *La Théologie du judéo-christianisme.* Paris-Tournai, 1958.
———. 'Exorcisme', DS 4/2 (1961) 1995–2004.
A. and C. Guillaumont. 'Démon dans la plus ancienne littérature monastique,' DS 3 (1957) 189–212.
A. J. Festugière. *Les moines d'Orient.* Vol I:23–39: the monk and demons. Paris, 1961.
P. P. Joannou. *Démonologie populaire-démonologie critique au XIe siècle. La vie inédite de S. Auxence par M. Psellos.* Wiesbaden, 1971.
A. and C. Guillaumont. Introduction to the *Traité pratique d'Evagre.* SCh 170 (1971) 94ff.
Garcia M. Colombas. 'Demonologia monastica', DIP 3 (1976) 440–42.

CUSTODY OF THE HEART, 242

Iréneée Hausherr. *La méthode d'oraison hésychaste*, Orientalia Christiana 9, fasc. 36 (1927) 134–42.
———. *Hésychasme. Étude de spiritualité*, OCP 22 (1956) 273–85 (*nepsis*); OCA 176 (1966) 225–37.

Robert Vernay. 'Attention', DS 1 (1937) 1058-77.
Michel Olphe-Galliard. 'La pureté de coeur d'après Cassien', RAM 17 (1936) 28-60.
Augustin George. 'Heureux les coeurs purs, ils verront Dieu.' *Bible et vie chrétienne* 12 (1956) 71-77.
Jacques Dupont. *Les béatitudes*. Bruges, 1954. Revised edition, Études bibliques 3:557-603 (bibliography). Paris, 1973.
Jean Claude Guy. 'Examen de conscience chez les Pères de l'Église', DS 4 (1961) 1801-7.
E. J. Agulles. *Bienaventurados los puros de corazón*. Valencia, 1965.
Juana Raasch. 'The Monastic Concept of Purity of Heart and its Sources', *Studia monastica* 9 (1966) 7-33, 183-213; 10 (1968) 7-55; 11 (1969) 269-314; 12 (1970) 7-41.
Pierre Adnès. 'Garde du coeur', DS 6 (1967) 100-17.
_____. 'Nepsis', DS 11 (1982) 110-18.

DISCERNMENT OF SPIRITS, p. 244

Arthur Cholet. 'Discernement des esprits', DThC 4 (1911) 1375-1415.
Irénée Hausherr. 'Direction spirituelle en Orient', DS 3 (1957) 1024-28: *diacrisis*.
Jacques Guillet. 'Discernement des esprits dans l'Ecriture', DS 3:1222-47.
Gustave Bardy. 'Discernement des esprits chez les Pères', DS 3:1247-54.
Francis Marty. 'Le discernement des esprits dans le *Peri Archon* d'Origène', RAM 34 (1958) 147-64, 253-74.
F. Digjan. 'La discrétion dans les Apophthégmes des Pères', *Angelicum* 39 (1962) 403-15.
Edouard des Places. Introduction to *Diadoque de Photicé*. SCh5ter (1966) 42-8.
Garcia M. Colombás. 'Discernimento degli spiriti (diacrisis)', DIP 3 (1976) 705-6.
For other bibliographies, see DS 3:1275, 1279ff, 1285, 1291.

EXAMINATION OF CONSCIENCE, p. 247

Jean Claude Guy. 'L'examen de conscience chez les Pères de l'Eglise', DS 4/2 (1961) 1801-7.
Atanas Liuma and André Derville. 'Examen particulier', DS 4/2:1838-49.

THE EIGHT EVIL THOUGHTS, p. 248

Otto Zöckler. *Das Lehrstück von der sieben Hauptsünden*. Munich, 1893.
P. Schulze. *Die Entwicklung der Hauptlaster und Haupttugenden von Gregor dem Grossen bis Petrus Lombardus*. Greiwald, 1914.
Johannes Stelzenberger. *Die Beziehungen der frühchristlichen Sittenlehre zur Ethik der Stoa*: 379-402. Munich, 1932.
Anton Vögtle. 'Woher stammt das Schema der Hauptsünden', *Theologisches Quartalschrift* 122 (1941) 217-37.

William M. Green. *Initium omnis peccati superbia*. Augustine on pride as the First Sin, University of California Publications in Classical Philology 13 (1949) 407-432.
Morton Bloomfield. *The Seven Deadly Sins*. East Lansing, Michigan, 1952.
Martin Steiner. *La tentation de Jésus dans l'interpretation patristique de saint Justin à Origene*. Paris, 1962.
Walter Völker. *Scala Paradisi. Eine Studie zu Johannes Climacus und zugleich eine Vorstudie zu Simeon dem Neuen Theologen*. Wiesbaden, 1968.
A. Guillaumont. Introduction to *Traité pratique d'Evagre*. SCh170 (1971) 55ff. English translation of Evagrius, with an Introduction and Notes, by J. E. Bamberger, *The Praktikos-Chapters on Prayer*, Cistercian Studies Series 4. Kalamazoo, 1958.
Heinrich Bacht. 'Logismos', DS 9 (1976) 955-57.

IMPURITY, p. 250

Bernard Dolhagaray. 'Fornication', DThC 6 (1920) 600-11.
Mystique et continence, Etudes carmélitaines. Paris, 1952.
Ermanno Ancilli. 'Lussuria', DESp 2 (1975) 1111-12.

SADNESS, p. 251

Michel Spanneut. *Le stoïcisme ...*, Index. p. 480: *lupē*.
H. Martin. 'Désolation', DS 3 (1957) 631-45.
―――――. 'Déréliction', DS3:504-17.
Robert Vernay. 'Découragement,' DS3:58-65.
M. Caprioli. 'Tristezza', DESp 2 (1975) 1919-20.
T. Goggi. 'Scoraggiamento'. *Ibid.*, 1191-2.

ACEDIA, p. 252

Gustave Bardy. 'Acedia', DS 1 (1937) 166-69.
H. Martin. 'Dégoût spirituel', DS 3 (1957) 99-104.
Joseph Mac Avoy. 'Endurcissement', DS 4/1 (1960) 642-52.

THE PASSIONS, p. 267

H. D. Noble. 'Passions' DThC 11/2 (1932) 2211-41.
Irénée Hausherr. *Philautie. De la tendresse pour soi à la charité*, OCA 137. Rome, 1952.
Jean Daniélou. *Platonisme et théologie mystique:* 50ff. Paris, 1944.
Wilhelm Michaelis. 'Pascho', in Kittel 5 (1954) 903-39.
Michel Spanneut. *Le stoïcisme ...* Index, p. 482: passions.
Lars Thunberg. *Microcosm and Mediator. The Theological Anthropology of Maximus the Confessor:* 244fff. Lund, 1965.
G. Presente. 'Passioni', DESp 2 (1975) 1406-10.

Bibliography

APATHEIA, p. 270

Max Pohlenz. *Vom Zorne Gottes. Eine Studie über den Einfluss der greichischen Philosophie auf das alte Christentum.* Göttingen, 1909.
J. K. Mozley. *The Impassibility of God.* Cambridge, 1926.
Gustave Bardy. 'Apatheia', DS 1 (1937) 727–46.
Walter Völker. *Fortschritt und Vollendung bei Philo von Alexandrien*, TU 49:126–38. Leipzig, 1938.
H. D. Pirre. 'Sur l'emploi des terms Apatheia et Eleos dans les oeuvres de Clément d'Alexandrie', *Revue des sciences philosophiques et théologiques* 27 (1938) 427–31.
_____. *Pitié ou insensibilité? Le témoignage de Clément d'Alexandrie.* Thuillies, 1939.
Pierre de Labriolle. 'Apatheia', *Mélanges... A Ernout*: 125–223. Paris, 1940.
Jean Daniélou. *Platonisme et théologie mystique. Essai sur la doctrine spirituelle de saint Grégoire de Nysse*, Théologie 2. Paris 1944. 2nd ed. 1954, pp. 61–6, 92–7.
Augustinus Dirking. 'Die Bedeutung des Wortes Apathie beim hl. Basilius dem Grossen', *Theologische Quartalschrift* 134 (1954) 202–12.
Th. Rüther. *Die sittliche Forderung der Apatheia in den beiden ersten christlichen Jahrhunderten und bei Klement von Alexandrien.* Freiburg-im-Breisgau, 1949.
Evangel Theodorou. 'Apatheia', in *Threskeutikē kai ēthikē enkyklopaideia.* vol. 2:138ff. Athens, 1963.
Evangelos G. Konstantinou. *Die Tugendlehre Gregors von Nyssa*: 138ff. Würzburg, 1966.
Pierre Thomas Camelot. 'Hellénisme', DS 7/1 (1969) 153–56.
A. Guillaumont. Introduction to *Traité Pratique d'Evagre le Pontique.* SCh170 (1971) 98–112.
Pierre Adnès. 'Impeccabilité', DS 7/2 (1971) 1614–20.
Tomaš Spidlík. 'Apatheia', DIP 1 (1974) 714–15.

THE WILL OF GOD, p. 283

Anton Michel. 'Volonté de Dieu', DThC 15/2 (1950) 3309–74.
Friedrich Wetter. 'Wille Gottes', LthK² 10:1161–63.
E. Jacquemin and X. Léon-Dufour. 'Volonté de Dieu', VTB (1970) 1381–86.

OBEDIENCE TO THE SPIRITUAL FATHER, p. 284

Jean Gribomont. 'Obéissance et Évangile selon saint Basile le Grand', *Vie Spirituelle.* Supplement 21 (1952) 192–215.
Adalbert de Vogüé. 'Le monastère, Église du Christ', *Studia anselmiana* 42:25–46. Rome, 1957.
_____. *La communauté et l'Abbé dans la Règle de Saint Benoît.* Paris-Bruges, 1961. English translation in two volumes, *Community and Abbot in the Rule of Saint Benedict*, Cistercian Studies Series 5/1 (1978), 5/2 (1985).
Konstantinos Mouratides. *L'obéissance monastique dans l'Église ancienne* (in Greek). Athens, 1957.

Joseph Lecuyer. 'Docilité au Saint-Esprit', DS 3 (1957) 1471–97.
Catherine Capelle. *Le voeu d'obéissance des origines au XIIe siècle*. Paris, 1959.
Pierre Salmon. *L'abbé dans la tradition monastique*. Paris, 1962. English translation, *The Abbot in Monastic Tradition*, Cistercian Studies Series 14 1972.
Georgii Florovskij. 'Poslusanie i svidetel' stvo' [*Obedience and Witnessing*], *Vestnik russkogo studentskogo christiankogo dviženija* 70–71 (1963) 18–28.
Oliver Rousseau, Michel Olphe-Galliard, *et alii*. *L'obéissance. Problèmes de vie religieuse*. 2nd ed. Paris, 1965.
Henri Rondet, *L'obéissance problème de vie, mystère de Foi*. Lyon, 1966.
Henri Holstein. 'Gouvernement spirituel', DS 6 (1967) 644–69.
Irénée Hausherr. *'L'obéissance religieuse.'* Toulouse, 1967.
Tomaš Špidlík. 'L'obedienza tra carisma e istituzione', *Vita monastica* 24 (1970) n. 100 pp. 36–49.
_____. 'Obedience in the Eastern Church Tradition', CIS, vol. 10/2: 69–74. Rome, 1979.
J. M. R. Tillard. 'Obéissance', DS 11 (1982) 535–63.

SPIRITUAL GUIDANCE, p. 284

Sergei Smirnov. *Duchovnyj otec v drevni vostočnoj Cerkvi* [The Spiritual Father in the Ancient Eastern Church]. Sergiev Posad, 1906.
_____. *Drevne-russkij duchovnik*. [The Spiritual Father in Ancient Russia]. Moscow, 1914.
Placide de Meester. *De monachico statu iuxta disciplinam byzantinorum*. Citta del Vaticano, 1942. See Index: *pater spiritualis*.
Irénée Hausherr. *Direction spirituelle en Orient autrefois*, OCA 144. Rome, 1955.
_____. 'La direction spirituelle chez les chrétiens Orientaux', DS 3 (1957) 1008–60 (bibliography).
Edouard des Places. 'Direction spirituelle dans l'antiquité classique', DS 3:1002–8.
M. Joseph Rouët de Journel. 'La direction spirituelle dans la Russie ancienne,' *Revue des Études Slaves* 38 (1961) 173–79.
Fairy von Lilienfeld. 'Anthropos Pneumatikos—Pater Pneumatophoros: Neues Testament und Aphophthegmata Patrum', *Studia Patristica* 5 TU 80:383–92. Berlin, 1962.
Nikolaj Arseniev. 'La direction spirituelle dans l'Église Russe', *Contacts* 38 (1967) 108–29.
Paul Evdokimov. 'La paternité spirituelle', *Ibid.*, p. 100–7.
Ermanno Ancilli. 'Direzione spirituale', DIP 3 (1976) 530–48.
Cuthbert Hainsworth. *Staretz Paisy Velichkovsky (1722–1794). Doctrine of Spiritual Guidance*. Rome, 1976.
Tomaš Špidlík. 'La direzione spirituale nell' Oriente cristiano', *Vita consacrata* 16 (1980) 502–14, 573–82.

THE DIVINE COMMANDMENTS, p. 286

David Amand. *L'ascèse monastique de saint Basile*. Maredsous, 1948.
C. H. Dodd. *'Gospel and Law'. The Relation of Faith and Ethics in Early Christianity'*. New York, 151

Bibliography 405

V. E. Hasler. *Gesetz und Evangelium in der alten Kirche bei Origenes. Eine auslegungsgeschichtliche Untersuchung.* Zurich, 1953.
Rudolf Schnackenburg. 'Gebote Gottes', LThK²:558–60.
Pierre Grelot. 'Loi', VTB (1970) 667–79.
Guy Bourgeault. *Décalogue et morale chrétienne. Enquête patristique sur l'utilisation et l'interprétation chrétienne du décalogue de c. 60 à c. 220,* Recherches 2, Paris: Desclée, 1971.
Jean Marie Aubert. 'Loi', *Catholicisme* 7 (1975) 995–1015.

EASTERN MONASTICISM, p. 287

Adolf Harnack. *Das Mönchtum, seine Ideale und seine Geschichte.* Leipzig, 1906.
Hal Koch. *Quellen zur Geschichte des Askese und des Mönchtums in der alten Kirche.* Tübingen, 1933.
Karl Heussi. *Der Ursprung des Mönchtums.* Tübingen, 1936.
Pierre de Labriolle. 'Les débuts du monachisme', in A. Fliche-V. Martin, *Histoire de l'Église,* vol. III:299–369. Paris, 1936.
David Amand. *Ascèse monastique de Saint Basile.* Maredsous, 1948.
André Ignace Mennessier. 'Conseils evangéliques', DS 2/2 (1953) 1592–1609.
Il monachesimo orientale. Atti del convegno di studi orientali a Roma 9–12 Aprile 1958, OCA 153 (1958).
Théologie de la vie monastique, Théologie 49. Paris, 1961.
Guiseppe Turbessi. 'Ascetismo e Monachesimo prebenedettino': 189–217 (bibliography). Rome, 1961.
―――――. 'Monachesimo', in E. Ancilli, ed. *Diz. encicl. di spiritualità,* vol. II:2131–38. Rome 1975.
Paul Evdokimov. 'Le monachisme interiorisé', *Le Millénaire de Mont Athos.* Vol I:331–52. Chevetogne, 1963.
K. Christou Panaghiotis. 'The Monastic Life in the Eastern Orthodox Church', in A. J. Philippou, ed. *The Orthodox Ethos:* 249–58. Oxford, 1964.
Archimandrite Sophrony. 'Principles of Orthodox Asceticism', *Ibid..,* 259–86.
Charil S. Tzogas. 'Monachismos,' in *Thesteutike kai ethike enkyklopaideia* 9 (1966) 18–35 (bibliography in Greek).
Tomaš Špidlík. 'Monasticism: Oriental since 1453', in *The New Catholic Encyclopedia* 9 (1967) 1043–48.
―――――. 'Das östliche Mönchtum und das östliche Frömmigkeitsleben', A. van Ivánka, J. Tyciak and P. Wiertz eds., *Handbuch der Ostkirchenkunde*: 543–68. Dusseldorf, 1972.
'Monachisme', DS 10 (1980) 1524–1617.
Tomaš Špidlík. 'Orthodoxe (Spiritualité)', DS 11 (1982) 972–1001.

VIRTUE, p. 288

Wilhelm Michaelis. *Die Entwickelungsstufen in Platos Tugendlehre.* Barmen, 1893.
H. Kalchreuter. *Die Mesotes bei und vor Aristoteles.* Tübingen, 1911.
Johannes Stelzenberger. *Die Beziehung der frühchristlichen Sittenlehre zur Ethik der Stoa*: 307–54. Munich, 1932.

Otto Bauernfeind. 'Arete' in Kittel 1 (1933 and 1957) 457–61.
F. van den Grinten. *Die natürliche und übernatürliche Begründung des Tugendlebens bei Clemens von Alexandrien.* Rome-Bonn, 1948.
A. Michel. 'Vertu', DThC 15/2 (1950) 2739–99.
Archbishop Michael [Konstantinides]. *Faith, Hope, Charity, Prayer* (in Greek). Athens, 1950.
Jacques Dupont. *Les Béatitudes.* Bruges, 1954.
Juan Alfaro. *Adnotationes ad tractatum de virtutibus.* Rome, 1959.
Evangelos G. Konstatinou. *Die Tugendlehre Gregors von Nyssa im Verhältnis zu der Antik-Philosophischen und Jüdisch-Christlichen Tradition,* Das östliche Christentum 17. Würzburg, 1966.
Grégoire de Nazianze, OCA 189:57–74. Rome 1971.

CHARITY, p. 295

G. Horn. 'L'amour divin. Note sur le mot "eros" chez S. Grégoire de Nysse', RAM 6 (1925) 278–89.
Salvatore Marsili. *Giovanni Cassiano e Evagrio Pontico. Dottrina sulla carita e contemplazione.* Rome, 1936.
Jozef Bliemel. *Agape im Frühchristentum. Eine ethisch-historische Untersuchung.* Rome, 1941.
Anders Nygren. *Eros und Agape, Gestaltswandlungen der christlichen Liebe.* Gütersloh, 1937. English translation by P. S. Watson, *Agape and Eros.* London, 1953.
Anastasy Welykyi. *Die Lehre der Väter des dritten Jahrhunderts von der Gottesliebe und Gottesfurcht.* (Diss.) Rome, 1948.
Gottfrid Quell and Ethelbert Stauffer. 'Agapao, agape, agapetos', in Kittel 1 (1933 and 1957) 20–55. In English, London, 1949.
Viktor Warnach. *Agape. Die Liebe as Grundmotiv der neutestamentlichen Theologie.* Düsseldorf, 1951.
Irénée Hausherr. *Philautie. De la tendresse pour soi à la charité selon saint Maxime le Confesseur,* OCA 137. Rome, 1952.
Jacques Farges and Marcel Viller. 'La charité chez les Pères', DS 2/1 (1953) 523–69.
Ceslas Spicq. *Agapè. Prolégomènes à une étude de théologie néotestamentaire.* Louvain-Leiden, 1955.
———. *Agapè dans le Nouveau Testament,* Études bibliques. 3 vols. Paris, 1958–1959.
Uta Ranke-Heinemann. 'Die Liebe als ein Motiv für die Entstehung des Mönchtums', *Münchener Theologische Zeitschrift* 8 (1957) 289–94.
William B. Frazier. *The Pre-eminence of Divine Mercy according to the Greek Fathers.* Rome, 1959.
Giovanni M. Cossu. 'Il motive formale della carita in S. Basilio Magno', *Bolletino della Badia greca di Grottaferrata* 14 (1960) 3–30.
J. Kabiersch. *Untersuchungen zum Begriff der Philanthropia bei dem Kaiser Julian.* Wiesbaden, 1960.
A. H. Armstrong and R. A. Markus. *Christian Faith and Greek Philosophy*: 79–96. London, 1960.
J. Colson. *Agapè, charité chez saint Ignace d'Antioche.* Paris, 1961.
Marguerite-Marie Laurent. *Realisme et richesse de l'amour chrétien. Essai sur Eros et Apagè,* Studia Regina Mundi 1. Rome, 1961.

Divo Barsotti. *La dottrina dell'amore nei Padri della Chiesa fino a Ireneo.* Milan, 1963.
John M. Rist. *Eros and Psyche: Studies in Plato, Plotinus and Origen.* Toronto, 1964.
_____. 'A Note on Eros and Agape in Pseudo-Dionysius', *Vigiliae christianae* 20 (1966) 235-43.
Jean Kirchmeyer. 'Grecque (Église)', DS 6:857ff.

PRAYER, p. 307

Eduard von der Goltz. *Das Gebet in der ältesten Christenheit.* Leipzig, 1901.
D. Genet. *L'enseignement d'Origène sur la prière.* Cahors, 1903.
Friedrich Heiler. *Das Gebet. Eine religionsgeschichtliche und religions-psychologische Untersuchung.* 5th ed., Munich, 1923. Rpt. Munchen-Basel, 1969 (bibliography). English translation by S. McComb and J. E. Park, *Prayer: A Study in the History and Psychology of Religion.* London, 1932.
L'oraison. Paris, 1947.
Jacob Muyser. *Un premier essai d'étude sur les vraies valeurs de la prière du moine copte et celle de son église d'après ce que nous possédons comme sources coptes les plus authentiques.* (Extract from *Les Cahiers Carmélitains*, 1950). Cairo, 1950.
La prière. Bruges, 1954.
Irénée Hausherr. 'Comment priaient les Pères', RAM 32 (1956) 33-58, 284-96.
_____. *Les leçons d'un contemplatif. Le Traité de l'Oraison d'Evagre le Pontique.* Paris, 1960.
_____. *Prière de vie — vie de prière.* Paris, 1964.
_____. *Hésychasme et prière*, OCA 176. Rome, 1966.
Elgraf Kovaleskij. *Technique de la prière.* Paris: Institut Orthodoxe Français Saint Denis, 1961.
Nikolaos G. Papadopoulos. 'La prière selon Origène (in Greek), in *GregPal* 45 (1962) 46-51, 124-29.
Joseph Nasrallah. 'La prière dans l'Église orthodoxe', *Études Franciscaines* 12 (Paris, 1962) 8-18.
Leonidas J. Philippidis. 'Prayer from the Religious and Psychological Point of View', *The Greek Orthodox Theological Review* 9 (1963) 29-49.
Albert Hamman. *La prière II. Les trois premiers siècles.* Tournai, 1963.
A. Vedernikov. 'Der heilige Johannes Klimakos as Lehrer des Gebetes', *Stimme der Orthodoxie* 4 (Berlin, 1964) 43-9; 5 (1964) 46-52.
Albert Plé, ed. *La prière.* 2nd ed., Paris, 1965.
La preghiera nelle Biblia e nella tradizione patristica e monastica.
Renato Boccassino, ed. *La preghiera* 3 vols. Rome-Milan, 1967.
Ermanno Ancilli. 'Preghiera', DESp 2 (1975) 1481-97.
Olivier Clément, B. Bobrinskij, E. Behr-Sigel, M. Lot-Borodine. *La douloureuse joie. Aperçus sur la prière personnelle de l'Orient chrétien*, Spiritualité orientale 14. Abbaye de Bellefontaine, 1974.
Wilhem Gessel. *Die Theologie des Gebetes nach 'De oratione' von Origenes.*
Špidlík. 'Ignatian Meditation and the Prayer of the Oriental Church', in V. V. ed., *Ignatian Spirituality*: 9-29. Rome, 1979.
_____. 'La prière en l'Église d'Orient', in *Tarnowskie studia teologiczne*: 115-128. Tarnow, 1981.

Michel Dupuy. 'Oraison (Oratio, Oracion)', DS 11 (1982) 831–46.
Aimé Solignac. 'Pater noster', DS 12:388–413.

THE PSALMS, p. 311

For the various commentaries on the psalms in the Fathers, see Werbeck, *Psalmen im Alten Testament*, in *Religion in Geschichte und Gegenwart*: col. 684ff. Tübingen, 1961.
Garcia M. Colombás. *Paradis et vie angélique*: 203ff. Paris, 1961.
Robert Langhe. *Le Psautier. Ses origines, ses problèmes littéraires, son influence*. Louvain, 1962.
Psaumes. DThC, Tables générales 3 (1972) 3820–25.

LITURGICAL PRAYER, p. 312

Nickolaj Vasil Gogol. *Razmyšlenija o Božestvennoj liturgii*. St Petersburg, 1902. English translation by Rosemary Edmonds, *The Divine Liturgy of the Eastern Orthodox Church*. London, 1960.
Sergei Bulgakov. *Le ciel sur la terre*. Munich, 1928.
_____. *The Orthodox Church*: 149–60. London, 1935.
Julius Tyciak. *Die Liturgie als Quelle östlicher Frömmigkeit*, Ecclesia Orans 20. Freiburg, 1937.
Michele Tarchnišvili. *Die byzantinische Liturgie als Verwirklichung der Einheit und Gemeinschaft im Dogma*, Das Oestliche Christentum 9. Würsburg, 1939.
Alphonse Raes. *Introductio in liturgiam orientalem*. Rome, 1947.
Boris Bobrinskij. 'Molitva i bogosluženije y žizni pravoslavnoj Cerkvi' (Prayer and the Liturgy in the Orthodox Church) in S. Verchovskoj, *Pravoslavije v žizni*: 241–73. New York, 1953.
Nikolaj Arseniev. 'Traits majeurs de la vie liturgique, contemplative et sacramentale', *Contacts* 14 (1962) 38–9, 135–38.
J. M. Sauget. *Bibliographie des Liturgies orientales* (1900-1960). Rome, 1962.
Tomaš Špidlík. 'La preghiera presso i popoli slavi,' in R. Boccassino, ed., *La preghiera*, Vol. 2:787–817. Milan-Rome, 1967.
Alexander Schmemann. *For the Life of the World. Sacraments and Orthodoxy*. Crestwood, New York, 1973.
J. Castellano. 'Liturgia', DESp 2 (1975) 1086–1104.
V.V. 'Liturgy et vie spirituelle', DS 9 (1979) 873–939.
Irénée Henri Dalmais. 'Les liturgies d'Orient', *Rites et Symboles*. Paris, 1980.

ICONS, p. 313

E. Trubetskoi. *Die religiöse Weltanschauung der altrussischen Ikonenmalerei*. Paderborn, 1972.
Sergei Bulgakov. *The Orthodox Church*: 161–67. London, 1935.
Georg Wunderle. *Um die Seele der heiligen Ikonen, Eine religions-psychologische Betrachtung*, Das östliche Christentum 3. Würsburg, 1947.

Leonid Ouspensky. *L'icône, vision du monde spirituel.* Paris, 1948.
―――――. *Essai sur la théologie de l'icône dans l'Église orthodoxe.* Paris, 1960. English translation, *Theology of the Icon.* Crestwood, New York, 1978.
Leonid Ouspensky and Vladimir Lossky. *Der Sinn der Ikonen.* Bern-Olten, 1952. English translation by G. E. H. Palmer and E. E. Kadloubovsky, *The Meaning of Icons.* Boston, 1952.
Heinz Skrobucha. *Von Geist und Gestalt der Ikonen*, Recklinghausen, 1961.
―――――. *Le message des Icônes.* Freiburg, 1966.
Pierre Scazzoso. 'Il probleme delle sacre icone', *Aevum* 43 (1969) 304–23.
Paul Evdokimov. *L'art de l'icône. Théologie de la beauté.* Bruges-Paris, 1970.
Tomaš Špidlík and Pierre Miquel. 'Icône'. DS 7/2 (1971) 1224–39 (bibliography).
Wilhelm Nyssen. 'Zur Theologie des Bildes.' *Handbuch der Ostkirchenkunde*, pp. 373–482. Bibliography, 803ff.
Michail Alpatov. *Le icone russe. Problemi di storia e d'interpretazione artistica.* Turin, 1976.
Christoph von Schoenborn. *L'icône du Christ. Fondaments théologiques élaborés entre le Ier et IIe Concile de Nicée* (325–787), Paradosis 14. Freiburg, Switz., 1976.
Tomaš Špidlík. 'L'icône, manifestation du monde spirituel', *Gregorianum* 61/3 (1980) 539–54.
―――――. 'Theologia dell' iconografia mariana', In *La Madre del Signore*, Parola spirito e vita, vol. 6:243–54. Bologna, 1982.

CHURCH-BUILDING, p. 314

Henri Leclercq. 'Église', DACL 4/2 (1921) 2220–38. 'Églises'. *Ibid.*, 2279–99.
Leonid Ouspensky. *Essai sur la théologie de l'icône.* Paris, 1960.
G. Bandmann. 'Kirche, Kirchenbau', in *Lexikon der christlichen Ikonographie* 2: col. 514–29. Freiburg/Br. 1970.
A. Pigna. 'Tempio'. DESp 2 (1975) 1841–44.

UNCEASING PRAYER, p. 315

Gerardo Békés. 'De continua oratione Clementis Alexandrini doctrina', *Studia Anselmiana* 14. Rome, 1942.
M. J. Marx. 'Incessant Prayer in the Vita Antonii', in *Antonius Magnus Eremita*, Studia Anselmiana 38:108–35. Rome, 1956.
Irénée Hausherr. '*Opus Dei*,' OCP 13 (1947) 195–218.
―――――. *Études de spiritualité orientale*, OCA 183:121–44. Rome, 1969.
―――――. *Noms du Christ et voies d'oraison.* OCA 157. Rome, 1960. English translation, *The Name of Jesus*, Kalamazoo, 1978.
―――――. 'La prière perpétuelle du chrétien', in *Laïcat et Sainteté*, vol. 2:111–166. Rome, 1965.
―――――. *Hésychasme et prière*, OCA 176:255–306. Rome, 1966.
Ermanno Ancilli. 'Presenza di Dio', DESp 2 (1975) 1498–1504.

ACOEMETI, p. 315

J. Pargoir. 'Acémètes', DACL 1 (1907) 307–21.
Siméon Vailhe. 'Acémètes', DHG 1 (1912) 274–82.
Venance Grumel. 'Acémètes', DS 1 (1937) 169–75.
Martin Jugie. 'Acemeti', *Enc. Catt.* 1 (1948) 211.
F. S. Pericoli Ridolfini. 'Alessandro l'Acemeta', Bibl. SS 1 (1961) col. 766–68.
Io Fontoules. '*Akoimēton Monē*', in *Thresteutike kai ethike enkyklopaideia* I (1962) col. 1216–17.
Tomaš Špidlík. 'Acèmeti', DIP 1 (1974) 88.

THE JESUS PRAYER, p. 316

Un moine de l'Église de l'Orient. *La prière de Jésus*. Chevetogne, 1947; (in *Irenikon*, 1951, 1959).
Heinrich Bacht. 'Das 'Jesus-Gebet, seine Geschichte und Problematik', *Geist und Leben* 24 (1951) 326–38.
Bernhard Schultze. *Der Streit um die Göttlichkeit des Namens Jesu in der Russischen Theologie*, OCP 17 (1951) 321–94.
_____. *Untersuchungen über das Jesus-Gebet*, OCP 18 (1952) 319–43.
Basile Krivocheine. 'Date du texte traditionnel de la "Prière de Jésus"', *Messager de l'Exarchat du Patriarche russe en Europe Occidentale* 7–8 (1951) 55–9.
E. Kadloubovsky and G. E. H. Palmer. *Writings from the Philokalia on Prayer of The Heart*. London, 1951.
I. Brjancanivnov. (Translated by Father Lazarus.) *On the Prayer of Jesus. From the Ascetic Essays of Bishop Ignatius Brianchaninov*. London, 1952.
W. Nölle. 'Hesychasmus und Yoga'. *Byzantinische Zeitschrift* 47 (1954) 95–103.
Kallistos II [Xanthopoulos]. *Das Herzensgebet. Mystik und Yoga der Ostkirche. Die Centurie der Monche Kallistus und Ignatius*. Munich, 1955.
Irénée Hausherr. *Noms du Christ et voies d'oraison*, OCA 157. Rome, 1960.
The Name of Jesus. Kalamazoo, 1978.
Per-Olof Sjögren. *Jesusbönen*. Stockholm, 1961. Translated by S. Linton, *The Jesus Prayer*. Philadelphia, 1975.
Kallistos Ware. *The Power of the Name. The Jesus Prayer in Orthodox Spirituality*. Oxford, 1974.
A. Zigmund-Cerbu. 'Lumières nouvelles sur le yoga et l'hésychasme', *Contacts* 26 (1974) 272–89.
Pierre Adnès. 'Jesus (Prière à)', DS 8 (1974) 1126–50.
Tomaš Špidlík. 'Esicasmo', DIP 3 (1976) 1306–10.
M. Basil Pennington. *Centering Prayer. Renewing an Ancient Christian Prayer Form*. New York, 1982.

CONTEMPLATION, p. 327

A. J. Festugière. *Contemplation et vie contemplative selon Platon*. Paris, 1936.
'*Contemplation...*', articles in DS 2/2 (1953) 1643–2193, especially col. 1762ff.

Bibliography

Irénée Hausherr. *Les leçons d'un contemplatif. Le traité de l'Oraison d'Evagre le Pontique*. Paris, 1960.
Henri Crouzel. *Origène et la 'connaissance mystique'*. Paris-Bruges, 1961.
Jean Kirchmeyer. 'Grecque (Église)', DS 6 (1967) 848–56.
Spidlík. 'La contemplazione nella spiritualita cristiana orientale', in *Enciclop. delle religioni* II:385–90. Florence, 1970

THE SENSES, p. 331

Nos sens et Dieu. Études Carmélitaines. 1954.
Michel Spanneut. *Le stoïcisme*... Index, p. 483: sens, sensus.
Henri Crouzel. *Origène et la connaissance mystique*. 273ff. Paris-Bruges, 1961.
Johannes B. Lotz. 'Sinn, Sinnlichkeit', LThK² 9:784–86.

THE NOUS, p. 332

A. H. Armstrong. 'The Plotinian Doctrine of NOUS in Patristic Theology', *Vigiliae Christianae* 8 (1954) 234–38.
Sargio Rendina. *La contemplazione negli scritti di S. Basilio Magno*. Rome, 1959.
E. von Ivánka. *Plato Christianus. Uebernahme und Umgestalltung des Platonismus durch die Väter*. Einsiedeln, 1964.
René Arnou. *Le désir de Dieu dans la philosophie de Plotin*. 2nd ed. Rome, 1967.
Pierre Thomas Camelot. 'Hellénisme', DS 7/1:145–64, especially 158ff.
Grégoire de Nazianze, OCA 189:25ff. Rome, 1971.
Pierre Thomas Camelot. 'Lumière, Étude patristique', DS 9:1149–58.
Aimé Solignac. 'NOUS' et 'Mens', DS 11 (1982) 459–69.

THEOLOGIA, p. 338

Pierre Battifol. 'Theologia, Théologie', *Ephemerides Theologicae Lovanienses* 5 (1925) 205–20.
M. Rothenhäusler. 'La doctrine de la "Theologia" chez Diadoque de Photiké', *Irénikon* 14 (1937) 536–53.
Yves Congar. 'Théologie', DThC 16/1 (1946) 341–502.
Werner Jaeger. *The Theology of Early Greek Philosophers*. Oxford, 1947.
───────. *Die Theologie der frühen griechischen Denker*. Stuttgart, 1953.
A. J. Festugière. *La Révélation d'Hermès Trismégiste*. Vol. 2:598–605 (appendix III). Paris, 1949.
R. Roques. 'Notes sur la notion de 'Theologia' chez le Pseudo-Denys l'Aréopagite', RAM 25 (1949) 200–12.
Victor Goldschmidt. 'Theologia', *Revue des Études Grecques* 63 (1950) 20–40.
Jean Plagnieux. *Saint Grégoire de Nazianze Théologien*: 168ff. Paris, 1952.
Jan Maria Szymusiak. *Eléments de théologie de l'homme selon Grégoire de Nazianze*: 7ff. Rome, 1963.
───────. *Grzegorz Teolog*: 212ff. Poznan, 1965
Grégoire de Nazianze, OCA 189·134ff. Rome, 1971.

MYSTICAL KNOWLEDGE, p. 338

Nikolaj S. Arseniew. *Ostkirche und Mystik*. Munich, 1925 and 1943. English Translation by A. Chambers, *Mysticism and the Eastern Church*. Crestwood, New York, 1979.
Hans Lewy. *'Sobria ebrietas. Untersuchungen zur Geschichte der antiken Mystik*. Beihefte zur Zeitschrift für die neutestamentische Wissenschaft und die Kunde der älterer Kirche, ZNW 9. Giessen, 1929.
Irénée Hausherr. *Ignorance infinie*, OCP 2 (1936) 351–62.
——————. *Hésychasme et prière*, OCA 176:38–49. Rome, 1966.
Henri Charles Puech. 'La ténèbre mystique chez le Pseudo-Denys l'Aréopagite et dans la tradition patristique, *Études Carmélitaines* 23 (1938) II, p. 33–53.
J. Lemaitre (I. Hausherr). 'Contemplation chez les orientaux chrétiens; mystique extatique', DS 2/2 (1953) 1862–72.
René Roques. 'Contemplation, extase et ténèbres chez le pseudo-Denys', DS 2/2:1885–1911.
Jean Daniélou. 'Mystique de la ténèbre chez Grégoire de Nysse'. DS 2/2: 1872–85.
——————. *La colombe et les ténèbres*. Paris, 1954
——————. Introduction to *From Glory to Glory: Texts from Gregory of Nyssa's Mystical Writings*, ed. and transl. by Herbert Musurillo: 3–78. New York, 1961.
Walter Völker. *Gregor von Nyssa als Mystiker*. Wiesbaden, 1955.
——————. *Kontemplation und Ekstase bei Pseudo-Dionysius Areopagita*. Wiesbaden, 1958.
Henri Crouzel. 'Grégoire de Nysse est-il fondateur de la théologie mystique? Une controverse récente', RAM 33 (1957) 189–202.
Maurice de Gandillac. 'Docte ignorance', DS 3 (1957) 1497–1501.
Jean Vanneste. *Le mystère de Dieu. Essai sur la structure rationelle de la mystique du Pseudo-Denys l'Aréopagite*. Louvain, 1959.
Several authors. 'Extase', DS 4/2 (1961) 2045–2189; especially J. Kirchmeyer. 'Extase' chez les Pères de l'Église', col. 2087–2113.
Henri Crouzel. *Origène et la 'connaissance mystique'*. Museum Lessianum. Section théologique 56. Paris-Bruges, 1961.
G. Widengreen. 'Researches in Syrian Mysticism. Mystical Experiences and Spiritual Exercises', *Numen* 8 (1961) 161–98.
Pierre Scazzoso. 'Rivelazioni del linguaggio pseudo-dionisiano intorno au temi della contemplazione e dell'estasi', *Rivista di filosofia neo-scolastica* 56 (1964) 37–66.
Vladimir Lossky. *In the Image and Likeness of God*: pp. 31–45. Crestwood, New York.
Andrew M. Greeley. *Ecstasy: A Way of Knowing*. Englewood Cliffs, N.Y. 1975.
V. V. 'Mystique', DS 10 (1980) 1889–1984.

THE GLORY OF GOD, p. 342

Kittel. 'Doxa', Kittel 2 (1935 and 1957) 236–258.
Z. Alszeghy and M. Flick. 'Gloria Dei', *Gregorianum* 36 (1955) 361–90.

A. Dupré la Tour. 'La Doxa du Christ dans les oeuvres exégétiques de Cyrille d'Alexandrie', *Recherches de Science religieuse* 48 (1960) 521-543; 49 (1961) 68-94.
Placide Deseille and Pierre Adnès. 'Gloire de Dieu', DS 6 (1967) 421-87.
Çarlo Skalicky. *La gloria nel vangelo di Giovanni*. Rome, 1970.
Špidlík. 'l'idéal du monachisme basilien', in P. J. Fedwick, ed., *Basil of Caesarea, Christian, Humanist, Ascetic*: 361-74. Toronto.
Hermann Jozef Sieben. 'Mneme Theou', DS 10 (1980) 1407-14.

INDEX OF USEFUL TEXTS

Holy Scripture, p. 5

Theophilus of Antioch, *Three Discourses to Autolycus*; SCh 20 (1948) II, 94–295; III, 206–271; ANF 2:94–110, 111–21 (sacred writings are superior to profane).
Irenaeus, *Against Heresies* IV.10.1-2; SCh 100 (1965) 490–97; ANF 1:474-74. (the son of God is everywhere throughout Scripture).
Basil, *Short Rules* 1.95; 235, 236; trans. W. Clarke, *The Ascetic Works of St Basil* (New York, 1925).
―――― . *Homily on Psalm* 1: PG 29:200–228; FCh 46 (1963) 151–64.
Cassian, *Conference* 8.3–5; SCh 54 (1958) 11–14; LNPF² 11:376–77; Index SCh 64 (1959) 236.
John Chrysostom, *Concerning the Statues* 1.1; PG 49:17ff; LNPF¹ 9:33lff.
Pseudo-Macarius, *Homily* 39: PG 39: PG 34:761; trans. George A. Maloney, *Intoxicated with God: The Fifty Spiritual Homilies of Macarius* (Denville, 1978) 195.
Staretz Leonid (d. 1841), in Stanislas Tyskiewicz and Theodore Belpaire, *Ascètes russes* (Namur, 1975) 154.

The Tradition of the Church, p. 6

Clement of Alexandria, *Stromata* I.1.1ff.; SCh 30 (1949) 43ff.; ANF 2:299ff (those who have instructed us, we call fathers).
Basil, *On the Holy Spirit* 27; SCh 17 (1945) 232ff; trans. D. Anderson (Crestwood, New York: St Vladimir's Press, 1980) 98ff.
Theodore the Studite. *Catechesis* 39; PG 99:561ff.
Ignatius Bryanchaninov, in Sergius Bolskafoff, *Russian Mystics* (Kalamazoo, 1977) 149 and 153 (reading the Fathers).

Wisdom, p. 22

Diadochus of Photice, *One Hundred Chapters* 6–11; SCh 5 ter (1966) 87–89; On Spiritual Knowledge and Discrimination: One Hundred Texts' G. E. H. Palmer, Ph. Sherrard and Kallistos Ware, eds. *The Philokalia. The Complete Text*, Volume 1 (London, 1979) 254–55.

'L'Office liturgique slave de la "Sagesse de Dieu"'. *Irénikon* 30 (1957) 164–188.
Staretz George the Recluse (d. 1836), in Tyskiewicz and Belpaire, *Ascètes russes* (Namur, 1957) 98ff.

Spiritual, p. 29

Basil, *On the Spirit* 16; SCh 17 (1945) 173ff; trans. Anderson (New York, 1980) 60ff.
Aphraates, *Demonstration* 6.14; Patrologia Syriaca 1 (1894) col. 293ff.; LNPF[2] 13:371ff.
Methodius of Olympus, *The Symposium: A Treatise on Chastity* 11:3; PG 18:216BC; SCh 95 (1963) 325ff.; ACW 27 (1958).
Seraphim of Sarov, in Ivan Kologrivof, *Essai sur la sainteté en Russie* (Bruges, 1953) 432–35.

Holy Spirit, p. 30

Basil, *On the Holy Spirit*; SCh 17bis (1968); trans. D. Anderson (New York, 1980).
Gregory of Nyssa, *On the Lord's Prayer* 3; PG 44:1155B–1157B; ACW 18 (1954) 21–84 (The Holy Spirit and the coming of the Kingdom of God).
Pseudo-Macarius, *Homily* 11; PG 34:544–56; Maloney, 77ff.
Symeon the New Theologian, *Catechetical Discourse* 33; SCh 113 (1965) 248ff.; trans. C. J. deCatanzaro (New York, 1980) 339ff.
The Russian text of the *Conversation of St. Seraphim of Sarov with Mototilov* was published in its entirety in *Russie et Église Universelle* (Brussels), n. 4, 5, and 6; A French translation may be found in I. Kologrivof, *Essai sur la sainteté en Russie* (Bruges, 1953) 432–435. [There is an English translation of it in Valentine Zander, *St. Seraphim of Sarov* (Crestwood, New York, 1975) 83ff.]
Vladimir Soloviev, *The Justification of the Good*, II.2.4; tr. N. A. Duddington (London, 1918) 166ff.

The Mystery of Christ, p. 34

Le mystère de Noël. Essential texts compiled and presented by Albert Hamman and France Quéré-Jaulmes. Lettres chrétiennes 8 (Paris, 1963).
Pseudo-Macarius, *Homily* 20 (PG 31:649–56) *Homily* 17 (624–33) *Homily* 44 (777–85); Maloney, 132, 118, 205.
Symeon the New Theologian, *Discourse* II; SCh 96 (1963) 242–56; deCatanzaro, 47–59 (Renouncing everything to find Christ). *Discourse* XXVIII: SCh 113 (1965) 152–54; de Cantanzaro, 295ff.
Vladimir Soloviev, *The Justification of the Good* II.3.3–7 (London, 1918) 186–95.

Devotion to Christ, p. 37

Gregorius Scholarius, *Precatio ad DNJXtum, Matutina, Meridiana et Vespertina:* PG 160:525–528.
Nersès Šnorhali, *Jesus Fils unique du Père:* ed. I. Kechichian; SCh 203 (1973).
Staretz George the Recluse, in Tyskiewicz and Belpaire, *Ascètes russes* (Namur 1957) 92–95.

Index of Useful Texts   417

The Imitation of Christ, p. 39

Basil, *Long Rules*, 3,5,7,16,43; trans. M. Monica Wagner, FC 9 (1950) 223ff.
Pseudo-Macarius, *Homily* 43.1–2; PG 34:722; Maloney,201.
Abba Isaiah, *Logos* 13; *Abbé Isaïe. Recueil ascétique. Introduction et traduction française por les moines de Solesmes*, Spiritualité Orientale, 7. (Etoilles, 1970) 114–19. *Logos* 22, p. 184ff. *Logos* 25, p. 232ff., *Logos* 27, p. 247ff.
Symeon the New Theologian, *Discourse* XX; SCh 104 (1964) 330–48; deCatanzaro, 231ff. (following Christ under the guidance of a spiritual father, in public life, at table, at the passion, in glory, in the light). *Discourse* 27; SCh 113 (1965) 118–26; deCatanzaro, 291–94.

God, p. 42

Irenaeus. Texts compiled and presented by Roger Poelman under the title, *De la plénitude de Dieu, Bible et la vie chrétienne (Maredsous, 1959)*.
Les chemins vers Dei. Texts compiled and presented by France Quéré-Jaulmes Albert Hamman. Lettres chrétiennes 11 (Paris, 1967).
Clement of Alexandria, *Exhortation to the Greeks* 5; SCh 2 (1941) 119–28; ANF 2:190ff. (the philosophers' opinions about God).
Vladimir Soloviev, *The Justification of the Good* III.10.10 (London, 1918) 437ff. (the religious principle of fatherhood).

The Most Holy Trinity, p. 44

John of Damascus, *De sancta Trinitate;* PG 94:9–18. *De hymno trisagio*; PG94: 21–62.
Gennadius Scholarius, *De Deo in Trinitate uno*; PG 16:467–596. *Disputatio cum amera Machumetis*; PG 16:322–328 (Images of the Trinity).
Gregory Palamas, in the French *Philocalie*, 269ff. (see chapter I,2, note 5).

Deification, p. 45

John Chrysostom, *Baptismal Instructions* I.1; SCh 50bis (1970) 108ff.; ACW 31 (1963).
Pseudo-Macarius, *Homily* 30; PG 34:721–728; Maloney, 171 (anyone who is to enter the kingdom must be born of the Holy Spirit).
Abba Isaiah, *Abbé Isaïe* (Etoilles, 1970) Index, 304ff.: the indwelling of God in the soul.
Symeon The New Theologian, *Catechetical Discourse* 8; SCh 104 (1964) 96ff.; deCatanzaro, 146ff. (The greatness of the sons of God).
Vladimir Soloviev, *The Justification of the Good* II.2.7, (London, 1918) 173ff.; II.2.10, 178ff. ('Have God within you').

The Image of God, p. 55

Origen, *First Principles* III.6.1; PG 11:333; ANF 4:344ff. *Homily on Genesis* 1.12–13; SCh 7 (1943) 78–84.

Athanasius of Alexandria, *Against the Heathen* I.2; SCh 18 (1946) 111–113; LNPF² 4:4–5.
Basil, *An Ascetical Discourse*: PG 31:869–881; FC 9 (1950) 207–15.
Gregory of Nyssa, *On the Making of Man* 16: SCh 6 (1943) 151–61; LNPF² 5:404–6.
Abba Isaiah, *Logos* 25; *Abbé Isaïe* (Etoilles, 1970) 214ff. (charity – the imprint of the true King).
Nicetas Stethatos, *On the soul*; SCh 81 (1961) 82ff.
Staretz Silouan, in Sergius Bolshakoff, *Russian Mystics* (Kalamazoo, 1977) 251ff.

Nature, p. 63

Basil, *Homily 9 on the Hexaemeron* 3–4; SCh 26 (1949) 496ff.; FC 46 (1963) 138–43.
Gregory Nazianzen, Index in PG 38: *natura*.
Abba Isaiah, *Abbé Isaïe* (Etoilles, 1970) Index, 307: nature and counternature.
Vladimir Soloviev, *The Justification of the Good* II.1.10 (London, 1918) 146ff. (the essence of morality is in itself one – the wholeness of man is inherent in his nature).
Nikolaj Berdiaev, *The Russian Idea*, trans. R. M. French (London, 1947), Chapter IV. The Problem of Humanism, 86–97.

The Happy Life, p. 64

Basil, *Long Rules* 17. *Short Rules* 193.
Abba Isaiah, *Logos* 16; *Abbé Isaïe* (Etoilles 1970) 126ff. (the joy coming to the soul desirious of serving God).
Theophane the Recluse, in S. Tyskiewicz and Th. Belpaire, *Ascètes russes* (Namur, 1957) 118.
V. Soloviev, *The Justification of the Good* I.6.1–7 (London, 1981) 114–31 (a critique of abstract hedonism).

The Salvation of the Soul, p. 66

John Chrysostom, *De salute animae*; PG 60:735–738.
Basil, *Praevia institutio ascetica*: PG 31:619–626; English trans. W. K. L. Clarke, *The Ascetic Works of Saint Basil* (London: SPCK, 1925).
Dorotheus, *Instruction* 12.124–137; SCh 92 (1963) 380–401; *Discourses and Sayings*, CS 33 (1977) 182–90.
Symeon the New Theologian, *Catechetical Discourse* II; SCh 96 (1963) 241–42; deCatanzaro, 47ff.
Seraphim of Sarov, in Tyszkiewicz and Belpaire, *Ascètes russes*, 66ff.

Progress in the Spiritual Life, p. 68

Origen, *Commentary on Matthew* 10.11: SCh 162 (1970) 178ff.; ANF, 10:419ff. (there are no different 'natures' of the souls of the wicked and the righteous).

Index of Useful Texts 419

Gregory of Nyssa, *The Life of Moses* II.305–314; SCh 1bis (1955) 129–31; trans. E. Ferguson and A. J. Malherbe (New York-Kalamazoo, 1978) 133ff.
Theodore the Studite, *Catechesis* 81; PG 99:615ff (*de amore erga profectum*).
V. Soloviev, *The Justification of the Good* II.2.6 (London, 1918) 170ff. (the necessity of spiritual progress). *Ibid*. 8, 174ff. (the higher degrees of morality do not abolish the lower).

The Consciousness of Grace, p. 71

Diadochus of Photice, *On Spiritual Knowledge: One Hundred Texts* 75–89; SCh 5ter (1966) 133–50; *The Philokalia, The Complete Text*, 1 (London, 1979) 278–88.
Mark the Ascetic, *De baptismo*; PG 65:985–1028. *Le lege spirituali*, PG 65:905–930.
Pseudo-Macarius, *Homily* 49; PG 34:812–816; Maloney, 224ff.
John Climacus, *Scala Paradisi* 18; PG 88:932–937; *The Ladder of Divine Ascent* (Boston: Holy Transfiguration Monastery, 1978) 124ff. (on spiritual insensibility).
Théophane le Reclus, Index 304.

Miracles, charisms, p. 74

Origen, *Commentary on Matthew* 10.19; SCh 162 (1970) 228–35; ANF 10:426–27 (faith and miracles).
John Chrysostom, *Concerning the Statues* 16.4; PG 49:167; LNPF[1].
Cassian, *Conference* 15; SCh 54 (1958) 209–20; LNPF[1] 11:445–449 (divine gifts).
Pseudo-Macarius, *Homily* 50; PG 34:816–21; Maloney, 226ff.
Apophthegmata: Bessarion 40, Macarius 2, 33, 38, Sisoes 7, 24, Or 2, 3; trans. B. Ward, *The Sayings of the Desert Fathers* (Oxford-Kalamazoo, 1975).

Visions, p. 74

Irenaeus, *Against Heresies* IV.20.9–11; SCh 100 (1965) 654–69; ANF 1:490–92.
Apophthegmata, The Anonymous Series, nn. 228–39; trans. B. Ward, *The Wisdom of the Desert Fathers* (Oxford: Fairacres Press, 1977) 62–65.
Diadochus, *On Spiritual Knowledge: One Hundred Texts* 36–40; SCh 5ter (1966) 105–08; *The Philokalia*, Vol. 1 (1979) 263–65.

Martyrdom, p. 75

Clement of Alexandria, *Stromata* IV.4.15; GCS 2:255; ANF 2:411–12 (daily martyrdom).
Origen, *Exhortation to Martyrdom*; PG 11:563–638; trans. L. Oulton and H. Chadwick, in *Alexandrian Christianity* (Philadelphia, 1954) 393–429.

Theodore the Studite, *Catechesis* 10; PG 99:522–523 (the martyrdom of daily life).
Other texts, in E. Malone, *The Monk and the Martyr* (Washington, 1950).

Christian Anthropology, p. 87

Lactantius, *L'ouvrage du Dieu Créateur*, SCh 212–14 (1974); *The Workmanship of God*, 54 (1965) 5–56.
Gregory of Nyssa, *On the Making of Man*; SCh 6 (1943); LNPF[2] 5:387–427. *On the Soul and the Resurrection;* PG 46:11–160: LNPF[2] 5:430–68.
Origen, *Esprit et feu*, vol. 1, *L'âme*. Texts compiled and presented by Urs von Balthasar (Paris, 1959). Italian trans., Milan, 1972.
Eusebius of Caesarea, *Praeparatio Evangelica* VII.4; SCh 215 (1975) English trans. E. H. Gifford (Oxford, 1903).
Nemesius, *De natura hominis*; PG 40:503–818; English trans. by W. Telfer, *Cyril of Jerusalem and Nemesius of Emesa* (London, 1955) 224–453.
Meletius, *De natura hominis*; PG 64:1075–1310.

Self-knowledge, p. 87

Origen, *In Canticum*. ed. W. A. Baehrens, GCS 33 (1925) vol. 3, 142ff.; English trans. R. P. Lawson, *Origen. The Song of Songs. Commentary and Homilies* ACW 26 (1957).
Basil, *Homilia in illud, Attende tibi ipsi*; PG 31: 197–218; *Homily on the Words, 'Give Heed to Thyself'*, FC 9: 431–46.
Theodoret of Cyrus, *Thérapeutique des maladies helléniques*; SCh 57 (1958) 252ff.
Symeon the New Theologian, *Theological and Ethical Treatises* 9.440ff.: SCh 129 (1967) 253.

Humility, p. 88

Basil, *Long Rules* 7, 10, 21, 22, 28, 30, 31, 41, 48. *On humility*; PG 31:525–540.
Apophthegmata. Anonymous Series, 165–203; *The Wisdom of the Desert Fathers*, 47–55.
Pseudo-Macarius, *Homily* 10; PG 34:510–44; Maloney, 75–76.
Diadochus, *On Spiritual Knowledge: One Hundred Texts* 95; SCh 5ter (1966) 157ff.: *The Philokalia*. 1 (1979) 292ff. (the two types of humility).
Dorotheus, *Instruction* 2.26–39; SCh 92 (1963) 186–207; *Discourses and Sayings*, 95–102.
John Climacus, *Scala Paradisi* 25; PG 88:988–1012; *The Ladder*
Martyrius Sahdônâ, *The Book of Perfection* II.10; CSCO 253, Syri 111, pp. 49–77 (sublime humility).

The Spiritual Sense, p. 94

Diadochus, *On Spiritual Knowledge: One Hundred Texts* 90–91; SCh 5ter (1966) 150–53; *The Philokalia*, vol. 1: 289–90 (the taste of God).

Ephrem, *Commentaire de l'évangile concordant* 7.3-12, SCh 121 (1966) 140-46 (to touch physically and to touch spiritually).
Symeon the New Theologian, *Theological and Ethical Treatises*; SCh 129 (1967), Index, 483ff.: *aisthesis*.

Conscience, p. 95

Irenaeus, *Against Heresies* IV.39.1-4; SCh 100 (1965) 960-74; ANF 1:522-23 (why the knowledge of good and evil).
Dorotheus of Gaza, *Instruction* 3.40-46; SCh 92 (1963) 208-18.; *Discourses and Sayings*, 105-7.
Abba Isaiah, *Logos* 4; *Abbé Isaïe* (Etoilles, 1970) 67ff. Analytical Index in CSCO 293, Syri 233 (1968) 484-85.
V. Soloviev, *The Justification of the Good* (London, 1918) 17ff, 37ff., 136ff.

The Soul, p. 96

Gregory of Nyssa, *On the Making of Man* 28ff.; SCh 6 (1943) 216-27; LNPF² 5:419ff. (the preexistence of souls).
Athanasius of Alexandria, *Against the Heathen* II.30-34; SCh 18 (1946) 171-78; LNPF² 4:20-22 (the existence of the rational soul).
Cassian, See the Index to E. Pichery, *Jean Cassien: Conférences* 3, SCh 64 (1959) 231.
Pseudo-Macarius, *Homily* 26; PG 34:676-693; Maloney, 147ff., (the dignity of the human soul). *Homily* 7.8; col. 528; p. 66 (the members of the soul).
Diadochus, *On Spiritual Knowledge: One Hundred Texts* 24-25; SCh 5ter (1966) 96-97; *The Philokalia*, vol. 1 (1979) 259.
Abba Isaiah, *Logos* 25, *Abbé Isaïe* (Etoilles, 1970), 212-14 (the soul must keep its nature). See *Ibid.*, 301, Index: soul and spirit.
Symeon the New Theologian, *Catechetical Discourse* 4; SCh 96 (1963) 369-72; deCatanzaro, 87-89 (the glory and dignity of the purified soul).
Tikhon Zadonsky, *Tvorenija* [*Works*], 3 ed., Moscow, 1875, vol. 3:305 (the dignity of the soul).

The Immortality of the Soul, p. 97

Le mystère de Pâques. Texts selected and presented by A. Hamman and F. Quéré-Jaulmes, Lettres chrétiennes 10 (Paris, 1965).

Freedom, p. 99

Gregory of Nyssa, *The Life of Moses* II.73-88; SCh 1bis (1955) 51-66; Ferguson-Malherbe, 70-74 (Providence and freedom).
Gregory of Nazianzus, *Oratio* 45.8; PG 36:632; *The Second Oration on Easter*, LNPF² 7:425.
Cassian, *Conference* 13; SCh 54 (1958) 147-81; LNPF² 11:426ff. (grace and freedom of the will).

Pseudo-Macarius, *De libertate mentis*, PG 34:935–968.
Symeon the New Theologian, *Catechetical Discourse* 5; SCh 96 (1963) 408–14; deCatanzaro, 100–18 (Jesus Christ sets us free): *Ibid.*, 28; SCh 113 (1965) 132–36; deCatanzaro, 295ff. (From the shadow of the law to the light of God).

The Heart, p. 103

Pseudo-Macarius, *De custodia cordis*; PG 34:821–908.
Theophane the Recluse, in Tyszkiewicz and Belpaire, *Ascètes russes*, 115ff.
Greek *Philokalia*, vol. 5, (Athens, 1963) Index, 233–35: *kardia*.

The Body, p. 107

Clement of Alexandria, *Paedagogos*, chapters 2, 5, 9, 10; SCh 158 (1970) 19ff., 71ff., 101ff., 107ff.; English trans. *Christ the Educator*, FC 23 (1953) 5ff.
Pseudo-Athanasius, *De corpore et anima;* PG 28:1431–1434.
Gregory of Nyssa, *On the Making of Man* 11–12; SCh 6 (1943) 121–34; LNPF[2] 5:396–99.
Cassian, *Conference* 4; SCh 42 (1955) 166–87; LNPF[2] 11:330–9 (on the lust of flesh and of the spirit).
Philoxenes of Mabbug, *Homilies*; SCh 44 (1956): Cf. Table of Ideas, 551ff.
Symeon the New Theologian, *Catechetical Discourse* 13: SCh 104 (1964) 109ff.; 25, SC 113 (1965), 50ff.; 27, 104ff. (deCatanzaro, 181ff., 267ff., 284ff.).
V. Soloviev, *The Justification of the Good.* I.2.4 (London, 1918) 47ff. (the three chief moments in the struggle of the spirit against the encroachments of the flesh).

Sex, p. 112

Origen, *Homily on Genesis* 1.14–16; SCh 7 (1943) 84–6: *Ibid.*, 13. 4: 222ff.
Gregory of Nyssa, *On the Making of Man* 17; SCh 6 (1943) 162–66; LNPF[2] 5:406–7.
La femme. Les grands textes des Pères. Compiled and presented by France Quéré-Jaulmes, Lettres chrétiennes 12 (Paris, 1968).

Illnesses, p. 113

Clement of Alexandria, *Paedogogos* 3.6; PG 8:620; FC 23:4.7.
Basil, *Long Rules* 55.
Diadochus, *On Spiritual Knowledge: One Hundred Texts*, SCh 5ter: 115–16; *The Philokalia*, 1 (1979) 268–69.
Philoxenes of Mabbug, *Homilies*; SCh 44 (1956), Table of Ideas, 558.

Death, p. 113

Gregory of Nyssa, *Life of Saint Macrina* 22ff.; SCh 178 (1971) 212ff.; *The Life of Macrina*, 58 (1966) 161–91.
John Chrysostom, *De consolatione mortis*; PG 56:293–306.

Index of Useful Texts

John Climacus, *Scala Paradisi* 6; PG 88:793–801 (the remembrance of death).
Symeon the New Theologian, *Catechetical Discourse* 21; SCh 104 (1964) 350–62; deCatanzaro, 238–42 (the blessed death of Antony, monk of Saint-Mamas).
Demetrius Cydonius, *De contemnenda morte*, PG 154:1169–1212.
V. Soloviev, *The Justification of the Good* II.1, 4 (London, 1918) 138ff.

The World, p. 125

Athenagoras, *A Plea for the Christians* 16; SCh 2 (1941) 104–7; ANF 2:136.
Origen, in Hans Urs von Balthasar, *Parole et mystère chez Origène* (Paris, 1957); Italian trans. *Il mondo, Cristo e la Chiesa* (Milan, 1972).
Athanasius of Alexandria, *Against the Heathen* III.35–47; SCh 18 (1946) 179–205; LNPF² 4:22–30 (the contemplation of God from the contemplation of the world).
Gregory of Nyssa, *On the Making of Man* 1; SCh 6 (1943) 83–9; LNPF² 5:388–90.
V. Soloviev, *The Justification of the Good* II.3.1 (London, 1918) 180ff. (the process of manifesting God in matter).

Divine Providence, p. 130

Socrates according to Xenophon, *Memorabilia* I.4; IV.3.
Plutarch, *Moralia: On the Delays of the Divine Vengeance (de sera numinis vindicta)*.
Seneca, *De providentia*.
Gregory of Nazianzus, *Carminum Liber* I.1,5 and 6; PG 37:424–453.
Gregory of Nyssa, *Contra Fatum*; PG 45:145–174.
John Chrysostom, *On Providence*: SCh 79 (1961).
Synesius of Cyrene, *The Egyptian Discourses or On Providence*; PG 66:1209–1282; English trans. by A. Fitzgerald, *The Essays and Hymns of Synesius of Cyrene*, 2 volumes. (London, 1930).
Theodoret of Cyrus, *Ten Discourses on Providence*, PG 83:555–774, French trans. by Y. Azéma (Paris, 1954); *id.*, *Thérapeutique des maladies helléniques* VI. 22ff., SC 57 (1958), 261ff.

The Problem of Evil, p. 135

Athanasius of Alexandria, *Against the Heathen* I.6; SCh 18 (1964) 118–21; LNPF² 4:6–7 (evil has no independent existence; man is the maker of evil).
John Chrysostom, *Concerning the Statues* 1.6ff. (PG 49:23ff.) 4, (59ff.), 15.1 (153ff.); LNPF¹ 9:333ff., 364ff., 438–9.
Cassian, *Conference* 8.6; SCh 54 (1958) 14; LNPF² 11:377 (nothing is created evil by God.)
Dionysius the Areopagite, *The Divine Names* IV.33; PG 3:8112ff. English trans. C. E. Rolt (London: SPCK, 1977) 128ff.
Maximus the Confessor, *Century III on Charity* 1–5; SCh 9 (1943) 123ff., English trans. P. Sherwood, ACW 21 (1955) 173–4 (the reasonable use of the soul's powers and of things; the demons are not evil by nature).

Suffering, p. 137

Origen, *Commentary on Matthew* 10.18; SCh 162 (1970); ANF 10:425–6 (the sufferings endured by the prophets).
Basil, *Quod Deus non est auctor malorum*, PG 31:329–353.
John Chrysostom, *Ad Stagirium a daemone vexatum*, PG 47:423–494.
_____ , *Lettre d'exil à Olympias et à tous les fideles* (*Quod nemo laeditur*), SCh 103 (1964). English trans., *A Treatise to Prove That No One Can Harm The Man Who Does Not Injure Himself*, LNPF[1] 9:271–84.
Abba Isaiah, *Logos* 21; *Abbé Isaïe* (Etoilles, 1970) 177ff. (through the Cross to perfect charity).
Maximus the Confessor, *Ad Thalassium, quaestio* 61; PG 90:625–641.

Eschatology, p. 143

Abba Isaiah, *Logos* 22; *Abbé Isaïe* (Etoilles, 1970) 186ff., (self-examination while thinking of the judgement to come): *Logos* 16:141ff. (preparing oneself for the Parousia and Judgement).
Nersès Snorhali, *Jésus Fils unique du Père*, SCh 203 (1973) 207ff., 858ff.
Theophane the Recluse, in Bolshakoff, *Russian Mystics* (Kalamazoo, 1977) 220ff.

Apokatastasis, p. 144

Gregory of Nyssa, *In illud: Quando sibi subiecerit omnia*, PG 44:1303–1316.
Cyril of Jerusalem, *De secundo Christi adventu*, PG 33:869–916.
Cyril of Alexandria, *De exitu animae et secundo Christi adventu*, PG 77:1071–1190.
Theophanes Cerameus, *De secundo Christi adventu*, PG 132:395–412.
Anthology of Byzantine liturgical texts illustrating the theme of Paradise; see Archdeacon Denis, *Fleurs de Paradis* (Rome, 1976).

Human Society, p. 151

Abba Isaiah, *Logos* 30 *Abbé Isaïe*, 281ff. (Poemen and his brothers: the conditions of living together peacefully).
V. Soloviev, *The Justification of the Good* III.2.1–2 (London, 1918) 220–27 (the individual and social consciousness). III.10.7, 426–32 (the unity of mankind).
Nicholas Berdyaev, *The Russian Idea*, trans. R. M. French, (London: The Centenary Press, 1947) chapter 3: Personality and World Harmony, 72–85, Chapter 5: The Social Theme, 98–127.

The Church, p. 157

John Chrysostom, *Eight Baptismal Catecheses* III.16; SCh 50bis (1970) 160ff.; English translation by P. W. Harkins, *Baptismal Instructions*, ACW 31 (1963).

Index of Useful Texts 425

Staretz Zosima († 1833), in T. Tyszkiewicz and Th. Belpaire, *Ascètes russes* Namur, 1957) 87–90.
V. Soloviev, *The Justification of the Good* III.10.8ff (London, 1918) 432ff.
Alexij Step. Chomiakov, in Tomaš Špidlík, *I grandi mistici russi* (Rome, 1977) 532ff.
Texts by the Greek Fathers on the Church; see DThC 4/2 (1911) col. 2177ff.

The Mother of God, p. 158

Corpus Marianum Patristicum, ed. S. Alvarez Campos (Bruges, 1970).

The Common Life, p. 160

Basil, *Long Rules* 7, 24, 35, 37, 42.
Abba Isaiah, *Logos* 5, *Abbé Isaïe* (Etoilles, 1970) 76–85.
Cassian, *Conference* 19; SCh 64 (1959) 37–55; LNPF[2] 11:439ff. (on the aims of the coenobite and hermit).

Friendship, p. 161

Cassian, *Conference* 16; SCh 54 (1958) 221–47; LNPF[2] 11:450–60 (on friendship).
John Chrysostom, *De sacerdotio* I; PG 48:623ff; trans. W. R. Stephens, *Treatise on the Priesthood*, LNPF[1] 9:33ff.
Basilian Monastic Constitutions, chapters 29–30; PG 31:141ff.

The Family, p. 162

John Chrysostom, *To A Young Widow On Marriage*, SCh 138 (1968); trans. W. R. Stephens, *Letter to a Young Widow*, LNPF[1] 9:118–28; *On Marriage and Family* (Crestwood, New York: St Vladimir's Seminary Press, forthcoming).
Abba Isaiah, *Logos* 25; *Abbé Isaïe*, 202–4 (a word to a young spouse).
Symeon the New Theologian, *Catechetical Discourse* 7; SCh 104 (1964) 48–84; deCatanzaro, 138–42 (the temptation of ties of kinship).

The State Society, p. 162

John Chrysostom, *Concerning the Statues* 6.1; PG 49:81ff.; LNPF[1] 9:381ff. (the fear of magistrates is beneficial).
Theophilus of Antioch, *To Autolycus* I.11; SCh 20 (1948) 82–85; ANF 2:92 (attitude toward the emperor: 'I will honor him; not by worshipping him, but by praying for him.').
Antiochus the Monk, *Homilia* 37; PG 89: 1549–1552: 'Adversus optimates et praefectos non esse contendendum'.
Eustathius of Thessalonica, *On the obedience owed to Magistrates*, PG 136:301–358.

V. Soloviev, *The Justification of the Good* III.10.11ff. (London, 1918) 440ff.
N. Berdyaeff, *The Russian Idea*, trans. R. M. French (London, 1947), chapter 7, 142–56 (anarchy).

Brotherly Love, p. 164

Antiochus the Monk, *Homily* 28 (PG 89:1528ff., on grumbling), *Homily* 29 (1529ff., on disparaging), *Homily* 30 (1533ff., on tale-bearing), *Homily* 31 (1536, on not being an informer or a troublesome censurer), *Homily* 32 (1537ff., on contradicting), *Homily* 40 (1557ff., on calumny), *Homily* 48 (1584, on not ridiculing another), *Homily* 49 (1585ff., that the neighbor should not be blindly condemned), *Homily* 50 (1588ff., on not causing scandal to anyone), *Homily* 51 (1589ff., on not bringing disgrace or dishonor on anyone, but instead wishing that they be changed), *Homily* 52 (1592ff., that evil should not be repaid with evil), *Homily* 53 (1597ff., that enmities should not at all be cultivated against anyone), *Homily* 56 (1604ff., against contention), *Homily* 57 (1605ff., on not hating anyone), *Homily* 58 (1608ff., on wishing for another's happiness and rejoicing in it), etc.

Not to Judge the Neighbor, p. 164

Dorotheus, *Instruction* 6.69–78; SCh 92 (1963) 268–87; CS 33:131–39, *Instr.* 8.89–95; 306–19; CS 33:149–55 (on resentment).
Apophthegmata, Anonymous Series 122–123; *The Wisdom of the Desert Fathers* (1977) 35–36.

Brotherly Correction, p. 165

Basil, *Long Rules* 7, 27, 28, 41, 46, 48, 50, 51, 52, 53. *Short Rules* 4, 7, 40, 46, 79, 81, 82, 99, 106, 149, 158, 165, 166, 177, 182, 189, 232.
John Chrysostom, *Eight Baptismal Catecheses* 6.14; SCh 50bis (1970) 222ff.; ACW 31 (1963).

Almsgiving, p. 167

Riches et Pauvres dans l'Église ancienne. Essential Texts compiled and presented by Albert Hamman, Lettres chrétiennes 6 (Paris, 1962).

Work, p. 168

Basil, *Long Rules* 37, 42. *Short Rules* 61.
Abba Isaiah, *Logos*; (Etoilles translation), 198ff.
_____, *L'Ascéticon*, CSCO 293, Syri 122, Index, 511: 'travail'.
Numerous texts are indicated in Lucien Daloz, *Le travail selon saint Jean Chrysostome* (Paris, 1959).

Index of Useful Texts

Apostolic Activity, p. 169

Basil, *Long Rules* 32 (with regard to visitors), 33 (with regard to the sisters), 36 (outside). *Short Rules*, 311, 312, 131.
Basilian Constitutions 9; PG 31:1369C–1372B (a monk should not desire the priesthood).
Cassian, see the Index to *Jean Cassien. Conférences*, SCh 64 (1959); 'enseignement', 236.
John Chrysostom, *De sacerdotio*, PG 48:633–692; for other texts by Chrysostom, see Ivo Auf der Maur, *Mönchtum und Glaubensverkündigung in den Schriften des hl. Johannes Chrysostomus* (Freiburg, Switz., 1959).

Education, p. 170

Clement of Alexandria, *Paedagogos* III.8.41; SCh 158 (1970) 91ff.; FC 23 (1953) 233ff.
Basil, *Long Rules* 15, 53. *Short Rules* 292.
John Chrysostom, *Sur la vaine gloire et l'éducation des enfants*, SCh 188 (1972). English translation, *Address on Vainglory and the Right Way of Parents to Bring up their Children*, in M. L. Laistner, *Christianity and Pagan Culture in the Later Roman Empire* (Ithaca: Cornell University Press, 1951).
V. Soloviev, *The Justification of the Good*. III.10.4–5 (London, 1918) 418ff.

Praxis, p. 177

Abba Isaiah, *Logos* 21, Etoilles translation, 170 (faith must be accompanied by works.)
Cassian, see the Index to the *Conferences*, SCh 64 (1959) 243: *praktike*.
Greek *Philokalia*, vol. 5, (Athens, 1963), Index, 310–11: *praxis*.

Asceticism, p. 179

Philoxenes of Mabbug, *Homily* 11; SCh 44 (1956) 373–428 (ascetic austerities).
Abba Isaiah, *Abbé Isaïe* (Etoilles, 1970), Index, p. 301: 'ascèse, mortification'.
V. Soloviev, *The Justification of the Good*. I.2.1–8 (London, 1918) 41–58 (the function of the ascetic principle in morality) III.2.3, 227ff.

Renunciation, p. 180

Basil, *Long Rules* 5, 6, 8, 9. *Short Rules* 2, 92, 94, 187, 188, 189, 190, 234, 237.
Abba Isaiah, *Logos* 15; *Abbé Isaïe*, 123–26.
Philoxenus of Mabbug, *Homily* 8; SCh 44 (1956) 221–24.
Dorotheos of Gaza, *Instruction* 1.1–25; SCh 92 (1963) 146–85; CS 33:77–93.
Theoleptus of Philadelphia, in the French *Philocalie*, 222–26 (renouncing memories and thoughts).

Mortification, p. 181

Basil, *Long Rules* 16, 17, 18, 19. *Short Rules* 90, 126, 129, 130, 131, 138, 139, 258.
Cassian, *Conference* 24; SCh 74 (1959) 169–206; LNPF[2] 11:533ff. (on mortification).
Theodore the Studite, *Catechesis* 120; PG 99:665–667 (crucified to the world).
Symeon the New Theologian, *Catechetical Discourse* 28; SCh 113 (1965) 130–32; deCatanzaro, 296ff. (being crucified to the world).

Abstinence, p. 182

Basil, *Short Rules* 128ff.
Basilian Constitutions 4 and 19; PG 31:1345ff, 1388ff.
Cassian, see Index, SCh 64 (1959) 230.
Staretz George the Recluse († 1836), in S. Tyszkiewicz and Th. Belpaire, *Ascètes russes* (Namur, 1957) 96–8.
V. Soloviev, *The Justification of the Good* I.2.8 (London, 1918) 57ff.

Purification, p. 182

Athanasius of Alexandria, *Against the Heathen* II.34: SCh 18 (1946) 177ff.; LNPF[2] 4:22 (the need for purification to attain to the knowledge of God).
Maximus the Confessor, in the French *Philocalie*, 258ff.
Isaac of Nineveh, *ibid.*, 100ff. (the phases of purification).

Sin, p. 183

Basil, *Short Rules* 4, 81, 82, 83, 294, 301 (the seriousness of sin). *Ibid.*, 45 (feigned ignorance makes the fault more serious).
Gregory of Nyssa, *On Virginity* 12.2; Sch 119 (1966) 405ff.; 58 (1966) 43ff. (freedom is the cause of evil).
Cassian, see Index, SCh 64 (1959) 241ff.: 'péché'.
Pseudo-Macarius, *Homily* 24.4ff; PG 34:664; Maloney, 140 (the leaven in the dough). *Homily* 28; col. 709–716; p. 165 (the calamity of the soul in whom, because of sin, Christ does not dwell). *Homily* 15.17; col. 585; p. 96 (whether grace remains after sin). *Homily* 45; col. 785–792; p. 209 (only Christ is able to heal man). *Homily* 40.7–8; col. 765–768; p. 197 (grace and sin co-exist together in the heart). *Homily* 2; col. 464–468; p. 34 (on the reign of darkness, that is, of sin).
Symeon the New Theologian, *Catechetical Discourse* 3; SC 96 (1963) 300–02; deCatanzaro, 66–67 (no sin is trifling).

Repentance, p. 189

Basil, *Long Rules*, Prologue, 6, 55. *Short Rules* 3, 4, 5, 6, 8, 10, 11, 12, 13, 17, 57, 177, 287, 288, 295.

Index of Useful Texts 429

John Chrysostom, *Ad Theodorum lapsum*, PG 47:277-316; *An Exhortation to Theodore After his Fall*, LNPF¹ 9:91ff. *Ad Demetrium monachum de compunctione* I, PG 47:393-410. *Ad Stelechium, et de compunctione* II; PG 47:411-492.
Cassian, *Conference* 20; SCh 64 (1959); LNPF² 11:496ff.
Mark the Ascetic, *De paenitentia*, PG 65:965-984.
Abba Isaiah, *Logos* 25 *Abbé Isaïe* (Etoilles, 1970) 223ff. *Logos* 21, pp. 162ff.
John Climacus, *Scala Paradisi* 5; PG 88:764-93.
Symeon the New Theologian, *Catechetical Discourse* 4 (SCh 96 [1963] 318ff.; deCatanzaro, 70ff.), 5, (374ff., deC., 90), 23, (SCh 113 [1965] 12ff.; deCat., 255ff.), 28, (138ff., deC., 295ff.), 30 (194ff., deC., 318), 32 (242ff., deC., 355.)
Seraphim of Sarov, in T. Tyszkiewicz and Th. Belpaire, *Ascètes russes* (Namur, 1957) 75.

Penthos, p. 193

Basil, *Long Rules*, Prologue, 37, 40, 52. *Short Rules* 16, 17.
Cassian, *Conference* 9; 26-30; SCh 54 (1958) 26-30; LNPF² 11:396ff.
Abba Isaiah, *Logos* 14, *Abbé Isaïe* (Etoilles, 1970) 119-123. *Logos* 23, 193ff.
Apophthegmata. Arsenius 41a, Evagrius 1, John the Dwarf 9, Macarius 12, 34, Poemen 26, 72, 39, 50, Or 1; *The Sayings of the Desert Fathers* (1975). the Anonymous Series 1-11, *The Wisdom of the Desert Fathers* (1975) 1-3.
John Climacus, *Scala paradisi* 7; PG 88:817-828.
Symeon the New Theologian, *Catechetical Discourse* 2 (SCh 96 [1963] 256-264; deCatanzaro, 47ff.), 5, (312-72; deC., 90ff.), 29, (SCh 113 [1965] 180-86; deC., 313ff.).

Flight from the World, p. 205

Basil, *Long Rules* 5, 6, 8, 32. *Sermo de renunciatione saeculi*, PG 31:625-648; English trans. M. M. Wagner, *An Ascetical Discourse and Exhortation on the Renunciation of the World*, FC 9 (1950) 15ff.
Cassian, *Conference* 3; SCh 42 (1955) 138-65; LNPF² 11:319ff. (on the three sorts of renunciations: of wealth, of past life, of visible things).
Pseudo-Macarius, *Homily* 5; PG 34:493-517; Maloney, 51 (on the great difference between Christians and men of this world). *Homily* 46; col. 792-96; Maloney, 212.
Philoxenes of Mabbug, *Homily* 9; SCh 44 (1956) 245-311.
John Climacus, *Scala Paradisi* 1; PG 88:632-53.
Martirius Sahdônâ, *Le livre de la perfection* II.5, CSCO 215, Syri 91, 51-66.

Poverty, p. 208

Riches et pauvres dans l'église ancienne. Texts compiled and presented by Albert Hamman, Lettres chrétiennes 6 (Paris, 1962).
Basil, *Long Rules* 8, 9, 18, 19, 20, 22, 41. *Short Rules* 85, 87, 91, 93, 143, 144, 145, 146, 187, 205, 284, 304, 305.

Diadochus of Photice, *On Spiritual Knowledge: One Hundred Texts*, 63–66; *The Philokalia*, vol. 1 (London, 1979) 272–75.
Apophthegmata Patrum, Antony 20, Arsenius 29, 20, Agathon 6, Theodore of Pherme 1, John the Persian 2, Isaac 7, Cassian 7, Pistamon, Serapion 2, Syncletica 5; *The Sayings of the Desert Fathers* (Oxford-Kalamazoo, 1975, 1984).
Symeon the New Theologian, *Catechetical Discourse* 9; SCh 104 (1964) 122–34; deCatanzaro 152ff.
V. Soloviev, *The Justification of the Good* III.7.1–10 (London, 1918) 326–61 (the economic question from the moral point of view).

The Solitary Life, p. 211

Apophthegmata, Antony 10, 11, Arsenius 1, 2, 7, 8, 21, 25, 28, Evagrius 2, Moses 7, Nilus 9, Poemen 43, 59, Sisoes 3.
Cassian, See Index; SCh 64 (1959) 244: 'solitude'.
Martyrius Sahdônâ, *Le livre de la perfection* I.3; CSCO 201, Syri 87, pp. 30–75 (the greatness of the rule of the solitary life). *Ibid.*, I.4; 105–18, 138–45.
Skhimnik Hilarion, *Na gorach Kavkaza*, in Sergius Bolshakoff, *Russian Mystics* (Kalamazoo, 1977) 244ff.

Hesychia, p. 211

John Climacus, *Scala Paradisi* 27; PG 88:1096–1129.
In the French *Philocalie*, p. 40ff. (*Apophthègmes*), 115ff (John Climacus), 288ff. (Callistus and Ignatius of Xantopoulos), 273ff. (Gregory Palamas).

The Eremitic Life, p. 212

Basil, Letter 2; PG 32:224–233; FC 13 (1951) 5–11.
Cassian, *Conference* 18; SCh 64 (1959) 10–36; LNPF[2] 11:479–89 (on the three sorts of monks). Index, SCh 64, p. 231.
Abba Isaiah, *Logos* 6, *Abbé Isaïe* (Etoilles, 1970) 86–88 (of those desirous of living in a good solitude.)
Numerous texts are indicated in Irénée Hausherr, *L'hésychasme. Étude de spiritualité*, OCP 22 (1956) 19ff.; OCA 176 (1966) 177ff.

Hospitality, p. 214

Basil, *Long Rules* 20, 32, 45. *Short Rules* 97, 155.
Apophthegmata, Cassian 1, 3; Moses 5, Poemen 51, 58.
Cassian, *Conference* 8.1; SCh 54 (1958) 9–10; LNPF[2] 11:375 (the hospitality of Abbot Serenus).
Symeon the New Theologian, *Catechetical Discourse* 9; SCh 104 (1964); de-Catanzaro, 150–60. *Discourse* 4; SCh 96 (1963) 334–40; deCatanzaro 76–89 (charitable monks who live daintily).

Silence, p. 215

Basil, *Long Rules* 13, 32, 45. *Short Rules* 47, 173, 208.
John Climacus, *Scala Paradisi* 11; PG 88:852–53.
Antiochus the Monk, *Homily* 16; PG 89:1476ff. *Homily* 22; 1501ff.
Symeon the New Theologian, *Catechetical Discourse* 12; SCh 104 (1964) 182–88; deCatanzaro, 177–79.

Abstaining from Laughter, p. 216

Pseudo-Chrysostom, *Ascetam facetiis uti non debere*, PG 48:1055–1060.
Staretz Leonid of Optino (†1841), in S. Tyszkiewicz and Th. Belpaire, *Ascètes russes* (Namur, 1957) 153.

Temperance, p. 217

Basil, *Long Rules* 16, 17, 18, 19, 20. *Short Rules* 128.
Apophthegmata, The Anonymous Series 12–30; *The Wisdom of the Desert Fathers* (1975) 3–7.
Martyrius Sahdônâ, *Le livre de la perfection* II.6; CSCO 215, Syri 91, 66–74.
Antiochus the Monk, *Homilia* 6; PG 89:1149–52.
Symeon Metaphrastes, *Sermo* 29; PG 32:1345–55.
Vie d'Hypatios, in A. J. Festugière, *Les moines d'Orient* (Paris, 1961–1965) vol. 2:43.

Chastity, p. 219

Basil, *Long Rules* 5, 14, 15.
Cassian, *Conferences* 12 and 19; SCh 54 (1958) 120–46; SCh 64 (1959) 53–55; LNPF² 11:489–96.
John Climacus, *Scala Paradisi* 15; PG 88:880–924.
Antiochus the Monk, *Homily* 20; PG 89:1492–96. *Homily* 69:1633–36.
V. Soloviev, *The Justification of the Good* I.1.1–2 (London, 1918) 25–32. I.2.6; 50ff. II.1.6; 141ff.

Marriage, p. 219

Gregory Nazianzen, *Oratio* 18.7ff.; PG 35:993; LNPF² 7:256. *Panegyric on his sister Gorgonia*, *Oration* 8; PG 35:789–817; FC 22 (1953) 101–18.
France Quéré-Jaulmes, *La Femme. Les Grands Textes des Pères*. Lettres chrétiennes (Paris, 1968): Gregory Nazianzus, 219–37; Gregory of Nyssa, *Vie de Macrine*, 244ff.; Clement of Alexandria, *Le Pédagogue* 3.1–2, 137ff.; James of Sarug, 307ff.
Symeon of Thessalonica, *De honesto et legitimo coniugio*, PG 155:503–16.
V. Soloviev, *The Justification of the Good* III.10.3–6 (London, 1918) 416–26.

Virginity, p. 220

John Chrysostom, *On Virginity*, SCh 125 (1966).
Gregory of Nyssa, *Treatise on Virginity*, SCh 119 (1966); English trans. by V. W. Callahan, FC 58 (1966) 6–75.
Methodius of Olympus, *Le banquet*, SCh 95 (1963); English trans. by Herbert Musurillo, *The Symposium: A Treatise on Chastity*, ACW 27 (1958).
Antiochus the Monk, *Homily* 21; PG 89:1496–1500.

Fasting, p. 223

The Church Fathers on fasting, see DS 8 (1974) 1175ff.
Martyrius Sahdônâ, *Le livre de la perfection* II.7; CSCO 215, Syr. 91, 75–92.
Nazarius of Valaam (†1809), in S. Tyszkiewicz and Th. Belpaire, *Ascètes russes* (Namur, 1957) 54–57 (the refectory).
Staretz Macarius (†1860), *Ascètes russes* 168ff. (to a mother about Lent).

Spiritual Warfare, p. 233

Cassian, see Index to the *Conferences*, SCh 64 (1959) 236ff: 'épreuves'.
Pseudo-Macarius, *Homily* 21; PG 34:656–60; Maloney, 135ff. *Homily* 3.4–6; 469–72; 38–39.
Diadochus, *On Spiritual Knowledge: One Hundred Texts*, SCh 5ter (1966) 154–57; *The Philokalia*, vol. 1 (1979) 290–92.
Abba Isaiah, *Logos* 21, *Abbé Isaïe* 178.
Dorotheos of Gaza, *Instruction* 13.138–48; SCh 92 (1963) 402–19; CS 33:192–200.
Symeon the New Theologian, *Catechetical Discourse* 3; SCh 96 (1963) 304–8; deCatanzaro, 68ff. *Discourse* 6; SCh 104 (1964) 22–8; deCatanzaro, 122–29 (living in the Holy Spirit involves violence).

Temptations, p. 234

Origen, *Commentary on Matthew* 11.5–6; SCh 162 (1970) 290–95; ANF 10:434–35.
John Chrysostom, *Ad Stagyrium a daemone vexatum*, PG 47:423–493. *Concerning the Statues* 15.2: PG 49:156ff.; LNPF[1] 9:439ff.
Pseudo-Macarius, *Homily* 16; PG 34:613–24; Maloney, 112–17. *Homily* 15.18ff.; 585ff.; Maloney, 99ff.
Abba Isaiah, *Logos* 16, *Abbé Isaïe*, 140ff. *Logos* 25, 211ff.
Martyrius Sahdônâ, *Le livre de la perfection* II.12; CSCO 252, Syr. 111, p. 96–124 (perfect constancy).
Symeon the New Theologian, *Catechetical Discourse* 7; SCh 104 (1964) 66–70; deCatanzaro, 136–42.
Staretz George the Recluse (†1836), in S. Tyszkiewicz and Th. Belpaire, *Ascètes russes* (Namur, 1957) 99–101.

The Demon, p. 234

Athenagoras, *A Plea for Christians* 24–27; SC 2 (1941) 24–27; ANF 2:141–43.
John Chrysostom, *Ad Stagyrium a daemone vexatum*, PG 47:423–93.
Cassian, *Conference* 8.7–25; SC 54 (1958); LNPF[2] 11:377–87.
Pseudo-Macarius, *Homily* 7.2; PG 34:524ff.; Maloney, 65ff.
Ephrem, *Hymnes sur le Paradis*, SC 137 (1968) 22ff.
Evergetinos, *Synagogē* I (Athens, 1957), chapter 39, 265–69; vol. 2 (1958) chapter 33, 299–302.

Attention, Sobriety, vigilance, p. 242

Dorotheos of Gaza, *Instruction* 10.104–22; SCh 92 (1963) 336–55; CS 33:163–71.
Apopthegmata patrum, Arsenius 9, 10, Agathon 2, 29b, Ammoes 1, 2, Alonios 1, 3, Bessarion 11, Evagrius 3, 4, Theodore of Enaton 3, Theonas, John the Dwarf 10, 11, 18, 20, Isidore 4, Cassian 6, Poemen 1, 165, 32, 65, Ammonas of Nitria 2, Titoes 3, Silvanus 4, 11, 16, Serapion 3, Hyperechius 7, Osiris 2; trans. B. Ward, *The Sayings of the Desert Fathers*. Anonymous Series 132–157, trans. B. Ward, *The Wisdom of the Desert Fathers*, p. 39–44.
Martyrius Sahdônâ, *Le livre de la perfection* II.13: CSCO 253, Scriptores Syri 111, 124–45.
Antiochus the Monk, *Homily* 61; PG 89:1616ff.
Philocalie, see Index; for example, Hesychius de Batos, 124ff.; Philothée le Sinaite, 145ff. In English translations, Hesychius the Priest, *On Watchfulness and Holiness*, *The Philokalia*. vol. 1 (London, 1975) 163–98; Philotheus of Sinai, *Forty Texts on Sobriety*, in *Writings from the Philokalia on Prayer of the Heart*, edd. E. Kadloubovsky and G. E. H. Palmer, (London, 1974) 323–40.

Custody of the Heart, p. 241

Basil, *Long Rules* 5. *Short Rules* 2, 22, 29, 80, 191, 195, 197, 306.
Pseudo-Macarius, *De custodia cordis* PG 34:821–41.
Numerous Texts in the French *Philocalie*. See Index, *The Philokalia, The Complete Text*, volumes 1–3.

The Discernment of Spirits, p. 244

Basil, *Long Rules*, 10, 43, 49. *Short Rules* 152.
Cassian, *Conference* 2; SCh 42 (1955) 109–37; LNPF[2] 11:307–18 (on discretion).
Apophthegmata, for example, Poemen 15, 20, 21, 31, 18, 22, 118, 23, 24, 25, 27, 29, 117, 91, 28, 33, 40, 45, 54, 67, 168; *The Sayings of the Desert Fathers* (1975) 137–64. The Anonymous Series, 84–121; *The Wisdom of the Desert Fathers*, 28–35.
Pseudo-Macarius, *De patientia et discretione*, PG 34:–865–89.

Abba Isaiah, *Logos*, 15, *Abbé Isaïe*, 148-52.
Diadochus of Photice, *On Spiritual Knowledge: One Hundred Texts* 26-35; SCh 5ter (1966) 97-105; *The Philokalia*, vol. 1 (1979) 259-64.
Symeon the New Theologian, *Catechetical Discourse* 28; SCh 113 (1965) 154ff.; deCatanzaro, 295ff.
Seraphim of Sarov, in S. Tyszkiewicz and Th. Belpaire, *Ascètes russes* (Namur, 1957) 74ff.

Examination of Conscience, p. 247

Basil, *Long Rules* 37.
Abba Isaiah, *Abbé Isaïe*, Index, 304.
Staretz George the Recluse (†1836), *Letters*, in S. Tyszkiewicz and Th. Belpaire, *Ascètes russes* (Namur, 1957) 101.
Nazarius of Valaam, *Ibid.*, 57ff.
Theophane the Recluse, *Ibid.*, 130ff.

Logismoi, p. 248

Cassian, *Conference* 5; SCh 42 (1955) 188-217; LNPF[2] 11:339-51 (on the eight principal faults). *Conf.* 7; SCh 242-77; LNPF 361-75 (on inconstancy of mind and spiritual wickedness).
Apophthegmata, Les Apophthegmes des Pères du Désert, (Begrolles, 1966) p. 419: 'Comment donc les Scétiotes plurent à Dieu dans la pensée antirrhétique'?
Isaac of Syria, *De cogitationibus*, PG 86-885-88.
John of Damascus, *De octo spiritibus nequitiae*, PG 95:79-86.
Nilus, *De octo spiritibus malitiae*, PG 79:1145-64. *De malignis cogitationibus*, col. 1199-1234. *De octo vitiosis cogitationibus*, col. 1435-72.

Gluttony, p. 249

Basil, *Short Rules* 17, 71, 72, 126.
Evagrius, *Praktikos* 7; SCh 171 (1971) 508-10; trans. J. E. Bamberger, CS 4 (1978) 17.
Cassian, *Institutes* 5; SC 109 (1965) 186-259; LNPF[2] 11:233-48.
Philoxenes of Mabbug, *Homily* 10, SCh 44 (1956) 321-72.
John of Damascus, *De octo spiritibus nequitiae*, PG 95:79-86.
Antiochus the Monk, *Homily* 3; PG 89:1440-41. *Homily* 5:1445-48.
Evergetinos, *Synagogē* II, 20 (Athens, 1958) 175-76: *lathrophagia*.

Impurity, p. 250

Cassian, *Institutes* 6; SCh 109 (1965) 260-89; Index *Conférences* SCh 64 (1954) 239: 'luxure'.
Philoxenes of Mabbug, *Homilies* 12 and 13; SCh 44 (1956) 429-541.
Antiochus the Monk, *Homily* 19; PG 89:1488-92.

Index of Useful Texts 435

Apophthegmata patrum: Antony 22, Gerontius, Cyrus 1, Matoes 8, Poemen 14, 62, Sarah 1, 2; *The Sayings of the Desert Fathers,* 31–83; The Wisdom of the Desert Fathers, 7–21.
Evergetinos, *Synagogē* II.25–31 (Athens, 1958) 199–274.

Avarice, p. 250

Cassian, *Institutes* 7; SCh 109 (1965) 290–233; LNPF[2] 11:248–57; see *Conférences* SCh 64 (1959) 232: 'argent, avarice'.
John Climacus, *Scala Paradisi* 16; PG 88:924–432.
Antiochus the Monk, *Homilies* 8–13; PG 89:1456–69.

Sadness, p. 251

Basil, *Short Rules* 192, 194 (sadness according to God and the world).
John Chrysostom, *Ad Stagyrium a daemone vexatum* II–III; PG 47:447–94.
Cassian, *Institutes* 9; SCh 109 (1965) 268–81; LNPF[2] 11:264–66.
Abba Isaiah, *Logos* 17, *Abbé Isaïe,* 148.
Antiochus the Monk, *Homily* 25; PG 89:1509–13.
Nil Sorsky, *Monastic Rule,* in Thomas Špidlík, *I grandi mistici russi* (Rome, 1977) 132–34.

Anger, p. 251

Basil, *Adversus eos qui irascuntur,* PG 31:353–72, English trans. 'Against those who are Prone to Anger', FC 9:447–61.
Cassian, *Institutes* 8; SCh 109 (1965), 334–67; LNPF[2] 11:257–64.
Diadochus of Photice, *On Spiritual Knowledge: One Hundred Texts* 62; SCh 5ter (1966) 121–23: *The Philokalia,* vol. 1 (1979) 272 (the usefulness of anger).

Acedia, p. 252

Cassian, *Institutes* 10; SCh 109 (1965) 282–425; LNPF[2] 11:266–75; see Index *Conférences,* SCh 64 (1959) 241: 'paresse spirituelle'.
Diadochus of Photice, *On Spiritual Knowledge: One Hundred Texts* 58, SC 5ter (1966), 118, *The Philokalia,* vol. 1, (1979), 270.
Abba Isaiah, *Logos* 17, *Abbé Isaïe,* 147.
Nil Sorsky, in T. Špidlík, *I grandi mistici russi* (Rome, 1977) 134–38.

Vainglory, p. 254

John Chrysostom, *Sur la vaine gloire et l'éducation des enfants* SCh 188 (1972) 64–97; English trans. *Address on Vainglory and the Right Way of Parents to Bring up Their Children,* in M. L. Laistner, *Christianity and Pagan Culture in the Later Rome Empire* (Ithaca: Cornell University Press, 1951).

Evagrius, *Praktikos* 13; SCh 171 (1971) 528-31; CS 4 (1978) 19-20. *De octo spiritibus* 15-16; PG 79:1160C-1161B.
Cassian, *Institutes* 11; SCh 109 (1965) 426-47; LNPF² 11:275-79.
Abba Isaiah, *Logos* 17, *Abbé Isaïe*, 145ff.
Apophthegmata patrum, Antony 14, 15, Arsenius 31, Eulogios 5, Zeno 1, Theodore of Pherme 3, 7, 9, Serapion 4, Moses 8, Poemen 5, 63, 56, Sisoes 1, 2; *The Sayings of the Desert Fathers*. *Anonymous Series*, 124-31, *The Wisdom of the Desert Fathers*, 36-38.
John Climacus, *Scala Paradisi* 22; PG 88:948-65.
Symeon the New Theologian, *Catechetical Discourse* 10; SC 104 (1964) 146-48; deCatanzaro, 165ff.

Pride, p. 254

Basil, *Long Rules* 21, 28, 29, 30, 31, 41. *Short Rules* 36, 56, 79, 247.
Evagrius, *Praktikos* 14; SCh 171 (1971) 532-35; CS 4 (1978), 20. *De octo spiritibus*, 17-19; PG 79:1161C-1164D.
Cassian, *Institutes* 12; SCh 109 (1965) 448-501; LNPF² 11:280-90.
John Climacus, *Scala Paradisi* 23; PG 88:965-80.
Antiochus the Monk, *Homilies* 44-47; PG 89:1569-81.

Love of Self, p. 255

Basil, *Long Rules* 7, 41. *Short Rules* 54, 86.
John Chrysostom, *Homilies on Timothy* 2; PG 65:1020ff.; LNPF² 13:479ff.
Maximus the Confessor, *Century II on Charity* 8 (SCh 9 [1943] 95; ACW 21 [1955] 153). III.56-58 (SCh 140; ACW 183-84).
Theophylactus of Bulguria, *In Epistolam 2 ad Timotheum*, PG 66:945ff.

Self-Will, p. 256

Basil, *Long Rules* 6, 41. *Short Rules* 60, 65, 96, 128, 129, 137, 298.
Abba Isaiah, *Logos* 22, *Abbé Isaïe*, 188-189; see Index, 310.
Vie de saint Dosithée, SCh 92 (1963) 122-45.
Theodore the Studite, *Catechesis* 128; PG 99:678-79.

The Passions, p. 267

Athanasius of Alexandria, *Against the Heathen* I.3-5; SCh 18 (1946) 113-118; LNPF² 4:5-6.
Gregory of Nyssa, *On the Making of Man* 18; SC 6 (1943) 167-72; LNPF² 5:407-9.
Dorotheos of Gaza, *Instruction* 11.113-23; SCh 92:356-79; CS 33:172-81.
Abba Isaiah, *Logos* 2.19 and 28, *Abbé Isaïe*, 47ff., 157ff., 258.
Symeon the New Theologian, *Catechetical Discourse* 5, 7 and 10; SCh 96 (1963) 402-66, SCh 104 (1964) 80-84, 148-50; deCatanzaro 90ff., 141ff., 162ff.

Apatheia, p. 270

Lactantius, *De ira Dei*; CSEL 27:66–132; English translation. *The Wrath of God*, 54 (1965) 61–116.
Gregory of Nyssa, *The Life of Moses* II.256–268; SCh 1 bis (1955) 114–17; Ferguson-Malherbe, 120–23 (beyond the passions).
Cassian, *Conference* 23; SCh 64 (1959) 136–168; LNPF² 11:519–31.
Abba Isaiah, *Logos* 23, *Abbé Isaïe*, 195–97.
John Climacus, *Scala Paradisi* 29; PG 88:1148–53.
Symeon the New Theologian, *Éthique* IV, VI; SCh 129:9–77, 212–155 (the power of the dispassionate). *Catechetical Discourse* 3 and 5; SCh 96:294–96, 466–68; deCatanzaro, 60ff., 90ff.

The Will of God, p. 283

Origen, *De oratione* 26; PG 11:500ff.; trans. R. A. Green, in *Origen: An Exhortation to Martyrdom, Prayer, and Selected Works*, (New York: Paulist Press, 1979) 114ff.
Basil, *Short Rules* 42.
Basilian Constitutions 19 and 22; PG 31:1388ff., 1401ff.
John Chrysostom, *Concerning the Statues* 18.3ff.; PG 49:185; LNPF¹ 9:459ff.
Abba Isaiah, *Logos* 27, *Abbé Isaïe*, 255ff. (to seek to do God's will in everything.

Obedience, p. 284

Basil, *Long Rules* Prologue, 6, 28, 29, 31, 41 (obedience); 24, 25, 26, 27, 30, 35, 43, 45, 50, 54 (the superior). *Short Rules* 98, 99, 104, 113, 152, 291.
Apophthegmata patrum The Anonymous Series, 158–64; *The Wisdom of the Desert Fathers*, 45–7.
Dorotheos, Letter 2; SCh 92 (1963) 498–505.
Vie de saint Dosithée, SCh 92 (1963) 122–45.
Diadochus of Photice, *On Spiritual Knowledge: One Hundred Texts* 41–42; SCh 5ter (1966) 108–10; *The Philokalia*, vol. 1 (1979) 265–66.
John Climacus, *Scala Paradisi* 4; PG 88:677–764. *Liber ad Pastorem*; 1164–1209.
Martyrius Sahdônâ, *Le livre de la perfection* II.11; CSCO 253, Syri 111, p. 77–96.
Symeon the New Theologian, *Catechetical Discourse* 18; SCh 104 (1964) 266ff.; deCatanzaro, 209ff. (choice and virtues of superiors).
Staretz Silouan, in S. Bolshakoff, *Russian Mystics* (Kalamazoo, 1977) 251.

Spiritual Guidance, p. 284

Basil, *Long Rules* 10, 26, 46; *Short Rules*, 227.
Symeon the New Theologian, *Catechetical Discourse* 26; SCh 113 (1965) 94–6; deCatanzaro, 283. *Ibid.*, 20 SCh 104 (1964) 330–48; deCatanzaro, 231–37.
Nazarius of Valaam (†1809), in S. Tyszkiewicz and Th. Belpaire, *Ascètes russes* (Namur, 1957) 59.
Evergetinos, *Synagogē* I.20–21 (Athens, 1957) 159–91.

438   Index of Useful Texts

The Divine Commandments, p. 286

Irenaeus, *Against Heresies* IV.12.5–13.3; SCh 100 (1965) 521–33; ANF 1:176–78. *Ibid.*, 14.3–15.2; SCh 546–59; ANF 479–80.
Basil, *De iudicio Dei*, PG 31:653–76, the Preface to 'on the judgment of God' in FC 9 (1950) 37–55.
Pseudo-Macarius, *Homily* 37; PG 34:749–57; Maloney 188ff. (the spiritual law).
Abba Isaiah, *Logos* 7, *Abbé Isaïe*, 92ff.
Symeon the New Theologian, *Catechetical Discourse* 5, SCh 104 (1964) 48–66; deCatanzaro, 90ff. 27; SCh 113 (1965) 100–26; deCatanzaro, 284–94.

The Monastic Life, p. 287

Basil, The *Long Rules* 14, 15 (the vow of chastity).
John Chrysostom, *Adversus oppugnatores vitae monasticae*, 33; PG 47:319–86. *Comparatio regis et monachi*, PG 47:387–92.
Cassian, *Institutes* 1; SCh 109 (1965) 34–55; LNPF² 11:201. *Ibid.*, 4; 118–85, LNPF 219–33 (of the training of those who renounce); Index. *Conférences*, SCh 64 (1959) 240: 'moine, monastère'.
Nilus, *De monachorum praestantia*, PG 79:1061–94.
Eustathios of Thessalonica, *De emendenda vita monachica*, PG 135:729–910.
Nazarius of Valaam (†1809), 'Instruction sur la vie monastique', in S. Tyszkiewicz and Th. Belpaire, *Ascètes russes* (Namur, 1957) 47–50.

Virtue, p. 288

Gregory of Nyssa, *Carminum Liber* I.II.9; PG 37:667ff.
Gregory of Nyssa, *The Life of Moses* II.287–90; SCh 1bis (1955) 123–24; Ferguson-Malherbe, 128–9 (the royal road).
Cassian, see Index *Conférences*, SCh 64 (1959) 245.
Pseudo-Macarius, *Homily* 40.1–2; PG 34:761–64; Maloney, 196.
Dorotheos of Gaza, *Instruction* 14.149–59; SCh 92 (1963) 420–45; CS 33 (1977) 201–11.
Abba Isaiah, *Logos* 7, *Abbé Isaïe*, 88ff. *Logos* 25, 216ff.
Symeon the New Theologian, *Catechetical Discourse* 4; SCh 96 (1963) 340ff; deCatanzaro, 70ff. 31; SCh 113 (1965) 224ff.; deCatanzaro, 329ff.
Vladimir Soloviev, *The Justification of the Good* I.5.1–7 (London, 1918) 92–113.

Charity, p. 295

Irenaeus, *Against Heresies* IV.12.1–3; SCh 100 (1965) 508–517; ANF 1:475–76 (the most important precepts of the law). *Ibid.* IV.13.4–14.2; SCh 536–57; ANF 478–79 (God is in want of nothing).
Basil, *Long Rules*, Prologue, 1, 2, 3, 5, 6, 8. *Short Rules* 157, 172, 211, 212, 213, 230, 282.
Cassian, *Conferences* 11; SCh 54 (1958) 100–19; LNPF² 11:415–22 (on perfection).

Index of Useful Texts 439

Pseudo-Macarius, *De charitate*, PG 34:908–36.
Diadochus of Photice, *On Spiritual Knowledge: One Hundred Chapters* 12–23; SCh 5ter (1966) 90–96; *The Philokalia*, vol. 1 (1979) 255–59.
Martyrius Sahdônâ, *Le livre de la perfection* II.4; CSCO 215, Syri 91, 31–51.
John Climacus, *Scala Paradisi* 30; PG 88:1153–64.
Symeon the New Theologian, *Catechetical Discourse* 1; SCh 96 (1963) 223–39; deCatanzaro, 41–46. *Ibid.*, 8; SCh 104 (1964) 88–96; deCatanzaro, 143–49.

Prayer, p. 307

Origen, *De oratione*, PG 11:415–562; English trans. Rowan A. Greer, *Origen: An Exhortation to Martyrdom, Prayer and Selected Works* (New York: Paulist Press, 1979) 81–170
Basil, *De gratiarum actione*, PG 31:217–38.
John Chrysostom, PG 50:773–86. Pseudo-Chrysostom, PG 64:461–66, PG 65:737–40.
Cassian, *Conferences* 9–10; SCh 54 (1958) 38–97; LNPF² 11:387–409.
Pseudo-Macarius, *De oratione*, PG 34:853–65. *Homily* 6.1–3; PG 34:517–20; Maloney, 61–62.
Nilus-Evagrius, *Treatise on Prayer*, PG 79:1165–1200. The French *Philocalie*, 44–45. Irénée Hausherr, *Les leçons d'un contemplatif* (Paris, 1960)
Eusebius of Alexandria, *De gratiarum actione*, PG 86:331–42.
John Climacus, *Scala Paradisi* 28, PG 88:1129–48.
John of Damascus, *Sacra Parallela* 7; PG 95:1436–56.
Callistus II of Xanthopoulos, *Chapters of Prayer* PG 147:813–18.
Callistus Telicoudes, *De oratione et attentione*, PG 147:827–32.
Symeon of Thessalonica, *De sacra precatione* PG 155:535–670.
Theophane the Recluse, *O molitve i trezvenii* [*On Prayer and Vigilance*] (Moscow, 1889).

On the Lord's Prayer, p. 307

Cyril of Jerusalem, PG 33:1117–24.
Gregory of Nyssa, PG 44:1119–94; English trans. by Hilda C. Graef, *The Lord's Prayer, The Beatitudes*, ACW 18 (1954).
John Chrysostom, PG 51:41–48.
Maximus the Confessor, PG 90:871–910.
Theophane the Recluse, *O molitve i trezvenii* (Moscow, 1889).

The Degrees of Prayer, p. 311

Nicephorus, ed., Irénée Hausherr, *La méthode d'oraison hésychaste*, Orientalia Christiana IX, 33 (Rome, 1927); the French *Philocalie*, 206ff. *The Art of Prayer* (London, 1966) 21ff.
Isaac of Nineveh, the French *Philocalie*, 107–10.
Theophane the Recluse, in T. Špidlík, *I grandi mistici russi* (Rome, 1977) 235ff.

Oral Prayer, psalmody, p. 311

Basil, Long Rules 37. *Short Rules* 43, 44, 147, 173, 238, 279, 281, 307.
Nicetas Stethatos, in the French *Philocalie*, 181ff.
Gregory of Sinai, *Ibid.*, 250-55, 261ff.
Agapet of Valaam, in T. Tysziewicz and Th. Belpaire, *Ascètes russes* (Namur, 1951) 59ff.

Prayer of the Heart, p. 311

Agapet of Valaam, in S. Tyskiewicz and Th. Belpaire, *Ascètes russes* (Namur, 1957) 60-63.
Theophane the Recluse, in S. Bolshakoff, *Russian Mystics* (Kalamazoo, 1977) 210ff.
Writings from the Philokalia on Prayer of the Heart, trans. E. Kadloubosvky and G. E. H. Palmer (London, 1979).

Pure Prayer, p. 312

Symeon the New Theologian, *Catechetical Discourse* 2; SCh 96 (1963) 270ff.; deCatanzaro, 56ff. (seeing the light and living in it).
Isaac of Nineveh, in the French *Philocalie*, 105ff.
Elias of Ecdidos, *Ibid.*, 169ff.

Liturgical Prayer, p. 312

Symeon the New Theologian, *Catechetical Discourse* 4; SCh 96 (1963) 326-34; deCatanzaro, 74ff. (attendance at offices is not enough).
Nicolas Cabasilas, *Explication de la divine liturgie* SCh 4bis (1967); translated M. Hussey-P. A. McNulty, *Commentary on The Divine Liturgy* (Crestwood, New York).
Symeon of Thessalonica, *De sacra liturgia*, PG 155:253-304.
Dimitry of Rostov, in S. Tyszkiewicz and Th. Belpaire, *Ascètes russes* (Namur, 1957) 25ff.
Nazarius of Valaam (†1809), *Ibid.*, 52-54.
John of Kronstadt, *Ibid.*, 176-86.
Theophane the Recluse, in T. Špidlík, *I grandi mistici russi*, (Rome, 1977) 241-45.

Icons, p. 313

Athanasius of Alexandria, *Against the Heathen* I.13; SCh 18 (1946) 136ff.; LNPF[2] 4: 11ff. (the folly of image worship.)
Etheria, *Journal de voyage* I, SCh 21 (1948) 170 (the letters of Abgar and Jesus); English translation by John Wilkinson, *Egeria's Travels* (London: SPCK, 1971)
John of Damascus, *De imaginibus orationes*; PG 94:1231-1420; English trans-

Index of Useful Texts 441

lation by D. Anderson, *On the Divine Images* (Crestwood, New York, 1980).
Symeon of Thessalonica, *Dialogue against heresies* 23; PG 155:113.
The Stoglav or *the Hundred Chapters* (Moscow Synod of 1551), French trans. by E. Duchesne (Paris, 1920).
Denis of Phourna, *Guide de peinture*, edd., M. Didron and P. Durand (Paris, 1845).

Prayer and Church-building, p. 314

Symeon of Thessalonica, *De sacro templo*, PG 155:305-365. *Expositio de divino templo*, 697-750.
Staretz Macarius (†1860), in S. Tyszkiewics and Th. Belpaire, *Ascètes russes* (Namur, 1957) 158ff. (prayer to the church).

Unceasing Prayer, p. 315

Basil, *Long Rules* 5, 6, 37, 44. *Short Rules* 21, 29, 33, 34, 37, 201, 202, 205, 294, 295, 306 (rememberance of God).
Cassian, *Conference* 10.10; SCh 54 (1958) 85-90; LNPF² 11:405-07.
Pseudo-Macarius, *Homily* 33; PG 34:741-44; Maloney, 182-83.
Apophthegmata, Antony 1, Arsenius 30, Bessarion 4, Isaiah 7, Macarius 19, Titoes 1.
Isaac of Nineveh, in the French *Philocalie*, 105ff.
Symeon the New Theologian, *Ibid.*, 173ff.
Nicetas Stethatos, *Ibid.*, 183ff.
Ignatius Bryanchaninov, in S. Bolshakoff, *Russian Mystics* (Kalamazoo, 1977) 150ff.

The Jesus Prayer, p. 316

Diadochus, *On Spiritual Knowledge: One Hundred Texts* 59-61; SCh 5ter (1966) 119-21; *The Philokalia*, vol. 1 (1979) 170-72.
In the French *Philocalie*, Symeon the New Theologian, 175ff; Gregory of Sinai, 249ff., Anonymous, 301ff. Nicodemus the Hagiorite, 310ff.
Ignatius Bryanchaninov, in S. Bolshakoff, *Russian Mystics* (Kalamazoo, 1977) 158ff.
The Russian Pilgrim, in T. Špidlík, *I grandi mistici russi* (Rome, 1977) 247-68.
On the Prayer of Jesus. From Ascetic Essays of Bishop Ignatius Brianchaninov. Translated by Father Lazarus (London, 1952).
The Art of Prayer. An Orthodox Anthology compiled by Igumen Chariton of Valaamo, translated by E. Kadloubovsky and E. M. Palmer (London: Faber & Faber, 1966).

Contemplation, p. 327

Theophilus of Antioch, *To Autolicus* I.5-7; SCh 20 (1948) 66-75; ANF 2:90-91.

Cassian, *Conference* 14; SCh 54 (1958) 182–208; LNPF² 11:435–45 (on spiritual knowledge).
Diadochus of Photice, *On Spiritual Knowledge*, 67–74; SCh 5ter (1966) 127–33; *The Philokalia*, vol. 1 (1979) 275–78 ('theology' and contemplation, the vicissitudes of contemplation).
Symeon the New Theologian, *Catechetical Discourse* 8; SCh 104 (1964) 98–100; deCatanzaro 147–48 (keeping the commandments as leading to the vision of God). 19 (SCh 326–328; deCantanzaro, 230, laying hold on God). 22 (SCh 364–92; deCatanzaro, 246–47, the light as the fruit of faith).
Seraphim of Sarov, in T. Tyszkiewicz and Th. Belpaire, *Ascètes russes* (Namur, 1957) 78ff. (the active and the contemplative life).

The Senses, p. 331

Gregory of Nyssa, *On the Making of Man* 10; SCh 6 (1943) 117–20; LNPF² 5; 395–96 (the mind works by means of the senses).
John Chrysostom, *Address on Vainglory and the Right Way of Parents to Bring up Their Children*; SCh 188 (1972) 144ff.; M. L. Laistner, *Christianity and Pagan Culture in the Later Roman Empire* (Ithaca, 1951).
Lactantius, *The Workmanship of God* 9; SCh 213 (1974) 157ff.; FC 54 (1965) 29 (are the senses truthful?).

Faith, p. 335

Basil, *Long Rules* Prologue, 28. *Short Rules* 21, 36, 38, 39, 248, 260.
Pseudo-Macarius, *Homily* 48; PG 34:808–12; Maloney, 221–23 (perfect faith in God).
Philoxenes of Mabbug, *Homilies* 2 and 3; SCh 44 (1956) 45–87.
Abba Isaiah, *Logos* 21, *Abbé Isaïe*, 170–72.
Martyrius Sahdônâ, *Le livre de la perfection* II.I; CSCO 215, Syri 91, 8–25.
Antiochus the Monk, *Homily* 1; PG 89:1432–37.

The Contemplation of Nature, p. 336

Athanasius of Alexandria, *Against the Heathen* II.30–34; SCh 18 (1946) 170–78; LNPF² 4; 20–22 (the contemplation of nature leads the soul to the knowledge of God.
John Chrysostom, *Concerning the Statues* 9.2ff.; PG 49:105ff.; LNPF¹ 9:399ff.
Abba Isaiah, *Logos* 12, *Abbé Isaïe*, 111–13 (examples of this type of contemplation: the treatment of wine, a figure of spiritual progress).
Tikhon of Zadonsk, in T. Špidlík, *I grandi mistici russi* (Rome, 1977) 61–67.

Mystical Prayer, p. 337

Gregory of Nyssa, *The Life of Moses* II.152–62; SCh 1bis (1955) 77–84; Ferguson-Malherbe, 91–95 (the mountain of divine knowledge, the darkness).
Symeon the New Theologian, *Catechetical Discourse* 14 (SCh 104:212–20;

deCatanzaro, 186ff., being amazed at the mysteries, to see God and only God), 15 (SCh 193-97; deCatanzaro, 193-97, the light of God), 16 (SCh 236-52; deCatanzaro, 198-203, ecstasy in the light), 17 (SCh 254-64; deCatanzaro, 204-08, the heights of contemplation), 23 (SCh 113:24-32; deCatanzaro, 258-260, mystical intoxication), 35 (SCh 304-356; deCatanzaro, 359-366, the mystical experience of grace), 34-36 (SCh 270-356; deCatanzaro, 347-78, at the threshold of total illumination).
Theophane the Recluse, in S. Bolshakoff, *Russian Mystics* (Kalamazoo, 1977) 215ff.

The Glory of God, p. 342

Basil, *Long Rules* 2, 17, 20, 55. *On the Holy Spirit* Chap. 24; SCh 17bis (1968) 448-55. trans. D. Anderson (Crestwood, New York, 1980) 86-89.
John Chrysostom, *Huit Catéchèses baptismales* 6.8.; SCh 50bis (1970) 219ff.; *Baptismal Instructions*, trans. P. W. Karkins, ACW 31 (1963) (what it means to do everything for the glory of God).
Pseudo-Macarius, *Homily* 47.1; PG 34:796ff; Maloney, 215ff. (the countenance of Moses — a figure of true glory).
Texts indicated in DS 6 (1967) 438ff.

TOPICAL INDEX

Abba, 285
Abode of the dead (*sheol*), 113
Absolution, 191
Acedia (sloth), 73, 252, 402, 435
Acoemeti (non-sleepers), 315, 410
Adoptive (sonship), 47, 370
African Fathers, 156, 211
Agape, 161, 298; *see:* love, charity
Almsgiving, 167, 193, 224, 390, 426
Amerimnia (tranquility), 209, 242, 318
Ammas, 112
Anamnesis (liturgical), 41
Anchorites, 213
Angels, cosmic function of, 235; the angelic life, 221, 224, 273; angelic state, 110
Anger, 251, 435
Animism, 129
Anthropology (semitic), 98; (christian), 87, 352, 376, 420
Antirrhesis (counter-argument), 243, 319
Apatheia (depression), 61, 100, 270, 403, 437; a. and love, 275; condemnation of a. by the West, 277; the sign of, 276
Apes mentis, 60, 379
Aphorism, 1
Apophthegm (saying), 1; *Apophthegmata Patrum* (Sayings of the Fathers), *see:* names index
Apokatastasis (restoration), 37, 144, 150, 386, 424
Apostolate of the monks, 169, 390, 427; service of the world, 166
Armenians, 19, 363
Asceticism, 22, 179, 354, 392, 427; martyrdom of conscience, 76; a. of the monks, 296
Attention of the heart, 107
Axioms on the virtues, 289

Baptism, and death, 139; repentance and second b., 189
Beatitude, *see:* eudemonism
Bible, *see:* Scripture
Blasphemy, 255
Body, 107, 380, 422; b. in antiquity, 107; aphorisms on the b. 111; bodily care, 113; bodily mortification, 223, 339; the b. of Christ in the church,

157; the demons use bodies, 111, 236; illnesses, 113, 381, 422; the b. instrument of the Spirit, 112; the b. and the salvation of the soul, 66; body-soul-spirit, 91; the b. as prison, tomb of the soul (*Sôma-Sêma*), 111, 122; the purity of the bodies, 219; renunciation of the flesh, 217; risen body, 272; the b. in scripture, 107; the b. spiritualized, 112; spiritual writers on the b., 112; union of body and soul, 110
Boskoi (grazing monks), 213
Brotherhoods (monastic), 59
Byzantine, 11, 361

Canon (iconographic), 3
Cardinal virtues, 293
Cardiognosis (understanding the secrets of the heart), 77, 284
Catynyctic, 354
Catanyxis (compunction), 185, 194, 354
Catharsis, see: purification
Cause, efficient, 55; examplary, 55
Cenobitism, 21, 212, 214
Centuries, 1, 11
Charismatic activities, 63, 75
Charismatism (of human nature), 63
Charity, 295, 406; *see:* love
Chastity, 182, 219, 393, 398, 431; preservation of, 222
Christ, the mystery of, 34, 366, 416; savior, 35, 366; light, 35, 367; unifier, 36, 368; mediator, 36, 368
Christological (the christian life), 34
Church, 157, 308, 387, 424; c. building, 314, 403, 441; C. Fathers, 7; the heavenly c., 158; image of the Trinity, 57; social union in Christ, 37; spirituality of, 21, 351; the tradition of, 6, 360, 415
Cloud (mystical darkness), 70, 340; *see:* contemplation
Commandments of God, 5, 405, 438; the first c., 290; obeying the c., 286; transgressing the c., 186
Common (life), *see:* cenobitism
Compunction, *see: Penthos*
Concordance of opposites (*concordia oppositorum*), 137

445

Confession, absolution of sin, 191;
acts of repentance, 193; disciplines
(*epitimies*), 192; sacramental repentance, 191
Connaturality (with God), 47
Conscience, 95, 341, 377, 421; examination of, 117, 247
Consolation, 245
Contemplation (*theōria*), 327, 410,
441; cloud and darkness, 336, 340;
the contemplative east, 328; the
comtemplative life (*bios theoretikos*),
142; contemplative spirituality, 352;
cont. and holiness, 77; the cont. of
nature (*theōria physikē*), 336;
definition of c., 327; ecstasy, 339;
the faculty of c., 331; effects of,
340; no true knowledge without
love, 334; the object of c., 329;
praxis leads to *theōria*, 333; progress
in c., 335; the c. of providence and
judgment, 339; various terms for c.,
327; *theologia*, 338,; transforming
c., 334, 341; c. of the visible and the
invisible, 337; vision of God, 338
Conversion, 190
Coptic, 13, 362
Correction (brotherly), 165
Corruptibility (human), 269
Cosmology (spiritual), 125, 127, 381
Cosmos, 127; the cosmic dimension
of sin, 188; the cosmic God, 129;
cosmic spirituality, 20, 353; cosmic
religion, 126; the c. vocation of
man, 140, 385; *see:* world
Cosmopolitanism (christian), 155
Counsels (evangelical), 287
Cultural (tradition), 8

Death, 113, 381, 422
Degrees of the spiritual life, 68
Deification (divinization-*theosis*), 8,
13, 45, 72, 103, 132, 235, 253, 351,
370, 417; the deified nous, 332
Demon, 233, 234; the power of, 235;
cosmic function of, 131, 132; noonday demon (*demonium meridianum*), 253
Dendrites (tree dwellers), 213, 396
Desolation, 245
Despair, 189
Destiny, *see: Fatum*
Devotion to Christ, 37, 38, 368, 369, 416
Dichotomy, 92, 93
Diorasis (discernment), 77, 78, 244, 284, 342, 401, 433

Disciplines (*Epitimies*), 192
Disinterestedness, 67
Docetism, 38, 110
Dualism, in eastern religions, 207;
orthodox reaction against, 109;
Platonic dualism, 207; *see:* body

East (christian), 2
Eastern spirituality, 351
Ecclesiology of the Fathers, 157
Education, 170, 391, 427
Eleutheria (structural freedom), 101
Encrateia (chastity), 182, 273
Enemy, 234, 400, 433; *see:* demon
Epektasis (stable movement), 71
Epiklesis (invocation), 33
Eremitic spirituality, 354; *see:*
solitude
Eros, 298; *see:* love
Eschatologism, 65, 207, 221, 355
Eschatology, 143, 372, 386, 424
Eternal (life), 65, 372
Eternity, 144
Ethiopians, 14, 362
Exagoreusis (manifestation of
thoughts), 246
Examination of conscience, 247,
401, 439
Example (*exemplum*), 41, 44, 51, 165
Exorcism, 236
Experience (spiritual), 20, 71
Eudemonism, 51, 64, 205, 290, 372,
419
Eudaimonia (the happy life, *vita beata*),
64, 290; *see:* Stoicism
Evil, 135; false opinions about the
origin of e., 136; the image of God
and evil, 61; physical and moral e.,
137; the problem of evil, 135, 384,
432; e. and Providence, 135
Evil thoughts, *see: Logismoi*

Faculties of the soul, 102
Faith, from f. to *Gnosis*, 335, 442; f.
and the pure life, 76
Family, 162, 389, 425
Fasting, 224, 399, 432
Father (God), 45; spiritual f. 285, 403
Fatalism, 136
Fatum (fate, *Moira*), 43, 98, 130, 146
Fear of God, 143
Feelings, 269; 'the school of feeling', 95; feelings of the heart, 106;
spiritual f., 20, 72, 94
Flesh (*sarx*), *see:* Body
Flight from divisions, 217; f. from
women and beardless youth, 222, 223

Flight from the world (*fuga mundi*), 205, 214, 395, 429; affective and effective, 211; various aspects of, 206; f. in cenobitism, 214
Fools for Christ, 165, 174, 277, 301, 396
Freedom from care (*Amerimnia*), 209
Freedom, christian, 99, 379, 421; the Greek concept of, 98; 'no one is harmed except by his own hand', 140; the spirit of f., 354; f. as a source of evil, 136; structural f. (*eleutheria*) and freedom of choice, 100
Free will, 101
Forgetting God, 209
Fornication, 250, 402, 434
Friendship (*philia*), 161, 388, 425

Georgians, 16, 363
Gluttony, 249, 434; see: Logismoi
Gnōsis, 10, 70, 114, 327, 343; g. and *apatheia*, 275; g. and charity, 296; from faith to g., 336; the higher g. (*gnōsis alēthinē*), 185; pseudo-gnōsis, 76, 77; true g., 76, 178, 208
Gnostic (the true g.), 76, 234, 375
Gnostics, 68
Gnostic heresies, 109, 127, 295, 329
God, in christian revelation, 43; in patristic thought, 369, 417; the cosmic God, 130; the glory of, 342, 413, 443; God in Greek thought, 42, 417; the impassibility of God, 272; his incomprehensibility, 329, 343, 347; the remembrance of God (*mnēmē theou*), 340; the vision of God, 338
Grace, 31, 68; the consciousness of grace, 71, 373, 419; g. and free will, 101
Greek (spiritual writers), 11
Growth (spiritual), 68
Guarding the Heart (*phylakē kordias, custodia cordis*), 242
Gyrovagi (roving monks), 213

Habit (monastic), 181
Happy (life), 64; see: *eudaimonia*
Hardening, 73
Hatred, 164
Heart, 103, 120, 379, 422; attention to, 107; the center of life, 105; custody of the h., 222, 242, 400, 433; the feelings of the h., 106; the importance of the h., in Eastern spirituality, 103; the point of contact between man and God, 104; the principle of human integration, 105; the h., in Scripture, 103; the spirituality of the heart, 20, 354
Hellenism, 9, 316
Heretics, anger against, 252; authors, 11
Hesychast, Hesychasm, 21, 25, 26, 161, 311, 318; 85, 211, 225, 227, 260, 395, 397, 407
Heterodox (authors), 11
Hierarchical (obedience), 285
History (of the world), 142, 386
Holiness, 34
Holy Spirit, 3, 30, 365, 366, 416; the Holy Spirit belongs to our 'self,' 94; comes from the outside, 94; his dynamic presence, 75; his effect on man, 32; life in the Spirit, 29; personal indwelling of, 30; 'the soul of the human soul,' 32,; the Spirit of God in action, 29
Homosexual (love), 223
Hospitality, 214, 430
Humility, 88, 255, 377, 420
Hymnography (sacred, Syrian), 15

Icon, 3, 313, 328, 408, 440
Iconographic (canon), 3
Iconography (byzantine), 114
Idiota (unlettered), 77, 85
Illness, 113
Ignorance (sin and ignorance), 185
Images, meditations upon i., 333; the veneration of, 20; the image of God, 55, 78, 371, 417; the distinction between i. and likeness, 58; the image in hellenistic philosophy, 55, 56; i. in Scripture, 55, 56; i. and sin, 61; the place of the i., 59; from i. to likeness, 57; i. in the Trinity, 56; world, the i. of God, 56
Imitation of Christ, 39, 40, 81, 89, 369, 417
Imitating the saints, 41
Immortality of the soul, 97
Impassibility of God, 272
Incomprehensibility of God, 329
Incorruptibility (*aphtharsia*), 98
Intellectualized spirituality, 19, 24
Irascible power (faculty) of the soul, 252, 267

Jesus Christ, 34; cosmic unity, 37; devotion to, 37; devotion to the humanity of Christ, 38; humanity of Christ, 57; the imitation of Christ, 39; the Jesus prayer, 316, 410, 441;

to live in Christ, 40; light, wisdom, 35; the model of humility, 89; titles (names) of, 34, 319; power against the demons, 237; recapitualation (*anakephalaiosis*), 35; Savior, 35; the unifying activity of Christ, 3; the virtues, participation in Christ, 290
Joy (of Pascha), 182, 210
Judaism, 8
Judaeo-Christian, 8, 360
Just suffering, 234, 318, 384

Kalyves, 213
Kathismaton (hermitage), 213
Kellia (cells), 213
Kenosis (humility, self-emptying), 84
Kinship (*syngeneia*), with God, 47
Knowledge, mere or simple, 2, 186, 330; true, 186; mystical, 338, 412

Ladder Hymns (*seblata*), 69
Ladder (spiritual), 69
Land of unlikeness, 188, 208
Laity, 214
Latrophagia (eating in secret), 250
Laughter, 216
Lavras, 209, 213, 397
Law, natural, 62; obeying the l., 285
Life, cenobitic, common, 160, 212, 388 425; l. in common, separated from the world, 214; eternal l., 64; l. in God, 29; the happy l., 64; natural l., 62; new l., 55; progress in the spiritual l., 64; public l., 207; the solitary, eremitical l., 211, 396, 430; the stages of l., (purgative, illuminative, unitive), 70
Light of Tabor, 13, 318, 338, 342
Literature (spiritual) of various churches, 11
Liturgy, 7; Ethiopian hymns, 14
Logion (rule), 5, 286
Logismoi (passionate thoughts, deadly sins), 212, 236, 238, 248, 274, 434; the degree of penetration of l. into the heart, 241; the eight evil thoughts, 248, 401; the elimination of thoughts, 242; method of fighting hostile thoughts, 243; *Philautia* (self-love), the root of all evil thoughts, 255
Logos, philosophic, 330; theory of *logos -pneuma*, 129, 130, 133; l. *theoteles* (the l. tending toward God), 330
Lordship of man, 61
Love of God, brotherly l. and the salvation of the soul, 165, 389, 426; charity manifested in martyrdom, 75; the christian teaching on, 297; the first commandment, 299; terms for love in Greek philosophy, 297; no true knowledge without love, 334; l. and *apatheia* 275; perfection in charity, 295
Love of neighbor, 300, 426; brotherly correction, 165, 426; the example of the christian life, 165; love of God and of neighbor, 152; love's universality, perpetuity and equality, 151, 153; practice of charity in monasteries, 169; the structure of love (*ordo amoris*), 153

Man, inner-outer, 90; the unity of body and soul, 91; microcosm, 141; man's concrete obligations in society, 164; *see also:* Dichotomy, Trichotomy
Manichaeism, 64, 147, 198
Manifestation of thoughts (*exagoreusis*), 246
Manuals (ascetic), 1
Mary, Ethiopian devotion to, 14; mother of God, 158
Marriage, 112, 219, 398, 431; second m., 221
Martyrdom, 75, 139, 375, 419; m. of conscience, 76; m. of virginity, 220
Matter (hyle), 127
Mechitarists, 16, 26
Mediator, 36
Meditate (*meletan*), 312, 316
Meditation, 6
Melancholy, a deadly sin, 251
Messalians, 11, 20, 24, 27, 31, 48, 61 64, 72, 74, 80, 84, 168, 183, 184, 197, 234, 241, 273, 274, 276, 279, 315, 374
Messianism (Russian), 156
Metanoia (repentance, change of mind), 190
Method of prayer (psychosomatic), 318
Microcosm, 90, 141, 385
Mingling (of soul and body), 110
Miracles, 74, 419
Mire (*borboros*), 111, 122, 188, 200, 225
Mixture (with God), 36, 47
Moderation, 88
Monastic (spirituality), 287, 353; Coptic m. writings, 14; the m. habit, 181; m. life, 287, 438
Monasticism, the common life, 160; Eastern m., 21, 287, 405
Mortification, 181, 428; bodily, m., 223

Topical Index 449

Mother of God, 158, 388, 425; devotion to, 158
Mother (spiritual), 112
Mysticism, 22; ecstasy, 339; origins of, 19

Nations (plurality of), 154
Natural law, 62, 133
Natural-supernatural, 63; s. virtue, 293
Nature, 63, 352, 371, 418; different meaning in East and West, 63; fallen nature (*natura lapsa*), 63; living according to n., 62; the unique n. of the human being, 90, 155
Neo-Platonism, 56, 92, 186
Nepsis (vigilance), 243, 319
Nest'azanie, 209
New Prophecy (Montanism), 77
Nous, mind, 95; reason, 104; the divine faculty, 310, 332; the purified and deified N., 332

Obedience, 284, 437
Old man (*senex, geron*), 69
Oikonomia (house management), 131; the divine o., 383; the economy of salvation, 142
Opus Dei (the work of God), 196, 197, 392
Opus divinum, 177
Orders, active and contemplative, 170

Paideia, divine, 139, human, 170
Parrhēsia (free speech, frankness), 100, 221, 254, 354
Participation, 47
Paschal (joy), 47, 63, 183, 240, 267, 402, 436; as seen by Eastern christian writers, 268; passionate thought, 239; philosophic theories about the p., 267; resisting the p., 275; transformation of the p., 267
Patristics, 11
Patrologies, 7
Peaceful state, 270
Pelagianism, 64, 101, 187, 277
Penitentials (*Exomologetaria*), Western, 192; Eastern, 202
Penthos (compunction), 150, 193, 251, 317, 354, 394, 429; cause of, 194; effects of, 196; ways of obtaining P., 196
Perfection (*teleosis*), 373
Peripatetics, 92

Philautia (love of self), 67, 82, 115, 201, 255, 265, 436
Philokalia, 13
Philosophy, attitude of the Fathers toward p., 10; Greek p., 9, 365; the philosophic life, 22; the problem of God in p., 42
Physikē theōria (the contemplation of nature), 70, 336
Pilgrim (Russian), 318
Pneuma, 365
Politeia (instruction), 5, 286
Poverty, 208, 395, 429
Praxis, 11, 66, 71, 177, 178, 183, 186, 392, 427; inner p., 237; p. leads to *theōria*, 11, 333; negative p., 179; positive p., 283; spiritual p., 19
Prayer, 307, 407, 439; p. answered, 309; the ascent of the mind to God, 104, 310; bodily p., 311; the body associated to p., 112; the p. of the Church, 7; p. in the church, 314; definition of p., 308; degrees and types of p., 311, 439; devotion to Christ, 37; p., a dialogue with God, 42; ejaculatory p., 316; p. and fasting, 224; p. of the heart, 311, 440; p. and works, 315; the Jesus prayer, 316, 441; liturgical p., 312, 408, 440; mental p., 311; the monastic rosary, 317; mystical p., 337, 443; the necessity of p., 307; psalmody, 311, 408, 440; psycho-somatic method, 318; pure p., 312, 440; p. of silence, 312; spiritual p., 311; p. in the Spirit, 33; the state of p., 105; p. of supplication, 309; treatises on, 1; unceasing p., 315, 409, 441; to whom do we pray? 307
Precepts, *see*: commandments
Pride (*hybris*), 254, 436
Primitive (spirituality), 18
Proairesis (freedom of choice), 100, 136
Probatio fidei (testing of faith), 234
Purgative (stage of life), 70
Purification, from sin, 182, 428; of the passions, 267
Progress in the spiritual life, 68, 373
Prophecy, 284; New Prophecy, 77
Prosbolē (suggestion), 241; *see* the mechanism of temptation, 241
Prosochē (attention), 243
Prospatheia (inclination, self-will), 240
Providence, divine, 99, 125, 130, 131, 383, 423; definition and purpose of, 132; p. and evil, 135; p. within evil,

137; p. and the demons, 235; personal p., 133; the surrender to p., 134, 209
Public (life), 207
Pythagoreanism, 179, 205, 216, 228, 277

Quietism, 234

Reading saints' lives, 41, 74
Recapitulation (*anakephalaiosis*), 35
Recluse, 213
Redemption, 35
Regeneration, 47
Relatives, 213
Remembrance of God (*mnēmē theou*), 340
Renunciation, 180, 205, 230, 427
Repentance, 170; a second baptism, 189, 394, 428
Resemblance, *see*; image
Responsibility of man, 99
Resurrection, 109, 144; of the flesh, 217
Rosary (monastic), 196
Russian tradition, 17, 364; r. Messianism, 156, 172; r. pilgrim, 318

Sadness, 196; a deadly sin, 251, 402, 435
Saints, 158, 308, 388; imitation of the s., 41; intercession of, 158
Salvation of the soul, 66, 111, 373, 418
Satiety (*koros*), 186, 191, 199
Sayings of the (Desert) Fathers, apophthegms, 1
Scandal, 5
Scripture, 5, 360, 415; inspiration of, 6; larger meaning of the term, 6; reciting s. from memory, 6; the spiritual sense of s., g, 94, 377; weapon against the demons, 237
Seculars, 214
Self-accusation, 89
Self-denial, 180
Selfishness (spiritual), 67
Self-knowledge, 87, 115, 376, 420
Self-love (*philautia*), 255, 436
Self-will, 256, 436
Semitic (theology), 9
Senses, 331, 411, 442; spiritual s., 94, 420
Sex, 112, 220, 380, 422
Silence, 215, 397, 431
Sin, 182, 428; sin is the absence of being, 184; consequences of, 188; cosmic s., 188; distinction between sins, 187; grave, venial, 187; s. as ignorance, 185; the image of God and evil, 61; offending God, 186; original sin, 183, 393; purification from s., 182; full responsibility for s., 184; the social dimension of s., 184; source of evil, 136; the state of sin, 183; the theology of sin, 393; the traces of s., 194; transgressing the commandments, 186; voluntary-involuntary, 185; s. of weakness, 185
Sinlessness, 276
Sketes (groups of cottages), 213
Soul, nature of, 96, 378, 421; the image of God, 60; immortality of, 97, 378, 421; parts and faculties of, 102, 266; the s. in Scripture, 92; salvation of the s., 66; the Spirit and the s., 94; spirituality of the s., 96
Sophiology, 129, 131, 382, 383
Spirit, the image of God, 60; the S. and the soul, 94
Spiritual, 29, 92; s. climate (Greek), 9; s. doctrine, 22; s. guidance, 284, 404, 427; s. sense, 44, 117; s. sociology, 151; s. theology, 1
Spirituality, of the cell, 210; characteristic traits of Eastern s., 351, 359; cosmic s., 20; ecclesiological s., 159; s. of the heart, 20, 354; intellectualized s., 19, 24; living dogma, 11; monastic s., 287; practical s., 18; primitive s., 18, 24; the s. of the soul, 96; trends in s., 17
Spiritualization, cosmic, 33; of the christian, 33
Sobriety, 242
Social, the s. dimension of s., 188; s. enslavement, 101; man a s. being, 151; s. obligations, 164
Sociology (spiritual), 151
Solitary life, 21, 207, 211; charity among the monks, 160; the solitude of the heart, 212
Sonship (adoptive), 47
Sources, 5
Stages of life, purgative, illuminative, unitive, 70
Starets (elder), 69
Startzy, 17, 284
State, 162; s. of disorder, 246; of prayer, 105; as human society, 162, 389, 424, 425
Statics (stationary monks), 213
Stoicism, 45, 56, 132, 233, 247, 251, 268, 341, 371, 377, 380, 390, 405; its views on the body, 108; its

Topical Index

classification of the disciplines, 70; its view on *prolepsis* (intuition), 332; of the moral life, 267, 273; of self-restraint, 182; of the unity of the soul, 103; of the unity of the virtues, 292, 293; of world order, 123; of Providence, 131; attacked by Justin Martyr, 99; some of their concepts radically innovated by Clement, 273; the cosmopolitanism useful to christian thought, 155
Strastoterpsi (those suffering a 'passion'), 139, 148
Stripping of self, 181
Stylitism, 213, 396
Suffering, 135, 274, 385, 424; benefits for the sinner, 137; Christlike s., 139; the s. of the just, 318
Supernatural, 63
Syndiasmos (coupling with an evil thought), 241
Synergeia (co-operation, synergism), 102
Syrian, 14, 363; S. Fathers, 17, 172

Tabor, light of, 13, 318, 338, 342
Teaching the truth, 166
Tears, 189, 193, 194
Temptation, its mechanisms, 241
Temperance, 217, 397, 431
Thanksgiving, 309
Theologia, 22, 42, 70, 336, 338, 411
Theology, of history, 9; primitive t., 9; spiritual t., 1
Theōria (spiritual knowledge), 11, 19, 66, 100, 101; t., the end of life, 19; t. *physikē*, 21, 70, 128, 336, 442; as the transforming vision, 59; *see*: contemplation
Time, 144
Tradition, 2, 6; the traditionalism of the Eastern churches, 7
Traditions (cultural), 8
Transformation through contemplation, 341
Trends (spiritual), in Eastern spirituality, 17
Trichotomy, 29, 32, 92, 93, 377
Trinity, divine activity *ad extra*, 31; Holy T., 44, 221, 351, 369, 417; image of the T., 57; the 'super-essential unity', 45
Tripartite division of the soul (Plato), 267
Tserkovnost' (a sense of Church), 157, 352
Typica, 5, 12, 247

Unanimity, 217
Union, the dialectic of the one and the many, 45; the 'super-essential unity', (*unitas super principum unitatis*) in the Trinity, 45; the unifiying activity of Christ, 36
Unitive (stage of life), 70

Vainglory (*vana gloria*), 254, 435
Vartaped, 169
Vigilance, (*nepsis*), 242, 433
Vice, 289; *see*: Logismoi
Virginity, 220, 398, 432
Virtue, 288, 405, 438; axioms on the virtues, 298; cardinal v., 293; the difficulty and ease of the virtuous life, 291; the division between virtues, 293; the genealogy of v., 294; the (golden) mean, 289; natural-supernatural, 293; oneness of the virtues, 291; the only good life, 289; v. as participation in Christ, 237, 290; v. its own reward, 290; v. of the soul and of the body, 288, 294
Vision, of God, 338
Visions, 74, 374, 419

War, visible and invisible, 233
Warfare, against demons, 235; against evil thoughts, 237; the necessity of, 234; spiritual w., 233, 400, 432
Watchfulness (*nepsis*), 243
Ways, the two w., 143
Western Fathers, 12, 162, 173, 351
Widowhood, 221
Will of God, 283, 403, 437
Wisdom, 22, 365, 415
Woman, fleeing from w., 222; women's spirituality, 23(n.11), 112
Word, service of the, 166
Work, 168, 175, 390, 426
World, 125; the w. in antiquity, 125; the beauty of the w., 127, 382, 423; man's cosmic vocation, 140; the deified w., 128; flight from the w., (*fuga mundi*), 205; history of, 142; law of, 133; the opinions of, 207; present-to come, 207; the purification and deification of the w., 141; in Scripture, 126, 382; unity of, 128; visible-invisible, 125, 207

Xeniteia (living as a stranger), 213, 397
Xerophagy (eating dry food), 224

Youths (beardless), 222

Zeal (biblical), 270

INDEX OF PROPER NAMES

Aalst, Patricius van der, 27 (n.7), 343
Abiy-Addi, Mario da, 363
Abramovič, 26, 123, 263
Adnès, Pierre, 25, 115,(n.19), 117 (n.11), 174(n.72), 280(n.56), 325 (n.44,51,56), 347(n.41), 369, 377, 396 398, 399, 401, 403, 410, 41
Aeby, Gervais, 366, 369
Aetius, 83(n.88)
Agaësse, Paul, 369, 379
Agapet the Deacon, 163
Agapet of Valaam, 440
Agapios Landos, 13, 25(n.14)
Agapit the Monk (Pečersk), 113
Agathon, Abba, 430, 433
Agouris, S., 369
Agulles, Estrada Juan, 401.
Albert, Micheline, 348
Albinus, 70
Alcain, José Antonio, 367
Alès, Adhémar d', 48
Alexander, P., 302
Alexij (Kuznecov), 396
Alexis of Moscow, 314
Alexis of Studios, 12
Alezeghy, Zoltan, 395, 412
Alfaro, Juan, 52(n.11), 359, 406
Allan, D. K., 389
Allers, R., 385
Alonios, Abba, 433
Alpatov, Michail, 409
Althaus, Heinz, 367
Alvares, T., 373
Alvares-Campos, Sergius, 425
Amadouni, Garabed, 176, 363, 391
Amand, David, 82, 121(n.6), 173(n.32), 175(n.118), 197(n.34), 200(n.8,53), 228(n.7,10,13), 229 (n.5), 230(n.55, 56), 231(n.67), 301(n.35,36,37,40), 305(n.35, 36), 383, 392, 404, 405
Ammann, Emile, 394
Ambrose, 81, 321(n.26), 382
Ammonas, Abba, 86(n.164), 203 (n.27), 212, 227(n.10,) 242, 291, 303(n.31,32)
Ammonas of Nitria, Abba, 433
Ammoes, Abba, 433
Anaxagoras, 19, 271

Anaximander, 385
Ancilli, Ermanno, 50(n.34), 79(n.21), 121(n.7), 172(n.16), 258(n.62), 261 (n.19), 357, 376, 374, 381, 383, 388, 396, 402, 404, 405, 407, 410
Anderson, D., 4, 415, 416, 440, 443
Ansaldi, J., 369
Antiochus the Monk, 174, 202(n.10), 425, 426, 431, 432, 433, 434, 435, 436, 442
Antoine, Charles, 390
Antonij, Metropolitan, 366
Antony, 1, 12, 41, 74, 76, 77, 81(n.31), 82(n.52), 85(n.129), 86(n.167), 89, 11, 115(n.32), 117(n.10), 122(n.35), 123(n.69), 180, 197(n.2), 203(n.29, 30), 212, 226(n.35), 227(n.10,26), 235, 240, 243, 244, 245, 246, 252, 257(n.32), 261(n.24,31,40), 262 (n.48), 263(n.29), 246(n.66,72,75), 265(n.92), 271, 273, 279(n.7), 288, 290, 291, 302(n.1), 303(n.30), 347 (n.14), 348(n.48), 349(n.14), 374, 409, 430, 435, 436, 441
Aphraates (Aphrahat), 15, 19, 31, 315 324(n.9), 416
Apollo, Abba, 152, 171(n.8)
Apophthegms (Sayings), 1, 12, 41, 59, 79(n.41), 82, 85(n.138), 115(n.32), 116(n.34), 117(n.13), 152, 171(n.8), 173(n.38, 45), 175(n.91), 197 (n.2, 5,6,7,), 199(n.17), 202(n.2), 210, 215-17, 222, 227(n.6,26), 228(n.16, 18,30), 255, 257(n.17), 260(n.6), 262(n.48,75), 266(n.113); 286, 303 (n.64)), 365, 419, 420, 426, 429, 430, 431, 433, 434, 435, 436, 437, 441
Apostolic Constitutions, 155, 171, 203 (n.24)
Aratos, 46
Aristides, 132, 147(n.65)
Aristotle, 39, 45, 46, 50(n.17), 52(n.3), 62, 64, 81(n.32), 92, 96, 115(n.18), 118(n.40), 142, 161, 173(n.42), 176 (n.140), 216, 228(n.23), 263(n.19), 265(n.105), 269, 278(n.23), 279 (n.4), 289, 291, 293, 297, 302(n.6,

12,13), 303(n.36,58), 304(n.19,22), 305(n.23), 329, 330, 343(n.22), 382, 386, 388, 405
Armstrong, Arthur Hilary, 406, 411
Arnim, Hans von, 80, 83(n.88), 119 (n.86), 145(n.8), 260(n.52), 262 (n.3), 264(n.53), 278(n.5,116), 280 (n.38), 302(n.7), 303(n.37,41), 304 (n.68), 348(n.3)
Arnobius, 51(n.46)
Arnou, René, 83, 145(n.5), 197(n.12,15), 198(n.2), 225(n.21), 305(n.44), 342 (n.1), 343(n.5), 344(n.6), 345(n.18, 37), 361, 392, 393, 411
Arrian, 52(n.30), 345(n.17)
Arroniz, José M., 378
Arseniev, Nikolaj Serg., 8(n.34), 173 (n.53), 364, 372, 382, 385, 389, 404, 408, 412
Artioli, E., 362
Assemani, Joseph Simon, 48(n.8), 81 (n.17), 200(n.6,61), 203(n.35), 229 (n.29,31), 346(n.50), 348(n.4)
Athanasius of Alexandria, 1, 12, (n.8), 32, 46, 57, 58, 64, 79(n.23), 81 (n.26), 85(n.149), 177, 179, 193, 196, 197(n.3,32), 229(n.21), 237, 258 (n.61), 259(n.13), 261(n.31,36, 40), 264 (n.66), 271, 279(n.8), 288, 302 (n.1), 303(n.30), 305(n.30), 347(n.14), 349(n.14), 371, 376, 387, 392, 418, 421, 423, 428, 436, 442, 440
(Pseudo-Athanasius, 231, 263
Athanasius of Sinai, 7, 57
Athenagoras, 110, 121(n.18), 132, 133, 147(n.68,71,72), 221, 230(n.41), 423
Attaliate, M., 12
Attalus the Martyr, 76
Attwater, Donald, 49(n.43), 231(n.65)
Aubert, Jean-Marie, 405
Aubin, Paul, 78(n.13)
Aubineau, Michel, 79(n.30), 122(n.25), 200(n63), 225(n32), 229(n.24), 370, 378, 380, 390, 399
Auf der Maur, Ivo, 176, 391, 427
Augoustinos Iordanites, 228(n.8)
Augoustinos Monachos, 197(n.4), 260 (n.7), 263(n.44)
Augustine, 44, 57, 64, 88, 101, 117 (n.19), 119(n.72), 198(n.53), 219, 242, 260(n.58), 277, 281(n.74), 315, 323(n.4), 324(n.8), 366, 377, 378, 380, 381, 387, 389, 391, 393, 394, 402
Aulén, Gustav, 50(n.11), 367
Auvray, Emmanuel, 85(n.151), 261 (n.47)

Auxence, St., 400
Azéma, Yvan, 146, 147(n.73), 413

Bacht, Heinrich, 23(n.9), 176(n.126), 324(n.19), 390, 410
Baehrens, Wilhelm A., 23(n.4), 245(n.5), 262(n.7)
Bailey, Derrick Sherwin, 380
Bainvel, Jean Vincent, 117(n.25)
Baker, John, 48(n.18), 360, 361
Balas, David L., 370
Baldry, Harold Caparne, 390
Balducelli, Ruggero, 389
Bamberger, J. E., 81(n.19), 264(n.60), 402, 434
Bandmann, G., 409
Barclay, W., 391
Bardy, Gustave, 28(n.34), 51(n.43), 121(n.10), 198(n.39), 261(n.22), 359, 370, 391, 392, 401, 402, 403
Bareille, Georges, 374
Barlaam and Joasaph, 17, 85(n.149)
Barnabas, Letter of, 150(n.28)
Barosse, T., 389
Barsanuphius, 5, 77, 167, 175(n.94), 195, 203(n.15), 227(n.25), 288(n.9), 246(n.49,50), 265(n.86), 284
Barsotti, Divo, 407
Bartelinck, G. J. M., 365
Barucq, André, 365
Basil the Great, 3, 5, 12, 16, 21, 23(n.16,17), 24(n.40,42,47), 27 (n.19,22), 28(n.27), 31, 32, 45, 48 (n.17,20,21,22,23), 49(n.31,36,40), 52(n.20), 67, 81(n.30), 82(n.48,54, 55,60), 83(n.81), 87, 89, 90, 99, 107, 108, 113, 115(n.3,7,8), 116(n.37,39), 117(n.6), 118(n.53), 119(n.56,65), 121(n.6,16), 122(n.29,30,35,36), 123 (n.61, 62), 128, 133, 134, 135-37, 145(n.20), 146(n.25,26,28,29,30,44), 147(n.2,3,76,77,81,82), 148(n.13,15, 20,29), 152, 160, 165-170, 171(n.4, 10), 172(n.29), 173(n.31,32,33,34, 35,39), 174(n.75,82), 175(n.28,108, 111,118,119,120,121), 176(n.132, 139), 177, 182, 187, 189, 197(n.8, 34), 198(n.51), 199(n.38,44,45), 200(n.8,53), 201(n.26), 202(n.47), 203(n.23,32,37), 208-12, 212-18, 223, 225(n.25), 226(n.34,38,39,40,47,55, 57,58,59,61,62), 227(n.2,4,5,6,7), 228(n.1,7,10,11,13,14,22,26,29,31, 32), 229(n.2,5,8,9), 230(n.45,49,55, 57), 231(n.66,67,68), 260(n.7), 273, 279(n.24), 286, 287, 299, 301(n.21,

Index of Proper Names 455

28,31,32,35,40), 302(n.41,42), 304
  (n.8), 305(n.35,37,40,41,42,43,45,
  46,47,48), 311, 313, 321(n.18), 322,
  (n.44), 323(n.28), 324(n.13), 331,
  344(n.17), 345(n.20), 347(n.15,17,
  22), 348(n.7), 349(n.9,16), 358, 360,
  368, 376, 382, 383, 387, 389, 390,
  392, 395, 399, 403, 404, 405, 406,
  411, 413, 415, 416, 417, 418, 420,
  422, 424, 425, 426, 427, 428, 429,
  430, 431, 433, 434, 435, 436, 437,
  438, 439, 440, 441, 442, 443
Basset, René, 227
Battifol, Pierre, 347(n.31), 411
Bauer, Johann B., 120(n.4)
Bauernfeind, Otto, 406
Baumgärtel, Friedrich, 379
Baumgartner, Charles, 371
Baumstark, Anton, 363
Bazelaire, Louis de, 115(n.6), 376
Beaucamp, Evode, 382
Beaulay, Robert, 26(n.31)
Beccari, Camillo, 362
Beck, Edmund, 26(n.22), 78(n.19), 81
  (n.17), 146(n.54), 147(n.59), 227
  (n.29), 229(n.30,31), 346(n.50)
Beck, Hans Georg, 361, 383
Bedjan, Paul, 83(n.84), 200(n.3), 220
  (n.51), 346(n.41
Behm, Johann, 379
Behr-Sigel, Elisabeth, 364, 407
Békés, Gerardo, 345, 409
Belinsky, Vissarion Georg, 37
Belpaire, Thédore, 364, 415, 416, 418,
  422, 425, 428, 429, 431, 432, 434,
  437, 438, 440, 441, 442
Benedetti, P., 200
Benedict, St., 197(n.17), 345(n.27), 403
Beneševič, Vladimir Vik., 25
Benoît, André, 258(n.58)
Benz, Ernst, 258(n.2), 343(n.13), 364,
  374, 384, 388
Berdiaev, Nikolaj Al., 123(n.70, 75),
  125, 137, 139, 145(n.4), 148(n.23,
  46), 149(n.51,52), 355(n.3), 376,
  379, 381, 418, 424, 426
Bergson, Henri, 84(n.107)
Bermejo, Aloysius, 366
Bernard, René, 79(n.23)
Bernard, St., 38, 349(n.19), 368, 377,
  385
Bernardi, Jean, 391
Bernhard, R. 371
Bernhardt, Joseph, 384
Berset, C., 372
Bertaud, Emile, 83(n.78), 322(n.46),
  373

Bertrand, Frédéric, 368
Bérulle, Cardinal, 51(n.61)
Bessarion, Abba, 419, 441, 433
Besse, Jean Martial, 227(n.17)
Bettencourt, Stephanus, 259(n.30,37),
  400
Beugnet, Auguste, 390
Bickel, Gustav, 230(n.35)
Biedermann, Hermegild M., 81(n.34),
  372, 376, 395
Biemel, W., 324(n.22)
Blakeney, E. H., 145(n.17)
Blanc, Cécile, 122(n.55)
Bläser, Peter, 379
Bliemel, Josef, 406
Blond, George, 393, 398
Bloomfield, Morton W. 263(n.16), 402
Bobrinskij, Boris, 51(n.65), 122(n.46),
  313, 366, 387, 407, 408
Boccassino, Renato, 172(n.14), 323,
  407, 408
Boethius, 44
Boettinger, L. A., 363
Bolšakov, T., 323(n.29)
Bolshakoff, Sergei, 364, 415, 418, 424,
  437, 440, 441, 443
Boman, Thorleif, 24(n.35)
Bonaiuti, E., 392
Bonnetsch, Nathanael, 147(n.68)
Boon, Amand, 176(n.137), 322(n.10)
Borne, Etienne, 384
Bornet, René, 347(n.21)
Bossuet, 105, 120(n.23)
Boularand, Ephrem, 82(n.51)
Bourassa, François, 375
Bourgeault, Guy, 405
Bourguet, Pierre, du, 26(n.33), 362
Bourguignon, Pierre, 256(n.33), 400
Bousset, Wilhelm, 117(n.13)
Bouyer, Louis, 32(n.32), 81(n.26), 257
  (n.35), 261(n.24), 359, 372, 375,
  384, 387, 397
Bovis, André de, 174(n.64), 380
Bowden, J., 385
Bradley, Bruce, 26(n.23)
Brancati, R., 384
Brandon, Samuel George F., 386
Bratsiotis, Panagiotis, 370, 371
Bréhier, Emile, 146(n.52), 225(n.5),
  279(n.6), 345(n.37)
Bremond, Jean, 399
Brjančaninov, Ignatii, 410, 441, 415, 441
Bromiley, Geoffrey, 358
Broudehoux, Jean-Paul, 398
Brouillard, René, 390
Broussaleux, S., 25(n.13)
Brox, Norbert, 367, 382

Brunet, Robert, 50(n.26)
Brunschwigg, L., 377
Buchanan, A. M., 81(n.35)
Bugge, John, 399
Bulgakov, Sergei Nikol, 51(n.65), 129, 166, 172(n.14), 174(n.84), 313, 319, 321(n.14), 322(n.20), 323(n.32,35, 43), 324(n.29), 365, 366, 368, 383, 388, 408
Bultmann, Rudolf, 24(n.32), 372, 375, 381
Burghard, Gladigow, 365
Burghardt, Walter, 80(n.53), 371, 378
Busiris, 197(n.26)
Bussini, François, 372
Butler, Cuthbert, 257(n.17), 348(n.53)
Butterworth, G. W., 79(n.34)

Cabasilas, Nicholas, 13, 25(n.13), 37, 40, 49(n.3), 74, 379, 440
Cacciamani, Giuseppe, 396
Caesarius Nazianzenus, 79(n.40)
Callahan, J. F., 382
Callahan, V., 150(n.33), 432
Callistus Cataphigiotes, 343(n.2)
Callistus Telicoudes, 439
Callistus II of Xanthopoulos, 439
Camelot, Pierre Thomas, 85(n.155), 121(n.7), 198(n.45), 229(n.24), 343(n.10), 361, 371, 375, 393, 398, 403, 411
Campenhausen, Hans von, 375, 397
Candillac, Maurice de, 412
Cantalamessa, Raniero, 381
Capelle, Cathérine, 404
Capizzi, Carmelo, 50(n.33)
Caprioli, M., 402
Carretto, Carlo, 325(n.41)
Carpentier, René, 377, 395
Casel, Odo, 349(n.12), 397
Cassian, John, 12, 21, 81(n.39), 82(n.65, 66), 83(n.99), 91, 116(n.49), 119(n.76), 123(n.69), 161, 173(n.40), 197(n.16), 213, 226(n.50), 227(n.14), 233, 234, 235, 236, 244, 249, 250, 256(n.5), 257(n.20,21,22), 258(n.54), 259(n.40), 261(n.25), 262(n.8), 263(n.14,20,24,30), 264(n.72), 265(n.90), 273, 288, 290, 294, 302(n.2,17), 304(n.67), 316, 321(n.33), 323(n.25), 324(n.14,20), 343(n.16), 345(n.38), 388, 391, 398, 401, 406, 415, 419, 421, 422, 423, 425, 427, 428, 429, 430, 431, 432, 433, 434, 435, 436, 437, 438, 439, 441, 442
Castellana, P., 397
Castellano, J., 408

Castro Albarrán, Alphonsus de, 380
Catret, Juan V., 397
Causse, A., 24(n.33)
Cauwenberge, Paul van, 362
Cavalcanti, E., 175(n.98)
Cavallera, F., 81(n.16, 369
Cavarnos, F. P., 303(n.40)
Cechetti, Igino, 227(n.23)
Celsus, 24(n.33), 27(n.18), 50(n.13), 116(n.38), 137, 162, 171(n.22,23), 174(n.57), 258(n.59), 321(n.9), 332, 344(n.8)
Cerfaux, Lucien, 51(n.55)
Cerulli, Enrico, 362
Chabot, Jean-Baptiste, 363
Chaadaev, Petr J., 37
Chadwick, Henry, 50(n.22), 419
Chadwick, Owen, 256(n.5), 343(n.11), 361
Chambers, A., 372, 412
Chambry, Emile, 321(n.35)
Chariton of Valaam, 441
Châtillon, Jean, 120(n.6), 377
Chênevert, Jacques, 387
Chetverikov, S., 364
Chevalier, Irénée, 369
Cholet, Jean-Arthur, 401
Chomiakov, Alexij S., 37, 157, 172(n.7, 13), 308, 321(n.13), 387, 425
Chosrov (Chosroès), 158, 172(n.10)
Christou Panaghiotis, 405
Chroust, A., 365
Chrysippus, 62, 140, 146(n.52), 264(n.53), 268
Cicero, 130, 146(n.48), 155, 171(n.33), 173(n.42), 330, 344(n.5), 388
Cioffari, C., 383
Clarke, W., 415, 418
Classen, Wilhelm, 24(n.31)
Claudian, J., 230(n.61)
Cleanthes, 62, 289
Clement of Alexandria, 10, 19, 24(n.44, 48), 46, 58, 62, 69, 76, 79(n.28,43), 80(n.2,6), 83(n.80,81), 85(n.155), 88, 90, 92, 93, 97, 98, 99, 103, 115(n.16,40,57), 118(n.31,32,54,55), 119(n.87), 122(n.23,27,31), 123(n.60), 129, 131, 132, 133, 144, 145(n.7), 146(n.35), 147(n.67), 155, 171, 175(n.98), 179, 182, 198(n.50), 199(n.20), 211, 216, 219, 226(n.3), 228(n.28), 229(n.12), 230(n.38), 234, 249, 256, 257(n.16), 262(n.3), 263(n.19), 266(n.114), 268, 272, 273, 274, 276, 278(n.12,16), 279(n.15,20, 22), 280(n.32,55), 293, 294, 295, 303(n.49), 304(n.73), 328, 335,

Index of Proper Names

343(n.11), 344(n.1,9), 345(n.27),
346(n.1,58), 358, 361, 365, 367, 371,
375, 377, 379, 380, 383, 384, 386,
389, 394, 398, 403, 406, 409, 415,
417, 419, 422, 427, 431
Clément, Olivier, 150(n.25,26), 385,
386, 407
Clement, I, II, 366
Clement of Rome, 132, 147(n.64), 295,
304(n.69), 358
Cobat, S., 202(n.52)
Cognet, Louis, 392
Cohn, Leopold, 348(n.3)
Colobos, Abba, 75, 429, 433
Colombás, Garcia M., 82(n.40), 83
(n.78), 229(n.31), 230(n.37), 231
(n.71), 256(n.3), 304(n.10), 360,
372, 399, 400, 401, 408
Colpe, Carstein, 375
Colson, Jean, 406
Coman, Joan G., 376
Congar, Yves, 78(n.2), 172(n.3), 360,
411
Conger, G. P., 385
Cornelis, Etienne, 375
Cornélis, H., 118(n.39), 387
Cossu, Giovanni M., 390, 406
Costanza, M., 367
Coste, Jean, 384
Cotelier, Jean-Baptiste, 262(n.51), 303
(n.33)
Cothenet, Edouard, 369
Couchoud, Paul-Louis, 24(n.34)
Courcelle, Pierre, 122(n.22), 377, 380
Courtonne, Yves, 146(n.30), 226(n.37),
227(n.2)
Crainic, N., 324(n.22)
Cristiani, Léon, 368
Crouzel, Henri, 24(n.46), 27(n.8), 49
(n.4), 79(n.25), 79(n.32,39), 80(n.51,
52,61,62,65,66), 82(n.59), 118(n.17,
36), 150(n.32), 200(n.58), 229(n.17),
230(n.48), 302(n.27), 342(n.1), 344
(n.15), 345(n.12,30), 346(n.53), 349
(n.8), 361, 365, 371, 375, 386, 398,
399, 400, 411, 412
Čuk, D. Alfonso, 379
Cullmann, Oscar, 118(n.39)
Cummings, Charles, 23(n.3), 301(n.30),
323(n.25), 368, 395
Cumont, Franz W. M., 118(n.39), 381
Cuttat, Jacques-Albert, 374
Cyprian of Carthage, 156, 171(n.39),
201(n.30), 220, 226(n.2), 321(n.37),
394
Cyprien (Kern), Archimandrite, 370
Cyril of Alexandria, 47, 50(n.24),
52(n.22), 53(n.43), 60, 80(n.53),
358, 366, 371, 376, 378, 413, 424
Cyril of Jerusalem, 49(n.34,35,36),
175(n.98), 371, 424, 439
Cyril Phileotes, 166, 174(n.75)
Cyrus, Abba, 435

Dadišo Quatraya, 15, 26(n.28), 67, 152,
174(n.75), 233, 275, 281(n.46)
Daele, A. van den, 52(n.24)
Daeschler, René, 265(n.102), 397
Dalmais, Irénée-Henri, 52(n.26), 370,
408
Daloz, Lucien, 175(n.106,117), 175
(n.113), 390, 426
Daniel the Stylite, 281(n.77)
Danassis, Antonis, 391
Daniélou, Jean, 25(n.25), 48(n.18), 53
(n.38,47), 81(n.13), 82(n.73), 83
(n.87,90), 115(n.10), 122(n.28), 146
(n.36), 149(n.7), 150(n.36,37,40),
201(n.34), 257(n.37), 258(n.56), 259
(n.30,37), 343(n.30), 344(n.14), 348
(n.58,59), 360, 361, 370, 373, 381,
386, 400, 402, 403, 412
Darrouzès, Jean, 2(n.10), 83(n.94)
Davids, E. A., 376
De Boer, S., 376
deCatanzaro, C. J., 25(n.9,13), 51(n.57),
84(n.120), 85(n.131), 416, 417, 418,
421, 422, 423, 425, 428, 429, 430,
431, 432, 434, 436, 437, 438, 439,
440, 442, 443
Deckers, A., 380
De Clercq, Charles, 25(n.3), 175(n.100),
264(n.57)
Dedering, Sven, 198(n.38)
de Fiores, Stefano, 359, 388
De Flore, 384
De Guibert, Joseph, 197(n.31,35), 388,
392, 397
Dejaifve, George, 305(n.39)
Delatte, Armand, 348(n.44), 390
Delehaye, Hippolyte, 397
Delhaye, Philipp, 377
de Mendieta, Amand, 399
Demetrius Cydonius, 423
Denis, Archdeacon, 424
Denis of Phourna, 441
Denziger, Henricus, 50(n.24), 52(n.19),
200(n.49)
Derville, André, 262(n.60), 263(n.17),
401
Deseille, Placide, 84(n.104), 349(n.19),
385, 400, 413
Des Places, Edouard, 230(n.40), 371
Deville, R., 265(n.98)

De Vries, Gulielmus (Wilhelm), 172 (n.4)
Dhorme, Edouard, 148(n.34), 257(n.13)
Diadochus of Photice, 12, 20, 27(n.16), 72, 73, 75, 79(n.33), 81(n.31), 84 (n.111,119), 115(n.33), 122(n.38), 198(n.12), 230(n.40), 244, 245, 257 (n.19), 261(n.26,29,39), 272, 280 (n.48), 297, 374, 401, 411, 415, 419, 420, 421, 422, 430, 432, 434, 435, 437, 439, 441, 442
Didache, 77, 150(n.28), 175(n.103)
Didascalia, 171(n.34)
Didot, Ambroise Firmin, 52(n.3)
Didron, M., 441
Didymus, 58
Diel, H., 83(n.88)
Diepen, Herman M., 376
Dietz, Matthias, 25(n.5)
Digjan, F., 401
Dillmann, August, 362
Dmitri of Rostov, 440
Diodore of Tarsus, 61, 79(n.46), 80 (n.60)
Diogenes Laertius, 304(n.68)
Diognetus (Epistle to), 53(n.42), 85 (n.143), 127, 145(n.16), 155, 171 (n.37,38), 226(n.1), 305(n.29
Dionysius of Phourna, 113
Dionysius, Pseudo-Areopagite, 45, 46, 70, 83(n.86), 297, 343(n.5), 344 (n.10), 407, 411, 412, 423
Dirkin, Augustinus, 279(n.24), 403
Disdier, Marie Théophane, 174(n.62)
Dittrich, Ottmar, 198(n.47)
Dmitrewski, M. von., 395
Dmitri of Rostov, 17
Dochner, Th., 52(n.7)
Dodo, Charles, Harold., 404
Dölger, Franz Jozef, 173(n.30), 361, 365
Dolhagaray, Bernard, 402
Doresse, Jean, 363
Dorotheus, 73, 77, 96, 115(n.24), 116 (n.35), 122(n.33), 152, 164, 171 (n.12), 174(n.65,66,83), 233, 247, 252, 256, 257(n.6,17,23,24), 259 (n.9,11,15,25,26,27,28,29), 260(n.4), 262(n.53,54,56), 263(n.23), 264 (n.67), 265(n.85,111,112), 266(n.113, 115,116,117), 301(n.13,20,23), 418, 420, 421, 426, 427, 432, 433, 436, 437, 438
Dörr, Friedrich, 27(n.16), 374
Dörries, Hermann, 24(n.52), 258(n.1), 345(n.15), 360, 374
Dosithy, 6, 23(n.13), 86(n.164), 436, 437

Dostoevsky, Fyodor M., 17, 140, 156, 188
Draguet, René, 23(n.9), 82(n.57), 171 (n.5), 257(n.10), 280(n.46)
Drewery, Benjamin, 366
Dublanchy, Edmondo, 202(n.53), 392
Dübner, Fr., 52(n.7)
Dubois, Yves, 368
Dubourg, P., 324(n.34)
Duchatelez, K., 384
Ducheshe, E:, 440
Duddington, N., 50(n.35), 416
Dugas, Ludovic, 388
Duhem, Pierre, 381
Dulaurier, Edouard, 363
Du Manoir, H., 383
Dümpelmann, Gottfried, 390
Du Plessis, P. J., 373
Dupont, Jacques, 117(n.10), 343(n.10), 377, 401, 406
Dupong-Somner, André, 85(n.142)
Dupré La Tour, A., 412
Dupuis, Jacques, 116(n.65,68), 365, 376, 378, 380, 387, 408
Durand, P., 441
Durmontier, J., 398
Durry, Marcel, 51(n.45)
Dvornik, Fr., 389

Eckhart, Meister, 79(n.49), 120(n.15)
Edmonds, Rosemary, 198(n.40), 322 (n.6), 408
Eliade, Mircea, 24(n.34), 149(n.19)
Elias, Abba, 197(n.6)
Elias of Ecdidos, 440
Eltester, F. W., 78(n.6)
Epictetus, 46, 52(n.30), 67, 108, 115 (n.3), 121(n.3), 130, 140, 145(n.6,7), 146(n.47), 225(n.2), 279(n.23), 300 (n.1), 345(n.17)
Ephrem, 15, 19, 30, 48(n.8), 50(n.36), 57, 63, 74, 143, 173(n.45), 189, 196, 200(n.6,7,61), 202(n.11), 203 (n.31,33), 220, 221, 229(n.30,31), (n.33,35), 292, 303(n.39), 335, 348 (n.4), 421, 433
Ephrem Mtsire, 16
Epiphanius, 59, 348(n.46), 374
Etheria, 440
Eugène (Mar), 176(n.128)
Eulogios, Abba, 436
Eunomius, 329
Eusebius of Alexandria, 245, 439
Eusebius of Caesarea, 85(n.146), 86 (n.162), 420
Eusebius of Emesa, 79(n.46)
Eustathius Antiochenus, 79(n.46)

Index of Proper Names

Eustathius of Sebaste (philosopher), 309(n.31), 286
Eustathius of Thessalonika, 223, 230 (n.59), 425, 438
Euthymius, St., 262(n.51)
Euthymius the Hagiorite, 16
Euthymius the Younger, 7
Evagrius, 12, 15, 19, 43, 57, 63, 69, 81 (n.31), 82(n.64), 83(n.89), 86(n.166), 89, 94, 95, 102, 103, 115(n.27), 119 (n.67), 121(n.13), 152, 153, 161, 171(n.6,17), 173(n.36), 178, 185, 197(n.16,20,21), 198(n.7), 199(n.36), 210, 226(n.47), 233-45, 248, 250, 252, 253, 254, 257(n.8,9,18,27,33), 258(n.3,5,6,7,44,45,46,47,48,52,53, 60), 259(n.12,32,40,43), 260(n.11, 13,47,50,51,53), 261(n.14,16,18,32, 33,34,35,37,44,45), 262(n.1,2,4,7, 10,11), 263(n.12,18,21,26,27,28,31, 33,37,38,39,47), 264(n.52,53,54,56, 59,60,61,62,63,64,65,68,77,78,80, 83), 265(n.87,90,99,101), 269, 273, 274, 276, 277, 278(n.2,14), 279 (n.21,23,25), 280(n.34,35,37,45,47, 51,63,64,65,66,67,68,69,70), 281 (n.72), 287, 294, 295, 301(n.33), 303(n.60,61), 304(n.14,15,75,76,80), 305(n.44,52), 315, 321(n.16,19,20, 26,28), 322(n.41), 323(n.1,2), 327, 333, 336, 338, 340, 341, 343(n.4, 17,28), 344(n.2,3,8), 346(n.2,4,5, 6,7,8,39,44,48), 347(n.13,14,25,28, 32,35,38), 348(n.5), 400, 402, 403, 406, 407, 411, 429, 430, 433, 434, 436
Evagrius the Scholastic, 213, 227(n.16)
Evdokimov, Paul, 6, 32, 49(n.39), 50(n.9), 58, 63, 79(n.27), 81(n.13, 14,20), 84(n.109), 88, 100, 115 (n.12), 119(n.57), 122(n.56), 129, 146(n.42,43), 163, 174(n.58), 335, 346(n.55), 359, 366, 368, 373, 380, 382, 387, 388, 404, 405, 409
Evergetinos, Paul, 7, 12, 24(n.29), 84 (n.127), 203(n.19,20,22), 283, 296, 300(n.3), 304(n.11), 322(n.42), 433, 434, 435, 437

Farges, Jacques, 406
Faricy, R., 380
Fascher, Erich, 367
Fay, Eugène de, 24(n.44)
Fedotov, Georgij Petr., 116(n.34), 364
Felici, S , 366, 387
Fedwick, P. J., 413
Fellowship of St. Alban and St. Sergius, 359

Ferguson, Everett, 259, 345(n.32), 419, 421, 437, 438
Ferlay, Philippe, 370
Fernandez, Domiciano, 388
Fernandez, R., 397
Festugière, André Jean, 52(n.4), 78 (n.12), 80(n.4), 83(n.85), 115(n.4), 118(n.26,48), 121(n.1,9), 123(n.66), 145(n.2,9), 146(n.48), 147(n.69), 171(n.36), 172(n.26), 197(n.11), 225 (n.27), 226(n.49), 230(n.50), 257 (n.39), 258(n.42), 281(n.77), 302 (n.4), 344(n.1), 347(n.29), 361, 365, 369, 372, 376, 377, 378, 380, 382, 383, 391, 400, 410, 411, 431
Fielden, F., 24(n.34)
Fisher, Héribert, 79(n.49), 120(n.15)
Fisher, J. A., 381
Fiske, Adele, 25(n.12)
Fitzgerald, A., 423
Flacelière, Robert, 173(n.47), 398
Flew, R. Newton, 373
Fliche, A.-Martin, V., 405
Flick, Maurizio, 412
Florensky, Pavel Al., 17, 129, 142, 146(n.49), 346(n.46), 365, 369, 376, 379, 381, 383, 385, 388, 393
Florovsky, Georgij Vas., 120(n.10), 146 (n.45), 360, 376, 380, 382, 386, 404
Floyd, W. E., 384
Foerster, Werner, 382
Fohrer, George, 365
Folliet, G., 323(n.4), 374
Fonk, Nicolas, 322(n.17), 373
Fontoules, Io., 410
Frangoulis, J. D., 365
Frank, L. S., 388
Frank-Duquesne, Albert, 385
Frankenberg, Wilhelm, 82(n.64), 119 (n.67), 257(n.27), 258(n.50), 260 (n.13), 261(n.18), 263(n.33), 264 (n.59), 321(n.16), 343(n.17), 345 (n.21), 346(n.2,4,5,6,7,8,48), 347 (n.13,35,38)
Frazier, William, 406
French, R. M., 123(n.75), 145(n.4), 148 (n.46), 322(n.9), 325(n.41), 379, 381, 418, 426
Fries, Heinrich, 28(n.37), 51(n.1), 52 (n.23), 357
Früchtel, Ursula, 382
Fumagalli, G., 362
Funck, Franz Xavier, 147(n.64), 171 (n.34), 174(n.68), 175(n.103), 203 (n.24), 304(n.2,74), 389

Gaïth, Jérôme, 119(n.59,65,66,67,69), 146(n.51), 172(n.2)

Galtier, Paul, 48(n.5,10), 49(n.29), 201 (n.31), 369, 379, 394
Gargano, I., 359
Garitte, Gérard, 364
Gass, Wilhelm, 383
Gaucheron, M., 197(n.27), 392
Gauthier, René-Antoine, 51(n.2), 81 (n.29), 372, 395
Gauvain, J., 325(n.41)
Gazet, Alardus, 388
Geiselmann, Joseph Rupert, 360
Genet, D., 407
Gennadius of Marseille, 248, 262(n.5)
Gennadius Scholarius, 417
George, Augustin, 373, 401
George the Hagiorite, 16, 416, 428, 432, 434
Germanus of Constantinople, 314
Germanus the Hagiorite, 210(n.39)
Gerontius, Abba, 435
Gertrude (Sister), 373
Gessel, Wilhelm, 407
Ghebreyesus, Job, 387
Giet, Stanislas, 82(n.55), 115(n.3), 123 (n.62), 173(n.35), 376, 389, 395
Gifford, E. H., 420
Gillet, Lev, 359
Gillet, Louis, 263(n.14)
Gillet, Robert, 385
Gillon, Louis Bertrand, 51(n.56)
Gilson, Etienne, 171(n.36)
Giovanelli, Germano, 396
Girad, Marc, 385
Girod, R., 384
Gnedič, P., 367
Godefroy, Louis, 230(n.43), 398
Godman, S., 359
Goegler, Rolf, 360
Goffi, T., 359
Goggi, T., 402
Gogol, Nikolaj Vasil, 198(n.40), 313, 322(n.6), 323(n.22), 408
Goguel, Maurice, 225(n.14)
Goldfrank, David M., 23(n.20), 26 (n.42), 322(n.45)
Goldschmidt, Victor, 146(n.33), 344 (n.5), 411
Goltz, Eduard von der, 407
Gomez, Anastasio, 202(n.9)
Gorce, Denys, 380, 398
Gordillo, Mauricio, 172(n.15), 198 (n.6), 388, 391
Gorgonia, St., 198(n.5), 431
Gorodetsky, Nadejda, 27(n.44)
Gössmann, F., 387
Graef, Hilda C., 80(n.59), 122(n.26,52), 200(n.59), 300(n.2), 371, 439

Graffin, François, 26(n.24,27,32), 118 (n.34)
Grant, Robert M., 150(n.39), 375
Graves, Charles, 366
Grébaut, E., 368
Greely, Andrew, 412
Green, A. A., 86(n.169)
Green, R. A., 437
Green, William M., 402
Greene, William Chase, 383
Greer, Rowan A., 227(n.5), 439
Grégoire, Réginald, 25(n.2), 84(n.107)
Gregorius Scholarius, 416
Gregory the Great, 12, 174(n.67,71), 249, 255, 265(n.100), 386, 390, 401,
Gregory of Nareg, 16, 26(n.35), 194, 203(n.12)
Gregory Nazianzen, 27(n.3,7,18), 28 (n.34), 34, 35, 40, 44, 49(n.5), 50 (n.16,18,23,25), 51(n.63,66), 52 (n.8), 64, 80(n.7), 81(n.11,12,24,25), 82(n.49), 83(n.81), 88, 92, 97, 104, 110, 111, 115(n.9), 116(n.55,56), 118(n.38,40), 121(n.19,20), 122 (n.21,24,45), 123(n.58,59,71,72,74), 132, 141, 145(n.1), 147(n.70), 149 (n.2,3,4,9), 150(n.22), 166, 171 (n.24,25), 172(n.29), 174(n.69,85, 87,88,89,133,176,289), 175(n.90,93, 95,96,97), 176(n.133), 179, 189, 197 (n.11,13,22), 198(n.3,5), 199(n.28, 35,47), 200(n.5,59), 225(n.20), 229 (n.28,30,32), 230(n.33,39), 233, 257 (n.7), 258(n.63), 261(n.41,42), 290, 291, 292, 293, 302(n.9,11,19,23,24), 303(n.46,47,48,50,51,56,60), 332, 343(n.7,21), 344(n.9,10,11), 345 (n.16,25,32,38), 346(n.45,52), 347 (n.31), 348(n.1,6), 349(n.18), 357, 367, 368, 369, 381, 385, 389, 392, 406, 411, 418, 421, 423, 431
Gregory of Nyssa, 12, 27(n.10), 48 (n.19), 57, 69, 70, 71, 78(n.15), 79 (n.38,40), 80(n.4,54,55,61,63), 81 (n.15), 83(n.81,87,90,99), 84(n.102, 103), 86(n.167), 88, 100, 101, 112, 115(n.13), 119(n.59,62,64,68,70), 121(n.9), 122(n.26,32,39,40,41,42, 47,49,50), 123(n.73), 131, 142, 146 (n.36,51), 149(n.8,18), 150(n.23,24, 33,34), 172(n.2), 175(n.98), 184, 185, 187, 194, 198(n.13,14,15), 199 (n.31), 200(n.59), 203(n.14), 219, 220, 229(n.10,15,32), 259(n.14), 268, 269, 274, 275, 278(n.18,19,25), 279(n.17), 280(n.36,41), 288(n.52), 290, 292, 298, 300(n.2), 302(n.5,14,

Index of Proper Names 461

15), 303(n.40,44,45), 305(n.28,34), 329, 336, 340, 344(n.4), 345(n.32), 347(n.11), 348(n.58,61), 349(n.13), 367, 368, 370, 371, 374, 376, 379, 381, 385, 386, 398, 399, 403, 406, 412, 416, 418, 419, 420, 421, 422, 423, 424, 428, 431, 432, 436, 437, 438, 439, 442
Gregory of Sinai, 12, 440, 441
Gregory Palamas, 13, 46, 53(n.37), 57, 78(n.20), 339, 342, 347(n.42), 360, 370, 376, 396, 417
Grelot, Pierre, 82(n.43), 145(n.14), 149 (n.13), 171(n.26,27), 365, 373, 382, 388, 405
Gribomont, Jean, 22(n.2), 28(n.27), 48 (n.4,10,15), 49(n.35), 174(n.81), 227(n.3,15), 301(n.28,31,32), 360, 374, 377, 388, 394, 395, 396, 403,
Grillet, Bernard, 399
Grilli, Albert, 225(n.24,27),
Grillmeier, Aloys, 24(n.37), 176(n.126), 301(n.15,16), 366, 390
Grinten, F. van den, 406
Gross, Jules, 370, 393
Grotz, Jozef, 394
Gruber, Gerhard, 372, 378
Grumel, Venance, 25(n.14), 324(n.6, 11), 410
Grundel, W., 146(n.50)
Grundmann, Walter, 198(n.46)
Grunwald, Constantin de, 364
Guidi, Ignazio, 202(n.48), 362
Guillaumont, Antoine, 26(n.18,26,28), 27(n.17), 52(n.12), 18(n.18), 83 (n.91), 119(n.85), 120(n.16), 121 (n.13), 197(n.20), 256(n.4), 257 (n.33), 258(n.51,66), 259(n.10,12, 30), 262(n.7,9), 263(n.13), 264 (n.59,60,70), 278(n.2), 279(n.26,27), 281(n.73), 301(n.33), 344(n.2,3,8), 362, 374, 380, 397, 400, 402, 403
Guillet, Jacques, 261(n.21), 321(n.34), 379, 401
Gunkel, Hermann, 348(n.45)
Guy, Jean-Claude, 257(n.17), 261 (n.25), 401

Haenschen, Ernst, 375
Hager, Fritz Peter, 384
Hainsworth, Cuthbert, 27(n.45), 404
Halkin, François, 201(n.29), 348(n.47)
Hamman, Albert, 300(n.2), 359, 407, 416, 417, 421, 426, 429
Hamon, Auguste, 380
Hamps, Vincenz, 365
Hanson, Richard P. C., 360

Hanssens, Jean-Michel, 258(n.57)
Harden, J. M., 362
Hardick, Lothar, 395
Harkins, P. W., 175(n.115), 424
Harl, Margherite, 51(n.60,62), 145 (n.22), 199(n.30,39,40), 345(n.31), 349(n.17), 367
Harnack, Adolf, 122(n.57), 197(n.7), 370, 405
Hart, F. J., 147(n.67)
Hartmann, Prosper, 375
Hasler, Victor Ernst, 405
Hauck, Friedrich, 388, 393
Hauschild, Wolf-Dieter, 366
Hausherr, Irénée, 2, 4, 23(n.3,9), 24 (n.29,30,38), 25(n.1,6,14,55), 26 (n.21,25), 27(n.1,12,14), 47(n.1), 48 (n.13), 50(n.38), 51(n.41), 80(n.68), 81(n.16), 82(n.53,68,69), 83(n.83, 97), 84(n.110,116,128), 85(n.130, 135,137,156,159), 115(n.27,31), 116 (n.61), 117(n.8), 121(n.45), 146 (n.27), 150(n.29), 171(n.14,21), 173 (n.36), 174(n.79), 196(n.1), 197 (n.35), 198(n.37,38,41), 199(n.17, 32), 200(n.4), 201(n.16,38,39,40), 202(n.1,10,41,50), 203(n.16,25), 225(n.26), 226(n.41), 227(n.9,10, 12), 228(n.25), 229(n.12), 260(n.1,9, 12,48), 261(n.46), 262(n.6), 263 (n.41), 265(n.102,107), 278(n.13), 279(n.28,29), 280(n.57), 300(n.3,7), 301(n.9,10,11,16,17,18,19,30), 302 (n.46), 303(n.33,36), 304(n.13,16), 305(n.25,27,49), 321(n.19,26,28), 322(n.41), 323(n.25), 324(n.20,21, 25,32,33,36,38,39), 325(n.47,55), 343(n.6,8,9,12), 345(n.27), 346 (n.40,42), 348(n.5,55), 349(n.10), 361, 363, 368, 372, 373, 374, 390, 392, 394, 395, 397, 399, 400, 401, 402, 404, 406, 407, 409, 410, 411, 412, 430, 439
Harvey, Wigan, 48(n.5), 85(n.145,156), 86(n.160), 116(n.63), 118(n.30,35, 46), 146(n.34,40)
Hayek, M., 363
Hebert, A. G., 50(n.11), 367
Hedde, René, 148(n.44)
Heiler, Friedrich, 387, 399, 407
Hemmerdinger, Demetrios, 26(n.22)
Hendrickx, Ephraem, 370
Hengel, M., 395
Herbigny, Michel d'., 81(n.35)
Herman, Emil, 25(n.8), 48(n.3), 118 (n.44), 300(n.6)
Hermas, Shepherd of, 22(n.1), 77, 295, 304(n.71)

Herodotus, 52(n.10)
Hertling, Ludwig von., 226(n.35)
Hertzsch, E., 397
Hesychius, 223, 230(n.58), 241, 243, 260(n.5,10), 272, 280(n.61), 297, 319, 433
Heussi, Karl, 197(n.6), 405
Hibbard, W., 360
Hieronymus Graecus, 27(n.13)
Hilarion of Aksubai, Schimnik, 430
Hillis, W. B., 378
Hippolytus, 145(n.24)
Hoffman, Paul, 123(n.67)
Hofmeister, Philip, 390
Holl, Karl, 348(n.46), 394
Holstein, Henri, 404
Homer, 52(n.29), 197(n.24,25), 297, 371
Horay, P., 384
Hörmann, Karl, 25(n.55)
Horn, G., 406
Hruby, Kurt, 360
Huebner, Reinhard, 367
Hufstader, Anselm, 83(n.97), 202 (n.1), 394
Hunger, Herbert, 389
Hussey, M., 440
Huve, J. C., 82(n.58)
Hyldahl, N., 24(n.43)
Hypatios, 226(n.49), 431
Hyperechius, Abba, 433

Ibn Saba, 216
Ignatius Bryanchaninov, 415, 441
Ignatius of Antioch, 46, 56(n.43), 75, 98, 109, 121(n.10), 122(n.43), 197 (n.28), 225(n.17), 268, 278, 279, 295, 304(n.79), 366, 368, 406
Ignatius of Loyola, St., 26(n.17), 325 (n.55)
Ilarion, Schimonach, 430
Iliadou, see: Hemmerdinger, 26(n.22)
Ioannou, P., 201(n.39), 399, 400
Irenaeus, 7, 30, 32, 36, 37, 48(n.5,26), 50(n.21), 52(n.27), 53(n.47), 57, 58, 60, 62, 68, 76, 77, 79(n.24,30,31, 46), 85(n.145,156), 93, 97, 109, 116, 118(n.30,34,35,46), 121(n.8,11), 129, 144, 146(n.34,40), 150(n.40), 172(n.28), 173(n.44), 304(n.3), 305 (n.28), 355(n.2), 370, 376, 378, 380, 382, 386, 407, 415, 417, 419, 421, 438
Isaac, Abba, 173(n.45), 264(n.83)
Isaac of Syria (of Nineveh), 11, 12, 15, 24(n.53), 26(n.30), 70, 82(n.67), 83 (n.84), 272, 275, 280(n.39), 321 (n.26), 333, 346(n.41), 428, 434, 439, 440, 441

Isaiah, Abba, 11, 24(n.54), 26(n.28), 69, 82(n.57), 89, 115(n.29), 171 (n.5), 174(n.75), 177, 208, 214, 226 (n.33), 228(n.8), 251, 257(n.10), 260(n.7), 263(n.44,46), 272, 280 (n.46), 295, 304(n.78), 417, 418, 421, 424, 425, 426, 427, 429, 430, 432, 434, 435, 436, 437, 438, 441, 442
Isidore, Abba, 433
Isokrates, 179
Ivánka, André von, 25(n.13), 344(n.4), 345(n.14), 358, 361, 367, 367, 389, 405, 411
Ivanov, Vjačeslav, 37, 201(n.15)

Jacamon, Sophia M., 463
Jackson, Blomfield, 4(n.6)
Jacquemin, E., 403
Jaeger, H., 148(n.34), 257(n.15), 262 (n.57), 379
Jaeger, Werner W., 302(n.15), 361, 365, 374, 391, 411
Jagu, A., 199(n.28), 300(n.1), 393
Jakovlev, V., 323(n.37)
Jamblichus Chaldicensis, 228(n.17)
James Bar Salibi, 15, 26(n.32)
James of Edessa, 15, 26(n.27)
James of Sarug, 15, 19, 26(n.24), 69, 189, 193, 200(n.3), 202(n.51), 431
James, William, 373
Janežič, Staukc, 27(n.44), 115(n.21)
Janin, Raymond, 26(n.36), 397
Janssens, Louis, 53(n.40), 371
Jaubert, Annie, 259(n.36), 360
Jenkinson, W. R., 371
Jerome, 109, 121(n.12), 273, 277, 281(n.73)
Jervell, J., 78(n.6)
Jetté, Fernand, 14(n.14), 120(n.24)
John, Abba, 213
John Chrysostom, 47, 53(n.41,43), 79 (n.46), 101, 115(n.22,26), 119 (n.71), 128, 131, 135-40, 143, 145 (n.18,19), 146(n.53,55,57), 147(n.6), 148(n.9,10,11,12,14,16,17,18,19,24, 27,28,30,32,33,41,42), 149(n.10,11, 12,14,47,48,49,50,56,57,58), 150 (n.31), 152, 162, 165, 167, 168, 169, 171(n.7,11), 173(n.43,44,48,49,50, 52), 174(n.73), 175(n.102,106,107, 112,114,115), 176(n.127,133,136, 140), 185, 189, 191, 192, 193, 196, 199(n.26), 200(n.9,10), 201(n.35), 202(n.3,42), 203(n.18,26,36), 219, 220, 222, 230, 247, 251, 255, 262 (n.55), 263(n.42,43,45), 265(n.94), 288, 293, 295, 302(n.44), 303(n.56),

Index of Proper Names 463

304(n.4,5,6), 305(n.27), 307, 309, 320(n.1), 321(n.27,32), 322(n.41,43), 323(n.29), 343(n.30), 347(n.33), 365, 366, 381, 382, 384, 385, 387, 389, 390, 391, 393, 395, 398, 399, 400, 415, 417, 418, 419, 422, 423, 425, 426, 427, 429, 432, 433, 435, 436, 437, 438, 439, 442, 443
John Climacus, 3, 12, 40, 41, 51(n.71), 69, 73, 76, 82(n.63), 83(n.79,98), 84(n.117), 89, 115(n.25,28,33), 116 (n.36), 122(n.37), 182, 191, 194, 198(n.44,52), 200(n.2), 201(n.14,24, 25,28), 202(n.4,10,48), 203(n.28), 218, 220, 222, 226(n.45,46,48), 229 (n.4,30), 230(n.45,46,50,51), 231 (n.69), 241, 242, 247, 250, 253, 258 (n.55), 260(n.55), 262(n.58,59), 263 (n.12,22,34,36), 264(n.55,62,78,81), 265(n.99), 272 303(n.42, 304(n.12), 396, 398, 402, 407, 419, 420, 423, 429, 430, 431, 435, 436, 437, 439
John Colobos, 85(n.139), 177, 197
John Moschus, 6, 12, 23(n.12), 63, 173 (n.44), 174(n.74), 200(n.1), 203 (n.13), 209, 210, 226(n.42,53), 228 (n.33), 23](n.53,54), 234, 257(n.28, 38), 258(n.64)
John of Dalyatha, 15, 26(n.31)
John of Damascus, 39, 51(n.48), 64, 85 (n.149), 102, 119(n.79), 122(n.48), 184, 201(n.38), 248, 252, 257(n.19), 260(n.49), 263(n.11), 264(n.58), 296, 302(n.45), 303(n.64,65), 308, 321 (n.17,21), 322(n.41), 343(n.15,25), 346(n.54), 347(n.33), 371, 376, 417, 434, 439, 440
John of Gaza, 203(n.15), 262(n.50)
John of Lycopolis, 198(n.38)
John Petritsi, 16
John of Pitra, 209
John, son of Abu Zakarija, 15, 26(n.33), 228(n.27
John, St., 193
John the Persian, 430
John the Prophet, Abba, 77
John the Solitary (of Apamea, Pseudo-John of Lycopolis), 15, 26(n.23), 69, 83(n.83), 174(n.79), 180, 195, 198 (n.38), 203(n.16,17), 251, 263(n.41), 269, 278(n.13,24), 346(n.40)
Johnston, William, 324(n.34)
Joly, R., 392
Joseph Hazzayâ, 83(n.77)
Joseph of Volokolamsk, 6, 17, 23(n.21), 26(n.42), 80(n.57), 81(n.36,37), 101, 119(n.74), 123(n.64), 163, 167,

172(n.12), 173(n.45), 174(n.59,60 76,77), 175(n.101), 197(n.10), 209, 215, 219, 225(n.18), 226(n.50,51), 228(n.15), 229(n.13), 230(n.35,52), 286, 287, 301(n.22,25,27,39), 303 (n.34), 311, 322(n.45), 323(n.40), 38, 358, 386, 395
Jossa, Giorgio, 386
Journet, Charles, 384, 395
Jugie, Martin, 119(n.75), 386, 410
Juliana of Lazarevskoe, 162
Julian the Apostate, 227(n.2)
Jungclausen, E., 325(n.41)
Jundt, Pierre, 305(n.27)
Justin Martyr, 10, 24(n.43), 62, 99, 118 (n.45), 147(n.65), 180, 198(n.36), 220, 229(n.20), 272, 302(n.180), 361, 366, 369, 382, 386, 402
Justinian, 5, 21, 163, 175(n.122), 343(n.14)

Kabiersch, J., 406
Kadloubovsky, E., 25(n.5), 26(n.17), 202(n.8), 258(n.52), 260(n.10), 314 (n.17,27), 360, 409, 410, 433, 440, 441
Kaiser, G. E., 390
Kalchreuter, H., 302, 405
Kallistos II Xanthopoulos, 410
Kalogirou, J., 374
Kannengieser, Charles, 366, 381, 387, 389, 391
Kant, Immanuel, 72, 120(n.31)
Karkins, P. W., 443
Karpp, H., 376
Karst, J., 363
Kartašev, Anton Vlad., 156
Kastolskij, D., 360
Kéchinian, Isaac, 26(n.35), 203(n.12), 416
Kekelidze, Korneli, 363
Kelly, John Norman, 49(n.30)
Kelly, R., 387
Kemmer, Alfons, 374, 397
Keseling, P., 392
Khalifé-Hachem, 24(n.53), 26(n.30), 345(n.33)
Khomiakov, see: Chomiakov, Alexij
Kiprian, see: Cyprien (Kern)
Kirchmeyer, Jean, 2, 26(n.38), 50(n.15), 53(n.41,44), 78(n.16), 79(n.23), 82 (n.44), 85(n.132,148), 126(n.22), 150(n.27), 199(n.30,34), 257(n.30), 264(n.79), 344(n.7), 367, 370, 371, 375, 379, 381, 407, 411, 412
Kittel, Gerhard, 50(n.19), 197(n.14), 198(n.46), 199(n.29), 278(n.1), 358

366, 380, 381, 382, 406, 412
Kleinknecht, Hermann, 50(n.19)
Klimenko, M., 364
Klostermann, Erich, 49(n.1), 197(n.30), 258(n.2), 280(n.32), 345(n.15)
Koch, Hal, 148(n.21), 201(n.26), 322(n.1), 383, 405
Koch, Robert, 51(n.53)
Koehler, Theodor, 388
Koester, Wilhelm, 373
Koetschau, Paul, 258(n.59)
Kologrivof, Ivan, 26(n.43,47), 37(n.45), 49(n.43,46), 82(n.62), 86(n.165), 123(n.63), 148(n.45), 149(n.53,54, 55), 173(n.41), 174(n.54), 197(n.33), 200(n.65), 225(n.16), 319, 325 (n.50), 364, 389, 416
Konstantinides, Michael, 406
Konstantinou, Evangelos G., 302(n.5), 398, 403, 406
Koreň, Antonio, 388
Korvin-Krasinski, Cyrill, 385
Kotter, B., 346(n.54)
Köttig, B., 172(n.9), 388, 397
Kovaleskij, Ergraf, 407
Kraft, R. A., 175(n.103)
Kretschmar, Georg, 375, 392, 397
Krivochéine, Basile, 325(n.42), 410
Kröger, M., 258(n.1), 345(n.15)
Krüger, Paul, 26(n.36), 376
Krumbacher, Karl, 361
Kuhn, Hulmut, 80, 372
Kutschbach, W., 302(n.10)
Kyriakos, 230(n.56)

Labriolle, Pierre de, 86(n.161), 403, 405
Lacan, M. F., 265(n.88)
Lactantius, 420, 437, 442
Ladner, Gerhart B., 121(n.9)
Ladomersky, Nicolas, 366
Laféteur, P., 398
Lafon, Ghislain, 373
Laistner, M. L., 176(n.103), 427, 435 442
Lamarche, Paul, 78(n.6)
Lamb, G., 176(n.135), 380, 391
Lampe, Geoffrey William H., 259(n.9), 366, 375
Lamy, Thomas-Joseph, 202(n.11), 230 (n.60), 399
Lang, David Marshall, 364
Langevin, G., 378
Langhe, Robert, 408
Langton, Edward, 400
Laurent, Marguerite-Marie, 305(n.32), 406
Laurentin, René, 388

Lawrence, G., 78(n.20), 396
Lanson, R. P., 116(n.43), 260(n.2), 420
Lebreton, Jules, 48(n.18)
Leclercq, Henri, 227(n.21,23), 388, 396, 397, 409
Leclercq, Jean, 373, 381
Lécuyer, Joseph, 82(n.76), 404
Le Déaut, Roger, 82(n.76), 360
Ledeur, Etienne, 369
Lefèvre, André, 120(n.4,20), 380
Legrand, Aimé, 199(n.28), 399
Leloir, Louis, 23(n.6), 363
Lemaire, Ph., 262(n.50), 203(n.15)
Lemaitre (Hausherr), J., 86(n.164), 117 (n.8), 146(n.27), 344(n.4,7,10), 345 (n.21,24,28,35), 347(n.10,36,37,38), 348(n.56,57), 371, 375, 377, 412
Lemoine, Eugène, 26(n.25)
Lèon-Dufour, Xavier, 116(n.45,53), 121 (n.4,5), 279(n.1), 344(n.32), 403
Lèonard, Augustin, 27(n.11), 84(n.105), 373
Leonardo da Vinci, 334
Leonid of Optino, 415, 431
Lepelley, Claude, 389
Lequien, Michel, 201(n.38)
Leroux, Jean-Marie, 391
Leroy, Julien, 28(n.28), 116(n.49), 262(n.52), 301(n.26)
Lesquivit, Colomban, 82(n.43), 145 (n.14), 149(n.13), 373, 382
Lettenbauer, Wilhelm, 172(n.45)
Leunclavius, 201(n.40)
Lewis, I. D., 51(n.45)
Lewy, Hans, 348(n.60), 412
Leys, Roger, 27(n.10), 78(n.15), 79 (n.40), 80(n.61,62), 81(n.15), 371
Lialine, Clement, 382, 396
Liber Gradum (The Book of Degrees), 69
Licknar, V., 364
Lieske, Aloysius, 368
Lightfoot, J. B., 85(n.143), 145(n.16), 171(n.37), 225(n.17), 226(n.1) 304(n.79)
Ligier, Louis, 393
Lilienfeld, Fairy von, 26(n.41), 27(n.47), 264(n.48), 365, 404
Linton, S., 410
Lisenko, A., 364
Littmann, Enno, 362
Litva, Alojz, 383
Liuma, Atanas, 262(n.6), 401
Lods, Marc, 375
Lohse, Bernard, 392, 399
Long, G. 115(n.3)
Losski, Nikolaj D., 149

Index of Proper Names 465

Lossky, Vladimir, 23(n.24), 25, 26, 38, 39, 60, 72, 79(n.48), 84(n.108,109), 87, 88, 114(n.1), 115(n.11), 172 (n.19,20,22), 201(n.22), 275, 359, 360, 367, 371, 387, 409, 412
Lot-Borodine, Myrrha, 49(n.8), 52(n.21), 53(n.38), 202(n.1), 370, 379, 394, 407
Lotz, Johannes B., 373, 411
Lovato, F., 362
Lowrie, D. A., 376
Lubac, Henri de, 23(n.4,12), 80(n.8), 117(n.71), 322(n.5), 344(n.16), 360, 371, 387
Luibheid, Colm, 115(n.25), 200(n.2), 303(n.42)
Lyonnet, Stanislas, 257(n.29), 365, 366
Lys, Daniel, 188(n.41)

Maas, Wilhelm, 369
Macarius, Abba, 419, 429
Macarius the Great, 122(n.34), 264 (n.75)
Macarius of Corinth, 13, 19
Macarius, Staretz of Optino, 441, 432
Mac Avoy, Joseph, 84(n.118), 389, 402
McComb, S., 397, 407
McGuckin, Paul, 25(n.9), 83(n.94), 117(n.7)
McKenzie, John L., 382
McNulty, P. A., 440
Macrina, St., 324(n.12), 431
Madosz, P. J., 368
Mainz, Barbara, 4(n.6)
Makarij, Metropolitan, 322(n.45)
Malak, Hanne, 362
Malatesta, E., 380
Malherbe, A. J., 80(n.4), 259(n.14), 345(n.32), 419, 421, 437, 438
Malingrey, Anne-Marie, 28(n.34), 148 (n.19), 149(n.49)
Malone, Edward, 85(n.150), 256(n.3), 375, 420
Maloney, George, 26(n.41), 48(n.12), 225(n.10), 280(n.58), 415, 416, 417, 419, 420, 421, 428, 429, 432, 433, 438, 439, 441, 442, 443
Mangenot, Joseph Eugène, 400
Manoir, Hubert du., 383
Mansi, D., 323(n.28)
Mansion, Augustin, 118(n.40)
Mantzarides, Georgios I., 53(n.37), 359, 360, 370
Manuel Paleologus, 202(n.10)
Marcellus, Abba, 63
Marchel, N., 369
Marcus Aurelius, 122(n.29), 126, 149 (n.50)

Margerie, Bertrand de., 370
Marie de l'Incarnation, 120(n.14)
Marin, Eugène, 391
Maritain, Jacques, 121(n.49)
Mark the Ascetic (or the Hermit), 72, 82(n.67), 194, 202(n.7,8), 266 (n.113), 276, 280(n.60), 419, 429
Markus, Robert Austin, 406
Marrou, Henri Irénée, 176(n.135), 380, 391
Marshall, J., 229(n.23)
Marsili, Salvatore, 197(n.16), 406
Martin, Jean-Pierre, 83(n.79), 366
Martinelli, M., 325(n.41)
Marty, Francis, 401
Martyrius Sahdônâ, 106, 120(n.27), 121 (n.50), 231(n.70), 312, 322(n.7), 335, 346(n.56,57), 363, 420, 429, 430, 431, 432, 437, 439, 442
Maraval, Pierre, 324(n.12)
Marx, Michael J., 409
Mason, A. J., 258(n.1)
Mason, M., 387
Matoes, Abba, 435
Matsagouras, E., 391
Mattingly, Harold, 85(n.149)
Maurer, Christian, 392
Maximus of Tyrus, 148(n.26)
Maximus the Confessor, 12, 37, 46, 52 (n.17), 58, 60, 79(n.26,47), 80(n.56, 58), 81(n.23), 132, 146(n.53), 147 (n.60,61,62,63,82), 149(n.5), 153, 154, 171(n.14,15,16,18,20), 200 (n.58), 207(n.28), 226(n.43), 229 (n.4), 238, 239, 240, 250, 255, 259 (n.18,19,20,21,22,23,24,33,35,41,42), 263(n.32), 265(n.91,95,96,102,108, 109,110), 178(n.26,27), 269, 272, 275, 276, 279(n.22,28), 280(n.40, 49,61,62), 295, 300, 304(n.77), 305 (n.49,50,51), 314, 315, 323(n.3), 336, 343(n.18), 344(n.10,11,12), 346(n.9), 347(n.28), 370, 372, 377, 381, 385, 386, 387, 393, 402, 423, 424, 428, 436, 439
Maxsein, A., 380
Mayer, Augustin, 371
Meany, James, 371
Mécérian, Johannes, 363
Meester, Placide de, 28(n.29), 404
Méhat, André, 199(n.20), 343(n.11), 386, 394
Mehl-Koehlein Herrade, 116(n.58)
Meinardus, Otto, 362
Melania, St, 112, 122(n.53), 175(n.91), 226(n.44), 235, 265(n.97), 258(n.41)
Meletius, 420

Melia, Elie, 395
Ménard, Jacques E., 304
Menas, Abba, 189
Mennessier, André-Ignace, 264(n.50), 405
Mensching, Gustav, 397
Merki, Hubert, 371
Merlin, Nicolas, 119(n.72)
Mersch, Emile, 386
Mesrob, 15
Methodius of Olympus, 49(n.33), 144, 147(n.68), 150(n.38,39), 220, 416, 432
Metz, Johannes Baptist, 365, 379, 380
Meyendorff, John, 25(n.12), 78(n.20), 227(n.13), 347(n.42), 362, 368, 376, 396, 398
Meyer, A., 385
Meyer, Robert T., 23(n.8), 122(n.33)
Meyer, Rudolf, 393
Michael (Konstantinides), 406
Michaelis, Wilhelm, 278(n.1), 302(n.5), 402, 405
Michaud, Eugène, 386
Michel, Anton, 302(n.16), 303(n.53), 389, 398, 403, 406
Michel, Maria Albert, 230(n.60), 399
Millar, L., 391
Mingana, Alphonse, 26(n.29), 83(n.77)
Miquel, Pierre, 264(n.79), 374, 409
Moeller, Edmond W., 381
Mohamed al-Birouni, 301(n.15)
Mollat, Donatien, 347(n.41), 377
Monden, Louis, 374
A Monk of the Eastern Church (Lev Gillet), 25(n.5), 324(n.23,24), 359, 410
Monod, V., 381
Montanus, 339
Moore, Lazarus, 115(n.25), 410, 441
Moraldi, Louis, 202, 384
Morey, Charles Rufus, 83(n.79)
Moses, Abba, 430, 436
Moschus, see: John Moschus
Mossay, Justin, 118(n.40), 381
Mouhama, Augustin, 386
Moulard, Anatole, 398
Mouratides, Konstantinos, 403
Mouroux, Jean, 27(n.11), 373, 384
Moutsoulas, Elias D., 370
Mozley, John Kenneth, 279(n.12), 403
Mueller, F., 48(n.19)
Mugnier, Francis, 397
Müller, G., 305(n.30), 386
Müller, M., 23(n.8), 84(n.100), 379
Mussner, Franz, 368
Musurillo, Herbert, 49(n.33), 83(n.87, 99), 122(n.32), 150(n.38,39), 305(n.34), 348(n.58), 399, 412, 432
Muyldermans, J., 258(n.48), 259(n.32), 264(n.56), 265(n.101)
Muyser, Jacob, 407

Naseby, M., 360
Nasrallah, Joseph, 407
Natali, Acain, 389
Nau, François, 85(n.136), 86(n.164), 118(n.34), 227(n.10), 228(n.17)
Nazarius of Valaam, 432, 434, 437, 438, 440
Nellas Panagiotis, 376
Nemeshegui, Peter, 369
Nemesius, 90, 420
Neri, Umberto, 25(n.13)
Nersis, Snorhali, 416, 424
Neville, G., 176(n.133)
Nicephorus the Monk, 80(n.60), 318, 345(n.38), 439
Nicetas Stethatos, 12, 73, 84(n.125,126), 260(n.13), 272, 418, 440, 441
Nicodemus of Naxos, the Hagiorite, 12, 13, 19, 26(n.17), 175(n.94), 202 (n.44), 203(n.15), 227(n.25), 228 (n.9), 262(n.94), 265(n.86), 300 (n.5), 324(n.17), 362, 441
Nicolas, Jean-Hervé, 150(n.28)
Nikon of the Black Mountain, 12, 25 (n.3), 163, 167, 175(n.100), 251, 264(n.57), 362
Nilus, Abba, 430
Nilus (Evagrius), 175(n.105), 231(n.68), 280(n.59), 339, 348(n.51), 434, 438, 439
Nilus of Sinai, 241
Nilus of Sora (Nil Sorsky), 17, 26(n.41), 161, 173(n.41), 209, 264(n.48), 364, 435
Nilsson, Martin, 24(n.34)
Noble, Henri-Dominique, 264(n.50), 402
Nock, Arthur Darby, 78(n.12), 147 (n.69), 172(n.26)
Nölle, W., 410
Normann, Friedrich, 367
Norris, Richard A., 382
Nowak, Edward, 146(n.55), 147(n.6), 148(n.13,22,27,37,39), 149(n.48), 385
Noye, Irénée, 325(n.43), 369
Nygren, Anders, 305(n.27,31), 406
Nyssen, Wilhelm, 409

Obolinskij, Serge, 383
Oldfather, W. A., 300(n.1)

Index of Proper Names   467

Oechslin, Raphaël-Louis, 392
Olerud, A., 385
Olphe-Gailliard, Michel, 117(n.5), 197 (n.29), 256(n.5), 257(n.34), 388, 392, 401, 404
Oltramare, A., 51(n.67)
O'Meara, J., 324(n.7)
Onasch, Konrad, 385
Onings, L., 150(n.35), 386
Orban, A. P., 382
Orbe, Antonio, 79(n.30), 86(n.160), 366, 370, 376, 378
Orfanickij, I., 366
Origen, 5, 10, 11, 12, 27(n.8,18), 32, 34, 36, 38, 40, 44, 49(n.37), 50 (n.13,22,36), 51(n.60), 57, 58, 59, 60, 61, 68, 69, 70, 76, 78, 79(n.25, 32,35,39,44), 80(n.57), 82(n.59,70, 71), 83(n.82,93), 84(n.100,101,116), 85(n.147), 86(n.100,169), 87, 88, 89, 90, 91, 93, 94, 96, 112, 116(n.38, 43,48,60,65), 117(n.5,71), 118, 121 (n.37), 122(n.44), 128, 137, 144, 145(n.22), 148(n.21), 153, 154, 161, 162, 167, 171(n.19,22,23), 172(n.11, 27), 173(n.37), 174(n.57), 175(n.92), 178, 179, 185, 186, 191, 194, 197 (n.17,30), 199(n.21,39), 201(n.26, 30,34,37), 202(n.5), 211, 220, 226 (n.4), 227(n.5), 229(n.17,18,19,35, 26,27), 230(n.34,35,38,46,47), 235, 236, 237, 238, 240, 242, 244, 248, 252, 255, 257(n.25), 258(n.2,40,43, 59), 259(n.17,30,37), 260(n.2,3,4), 262(n.7), 265(n.93), 272, 273, 274, 279(n.13,14), 280(n.32), 291, 300 (n.2), 302(n.26.27.29), 303, 305 (n.38), 307, 311, 312, 315, 321(n.8, 9,10,11,12,26,30,31,33), 322(n.1), 324(n.7,10), 328, 330, 331, 333, 335, 337, 341, 342, 344(n.8,12,13,15), 345(n.12,30,31,36,37), 346(n.1,3, 39,53,59), 347(n.16,23,24,28), 348 (n.52), 349(n.8,11,17), 360, 361, 365, 366, 367, 368, 369, 370, 371, 372, 373, 375, 376, 377, 378, 380, 381, 382, 383, 384, 386, 387, 389, 393, 394, 398, 399, 400, 401, 402, 405, 407, 411, 417, 418, 419, 420, 422, 423, 424, 432, 437, 439
Orlov, Alexander, Serg., 174(n.55)
Ormanian, Malachy, 363
Ortiz de Urbina, Ignacio, 49(n.30), 363
Osiris, Abba, 433
Otto, Stephan, 372
Ouince, René d', 381
Oulton, J. E. L., 50(n.22), 419

Oury, Guy, 185(n.157)
Ouspensky, Leonid, 313, 323(n.27,33, 34,38,42,44,45), 409
Outtier, Bernard, 203(n.15), 262(n.50)
Pachomius, 21, 176(n.137), 201(n.29), 257(n.17), 322(n.10), 348(n.47)
Pacourianos, 12
Padelford, F. M., 24(n.47)
Paisius Velichkovsky, 17, 27(n.45), 135, 244, 261(n.30
Palladius, 12, 23(n.8), 122(n.33), 348 (n.53)
Palmer, G. E. H., 25(n.5), 26(n.17), 202(n.8), 260(n.10), 324(n.17), 360, 362, 409, 410, 415, 433, 440, 441
Pallmer, William, 176(n.125)
Pambo, Abba, 166, 173(n.91), 226(n.52)
Panaetius, 62
Papadoulos-Kerameus, Athanasios, 84 (n.113), 200(n.4), 228(n.21)
Papadoulos, Nikolaos, 407
Paparozzi, M., 396
Paracelsus, 385
Parain, Brice, 146(n.49)
Pargoire, Jules, 410
Parisot, Jean, 48(n.15)
Park, J. E., 397, 407
Parmenides, 45
Pascal, Pierre, 325(n.40)
Paschen, Wilfried, 393
Patterson, Lloyd G., 386
Paulus, J., 384
Pax, Elpidius, 374
Pechersky Paterikon, 17, 113, 123(n.63), 263(n.35)
Pegon, Joseph, 394
Pelagius, 264(n.72)
Pelikan, Jaroslav, 378, 381
Pellegrino, Michele, 371, 375
Peña, I., 397
Penco, Gregorio, 365, 388
Pennington, Basil, 410
Pepin, Jean, 382
Pericoli-Ridolfini, Francesco S., 410
Périer, Jean, 228(n.27)
Perridon, Johannes F. Th., 399
Perruchon, Jules, 202(n.48)
Perzold, H., 376
Peter of Damascus, 195
Peter the Iberian, 86(n.163
Petit, Françoise, 384
Pétré, Hélène, 51(n.68), 389
Petschenig, Michael, 257(n.22), 265 (n.90)
Peursen, Cornelis A. von, 377
Pezos the Hieromonk, 201(n.39)

Philaret of Moscow, 130, 342, 349 (n.19), 367
Philemon, Abba, 317, 345(n.38)
Phileotes, Cyril, 174(n.86)
Philippe de la Trinité, 384
Philippidis, Leonidas J., 407
Philippou, A. J., 405
Philips, Gérard, 48(n.10)
Philokalia, 12, 13, 19, 25, 38, 79(n.33), 84(n.14,119), 85(n.141), 115(n.33), 120(n.3), 122(n.38), 171(n.12), 198 (n.12), 202(n.8), 203(n.21), 228 (n.12), 230(n.58), 257(n.19), 258 (n.52), 259(n.43), 260(n.7,8,49,56), 261(n.14,29,32,44), 262(n.1,4), 265 (n.91,05), 272, 278(n.27), 279(n.9), 280(n.59,61,62), 302(n.45), 305 (n.52), 317, 323(n.1), 325(n.45), 345(n.38), 346(n.41,44), 362, 415, 417, 419, 420, 421, 427, 428, 430, 432, 433, 434, 435, 439, 440, 441
Philo of Alexandria, 50(n.19), 57, 58, 62, 79(n.22), 87, 88, 91, 95, 99, 115 (n.10), 117(n.18), 118(n.50), 133, 141, 149(n.7), 179, 182, 198(n.48, 49), 243, 255, 259(n.9), 261(n.15), 265(n.106), 271, 274, 279(n.6), 280 (n.31), 289, 290, 292, 294, 299, 302 (n.8,28), 303(n.22,38,52), 341, 348 (n.3), 373, 382, 403
Philostratus, 225(n.3)
Philotheus, 241
Philotheus Coccinos, 13, 201(n.39), 228 (n.21)
Philotheus of Sinai, 242, 433
Philoxines of Mabbug, 15, 26(n.25), 69, 70, 74, 75, 77, 85(n.159), 206, 225 (n.9), 296, 304(n.16), 341, 346(n.42), 348(n.54), 349(n.10), 422, 427, 429, 434, 442
Photius, 376
Physiologus, 347(n.18)
Pichery, E., 421
Pichler, Theodorich, 399
Pieper, Josef, 360
Pierce, C. A., 377
Pigna, A., 409
Pirre, D. D., 280(n.33), 403
Pistamon, Abba, 430
Pitra, Johannes Bapt., 176(n.124), 229 (n.18)
Places, Edouard des, 27(n.16), 53(n.45), 261(n.26), 348(n.44), 384, 401, 404
Plagnieux, Jean, 175(n.90), 411
Plato, 27(n.18), 36, 39, 42, 43, 45, 46, 52(n.4), 56, 58, 62, 70, 78(n.11), 80 (n.9,10), 88, 91, 92, 93, 97, 98, 102,
193, 104, 108, 109, 118(n.37), 120 (n.12), 121(n.1,2), 122(n.22,24,30), 123(n.69), 125, 138, 142, 145(n.1,5), 148(n.35,36), 171(n.3), 176(n.140), 197(n.11,12), 198(n.2), 199(n.29), 205, 207, 208, 225(n.4,27), 234, 257 (n.12,14), 265(n.103,104), 278(n.25), 288, 290, 291, 293, 298, 302(n.4,5, 10,20,21,28), 303(n.35,57,60), 304 (n.20,21), 305(n.44), 310, 321(n.35), 330, 331, 333, 338, 343(n.23), 344 (n.1,6), 345(n.13,18), 347(n.30), 361, 381, 383, 384, 385, 403, 405, 407, 410, 411
Plé, Albert, 407
Plessis, P. J. du, 82(n.46)
Plethon, Gregory, 294, 303(n.63)
Pliny the Younger, 38, 51(n.45)
Plotinus, 45, 56, 78, 91, 92, 109, 116 (n.47), 178, 197(n.15), 198(n.2), 205, 225(n.5,6), 345(n.37), 392, 393, 407, 411
Plumpe, Joseph C., 387
Plus, Raoul, 398
Plutarch, 52(n.7), 83(n.88), 228(n.19), 423(pseudo-plutarch), 147(n.4)
Podipara, Placid I., 363
Podskalsky, Gerhard, 396
Poelman, Roger, 417
Poemen, Abba, 193, 202(n.2), 216, 228 (n.16), 260(n.6), 266(n.113), 303 (n.64), 424, 429, 430, 433, 435, 436
Pohlenz, Max, 80(n.1,2), 118(n.47), 119(n.86), 278(n.3), 403
Poladian, T., 363
Polycarp, 51(n.43), 174(n.68), 197 (n.28), 304(n.70)
Pond, K., 397
Porphyry, 205, 231(n.67)
Poschmann, Berhard, 201(n.30), 394
Poseljanin, E., 23(n.7), 364
Posidonius, 92
Potterie, Ignace de la, 53(n.44), 199 (n.41), 366
Pourrat, Pierre, 379
Pousset, Edouard, 379
Prat, Ferdinand, 116(n.59), 304(n.18)
Preisker, Herbert, 398
Presente, G., 402
Prestige, George L., 48(n.18), 369
Preuschen, E., 344(n.13)
Prévot, P., 383
Proclus, 27(n.18), 331, 344(n.7)
Prosper, St., 119(n.76)
Prümm, Karl, 82(n.46), 373
Psellos, M., 400
Pseudo-Athanasius, 225(n.15), 422

Index of Proper Names

Pseudo-Barnabas, 304(n.2,74)
Pseudo-Basil, 49(n.32)
Pseudo-Caesarius, 55
Pseudo-Chrysostom, 431, 439
Pseudo-Clementine *Hom.*, 79(n.46)
Pseudo-Macarius, 11, 20, 31, 47, 48 (n.11), 53(n.49), 58, 64, 74, 81 (n.24), 102, 106, 121(n.39), 172 (n.29), 178, 183, 197(n.9), 198 (n.10), 225(n.10), 233, 237, 257 (n.26), 258(n.1,55), 259(n.45), 276, 280(n.58), 297, 303(n.42), 345(n.15), 374, 415, 416, 417, 419, 420, 421, 422, 428, 429, 432, 433, 438, 439, 441, 442, 443
Pseudo-Plutarch, 342(n.2)
Pseudo-Rufinus, 264(n.72)
Puech, Henri Charles, 147(n.8), 376, 384, 412
Pusey, Philipp Edward, 52(n.22), 53 (n.43), 358
Pythagoras, 108, 216, 277

Quéré-Jaulmes, France, 416, 417, 421, 422, 431
Quell, Gottfried, 406

Raabe, Richard, 86(n.163)
Raasch, Juana, 393, 401
Raes, Alphonse, 229(n.14), 408
Rahmani, Ignatius, 50(n.36), 229(n.30), 230(n.33,35)
Rahner, Hugo, 228(n.24), 374, 387, 396
Rahner, Karl, 52(n.13), 117(n.5), 370, 375, 377, 379, 392, 394
Rainborough, T., 360
Rancillac, Ph., 172(n.1), 387
Ranke-Heinemann, Uta, 375, 400, 406
Ratzinger, Joseph, 172(n.25), 368, 373
Rauer, Max, 345(n.36,37)
Ravier, A., 364
Rayez, André, 83(n.78), 364, 373, 374, 398
Refoulé, F., 263(n.31), 379
Refoulé, R., 118(n.41)
Régamey, Pie-Raymond, 231(n.63), 384
Reginald, M., 391
Regnault, Lucien, 24(n.54), 50(n.10), 203(n.15), 227(n.25), 228(n.9), 262(n.50)
Reichart, G., 78(n.5)
Reifferscheid, August, 51(n.46)
Reitzenstein, Richard, 279(n.8)
Remmers, J. G., 370
Renaud, Bernard, 279(n.1)
Rendina, Sergio, 411
Reumann, J., 384

Rey, Bernard, 78(n.9)
Reypens, Leonce, 118(n.26), 378
Rezáč, Joannes, 176(n.131,138), 301 (n.24), 391, 396, 400
Richardson, Ernest, C., 262(n.5)
Richter, G., 379
Ridouard, André, 321(n.34)
Riemann, D., 386
Riou, Alain, 387
Rist, John, 407
Rius-Camps, Jozef, 116(n.60), 370
Rivière, Jean, 366, 392
Robilliard, Jean-Augustin, 51(n.47)
Robin, L., 304(n.20), 305(n.44)
Robinson, A., 147(n.65)
Rocco, U., 398
Rohde, Erwin, 378
Roldanus, J., 197(n.32), 279(n.8), 303 (n.30), 376, 392
Rolt, C. E., 52(n.24), 343(n.4), 423
Rondet, Henri, 393, 394, 390, 398, 404
Roques, R., 83(n.86), 375, 411, 412
Rordorf, W., 375
Roschini, Gabriele, M., 384
Rothenhäusler, M., 411
Rotureau, Gaston, 378
Rouët de Journel, M-Joseph, 364, 404
Rougier, Louis, 24(n.330)
Rousseau, O., 390, 404
Roy, Léon, 226(n.36)
Rubens-Denval, 363
Rundmann, Remigius, 390
Rüsche, Franz, 325(n.52), 378
Ruf, Ambrosius Karl, 393
Rufinus, 60
  Pseudo-Rufinus, 264(n.72)
Rupp, Jean, 387
Russell, Norman, 23(n.8), 115(n.25), 200(n.2), 259(n.32), 303(n.42)
Russian Pilgrim, 318
Russier, Jeanne, 384
Rüther, Theodor, 279(n.15,20), 280 (n.55), 403

Sabas, St., 223, 230(n.56), 236, 258 (n.42)
Sabas the Younger, 216
Salama, Abuna, 14
Salaville, Sévérien, 49(n.38), 50(n.28,39), 172(n.10), 322(n.10), 368
Salmon, Pierre, 404
Sarah, Amma, 435
Sargologos, Etienne, 174(n.75,86)
Sauget, Joseph-Marie, 408
Savramis, Demosthenes, 395
Sawhill, J. A., 400
Scazzoso, Piero, 409, 412

Schaeder, Hans, 172(n.45)
Schaefer, Karl Th., 368
Schaerer, René, 379
Scharbert, Josef, 147(n.5)
Scharl, Emmeran, 367
Scheffczyk, Leo, 200(n.50), 382, 383, 394
Schenkl, H., 52(n.30), 345(n.17)
Scherwood, P., 386
Schillebeeckx, Edward, 366
Schierse, Franz-Josef, 50(n.20), 368, 372
Schlier, Heinrich, 379
Schmaus, Michael, 52(n.18), 394
Schmemann, Alexander, 385, 394, 408
Schmitt, J., 225(n.7)
Schnackenburg, Rudolf, 405
Schneider, A. M., 361
Schoenborn, Christoph von, 409
Schoeps, H. J., 360
Schoonenberg, Piet, 199(n.42)
Schneider, A., 345(n.15)
Schubert, V., 383
Schulz, Hans Joachim, 123(n.68)
Schultze, Berhard, 50(n.9), 172(n.46), 325(n.48), 367, 368, 369, 376, 383, 396, 410
Schulze, P., 401
Schwanz, Peter, 371
Schwarz, M. 27(n.45)
Schweizer, Eduard, 377, 380
Scrima, André, 26(n.16), 172(n.1)
Scupoli, Lorenzo, 13, 244, 324(n.17)
Seckler, Max, 24(n.50)
Secondin, B., 359
Séjourné, Paul, 388
Semmelroth, Otto, 48(n.7,9), 373
Seneca, 70, 123(n.69), 130, 146(n.50), 251, 256(n.2), 264(n.51), 271, 279 (n.5), 380, 423
Seraphim of Sarov, 5, 34, 416, 418, 429, 434, 442
Seraphim (Sobolev), 382
Serapion, Abba, 430, 433, 436
Sergius of Radonezh, 364
Serpinet, A., 349(n.19)
Serr, Jacques, 322(n.12)
Serra, Mario, 389
Sevčenko, J., 174(n.62)
Severianus of Gabala, 79(n.46)
Severus of Antioch, 260(n.5)
Sheed, R., 372
Shein, J. L., 120(n.2)
Sherrard, Philip, 25(n.5), 362, 415
Sherwood, P., 171(n.14), 225(n.28), 423
Sieben, Hermann Josef, 400, 413
Siewerth, Gustav, 379
Silouan, Staretz, 418, 437

Silvanus, Abba, 433
Silvester, Russian Priest, 162
Simon, M., 393
Simonetti, Manlio, 375
Simonides of Ceos, 118(n.48), 216
Simonin, Henri-Dominique, 383
Siniscalco, Paolo, 386
Sisoes, Abba, 116(n.34), 419, 430, 436
Siwek, Paul, 384
Sjögren, Per-Olof, 410
Skabanovič, N., 391
Skalicky, Carlo, 367, 413
Skovorodà, Grigorij S., 37
Skrobucha, Heinz, 409
Smirnov, Sergei, 202(n.44), 390, 394, 404
Smirnova, Y., 149(n.52)
Smolitsch, Igor, 25(n.5), 364
Socrates, 87, 137, 234, 288, 297, 377, 423
Socrates, historian, 229(n.11), 349(n.14)
Sodano, Angelo, 148, 395
Sokolov, Joan Iv., 123(n.62), 391
Solignac, Aimé, 116(n.47), 118(n.39), 355(n.1), 362, 372, 375, 379, 408, 411
Soloviev, Vladimir, 17, 37, 49(n.43), 50 (n.35), 81(n.35), 110, 114, 121 (n.14), 123(n.76), 129, 140, 149 (n.1), 156, 171(n.40,41,42,43), 172 (n.47), 220, 224, 229(n.23), 343 (n.19), 416, 417, 418, 419, 421, 422, 423, 424, 425, 426, 427, 428, 430, 431, 438
Sopatrus, Abba, 59
Sophronius of Jerusalem, 314
Sophrony, Archimandrite, 398, 405
Soury, Georges, 148(n.26)
Spáčil, Theophil, 120(n.31)
Spanneut, Michel, 24(n.31), 49(n.41), 51(n.2), 80(n.1), 82(n.61), 86(n.160), 114(n.1), 116(n.64), 118(n.30,46,49, 52,55), 119(n.83,87), 121(n.18), 145 (n.3,10,11,12,17), 146(n.31,32,36, 37,38,39,46), 147(n.66,67,74,75,78), 148(n.25), 149(n.6), 171(n.28,29,30), 199(n.28,30), 229(n.16), 230(n.41), 257(n.36), 278(n.4,6,11), 379(n.12), 280(n.50,54), 325(n.53), 342(n.1), 343(n.24,26), 344(n.1,2,5), 345 (n.14,19), 347(n.12), 358, 361, 379, 383, 386, 402, 411
Spetsieri, 280(n.39)
Spicq, Ceslas, 406
Špidlík, Tomáš, 23(n.2,9,10,17,18,20), 25(n.8), 26(n.42), 27(n.1,3,15,18, 19,46), 28(n.34), 48(n.11,14,17,27),

Index of Proper Names 471

49(n.37), 50(n.16,18,23,34), 52(n.8, 14), 79(n.21), 80(n.50,57), 81(n.30, 36,37), 82(n.48,54), 84(n.104,111, 112,115,122,124), 85(n.157), 115 (n.3), 116(n.37,39,50,56,62), 117 (n.1,72), 118(n.38), 119(n.56,61,65, 74,80,82,88), 120(n.10,11,17), 121 (n.7,15,20,43), 122(n.28,31,45), 123 (n.64), 146(n.26), 147(n.1,7,6,79, 82), 148(n.20,29,45), 149(n.2,3,4, 20), 150(n.22), 170(n.1), 172(n.6,14, 16,24), 173(n.34,45,49,53), 174 (n.60,76,77,80,87), 175(n.97,101, 108), 176(n.123,129,132,134,138), 197(n.10,13), 198(n.3,8), 199(n.16, 19,22,24,26,35,38,44,45), 200(n.48, 51,52,53,60,62,64,68), 201(n.19,26), 225(n.11,12,16,18), 226(n.39,50,51, 57,58), 227(n.17,20,24), 228(n.15, 20,29,32), 229(n.13,22), 230(n.35, 52,60), 257(n.19), 258(n.62), 259 (n.45), 260(n.46,57), 261(n.17,19, 27,38), 264(n.49,58), 265(n.112), 278(n.15), 281(n.71,75,76), 301 (n.13,14,22,25,27,29,39), 302(n.9, 42), 303(n.34), 305(n.33,37,41,46), 321(n.4,5,6), 322(n.3,4,11,13,15,40), 323(n.23,24,26,40), 324(n.6,13,16, 20,31,35), 325(n.42,57), 343(n.7,21, 27), 344(n.9,10,11,17), 345(n.25,32), 346(n.45,52), 347(n.17,22,31), 348 (n.1), 349(n.7), 357, 358, 359, 362, 364, 366, 368, 369, 372, 374, 376, 377, 379, 380, 381, 382, 383, 385, 386, 387, 388, 390, 391, 392, 395, 396, 397, 398, 399, 403, 404, 405, 406, 407, 408, 409, 410, 411, 413, 419, 425, 435, 439
Spitzer, L, 146(n.31)
Staats, Reinhart, 374
Stählin, W., 83(n.80), 228(n.28), 257 (n.16), 266(n.114), 279(n.21), 344 (n.9), 343(n.11), 380
Staniloe, Dimitry, 376
Staretz, Leonid, 415
Stauffer, Ethelbert, 406
Stead, Julian, 50(n.32)
Steely, John, 375
Steidle, Basilius, 374, 375
Steiner, Martin, 402
Stelzenberger, Johannes, 117(n.15,19), 303(n.37, 365, 371, 377, 380, 398, 401, 405
Stephanou, E., 121(n.9)
Stephen bar Soudaili, 15, 26(n.26)
Stephens, W. R., 425
Stiernon, D., 362, 396

Stockmeier, P., 384
Stoffels, Joseph, 53(n.53)
Stogogliou, George A., 359
Strathmann, Herman, 359
Suarez, 321(n.15)
Sumption, Jonathan, 397
Susemihl, Franz, 303(n.58), 305(n.23)
Suttner, Ernst Christoph, 387
Suvorov, N., 202(n.49)
Sylvester the Priest, 323(n.37)
Symeon Metaphrastes, 134, 147(n.80), 431
Symeon of Mesopotamia, 24(n.52), 374
Symeon of Thessalonica, 13, 314, 323 (n.41), 440, 441
Symeon the New Theologian, 5, 7, 12, 27(n.13), 46, 71, 73, 84(n.120), 117 (n.7,12), 182, 196, 198(n.44), 201 (n.23,25), 215, 283, 288, 296, 302 (n.3), 304(n.7), 376, 396, 402, 416, 417, 418, 420, 421, 422, 423, 425, 428, 429, 430, 431, 432, 434, 436, 437, 438, 439, 440, 441, 442
Symeon the Studite, 215
Syncletica, St., 303, 430
Synesius of Cyrene, 423
Szabó, Ladislas, 198(n.1)
Szylkarski, Vladimir, 368
Szymusiak, Jan Maria, 411

Taleleus, Abba, 194
Tamisier, Robert, 380
Tarchnišvili, Michele, 364, 408
Tatian, 118(n.27), 150(n.36)
Teichtweier, Georg, 393
Telfer, W., 420
Tertullian, 24(n.39), 51(n.43), 144, 155, 171(n.35), 378, 382
Terzoli, Riccardo, 372, 387
Thales of Miletus, 45
Theodore of Ancyra, 52(n.28)
Theodore of Enaton, Abba, 433
Theodore of Mopsuestia, 79(n.46)
Theodore of Pherme, 197(n.5), 430, 436
Theodore the Studite, 7, 12, 25(n.6), 76, 81(n.38), 123(n.65), 165, 173 (n.45), 174(n.78), 189, 200(n.4), 209, 235, 246, 257(n.30), 261(n.47), 343(n.25), 392, 415, 419, 420, 428, 436
Theodoret of Cyrus, 12, 64, 80(n.60), 81(n.21,23), 85(n.133), 146(n.53), 147(n.73), 148(n.31), 152, 171(n.9), 175(n.116), 225(n.8,30), 227(n.19), 296, 297, 304(n.9), 333, 345(n.28), 374, 420, 423
Theodorou, Euang., 403

Theoleptus of Philadelphia, 427
Theonas, Abba, 433
Theophane the Recluse, 1, 4(n.2), 17, 23(n.9), 25(n.5), 27(n.15,46), 28 (n.32), 32, 33, 48(n.11,14), 49(n.37, 42,44,45), 53(n.49), 73, 80(n.50), 84(n.111,112,114,115,122,123,124 125), 91, 93, 94, 102, 104, 105, 106, 107, 110, 116(n.50,62), 117(n.1,72), 119(n.80,82,88), 120(n.8,11,22,35, 36), 121(n.15,41,42,43,47,48), 172 (n.6), 183˜8, 190, 198(n.8), 199 (n.16,18,22,23,24,26,27,37), 200 (n.48,51,52,60,64), 201(n.22), 206, 225(n.11,12), 241, 244, 259(n.45), 260(n.46,57), 261(n.27,38), 264 (n.49), 268, 269, 278(n.15,20), 281 (n.71), 305(n.33), 307, 309, 311, 312, 316, 317, 318, 320(n.2), 321 (n.3,4,5,6,23,24,25,26), 322(n.2,3, 4,11,13,15,17,18,19,40), 323(n.23, 24), 324(n.16,20,27,31,35), 325 (n.42,57,59,60), 339, 340, 347, 348 (n.50), 358, 372, 374, 377, 380, 418, 419, 422, 424, 434, 439, 440, 443,
Theophanes, Cerameus, 202(n.6), 424
Theophilus, Georgian, 16
Theophilus of Antioch, 144, 147(n.64), 150(n.39), 272, 279(n.11), 415, 425, 441
Theophrastes, 265(n.89)
Theophylactus of Bulgaria, 436
Thomas Aquinas, 51(n.56), 96, 104, 118(n.29), 120(n.6), 121(n.49), 198 (n.9), 216, 228(n.24), 278(n.7,8,9), 288, 294, 295, 303(n.62), 304(n.1), 321(n.15), 383
Thunberg, Lars, 50(n.31), 149(n.5), 370, 372, 377, 381, 385, 387, 393, 402
Tikhon of Zadonsk, 17, 115(n.21), 337, 347(n.19), 421, 442
Tillard, J. M. R., 404
Tisserant, Eugène, 363
Tithoes, Abba, 44, 75, 433
Tolstoj, A., 174(n.54)
Tolstoy, N., 230(n.60), 399
Toombs, L. E., 393
Tougard, A., 261(n.47)
Traets, Charles, 367
Trajan, 38
Trembelas, Panagiotis, N., 190, 191, 201(n.11,12,13,36), 202(n.45,56), 393, 395
Trilling, Wolfgang, 373
Trouillard, Jean, 393
Trubetzkoi, E., 408
Truhlar, Karel Vladimir, 368

Tschiżewskij, Dmitry, 26(n.40), 123 (n.63), 263(n.35)
Tugij, I., 48(n.6)
Turbessi, Giuseppe, 392, 405
Turcu, I., 371
Turner, Cuthbert Hamilton, 372
Turner, H. E. W., 367
Tyciak, Julius, 358, 367, 389, 405, 408
Tyszkiewicz, Stanislas, 172(n.5), 200 (n.54), 364, 415, 416, 418, 422, 428, 429, 431, 432, 434, 437, 438, 440, 441, 442
Tzogas, Charil S., 405

Ueding, Leo, 176, 390
Uspenskij, *see*: Ouspensky

Vacant, Jean-Michel Alfred, 202(n.43), 394
Vailhé, Simeon, 397, 410
Van den Eynde, Damien, 391
van den Grinten, F., 406
Vanhoye, Albert, 83(n.96), 373
Vanneste, Jean, 412
Vannucci, Giovanni, 25(n.5)
Vedernikov, A., 407
Veilleux, Armand, 201(n.29), 322 (n.10)
Velat, Bernard, 343
Velichkovsky, Paisii (Paisius), 135, 364
Verbeke, Gerard, 47(n.1), 377
Verchovskoj, Sergei, 51(n.65), 120(n.4), 122(n.46), 172(n.44), 323(n.21), 389, 408
Vermeersch, Arthur, 321(n.15)
Vernay, Robert, 401, 402
Viller, Marcel, 26(n.17), 197(n.29), 261 (n.23), 264(n.50), 374, 375, 379, 406
Vischer, Lukas, 388
Vizmanos, Francisco de, 399
Vögtle, Anton, 382, 401
Vogüé, Adalbert de, 256(n.3), 391, 400, 403
Volk, Hermann, 382
Völker, Walter, 82(n.70), 84(n.10), 85 (n.155), 117(n.18), 149(n.8), 175 (n.92), 199(n.21,25), 226(n.3), 229 (n.32), 279(n.20), 302(n.28), 346 (n.53), 373, 375, 396, 402, 403, 412
Vökl, Richard, 390
von Balthasar, Hans Urs, 83(n.89), 147 (n.82), 347(n.28), 382, 386, 387, 420, 423
von Campenhausen, Hans, 359
Vööbus, Arthur, 363
Vorgrimler, V., 201(n.32,33)

Index of Proper Names 473

Vornicescu, N., 371
Vukovič, S., 399
Vyšeslavcev, Boris P., , 103, 119(n.1), 120 (n.21), 334, 346(n.47), 379

Wagner, F., 368
Wagner, M. Monica, 176(n.139), 226 (n.40), 417, 428, 429
Wagner, Reinhard, 375
Waldmann, M., 377
Wall, Barbara, 359
Wallis Budge, Ernest, A., 362
Ward, Benedicta, 419, 433
Ware, Kallistos, 25(n.5), 362, 410, 415
Warkotsch, Albert, 361
Warnach, Viktor, 116(n.58), 170(n.2), 406
Watson, Philip S., 305(n.27), 406
Way, A. C., 199(n.43)
Weil, Raymond, 386
Weiss, Karl, 391
Welykyi, Anastasij, 406
Wendland, Paul, 348(n.3)
Wenger, Antoine, 262(n.55)
Wenner, Francis, 256(n.3)
Werbeck, Wilfrid, 408
Werner, Francis, 400
Wetter, Friedrich, 403
Wey, H., 400
Wheeler, Eric P., 115(n.24)
Widengreen, Geo., 412
Wiener, Claude, 305(n.24,26)
Wiertz, Paul, 358, 367, 389, 405
Wilckens, Ulrich, 365
Wilkinson, John, 440
Willwoll, Alexander, 392
Wilson, H. A., 150(n.34)
Windisch, Hans, 392
Wolfson, Harry Austyn, 118(n.50), 361
Wolters, Clifton, 324(n.34)
Wood, S., 171(n.32), 228(n.28)
Woodward, George Ratcliffe, 85(n.149)
Wulf, Friedrich, 392
Wunderle, Georg, 359, 389, 396, 408
Wytzes, J., 383, 384

Xanthopoulos, Callistus and Ignatius, 13, 272, 410, 430
Xenophon, 114(n.2), 423

Yamshchikov, S., 149(n.52)
Yannaras, Ch., 376
Yannoulatos, A., 391
Yeomans, William, 263(n.17)

Zagiba, Franz, 23(n.20)
Zander, Leon Λ., 383, 388
Zander, Valentine, 416
Zankow, Stefan, 81(n.34), 372
Zanutto, S., 362
Zar'a Yakob, 14
Zarin, Sergei Mich., 28(n.36), 116 (n.65)
Zedda, S., 371
Zeňkovsky, B., 129, 376, 378
Zeňkovsky, V. V., 378, 379
Zeno, Abba, 436
Zeno the Stoic, 62, 129, 277, 348(n.3)
Zeoli, A., 379
Ziadé, Ignace, 363
Ziegler, Adolf Wilhelm, 389
Ziegler, Jozef G., 51(n.42), 117(n.11); 372
Zielinski, T., 24(n.34)
Zigmund-Cerbu, A., 410
Zincone, S., 395
Zissis, Th. N., 382
Zöckler, Otto, 401
Zonaras, J., 229(n.18)
Zoras, G. 397
Zossima, Staretz, 425

www.ingramcontent.com/pod-product-compliance
Lightning Source LLC
Chambersburg PA
CBHW051415290426
44109CB00016B/1307